# CONCEPTIONS OF DATA PROTECTION AND PRIVACY

This open access book offers a clear and concise overview of leading conceptions of data protection and privacy, exploring their social value through philosophical theorisations and European and US-American legal perspectives.

Featuring prominent experts and emerging scholars, the book presents diverse understandings to showcase the multifaceted interests and values embedded in the concepts of data protection and privacy. It links philosophical and legal perspectives on privacy to historical and contemporary rights struggles. The book also addresses privacy challenges posed by the digital revolution, including advances in AI, and recent efforts to safeguard privacy.

Aimed at scholars, researchers, and students in law and philosophy, the book covers key theoretical and legal positions on privacy and data protection. Legal practitioners will find insights into landmark EU and US constitutional decisions, such as the German Constitutional Court's *Census Decision* and *Carpenter v United States*. Additionally, it is valuable for anyone seeking to understand the legal and philosophical foundations of globally influential regulations like the GDPR and the AI Act.

**Hart Studies in Information Law and Regulation: Volume 5**

**Hart Studies in Information Law and Regulation**

**Series Editors**

Tanya Aplin (General Editor)
Perry Keller (Advisory Editor)

This series concerns the transformative effects of the digital technology revolution on information law and regulation. Information law embraces multiple areas of law that affect the control and reuse of information, data and digital tools – intellectual property, data protection, privacy, freedom of information, state security, tort, contract and competition law. 'Regulation' is a similarly extensive concept in that it encompasses legal and non-legal modes of control, including technological design and codes of practice.

The series provides cross-cutting analysis and exploration of the complex and pressing issues that arise in a society where digital infrastructures are now pervasive and when massive volumes of digital information are shared globally. These issues include access to data; sharing, reuse, and governance of data; open source and public sector data; the legitimacy and transparency of training data; propertisation of data and digital tools; freedom of expression and information access rights; privacy rights and data protection regimes; and the role of the state and private entities in safeguarding the public interest in the uses of data.

In the spirit of representing the diverse nature of its topics, the series embraces various methodologies: doctrinal, comparative, empirical, theoretical, historical and socio-legal, and particularly welcomes monograph proposals.

The series is especially open to perspectives from jurisdictions or regions which have traditionally been underrepresented in the scholarly literature.

**Recent titles in this series:**

*Constitutionalising Social Media*
Edited by Edoardo Celeste, Amélie Heldt and Clara Iglesias Keller

*Cybersecurity, Privacy and Data Protection in EU Law: A Law, Policy and Technology Analysis*
Maria Grazia Porcedda

*Critical Reflections on the EU's Data Protection Regime: GDPR in the Machine*
Edited by Róisín Á Costello and Mark Leiser

*Big Data for the Public Good: Regulating Access to Public Sector Big Data for Research and Innovation*
Stergios Aidinlis

*Conceptions of Data Protection and Privacy: Legal and Philosophical Perspectives*
Edited by Elisa Orrù and Ralf Poscher

# Conceptions of Data Protection and Privacy

*Legal and Philosophical Perspectives*

Edited by
Elisa Orrù
and
Ralf Poscher

•HART•
OXFORD • LONDON • NEW YORK • NEW DELHI • SYDNEY

HART PUBLISHING

Bloomsbury Publishing Plc

Kemp House, Chawley Park, Cumnor Hill, Oxford, OX2 9PH, UK

1385 Broadway, New York, NY 10018, USA

Bloomsbury Publishing Ireland Limited, 29 Earlsfort Terrace, Dublin 2, D02 AY28, Ireland



First published in Great Britain 2026



Open access was funded by the Max Planck Institute for the Study of Crime, Security and Law.



A catalogue record for this book is available from the British Library.

A catalogue record for this book is available from the Library of Congress.

Library of Congress Control Number: 2025949170

ISBN: HB: 978-1-50998-372-8
ePDF: 978-1-50998-374-2
ePub: 978-1-50998-373-5

Typeset by Compuscript Ltd, Shannon

# ACKNOWLEDGEMENTS

Many of the contributions and ideas presented here were discussed at a two-day conference held at the Max Planck Institute for the Study of Crime, Security and Law in Freiburg, Germany, in July 2024. The conference was a unique opportunity to discuss the closely related issues of data protection and privacy, which are neither easily defined nor neatly categorised – either theoretically or doctrinally. We would like to thank all participants, both speakers and attendees, for the unprecedented and stimulating discussions and exchanges. Special acknowledgement is due to the conference participants and book contributors who, despite having divergent and often strongly conflicting political views, accepted our invitation. Needless to say, their contribution to this volume does not in any way imply endorsement of each other's positions. We acknowledge that the exchange of ideas and discussion on a topic that is contentious in more than one dimension required tolerance on all sides, and we are thankful and glad that we could facilitate the dialogue.

Our gratitude is also owed to Joern Roeder and Jonathan Pirnay, who kindly granted us permission to use a reproduction of their artwork on the book cover. Furthermore, we are grateful to Jasmin Lutz and Layla Murmann from the Max Planck Institute for the Study of Crime, Security and Law for their editorial support during the manuscript's preparation. We thankfully acknowledge Chris Harrison's professional support in copy-editing the manuscript. Lastly, we would like to express our sincere gratitude to the editors of the series Hart Studies in Information Law and Regulation, Tanya Aplin and Perry Keller, for their enthusiastic acceptance of our book proposal and their valuable feedback, as well as to the staff at Hart Publishing, particularly Verity Stuart, Roberta Bassi, and Linda Goss, for their professionalism and guidance throughout the editorial process.

# CONTENTS

PART III
EUROPEAN PRIVACY AND DIGITAL LAW: THE ROLE OF TRUST AND OF THE TRANSATLANTIC DIGITAL ECONOMY



PART IV
DATA PROTECTION AS A PROCEDURAL LIMITATION OF PUBLIC POWER, AND THE POWER TO DELIMIT THE PUBLIC AND THE PRIVATE



PART V
PRIVACY IN SOCIETY: TECHNOLOGY CHALLENGES, INDIVIDUALS' AUTONOMY AND FREEDOM

# CONTRIBUTORS

**Marion Albers** is Professor of Public Law, Information and Communication Law, Health Law and Legal Theory at Hamburg University. She received her diploma in sociology with a theoretical thesis on the information society. Her doctoral thesis in law focused on crime prevention and law enforcement, and her postdoctoral thesis on the reconceptualisation of informational self-determination. She has served as an assistant at the Federal Constitutional Court, an expert of the German *Bundestag*'s Advisory Committee on Ethics and Law in Modern Health Care, and a member of the German Council for Scientific Information Infrastructures. Her areas of research include fundamental rights, information law and data protection, internet and media law, biolaw, police law, and the law of intelligence services. Albers is involved in several, partly interdisciplinary projects dealing with legal aspects of data protection and data governance, freedom of information, surveillance, and biotechnologies.

**Anita L Allen**, JD, PhD, is the Henry R. Silverman Professor of Law and Professor of Philosophy at the University of Pennsylvania. Her prolific academic career includes groundbreaking research on the intersection of law, ethics, and technology. She has published six books and over 130 articles. Her influential advocacy, scholarship, and service have garnered numerous honours and awards, including membership to the American Academy of Arts and Sciences, the National Academy of Medicine, and the American Philosophical Society. She has been awarded the Lifetime Achievement Award of the Electronic Privacy Information Center and the Privacy Award of the Berkeley Law and Technology, along with the Hastings Center Bioethics Founders Award and the Quinn Prize for Service to Philosophy by the American Philosophical Association. She delivered the 2024 H.L.A Hart Memorial Lecture at Oxford University and is currently Laurance S. Rockefeller Visiting Professor for Distinguished Teaching at Princeton University.

**Claire Boine** is a postdoctoral fellow specialised in AI law at the Washington University Law School and an AI For Humanity Fellow at Mila Quebec. Receiving a PhD in technology law from the University of Ottawa, a Masters in Public Policy from Harvard Kennedy School, and her J.D. in EU law from Nantes University, Claire is an expert of General Purpose AI regulation and has consulted for several governments on the topic. Before the release of ChatGPT, Claire published the first law journal article arguing that GPT-3 and General Purpose AI systems were not regulated under the AI Act. She has also worked on diverse AI law topics such as AI and democracy, algorithmic bias, AI and gender, and AI-enabled manipulation.

**Gabriele Britz**, born in 1968, studied law and obtained her doctorate in Frankfurt am Main in 1993 with a thesis on local energy supply under national and European law

(‘*Örtliche Energieversorgung nach nationalem und europäischem Recht*’). She habilitated in 2001 on the topic of cultural rights and the constitution – on the legal approach to cultural difference (‘*Kulturelle Rechte und Verfassung – Über den rechtlichen Umgang mit kultureller Differenz*’). From 2001 to 2024, Britz was Professor of Public Law and European Law at Justus Liebig University Giessen. Since 2024, she has been Professor of Public Law, in particular Constitutional Law, at Goethe University Frankfurt. She was a judge on the First Senate of the Federal Constitutional Court from 2011 to 2023.

**Lea Despotis** works as the Program Coordinator at the Cordell Institute at Washington University School of Law. She earned her bachelor's degree in Political Science, Legal Studies, and Design from Washington University. Currently, she is pursuing a law degree at Duke University School of Law, specialising in data privacy, artificial intelligence, and cybersecurity law. As a former Speech, Privacy, and Technology intern at the American Civil Liberties Union (ACLU) for two years and a member of technology policy groups, she has contributed to campaigns related to surveillance and biometric technologies, social media regulation, and state privacy legislation.

**Johannes Eichenhofer** is the Professor for Public Law, Information and Migration Law at Leipzig University. Previously, he held stand-in professorships at the universities of Freiburg, Karlsruhe, Bochum, and Bielefeld, where he habilitated in 2020. The topic of his habilitation thesis, published in 2019, is *e-Privacy – Theory and Dogmatics of European Privacy Protection in the Internet Age*. In this work, he reconstructs European privacy protection law as a concept based on two pillars, namely self-determination and trust protection. In his recent work he applied this ‘trust based approach’ to other fields of digital law such as AI Regulation.

**Severin Engelmann** is a Postdoctoral Associate in the Information Science Department at Cornell University and Cornell Tech. His research examines the normative dimensions of AI that infer, classify and simulate people in socio-technical systems such as large language models, facial processing tools and social media. His work has been published in venues such as ACM FAccT, ACM AIES, ACM EAAMO, ACM CHI, and First Monday, and has been featured in outlets including *TechCrunch* and *The Washington Post*. He holds a PhD in Computer Science and an MA in Philosophy of Technology from the Technical University of Munich.

**Theodore Furchtgott** is an attorney at a New York law firm. He earned his J.D. from Stanford Law School, his M.Phil in mediaeval history from the University of Cambridge, and his A.B. in history from Princeton University. Mr Furchtgott clerked for Judge Timothy Tymkovich on the United States Court of Appeals for the Tenth Circuit and for Judge Daniel Domenico on the District of Colorado.

**Gloria González Fuster** is a Research Professor at Vrije Universiteit Brussels (VUB)'s Faculty of Law and Criminology, and Director of the Law, Science, Technology and Society (LSTS) Research Group. She holds a research position on ‘Digitalization and a Europe of rights and freedoms’, and teaches classes on privacy and data protection law and on the topic ‘*Bruxelles: La ville et le droit*’. González Fuster also lectures at the University of Göttingen and is a member of the EUTOPIA interdisciplinary learning community ‘Fairness, Accountability, Transparency, and Ethics in Data

Processing' (FATE). In addition, González Fuster is the principal investigator of the project 'Articulating Law, Technology, Ethics and Politics: Issues of Enforcement and Jurisdiction of EU Data Protection Law under and beyond the General Data Protection Regulation (GDPR)' (ALTEP-DP), and member of the European Commission's Multi-Stakeholder Expert Group Supporting the Implementation of the GDPR.

**Neil M Gorsuch**, Associate Justice, was born in Denver, Colorado, on 29 August 1967. He and his wife, Louise, have two daughters. He received a B.A. from Columbia University, a J.D. from Harvard Law School, and a D.Phil. from Oxford University. He served as a law clerk to Judge David B Sentelle of the United States Court of Appeals for the District of Columbia Circuit, and as a law clerk to Justice Byron White and Justice Anthony M Kennedy of the Supreme Court of the United States. From 1995 to 2005, he was in private practice, and from 2005 to 2006 he was Principal Deputy Associate Attorney General at the US Department of Justice. Gorsuch was appointed to the United States Court of Appeals for the Tenth Circuit in 2006. He served on the Standing Committee on Rules for Practice and Procedure of the US Judicial Conference, and as chairman of the Advisory Committee on Rules of Appellate Procedure. He taught at the University of Colorado Law School. President Donald J Trump nominated him as an Associate Justice of the Supreme Court, and he took his seat on 10 April 2017.

**Woodrow Hartzog** is a Professor of Law and Class of 1960 Scholar at Boston University School of Law. He is also a Faculty Associate at the Berkman Klein Center for Internet & Society at Harvard University, a Non-resident Fellow at The Cordell Institute for Policy in Medicine & Law at Washington University, and an Affiliate Scholar at the Center for Internet and Society at Stanford Law School. Hartzog is the author of *Privacy's Blueprint: The Battle to Control the Design of New Technologies*, published in 2018 by Harvard University Press, and the co-author of *Breached! Why Data Security Law Fails and How to Improve It*, published in 2022 by Oxford University Press.

**Paul de Hert** is a Professor at the Vrije Universiteit Brussels (VUB), where he holds the Chair of International, European and Belgian Criminal Law. He is also Associate Professor teaching Privacy and Data Protection at Tilburg University (TILT). He was Director of the research group Law Science Technology & Society (LSTS) at the Vrije Universiteit Brussels. He is now Director of the Department of Interdisciplinary Studies of Law and Director of the research group on Fundamental Rights and Constitutionalism (FRC). Paul de Hert's work addresses problems in the area of privacy and technology, human rights, and criminal law. His publications include books such as *Data Protection and Privacy In Transitional Times* (Matsumi, de Hert et al., Hart Publishing 2023). A human rights approach combined with a concern for theory is the common denominator of all his work. De Hert is series editor of the *Computers, Privacy and Data Protection* series and board member of several Belgian, Dutch and other international scientific journals, such as *Computer Law & Security Review*.

**Nikolaus Marsch** has held the Chair of German and European Public Law and Comparative Law at Saarland University since 2019; he was previously Director of the Institute for Business and Information Law at the Karlsruhe Institute of Technology

(KIT) and a research assistant at the Institute for Media and Information Law at the University of Freiburg. Nikolaus Marsch is the editor of a commentary on the GDPR and the German Federal Data Protection Act and the author of a monograph on the fundamental right to data protection in the EU Charter of Fundamental Rights. In addition to data protection law and media law, his main research interests lie in German-French comparative law and administrative court procedural law.

**Johannes Masing** has been Professor of Law at the University of Freiburg since 2007. He served as a justice of the German Federal Constitutional Court from 2008 to 2020. From 1998 to 2007, he was a Professor in Augsburg. Before, he clerked at the German Federal Constitutional Court from 1992 to 1996. He studied law, philosophy, and piano in Freiburg (habilitation in 1997, doctoral exam in 1996, law exams in 1989 and 1985; piano degrees in 1986 and 1983). Born in 1959, he grew up in Hamburg. Today, his research focuses on constitutional law, in particular from a transnational and comparative perspective. He has been a visiting scholar at Michigan Law School, Ann Arbor, Pennsylvania Law School, Philadelphia (US), the Jagellonian University, Krakow (Poland), and several times at Paris I, II and Lyon III (France). Masing was awarded the Prix Gay Lussac-Humboldt in 2008. He is a member of the Academia Europaea. In 2020, he was recognised with the Grand Cross of the Order of Merit of the Federal Republic of Germany. The University Jean Moulin (Lyon III) awarded him an honorary doctorate in 2022.

**Tobias Matzner** is Professor for Digital Cultures at Paderborn University in Germany. He studied computer science and philosophy in Karlsruhe, Rome, and Berlin and holds a PhD in philosophy from the Karlsruhe Institute of Technology. Before joining Paderborn University, he worked at the International Centre for Ethics in the Sciences and Humanities in Tübingen and as a Feodor Lynen Fellow at the New School for Social Research in New York. His research is located at the intersection of theories of technology and the digital, as well as political thought and critical theories. Recent publications include the monograph *Algorithms: Technology, Culture, Politics* (Routledge 2024), and he is one of the editors of the *Routledge Handbook of Political Phenomenology* (Routledge 2024).

**Helen Nissenbaum** is the Andrew H. and Ann R. Tisch Professor of Information Science and the founding director of the Digital Life Initiative at Cornell Tech. Her research spans issues of bias, trust, security, autonomy, and accountability in digital systems, most notably, privacy as contextual integrity. Professor Nissenbaum's publications include the books *Obfuscation: A User's Guide for Privacy and Protest*, with Finn Brunton (MIT Press, 2015) and *Privacy in Context: Technology, Policy, and the Integrity of Social Life* (Stanford, 2010). These, along with numerous research articles, have been translated into seven languages. Professor Nissenbaum received the 2014 Barwise Prize from the American Philosophical Association and the IACAP Covey Award for computing, ethics, and philosophy. She has also contributed to privacy-enhancing free software, such as TrackMeNot (designed to prevent the profiling of web search histories) and AdNauseam (designed to counter profiling based on ad clicks).

**Elisa Orrù** is a Senior Researcher at the Max Planck Institute for the Study of Crime, Security and Law and Associate Professor at the University of Freiburg. She holds a

Doctorate in law from the University of Pisa and habilitated in philosophy at the University of Freiburg. Previous positions include research fellow at the Max Planck Institute for Comparative Public Law and International Law in Heidelberg and at the Centre for Human Values at Princeton University. Her research focuses on digitalisation, privacy and data protection as well as data ethics and the ethics of artificial intelligence. Her publications include the monograph *Legitimität, Sicherheit, Autonomie: eine philosophische Analyse der EU-Sicherheitspolitik im Kontext der Digitalisierung* (Legitimacy, security, autonomy: a philosophical analysis of EU security policy in the context of digitalisation), published by Nomos in 2021 and the co-edited volume *Rethinking Surveillance and Control. Beyond the 'Security vs. Privacy' Debate* (2017).

**Maria Grazia Porcedda** is Associate Professor in Information Technology Law and a Fellow of Trinity College Dublin, Ireland. She carries out research on cybercrime, cybersecurity, data protection, privacy, surveillance, and systemic factors that shape IT law. Her monograph *Cybersecurity, Privacy and Data Protection in EU Law* (Hart Publishing, 2023) is the first major work on this topic. Porcedda is a collaborator with the SFI ADAPT Centre, a member of the European Data Protection Board's support pool of experts and serves on VIGILANT's ethical advisory board. She trained at the EDPS and the OECD and previously worked at the University of Leeds, the European University Institute (where she gained her PhD) and the University of Namur.

**Ralf Poscher** is Director of the Department of Public Law at the Max Planck Institute for the Study of Crime, Security and Law in Freiburg and Honorary Professor at the University of Freiburg. From 2009 to 2019, he held the Chair of Public Law and Legal Philosophy at the University of Freiburg. He has been a research fellow at the European University Institute, held guest professorships at the universities of Osaka, Seoul, Lyon, Paris II, Rome III, and was a member of the Institute for Advanced Study in Princeton from 2007 to 2008. His research focuses on public security law, fundamental rights, and legal theory. His publications in English include a volume on vagueness and law, a series of articles on legal hermeneutics, and publications on constitutional law, including the handbook *Constitutional Law in Germany* and articles on the right to data protection. He headed the *Periodic Surveillance Barometer for Germany* project, which aims to identify and quantify the cumulative impact on privacy of various surveillance activities undertaken by security and prosecution agencies.

**Beate Rössler** is Professor of Philosophy at the University of Amsterdam. She formerly taught philosophy at Leiden University, the Free University, Berlin, and at the University of Bremen. She had fellowships and visiting professorships at the Institute for Advanced Study (*Wissenschaftskolleg*) in Berlin, at the Center for Agency, Value, and Ethics at Macquarie University, Sydney, at the University of Melbourne Law School, and at New York University. She is a co-editor of the *European Journal of Philosophy* and a member of various advisory boards, among them the International Scientific Board of the Institute for Social Research. Rössler is a member of the Göttinger Akademie der Wissenschaften, of the European Academy, and of the American Academy of Arts and Sciences. She has published widely on topics in ethics, social and political philosophy, including *The Value of Privacy*, Polity 2004. Her most recent book is *Autonomy. An Essay on the Life Well Lived* (2022 with Polity).

**Neil Richards** holds the Koch Distinguished Professorship at Washington University School of Law, where he co-directs the Cordell Institute for Policy in Medicine and Law. He is also an affiliate scholar with the Stanford Center for Internet and Society and the Yale Information Society Project, a Fellow at the Center for Democracy and Technology, and a consultant and expert in privacy cases. Professor Richards serves on the board of the Future of Privacy Forum and is a member of the American Law Institute. He writes, teaches, and lectures about the regulation of the technologies powered by human information that are revolutionising our society. He is the author of *Why Privacy Matters* (Oxford University Press, 2022) and *Intellectual Privacy* (Oxford University Press, 2015). His award-winning writings on privacy and civil liberties have appeared in a wide variety of media, from the *Harvard Law Review* and the *Yale Law Journal* to *The Guardian*, *WIRED*, and *Slate*.

Judge **Timothy Tymkovich**, of Denver, Colorado, was nominated to the Tenth Circuit Court of Appeals by President George W Bush and confirmed in April 2003. Since he has been on the Court, he has served as Chief Circuit Judge, 2015–22; Chair of the US Judicial Conference's Committee on Judicial Resources, 2011–15; the Judicial Conference Workplace Conduct Working Group; Cybersecurity Task Force; Chair of the US Judicial Conference's Committee on Judicial Conduct and Disability, 2025–28; and the Foreign Intelligence Surveillance Court of Review since November 2023. He previously taught Election Law at the University of Colorado School of Law. He is a member of the Doyle Inn of Court, the American Law Institute, and the International Society of Barristers. Judge Tymkovich also represented the United States in four judicial education programs in Ukraine prior to the Russian invasion in 2022.

# Data Protection and Privacy: Digitalisation, Power, and the Transatlantic Divide

RALF POSCHER AND ELISA ORRÙ

This book is devoted to exploring the concepts of data protection and privacy. It addresses the fundamental questions of what is meant by the concepts of privacy, data protection, and the right to informational self-determination, and what values, goods, or interests they are purported to protect. To answer these questions, the book draws on philosophy, legal theory, and case law, providing an in-depth analysis of philosophical understandings as well as United States, European, and German jurisprudence.

135 years after the first legal definition of privacy by Samuel Warren and Louis Brandeis as 'the right to be left alone'[1] and 50 years after Judith Jarvis Thomson's radical critique of that right,[2] it has become more urgent than ever to reflect on the meaning of privacy and reaffirm the importance of the family rights associated with it. At the heart of Thomson's irritation was the ambiguity surrounding common understandings of the right to privacy. She observed that privacy seemed to refer to many different rights and that a violation of privacy could always be explained as a violation of other rights: 'The wrongness of every violation of the right to privacy can be explained without ever once mentioning it.'[3] In the interest of clarity, Thomson argued, we should abandon the concept of privacy as a separate right and instead focus on the other rights that are directly violated. Today, we can consider ourselves fortunate that we have not abandoned the protection of a specific right to privacy. Thomson's assertion that privacy means many different – and often disparate – things remains true, however, and can be extended to the right to data protection. This book analyses this complexity of meanings and conceptualisations. However, rather than seeing the different meanings of privacy and data protection as a shortcoming to be overcome by bringing them under a single overarching taxonomy, we aim to highlight the richness of these multifaceted concepts. Building on the expertise of distinguished academics and judges, past and

[1] SD Warren and LD Brandeis, 'The Right to Privacy' (1890) 4 *Harvard Law Review*, reprinted as 'The Right to Privacy [the Implicit Made Explicit]' in FD Schoeman (ed), *Philosophical Dimensions of Privacy: An Anthology* (Cambridge, Cambridge University Press, 1984) 75–103.

[2] JJ Thomson, 'The Right to Privacy' (1975) 4 *Philosophy & Public Affairs* 295–314.

[3] ibid 133.

present, this book offers unique insights on leading conceptions of privacy and data protection.

While our interest is primarily conceptual, understanding the real-world implications of privacy and data protection is also paramount. The relationship between the European Union (EU) and the United States (US), for instance, has been marked by deep disagreement over data protection and privacy law, with very practical consequences for the exchange of data. In 2015, the Court of Justice of the European Union (CJEU) first invalidated the Safe Harbor agreement between the EU and the US, which was designed to ensure adequate protection for data flowing from the EU to the US.[4] The CJEU found that it did not in fact ensure an adequate level of protection, with the result that personal data was no longer allowed to flow from the EU to the US. Safe Harbor was quickly replaced by Privacy Shield, which was again challenged before the CJEU and annulled in the 2020 *Schrems II* decision,[5] once again leaving institutions and companies scrambling to regulate the cross-border transfer of data. For the time being, the new EU–US Data Privacy Framework is in place; it was approved by the European Commission in July 2023, thus allowing the transfer of personal data from the EU to the US on the basis of Article 45 of the EU's General Data Protection Regulation (GDPR).[6] However, the validity of this new transatlantic framework is being questioned by critical voices within the EU.[7] More dramatically still, the rise of authoritarian and nationalist trends in both the EU and the US increasingly calls into question the effective protection of fundamental rights in general and of privacy and data protection in particular.

Some of the difficulties involved in the EU and the US reaching a consensus on data protection are likely rooted in their different legal cultures. The EU's approach to data protection regulation follows the continental tradition of systematic, wide-ranging codifications, such as the GDPR, which provides a comprehensive approach to regulating present and future matters of data protection across the board. This approach contrasts sharply with the common law tradition in the US, which is based on a more reactive or case-by-case approach to the law – waiting for problems to arise and then addressing them through judicial decisions rather than anticipating and proactively setting a system of rules in place.

Both the EU and the US have a complex web of legal instruments for privacy and data protection, spanning constitutional law, legislation, and judicial interpretations. These different approaches result in divergent codification and legal interpretations in the US and in Europe. Several chapters of this book explore one or more of these levels of regulation, examining and discussing their complexity. While detailed analyses and comparisons can be found therein, it is useful to recall a few fundamental differences

[4] Case C-362/14 *Maximillian Schrems v Data Protection Commissioner* ECLI:EU:C:2015:650.

[5] Case C-311/18 *Data Protection Commissioner v Facebook Ireland Limited and Maximillian Schrems* ECLI:EU:C:2020:559.

[6] Regulation (EU) 2016/679 of the European Parliament and of the Council of 27 April 2016 on the protection of natural persons with regard to the processing of personal data and on the free movement of such data, and repealing Directive 95/46/EC (General Data Protection Regulation) [2016] OJ L119/1.

[7] See European Parliament, Procedure File: 2023/2501(RSP) *Legislative Observatory* oeil.secure.europarl.europa.eu and 'European Commission gives EU-US data transfers third round at CJEU' (Noyb, 10.06.2023), noyb.eu/en/european-commission-gives-eu-us-data-transfers-third-round-cjeu.

between these legal systems at this juncture. Firstly, the level of constitutional protection varies considerably. While the US Constitution does not explicitly recognise a right to privacy or data protection, both the EU Charter of Fundamental Rights and the European Convention on Human Rights do so in Europe. However, this does not mean that the US Constitution does not allow for the protection of privacy rights. In fact, the Supreme Court of the US has derived constitutional protection of privacy from the Fourth and Fourteenth Amendments. The Fourth Amendment protects citizens against unreasonable searches of 'persons, houses, papers, and effects' by government authorities. The US Supreme Court's interpretations of this constitutional principle have given rise to the well-known 'reasonable expectation of privacy' doctrine. As several chapters in this volume also note, this doctrine has limitations of its own, however, and the Fourth Amendment only provides protection against government activities, thus excluding potential infringements of privacy perpetrated by private actors.[8] By contrast, the Fourteenth Amendment was used by the Supreme Court to establish a general right to informational privacy in the *Whalen v Roe* case.[9] However, it still remains unclear whether or not such a right is enshrined in US constitutional law.[10] In Europe, the protection of privacy and personal data is firmly anchored in constitutional law. Article 8 of the European Convention on Human Rights establishes the right to respect for private and family life. This right is also protected by Article 7 of the EU Charter of Fundamental Rights, which additionally recognises the protection of personal data as a fundamental right, as set out in Article 8. Finally, the German Basic Law protects the inviolability of the home (Article 13) as well as the privacy of correspondence and the confidentiality of postal and telecommunications communications (Article 10). There is no explicit right to the protection of personal data recognised by the German Basic Law. In its well-known Census Decisions of 1983, however, the German Federal Constitutional Court derived such a right from the constitutional principle of a general right to personality.[11] The right to informational self-determination is now a well-established constitutional principle in German law, but it remains controversial; ongoing debates on its nature, as evidenced by several contributions to this book, demonstrate the complexity and uncertainties surrounding this principle.

These different conceptualisations also influence interpretations of the relationship between privacy and data protection. Data protection and privacy can be understood either as separate rights or as two aspects of the same underlying right. Traditionally, in the law of the US, they are conflated into one right (the right to privacy), while in the EU they have been recognised as two distinct rights. The concept of the right to informational self-determination adds another layer of complexity to the picture by raising the question of its relationship to privacy and data protection.

[8] KN Peifer and PM Schwartz, 'Transatlantic Data Privacy Law' (2017) *The Georgetown Law Journal* 106, 133.

[9] 429 U.S. 589, 605–06 (1977).

[10] Peifer and Schwartz (n 8) 133; F Bignami, 'European versus American Liberty: A Comparative Privacy Analysis of Antiterrorism Data Mining' (2007) *Boston College Law Review* 48, 625. However, it should be noted that some US states grant constitutional privacy protection against infringements by private actors. For example, see the decision of the California Supreme Court in *Athletic Assn.*, 7 Cal. 4th 1 (1994).

[11] BVerfGE 65, 1 [1983] – *Volkszählungsgesetz.*

At the level of statutory law, some basic differences can also be identified between the US and European legal systems. The most fundamental difference likely lies in the sector-specific versus overarching approach to privacy legislation. The US's Privacy Protection Act of 1974 remains the primary legislative basis for government regulation of personal data processing.[12] However, the US has explicitly decided not to pursue omnibus privacy legislation for data processing in the private sector.[13] Consequently, a privacy law that protects individuals across the board is lacking in the US, and protection is instead granted by legislation targeting specific market sectors. Conversely, in Europe, national legislation such as the German Federal Data Protection Act of 1977 (BDSG) has long been in place, and the EU's GDPR, which superseded the Data Protection Directive in 2018, now provides a unified framework for data protection in the digital economy. At its core, the fundamental principle of data privacy law in the EU is that processing must be based on a legal ground, as set out in Article 6 of the GDPR. This means that, by default, any processing of personal data requires a legal basis to be permitted. In the US, by contrast, such a requirement does not exist, and the governing principle is that of the free flow of information. From this perspective, any processing is permitted unless explicitly prohibited by law.[14] This core divergence was efficaciously summarised by Anu Bradford, who contrasted the rights-based EU approach to the regulation of digital technologies with the market-based approach of the US.[15]

None of these approaches offers a one-size-fits-all solution, as each has its own strengths and weaknesses. First, the fact that data protection in the US is conceptualised on the idea of privacy seems to necessitate that all data protection issues be framed as privacy issues. This is not a straightforward task in all instances. One example is the collection of data by security agencies at public assemblies, which challenges traditional notions of privacy: after all, why should registering attendance at a public meeting be regarded as a matter of privacy, given that the participants intentionally want to be seen as engaging in public discourse? Second, in contrast, an advantage in Europe may be that it has better conceptual resources to deal with data protection issues than the US. By developing the right to informational self-determination, as the German Federal Constitutional Court has done, or by guaranteeing a separate right to data protection, as the EU Charter of Fundamental Rights does in its Article 8, the EU and its Member States' legal systems seem better equipped to acknowledge that data protection is not just about privacy. Moreover, the European approach treats every instance of data processing as a violation of a fundamental right to data protection. This has the advantage that all forms of personal data processing are subject to legal scrutiny, and, given the inferential powers of modern data processing, not distinguishing between different types of data or data processing may seem justified. The disadvantage, however, is that this approach has led to an excessively formalistic practice of data processing regulation and consent requirements that, at least sometimes,

[12] Privacy Act of 1974, 5 U.S.C. § 552a (2000 & Supp. IV. 2004).
[13] Peifer und Schwartz (n 8) 156.
[14] Peifer und Schwartz (n 8) 137.
[15] A Bradford, *Digital Empires. The Global Battle to Regulate Technology* (Oxford, Oxford University Press 2023).

border on the absurd. The neologism 'consent spam', for example, captures very well the experience of cookie policies when surfing the web in the EU. With its focus on rigorous compliance with regulations, the EU's overly formalistic approach to data protection seems to have lost sight of its underlying purpose of protecting individuals' rights. And it is easy to imagine that EU representatives may struggle to explain to their American counterparts the underlying substantive values and principles that drive their data protection policies.

Such reflections on the transatlantic relationship on privacy and data protection issues are an important thread that runs throughout the book. Throughout the chapters, a dialogue unfolds between Europe and the US, spanning constitutional understandings, philosophical debates, case law, and recent regulations.

A second thread concerns the challenges of digitalisation and artificial intelligence for data protection and privacy. There is a common understanding that, while data protection and privacy have always been contested concepts, recent technological developments are subjecting them to new and intense pressure. As technological developments have exponentially increased the ability of states and corporations to collect and process personal data and intrude into the most private spheres of life, there have been calls to both abandon privacy and data protection as outdated concepts and provide greater protection to privacy and personal data. Against the backdrop of this book, the discussion on digitalisation and artificial intelligence highlights the need for sharper – or new – conceptualisations.

The third thread that emerges throughout the book is a reflection on how privacy and data protection shape power relations within society and between individuals, corporations, and public authorities. Privacy and data protection are often conceptualised as individual rights – as such, they are a way of redistributing power among political and legal entities and contribute to limiting state power. But subjective rights can also enhance the protection of individuals from the handful of powerful corporations that almost completely control digital markets and services. Relying on the individual to enforce data protection and privacy, however, would be ineffective; as a matter of fact, public authorities are required to put in place structural mechanisms that enable individuals to make effective use of their privacy and data protection rights. At a more fundamental level, privacy considerations also shape power relations before they are formalised into law: the very definition of what is public and what is private is an exercise of power. Furthermore, the smoke shield of 'privacy' can be used to obscure unjust and oppressive practices, including systemic injustices and human rights abuses, blurring the lines between legitimate and non-legitimate uses of power.

Each of the contributions collected in this book considers several aspects of the three aforementioned thematic threads: (1) reflections on the transatlantic relationship on privacy and data protection issues, (2) the challenges of digitalisation for data protection and privacy, and (3) a reflection on how privacy and data protection shape power relations. This thematic overlap did not lend itself to the allocation of individual chapters to a specific topic. Nonetheless, we have organised the chapters into five sections, each presenting a broad thematic focus related to one of the three threads. The first two sections address fundamental questions about the meaning of privacy and data protection (Part I) and how these are codified and interpreted in constitutional law

(Part II). These two sections provide a foundation for understanding the deeper origins of controversies and convergences surrounding privacy and data protection on both sides of the Atlantic and thus contribute to the first thematic thread. Part III connects the theoretical and constitutional discussions of the first two sections with an examination of recent legislation that effectively intertwines all three thematic threads of the book. The regulation of transatlantic digital markets indeed involves issues relating to the relationship between the EU and the US, power imbalances between technology companies and users, and the specific challenges posed by digitalisation. Part IV focuses on power relations and the role of privacy and data protection in shaping them, thus contributing specifically to the development of the third thematic thread. Finally, Part V returns to the themes introduced in Part I by discussing the fundamental importance of privacy and data protection for related values, such as the integrity of social life, individual autonomy, and personal freedom – with a focus on digital technologies (second thread) and power distribution in society (third thread). Beyond this overall structuring, the topics are interconnected and intersect throughout the book, as the summaries of the individual chapters below illustrate.

Part I is a conceptual exploration of the nature of privacy and data protection rights and the interests they seek to protect. Anita Allen's opening chapter addresses fundamental questions relating to theoretical and practical approaches to these rights. The main thrust of her contribution is an analysis of the very usefulness of defining privacy at the intersection of philosophy, legal theory, and societal implications. After reviewing widely used definitions of privacy, namely control and restricted access (the latter the one once put forward[16] and still favoured by the author), she concludes that philosophers and legal theorists need to accept that privacy is an inherently contested concept. Rather than either criticising privacy for being a vague concept or indulging in abstract definitional disputes, Allen argues that theorists should engage in 'critical definitional facilitation': a process of making explicit the deeper values whose protection is at stake when people assert a claim to 'privacy', and thereby also supporting those claims against critiques of vagueness that ultimately seek to undermine more fundamental claims to justice, equal participation, and freedom. Against this background, Allen concludes by assessing contemporary claims by African Americans and other groups in the US who frame privacy as a 'civil right'.

Marion Albers, in the second chapter, aims to identify and conceptualise the protected interests in data protection law and the complex bundle of rights it safeguards, including privacy, data protection, and informational self-determination. She unravels the complex subject matter of data protection law by differentiating between the concepts of data, information, knowledge and processing. Albers proposes a multi-layered approach to data protection that requires sophisticated regulation, takes into account the specific challenges posed by digital technologies, and allows data protection law to be productively combined with data and information law. At its core, and despite its name, data protection law does not protect 'data' but aims to protect individuals and, by extension, broader principles such as democracy. Data protection, Albers argues, is the right of individuals to the protection of personal data concerning them

[16] A Allen, *Uneasy Access: Privacy for Women in a Free Society* (Totowa, Roman and Littlefield, 1988).

and therefore requires regulation that imposes affirmative obligations on the public authorities to make data protection effective.

Johannes Masing offers a nuanced commentary on Albers' transversal analysis of different legal systems through the lens of German constitutional law. He observes that German case law already satisfies, albeit often only implicitly, two of Albers' key criteria: the distinction between data and information, and a multi-layered, multi-dimensional, multifaceted, and multifarious approach to data protection. In contrast to Albers' emphasis on shifting towards a more structural approach, Masing stresses the importance of maintaining a strong focus on individual protection in data protection law. In his view, the right to data protection is similar to all other fundamental rights in that it serves individual freedom, understood as the freedom to develop one's personality.

The fundamental question of which specific interests are protected by data protection is also at the centre of Ralf Poscher's contribution. Based on an analysis of German and European case law, Poscher argues that data protection does not protect against actual violations, but rather against abstract dangers that could materialise and lead to violations of other fundamental rights, such as freedom of expression and freedom of association. Data protection is therefore better understood as a preventive reinforcement of other rights and freedoms guaranteed by the constitution. Poscher concludes by fleshing out his understanding of data protection as a preemptive right that anticipates and prevents potential harms and exploring its legal and practical implications for information technologies and AI-driven data processing.

Part II continues the reflection on the nature and the protected interests in privacy and data protection law by connecting theoretical insights to constitutional decisions in Germany and the US, as well as to the codification of these rights in European law(s). Drawing on landmark decisions of the German Federal Constitutional Court, Gabriele Britz examines the material interests protected by the right to informational self-determination. She identifies freedom of action and communication, especially in the political sphere, as the primary material goods targeted by data protection law. Another layer of protection serves to prevent the misuse of collected data, the development of the individual's personality, the individual's ability to shape other people's perceptions of him or her as well as one's own self-perception, and protection against discrimination. The 1983 decision of the German Federal Constitutional Court,[17] in which the right to informational self-determination was first articulated, is still highly influential at the European level to this day. However, Britz sees major future developments in general data protection more likely taking place at the European level than at the national level.

Gloria González Fuster elaborates on the complex and diverse roots of European data protection law. She demonstrates that European data protection law has been influenced by multiple national perspectives, including but not restricted to German doctrine. She also shows that EU data protection law was significantly shaped by interactions with and influences from the US during the formative period of the 1970s and 1980s. This complex genesis is also at the root of common misconceptions about

[17] BVerfGE 65, 1 [1983] – *Volkszählungsgesetz.*

European data protection law, especially those centred on the relationship between data protection and privacy. Crucially, in order to be properly conceptualised, Gonzalez Fuster argues that data protection must be understood as a concept distinct from privacy, and any attempt to explain data protection in comparison or opposition to privacy can be problematic, as it risks mischaracterising both concepts.

The second half of Part II focuses on the US's constitutional framing of the right to privacy, which also encompasses data protection. Neil Gorsuch's 2018 dissent in *Carpenter v United States*,[18] reprinted in this book, reviews landmark Supreme Court decisions and argues for a narrow interpretation of the Fourth Amendment to the US Constitution. The US's standard constitutional understanding is based on the 'reasonable expectation of privacy' test, which the dissent argues is flawed due to its overreliance on judicial discretion and subjective interpretation. An approach that subsumes privacy rights under a property-like understanding would, according to Gorsuch, allow for greater protection of personal information.

Timothy Tymkovich and Theodore R. Furchtgott also defend a 'trespass-driven' understanding of privacy. They review recent US Supreme Court cases that deal with new search methods supported by digital technologies. Because of their intrusiveness, these new methods challenge previous mechanisms for constraining government activity. By examining the text and history of the Fourth Amendment, the authors provide a systemic basis for analysing the Supreme Court's assessment of government intrusion in the Internet age. This reading allows digital information to be viewed as analogous to private papers, which have historically been protected from government surveillance. In an era of pervasive digital surveillance, the authors conclude that personal information is better protected from government surveillance by a narrow reading of the Fourth Amendment.

Part III revisits the theme of transatlantic influences between EU and US law by assessing EU privacy and digital law in the context of reciprocal digital markets. This part investigates the specific EU approach taken in recent legislation, such as the GDPR and the EU Artificial Intelligence Act (AI Act)[19] – aimed at enhancing trust – and scrutinises the role of digital service providers and technology (tech) companies – usually based in the US – within the EU regulatory framework. Maria Grazia Porcedda highlights the powerful position afforded to United States corporations by the complex regulatory ecosystem of EU data protection law. This influence stems from both the complex evolution of European data protection law and the specific design of the GDPR, which allocates co- or meta-regulatory tasks to technology developers and delegates regulatory power to standardisation mechanisms. Porcedda concludes that tech companies wield considerable influence over individuals' personal data and online activities (hence, their digital rights), which necessitates greater involvement on the part of EU regulators in the development of digital technology and infrastructure.

[18] *Carpenter v United States*, 585 US 296 (2018).

[19] Regulation (EU) 2024/1689 of the European Parliament and of the Council of 13 June 2024 laying down harmonised rules on artificial intelligence and amending Regulations (EC) No 300/2008, (EU) No 167/2013, (EU) No 168/2013, (EU) 2018/858, (EU) 2018/1139 and (EU) 2019/2144 and Directives 2014/90/EU, (EU) 2016/797 and (EU) 2020/1828 (Artificial Intelligence Act) [2024] OJ L2024/1689.

Johannes Eichenhofer examines the notion of trust, as encapsulated in EU privacy and digital law, as a way of rebalancing these power relations. Already central to the US doctrine of 'reasonable expectation of privacy', the notion of trust has come to the fore in recent European privacy legislation, including the GDPR and the AI Act. By embracing the trust paradigm, Eichenhofer proposes a new conceptualisation of privacy, shifting from a focus on the individual to a more relational perspective. In the digital world, the dependence of individuals on others and on the companies that provide digital services makes them particularly vulnerable; individuals are particularly at a disadvantage when interacting with tech companies due to the power imbalance between them. Under these conditions, Eichenhofer sees the main goal of privacy law as preserving users' trust in the face of the opaque conditions of data processing on the Internet.

Neil Richards, Woodrow Hartzog, Claire Boine, and Lea Despotis, in their chapter, share with Eichenhofer the understanding that most of the recent EU digital regulation is aimed at enhancing trust. They build on earlier work by Richards and Hartzog,[20] according to which the essence of the value of privacy lies in protecting relationships of trust and ensuring that data sharing and data processing are carried out in accordance with these relationships. However, they are critical of the effectiveness of the current EU effort. In their view, EU regulation takes an overly negative approach; it is aimed at mitigating harm rather than building positive relationships between users and tech companies. In order to support positive obligations in the digital environment, the authors suggest that EU digital law should be based on four principles drawn from fiduciary law: discretion, honesty, protection, and loyalty.

Power relations are also at the centre of the contributions in Part IV of this book. In this part, though, the main concern shifts from the power imbalances between tech companies and individuals to the relationship between the public sphere (and powers) and its relationship to the private. Introducing the concepts of opacity, transparency, and obscurity, Part IV explores the ways in which privacy and data protection can shield individuals from public power as well as the power dynamics between what is private and what is public – and thus subject to public scrutiny. Paul de Hert's contribution interprets privacy rights as tools of 'opacity', in contrast to data protection rights, which are interpreted as tools of 'transparency'. The former aims to make individuals opaque to state power; the latter structurally aims to make power transparent by regulating how personal data can be legitimately processed and by creating accountability mechanisms. Data protection is thus seen as an integral part of due process rights, which reinforce the rule of law by ensuring throughput legitimacy and focusing on distinctive criteria such as transparency and accountability.

In a similar vein, Nikolaus Marsch contends that the individualistic framing of the right to data protection is primarily due to procedural rather than substantive issues. Based on a review of key decisions of the European Court of Human Rights (ECtHR), he argues that fundamental rights to data protection can be understood as a means of controlling the power of the digital state. This fundamentally calls for a legal basis for

[20] N Richards and W Hartzog, 'Taking Trust Seriously in Privacy Law' (2015) 19 *Stanford Technology Law Review* 19 431.

any data processing activity on the part of the state, the main aim being to regulate and limit such processing; individuals who assert their privacy rights are not so much defending their sphere of freedom as they are defending the rule of law. Data protection law, according to Marsch, can essentially be interpreted as a kind of digital separation of powers within the state's administration.

While limiting public power is a key aspect of data protection law, privacy and data protection are about more than merely shielding the private sphere from public intrusion. Woodrow Hartzog's chapter puts forth that it would be counterproductive and misleading to see personal information as needing protection only when not in the public domain. He addresses two misconceptions: The first is that 'public information' is an established and objective concept; in fact, 'public' is not clearly defined either in theory or in law, and it is used in an inconsistent and prescriptive manner. The second misconception stems from a failure to recognise that there are zones of obscurity even in the public sphere; information in the public sphere can still be obscure if there are high transaction costs involved in finding or understanding it. The legal framework, Hartzog argues, should recognise and better protect obscurity as a valuable form of privacy.

Beate Rössler enriches the reflections on power imbalance, the public sphere, and the private sphere by pointing out that drawing the boundaries of privacy is itself a matter of public concern and a way of exercising power. Drawing on her previous work and the identification of three different spheres of privacy (decisional, informational, and local),[21] she reflects on 'repressive privacy' practices and the use of the 'woke' rhetoric as a setback to the emancipatory attempt to make previously private aspects of individuals' lives public. Struggles for liberation from oppressive and discriminatory practices, Rössler observes, are also a way of bringing supposedly 'private' issues into the public sphere. Drawing on feminist philosophy and discourses of privacy on the Internet, Rössler further discusses how our social understanding of the private sphere has changed in the wake of societal debates, making privacy part of the dynamic between power and liberation in the Internet age.

Finally, Part V reflects on the value of privacy and data protection in society and on the relationship between privacy, autonomy, and freedom. The contributions in this part share a common understanding of privacy as a value deeply rooted in society. They do not dissociate privacy from the individual, but conceive of human subjects as fundamentally socially embedded and interdependent beings. From this vantage point, Helen Nissenbaum and Severin Engelmann build on Nissenbaum's theory of privacy as contextual integrity[22] to address the challenges posed by AI-driven inference techniques. They refute privacy nihilism, ie, the allegation that stricter protection of sensitive data is pointless because AI tools can supposedly infer sensitive information from any type of data. The authors contend that it is indeed still expedient to protect privacy from the inferential power of AI, but to succeed, protection strategies must focus not only on the type of data, but also on the actors sharing the data and the purposes for which they are used.

[21] B Rössler, *The Value of Privacy* (Cambridge, Polity Press, 2005).
[22] HF Nissenbaum, *Privacy in Context: Technology, Policy, and the Integrity of Social Life* (Stanford, Stanford Law Books, 2010).

Building on the idea of the integrity of social contexts, Elisa Orrù questions whether this idea can shed new light on the relationship between privacy and individual autonomy. Autonomy is often seen as the most fundamental value that privacy seeks to protect. However, it has been noted that legal understandings of privacy often rely on an oversimplified account of the autonomous 'self'. In order to make sense of the interplay between individuals' self-relatedness and sociality, Orrù proposes a contextual conception of autonomy that builds on socio-relational understandings of personal autonomy. According to this understanding, autonomy is not in absolute opposition to heteronomous influences. Rather, it can be conceptualised as a net of norms that distinguish legitimate from illegitimate heteronomous influences in particular social contexts. This interpretation also makes it possible to identify the specificity of the challenges that digitalisation and AI pose to autonomy, namely the blurring of social contexts that were previously relatively separate.

Tobias Matzner, in the concluding chapter, also focuses on the complex relationship between privacy and autonomy, but he rejects the idea that the value of privacy must be understood solely in relation to its contribution to autonomy. Engaging with critiques of privacy and autonomy, Matzner acknowledges the ambivalence and shortcomings of both concepts and instead posits that the emphasis on autonomy overly restricts the scope of what makes privacy worth protecting. Rather than reworking the concept of autonomy to incorporate these limitations, as recent relational approaches to autonomy have attempted to do, Matzner argues that the value of privacy is better understood as a mechanism for moderating heteronomous influences. Privacy essentially safeguards the possibility for change – regardless of whether that change is autonomously directed or not. The value of privacy can thus be defended independently of the stance taken on autonomy.

The contributions that comprise this book offer an in-depth reflection on the meaning and value of data protection and privacy in today's world. The book draws on a kaleidoscope of approaches, united in their search for answers to fundamental theoretical and practical questions. Still, the different conceptualisations collected here each retain their distinctiveness and are sometimes characterised by deep disagreement. As editors, we have not attempted to reduce this complexity, but rather believe that the existing divergence in the conceptualisation of privacy and data protection reveals the richness of these multifaceted concepts and that this diversity can ultimately refine our understanding and addressing of the challenges and controversies surrounding them. Firmly anchored in current legal and social developments, including technological advances and societal struggles, the book is intended to be a source of inspiration for all those who believe that the cause of privacy and data protection is worth advancing.

# PART I

# Privacy and Data Protection: The Value of Definitions and the Protected Goods

# 1

# Defining Away Our Privacy

ANITA L ALLEN

## I. Introduction

Privacy is imperilled. The protection of personal privacy reigns among the chief objectives of data protection. Privacy norms and rules include those that govern the flow of data and information – their collection, access, sharing, storage and security.[1] These norms and rules allocate social power among competing individuals, governments and businesses.[2] But what exactly is privacy? And do we need a definition? Technology developers have certainly not slowed their pace waiting around for academics to come up with the perfect one.

A category of definitions popular in the digital policy arena identifies privacy with control over personal information, and data privacy with data subjects' control over data.[3] Yet, as I describe below, for many years now and on a variety of conceptual, practical and moral grounds, scholars have grown critical of the popular definitions of privacy as information or data control.[4]

[1] See generally N Richards, *Why Privacy Matters* (Oxford, Oxford University Press, 2021). See also H Nissenbaum, *Privacy as Context* (Palo Alto, Stanford University Press, 2009).

[2] C Veliz, *Privacy is Power* (London, Penguin Random House, 2020).

[3] See C Fried, *An Anatomy of Values* (Cambridge, Harvard University Press, 1970) 140 ('Privacy … is the control we have over information about ourselves'); AF Westin, *Privacy and Freedom* (New York, Atheneum, 1967/1970) 7 (defining privacy as 'the claim of individuals, groups, or institutions to determine for themselves when, how, and to what extent information about them is communicated to others').

[4] For philosophical and legal criticism of control-based theories of privacy see, eg, C Veliz, *The Ethics of Privacy and Surveillance* (Oxford, Oxford University Press, 2024) 50–9; Richards (n 1) 90–100; B Lundgren, 'A Dilemma for Privacy as Control' (2020) 24 *The Journal of Ethics* 165–75; W Hartzog, *Privacy's Blueprint: the Battle to Control the Design of New Technologies* (Cambridge, Harvard University Press, 2018) 95–100; AE Waldman, *Privacy as Trust: Information Privacy for an Information Age* (Cambridge, Cambridge University Press, 2018) 29–33; K Macnish, 'Government Surveillance and Why Defining Privacy Matters in a Post-Snowden World' (2018) 35 *Journal of Applied Philosophy* 417, 418; D Solove, 'Introduction: Privacy, Self-Management and the Consent Dilemma' (2013) 126 *Harvard Law Review* 1880; PM Schwartz, 'Internet Privacy and the State' (2000) 32 *Connecticut Law Review* 815, 818–34. *Cf.* SA Elvy, 'Paying for Privacy and the Personal Data Economy' (2017) 117 *Columbia Law Review* 1369 (demonstrating that payment-for-data schemes offer inequitable and illusory control to internet users).

As Beate Rössler has observed, there are multiple histories of privacy discourse, with distinct such histories in Europe as compared to the US.[5] Definitional debates about privacy in the US date back to the 1970s and 1980s, before the digital era gave them special relevance. Those early debates were driven by concerns that included medical decision-making, abortion, research ethics, LGBTQ rights and wiretapping. I was among the earliest philosophers to consider and reject the privacy-as-control paradigm.[6] Nearly 40 years ago I argued that certain other definitions are more plausible than those equating privacy with control. Moreover, influenced by Israeli legal theorist Ruth Gavison and Swedish-American philosopher Sissela Bok, I contributed a defence of an alternative 'restricted access' account of privacy to the literature. My account characterised privacy as what I then termed an 'umbrella' concept encompassing various modes of inaccessibility to others' senses and devices, including seclusion, solitude, confidentiality, secrecy, anonymity, and reserve.[7]

Some philosophers in the US – and the UK – have continued to produce 1970s and 1980s-style definitional analysis.[8] However, my work on privacy has long shifted away from freestanding prescriptive definitional analysis aimed at dictating proper or clarifying usage supposedly to improve normative assessment of policy and practice and guide the law.[9] Some of my recent work questions whether scholars should continue to prescriptively define privacy at all;[10] who benefits from particular definitions of privacy and privacy laws;[11] and whether characterising privacy as a 'civil right' makes for better law.[12] In this chapter I knit together ideas advanced in my law and philosophy work over time to explain why I am not now tempted to revert to foregrounding purely philosophical debates over whether privacy should be defined in part or overall as information/data control,[13] despite the continued popularity of designating personal information and/or data control as the central point of data protection laws.

[5] B Rössler, *The Value of Privacy* (Cambridge, Polity Press, 2005) 3–4.

[6] AL Allen, *Uneasy Access: Privacy for Women in a Free Society* (Totowa, Roman and Littlefield, 1988) 1–35. See also Allen, 'Privacy-as-Data Control: Conceptual, Practical, and Moral Limits of the Paradigm' (2000) 32 *Connecticut Law Review* 861. Lundgren (n 4) 165–75 misattributes a data control theory to me, curiously citing Allen, 'Privacy-as-Data Control' in which I explicitly reject control-based theories, and seemingly unaware of my criticism of control-based theories in favour of restricted access theories in Allen, *Uneasy Access* ch 1.

[7] Allen, *Uneasy Access* (n 6) 1–35. Cf. R Gavison, 'Privacy and the Limits of the Law' (1980) 89 *Yale Law Journal* 421; S Bok, *Secrecy: On the Ethics of Concealment and Revelation* (New York, Vintage Books, 1983). Also influenced by Rössler (n 5) 8 (defining privacy as 'control of access' to something deemed private).

[8] See, eg, Veliz (n 4) 50–9. *Cf.* L Menges, 'Three Control Views on Privacy' (2022) 48 *Social Theory and Practice* 69, assessing three theories of privacy defined as data control. Defining privacy partly by reference to data control, see HT Tavani, 'Philosophical Theories of Privacy: Implications for an Adequate Online Privacy Policy' (2007) 38 *Metaphilosophy* 1–22. *Cf.* Rössler (n 5) 2–10.

[9] See eg, recent articles cited below n 10 and n 11, AL Allen, *Unpopular Privacy: What Must We Hide* (New York, Oxford University Press, 2011), challenging libertarian assumptions about privacy as choice; and AL Allen, *Why Privacy Isn't Everything: Feminist Reflections on Personal Accountability* (Totowa, Roman and Littlefield, 2003), arguing that some accountability for otherwise private life is commonplace and warranted.

[10] AL Allen, 'Privacy, Critical Definition, and Racial Justice' in E Lepore and L Anderson (eds), *Oxford Handbook of Applied Philosophy of Language* (Oxford, Oxford University Press, 2024).

[11] AL Allen, 'Dismantling the "Black Opticon": Privacy, Race Equity, and Online Data-Protection Reform' (2022) 131 *Yale Law Journal Forum* 907; AL Allen and J Rothman, 'Postmortem Privacy' (2024) 123 *Michigan Law Review* 285; AL Allen, 'Protecting One's Own Privacy in the Big Data Economy' (2016) 130 *Harvard Law Review Forum* 7.

[12] AL Allen and C Muhawe, 'Is Privacy Really a Civil Right' (2024) 40 *Berkeley Technology Law Review* 1.

[13] Foregrounding the definitional debates, see works cited above n 4.

## II. Privacy as Data Control

Some of the earliest definitional accounts of privacy in the US characterised it as 'control over information'.[14] Most of these accounts were intended as *general* accounts of privacy, not merely accounts of *information or data* privacy. Conceptualising privacy as control over information/data presupposes a population, perhaps mythical, empowered to control information/data about themselves in the interest of self-determination and autonomy. At the moment, the African American population of the US is certainly not such a population.[15] Nor are immigrants, refugees and asylum seekers within US borders.[16]

Since the emergence of the internet, there has been a keen interest in how to define the privacy at stake in digital technology contexts. Twenty-five years ago, from a legal perspective, Paul Schwartz observed with concern that just about everyone accepted the definition of privacy as control over information/data.[17] Like Schwartz before him, Neil Richards is sceptical about what he dubs the pervasive 'privacy-control paradigm', which 'conceives of privacy as a personal right to control the use of one's data' and 'seeks to place the individual at the center of decision-making about personal information use'.[18] Richards detects a ubiquitous 'lionisation' of control concepts that are embedded, for example, in the Fair Information Practice Principles, the US Privacy Act of 1974, the California Consumer Privacy Act of 2020, and the EU's GDPR and its official commentary.[19]

The control paradigm of 'staggering' consensus[20] that Paul Schwartz challenged at the turn of the twenty-first century – which was before the rise of social media platforms and algorithmic analytics – is even more clearly problematic today. In my year 2000 colloquy with Schwartz, I presented the paradigm as a set of three perspectives.[21] First, there is the thesis that the term 'privacy' means control (or rights of control) over the use of personal data or information; second, that the expression 'right to privacy' means the right or claim to control the use of personal data or information; and, third, that the central aim of privacy regulation should be promoting individuals' control (or rights of control) over personal data or information. The three theses are logically independent. A person who believes that 'privacy' means data control might also believe, with complete logical consistency, that privacy regulation should not have as its central aim promoting individuals' control over personal data or information. For example, one who embraces Beate Rössler's philosophical definition of privacy as the capacity to 'control the access to something' is not automatically committed to the belief that there should be government regulations that

[14] See Fried (n 3) 140; Westin) (n 3) 7. *Cf* Richards (n 1) 90; Rössler (n 5) 7, citing examples of control-based theories by American philosophers as well as lawyers.

[15] See Allen, 'Dismantling the "Black Opticon"' (n 11) 907.

[16] See Allen and Muhawe (n 12).

[17] Schwartz (n 4) 815, 818–34. See Allen, *Uneasy Access* (n 6) 8–34 *passim*, evaluating early control-based definitions of privacy and their competitors. *Cf.* PM Schwartz, 'Property, Privacy, and Personal Data' (2004) 117 *Harvard Law Review* 2056–128.

[18] Richards (n 1) 90–9.

[19] ibid.

[20] Schwartz (n 4) 820.

[21] For my invited assessment of Schwartz from which I herein liberally draw, see Allen, 'Privacy-as-Data Control' (n 6) 861–75.

allocate control of personal data to individuals.[22] Moreover, a person who believes that 'privacy' means data control and that 'the right to privacy' means the right to data control is not logically committed to the beliefs that there is or should be a right to privacy and that privacy regulation should aim at rationally optimising or otherwise promoting 'informational self-determination through individual stewardship of personal data'.[23]

By the year 2000 I was ready to outright reject the paradigm in the law, based on three categories of objections I labelled conceptual, practical and moral.[24] I will briefly repeat those objections, noting that Richards has elaborated similar objections to the control paradigm for a new generation with pertinent examples from contemporary trends and practices barely imaginable to me in 2000, arguing that control is 'overwhelming', 'illusory', and 'insufficient'.[25]

*Conceptual objections.* I first voiced philosophical objections to the privacy-control paradigm when I pointed to problems in Alan Westin's landmark 1967 book, *Privacy and Freedom.*[26] Westin offered several control-themed conceptualisations of privacy in the book, but the one that is most often quoted was: 'Privacy is the claim of individuals, groups, or institutions to determine for themselves when, how, and to what extent information about them is communicated to others.'[27] I argued that Westin's characterisation was too narrow.[28]

Information control as a 'general' definition of 'privacy' is indeed too narrow because it simply ignores common meanings. Privacy claims in opposition to government interference with personal medical decisions, such as the termination of pregnancy, a major concern for American women then and now, are about decisional autonomy, not only information control. Moreover, when Americans say they want privacy, they may be interested in conditions of solitude, repose, or intimacy rather than control over facts about themselves. Today it is clear that privacy-denominated claims in opposition to targeted oversurveillance of African Americans are less about control than freedom from discrimination and targeted exploitation.

A conceptual reason to reject definitions of information/data privacy as control is that control over personal information/data is neither necessary nor sufficient for states or conditions of privacy to obtain. Possessing control over personal information or data does not entail having privacy. The person in control of their data might elect to share personal information with others, and many do.[29] In fact, one of the reasons the control paradigm is so popular is that it allows the business sector to claim that notice and consent adequately address consumer privacy by enabling consumers to choose and, in that sense, control whether to keep or give up privacy. Philosophers

[22] Rössler (n 5) 8.

[23] Schwartz (n 4) 864. *Cf.* DN MacCormick, 'Privacy: A Problem of Definition?' (1974) 1 *British Journal of Law and Society* 75–8, distinguishing, in response to a famous report, the issue of what privacy means from the issue of whether the law ought to afford rights of privacy.

[24] Allen, 'Privacy-as-Data Control' (n 6) 865–872.

[25] Richards (n 1) 92–9. But see Rössler (n 5) 4–10, defining privacy in combined control and access terms in support of a general theory of its value.

[26] Allen, *Uneasy Access* (n 6) 8.

[27] Westin (n 3) 7.

[28] Allen, 'Privacy-as-Data Control' (n 6) 866.

[29] ibid 867.

debate whether privacy is having the choice or being in the existential condition. I have voted for the latter.[30]

I concede that 'control over information/data' (by some entity or technology or the other) describes one of the issues at play in policy debates about the digital economy. However, even for purposes of discussing issues tied to digital life, there are reasons to be wary of definitions of privacy that reduce it to data control, as further explained below. Moreover, a concept other than control may more adequately capture the sense of 'privacy' at issue in online and other digital economy contexts. Restricted access might do the trick or, as many would contend, contextual integrity.[31]

*Practical Objections.* A second category of objections is practical. These objections are especially resonant in view of near-ubiquitous smartphone and internet usage and black box AI, and are very widely discussed by legal scholars.[32] We are responsible for what we can control,[33] but there is much we cannot control.[34] As we browse the internet, use social media platforms, and transact online business, we disclose a great deal of information, sometimes knowingly, sometimes unknowingly. The privacy-control paradigm provides ideological support for notice and consent regimes, now widely rejected for overreliance on rituals of consent rather than genuinely informed consent. Opt-out consent regimes are especially dubious. It is pointless or merely symbolic to ascribe data or information control if it turns out that control does not obtain.

*Moral Objections.* A final category of objections is moral or ethical. Let us suppose that privacy is indeed the basis of a morally compelling human right. This is a widely accepted point of view, advanced philosophically, for example, by Beate Rössler, who links intrinsically valuable privacy to a robust brand of autonomy.[35] Ideally such rights would be protected by law. The control paradigm shades the reality that in some policy contexts it is morally wrong to insist on individual control over personal data, because people may want too little privacy or be indifferent to their privacy. In these contexts people could use data control attributed to them to give up forms of privacy vital to their objective interests, from a human rights or liberal democracy perspective.[36] Of equal concern is that individuals may share data in ways that are not compatible with the vital interests of others, including family members to whom they are ethically accountable or have moral duties,[37] or the interests of the greater society. Unless people want data privacy, neither government nor private sector policies aimed at individual data control and individual stewardship of personal information can ensure adequate

[30] Allen, *Unpopular Privacy* (n 9), challenging some libertarian assumptions about privacy as requiring choices.

[31] Allen, *Uneasy Access* (n 6), (defending a restricted definition); Nissenbaum (n 1) (defending a contextual integrity account of privacy as norms of data flow).

[32] See, eg, Waldman (n 4) 29–33; F Pasquale, *The Black Box Society: The Secret Algorithms that Control Money and Information* (Cambridge, Harvard University Press, 2015); Richards (n 1) 93–6; Solove (n 4) 1880; Hartzog (n 4) 95–100.

[33] AL Allen, 'An Ethical Duty to Protect One's Own Privacy?' (2013) 65 *Alabama Law Review 845.*

[34] *Cf.* Solove (n 4) 1880.

[35] Rössler (n 5) 3–4; Rössler, *Autonomy: An Essay on the Life Well-lived* (New York, John Wiley & Sons, 2021).

[36] Allen, *Unpopular Privacy* (n 9).

[37] Allen, *Why Privacy Isn't Everything* (n 9).

privacy. We must be open to the idea that personal privacy is a good, even for those who do not want it, and therefore that efforts should be made through education and nudging to alter preferences or even to 'coerce' privacy.[38] For these reasons neither privacy as such nor information/data privacy should be definitionally reduced to information/data control.

## III. Other Approaches to Definition

Rejecting the conceptualisation of privacy as data control does not mean we have no way to understand data privacy or no way to deploy data protection in its name. We are not left out in the cold. The rejection merely opens the door to other approaches.[39] These approaches may imply that our data protection laws purporting to protect privacy must do something more or different than giving consumers an array of putative 'choices' by means of which they putatively control their data. Our risks and consequences are opaque.

What are alternative approaches? Over the decades many philosophers have adopted some form of the account that defines privacy as conditions of restricted access to people and information about them. A recent book by Carissa Veliz seeks to marry the restricted access and control theories into what she terms a 'hybrid' theory, which she commends for addressing the privacy problems associated with new technology.[40] Understanding data privacy as a matter of restricting and restricted access to data, some of the restricting could be via controls placed in the hands of individuals (such as the ability to build a backyard fence), and other restrictions could result from the legitimate decisions of other parties and government (such as through laws prohibiting health care providers from revealing confidences stored in electronic medical records). As noted, in my early work I advanced a general-purpose definition of privacy as restricted access.[41] I no longer subscribe without qualification to my definition or to the project of definition but believe my definition was and is stronger than some.[42]

The general appeal of restricted access definitions is that they exploit a strong practical link between protecting privacy and physical and normative conditions regulating and preventing inaccessibility. 'Privacy' is commonly used to denote conditions of restricted access in the senses of seclusion, solitude, anonymity, confidentiality, secrecy, reserve, and modesty. My variant construing privacy as a neutral condition (not a value) enables varied and opposing normative assessments. But restricted access accounts have drawbacks. They do not put data subjects in the driver's seat as control definitions do. They do not inherently capture the intuition held by some that privacy typically refers to a positive value, something wanted. They do not inherently capture

[38] AL Allen, 'Coercing Privacy' (1999) 40 *William & Mary Law Review* 723.
[39] See, eg, B van der Sloot, *Privacy as Virtue: Moving Beyond the Individual in the Age of Big Data*, Human Rights Research Series 81 (Cambridge, Intersentia, 2017) 29.
[40] Veliz (n 4) 50–9.
[41] Allen, *Uneasy Access* (n 6) 1–35.
[42] ibid.

the intuition that privacy's meaning relates to intimacy. They do not easily capture 'decisional' senses of privacy as freedom from government interference, a particularly significant drawback for me.

Prominent US-based privacy law scholars recommend other approaches to characterising privacy, and I would cite Ari Waldman's work on trust in this regard,[43] along with work by Neil Richards and Woodrow Hartzog.[44] Helen Nissenbaum's approach, characterising privacy in terms of contextual integrity, has been highly influential, drawing attention to context-specific norms of appropriateness and distribution in data flow rather than individual control of data. In her theory, a privacy violation occurs when information is shared or accessed in a way that violates the established norms of a context. This breach might occur should an unauthorised person access or misuse personal information. Contextual integrity points to the need to develop privacy policies and laws that are sensitive to the specific needs and norms of different circumstances.

Philosophical debates about the meaning of privacy will doubtless continue as new generations of scholars seek to place themselves in conversation with older generations by adopting, tweaking, or rejecting their conceptualisations. We must take care, however, not to think of ourselves as (merely) a community of definitional sophisticates, searching for a universally embraceable definition of privacy devised through incremental critiques and improvements of the old ones. There is simply too much variation in the use and meaning of the term 'privacy' in English and other languages; variation in the purposes for undertaking the task of definition; and variation in approaches to the task of definition to expect definitional consensus.[45] In my most recent work, I propose and demonstrate a very different way of thinking about the task of definition, being cognisant of politics and aiming at justice facilitation.

## IV. Something New – Critical Definitional Facilitation

Logically prior to the question of *how* to define privacy is the question of *whether* to define it. Moreover, as we consider whether and how to define privacy, we should also concern ourselves with *who stands to benefit* from which definitions and approaches to definition. I broached these questions long ago, briefly pointing to 'ways in which the choice of a theoretical definition can have practical import'.[46]

*Whether to Define Privacy*. Today, prescriptive definitional accounts of privacy dictating privacy's meaning proliferate, as they did in the 1970s for an earlier generation.[47] Some are linked to advocacy for better regulation of consumer and citizen data in the digital economy, but few are focused on the profound costs of digital life for

[43] Waldman (n 4) 29–33.
[44] Richards (n 1) 90–100; Hartzog (n 4) 95–100.
[45] I elaborate these three kinds of variation in Allen, *Uneasy Access* (n 6) 5–10.
[46] ibid 4.
[47] See, eg, Veliz (n 4), defending a 'hybrid' control and restricted access definition of privacy, with practical aims.

people in historically marginalised groups.[48] There is clear instrumental value in merely stipulating definitions of privacy for narrow practical purposes such as drafting a health information protection law or a social media platform use policy. But I have grown sceptical of the value of ambitiously prescribing general analytic definitions. Why do it?

Some philosophers will insist that philosophical clarity for its own sake is a good thing; others will insist that one cannot illuminate the value of privacy without first understanding what privacy is; still others will insist that a sound definition of privacy is needed to clear up the confusion and disarray they see in law and policy. I will not deign to tell other scholars how they ought to spend their time. I will assert, however, that the definitions concocted by analytic philosophers can be impractically technical and abstruse. But it is even more troubling to me that the conceit of trying to make privacy talk tidy for the sake of clarity and rigour seems to sideline the 'who benefits from which definitions' question explained below. That question is of paramount importance, far more important in my view than reified definitional scholasticism. Putatively politically neutral and neutral-seeming prescriptive conceptual analysis of privacy dictating ideal uses can only take us so far.

Rather than engage in prescriptive analysis to 'fix' privacy talk deemed confused, vague, or misguided, theorists should accept that the concept of privacy is and will be definitionally contested and own up to the political struggles embedded in privacy disagreements. With this in mind, I suggest a new direction for philosophers and legal theorists. We might aim to articulate what is at stake when speakers deploy 'privacy' discourse first and then seek to do the work of making deep normative values, such as freedom, respect, civil participation, and anti-discrimination, real.

Advancing beyond prescriptive definitional analysis, I now believe there is a more fruitful and urgent type of definitional work to be performed by philosophers and legal professionals. I call this alternative intellectual work 'critical definitional facilitation', a set of tasks motivated by the recognition that there are discernible political dimensions to privacy discourse in the everyday world, including inside 'ivory tower' research and within the elite federal courts.[49] Critical definitional facilitation focuses on earnest efforts to understand what speakers mean when they appeal to the language of privacy to press their claims and then judging the justice of those substantive claims.[50]

Critical definitional facilitation eschews telling people how to talk and focuses instead on helping people and communities solve problems. Our taxonomies of privacy have more value as descriptions of actual usage rather than ideals of proper usage.[51] Theorists might excavate what people are seeking through privacy discourse and do something practical about it, if they can. For example, applied philosophers of language

[48] But see ibid.
[49] Allen (n 10).
[50] Allen (n 10).
[51] It can be useful to have a taxonomic vocabulary for distinguishing the many uses of the term 'privacy'. Toward that end, I often teach my law students to recognise the six forms of privacy found in US law: physical, informational, decisional, associational, proprietary and intellectual. See AL Allen and M Rotenberg, *Privacy Law and Society* (Minneapolis, Thomson West, 2016). There can be better and worse taxonomies, and many admire, as among the best, DJ Solove, *Understanding Privacy* (Cambridge, Harvard University Press, 2010).

could facilitate an understanding of how the recent anti-racist, anti-surveillance movements use the discourse of privacy to express opposition to monitoring, surveillance, flawed racial recognition technologies, and inequitable uses of our data toward algorithms that make decisions based on stereotypes of criminality, irresponsibility, and threat. Commentators in the last decade warn of surveillance capitalism, algorithms of oppression, and the New Jim Code.[52] 'Critical definitional facilitation', as I term it, foregrounds practical politics, methodologically legitimating important concerns about, for example, bodily integrity, autonomy, and government interference that are commonly framed as privacy concerns because of their close relationship to personhood, personality, and the intimacies that make us more fit for social roles and the responsibilities of citizenship.

I do not claim that a use of privacy discourse should never be challenged. Terms can be misused. (Let us not start calling onions ovens.) Moreover, there will be contexts in which the best move would be to replace arguments using the language of privacy with arguments that are likely to be more effective under the circumstances.

*Who Benefits from Privacy Disparagement?* Madison Powers has observed, and I agree, that 'conceptual positions can serve strategic political interests' and that 'conclusions on definitional matters may be motivated partly by partisan positions on the underlying substantive issues, such as abortion, or by doctrinal disagreements about methods of constitutional adjudication, rather than by concerns about philosophical clarity'.[53] Academic theorists may genuinely believe they can clearly 'define' privacy and its value without taking sides in political controversies related to gender, race, intimate same-sex relationships, contraception, abortion, criminal procedure and discriminatory targeted surveillance. But they cannot. The concept of privacy is enmeshed in politics. And the politics are not effectively cloaked or disguised as neutral armchair intellectual debates about conventional and ideal uses of words.

Many academics and others have readily bought into what I have termed the 'intractable vagueness thesis'.[54] This is the disparaging characterisation of privacy discourse as hopelessly vague, ambiguous, and dispensable. Seeking to silence and demean privacy talk as muddled and confused, the intractable vagueness thesis has needlessly hampered liberal, progressive, and critical agendas of racial, sexual, and reproductive equality.[55] It has created noise that has impaired efforts to criticise and hold accountable profit-seeking innovators, personal-data-dependent businesses and Big Tech platforms. It has enabled federal judges to launch a privacy disparagement juggernaut serving the interests of the political right that began in the 1960s and 1970s. Conservative federal judges, including the late Federal Court of Appeals Judge Robert Bork, and Supreme Court Justices Antonin Scalia, William Rehnquist and Clarence Thomas, paved the way for Justice Neil Gorsuch and others who are

[52] S Zuboff, *The Age of Surveillance Capitalism* (New York, Public Affairs, 2019); R Benjamin, *Race After Technology: Abolitionist Tools for the New Jim Code* (Cambridge, Polity Press, 2019) 108, 124, 125, 127; SU Noble, *Algorithms of Oppression: How Search Engines Reinforce Racism* (New York, NYU Press, 2018) 160, 169.

[53] M Powers, 'A Cognitive Access Definition of Privacy' (1996) 15 *Law and Philosophy* 369, 371.

[54] AL Allen, 'Synthesis and Satisfaction: How Philosophy Scholarship Matters' (2019) 20 *Theoretical Inquiries in Law* 343.

[55] Allen (n 10) 353.

outright foes or at best unsteady friends of privacy jurisprudence. Judge Robert Bork was infamous for his opposition to constitutional privacy rights. Bork characterised privacy jurisprudence as 'intellectually empty', 'utterly specious', 'unprincipled' and 'unconstitutional'.[56]

The disparagement of what women, marginalised groups, and their advocates label their 'privacy' has been of particular concern to me. It calls for an overt focus on the politics of privacy discourse. One way to view the recent privacy-and-civil-rights movement in the US – notable for evolving sufficiently coherently without a singular definition of 'privacy' at its core – is as a political countermove to privacy disparagement.[57] If privacy and data protection law is to help at all, we need new, better, and inclusive such law, which some would frame as civil rights law.[58]

*Privacy Discourse and the Politics of Privacy.* A polarised, politically dysfunctional American society is beset by disturbing trends relating to decisional and informational privacy rights. Our law courts have a vital role to play in the protection of rights and interests, but the public is losing confidence. Blatant partisan politics now often determine who is appointed to life-tenure positions on the federal courts. Ethical concerns over the behaviour of Supreme Court justices are at an all-time modern high, amidst revelations that Justices Clarence Thomas and Samuel Alito improperly accepted and concealed lavish gifts from wealthy individuals.

One especially disturbing US trend is the ongoing regressive judicial assault in the US on constitutional privacy doctrines that since the mid-twentieth century had gradually improved the lives of women, LGBTQ people and other often vulnerable Americans.[59] Some would associate Donald Trump appointee Supreme Court Justice Neil Gorsuch and his former judicial colleague Tenth Circuit Court of Appeals Judge Timothy Tymkovich with a regressive trend.

As Solicitor General of Colorado, Judge Timothy Tymkovich unsuccessfully defended the constitutionality of provisions of the Colorado State Constitution denying lesbian, gay and bisexual citizens the right to seek legal protection against discrimination.[60] The judge has defended the stance that a major retail employer of thousands can deny health insurance coverage mandated under the Affordable Care Act (nicknamed 'Obama Care') for reproductive services simply because of the owner's personal religious beliefs.[61] Judge Tymkovich has also defended the notion that businesses offering bakery and website design services to the general public in his state may turn away would-be customers based on their LGBTQ sexual orientation.[62]

[56] Allen (n 10) 351.

[57] Allen and Muhawe (n 12).

[58] ibid.

[59] ibid. *Dobbs v Jackson*, 597 US 215 (2022), Thomas, J., concurring ('we should reconsider all of this Court's substantive due process precedents, including *Griswold* [decriminalising access to birth control], *Lawrence* [decriminalising same sex sex], and *Obergefell* [striking down marriage laws against same sex marriage], because any substantive due process decision is "demonstrably erroneous"').

[60] See *Romer v Evans*, 517 US 620 (1996).

[61] See *Hobby Lobby Stores v Sebelius*, 723 F.3d 1114 (10th Cir 2013), one of a series of cases brought seeking to gut a health law – unpopular with some conservative activists and lawmakers – that made health insurance available to low-income and middle-income Americans.

[62] See *Masterpiece Cakeshop v Colorado Civil Rights Commission*, 370 P.3d 272 (2015), *cert granted* 137 S. Ct. 2290 (2017), decided 584 US 617(2018); and see *303 Creative LLC v Elenis*, 6 F.4th 1160 (10th Cir 2021) (Tymkovich, J.J, dissenting).

A conservative majority of the Supreme Court that included Justice Neil Gorsuch, agreed with Judge Tymkovitch.[63]

Justice Gorsuch joined the majority in *Dobbs v Jackson*, the case overturning federal abortion privacy protections.[64] Justice Gorsuch and most of his conservative colleagues on the Court (but not Chief Justice Roberts) dissented from a key privacy decision of the Court in *Carpenter v United States*, which held that law enforcement must obtain a search warrant before collecting cell site location data from service providers.[65] Justice Gorsuch and Judge Tymkovich would have us abandon capacious Fourth Amendment 'expectation of privacy' rationales in relation to government acquisition of cell-site location data obtained from service providers. They assert that the Fourth Amendment warrant requirement was established in recognition of safeguarding property, including incriminating 'papers', an ironic revert to the eighteenth century in the name of a digital age whose needs all agree the courts must service.

## A. What Privacy Talk Can Accomplish

Privacy protection has been called for as urgent protection from fundamental assaults on freedom, dignity, and autonomy.[66] New significance can thus be attached to the fact that the judge who created the positive legal right to privacy tort in the US in 1905 arrestingly characterised the deprivation of privacy as a kind of involuntary servitude.[67] In his ruling, Judge Andrew Jackson Cobb pointed out that the victim of privacy invasion is 'no longer free, and that he is in reality a slave, without hope of freedom, held to service by a merciless master'.[68] As someone whose third great-grandparents were enslaved in Cobb's state of Georgia, his analogy holds special meaning to me.

People often use privacy discourse today to communicate that deep, personal, and politically urgent matters are at stake. When the US Supreme Court recognised that privacy in group association is necessary for groups to freely and safely associate,[69] it enabled the NAACP, an African American civil rights organisation, to advance desegregation efforts in a racist state of Alabama.[70] The 'privacy' Black people are complaining about today relates to freedom from oppressive observation, surveillance, harassment, and violence by officials. Also of concern to Black people today is freedom from interference in family and intimate life, concealment and disclosure on social media platforms, privacy in healthcare and at work, and greater algorithmic transparency and accountability.

The future of privacy is one of the most widely voiced concerns arising from digital life. Data gathering, storage, aggregation, and algorithmic analysis are routine in the business and government sectors. Highly sensitive information and tiny bits of data

[63] See *303 Creative LLC v Elenis*, 600 US 570 (2023).
[64] *Dobbs v Jackson* 597 US 215 (2022).
[65] *Carpenter v United States*, 585 US 296 (2018).
[66] See generally Rössler (n 5).
[67] AL Allen, 'Natural Law, Slavery and the Right to Privacy Tort' (2012) 81 *Fordham Law Review* 1187.
[68] *Pavesich v New England Life Ins. Co.* (122 Ga. 190 (Ga. 1905)).
[69] *NAACP v Alabama*, 357 US 449 (1958).
[70] Allen (n 10) 365.

about quotidian behaviours are market commodities and political assets. In this context, alarms are sounded about a 'weaponisation' of technology.[71] Here and now, being wise to the politics of privacy discourse matters, and we cannot stand for academics or judges defining away our privacy.

Nor can we allow revenge pornographers, social media companies, online retailers, or government actors to silence complaints about the loss of information/data privacy by claiming that information/data they have taken charge of was shared consensually by data subjects exercising their control. The claim that there can be no 'privacy' rights in 'public' places defines away privacy. 'Privacy in public' is treated as a simple oxymoron foreclosing substantive privacy objections to the deployment of, for example, facial recognition technology and drone surveillance. Similarly, it is claimed that there can be, by definition, no 'privacy' rights respecting the 'deidentified' information sought after by researchers, pharmaceutical companies, or social tracking data aggregators. De-identification supposedly takes the personal and the private out of the equation, by definition. In these and other ways, assertions about the meaning of privacy are designed to shut down the opponents of controverted government and business practices. But they are not, in fact, showstoppers.

### B. New Questions

So, what questions about the concept of privacy really matter today? Focusing on the EU and its GDPR, a question that seems to matter greatly is whether data protection regulations in Europe overemphasise giving consumers choices, based on the problematic belief that privacy should be defined simply as control over information/data. Analogous questions can be raised about the recent outcrop of US consumer privacy law and policy. I have explained why privacy-as-control won't do, and I am proposing to also focus elsewhere, on different questions.

## V. A Privacy-and-Civil-Rights Movement

A question worth asking on behalf of African Americans and others who face privacy-related discrimination in daily life is whether privacy is a civil right. Christopher Muhawe and I have sought to explain how and why privacy was never much considered a 'civil right' in the US, but now, in just the last decade, it suddenly is. Danielle Citron has pushed the claim, defending intimate privacy as a civil right.[72] Dozens of state, local, and federal government officials, researchers and civil society groups

[71] *Cf.* C Foucek, 'Is Data Privacy a Privilege: The Racial Implications of Technology Based Tools in Government' (Techdirt, 24.06.2020), www.techdirt.com/2020/06/24/is-data-privacy-privilege-racial-implications-technology-based-tools-government/; Zuboff (n 52); N Leong, 'Racial Capitalism' (2013) 126 *Harvard Law Review* 2151; D Bigo, 'Globalized (In)security, the Field and the Banopticon' in D Bigo and A Tsoukala (eds), *Terror, Insecurity and Liberty: Illiberal Practices of Liberal Regimes after 9/11* (London, Routledge, 2008) 10–48.

[72] D Citron, *The Fight for Privacy: Protecting Dignity, Identity and Love in the Digital Age* (New York, W.W. Norton, 2022).

now assert that privacy is a civil right or a right that protects or is protected by civil rights.[73]

The term 'civil rights' has a specific set of denotations and connotations in the US that it does not have in other countries.[74] In the US, statutory 'civil rights' protect individuals from discrimination and unfair treatment in areas such as voting, employment, education, housing, and public accommodations. These civil rights are deemed essential to democracy, shielding individuals from discrimination based on race, sex, gender, national origin, disability, veteran status, religion, sexual orientation, or other personal characteristics. A pivotal chapter in this quest for civil rights was the mid-twentieth-century African American Civil Rights Movement, which remains significant in American history. A growing trend now links the concept of privacy to the civil rights ideal, arguing that privacy is a civil right or, at the very least, a vital protector of civil rights. (Traditionally, privacy has been regarded as a 'civil liberty', which shields individuals from government interference, such as freedom of speech and the freedom to practice one's religion. In contrast, civil rights protect individuals, inter alia, from discrimination by both public and private entities in a well-functioning democracy.) Advocates for privacy as a civil right draw on the values and achievements of the Civil Rights Movement to combat discrimination and inequality associated with technology in government, business, and social life.

Designating privacy as a civil right is a response to wrongs Americans are experiencing in light of the digital economy and lifestyles. As described in 'Dismantling the Black Opticon',[75] discriminatory over-surveillance, exclusion, and predation plague online transactions. The first element of the Black Opticon, over-surveillance, can be traced back to the concept of the panopticon, as described by Jeremy Bentham and Michel Foucault, where power is exercised through self-disciplining awareness of observation. Observation can be aimed at control or detecting predicted deviant or criminal behaviour. The second element, the banopticon, borrows from European scholar Didier Bigo and represents the exclusion of groups to the sidelines of opportunity, placing people outside the boundaries of civil society. For example, if a Facebook housing ad excludes Black individuals through targeted algorithms, it represents discriminatory exclusion from opportunities available to others. The third element, the conopticon, refers to scams and predatory practices targeting people of colour, such as high-interest payday loans and pyramid schemes that exploit the vulnerabilities of African Americans.

Strengths of depicting privacy as a civil right include that it signals that privacy/data protection should be an important priority for positive law. It also signals that racial and other group-based discrimination can be/should be addressed through privacy/data protection rights. It divorces the case for privacy/data protection in the digital economy from purely libertarian values and marries it to equity values. It is consonant with EU dignity and human rights norms. In a society marked by increased

[73] Allen and Muhawe (n 12).

[74] See generally R West, *Civil Rights: Rethinking their Natural Foundation* (Cambridge, Cambridge University Press, 2019). West argues that civil rights potentially protect civil participation and the flourishing of human capabilities, as well as freedom from discrimination.

[75] Allen 'Dismantling the "Black Opticon"' (n 11).

personal data collection, analytics, and surveillance, combining civil rights and privacy discourses is compelling. Discrimination stemming from digital technology and AI applications implicating traditional civil rights concerns such as equal employment opportunities, voter rights, and education access has made the appeal to civil rights discourses and strategies attractive.

Weaknesses of depicting privacy as a civil right are that in the US context privacy is not closely tied to core priorities of the Black Civil Rights Movements or its history.[76] As Christopher Muhawe and I explain, the relationship between privacy rights and minority civil rights has been complex, with instances of ambivalence, condemnation, and celebration. Thus, pairing them today cannot be presumed as straightforward. Alliances sought by civil rights and other civil society groups and lawmakers require costly compromises – eg, re pre-emption, private rights of action, and strong-handed regulation of Silicon Valley.

A paramount worry is whether newly enacted comprehensive data protection laws at the state or federal level in the US will advance the privacy interests by addressing urgent digital economy problems. It remains to be seen. The overhyped state laws nominally inspired by the GDPR grow in number but are weak. Nearly half the states have consumer privacy laws adopted in the past five years or so. No federal Bill introduced into Congress for comprehensive data protection laws, including those calling for a federal data protection agency and anti-discrimination practices in consumer data processing, has been enacted. At least in the US context, adequate data protection laws protecting data privacy – however defined or conceived – remain aspirational.

## VI. Conclusion

How do we define privacy? A logically prior question is *whether* we should define privacy and *who* will benefit from what definitional approaches. With these atypical challenges and questions as the backdrop, I have considered whether privacy is best defined as control over information or data. In academic, legal and policy circles, a remarkably pervasive and hotly contested definition would have us suppose that indeed privacy is best defined in terms of control. Many competing definitions have been proffered, so many that some have concluded that privacy is an 'essentially contested' or even vacuous concept.[77] Following WB Gallie, concepts are 'essentially contested' when their users fall into endless, unresolvable disputes about proper uses.

The perspectives that privacy is a contested or even empty concept are not among my reasons for criticising control-based definitions of privacy. I have criticised control-based definitions for decades because they are conceptually, pragmatically, and morally problematic. Although I once defended 'restricted access' definitions of privacy and still find them superior to control-based definitions, I have backed off from the enterprise of analytic definitional prescription. This enterprise can devalue, or obscure the value

[76] Allen and Muhawe (n 12).

[77] DK Mulligan, C Koopman and N Doty, 'Privacy is an Essentially Contested Concept: A Multi-dimensional Analytic for Mapping Privacy' (2016) 374 *Philosophical Transactions of the Royal Society A: Mathematical, Physical and Engineering Sciences* 2083.

of, the non-ideal privacy talk often utilised by laypeople and advocates in attempts to express and advance urgent just causes.

When Americans talk about their privacy, they are not talking nonsense, as privacy disparagers will contend. More strenuously than ever, I reject privacy disparagement both because it is philosophically needless and because it is a favourite rhetorical and jurisprudential strategy within right-wing American politics and the ultra-partisan judiciary for undercutting vital claims advanced on behalf of women, LGBTQ people, and everyone. In the context of digital life, when people say they want more privacy and that it is they themselves who should be controlling who can collect, store, analyse, process, and share information/data about them, they should not be dismissed as muddled. Moreover, they need not be read as *defining* privacy as control. Without analytically and prescriptively defining privacy as control, we can undertake what I call 'critical definitional facilitation'. This new methodology commends respectfully listening to claims expressed in privacy discourses and judging the possibility, ethics, and justice of enabling worthy claims through civil rights law, constitutional law or other practical mechanisms.

# 2

# Conceptualising the Protected Interests in Data Protection Law

MARION ALBERS

## I. Introduction

How to conceptualise the interests of individuals to be protected with respect to the handling of personal data and information is a key issue in the development of information and data law. The more society becomes digitalised, data-driven, and dependent on cross-border data flows, the more attention is drawn to this area of law.[1] However, the approaches taken are very different, not least when comparing Europe and the US. At the same time, approaches are in a state of flux, and fresh ideas are needed. This chapter argues that data protection addresses a highly complex subject matter with its own set of characteristics. Therefore, it must be conceived as a novel, distinct facet of fundamental rights protection. More precisely, based on a functional cooperation of fundamental rights at different levels, data protection comprises a bundle of multi-layered, multi-dimensional, and multi-faceted provisions and rights to which all fundamental rights can contribute with their substantive particularities. Against this background, the 'right to the protection of personal data' now enshrined in some fundamental rights catalogues proves to be a fruitful, although not indispensable, step forward as a pillar to be developed in an interplay with other fundamental rights.

My contribution will first provide a brief overview of the backgrounds (II.). The idea of data protection has, to some extent, evolved from the idea of privacy. But it is also distinct from it. In today's environment – the Internet, digitalisation, AI – we are dealing with digital data, and I will introduce the essential understanding of data and personal data in the context of data protection law to provide the foundations for further considerations. We will then take a look at the familiar but fuzzy concepts of the right to privacy, the right to informational self-determination, and the right to the protection

[1] See the manifold articles in M Albers and IW Sarlet (eds), *Personality and Data Protection Rights on the Internet* (Dordrecht, Springer (Ius Gentium), 2022).

of personal data (III.). The analysis of both the backgrounds and the achievements and limitations of these different concepts leads to my own approach (IV.). Data protection deals with a highly complex distinct subject matter, and any sufficiently well-thought-through legal approach points to multi-layered, multi-dimensional, and multifaceted guarantees and rights as well as to sophisticated doctrinal constructions. These insights enable us to comprehend the protected interests of data subjects as a bundle of provisions and rights in a multi-layered approach that includes, at a basic level, provisions and rights for appropriate regulation, and, at a second level, further requirements arising from content-specific fundamental rights. Such an approach is a prerequisite for developing data protection law in a reasonable way and for coordinating it with other legal regulations, for example, with the overarching European data and digital strategy. The chapter closes with a summary and an outlook (V.).

## II. Backgrounds

### A. Data Protection in the Digitalised Society

The idea of data protection has some of its roots in the idea of privacy, and this concept in turn has a very colourful history. Its traditional understanding has been shaped by several guiding dichotomies:[2] the contrasting of privacy and the state,[3] the distinction between privacy and publicness,[4] and the differentiation between the individual's private matters and the spheres of decision and influence (also) open to others.[5] A closer scrutiny quickly reveals the numerous premises and the complexity of the converse terms. Nonetheless, a basic understanding emerges: 'Privacy' assigns something to a person or a group of persons as their own concern and establishes limits to others' access to it. Over time, and more controversially, the range of issues that privacy addresses,[6] the mechanisms of allocation as one's own, and the concept of access have been understood in an increasingly abstract and broad way. Topics include personal communications, documents and data, 'access' comprises informational

[2] *Cf* M Albers, 'Privatheitsschutz als Grundrechtsproblem' in S Halft and H Krah (eds), *Privatheit. Strategien und Transformationen* (Passau, Stutz, 2013) 15 (20).

[3] This dichotomy is constitutive for liberal thought. *Cf* B Rössler, *Der Wert des Privaten* (Frankfurt am Main, Suhrkamp, 2001) 27 ff.

[4] The concept of 'publicness' is conceived in a variety of ways. See J Weintraub, 'The Theory and Politics of the Public/Private Distinction' in J Weintraub and K Kumar (eds), *Public and Private in Thought and Practice. Perspectives on a Grand Dichotomy* (Chicago, University of Chicago Press, 1997) 1 (1 ff); N Bobbio, 'The Great Dichotomy: Public/Private' in N Bobbio, *Democracy and Dictatorship* (Cambridge, Polity Press, 1989) 1 (17). *Cf* also with criticism R Geuss, *Public Goods, Private Goods* (Princeton, Princeton University Press, 2001).

[5] This differentiation is linked to one's individuality, but is not identical to it.

[6] Varying across cultures and historical epochs, the range of issues include the body, facets of the personality, religious convictions and conscience, spaces such as place of residence, property, close relationships such as partnership and family, confidential documents, communications only to specific addressees, or personal data. *Cf* with a broad historical overview the contributions in P Ariès et al, *Histoire de la vie privée*, (Paris, Seuil, 1985–1987). *Cf* also R Gavison, 'Privacy and the Limits of Law' (1980) 89 *Yale Law Journal* 421, 440 ff.

measures,[7] and 'limits to access' extend to boundaries based on social expectations of expectations.[8]

When the idea of data protection began to emerge in the 1960s and 1970s, privacy discourses already provided a variety of starting points. Moreover, in a more or less clear distinction from these, data protection was initially conceived with concepts of its own that not only emphasised the relevance of all individual rights but also considered the institutional or societal handling of (personal) data as such in need of regulation.[9] The socio-technical stimulus – automated data processing in large computer systems – could certainly have created the conditions for the development of overarching regulatory concepts. But the first attempts at a complex regulation quickly took a turn towards an individual-rights approach. One of the reasons for this was particular references to the discourses on privacy, which for their part have been specifically narrowed down. For example, in 1972, Wilhelm Steinmüller and other German scholars proposed an individual-rights-orientated, phase-specific approach to data protection,[10] following Westin's idea to define the right to privacy as 'the claim of individuals, groups, or institutions to determine for themselves when, how, and to what extent information about them is communicated to others'.[11] From the Federal Constitutional Court's census ruling in 1983 onwards, data protection and its principles have been significantly influenced by the right to informational self-determination.

Since the beginning of the current millennium, we have been experiencing a very profound social change that extends to ontologies. This change is once again prompted by novel socio-technical arrangements, particularly in connection with the internet as an infrastructure, digitalisation, and AI. Areas of life are subject to datafication, activities are becoming data-driven, and communications are characterised by 'virtual contingency'[12] due to the autonomous contribution of machine data processing. In response to this societal change, a series of new regulations of data, technologies and infrastructures enters the scene. In Europe, this is the European Union's data and digital strategy for 'shaping Europe's digital future'.[13]

[7] See the description of 'privacy' by S Bok, *Secrets – On the Ethics of Concealment and Revelation* (New York, Pantheon Books, 1982) 10 f: 'the condition of being protected from unwanted access by others – either physical access, personal information, or attention'.

[8] *Cf* H Nissenbaum, *Privacy in Context. Technology, Policy, and the Integrity of Social Life* (Stanford, Stanford University Press, 2010) 74 ff.

[9] See G González Fuster, ch 6 in this volume. For the early discussion in Germany see M Albers, *Informationelle Selbstbestimmung* (Baden-Baden, Nomos, 2005) 113 ff.

[10] W Steinmüller et al, *Grundfragen des Datenschutzes*, Bundestags-Drucksache VI/3826 (1972). Admittedly, this approach was part of an overarching concept in that expertise, but the overarching elements have been lost in subsequent developments. See F Bieker, *The Right to Data Protection: Individual and Structural Dimensions of Data Protection in EU Law* (The Hague, TM Asser Press, 2022) 180 ff.

[11] AF Westin, *Privacy and Freedom*, 6th edn (New York, Atheneum, 1970) 42.

[12] See E Esposito, 'Artificial Communication? The Production of Contingency by Algorithms' (2017) 46(4) *Zeitschrift für Soziologie* 249 (257 ff).

[13] For the foundations see in particular: Communication from the Commission to the European Parliament, the Council, the European Economic and Social Committee and the Committee of the Regions 'European Interoperability Framework – Implementation Strategy' [2017] COM(2017) 134 final; 'Towards a common European data space' [2018] COM(2018) 232 final; 'Shaping Europe's digital future' [2020] COM(2020) 67 final; 'A European strategy for data' [2020] COM(2020) 66 final; 'European Commission digital strategy. Next generation digital Commission' [2022] COM(2022) 4388 final; White Paper 'On Artificial Intelligence – A European approach to excellence and trust' [2020] COM(2020) 65 final.

This strategy covers the regulations on digital markets and digital services,[14] the regulation on a framework for the free flow of non-personal data,[15] open data concepts,[16] the Data Governance Act[17] and common European sector-specific data spaces[18] that, among other things, create a framework for 'data altruism',[19] the Data Act that revolves around ensuring that personal and non-personal data generated in the context of the Internet of Things is made available for use by various stakeholders,[20] and, last but not least, harmonised rules on artificial intelligence.[21] Some of these new regulations come along with new principles such as data sharing or making data available for their reuse in various contexts. Actually, they are fuelling pressure for change on the familiar data protection regulations.[22] Nevertheless, these are classified

[14] Regulation (EU) 2022/1925 of the European Parliament and of the Council on contestable and fair markets in the digital sector (Digital Markets Act) [2022] OJ L265/1; Regulation (EU) 2022/2065 of the European Parliament and of the Council on a single market for digital services (Digital Services Act) [2022] OJ L277/1. Their provisions concern the regulation of gatekeepers including their handling of data or obligations of online platforms, for example, with regard to user-generated illegal content. In addition, the aim of these strategies is to establish a common European data space or sector-specific data spaces, the design of which is intended to unlock the potential of digitisation.

[15] See Regulation (EU) 2018/1807 of the European Parliament and of the Council on a framework for the free flow of non-personal data in the European Union [2018] OJ L303/59, and the Commission's Guidance on the Regulation on a framework for the free flow of non-personal data in the European Union (2019), which in particular deal with the demarcation from the regulations on personal data in the GDPR [2019] COM(2019) 250 final.

[16] The respective regulations aim to ensure that certain data sets and documents in the public sector are made available in open, machine-readable, accessible, findable and reusable formats, and may be reused in the private sector, subject to conditions if necessary; see Directive 2019/1024/EU of the European Parliament and of the Council on open data and the re-use of public sector information [2019] OJ L172/56; for delimitation in the above context, see art 2(1)(h) on its scope.

[17] Regulation (EU) 2022/868 of the European Parliament and of the Council on European data governance and amending Regulation (EU) 2018/1724 (Data Governance Act) [2022] OJ L152/1.

[18] See, eg, the intended Regulation on the European Health Data Space in its last version of the draft after consensus has been reached in the trilogue procedure, European Parliament legislative resolution on the proposal for a regulation of the European Parliament and of the Council on the European Health Data Space ([2024] COM(2022)0197 – C9-0167/2022 – 2022/0140(COD)), www.europarl.europa.eu/doceo/document/TA-9-2024-0331_EN.html.

[19] Data subjects provide data for specified (research) purposes by means of consent. Complementing the Open Data Directive, the reuse of sensitive data is facilitated under certain conditions, first of all through the implementation of technological data protection concepts. New institutions such as data intermediaries, ie, data sharing services that can also operate in the sense of 'data trustees', and data altruistic organisations are given a key role with regard to, among other things, ensuring data protection rights.

[20] See the Regulation 2023/2854/EU of the European Parliament and of the Council on harmonised rules on fair access to and use of data (Data Act) [2023] OJ L1/71. To achieve this goal, data owners must adhere to and ensure certain conditions for data processing. Above all, users of products or related services are to be enabled to use the data that is generated by their use (user-generated data), to share it with third parties or demand direct access for third parties. Subject to the specified criteria, data access is opened up for the benefit of public bodies. All in all, the knowledge and value creation potential of this data shall be exploited in a productive manner.

[21] Regulation (EU) 2024/1689 of the European Parliament and of the Council laying down harmonised rules on artificial intelligence […] (Artificial Intelligence Act) [2024] OJ L, 12.7.2024.

[22] These include above all the General Data Protection Regulation (GDPR) – Regulation (EU) 2016/679 of the European Parliament and of the Council on the protection of natural persons with regard to the processing of personal data and on the free movement of such data, and repealing Directive 95/46/EC (General Data Protection Regulation) [2016] OJ L119/1 – which is supplemented by the Data Protection Directive for Police and Criminal Justice – Directive 2016/680 of the European Parliament and of the Council on the protection of natural persons with regard to the processing of personal data by competent authorities for the purposes of the prevention, investigation, detection or prosecution of criminal offences or the execution of criminal penalties, and on the free movement of such data, and repealing Council Framework Decision 2008/977/JHA

as a first fundamental pillar intended to provide a 'framework for trust in the digital environment'.[23] Personal data is explicitly a key factor upon which the legal regimes are built and are delineated. Let us now take a brief look at this core element of data protection: personal data.

## B. Personal Data in Context

### i. *What is Data?*

Although personal data is a core element of data protection, it is far from sufficiently clear what the concept of data is and what is or is not covered by it. Therefore, I am briefly introducing the subject matter in order to lay the foundation for further considerations.

The etymological root, with regard to which data presents itself as something 'given', creates an extraordinarily broad starting point for the understanding of the term 'data', and this understanding varies according to historical epoch, perspective, and framing. Data is a construction[24] and 'sociotechnological in nature',[25] because it, its storage forms, and the data formats in which data is embodied are shaped by technologies, media, and infrastructures. While in a certain phase 'data' was often linked to the evolution of science, experimentation, and measurement,[26] today they are a multifaceted element of the 'onlife world' as binary digital units which are, depending on the technology, manifested in dual electrical, optical or electromagnetic (voltage or light) states.

No surprise, modern approaches choose a very abstract level:

> [...] the general definition of a datum is: Dd) datum = def. x being distinct from y, where x and y are two uninterpreted variables and the relation of 'being distinct', as well as the domain, are left open to further interpretation.[27]

This seems to be too abstract to be useful. But such an approach can capture different levels of abstraction and different reference points. Such a highly abstract approach is also necessary and suitable for grasping 'digital data' against the background of digitalisation and AI.

As the concept of data is a construction, the various scientific disciplines each take their own approach. Concepts of 'data' are described in multifarious and discipline-dependent ways.[28] The law does not simply borrow descriptions like those approaches in

[2008] OJ L119/89, by the e-privacy Directive – Directive 2002/58/EC of the European Parliament and of the Council concerning the processing of personal data and the protection of privacy in the electronic communications sector [2002] OJ L201/37, and by numerous further sector-specific legal acts.

[23] Communication from the Commission 'Towards a common European data space' [2018] COM(2018) 232 final, p 1.

[24] R Kitchin, *The Data Revolution* (Los Angeles, Sage, 2014) 2 ff; S Leonelli, 'The Philosophy of Data' in L Floridi (ed), *The Routledge Handbook of Philosophy of Information* (London, Routledge, 2016) 192 (192 ff).

[25] R Kitchin, *Data lives: How Data are Made and Shape our World* (Bristol, Bristol University Press, 2021) 5.

[26] *Cf* also D Rosenberg, 'Data before the Fact' in L Gitelman (ed), *"Raw Data" is an Oxymoron* (Cambridge (MA), MIT Press, 2013) 33 (36).

[27] L Floridi, *Information. A Very Short Introduction* (Oxford, Oxford University Press, 2010) 23.

[28] ibid 19 ff.

computer science might use. Instead, it builds on different types of description patterns to cover the spectrum of regulatory needs and cases, takes them up in a legally specific way, and reformulates them with a view to the legally justified need for protection. What is meant by 'data' in the juridical context is, to a certain extent, a legal construction in itself. Since the concept of data is such an abstract one, there may be different descriptions even in different areas of law, such as data protection law, copyright law, or patent law. For example, we have different legal definitions in the GDPR on the one hand[29] and in the Data Governance Act and Data Act on the other[30] – all of them not well thought through, but not necessarily inconsistent, because they can be explained from their specific legal context.

### *ii. Data in Data Protection Law*

The aim of data protection law is not the protection of data but of the persons to whom the data refers. This is reflected in its focus on 'personal data'.[31] How data is to be understood in data protection law must be approached by simultaneously considering 'personal data'.

Personal data is understood as data concerning the individual.[32] That means that its content refers to a particular natural or, depending on the legal system, also other legal person. However, such content is neither an intrinsic property of data nor is it attached to it like a label. It is an achievement attributing meaning to data. Two key questions are hidden in the 'person-relatedness': When does data refer to a *specific* person, and when does data *refer* to a person?

Data protection law responds by defining that the data must relate to either an identified or an identifiable person.[33] Data such as the personal name and data that is regularly linked to it, such as the address, date of birth, marital status, social security and tax identification numbers, fingerprints, or portrait photographs, are illustrative examples. Even with these simple examples, it quickly becomes clear that it must be answered which identifiers specify a person and that, if necessary, a connection between particular data and identification data must be drawn. Such a connection may be readily available in a given situation, but it may also only be possible by means of a number of steps, the relevance of which must be legally assessed with regard to the identifiability of a person. Prior or additional knowledge that some people might have can enable them to associate data that is not readily assignable on its own with a specific person.[34] If a reference to the person to be protected can only be established via

[29] Art 4 no 1 GDPR: '"personal data" means any information relating to an identified or identifiable natural person ("data subject") […]'.

[30] Art 2 no 1 DGA and 2 no 1 DA: '"data" means any digital representation of acts, facts or information and any compilation of such acts, facts or information, including in the form of sound, visual or audiovisual recording […]'.

[31] See, eg, art 2(1) GDPR.

[32] See, eg, art 8(1) CFR: 'Everyone has the right to the protection of personal data concerning him or her.'

[33] Art 4 no 1 GDPR.

[34] See also the breadth of the term 'personal data' ECJ, Judgment Case C-582/14 *Breyer* ECLI:EU:C:2016:779, [2016] § 32 ff; Judgment Case C-434/16 *Nowak* ECLI:EU:C:2017:994, [2017] Rn. 27 ff; Judgment Case C-579/21 J.M. ECLI:EU:C:2023:501, [2023] §§ 41 ff. *Cf* also the overly broad approach of the art 29 Data Protection Working Party, Opinion 4/2007 on the concept of personal data, 01248/07/EN WP 136.

several activities involving a variety of parties, it can be quite difficult to decide under which conditions the person in question can be regarded as 'identifiable' in relation to which party. Many courts have struggled with the categorisation of IP addresses,[35] and the ECJ, in a recent illustrative decision, also with that of vehicle identification numbers.[36] The considerations already result in a very broad spectrum of data that can be linked to a person and then provide information about them.

Moreover, the identifiability of a person in a given situation or the much-discussed problem of re-identification are not the only issues. In light of its aims of protection and governance, data protection law does not only cover situations or activities in which a connection between data and particular persons actually exists or might be created by identifying steps. It also aims at preventing in advance legally undesirable connections between particular data and persons, the resulting knowledge about a person, and its potential disadvantageous use. Hence, it has to be more or less future-orientated and applicable prior to risks that have become manifest. The specification of personal data and the question of whether a person is identifiable therefore involve not only a substantive dimension, which may eventually be relational with respect to different parties, but also a temporal dimension. The possibility of referring data to persons over time and in contexts not yet foreseeable – data generated anew as personal data at a later point in time – must be considered to a certain extent. Under the conditions of a data-driven society and economy, data is constantly linked to persons in new and unpredictable ways. However, it cannot be sufficient for activating protection that somebody might link data to a person somehow at some point in time. Otherwise all data would have to be classified as personal data. Data protection law would be overinclusive and end up being a 'law of everything'.[37]

From these difficulties associated with the description and delimitation of personal data, we can draw several conclusions. Beyond pure identification data, the answer to the question of which data relates to a person requires a description of the quality that the relationship between the data and the person concerned must have, as well as a description of the contexts in which the handling of data and information takes place. In both respects, evaluative judgements and assumptions of probability come into play. To a considerable extent, prognoses and typifications may enter the picture. The personal-relatedness of data is rarely determined by looking at a single piece of data separately but rather with a view to the information and the knowledge that can be produced, to the overarching context, under certain circumstances to different relationships and participants, and through evaluative decisions.

The answers to the question of when data is personal are just as legally constructed as the concept of data. The understanding and delimitation of 'personal data' must be conceptualised against the background of the protected interests, which are the reason for data protection. Thus, it is not a seemingly easily detectable personal-relatedness of data as such that justifies the protection of data subjects. It is *the other*

[35] See, eg, the judgment of the Canadian Supreme Court, *R v Bykovets*, (2024) SCC 6, which is controversial concerning how to determine the information content of IP addresses.

[36] ECJ, Judgment Case C-319/22 *Gesamtverband Autoteile-Handel e. V.* ECLI:EU:C:2023:385, [2023] § 44 ff.

[37] N Purtova, 'The Law of Everything. Broad Concept of Personal Data and Future of EU Data Protection Law' (2018) 10 *Law, Innovation, and Technology* 40.

*way around*: the reasons for protection make it possible to determine the personal-relatedness of data. Hence, the necessity of substantiating data protection interests – in more depth than a mere remark about a personal-relatedness of data – does not vanish. Such an approach is not only normatively convincing. It enables us, for example, to find solutions for scenarios that occur more frequently with the Internet of Things: data refers to several people in different ways, so that legal positions must be justified in more detail.

### *iii. Understanding 'Personal Data' within a Network of Basic Elements*

At this point, it has already become clear that, from a constitutional and legal perspective, data protection deals with a highly complex subject matter. It is not about data as such. We must expand this isolated view by including further elements, in particular at a basic level the element of information, in the structural dimension knowledge, in the temporal dimension the flow of data and information, and in the broader context decisions, actions, and their consequences. Data protection aims at regulating data processing and data architectures but also at regulating the production of information and knowledge, at influencing the decisions based on such knowledge, and at preventing adverse consequences for the individuals affected.

It is of utmost importance for the understanding of data protection law that data and information must not be seen as if they were synonymous.[38] If their differentiation is considered to be irrelevant, neither the characteristics of data protection law nor the challenges it faces can be worked out. This is true even though legal definitions and some scholarly contributions might not reflect this in the required manner.

Data protection law addresses data, on the one hand, as an *objectified entity* that is characterised by a *specific technology-dependent materiality*. Data might be described as characters, symbols, or binary digital units that are stored in a certain format on a data carrier, including written documents or videos as well as data digitally stored on hard drives or mobile data storage devices. On the other hand, data protection law addresses data – and more precisely: personal data – because it can acquire informational significance in social contexts. Data is relevant as 'potential information'. This is to be understood more or less abstractly; as we have seen, it does not mean that there are fixed intrinsic meanings associated with the data. Furthermore, data can be decoupled from its potential informational significance to a certain extent; it can be identified as a distinct entity and become the subject of law even if it contributes to information and knowledge only in conjunction with other data or processing procedures. Data is often less important as a single piece of data but rather as part of data processing or data architectures. Without any potential informational significance, however, the legal relevance required in the context of data protection law is lacking.

In contrast to data, pieces of information are *elements of meaning* that may be based on data (or on observations or communications) and are then created by

[38] More closely Albers (n 9) 87 ff.

interpretations which take place in a particular social context.[39] Information is context-dependent in an elementary way. Although this insight may be well-established today, people hardly face up to the difficulties this entails for legal regulation. In the structural dimension of such context, *knowledge* – founded upon texts, files, archives, registers, databases, or expert systems, but also upon institutional, organisational or procedural arrangements – makes interpretation possible and limits the possibilities of interpretation.[40] In the temporal dimension, data as well as information is constantly generated anew and altered during *processing operations* or *flows of data and information*. Information and knowledge are increasingly recognised and worked out as distinct topics of law. They are also crucial factors in decision-making; they serve as bases for certain decisions and actions. Such decisions have consequences and may have an adverse effect on the person to whom the data and information refer. If disadvantages are normatively undesirable and unjustified, protection against such disadvantages – or even against the mere risk of such disadvantages arising – is one of the reasons for data protection. There are other reasons that can be elaborated on in the determination of protected interests. At this point, it should only be made clear that understanding data protection requires thinking in social relations, in overarching contexts and in processes. The scope and form of considering social contexts depend on how relatively loose or condensed the relationship between data and knowledge and actions and decisions is in the focused context.

As a result, data must be conceived of within a network of several basic elements. It is one, but not the only reference point. At the same time, these analyses have shown at what fundamental level we are working when regulating data and information.[41] It is as fundamental as regulating decisions or actions.

## III. Familiar, but Fuzzy and Manifold Foundations of Data Protection Interests

Now that we have arrived at regulation, the next section analyses the familiar, but fuzzy foundations of data protection interests that are acknowledged at a constitutional level. How data protection interests are identified and described depends, of course, on the legal system and legal culture of the country concerned, on what is enshrined in the Constitution, or on the relationship between the legislature and the courts. Last but not least, constitutional concepts are always characterised by an interplay of substantive as

[39] Data and information are above all not synonyms because, although data as a basis for information may provide information, it presupposes far more than just data. Information cannot be described without observing knowledge structures, processes and the broader social context in which it arises.

[40] In more detail and with further references M Albers, 'Umgang mit personenbezogenen Informationen und Daten' in A Voßkuhle, M Eifert and C Möllers (eds), *Grundlagen des Verwaltungsrechts* vol I, 3rd edn (Munich, Beck, 2022) § 22 Rn 8 ff.

[41] These considerations also imply that it is always necessary to think through, in the context of the relevant norms, what normative role the terms 'data' or 'information' play and what exactly is therefore meant by them. *Cf* D Hallinan and R Gellert, 'The Concept of "Information": An Invisible Problem in the GDPR' (2020) 17(2) *SCRIPTed* 269 ff.

well as doctrinal and methodological considerations. Nevertheless, raising awareness of achievements and shortcomings of approaches can be fruitful.

Among the familiar foundations of data protection interests are the right to privacy, the right to informational self-determination, and the right to the protection of personal data. Rights to privacy are the bedrocks of broad debates and judicial decisions in the US as well as in some other countries, such as Canada, India, or South Africa. The understanding of the scope of protection of article 8 ECHR, the right to respect for private life, home, and correspondence, has been gradually extended to include data protection interests. The right to informational self-determination is a German peculiarity, but one that has attracted worldwide attention. The European Charter of Fundamental Rights – as a more recent codification that endeavours to meet the needs of modern society – guarantees everyone the right to the protection of personal data concerning him or her. The following sections analyse these legal foundations with a primary view to case law and aim at identifying achievements, weaknesses, and challenges. Our overview of case law begins with the US, a cradle of a 'right to privacy'.

## A. Right to Privacy

### *i. Approaches and Developments in Case Law*

To what extent 'privacy' is a suitable description of protected interests and how rights to 'privacy' must then be conceptualised in detail is part of a broad debate in the US. In reaction to media intrusions, the famous article by Warren and Brandeis in 1890 advocated the recognition of a right to privacy, shaped as a 'right to be let alone',[42] as part of tort law and thus put the idea on the map. While the term 'privacy' is not explicitly used in the text of the US Constitution, there are various approaches in the jurisdiction to anchor its more or less specified protection with regard to guarantees of primarily the First,[43] Fourth,[44] Fifth,[45] and Fourteenth[46] Amendments in a way that these guarantees have privacy as their underlying idea, and that this, in turn, lends itself to a methodologically broad interpretation of their subject matter and scope.[47]

[42] SD Warren and LD Brandeis, 'The Right to Privacy' (1890) 4/5 *Harvard Law Review* 193.

[43] 'Congress shall make no law respecting an establishment of religion, or prohibiting the free exercise thereof; or abridging the freedom of speech, or of the press; or the right of the people peaceably to assemble, and to petition the Government for a redress of grievances.'

[44] 'The right of the people to be secure in their persons, houses, papers, and effects, against unreasonable searches and seizures, shall not be violated, and no Warrants shall issue, but upon probable cause, supported by Oath or affirmation, and particularly describing the place to be searched, and the persons or things to be seized.'

[45] 'No person shall […] be deprived of life, liberty, or property, without due process of law […].'

[46] '[…] nor shall any State deprive any person of life, liberty, or property, without due process of law […].'

[47] Methodologically partly with references to the Ninth Amendment: 'The enumeration in the Constitution, of certain rights, shall not be construed to deny or disparage others retained by the people.' See Justice Goldberg Concurring Opinion in *Griswold v Connecticut* 381 US 479, 489 ff (1965).

In several judgments of the US Supreme Court, these possible approaches have been worked out with regard to more closely specified individual decisions and relationships 'lying within the zone of privacy created by several fundamental constitutional guarantees […]'.[48] In the landmark judgment *Roe v Wade*, the Court held that 'a right of personal privacy, or a guarantee of certain areas or zones of privacy, does exist under the Constitution'.[49] This hereafter acknowledged 'right of personal privacy includes the interest in independence in making certain kinds of important decisions'.[50] Such decisional privacy is not assigned solely to liberty[51] because it is not about freedom of decision as such but about an even stronger protection for the 'most intimate and personal choices a person may make in a lifetime, choices central to personal dignity and autonomy'.[52] The allocation of decision-making options is linked to certain spaces or topics and is inspired by the traditional differentiation between the individual's private matters and the spheres of decision and influence (also) open to others.

Privacy as a protected interest has been further outlined by interpreting the 'right of the people to be secure in their persons, houses, papers, and effects, against unreasonable searches and seizures', established in the Fourth Amendment, and by specifying which spaces and objects are protected against what. The protection of the (relative) inviolability of the home as the spatial sphere of private life, which is delineated in terms of its functions as well as physical boundaries (for example, walls or fences), is a classic paradigm case. The protection of the secrecy of telecommunications can also be captured by using spatial metaphors, which address the network of communication relationships that are created via the use of certain communications technologies and services. Over time, the jurisdiction has moved away from restricting the protected good to 'material things – the person, the house, his papers, or his effects […]'[53] characterised by corporeal, material, or physical features and boundaries and regularly existing possibilities of control. Likewise, the understanding of what 'searches and seizures' are has been dissociated from the notion that an 'entry of the houses'[54] would be required for the approval of a relevant encroachment. In response to changes in the way society communicates, the US Supreme

[48] 381 US 479, 485.

[49] *Roe v Wade*, 410 U.S. 113, 152 (1973), and the Court stated in the following (at 153) that this 'right of privacy, whether it be founded in the Fourteenth Amendment's concept of personal liberty and restrictions upon state action, as we feel it is, or, as the District Court determined, in the Ninth Amendment's reservation of rights to the people, is broad enough to encompass a woman's decision whether or not to terminate her pregnancy.' Recently, this decision has been overruled by the US Supreme Court's judgment *Dobbs v Jackson Women's Health Organization*, 597 U.S. 215 (2022), with as yet not fully foreseeable ramifications.

[50] *Whalen v Roe*, 429 U.S. 589, 599 f (1977); *Carey v Population Services International*, 431 U.S. 678, 684 (1977).

[51] See, however, the sophisticated argumentation with some well-justified criticism of J Bellin, 'Pure Privacy' (2021) 116 *Northwestern University Law Review* 463, 477 ff, 481 ff.

[52] *Planned Parenthood of Southeastern Pa. v Casey*, 505 U.S. 833, 851 (1992).

[53] In *Olmstead v United States* 277 U.S. 438 (1928), the question before the Court was whether the use of evidence of private telephone conversations, intercepted by means of wiretapping, amounted to a violation of the Fourth and Fifth Amendments. In a 5:4 decision, it was held that there was no violation of the Fourth and Fifth Amendments. Chief Justice Taft wrote the majority judgment, holding that (at 464): 'The Amendment itself shows that the search is to be of material things – the person, the house, his papers, or his effects …'.

[54] See for the 'trespass doctrine' *Olmstead v United States*, 277 U.S. 438, 464 (1928). See also the dissent of Justice Brandeis in this respect.

Court reached the landmark decision '*Katz v United States*':[55] An enclosed public telephone booth is an area where a person has a constitutionally protected reasonable expectation of privacy, and eavesdropping activities of governmental agencies constitute a 'search and seizure' within the meaning of the Fourth Amendment that extends as well to the recording of oral statements.

For the subsequent case law, profound rearrangements, abstractions, and novel key concepts are crucial, especially the argumentation that 'the Fourth Amendment protects people, not places',[56] along with the 'reasonable expectation of privacy' test,[57] which places the emphasis on social relationships as well as on the boundaries that arise through them, and the extended understanding of encroachments. Substantive approaches based on traditional images of the safeguarded person or house are supplemented by functional approaches: the protective function is the guarantee of privacy, and what fulfils the functions of such privacy under the given social conditions, based on expectations of privacy that society acknowledges as reasonable, should be safeguarded. On the one hand, this leads to flexibility, but on the other hand, to a loss of legal certainty. This is because descriptions of social contexts and functional relations depend on the predefined theoretical framework and theoretical assumptions, for example, a theory of the individual and individuality.[58] The extension of the scope of protection goes hand in hand with an expanded understanding of 'search and seizures'. To a certain extent, the permissibility of these encroachments has always indicated that fundamental rights can include a protection against data collection; however, their traditional understanding was linked to certain activities against which a high level of protection is explainable due to the intrusiveness of the methods or the risks of their use regarding protected interests.[59] A more abstract understanding of search and seizures makes it possible to include new activities and methods made possible by technological developments as well as further encroachments of an informational nature. In turn, this leads to a loss of criteria that limit the spectrum of encroachments covered and of legal certainty. The subsequent case law illustrates the adaptability to social and technical developments as well as constant discussions regarding both the underlying legal approaches and the subsumption of the specific circumstances of the cases.[60]

[55] *Katz v United States*, 389 U.S. 347 (1967). Charles Katz was a gambler who used a public telephone booth to transmit illegal wagers. Unbeknownst to Katz, the FBI, which was investigating Katz's activity, was recording his conversations via an electronic eavesdropping device attached to the exterior of the phone booth. Subsequently, Katz was convicted based on these recordings. He challenged his conviction, arguing that the recordings were obtained in violation of his Fourth Amendment rights.

[56] *Katz v United States*, 389 U.S. 347, 351 (1967).

[57] In the following, the 'reasonable expectation of privacy' has become a pivotal pattern of argumentation and been relied on by various other jurisdictions while developing the right to privacy.

[58] *Cf* Gavison (n 6) 445.

[59] *Cf* also the dissent of Justice Alito, joined by Justice Thomas, *Carpenter v United States*, 585 U.S.____ (2018), 10 f.

[60] For example, whether 'reasonable expectations of privacy' can be recognised, is addressed in *United States v Miller*, 425 U.S. 435 (1976), in *Minnesota v Olson*, 495 U.S. 91 (1990), or in *Minnesota v Carter*, 525 U.S. 83 (1998). Whether there is a 'search' under the Fourth Amendment, is discussed with regard to an installation and use of a pen register in *Smith v Maryland*, 442 U.S. 735 (1979), to the thermal imaging of the house in *Kyllo v United States*, 533 U.S. 27 (2001), or to a GPS tracking device on a vehicle in *United States v Jones*, 565 U.S. 400 (2012). See also *Riley v California*, 573 U.S. 373 (2014), for the search and seizure of digital contents of a cell phone.

This becomes particularly evident in *Carpenter v United States*.[61] In this landmark ruling, the majority highlighted that the conception of the Amendment has been expanded 'to protect certain expectations of privacy', which could be positively assessed for cell site location information in light of their informative content and regardless of the fact that this data is held and retrieved by the wireless carrier.[62] The four dissents presented a variety of arguments, which spanned from fundamental criticism of the 'Katz' test[63] to the insistence on 'accepted property principles as the baseline for reasonable expectations of privacy'[64] up to the proposal to revisit the 'kind of legal interest' that 'is sufficient to make something *yours*' and 'the source of law that determines that' in order to also give room for legislative participation.[65]

Beyond the Fourth Amendment, the informational dimension of the right to privacy is addressed to a certain extent by using the idea of a zone of privacy created by several fundamental constitutional guarantees. The judgment '*Whalen v Roe*' was the starting point for differentiating kinds of interests which are covered by this protection,[66] even though the grounds of this judgment were fluctuating when locating these interests within the Constitution.[67] Besides the interest in independence in making certain kinds of important decisions, the individual interest in avoiding disclosure of personal matters was identified.[68] In the following, the informational dimension of privacy was of broader relevance in '*NASA v Nelson*', a case that dealt with NASA's background checks of contract employees.[69] The majority judgment chose to assume that a privacy interest of constitutional significance was at stake, but considering the legal safeguards, it concluded that there was no violation.[70] This line of reasoning was sharply criticised by the concurring opinions.[71] Their findings instead were that there is no constitutional right to 'informational privacy'.

Despite the recognition of different kinds of interests in the case law of the US Supreme Court, 'privacy' offers only limited, mostly accessory informational protection. Although some of the decisions address digital devices or advanced surveillance methods,[72] there is little success in developing sophisticated concepts of the protection

[61] Timothy Carpenter was charged with several crimes after wireless carriers handed over the cell site location information generated by his phone to the FBI and these data supported the suspicion that he had been involved in these crimes, *Carpenter v United States*, 585 U.S. ____ (2018).

[62] *Carpenter v United States*, 585 U.S. ____ (2018), p 5; *cf* for the protection of 'a person's expectation of privacy in his physical location and movements' pp 7 ff and for the discussion of the former 'third-party doctrine' pp 9 ff.

[63] See the dissent of Justice Thomas in *Carpenter v United States*, 585 U.S. ____ (2018).

[64] Dissent of Justice Kennedy, joined by Justice Thomas and Justice Alito, *Carpenter v United States*, 585 U.S. ____ (2018) p 22.

[65] Dissent of Justice Gorsuch, *Carpenter v United States*, 585 U.S. ____ (2018), p 13.

[66] *Whalen v Roe*, 429 U.S. 589 (1977) dealt with obligations of health care providers to store the private information of patients who received prescriptions for drugs.

[67] C Shachar and C Zubrzycki, 'Informational Privacy After *Dobbs* (2023) 75 *Alabama Law Review* 1, 12 ff.

[68] *Whalen v Roe*, 429 U.S. 589 (1977), at 598 f. See also with partly different considerations, *Nixon v Administrator of General Services*, 433 U.S. 425(1977) at 457.

[69] *NASA v Nelson*, 562 U.S. 134 (2011).

[70] Many questions remain unclear in the grounds, *cf* CP Moniodis, 'Moving from Nixon to NASA: Privacy's second strand – A right to informational privacy' (2012) 15 *Yale Journal of Law & Technology* 139, 157 ff.

[71] Concurring opinion of Justice Scalia, joined by Justice Thomas.

[72] See, eg, the reasoning in *United States v Jones*, 565 U.S. 400 (2012), in *Riley v California*, 573 U.S. 373 (2014), and in *Carpenter v United States*, 585 U.S. ____ (2018).

that is constitutionally guaranteed. As the grounds of the recent judgment '*Dobbs v Jackson Women Health Organization*' may illustrate,[73] the reasons for this have to do with the limits of the legal anchors and the methodological strategies. Catchphrases such as 'dignity versus liberty'[74] cannot capture the entire background and would be an exaggeration.

A more elaborated development of a constitutional right to privacy can be found in the case law of the Canadian Supreme Court. This is true, although the guarantees this Court refers to – most notably Section 8 and also Section 7 of the Canadian Charter of Rights and Freedoms[75] – are quite similar to those in the US. The understanding of the Charter as a 'purposive document'[76] whose spirit 'must not be constrained by narrow legalistic classifications based on notions of property'[77] leads to an abstract and broad understanding of Section 8 in the sense of a 'right to privacy'[78] that is shaped by the 'underlying values of dignity, integrity and autonomy'.[79] The pattern of 'reasonable expectations of privacy' has been essential for this understanding[80] and normatively assessed with a view to the 'totality of circumstances'.[81] The approach is sufficiently flexible to allow a distinction to be made between 'types of privacy interests – territorial, personal, and informational'.[82] Informational privacy interests are then described primarily as interests in the confidentiality, non-disclosure, non-dissemination or individual control of information, especially but not only in the case of intimate details on the individual's lifestyle and personal choices.[83] Recent judgments go further, differentiating privacy as secrecy, as control and as anonymity,[84] and pointing to 'informational self-determination'.[85] Some cases give rise to the development of more specific considerations which reflect the characteristics of information.

[73] *Dobbs v Jackson Women Health Organization*, 597 U.S. 215 (2022). The majority judgment emphasises that the reasons for overruling *Roe v Wade* and *Planned Parenthood v Casey* are partly of substantial nature, but above all, it is the methodological approach that is being subjected to a fundamental criticism, with as yet not all impacts predictable. For the discussion see, eg, S Kamin, 'Katz and Dobbs: Imagining the Fourth Amendment Without a Right to Privacy' (2022) 101 *Texas Law Review Online* 80.

[74] *Cf* JQ Whitman, 'The Two Western Cultures of Privacy: Dignity versus Liberty' (2004) 113 *Yale Law Journal* 1151.

[75] Section 8 states: 'Everyone has the right to be secure against unreasonable search or seizure.' Section 7 guarantees that 'Everyone has the right to life, liberty and security of the person and the right not to be deprived thereof except in accordance with the principles of fundamental justice.'

[76] See the methodological considerations in *Hunter et al v Southam Inc.*, [1984] 2 S.C.R. 145, 155 ff, 156 (for the citation).

[77] *R. v Dyment*, [1988] 2 S.C.R. 417, at 15.

[78] See as a landmark decision *Hunter et al. v Southam Inc.*, [1984] 2 S.C.R. 145, 155 ff.

[79] *R. v Plant*, [1993] 3 S.C.R. 281.

[80] *Hunter et al. v Southam Inc.*, [1984] 2 S.C.R. 145, 155 ff; *R. v Dyment*, [1988] 2 S.C.R. 417, at 15; *R. v Plant*, [1993] 3 S.C.R. 281.

[81] *R. v Tessling*, 2004 SCC 67, at 31 ff.

[82] *R. v Spencer*, 2014 SCC 43, at 35; see also *R. v Dyment*, [1988] 2 S.C.R. 417, at 19 ff; *R. v Tessling*, 2004 SCC 67, at 20 ff.

[83] *R. v Dyment*, [1988] 2 S.C.R. 417, at 31 ff.

[84] *R. v Spencer*, 2014 SCC 43, at 38.

[85] *R. v Jones* 2017 SCC 60, at 39, quoting *R. v Dyment* and the report of the Task Force, Privacy and Computers, 1972, 13, 'all information about a person is in a fundamental way his own, for him to communicate or retain for himself as he sees fit'. See also *R. v Bykovets*, 2024 SCC 6, at 32. See further *R. v Tessling*, 2004 SCC 67, at 23, quoting Westin (n 11) 7: 'the claim of individuals, groups, or institutions to determine for themselves when, how and to what extent information about them is communicated to others'. *Cf* for the jurisdiction of the German FCC section III.B of this chapter.

The landmark decision '*R. v Dyment*' notes that if 'the privacy of the individual is to be protected, we cannot afford to wait to vindicate it only after it has been violated'.[86] It also highlights that 'situations abound where the reasonable expectations of the individual that the information shall remain confidential to the persons to whom, and restricted to the purposes for which it is divulged, must be protected',[87] implying a pivotal role of purpose specification and purpose limitation in the processing of data and information. Cases on the Internet have led to a further differentiation of informational privacy in interests such as secrecy, control, or anonymity. The recent judgment '*R. v Bykovets*' underlines that the subject matter of the protection revolves around information, not just data, and the dispute between majority opinion and dissents centres on the problem of determining the information content of IP addresses.[88] Nevertheless, the informational protection is repeatedly referred back to the underlying, albeit highly abstractly interpreted, 'protection against unreasonable search and seizure'. All in all, specific patterns and limitations shape the 'right to privacy' derived from Section 8 of the Canadian Charter of Rights and Freedoms, even if the Canadian Supreme Court goes considerably further in developing informational protection as compared to the US Supreme Court.

The recognition of a constitutional right to privacy in the jurisprudence of the Supreme Court of India also provides some insight. The text of the Constitution of India does not explicitly mention 'privacy'. Nevertheless, following an open methodological approach, including 'borrowing', the Supreme Court has derived a multi-layered and multi-dimensional right to privacy in its comprehensive '*Puttaswamy-I*-verdict' and reaffirmed this recognition in the '*Puttaswamy-II* case'.[89] Both judgments dealt with the constitutionality of the Aadhaar project, a centralised nationwide identification system based on biometric technology. The Court highlights that privacy 'constitutes the foundation of all liberty' and 'lies across the spectrum of protected freedoms'.[90] In its conclusions, it anchors the right to privacy on a broad foundation:

> [p]rivacy is a constitutionally protected right which emerges primarily from the guarantee of life and personal liberty in art 21 of the Constitution. Elements of privacy also arise in varying contexts from the other facets of freedom and dignity recognized and guaranteed by the fundamental rights contained in Part III.[91]

[86] *R. v Dyment*, [1988] 2 S.C.R. 417, at 23: 'This is inherent in the notion of being *secure* against unreasonable searches and seizures.'

[87] *R. v Dyment*, [1988] 2 S.C.R. 417, at 22, 29 ff. In this case, the appellant had a traffic accident. A doctor collected a vial of free-flowing blood for medical purposes without the appellant's knowledge or consent. Later on, he handed the blood sample over to a police officer. The appellant was subsequently charged and convicted of impaired driving.

[88] *R. v Bykovets*, 2024 SCC 6.

[89] *Justice KS. Puttaswamy (Retd) v Union of India*, Judgment on 24 August 2017, Writ Petition (Civil) No 494 of 2012; (2017) 10 SCC 1; AIR 2017 SC 4161; and *Justice KS. Puttaswamy (Retd) v Union of India*, Judgment on 26 September 2018, AIR 2018 SC (SUPP) 1841, 2019 (1) SCC 1. While the right to privacy is recognised as a fundamental right in the *Puttaswamy-I*-decision, the Aadhar scheme has nevertheless been held constitutional in *Puttaswamy-II*.

[90] *Puttaswamy-I*, Part R (243, 244; Chandrachud J).

[91] *Puttaswamy-I*, Part T (266; Chandrachud J). Already in earlier case law, the right to life enshrined in art 21 of the Constitution has been interpreted as a basic right to a decent existence and has been given an expansive scope. *Cf* also regarding the jurisdiction of the Supreme Court of Pakistan S Aftab, *Comparative Perspectives on the Right to Privacy* (Dordrecht, Springer, 2024) 99 ff.

Different strands are covered, among others, informational privacy.[92] It is in line with the multi-layered and broad approach that the right to privacy is not only conceptualised as a right of defence against encroachments. It also includes duties of the state and mandates it to 'put in place a positive regime'.[93] Since the Aadhaar project raises many questions that are genuine data protection issues beyond common notions of privacy, it is particularly interesting that the Court, after addressing the characteristics of data and information, notes that 'apart from safeguarding privacy, data protection regimes seek to protect the autonomy of the individual [...] and the principle of non-discrimination'.[94]

What shape does a right to privacy take when it is explicitly enshrined in constitutional codifications? Textually and systematically, the protection under the right to privacy is usually placed in more traditional contexts of home, correspondence, or property, as well as search and seizures. An example of this is Section 14 of the Bill of Rights in the Constitution of the Republic of South Africa, 1996.[95] However, the anchoring of the right to privacy in the form of a general term – in conjunction with doctrinal and methodological considerations – allows the Constitutional Court of South Africa to develop this right relatively independently. The Court underlines the interrelationships between privacy, dignity, autonomy, and equality, as well as, in some cases, other freedom rights that are also affected, for example, the rights to freedom of expression and the media.[96] Nevertheless, 'privacy' implies certain patterns of thought, such as the juxtaposition of privacy and publicity, the differentiation of more or less personal realms, or the emphasis on an individual right to decide on disclosure. To a certain extent, such thought patterns are also at work when it comes to the issues of data protection.[97]

Article 8 of the European Convention on Human Rights (ECHR) expressly provides for the right of everyone to respect for his or her private life and correspondence.[98] Since the European Court of Human Rights (ECtHR) sees itself as the pivotal European court in the field of international law and as part of a network between the signatory states and the European courts within which these courts and their

[92] See *Puttaswamy-I*, Part S (246 ff; Chandrachud J).

[93] *Puttaswamy-II*, Part G (232; Chandrachud J, dissenting); *cf* also *Puttaswamy-I*, Part S (p 254; Chandrachud J).

[94] *Puttaswamy-I*, Part S (246 ff, 252; Chandrachud J).

[95] Section 14 of the Bill of Rights provides that everyone has the right to privacy, which includes the right not to have: (a) their person or home searched; (b) their property searched; (c) their possessions seized; or (d) the privacy of their communications infringed.

[96] *Cf Amabhungane Centre for Investigative Journalism NPC and Another v Minister of Justice and Correctional Services and Others; Minister of Police v Amabhungane Centre for Investigative Journalism NPC and Others* (CCT 278, 279/19) [2021] ZACC 3, at 112 ff.

[97] *Cf* the judgments *Bernstein and Others v Bester NO and Others* (CCT 23/95) [1996] ZACC 2, at 56 ff; *NM and Others v Smith and Others* (CCT 69/05) [2007] ZACC 6, at 32 ff; *Amabhungane Centre for Investigative Journalism NPC and Another v Minister of Justice and Correctional Services and Others; Minister of Police v Amabhungane Centre for Investigative Journalism NPC and Others* (CCT 278, 279/19) [2021] ZACC 3, at 23 ff.

[98] 'Everyone has the right to respect for his private and family life, his home and his correspondence. There shall be no interference by a public authority with the exercise of this right except such as is in accordance with the law and is necessary in a democratic society in the interests of national security, public safety or the economic well-being of the country, for the prevention of disorder or crime, for the protection of health or morals, or for the protection of the rights and freedoms of others.'

decisions increasingly interact,[99] it has moved away from the traditional understanding of the ECHR in terms of international minimum standards. According to its case law, article 8 ECHR protects a broad spectrum of interests.[100] Besides the protection of personal activities, decisions or spatial areas, which always included social relationships and public activities to a certain extent, protection was gradually developed with regard to the handling of personal information and data. The initial judgments dealt with traditional cases of phone surveillance and, thus, the right to respect for correspondence. In such cases, first guidelines were developed, for example, that business connections are covered by protection if reasonable expectations of privacy protection can be recognised, or that an impairment does not depend on whether and to what extent recordings are subsequently used or whether concrete disadvantages have arisen – an argumentation pattern that has always existed in cases of telecommunications surveillance as a typifying approach. The informational protection of the right to respect for the 'private life' was to some extent based on these initial guidelines, not least because the data processing steps that followed the interception were subsumed under this right.[101] The protection extends to data that originates within a private sphere. To a certain extent, it can also cover data that is publicly accessible, for example, in the event of systematic collection and storage by public authorities, or in the case of a compilation, use, or other form of processing of personal data that the data subject would not reasonably expect. In the subsequent case law, the focus has increasingly shifted from the private sphere as the source of the data to its informational content. A wide range of data has been classified as belonging to private life, such as tax data, medical data and information, data on the health or sexual life of somebody, personal data revealing political opinions, such as information about participation in peaceful protests, the IP address or geolocation data insofar as it can be related to individuals, a person's image and biometric data, but also photos and video recordings or DNA samples as data carriers.[102] Data processing steps are differentiated and, if necessary, independently assessed as an intrusion.[103] In principle, the Court upholds the presumption that the collection, recording, use, or publication of private life can constitute an impairment, regardless of whether the

[99] M Albers 'Höchstrichterliche Rechtsfindung und Auslegung gerichtlicher Entscheidungen' in G Lienbacher, B Grzeszick and C Calliess et al (eds), *Grundsatzfragen der Rechtsetzung und Rechtsfindung*, VVDStRL vol 71 (Berlin, de Gruyter, 2012) 257 (272 ff, 287 ff).

[100] For a comprehensive overview of the case law see ECtHR, Guide on art 8 of the European Convention on Human Rights, right to respect for private and family life, home and correspondence (last update: 5.11.2024), www.ks.echr.coe.int/web/echr-ks/article-8-all-updates; ECtHR, Factsheet – Personal data protection (last update: February 2024), www.echr.coe.int/documents/d/echr/fs_data_eng.

[101] *Cf* ECtHR, No 27798/95 *Amann* ECLI:CE:ECHR:2000:0216, [2000] §§ 44 ff, 64 ff.

[102] *Cf*, ECtHR Case No 20383/04 *Khmel* ECLI:CE:ECHR:2013:1212, [2013] §§ 41 ff, 49; Case No 931/13 *Satakunnan* ECLI:CE:ECHR:2017:0627, [2017] §§ 133 ff; No 66490/09 *Mockutė* ECLI:CE:ECHR:2018:0227, [2018] §§ 93 f; No 62357/14 *Benedik* ECLI:CE:ECHR:2018:0424, [2018] §§ 100 ff, 107 ff; No 50001/12 *Breyer* ECLI:CE:ECHR:2020:0130, [2020] §§ 76 ff; No 75229/10 *Dragan Petrović* ECLI:CE:ECHR:2020:0414, [2020] §§ 69, 79; Nos 3153/16 and 27758/18 *Drelon* ECLI:CE:ECHR:2022:0908, [2022] §§ 79 ff; No 11519/20 *Glukhin* ECLI:CE:ECHR:2023:0704, [2023] §§ 64 ff.

[103] ECtHR, No 20383/04 *Khmel* ECLI:CE:ECHR:2013:1212, [2013] §§ 40 ff; No 42788/06 *Surikov* ECLI:CE:ECHR:2017:0126, [2017] §§ 75, 84 ff; No 931/13 §§ 134 ff.

data is sensitive or whether the data subject has suffered specific disadvantages.[104] However, potentially detrimental consequences do play a role in the overall assessment of protection.[105] When such effects are taken into account, other freedoms may become relevant as well, for example, the freedom of expression.[106]

The ECtHR specifies more detailed requirements for the necessary legal basis in a very differentiated manner, depending on the context and dimension of protection, while recognising the more or less far-reaching margin of appreciation of the signatory states. For example, state surveillance measures, especially if they are secret at certain stages, require a series of coordinated minimum legal precautions.[107] And the state does not adequately fulfil its duty to protect unless it ensures respect for private life among private individuals by creating a legal framework that takes account of the different protection interests in a particular context.[108] article 8 ECHR can also provide (limited) rights of knowledge, such as the right to information or access to files with regard to personal data or documents held by the authorities.[109]

### *ii. Achievements and Shortcomings of Privacy as Protected Interest*

Irrespective of whether the constitutional protection of (respect for) privacy is explicitly enshrined or derived from other fundamental rights, its long and rich tradition as an idea makes it easier to address it as a subject matter of fundamental rights protection at different levels and in different contexts. The heterogeneous framings and the shifting meanings of privacy also make it easier to refer to seemingly established views, just as they are often the reason for talking past one another. How constitutional provisions are interpreted in terms of a 'right to privacy' depends, of course, on the legal system and culture, as well as on the role and self-understanding of the courts, and not only on substantive but also on doctrinal and methodological considerations. Nevertheless, some achievements and weaknesses of privacy as a protected interest when it comes to constitutionalising data protection can be identified, which emerge as issues across jurisdictions.

In terms of content, it is a particular achievement that the right to (respect for) privacy can be applied to very different and wide-ranging subject matters of protection.[110]

[104] ECtHR, No 28 341/95 *Rotaru* ECLI:CE:ECHR:2000:0504, [2000] §§ 42 ff; No 44 647/98 *Peck* ECLI:CE:ECHR:2003:0128, [2003] §§ 57 ff; No 62 332/00 *Segerstedt-Wiberg* ECLI:CE:ECHR:2006:0606, [2006] §§ 69 ff; No 30 562/04 *S. and Marper* ECLI:CE:ECHR:2008:1204, [2008] §§ 58 ff; No 11519/20, 67 ff. See also for a legal obligation of Telegram to decrypt Internet communications if they are encrypted No 33696/19 *Podchasov* ECLI:CE:ECHR:2024:0213, [2024] § 58.

[105] ECtHR, No 931/13, § 137; No 50001/12, §§ 74 ff; No 11519/20, §§ 65 ff; No 33696/19, § 51 ff.

[106] See ECtHR, Nos 58170/13, 62322/14 and 24960/15 *Big Brother Watch* ECLI:CE:ECHR:2018:0913, [2021] §§ 442 ff.

[107] ECtHR, No 47143/06 *Zakharov* ECLI:CE:ECHR:2015:1204, [2015] §§ 228 ff, Nos 58170/13, 62322/14 and 24960/15, §§ 322 ff; No 70078/12 *Ekimdzhiev* ECLI:CE:ECHR:2022:0111, [2022] §§ 291 ff; No 33696/19, §§ 63 ff.

[108] *Cf* ECtHR, No 61496/08 *Bărbulescu* ECLI:CE:ECHR:2017:0905, [2017] §§ 115, 120 ff.

[109] *Cf* ECtHR, No 10 454/83 *Gaskin* ECLI:CE:ECHR:1989:0707, [1989] § 37; No 62 332/00, §§ 99 ff; No 12 504/09 *Yonchev* ECLI:CE:ECHR:2017:1207, [2017] §§ 46 ff.

[110] *Cf* D Solove, *Understanding Privacy* (Cambridge (MA), Harvard University Press, 2008) 45: 'umbrella term'. *Cf* also more closely BJ Koops, B Newell, T Timan, I Skorvanek, T Chokrevski and M Galič, 'A Typology of Privacy' (2017) 38 *University of Pennsylvania Journal of International Law*, 483, 491 ff; Aftab (n 91) 39 ff.

On the one hand, this is due to its level of abstraction. In line with the basic dichotomies that have shaped the traditional understanding of privacy, some lines of reasoning take a very fundamental approach by emphasising that privacy is a crucial value for a liberal society and, in the sense of a precondition, essential for the exercise of other freedoms.[111] On the other hand, the concept of a private 'sphere' can cover different facets of protection, for example, personal decisions, particular spatial areas, and also the content of conversations or data that arise in or can be attributed to that private sphere. As we have seen: 'Privacy' assigns something to a person or a group of people as their own concern and sets limits on others' access to it. The attribution already made in the concept – in particular, of data to the individual[112] – reduces the burden of giving reasons for protection needs. Just as the protected interests do not have to be specified in detail, it is not necessary to specify impairments and to break down precisely to what extent the person in question is actually exposed to disadvantages. As we have seen, the ECtHR even emphasises that an impairment does not depend on whether concrete disadvantages have arisen. The data subject as a fundamental rights holder has a protected negative-liberty status based on the principle of non-interference in the private sphere, which can be applied to various forms of intrusions, including the acquisition of data, information, and knowledge about the right-holder. Such an approach does not need to be more closely aligned with the characteristics of this particular subject matter to which the protection is extended. Provided that more detailed aspects of protection or of impairments are addressed, particularly in the balancing of interests, interdependencies between data protection and freedoms of decisions or behaviour that might be protected by specific fundamental rights show up.[113] In this sense, the right to privacy always points beyond itself.

Following traditional patterns for the development and justification of data protection has its disadvantages as well. Insofar as some courts, due to their doctrinal and methodological approach, are rather reluctant to make more extensive interpretations, the protection with regard to the handling of data and information is understood as an extension and more or less accessory to traditionally protected freedoms or at best one facet of protection among others. It is not explicitly information- and data-orientated but rather based on the assumption that data shares the privacy of the personal sphere from which they originate. Consequently, it is more or less designed as a sphere-related 'defence formula'. Difficulties arise already if data acquires an informational content that calls for protection only in the context of its further processing or use, for example, through the linking of data or additional knowledge. The paradigm of a private sphere directs attention primarily to the collection of data (as an intrusion into the personal

[111] See, eg, the Supreme Court of Canada, *R. v Dyment*, [1988] 2 S.C.R. 417, at 17 (quoting Westin, (n 11) 349 f): '[…] society has come to realize that privacy is at the heart of liberty in a modern state […] Grounded in man's physical and moral autonomy, privacy is essential for the well-being of the individual.'; and the Supreme Court of India, *Puttaswamy-I*, Part R (243, 244).

[112] *Cf* the dissent of Justice Gorsuch, *Carpenter v United States*, 585 U.S. ____ (2018), 13, with the proposal to revisit the 'kind of legal interest' that 'is sufficient to make something *yours*'.

[113] For example: Constitutional Court of South Africa, *Amabhungane Centre for Investigative Journalism NPC and Another v Minister of Justice and Correctional Services and Others; Minister of Police v Amabhungane Centre for Investigative Journalism NPC and Others* (CCT 278, 279/19) [2021] ZACC 3, at 112 ff; ECtHR, Nos 58170/13, 62322/14 and 24960/15, §§ 442 ff.

sphere) and the requirements for its justification, for example, a search warrant. The subsequent data processing steps receive only limited attention and are not appropriately assessed in terms of their own potentially detrimental consequences. Insofar as other courts see their role as a proactive one and understand the relevant codification in the sense of a 'living constitution', they arrive at very sophisticated multi-layered and multi-dimensional conceptions, which also set a demanding task for the legislature. While the lines of reasoning are problem-orientated, they may be criticised for not being sufficiently grounded in the provisions, especially since the concept of privacy itself is under constant criticism.[114] In addition, to some extent, traditional patterns of thought still have an impact on the conceptions. The focus on 'privacy' runs the risk of failing to adequately develop the protected interests of data subjects and data protection law. References to informational self-determination, such as we find in some of the court decisions, are therefore not surprising.

At this point we can move on to the right of personality and the right to informational self-determination. In the jurisprudence of the German Federal Constitutional Court, this right has been developed not least in response to the weaknesses of the formerly recognised right to respect for privacy. It is tailored to the purpose of providing protection to the individual with regard to the handling of personal data and information.

## B. Right to Personality and Informational Self-Determination

German law is famous for the development of a protected interest that has attracted worldwide attention: 'informational self-determination'. I would prefer to call it 'informational autonomy' because 'informational self-determination' is just a poor translation. However, this term is established, and therefore, I will stick to it.

### *i. Approaches and Developments in Case Law*

The Federal Constitutional Court derived the 'right to informational self-determination' from article 2(1) in conjunction with article 1(1) of the Basic Law[115] in its decision concerning the census ('*Volkszählungsurteil*') taken in 1983.[116] The wording of these fundamental rights does not explicitly provide for a 'right to informational self-determination'. Instead, it refers to the protection of the free development of one's personality and to the inviolability of human dignity.

In our context, it is of particular interest that article 2(1) in conjunction with article 1(1) of the Basic Law has long been interpreted in the case law of the Federal Constitutional Court primarily as a 'right to respect for privacy'. Scholarly contributions

[114] See, eg, Bellin (n 51).

[115] Art 2 Basic Law: 'Everybody shall have the right to the free development of his or her personality […]'; art 1 Basic Law: 'Human dignity shall be inviolable. To respect and to protect it shall be the duty of all state authority.'

[116] Decisions of the FCC (BVerfGE) vol 65, 1. See also G Britz, ch 5 in this volume.

and an inspirational glance at American case law have contributed to the derivation of this right. In its early case law, the Federal Constitutional Court originally conceived of 'privacy' employing the spatial imagery of areas of retreat walled off from the outside world or situations for interaction and communication that are to remain, in principle, free of undesired inspection. Subsequently, issues were included that are typically classified as 'private' due to their information content. As a result, the right to respect for privacy has covered many constellations: the protection of medical files stored at the doctor's workplace from access by security authorities,[117] the use of secret tape recordings in a civil court proceeding,[118] the publishing of a fictitious interview about private matters in the press,[119] or a television movie about a murder in which the criminal, who has since been released, can be identified (the famous '*Lebach*-case').[120]

But then the '*Eppler*-case' resulted in a turning point.[121] In this case of an alleged public statement on a public matter, the FCC reached the conclusion that 'the right to respect for privacy' was not a suitable approach to grasp the problems of the case appropriately. Instead, the 'general right of personality' was derived from article 2(1) in conjunction with article 1(1) of the Basic Law.[122] This development is facilitated by the fact that the wording of article 2(1) of the Basic Law promises everyone the right to freely develop their personality. In the '*Eppler*-decision', the Court held that, in principle, individuals should be able to decide for themselves how they wish to present themselves to third parties or to the public, and whether and to what extent third parties may dispose of their personality.[123] Although the case was about statements falsely attributed to one's person, this description of the scope of protection has been understood as if the general right of personality provided a right that people see you the way you want to be seen. This paved the way for the right to informational self-determination.

According to the '*Census*-judgment', the right to informational self-determination confers on the individual the authority to, in principle, determine for themselves the disclosure and use of their personal data.[124] Individuals have the right to decide for themselves whether and how their personal data is to be revealed and used; in other words, they have a right to self-determination about the processing of data relating to them. An analysis of the broader background, previous case law, and academic debate can explain very well how the Federal Constitutional Court arrived at this subject

[117] BVerfGE 32, 373 [1972] – *Ärztliche Schweigepflicht (Medical Confidentiality)*; 44, 353 [1977] – *Durchsuchung Drogenberatungsstelle (Search of drug counseling center).*

[118] BVerfGE, 34, 238 [1973] – *Tonband.*

[119] BVerfGE 34, 269 [1973] – *Soraya.*

[120] BVerfGE 35, 202 [1973] – *Lebach.*

[121] BVerfGE 54, 148 [1980] – *Eppler*. Erhard Eppler, a well-known member of the Social Democratic Party of Germany, was blamed for making a public statement on a public matter which he proved he had not made in this way and requested injunctive relief.

[122] BVerfGE 54, 148, 153 ff.

[123] BVerfGE 54, 148, 155.

[124] BVerfGE 65, 1, 43 [1983] – *Volkszählungsurteil.* Analysing the decision and its background Albers (n 9), 151 ff. Limitations to this broadly defined scope of protection – see Britz (n 116) – are considered by the court only when looking at the possibilities of restricting protection on the basis of the legal reservation, see BVerfGE 65, 1, 46 ff.

matter to be protected. The precursor of the right to informational self-determination, the right to respect for privacy, drew the same criticism in Germany as it did in the US-American privacy debate. The first point of criticism emphasised the relativity of the sphere of personal privacy: it could be described only in terms 'relative' to those receiving information.[125] Therefore, what was to be protected was not a predetermined sphere, but the capacity of the individual to decide to whom to disclose which information. Alan Westin formulated this idea in these terms as early as 1972.[126] The second point of criticism highlighted the fact that the need for protection was less about the private sphere as the context in which certain data emerges but rather about which information could be derived from data obtained and how that information could be used.[127] In other words, what is decisive is not the context the data originates from but rather the context in which the information is used. The Federal Constitutional Court responded to these central points of criticism by developing a right with a scope of protection which centres on individual decision capacities as well as on the context of use of personal data.[128] It also took up the acknowledged constitutionally protected goods of autonomy and freedom of decision and action, arguing as follows: free decision and action are possible only under certain circumstances. If people are unsure whether deviating behaviours may be stored as information and used to their disadvantage, they will try not to attract attention by such behaviour and will no longer be free to act at will.[129] That is why the protection of fundamental rights must cover the protection against information and data processing by the state. The Federal Constitutional Court concluded that, just as people can decide about their actions, they also have the right to determine how 'their' personal data will be processed. The protected persons also have the right to know by whom and for what purposes personal data referring to them are processed,[130] but that right is accessory in the context of the concept.

In the course of its case law, the FCC has long maintained a scope of protection defined in this way and, using it as a starting point, has developed a wide range of requirements with which statutory law must comply. These include the principles of purpose specification and purpose limitation, thresholds for the permissibility of data processing steps, and data security standards. Particular requirements can usually be traced back to the challenges raised by the case. The doctrinal reference point is often

[125] See B Schlink, 'Das Recht der informationellen Selbstbestimmung' (1986) 25 *Der Staat* 233, 242; D Solove, *The digital person* (New York and London, NYU Press, 2004) 212 f.

[126] AF Westin, *Privacy and Freedom*, 6 edn (New York, Atheneum, 1970) 42.

[127] See S Simitis, 'Chancen und Gefahren der elektronischen Datenverarbeitung' [1971] *Neue Juristische Wochenschrift (NJW)* 673, 680.

[128] For literary sources of the Court's decision see H Heußner (former judge at the BVerfG preparing the Census Decision), 'Das informationelle Selbstbestimmungsrecht in der Rechtsprechung des Bundesverfassungsgerichts' [1984] *Die Sozialgerichtsbarkeit (SGb)* 279, 280 f. Amongst others, the ideas of Westin have been received by the members of the Court, see E Benda (former President of the BVerfG participating at the Census Decision), 'Privatsphäre und "Persönlichkeitsprofil". Ein Beitrag zur Datenschutzdiskussion' in Leibholz, Faller, Mikat and Reis (eds), *Menschenwürde und freiheitliche Rechtsordnung* (Tübingen, Mohr Siebeck, 1974) 23, 32.

[129] BVerfGE 65, 1, 43.

[130] BVerfGE, 65, 1, 46.

the principle of proportionality, although it may not be the most appropriate reference point for some requirements.

In the aforementioned version of a right of individuals to decide whether and how 'their' personal data is to be disclosed and used, the right to informational self-determination was quite firmly established for a long time. But meanwhile, this version is in flux. It already has been modified to a certain extent. The FCC has thus reacted to scholarly criticism as well as to changes in its own case law on the right to respect for privacy and the general right of personality.[131] For instance, the Court clarified in its '*Caroline I*-judgment' that

> [...] the general right of personality does not confer to the individual the right to be portrayed by others only as he or she views him- or herself or only as he or she wants to be perceived [...] Such a broad protection would not only exceed the aim of protection, i.e. to avoid risks to the development of an individual's personality, but would also extend far into third parties' sphere of freedom.[132]

Thereby a pattern of argumentation has been abandoned that contributed to the definition of the scope of protection of the right to informational self-determination.[133] In relation to the state, the problem has arisen in cases such as electronic profiling and searches or automatic licence plate recognition that personal data is collected but quickly and automatically sorted out and deleted, raising the question of whether this is relevant to the scope of protection and may amount to an encroachment. In such cases, the Court has partially modified the protective functions and the scope of protection of the right to informational self-determination in a more or less well-thought-out manner.[134] In the '*Right to be Forgotten I*-judgment' of 2019, the Court has undertaken significant changes: Between private parties,[135] the right to informational self-determination provides the individual

> the possibility of influencing, in nuanced ways, the context and manner in which their data is accessible to and can be used by others, thus affording the individual considerable influence in deciding what information is available on them.[136]

Further elaboration of the right to informational self-determination continues to progress.

[131] For these changes see BVerfGE 97, 125, 146 ff [1998] – *Caroline I*; 97, 391, 403 ff; 101, 361, 382; 120, 180, 199.

[132] BVerfGE 101, 361–396 [1999] – *Caroline II*, para 70, www.bverfg.de/e/rs19991215_1bvr065396en.html.

[133] *Cf* M Albers, 'Grundrechtsschutz der Privatheit' [2010] *Deutsches Verwaltungsblatt (DVBl)* 1061, 1065 f.

[134] See BVerfGE 115, 320, 342 ff [2006] – *Rasterfahndung II*; 120, 378, 398 [2008] – *Automatisierte Kennzeichenerfassung*; 150, 244 [2018] – *Kennzeichenkontrolle Bayern* Rn 41 ff.

[135] The relationship between private parties is covered by fundamental rights via acknowledged third-party effects ('*Drittwirkung*'), however, an individual right to decide on the disclosure and use of personal data has always created substantial and doctrinal problems. See L Schertel Mendes, *Schutz vor Informationsrisiken und Gewährleistung einer gehaltvollen Zustimmung: Eine Analyse der Rechtmäßigkeit der Datenverarbeitung im Privatrecht* (Berlin, De Gruyter, 2015) 44 ff. *Cf* also for the doctrine of the '*Drittwirkung*' M Albers, 'L'effet horizontal des droits fondamentaux dans le cadre d'une conception à multi-niveaux' in Hochmann and Reinhardt (eds), *L'effet horizontal des droits fondamentaux* (Paris, Éditions Pedone, 2018) 177 ff.

[136] BVerfGE 152, 152–215 [2019] – *Recht auf Vergessen I*, Headnote 3 and Rn 83 ff, www.bundesverfassungsgericht.de/SharedDocs/Entscheidungen/EN/2019/11/rs20191106_1bvr001613en.html.

### *ii. Achievements and Weaknesses of Informational Self-Determination as Protected Interest*

The right to informational self-determination reaches far beyond the classical understanding of the right to respect for privacy. Its core element is a relatively abstract individual right to make decisions ranging from disclosure of data to their processing and to their use. This scope of protection is characterised by an approach that places the handling of personal data and information as such at the centre of attention. The protection provided is no longer derived from and no longer dependent on otherwise protected interests – such as 'privacy' – that have particular definitions and delimitations. It is an area in its own right. This opens up the possibility that the protection is being tailored appropriately to the subject matter. The protection directly aimed at the handling of personal data and information and the possible extension to a wide range of protection requirements that already exist or may arise in the future are an important step forward that the right to informational self-determination has brought.

Despite these achievements of the novel approach to protection requirements, there are shortcomings in the FCC's definition of the scope of protection. As explained, the approach opens up the possibility that the protection is being tailored appropriately to the subject matter. But this is precisely what the Court fails to do. The Court adheres to traditional patterns of thought with regard to both content and doctrine. In terms of content, the Court is guided by the familiar patterns used to describe freedom of decision and action, or property rights. After all, these patterns of free decision and action have been referred to in the argumentation of the census judgment's grounds in order to support the development of the right to informational self-determination. Additionally, even though the right to informational self-determination is derived from the right to the free development of personality and from human dignity, its scope of protection is to a certain extent shaped like a property right.[137] Similar to some US-American conceptions of privacy, informational self-determination is primarily thought of as a right of control over personal data.[138] Such an approach does not do justice to the distinct categoriality and characteristics of data, information and knowledge. It entails ontic ideas, as if data or even information were a kind of ball that can be held or passed on and that does not change in the process. It is no coincidence that the scope of protection of 'informational' self-determination relates to data, not information. The fact that others, be they government agencies or private individuals, are structurally involved with their own activities of interpreting, processing, and

[137] Sometimes it is emphasised that the BVerfG also stated: 'The individual does not have a right in the sense of an absolute, unlimitable mastery over "his/her" data; he/she is rather a personality that develops within a social community and is dependent upon communication', BVerfGE 65, 1, 43, 46. However, these grounds refer to the reservation allowing to limit the scope of protection by means of statutory rules. They do not alter the shaping of the scope of protection.

[138] The ideas of Westin (n 126) 42, which the BVerfG adopted, have also been cited in some rulings of the Canadian Supreme Court. See also C Fried, 'Privacy' (1968) 77 *Yale Law Journal* 475, 482, 483: 'Privacy [...] is the *control* we have over information about ourselves [...] is control over knowledge about oneself.' For more on these ideas and their critique, see A Allen, ch 1 in this volume.

creating constantly changing data and information is lost.[139] In its case law, the Court does occasionally address the informational content of data and the informational consequences in the social relations between the parties involved when it comes to discussing the impairment of the right to informational self-determination or to the balancing of interests required by the principle of proportionality.[140] However, as long as the scope of protection continues to be defined in its flawed conception, the Court's deliberations lack substantive and doctrinal consistency.

In terms of doctrine, the Court is guided by the familiar patterns of protection against encroachments. That means that the fundamental right's scope of protection is interpreted as safeguarding individual freedom (traditionally understood in a liberal way) against any impairments unless they are covered by statutory provisions which meet the principle of clarity and certainty, the principle of proportionality, and all other relevant constitutional requirements. This doctrinal approach results in specific forms of describing the subject matters or interests which are to be protected by fundamental rights as well as in specific functions and features regarding the statutory provisions. In particular, the idea is lost that an appropriate regulation of the handling of personal information and data must be multi-layered as well as manifold and requires a multitude of regulatory tools. Since the doctrinal approach leads to a limited perspective, the wide range of requirements that the Court has nevertheless developed in the course of its jurisprudence[141] is often not sufficiently linked to the scope of protection and can be better explained in terms of reasonable solutions to the challenges of the case. Relatively free-standing judicial findings raise problems not only of doctrinal consistency but also of the role and legitimacy of the courts. It simply does not work to comprehend a fundamental right's scope of protection merely in terms of its function to activate 'the fundamental need to justify [...] data processing' or 'to create a starting point for a process that requires legal structuring with regard to the free development of personality'.[142]

The right to informational self-determination is quite popular in other countries' jurisdictions, as well as within the international scientific community. But we must be aware that the FCC, as I have mentioned above, has modified the scope of protection of this right in recent decisions. It has revised its approach only to a very limited extent in the state-citizen relationship, but more significantly in the relations between private individuals. The description of the scope of protection in these relations has been left rather vague, and the sharp distinction between the statements on the state-citizen relationships and those on the relations between private parties reveals an overly traditional understanding of the state. The interplay with the Charter of Fundamental Rights of the European Union, which is not only based on factual influences but is also doctrinally justified,[143] opens up opportunities for the necessary further development of fundamental rights.

[139] For a detailed analysis and critique, see Albers (n 9) 151 ff, 234 ff, 280 ff.
[140] This is emphasised by J Masing, ch 3 in this volume.
[141] See above III.B.i. and Masing (n 140).
[142] Masing (n 140).
[143] *Cf* Albers (n 99) 287 ff.

## C. Right to the Protection of Personal Data

Aiming at being a modern charter covering contemporary challenges,[144] article 8(1) of the Charter of Fundamental Rights of the European Union (CFR) offers everyone a specific right to the protection of personal data concerning them.[145] Article 8(2) and (3) CFR point in part to the possibility of shaping or restricting the fundamental right via statutory regulations and in part contain guidelines for such regulations.[146] The explicit enshrinement of a right to the protection of personal data has been the model for the new similar anchor in article 5 LXXIX of the Constitution of the Federative Republic of Brazil.[147] Article 8(1) CFR stands alongside the protection of article 7(1) CFR, the right to respect for private and family life, home, and communications. Does that novel fundamental right advance the constitutional landscape and offer answers to the question of how to unfold the protected interests of data subjects?

### *i. Approaches and Developments in Case Law*

In its initial decisions, the ECJ stated that article 8 CFR was 'closely linked' to article 7 CFR[148] and did not differentiate in more detail between the two fundamental rights.[149] Specific difficulties in distinguishing between the scope of protection of article 7 CFR on the one hand and article 8 CFR on the other arise for doctrinal reasons: article 52(3) CFR grants the rights of the Charter the same meaning and scope as the corresponding Convention rights, and article 7(1) CFR corresponds to article 8(1) ECHR, which is the foundation of data protection in the case law of the ECtHR. In its landmark '*Tele2 Sverige*-judgment', the ECJ does not address all the questions arising, but at least it explains that 'Art. 52(3) CFR does not preclude Union law from providing protection that is more extensive than the ECHR' and that

[144] See also F Picod, C Rizcallah and S Van Drooghenbroek (eds), *Charte des droits fondamentaux de l'Union européenne*, 3rd edn (Édition Bruylant, Bruxelles, 2023) art 8 Rn. 1.

[145] Art 8(1) CFR states: 'Everyone has the right to the protection of personal data concerning him or her.' The right to the protection of personal data concerning him or her is also anchored in art 16(1) TFEU. The difficulties in reconciling art 16(1) TFEU, arts 8, 52(1) and 52(2) CFR can be resolved by a teleological reduction of art 52(2) CFR. *Cf* ECJ (Grand Chamber) of 26 July 2017, Opinion 1/15, PNR, § 120.

[146] These sections read: '(2) Such data must be processed fairly for specified purposes and on the basis of the consent of the person concerned or some other legitimate basis laid down by law. Everyone has the right of access to data which has been collected concerning him or her, and the right to have it rectified. (3) Compliance with these rules shall be subject to control by an independent authority.'

[147] According to the amendment of this article in 2022, 'under the terms of the law, the right to protection of personal data is ensured, including in digital media'. See for the preceding development until the landmark ruling of the Brazilian Supreme Court on 7 May 2020, that paved the way for Congress to pass the constitutional amendment I Sarlet, 'The Protection of Personality in the Digital Environment' in Albers and Sarlet (n 1) 133 (137 ff).

[148] ECJ, Judgment (Grand Chamber) Case C-92, 93/09 *Schecke* ECLI:EU:C:2010:662, [2010] § 47.

[149] See ECJ, Judgment (Grand Chamber) Case C-92, 93/09, §§ 45 ff; Judgment (Grand Chamber) Case C-468, 469/10 *ASNEF/FECEMD* ECLI:EU:C:2011:777, [2011] §§ 41 ff. For more in-depth analyses of earlier case law P de Hert and S Gutwirth, 'Data Protection in the Case Law of Strasbourg and Luxemburg: Constitutionalisation in Action' in Gutwirth, Poullet, de Hert, de Terwagne and Nouwt (eds), *Reinventing Data Protection?* (Berlin, Springer, 2009) 3 (29 ff).

article 8 CFR 'concerns a fundamental right which is distinct from that enshrined in art 7 of the Charter and which has no equivalent in the ECHR'.[150]

However, the Court's interpretation of the scope of protection under article 8 CFR does not provide much substance. The '*Digital Rights Ireland*-judgment' indicates that article 7 CFR protects private life in a substantive sense, while article 8 CFR focuses on the processing of personal data in a way that is not limited to private life and sets its own requirements, for example, in terms of data security or in terms of protecting personal data against the risk of abuse and against any unlawful access and use.[151] The constituent elements of article 8(1) CFR are 'personal data' and their processing, irrespective of whether the information that can be obtained from the data is of a sensitive nature or whether any detrimental effects have been suffered.[152] Data processing phases are differentiated and assessed separately – not in isolation, however, but as relatively independent elements of a processing sequence.[153] In a closer context, the protected interests of data subjects are occasionally specified, such as the need for protection against comprehensive profiling or constant surveillance, against expectation-mediated constraints on actually protected behaviour, against the undermining of professional secrecy or informant protection, or against data misuse.[154] When developing these protected interests, the ECJ takes into account other fundamental rights of the European Charter as well as interests protected under secondary or national law.[155] This is quite convincing if we associate article 8 CFR with a bundle of protected interests and with requirements that are first and foremost directed at legislation, which must consistently develop an appropriate data protection regime and coordinate it with other legal regimes. It is in line with this approach that the ECJ recognises different dimensions of protection, ie, besides rights of defence against encroachments, also duties to protect or, not quite clearly, an indirect horizontal effect in the relationship between private individuals.[156]

Where appropriate, the ECJ points to the provisions of article 8(2) and (3) of the CFR for guidelines. In addition, it bases many requirements on the principle of

[150] ECJ, Judgment (Grand Chamber) Case C-203/15 and Case C-698/15 *Tele2 Sverige* ECLI:EU:C:2016:970, [2016] § 129.

[151] ECJ, Judgment (Grand Chamber) Case C-293/12 and Case C-594/12 *Digital Rights Ireland Ltd* ECLI:EU:C:2014:238, [2014] §§ 29 f, 40, 54.

[152] ECJ, Judgment (Grand Chamber) Case C-511, 512 and Case 520/18, *Quadrature du Net* ECLI:EU:C:2020:791, [2020] § 115; Judgment (Grand Chamber) Case C-623/17, *Privacy International* ECLI:EU:C:2020:790, [2020] § 70.

[153] ECJ, Judgment (Grand Chamber) Case C-293/12 and Case C-594/12, §§ 34 f; Judgment (Grand Chamber) Case C-136/17 GC and Others ECLI:EU:C:2019:773, [2019] § 36; Judgment (Grand Chamber) of 21 March 2024, Case C-61/22, *RL* ECLI:EU:C:2024:251, [2024] §§ 70 ff. See also, emphasising that data and information is addressed while it flows, E Orrù, 'Privacy: Scepticism, Normative Approaches and Legal Protection. A Review of the Theoretical Debate and a Discussion of Recent Developments in the EU' (2022) 52 *DPCE online* 2, 779 (798).

[154] *Cf* ECJ, Judgment (Grand Chamber) Case C-131/12 *Google Spain* ECLI:EU:C:2014:317, [2014] § 80; Judgment (Grand Chamber) Case C-136/17, § 36; Judgment (Grand Chamber) Case C-511, 512 and Case 520/18, §§ 106 ff; Judgment (Grand Chamber) Case C-623/17 §§ 50 ff.

[155] See ECJ, Judgment (Grand Chamber) Case C-362/14, § 72; Judgment (Grand Chamber) Case C-511, 512 and 520/18, §§ 87 ff; Judgment (Grand Chamber) Case C-623/17, §§ 30 ff.

[156] See also O Tambou, *Manuel de droit européen de la protection des données à caractère personnel* (Édition Bruylant, Bruxelles, 2020) 22. For the problem of horizontal effects see J Reinhardt, 'Realizing the Fundamental Right to Data Protection in a Digitized Society' in Albers and Sarlet (n 1) 55 (58 ff).

proportionality, from which it takes a limitation of the restrictions on the protection of personal data 'to what is absolutely necessary'[157] – a catchword from which a range of different precautions to be defined in the event of restrictions is then developed in a not necessarily stringent deduction. The requirements and precautions range from system design provisions and thresholds for the respective processing phase to reservations for judicial review or data security requirements to the right of notification in case of intervention.[158]

The case law of the ECJ thus reveals a multi-dimensional and multifaceted conception of the statements of article 8 CFR, without these already being substantively and doctrinally established. However, a coherent concept cannot be expected either. Not only does the ECJ often remain apodictic in its reasons for its decisions against the background of the different legal cultures in the Member States, but it also cannot take on a role that is completely centralised and hierarchical. There is a need for interplays between the courts in the multi-level system. This is due to the fact that the statements of the fundamental right to the protection of personal data need to be contextualised as soon as we seek to fill it with substance.

### *ii. Achievements and Challenges of the Right to the Protection of Personal Data as Protected Interest*

The right to the protection of personal data places the handling of data and information at the centre of its scope of protection. As a novel right that responds to the challenges of modern society, it is hardly surprising that it has triggered extensive debates among the legal community. Since these debates are to some extent guided by substantial and doctrinal preconceptions that differ from one Member State to another, they vary and diverge quite widely.

On the basis of the previous analysis, it can be stated that the right to the protection of personal data anchored in article 8 CFR is a relatively independent right and not exhausted by a reference to the protection of the respect for private life provided by article 7 CFR. It is also not analogous to the right to informational self-determination. It is not based on the idea of control as an underlying concept and does not provide blanket protection for 'control over one's own data'. Nor is it primarily to be understood as a prohibitive right. On the contrary, it is formulated in such a way that it allows us to move away from the traditional substantive and doctrinal patterns of thought and to break new ground. As a right to protection, article 8(1) CFR can be developed multifariously, as is also shown by paragraphs 2 and 3. It points to the need for shaping and the multifunctional role of legislation, but also to the role of those involved in its implementation. Although it is true that existing secondary data protection legislation has

[157] Settled case law, eg, ECJ, Judgment (Grand Chamber) Case C-746/18 *H. K.* ECLI:EU:C:2021:152, [2021] §§ 38 ff.

[158] ECJ, Judgment (Grand Chamber) Case C-293/12 and Case C-594/12, §§ 53 ff, 68; Judgment (Grand Chamber) Case C-362/14, §§ 91 ff; Judgment (Grand Chamber) Case C-136/17, §§ 49 ff; Judgment (Grand Chamber) Case C-511, 512 and 520/18, §§ 105 ff; Judgment (Grand Chamber) Case C-746/18, §§ 51 ff; Judgment (Grand Chamber) Case C-61/22, §§ 75 ff; Judgment (Full Court) Case C-470/21 *Quadrature du Net* ECLI:EU:C:2024:370, [2024] §§ 67 ff; Judgment (Grand Chamber) Case C-548/21, §§ 84 ff.

played a certain role in the genesis of the right to the protection of personal data,[159] its references to legislation need to be understood dynamically. It is suitable for initialising a complex legal framework that is also designed to be constantly adapted.

However, article 8 CFR remains relatively vague in terms of the protected interests. Its wording merely points to the individual's right to the protection of personal data concerning them and offers some more or less eclectic guidelines in paragraphs 2 and 3. The vagueness of the guidelines, together with the fact that activities are shifting increasingly to the Internet and conflicts are becoming datafied, is leading to an ever-expanding scope of protection in case law. Against this background, the right to the protection of personal data tends to turn into a 'super-fundamental right' within the realm of a 'law of everything'.[160] To avoid this, there have been numerous attempts by jurisprudence and scholarship to clarify what exactly is meant by data protection and what the right to the protection of personal data aims to achieve in contrast to other rights. If, for example, article 7 CFR is interpreted in the case law of the ECJ as protecting private life in a substantive sense, while article 8 CFR focuses on data security or risks of unlawful access and abuse of personal data, or if the right to the protection of personal data is conceptualised as a procedural right, solutions are sought in a functional combination of both rights. But this combination is usually conceived as an additive juxtaposition. Such an additive juxtaposition is not feasible and falls short because it does not succeed in convincingly distinguishing between the scopes of protection of privacy on the one hand and data protection on the other. Furthermore, it is recognised that the right to the protection of personal data also has close interdependencies with other freedoms that contribute substantive aspects. But references to other fundamental rights, such as freedom of expression, remain vague. Again, the relationship between the right to the protection of personal data, the right to privacy, and other substantive freedoms is not convincingly elaborated either in terms of content or doctrine.

## IV. Conceptualising Data Protection Interests as a Bundle of Provisions and Rights in a Multilayered Approach

In the following, the considerations on the backgrounds, in particular on the network of basic elements, and the insights from the case law, where partly parallel and time and again more or less convincing solutions can be found, will be brought together. It has become obvious that we need to leave behind approaches that do not do justice to the subject matter. How this can be realised in detail depends on the legal system, on what is enshrined in the Constitution, and on doctrine and methodology. But in the first step, some notes on the essentials of appropriate legal approaches and then an overarching meta-conception shall be introduced.

[159] *Cf* the Explanations on art 8, Explanations relating to the Charter of Fundamental Rights [2007] OJ C303/17.

[160] Purtova (n 37).

## A. Essentials of Appropriate Legal Approaches

### *i. Data and Information as Distinct Content of Fundamental Rights Protection*

The first finding that can be made in the light of the characteristics of the subject matter, but also in the light of case law, is that protection with regard to the handling of information and data concerning individuals must be conceived as a novel, distinct facet of fundamental rights protection. In the case law on the right to privacy, courts emphasise occasionally that the information and data dimension is a distinct facet. Moreover, such an acknowledgement is the convincing achievement of the FCC's development of the right to informational self-determination and of the enshrinement of a right to the protection of personal data. The fact that there are cross effects between the information and data-related dimension of protection and other facets of fundamental rights protection – protection of decisions, actions, spaces, property – does not undermine this finding.

We cannot assume that it is impossible to develop any rights in this respect. Nor are such rights to be understood as merely accessories to the familiar scopes of protection.[161] On the contrary, developing out data protection interests as a facet of fundamental rights is capable of broadening our narrow notions of protected interests and the philosophical traditions behind them.

### *ii. Multi-Layered, Multi-Dimensional and Multifaceted Guarantees and Rights*

Keeping in mind at what a fundamental level we are dealing with and that a network of fundamental categories is being addressed – data, information, knowledge, processes as data and information flows, and communication – it would be naïve to think that protection of personal data and information could be described in terms of a uniform protected good. The requirement of multi-layered, multi-dimensional, and multifaceted guarantees and rights becomes apparent at many points across the jurisdictions.

The most significant and also most challenging insight is the necessity of a multi-layered conception. At first glance, an extension of the notion of freedom anchored in each fundamental right to the handling of data and information might seem like a good idea. In other words, to embed the protected interests in the context of the entire constitutional law and to search for them at the level of each individual fundamental right. At times, particular guarantees have already been drawn upon. The European

[161] Despite the interrelationships with other facets of fundamental rights protection, it would be misleading to understand protection with regard to the handling of information and data in purely instrumental terms. Of a different opinion G Britz, 'Informationelle Selbstbestimmung zwischen rechtswissenschaftlicher Grundsatzkritik und Beharren des Bundesverfassungsgerichts' in W Hoffmann-Riem (ed), *Offene Rechtswissenschaft* (Tübingen, Mohr Siebeck, 2010) 562, 569 ff; R Poscher, 'Die Zukunft der informationellen Selbstbestimmung als Recht auf Abwehr von Grundrechtsgefährdungen' in Gander et al (eds), *Resilienz in der offenen Gesellschaft* (Baden-Baden, Nomos, 2012) 167, 178 ff. Slightly broader accentuated Britz (n 116).

Court of Justice mentions the freedom of expression quite regularly. The freedom of assembly has been acknowledged as being relevant in the case of surveillance by intelligence services. The right to mental integrity could be interpreted with regard to the use of certain neurotechniques.

However, if all the possible specific scenarios of the handling of personal data and information are considered, the application of content-specific guarantees turns out to be full of prerequisites. We are not confronted with a single act of intervention but with processes. The contents of the information and the consequences of their use depend on the respective purpose. As data protection is primarily future-orientated, and aims at avoiding harms beforehand in a way that 'we cannot afford to wait to vindicate it only after it has been violated',[162] we must be able to describe to a certain extent which data are collected and how they are altered and linked with one another, which information could be derived from certain data, for which purposes it is used, and which disadvantageous consequences the individual might have to expect. It is therefore necessary to work out the relevant context and to break down the processes of handling information and data to the necessary extent by means of descriptions and prognoses. These prerequisites are not given without further ado.

This problem, which arises from the subject matter we address, can be resolved by distinguishing between two or more levels at which the constitutional requirements are to be developed. Fulfilling the requirements at the basic level can create the conditions that enable us to apply particular guarantees at the second level. From a doctrinal perspective, this can be described as a *cooperation of coordinated fundamental rights within a multilayered conception of guarantees and rights*. Within such a multilayered conception, certain interests of the data subject to be protected must or can be addressed at a basic level and resolved there, in particular through appropriate regulation, while more concrete protection interests that emerge in particular contexts, which, thanks to this regulation, can be described with a sufficient degree of accuracy, may be covered by the guarantees of the specific fundamental rights.

Second, guarantees and rights must be multidimensional. They have to be more diverse than the traditional concept of protection against encroachments because the data subject is to be protected with regard to personal information and data which are generated and processed by others in particular contexts. As has just been explained, appropriate regulation at a basic level is necessary; at this level the state is anything but kept out. Beyond that, protection directed solely at defending against and refraining from processing personal data is insufficient because the data subject may also be interested in personal data being made available so that agencies or private persons have the information at their disposal which they need for a correct decision. And it is just as important that the data subject is informed about the processing of personal data and information and can influence it. Hence, individuals need not only 'negative' or defensive rights but also 'positive' or enabling rights to regulation, to know, to obtain information, to participate, or to exert influence.

[162] Judgment of the Canadian Supreme Court, *R. v Dyment*, [1988] 2 S.C.R. 417, at 23: 'This is inherent in the notion of being *secure* against unreasonable searches and seizures.'

Third, guarantees and rights must be multi-faceted in the sense that their appropriately extended concept of freedom includes a variety of protected interests, each of which has its own characteristics. Protection of fundamental rights in terms of the way in which government agencies or other private parties handle personal information and data is different from the legally protected interests with which we are familiar in the traditional understanding of fundamental rights. The subject matter of protection is not a person's freedom of behaviour or decision, and protection of personal data is also not primarily about protecting a private sphere or what is already existing from informational access by others. People are to be protected with regard to the data and information concerning them as well as to the knowledge developed by others about them and against the repercussions or adverse effects this information and knowledge has or may have. But already, due to the mere fact that data and information are handled and interpreted, government agencies or other private persons are structurally involved in the processing of personal data and information. From a general perspective, ie, leaving aside the special cases, personal data cannot be assigned to the person in question like an object belonging to them. Individualistic patterns of assignment fall short.[163] Reasoning why and to what extent the person to whom data, information, and knowledge refer is to be protected must rather be made from a supraindividual perspective. The protected interests of data subjects have to be conceptualised with regard to the sociality of the individual and to structurally involved counterparts. Hence, they require their own separate patterns of description.

### *iii. Sophisticated Doctrinal Constructions and Methodologies*

The understanding of fundamental rights as multi-layered, multi-dimensional, and multifaceted guarantees and rights is not conceivable without sophisticated doctrinal constructions and methodologies. Classical notions based on a bourgeois-liberal approach and the complementary doctrine that fundamental rights are merely rights of defence against encroachments have dysfunctional prerequisites and limitations.[164] If we fall back on them, we will fail to work out data protection interests and the required regulation appropriately. As has been explained, this is why the right to privacy in case law often falls short of what is needed. But by now, extensions of the functions of the fundamental rights and of the scope of their protection, which go beyond the traditional understanding of fundamental rights, are recognised in many countries. Modern codifications reflect the diversity of dimensions of protection in their catalogues of fundamental rights. Additionally, guarantees of fundamental rights are open to interpretation. By means of sufficiently sound and sophisticated methodologies, they permit an elaboration of diverse dimensions of protection, including positive obligations of the

[163] This does not mean that it is not possible to grant decision-making rights to individuals – but it is one of the means of implementation, not the general overarching approach to understanding data protection rights.

[164] More closely M Albers, 'Realizing the Complexity of Data Protection' in Gutwirth and Leenes and De Hert (eds), *Reloading Data Protection. Multidisciplinary Insights and Contemporary Challenges* (Dordrecht, Springer, 2014) 213 (216 f).

state to provide a regulatory framework and to protect individuals through legal rules and actions.

### *iv. Various Functions of Statutory Regulation and Legal Norms*

Last but not least, if guarantees and rights have to be understood as multi-layered and multidimensional, legislation is addressed in different roles. It must not only create positive rights of the data subject to know about or to exert influence on the processing of personal data and information but also provide for an appropriate legal framework at a basic level. Legal norms do not only limit freedoms; they can also create freedoms in the first place, make them concrete, and influence their social conditions and prerequisites. The resulting variety of relationships between fundamental rights and statutory regulation can be elaborated in a very nuanced way. The point is not reduced to the idea that a legal basis in the sense of the traditional concept of a defence against encroachments needs to be provided for.[165] On the contrary, developing sophisticated approaches to regulation and its functions is essential. Further considerations can also lead to novel approaches to the understanding of law as such.

## B. Cooperation of Fundamental Rights at Different Levels

In summary, data protection rights can be developed from an interplay of fundamental rights within the framework of a multi-layered concept. Such an interplay should not be conceived as an additive juxtaposition. Rather, it must be understood as a *functional cooperation* of fundamental rights at *different* levels. This results in a bundle of multi-layered, multidimensional, and multi-faceted provisions and rights to which all fundamental rights with their substantive particularities can contribute.

### *i. Basic Level: Provisions and Rights to Appropriate Regulation*

At a basic level, data protection responds to risks and harms that have been addressed since the emergence of new technologies in the 1970s and have increased even further with the internet. In a rough summary, the crucial problems centre around a potentially all-encompassing, unlimited, and non-transparent processing of personal data and information by the state or other private parties. These problems are, of course, a question of individual freedom in sociality, but they also point beyond that.[166] Orwell's 'Big Brother', Bentham's 'Panopticon', and Kafka's 'The Trial' might be illustrative as widely known, culturally anchored metaphors that – despite these narratives being rooted in quite different contexts – take up different facets of the dangers just mentioned above. In addition to these state-centred works, more recent novels, such as Dave Eggers' 'The Circle', might be added with a view to social networks.

[165] *Cf* Masing (n 140).
[166] *Cf*, however, the critical remarks made by Masing (n 140).

Daniel Solove has shown that the well-known Big Brother metaphor effectively captures certain data protection problems, but that it is the Kafka metaphor that illustrates those elements of threats to privacy which deal with certain data collection and circulation by others

> without having any say in the process, without knowing who has what information, what purposes or motives those entities have or what will be done with that information in the future.[167]

The very beginning of the work gives a sense of how threatening this can be: 'Someone must have slandered Josef K., for one morning, without him having done anything wrong, he was arrested. Why so, he asks the guards, and receives the terse reply: We are not appointed to tell you that.'

These considerations point to the fact that, at the basic level, there are already multifarious threats that data protection shall countervail. In the first place, they call for the establishment and implementation of a legal framework guaranteeing that the handling of personal information and data is not largely unbound, unlimited, opaque, or beyond any possibility of affected individuals to influence procedures or results. Additionally, as we have already seen, the legal framework at the basic level also has the function of ensuring that contextually definable risks that the data subjects may face are recognisable and describable and of creating the conditions for the applicability of specific fundamental rights. Thus, *substantially*, the regulations directed by certain constitutional guidelines must ensure that data and information flows and contexts of data processing are limited and structured, that data subjects have certain rights of knowledge and of influence, or that there are appropriate institutional provisions. *Functionally*, the regulations must create the conditions that make it possible to apply specific guarantees and ensure, for example, that risks to specific protected interests can be identified and countered in due time.

But is this level and are these requirements covered by fundamental rights and, more closely, by individual rights? That depends, of course, on the legal system in question and on its constitutional provisions, doctrines, and methodologies. It is conceivable that it is up to the legislator to decide whether and to what extent a legal framework is created on the basis of which specific fundamental rights can then be applied and unfolded in a way that reflects the subject matter appropriately. However, in principle, there is no reason to assume that fundamental rights are not suitable for covering this basic level.

In scholarly approaches as well as in the case law of courts, a level that is more foundational than cases that can be contextually delineated is recognised and addressed to a certain extent. It is reflected, for example, in the numerous considerations on the relationship between data protection and a democratic order. Data protection is seen as a factor in, or even a prerequisite for, enabling a democratic order to exist.[168] This presupposes, of course, that it is understood not as individual control over personal

[167] D Solove, 'Privacy and Power: Computer Databases and Metaphors for Information Privacy' (2001) 53 *Stanford Law Review* 1393, 1426.

[168] See for references to the democratic order BVerfGE 65, 1, 43.

data, but as multilayered, multidimensional, and multifaceted.[169] But even without these references to democracy, some courts have pointed out that privacy, or the right to respect for privacy, which has been extensively elaborated in some jurisdictions, is at the heart of liberty in a modern state and a condition for the enjoyment of other rights or non-discrimination.[170] However, as the right to privacy covers many facets, from preconditions to various protected interests in very specific case constellations, and as the content of the protection is more or less blurred, this cannot be addressed with the necessary accuracy.

Greater clarity and effectiveness can be achieved if these interests of the data subject at this basic level are assigned to a specific fundamental right and its protective content is developed accordingly. With regard to German law, this is possible in view of article 2(1) in conjunction with article 1(1) of the Basic Law if we leave behind the version of the right to informational self-determination that was established by the census ruling and which is now in flux anyway and develop a more complex conceptualisation of the safeguards and individual rights provided by this fundamental right.[171] Even better suited to such an approach is the right of individuals 'to' the 'protection' of personal data concerning them.

The right to the protection of personal data offers the opportunity to work out the content of the protection and the protected interests of the data subjects independently with a fresh approach in terms of content and doctrine, and thus in accordance with the subject matter.[172] Such a right can be interpreted in such a way that it provides regulatory and protective requirements that primarily apply at a basic level prior to constellations that can be contextually delineated and addresses certain protection needs of the data subjects at a first-layer level. Regarding article 8(1) CFR, these considerations are consistent with the fact that article 8(2) and (3) CFR lay down a number of requirements, although these are a rather unsystematic compilation of several factors of different provenance, which do not exhaustively describe the core of the right to the protection of personal data. Article 8 CFR primarily addresses the legislator with a complex set of provisions and, to a certain extent, corresponding individual rights aimed at ensuring that the substantive and functional requirements, as explained above, are met through appropriate regulation.[173]

[169] *Cf* also from an overarching point of view, P de Hert and C Cocito, 'The Added Value of Data Protection within the Framework of Digital Constitutionalism in Europe' in De Gregorio (ed), *The Oxford Handbook of Digital Constitutionalism* (Oxford, Oxford University Press, 2024).

[170] See as examples from our analysis of the case law Supreme Court of Canada, *R. v Dyment*, [1988] 2 S.C.R. 417, at 17; Supreme Court of India, *Puttaswamy-I*, Chandrachud, J, Part R (243, 244); Constitutional Court of South Africa, *Amabhungane Centre for Investigative Journalism NPC and Another v Minister of Justice and Correctional Services and Others; Minister of Police v Amabhungane Centre for Investigative Journalism NPC and Others* (CCT 278, 279/19) [2021] ZACC 3, at 112 ff.

[171] Albers (n 9) 454 ff. This approach to art 2(1) in conjunction with art 1(1) of the Basic Law is not prior to individual rights but addresses a level precedent to concrete cases covered by specific fundamental rights. It is also at this level that both safeguards and individual rights can be developed.

[172] See also the considerations of P de Hert, ch 12 in this volume, (section VII).

[173] This coincides with many elaborations in the literature – even if they each have their own approaches to a certain extent – that distinguish the right to respect for private life from the right to the protection of personal data and highlight that the latter stipulates that a regulatory framework involving a multi-dimensional set of rules be established, see, eg, P De Hert and S Gutwirth (n 149) 3 ff; M Tzanou, *The Fundamental Right to Data Protection* (Oxford, Hart Publishing, 2017) 7 ff; M von Grafenstein, 'Refining the Concept of the Right

This is not done with any regulation. In particular, and as a non-exhaustive outline, legislation must safeguard that the handling of personal information and data is not unrestricted, unlimited and opaque. It must also provide that risks to specific protected interests of data subjects can be identified and countered in a timely manner. Data subjects must have the opportunity to obtain sufficient knowledge of and influence over the processing of data and information relating to them. Given the inherent limitations of rights-based approaches alone, a number of obligations must be imposed on persons or entities that handle personal information and data. Institutional safeguards and control mechanisms must be added.[174]

Under these circumstances, the pertinent fundamental rights must be interpreted as provisions and rights that are directed at requiring legislation to achieve certain goals and fulfil certain functions. On the one hand, they do not lay down a definite program that simply has to be carried out. Rather, the legislator has a margin of appreciation in the choice of the specific legal measures and instruments, as long as the goals and functions set forth in the Constitution are achieved with the regulation created. On the other hand, precisely because the fundamental rights demand such a result, they would fall short if they were limited to merely vague statements. The problem of the extent to which it is possible to develop provisions and rights that are sufficiently clear to be effective as constitutionally binding from the textually relatively vague fundamental rights is one of the core questions of all interpretations of fundamental rights that go beyond the 'classical' defence against encroachment.

The challenges can be handled if we understand the pertinent fundamental rights in such a way that they consider the regulatory choices of the legislation and are constantly reapplied at more specific stages with more concrete requirements. Thus, as long as there is no legislative framework, fundamental rights requirements initially start with relatively vague provisions and rights. Then, at a second stage, they are conditioned in the sense that they are based on the legislator's regulatory choices of a specific framework and set more specific, concrete provisions for its rules and regulations. In the case law of the German Federal Constitutional Court, there are illustrative examples of such an approach in the areas of the guarantee of property, of the freedom of the press, and, above all, of the freedom of broadcasting.[175] As a result of such a process

to Data Protection in Article 8 ECFR Part I' (2020) 6 *European Data Protection Law Review* 509, 514 ff; M von Grafenstein 'Refining the Concept of the Right to Data Protection in Article 8 ECFR Part II' (2021) 7 *European Data Protection Law Review* 190, 191 ff; and 'Refining the Concept of the Right to Data Protection in Article 8 ECFR Part III' (2021) 7 *European Data Protection Law Review* 373, 374 ff; P Vogiatzoglou and P Valcke 'Two Decades of Article 8 CFR: A Critical Exploration of the Fundamental Right to Personal Data Protection in EU Law' in E Kosta, R Leenes and I Kamaras (eds), *Research Handbook on EU Data Protection Law* (Cheltenham and Northampton, Edward Elgar, 2022) 11 ff.

[174] *Cf* Albers (n 164) 229 ff. *Cf* also with partly different considerations, N Marsch, *Das europäische Datenschutzgrundrecht: Grundlagen, Dimensionen, Verflechtungen* (Tübingen, Mohr Siebeck, 2018) 127 ff; L Dalla Corte, 'A Right to a Rule: On the Substance and Essence of the Fundamental Right to Personal Data Protection' in D Hallinan, R Leenes, S Gutwirth and P de Hert (eds), *Data Protection and Privacy: Data Protection and Democracy* (Oxford, Hart Publishing, 2020) 27 (38 ff).

[175] See, eg, the landmark judgment *FRAG* of 1981, BVerfGE 57, 295 (319 ff) [1981] – *Rundfunkentscheidung (Broadcasting freedom judgement).* Initially, the fundamental right that safeguards broadcasting freedom provides merely general requirements, but no particular model of how to regulate and organise broadcasting. However, if the legislator chooses, for example, a dual model of public and private broadcasting, the guarantee of the freedom of broadcasting sets out more detailed guidelines based on the model chosen by the legislator.

of interpretation, the relation between the pertinent fundamental rights and statutory legislation can be described as being shaped in a way that secondary legislation impacts 'the content of the fundamental right, which is therefore destined to be constantly in flux and evolution'.[176] However, the relation is neither reverse nor a circle. It is important to note that the relative hierarchy between fundamental rights requirements and legal regulations always continues to exist. Altogether, the interplay between fundamental rights and statutory regulations in the field of data protection becomes extremely challenging.

Since the fundamental right to the protection of personal data understood in this way requires, from a functional point of view, that the regulations at the basic level create the conditions that make it possible to apply specific guarantees, it points beyond itself to the spectrum of other fundamental rights.[177] It sets the stage for them to enter the scene.

### *ii. Second Level: Data Protection Rights from Content-Specific Fundamental Rights*

At a second level, content-specific fundamental rights can enter the picture. This applies to all possibly relevant guarantees: rights to mental integrity, to freedom of thought, conscience and religion, to freedom of expression, to freedom of assembly, or to freedom to choose an occupation. In the concept outlined here, if the right to privacy is established alongside a right to the protection of personal data, it can also be given specific content. The factual fundamentals already suggest the recourse to a broad normative basis to concretise fundamental rights requirements. The jurisprudence of the courts, as shown, has in principle recognised the relevance of the specific fundamental rights.[178] However, specific freedoms are often mentioned only in passing. It is not worked out exactly under which conditions they actually apply and how.

Whether, when, and how they are to be applied can be more clearly and precisely defined by considering that the ability to describe all relevant risks to data subjects that may or are likely to arise and the specific interests to be protected requires basic regulations at the first level. If such regulations exist and if we can then describe in more detail the contexts in which the handling of personal information and data takes place, the purposes, the players involved, and the procedures, potential context-specific harms and the particular interests of the data subject to be protected show up. Under these circumstances, specific fundamental rights tailored to particular contexts and risks can be referred to. We can interpret them in a problem-orientated way from a supraindividual perspective, keeping in mind the characteristics of data, information, and

[176] Y Ivanova, 'The Role of the EU Fundamental Right to Data Protection in an Algorithmic and Big Data World' in D Hallinan, R Leenes, S Gutwirth and P de Hert (eds), *Data Protection and Privacy: Data Protection and Artificial Intelligence* (Oxford, Hart Publishing, 2021) 145, 151.

[177] In the European multi-level system, the relationship between the EU and its Member States must additionally be addressed, which includes the relationship between the fundamental rights enshrined in the EU Charter and those in the Member States' constitutions. This adds another layer of complexity to the picture, but this will not be discussed in this text.

[178] See nn 90, 91, 106, 155.

knowledge. Provisions and individual rights can be applied exactly where and insofar as a need for protection can be identified. This results in a broad, dynamic, and procedural concept of data protection rights derived from specific fundamental rights.

Legislation regulates the given situation with regard to additional protected interests and can restrict these if necessary. The result is not only a sophisticated arrangement of fundamental rights but also a sophisticated picture of the legal regulations guided by various fundamental rights provisions. This does not have to result in lots of regulations. A specific statutory rule may be shaped by a multitude of different provisions of fundamental rights. This is not unusual, especially not in the multi-level system between the EU and the Member States. In the bigger picture, developing data protection law becomes even more challenging, and this is what I will discuss now in closing.

## C. Developing Data Protection Law

Data protection places high demands on law, and regulatory concepts are complex on their own terms. This is all the truer as regulations are shaped not only by fundamental rights and the requirements they impose but also by legal policy. Even if individual rights are developed in a way that reflects the characteristics of data and information and is problem-orientated, they are and should be only a small component of a much larger architecture.[179]

Statutory rules and legal positions of data subjects must be founded on the diverse functions and diverse forms of law. Regulation concepts must include a wide range of constituent elements which utilise the entire spectrum of legal forms and instruments, and in addition, they have to be interwoven. As an innovative and highly dynamic field, data protection law needs to be, in terms of legal theory, 'reflexive law' and, from a doctrinal point of view, a mixture of stability and dynamics. This is reflected, for instance, in the delegation of legislative competences, in the use of legal terms which are vague and in need of being concretised, in normative references to dynamically adapted technical standards, in rules allowing for experimentation, in evaluation procedures, or in other tools to ensure the capacity to learn and develop. In many respects, the appropriate use of insights from other disciplines or interdisciplinary approaches is needed.[180] The emerging variety of regulatory concepts is also compatible with a less legislation-centred understanding of law and regulation. From a political science point of view, it has been analysed how the substance of data protection law is made concrete by the interactions among different actors – the legislative, executive, and judicial branches; data protection agencies; data users; and data subjects. An appropriate normative conception has to be responsive to the interplay of actors generating and concretising law whilst, at the same time, keeping the normative perspective. Last but not least, it is essential to embed data protection rules and rights in overarching contexts and to coordinate them appropriately with other legal regimes.

[179] D Solove, 'The Limitations of Privacy Rights' (2023) 98 *Notre Dame Law Review* 975, 977 ff.
[180] See, eg, A Schimke, *Netz-Gedächtnis und Recht* (Tübingen, Mohr Siebeck, 2025).

How (personal) information and data may be processed has always been regulated, to some extent and from certain perspectives, by various legal regimes such as media law or tort law. The resulting need for coordination between the rules of these regimes and data protection law is increasingly evident, and this is a very challenging task.[181] The same applies to the series of regulations within the EU Data and Digital Strategy. Data protection is, and must be, an integral part of this overall strategy. However, as the GDPR is, to some extent, path-dependent[182] and sticks to traditional patterns of data protection that are not compatible with some of the other regulatory concepts, it cannot remain entirely untouched.[183] As a prerequisite, the fundamental rights and protected interests of data subjects must also be rethought and reconceptualised.

## V. Summary and Outlook

This chapter began by drawing attention to the fact that data protection law deals with a highly complex subject matter involving (personal) data, information, knowledge, or processing and, in the broader context, also decisions, actions and their consequences. It aims at protecting individuals, and, in addition, connections to normative principles such as democracy can be identified. The complexity of the issue highlights the challenges that arise not only in the detailed elaboration of data protection law but also in the conceptualisation of the interests to be protected. In this respect, privacy is still a keyword around the world, and the right to privacy is a normative anchor that is, in various formulations, explicitly codified in constitutions or derived from them through interpretation. However, one of the findings of our analysis of case law is that privacy, particularly in law, is burdened with traditional substantive and doctrinal implications that hamper a suitable conceptualisation of data protection. That is why the 'right to the protection of personal data', which has recently been established in some fundamental rights catalogues, offers a fresh opportunity to appropriately conceive and develop such protection in an interplay with other fundamental rights.

Data protection responds to threats to freedom and needs for protection that require their own separate patterns of description. The ensemble of fundamental rights calls for developing a multi-dimensional and manifold bundle of provisions and rights within the framework of a multi-layered conception. This bundle includes, at a basic level, provisions and rights for appropriate regulation, and, at a second level, further

[181] See A Schimke, 'Forgetting as a Social Concept. Contextualizing the Right to Be Forgotten' in Albers and Sarlet (n 1) 179 (190 ff).

[182] Following the path taken by the Convention No 108 for the Protection of Individuals with regard to Automatic Processing of Personal Data from 1981 and the EU Data Protection Directive from 1995, see also RD Veit, *Einheit und Vielfalt im europäischen Datenschutzrecht* (Tübingen, Mohr Siebeck, 2023) 103 ff.

[183] In principle, the Commission assumes that the existing data protection regulations, as one of the pillars of its data and digital strategy, can be reconciled relatively seamlessly with the new regulations. *Cf*, eg, Communication from the Commission to the European Parliament, the Council, the European Economic and Social Committee and the Committee of the Regions 'A European strategy for data' [2020] COM(2020) 66 final. See also art 1(3) Data Governance Act, art 1(3) Data Act. A closer analysis, however, reveals various inconsistencies, incompatibilities and reform requirements.

requirements and rights arising from content-specific fundamental rights. It must be open to continuous revision and constantly adapted to societal change and new threats.

At present, one of the key legal challenges is how data protection law can be convincingly included as part of a comprehensive data and information law, as it is now being addressed in numerous regulations related to the Internet or artificial intelligence. Only a properly tailored approach to data protection interests and data protection law can be reasonably coordinated with other areas of law.

# 3

# Commentary on Marion Albers

JOHANNES MASING

Marion Albers presents a sophisticated analysis of the challenges surrounding effective data protection guided by legal theory. Based on this, she calls for a fundamental restructuring of constitutional data protection: According to her, this restructuring must be based on the distinction between data and information, must be guaranteed as protection at various layers that are multidimensional and multifaceted, and requires regulation that seeks distance from the idea of individual protection. The depth of theoretical insight into the demands of modern data protection is truly remarkable.

I will not delve into the case law analysis that Marion Albers provides at the beginning of her text, particularly in the written version. However, it is important to emphasise that this analysis is beneficial in its own right. She not only compiles various legal foundations in the US and Europe – protection of property against intrusion, privacy, and the right to informational self-determination – but also considers case law from Canada and India, for example. This provides an overview that is not easily found elsewhere. Certainly, one might question whether the line of cases could at some point be analysed more precisely; for example, the *Katz* case of the Supreme Court of the United States seems to me to have been significantly narrowed over time and on the verge of being overruled, and the case law of the European Court of Human Rights has moved further from the starting point of privacy than has been developed in the text. Nevertheless, this compilation is very helpful.

However, the thrust of the paper is, of course, the call for a comprehensive new conceptualisation of constitutional data protection. This demand is set as a task for the courts and contrasted with their current case law. It is based on a careful analysis, developed at a high level of abstraction, of the challenges to functional data protection in our time.

To summarise my comments, I consider this analysis to be largely convincing at the level of abstraction at which it is presented. However, I wonder whether the case law is not already much closer to these requirements than Marion Albers suggests – in fact, I think it largely meets them, at least in Germany.

# I. Data and Information

This starts with the requirement of a distinction between data and information. In fact, an analytical distinction can be made between the two, and data protection can only be meaningfully conceived and regulated with regard to information that is actually or potentially linked to data. However, the case law takes this into account – at least in substance. I believe that this is true for all European courts, at least. The case law aims to guarantee the free development of personality in view of the interaction between data processing and the *information* that can be obtained by data processing – actually or potentially.[1] The central category of *purpose*, a pillar of data protection requirements, is an expression of this.

Indeed, case law does not make the distinction between data and information as the conceptual starting point for its tests and balancing. Nonetheless, this does not mean that the information-related relativity of the need for protection is not taken into account. Certainly, the Court understands the term 'data' in a comprehensive manner (as people colloquially do). It thereby considers that the relationship between data and information is volatile, unstable, and dependent on specific situations; that it is therefore difficult to grasp, potentially resulting in risks for the development of personality. Data processing is therefore subject to justification requirements in a broad sense, and the understanding of an infringement of fundamental rights is therefore independent of an analysis of the relationship between information and data in a specific situation. However, the Court then evaluates the informational impact of data processing thoroughly when it considers the question of justification of the infringement, notably when it comes to the proportionality test.

This is all the more adequate when data protection is understood as a distinct right in and of itself. It is, indeed, not only to be understood as a preliminary protection against subsequent infringements of other fundamental rights but also as a stand-alone guarantee of an inner freedom against the menace of unbound information that gives others power over oneself.[2]

# II. First Layer of Data Protection

Marion Albers demands *a first layer of data protection* that is prior to individual fundamental rights. This is also largely consistent with existing case law – at least with

[1] See, eg, BVerfGE 125, 260 paras 190, 252 [2010] – *Vorratsdatenspeicherung*.

[2] See BVerfG when it refers to the diffuse fear of being observed BVerfGE 125, 260 paras 212, 242, 313 or the freedom not to be monitored without cause, see BVerfGE 150, 244 para 51 [2018] – *Kfz-Kennzeichenkontrolle II*; 'With this measure, the persons concerned are checked against whether they or the objects with them are sought by the authorities. At the same time, they may only continue their journey unhindered on the condition that the police records do not contain relevant information on them. In view of this, it is not just the consequences of the measure, but the measure as such that results in an impairment to the freedom of the persons concerned. It is integral to a free society that anyone may in principle move freely, without having their movements arbitrarily registered by the state, without having to prove their integrity as law-abiding citizens, and without the feeling of constantly being under surveillance .... The possibility that a person could be registered at any time and in any place without noticing it and checked against police search lists or otherwise appear in data records would be incompatible with this principle'.

German case law – and includes the idea that it ultimately leads to certain regulatory requirements.

## A. In the Context of the Public Sector

Let me begin by demonstrating this in the context of the public sector. The right to informational self-determination provides a basic legal structure for data processing by public authorities. This means that any processing of personal data is understood as an infringement of fundamental rights – a central point. This does not imply that the data is assigned to the individual as their own and that it is at their free disposal – even if the case law contains imprecise and misleading formulations in this regard. The important point of this understanding lies in the fundamental need to justify the corresponding data processing. This requires specific legal bases, ie, transparent rules that define the exact purposes of the collection and processing of data.[3]

Any processing for purposes other than those initially specified requires a new legal basis. Once the purpose has been fulfilled, the data (and the information it contains) must be deleted.[4] Data protection is therefore not conceived as protection against one-off interventions, but rather as a process. Furthermore, there are requirements for access and rectification rights as well as for supervisory control by independent data protection officers.[5] In cases where the significance of the data processing is deemed to be high, additional obligations, such as notification duties, prior judicial approval, and other requirements from a modular, pre-structured arsenal of protection mechanisms, may be imposed.[6] Gabriele Britz mentioned more of them.[7]

This structuring of data protection applies in general and across all fundamental rights. It is true that other fundamental rights also offer protection against data processing, such as in particular the secrecy of telecommunications (article 10 GG[8]) or the protection of the home (article 13 GG).[9] Correspondingly, freedom of religion or freedom of assembly, for example, can also offer protection against data processing, and it is likely that almost all fundamental rights can provide such protection. However, the aforementioned structures are regarded as a common basis. In Marion Albers' terms, they constitute the first layer, which is then specifically supplemented on a further level by additional requirements of the various fundamental rights.

## B. In the Relation between Private Actors

The Court has not worked out such rules in the same detail yet for relationships between private actors. However, horizontal effects of fundamental rights are

[3] See, eg, BVerfGE 141, 220 para 105 [2016] – *Bundeskriminalamtgesetz I*; Bundesverfassungsgericht, Judgment of 1 October 2024, 1 BvR 1160/19 para 90 – *Bundeskriminalamtgesetz II*.

[4] See BVerfGE 141, 220 para 105; BVerfG, 1 BvR 1160/19 paras 43, 187 f.

[5] Already BVerfGE 65, 1 [1983] – *Volkszählung*.

[6] See, eg, BVerfGE 141, 220 para 105.

[7] See above.

[8] Grundgesetz für die Bundesrepublik Deutschland (GG) 1949.

[9] See, eg, BVerfGE 141, 220 para 105; see also BVerfGE 120, 274 [2008] – *Onlinedurchsuchung*.

generally recognised, and there is already some case law applying this to the right of informational self-determination.[10] As data protection in this respect is about balancing mutual freedom, such structures cannot be formalised and uniform in the same way. Rather, the different areas of life must be taken into account in a differentiated manner, whereby particular attention must be paid to power imbalances.[11] Here in particular, the requirements can have a wide range of different dimensions and be multifaceted – as Marion Albers demands. Constitutional data protection is first and foremost embedded in ordinary law, with the General Data Protection Regulation and numerous other legal acts, including the Digital Services Act and the Digital Markets Act, representing key examples. However, it is part of our general understanding of fundamental rights that both this framework and its interpretation are subject to constitutional requirements.[12] Thereby we take into account the multi-dimensional nature of legal relationships as well as the procedural nature of communication processes. Hence, case law already imposes transparency and procedural requirements on private parties.

The Court has expressly stated that horizontal data protection requirements may arise in particular in the context of the monopoly or market power of dominant providers.[13] As with the case of the public sector, this is not just a matter of punctuated defence against interference, but also a matter of positive rights, such as the right to information and the right to intervene. Indeed, the formal basis of such requirements often lies in the justification of a specific infringement of fundamental rights at the outset. However, this only shows that the necessity for justification is rightly considered broadly – namely, before the distinction between data and information. As I previously stated, this is not based on the idea that personal data is substantially assigned to the individual for their own disposal, but rather on the aim to create a starting point for a process that requires legal structuring with regard to the free development of personality.

To summarise: Fundamental right requirements for data protection are indeed multi-layered, multidimensional, multifaceted and multifarious. Consequently, constitutional protection does not need to be completely redesigned. What Marion Albers demands has in substance already been realised – at least according to German case law. It is another issue, of course, that this protection must be further specified and expanded, especially for many conflicts specific to the age of information – above all in the private sector.

## III. Prerequisite for a Democratic Order

I am less concerned with the question of whether data protection should also be conceived as a prerequisite for a democratic basic order than Marion Albers.

[10] BVerfGE 152, 152 [2019]– *Recht auf Vergessen I.*

[11] See BVerfGE 152, 152 para 77; see also BVerfGE 128, 226 para 58f [2011] – *Fraport*; BVerfGE 148, 267 para 33 [2018] – *Stadionverbot.*

[12] See, eg, T Kingreen and R Poscher, *Grundrechte Staatsrecht II*, 39th edn (Heidelberg, C.F Müller, 2023) 134 f; J Ipsen, *Staatsrecht II Grundrechte*, 24th edn, (München, Valen, 2021) 87 ff; T Barczak, 'Art. 2 I' in F Brosius-Gersdorf (ed), *Dreier Grundgesetz Kommentar*, 4th edn (Tübingen, Mohr Siebeck, 2023) 353 ff.

[13] BVerfGE 128, 226; BVerfGE 148, 267; BVerfGE 152, 152.

Data protection in the broad sense understood today determines communication structures. It seems obvious to me that this is a foundation of the democratic order. Just as the requirements for freedom of expression[14] are also determined by their significance for democratic debate, the constitutional requirements for fundamental data protection should be determined in light of the principle of democracy as well.

## IV. Individual Protection

Another question is how far data protection should move away from the idea of individual protection, as Marion Albers suggests. On this point I am rather sceptical. The protection of fundamental rights axiomatically serves individual freedom. This is the essential premise underlying the concept of fundamental rights in general and, indeed, represents the overarching objective of the constitutional legal system as a whole. It is true that data protection cannot be conceived as a defence against intrusions into one's personal domain. Data protection cannot be understood as a right that 'assigns something to a person … as their own concern establishing limits to others' access to it'.[15] If Albers' objection is limited to this, I agree. However, case law has long since moved away from this understanding. Indeed, it is true that old definitions, which are poorly formulated but are repeated again and again out of respect for the census ruling, are misleading in this sense. However, if the decisions are read carefully, it is abundantly clear that this is not the basis of data protection case law.

However, the case law on data protection is an application and interpretation of fundamental rights and therefore relates to individual freedom. It protects the free development of the personality from dangers arising from the processing of data (and information) relating to it, including its chilling effects. The processing of personal data is regarded as an infringement on fundamental rights, as it encroaches upon the individual's right to have such data processed only within a legally regulated framework that provides protection against the unbalanced power of others through data processing. Data protection as a protection of fundamental rights must be linked to a substantial notion of freedom. That is the development of the individual as a free personality.

## V. Conclusion

Indeed, the question of the protection of private freedom reveals a problem of Marion Albers' overall approach: Albers develops data protection law abstractly from a legal-theoretical perspective as the creation of functionally adequate regulations for data processing. These are developed largely detachedly from concrete guarantees of fundamental rights and categories of fundamental rights – and in some cases even in explicit opposition to them. The leap into positive law is then made with recourse to

[14] See, eg, BVerfGE 7, 198 [1958] – *Lüth*; BVerfGE 124, 300 para 97 [2009] – *Wunsiedel*.
[15] *Cf* Albers, above.

the fundamental right to data protection as guaranteed in article 8 of the Charter of Fundamental Rights.[16] However, what this data protection is supposed to materially achieve remains unclear. Consequently, the discussion of data protection only refers to itself. Without a link to concrete rights to freedom or, at the very least, specific problem constellations of individual freedom, the demands remain abstract and anaemic: According to Marion Albers, data protection should be multi-layered, multidimensional, and multifaceted; it should be designed in a processual way and ensure by means of sophisticated doctrinal constructions and methodologies that data processing is not unbound, unlimited, or opaque. All this may be the case, but an implication of what the inner idea of data protection should be is not perceptible. The notion of freedom in data protection is not given any substantive contours. I suppose the idea of data protection as a prerequisite for the free development of personality is ultimately also in the unspoken background of Marion's concept. So, ultimately, we may be quite close. However, this is not addressed.

In conclusion, I am not convinced that there is a need for a fundamental restructuring of data protection, nor does the paper try to substantiate data protection – perhaps it even deliberately opposes such attempts. However, it offers a high level of the numerous interconnections and different perspectives that are crucial in ensuring data protection. At the same time, it imparts a better understanding of existing case law.

[16] Charter of Fundamental Rights of the European Union [2016] OJ C202/2.

# 4

# Resubstantivising Data Protection Rights

RALF POSCHER*

The US and Europe face different challenges when it comes to data protection, and these differences contribute to the transatlantic data exchange issues mentioned in the introduction to this volume.[1] To date, issues of data protection can only be discussed as issues of privacy in the US, at least at a constitutional level. Yet the current state of data collection and automated processing not only presents economic implications but also impacts virtually all aspects of our daily lives. This makes it somewhat paradoxical that every individual interest influenced by modern IT systems is compelled to fit within the rigid framework of the right to privacy, just to be able to initiate a legal discussion about corresponding fundamental rights questions. This inconsistency indeed poses a substantial challenge and has given rise to a plethora of privacy conceptions, some of which attempt to frame some of the most public activities, such as public protests, as private to protect them against state surveillance and data collection.

Europeans have the conceptual advantage of distinguishing between a right to privacy and rights to data protection. They are thus not forced to turn every data protection issue into a privacy matter. The right to data protection gives them conceptual scope to accommodate data protection issues that cannot – at least not easily – be construed as pertaining to people's privacy. Europe's challenge, on the other hand, is to account for the substance of the right to data protection. While at least the core substance of the right to privacy is straightforward, ie, a right to be left alone and unobserved by intrusive third parties to leave some space for developing one's personality without being confronted with the perceptions of others,[2] things are much less clear-cut for the right to data protection.

* This contribution relies in large parts on two previous articles: R Poscher, 'The Right to Data Protection: A No-Right Thesis' in R Miller (ed), *Privacy and Power* (Cambridge, Cambridge University Press, 2017) 129–142; R Poscher, 'Artificial Intelligence and the Right to Data Protection' in S Vöneky, P Kellymeyer, O Mueller, W Burgards (eds), *The Cambridge Handbook of Responsible Artificial Intelligence* (Cambridge, Cambridge University Press, 2022) 281–290.

[1] See R Poscher and E Orrù, introductory chapter to this book.

[2] SD Warren and LD Brandeis, 'The Right to Privacy' (1890) 4 *Harvard Law Review*, see groups.csail.mit.edu/mac/classes/6.805/articles/privacy/Privacy_brand_warr2.html.

# I. The Original Property-Rights Conception of Data Protection

During the initial phases of its data protection jurisprudence, the German Federal Constitutional Court played a leading role in establishing the right to data protection, not only in Germany, but also in a European context.[3] To start with, it linked the 'right to informational self-determination' to what can be understood as a property-rights conception of personal data.[4] The Court held that every individual has the 'right to determine himself, when and in which boundaries personal data is disseminated' – just as an owner has the right to determine for themselves when to allow someone to use their property.[5] This notion, which appears illusory even in an analogue world, has often been ridiculed as naive given our contemporary, technologically interconnected, and socially networked reality, in which a vast amount of personal data is disseminated and exchanged at all levels almost all the time.[6] Data simply does not possess the kind of exclusivity that would justify drawing a parallel with property ownership.[7]

The German Constitutional Court seems to have recognised this. While it never explicitly revoked the property parallelism, it made use of this formula less and less frequently over the years, and stopped referring to it altogether in more recent decisions.[8] However, despite a general consensus that the right to data protection is, in substance, not akin to a property interest in one's personal data, the right to data protection is nevertheless formally treated as if it were a property right. In the same way that any non-consensual use of one's property by someone else is regarded as a property rights infringement, any unauthorised use – gathering, storage, processing, and transmission – of personal data is viewed as an infringement of the right to data protection. This formalist conception of data protection is not only still prevalent in the German context, but the European Court of Justice (ECJ) perceives of the right to data protection in much the same way under article 8 of the Charter of Fundamental Rights of the European Union (CFR). For example, the ECJ has confirmed that data

[3] M Albers, 'Realizing the Complexity of Data Protection' in S Gutwirth, R Leenes and P De Hert (eds), *Reloading Data Protection* (Dordrecht, Springer, 2014) 217 (hereafter Albers, 'Complexity'); K Vogelsang, *Grundrecht auf informationelle Selbstbestimmung?* (Baden-Baden, Nomos, 1987) 39–88.

[4] There is a certain parallel between this conceptualisation of the right to privacy and its scope under the US Supreme Court's early Fourth Amendment jurisprudence: Before *Katz v United States* 389 US 347 (1967), the Supreme Court applied the Fourth Amendment only to the search and seizure of a citizen's personal property and effects (see, eg, *Olmstead v United States* 277 US 438 (1928); it was thus tied in substance to a property right.

[5] Albers, 'Complexity' (n 3) 219.

[6] M Albers, 'Information als neue Dimension im Recht' (2002) 33 *Rechtstheorie* 61 (81) (hereafter Albers, 'Information'); K Ladeur, 'Das Recht auf informationelle Selbstbestimmung: Eine Juristische Fehlkonstruktion?' (2009) 62 *DÖV* 45 (46–47).

[7] *Cf* J Fairfield and C Engel, 'Privacy as a Public Good' in RA Miller (ed), *Privacy and Power: A Transatlantic Dialogue in the Shadow of the NSA-Affair* (Cambridge, Cambridge University Press, 2017).

[8] Eg, BVerfGE 120, 351 (360) [2008] – *Steuerliche Auslandsdaten*; BVerfGE 120, 378 (397–398) [2008] – *Automatisierte Kennzeichenerfassung*.

retention as such constitutes an infringement, irrespective of whether any substantive inconvenience has been caused:

> It should be made clear, in that regard, that the retention of traffic and location data constitutes, in itself, … an interference with the fundamental rights to respect for private life and the protection of personal data, enshrined in Articles 7 and 8 of the Charter, irrespective of whether the information in question relating to private life is sensitive or whether the persons concerned have been inconvenienced in any way on account of that interference.[9]

According to this traditional view, each and every instance of the processing of personal data infringes the respective right – just as the use of physical property would be an infringement of the property right.[10] For instance, if my name, licence plate, or phone number is registered, this counts as an infringement; if they are stored in a database, this counts as another infringement; and if they are combined with other personal data, such as location data, this is considered yet another infringement.[11] So even though the right to data protection is no longer regarded as an actual property right, its formal structure still corresponds to one.

## II. The Hollow Shell of a Right

Such a strictly formal conception of the right to data protection makes the issue of its substance ever more pressing: If European data protection does not protect personal data as a property right, then what kind of substantive interest does it actually protect? If the answer simply revolves around a formal interest in any kind of personal data processing, without the ability to identify a specific substantive interest connected to it, what we are left with is merely the hollow shell of a right. We have a right that protects; we know how it formally works, but we do not know what it substantively protects. It is easy to see that such a model is hard to explain to our partners across the Atlantic.

Yet the purely formal character of the right to data protection does not only raise conceptual concerns but also very practical ones. If every single act of processing personal data is considered a fundamental rights infringement, the latter quickly add up. Given the processing power of modern CPUs, we are easily confronted with millions of fundamental rights infringements occurring in split seconds. This, however, seems a rather disproportionate way of conceptualising the actual data processing issues at hand – one that nevertheless persists and is routinely applied to modern forms of data collection. Take for example automated licence plate recognition, whereby an initial infringement occurs when scanners are used to collect licence plate data, another one

[9] CJEU, Joined Cases C-511/18, C-512/18 and C-520/*18 La Quadrature du Net and Others v Premier ministre and Others* ECLI:EU:C:2020:791, [2020] para 115 (hereafter CJEU, *La Quadrature du Net*).

[10] Albers, 'Complexity' (n 3) 219.

[11] BVerfGE 100, 313 (366) [1999] – *Telekommunikationsüberwachung*; BVerfGE 115, 320 (343–344) [2006] – *Informationelle Selbstbestimmung*; BVerfGE 125, 260 (310) [2010] – *Voratsdatenspeicherung*; BVerfGE 130, 151 (184) [2012] – *Telekommunikationsgesetz*; BVerfGE 150, 244 (265–266) [2018] – *Kfz-Kennzeichenkontrollen*.

when this information is checked against stolen car databases,[12] etc. How should these millions upon millions of fundamental rights infringements be tracked and dealt with forensically?

However, such a formalist conception does not only lead to an excessive amount of fundamental right infringements; it is also impossible to apply to data processing by systems relying on artificial intelligence (AI). AI technology is driven by self-learning mechanisms,[13] which can adapt their programmed algorithms in response to data input.[14] Importantly, while such algorithms may be initially transparent to their creators,[15] once a system has undergone hundreds, thousands, or even millions of iterations of recursive, self-evolving patterns, even the system programmers may lose track of how specifically certain data were processed, which inferences were drawn from which data correlations, and how particular data were weighted.[16] The self-adaptive 'behaviour' of at least certain types of AI technologies consequently leads to a lack of transparency. This phenomenon is often referred to as the black box issue of AI technologies.[17]

This poses a problem for a strictly formalist approach to data protection. The method is rooted in the necessity to justify each and every instance of personal data processing as an infringement of fundamental rights. In AI systems, however, we do not know which specific personal data are used, or how many times they are processed and cross-analysed with what types of other data.[18] This makes it impossible to apply the strictly formalist approach to determine the occurrence, frequency, and type of infringements on a right to data protection conceived in such a manner. AI's lack of transparency seems to rule this out. Thus, AI creates problems for the strictly formalist understanding and treatment of the right to data protection due to its lack of transparency.[19] These issues are mirrored in the transparency requirements of the General Data Protection Regulation (GDPR), which predominantly relies on the conventional understanding of the fundamental right to data protection.[20] However, according to article 2(7) of the AI

[12] BVerfGE 120, 378 (400–401); BVerfGE 150, 244 (266).

[13] H Surden, 'Machine Learning and Law' (2014) 89 *Washington Law Review* 87 (88–90) (hereafter Surden, 'Machine Learning'); W Hoffmann-Riem, 'Verhaltenssteuerung durch Algorithmen – Eine Herausforderung für das Recht' (2017) 142 *AöR* 3 (hereafter Hoffmann-Riem, 'Verhaltenssteuerung'); W Hoffmann-Riem, 'Artificial Intelligence as a Challenge for Law and Regulation' in T Wischmeyer and T Rademacher (eds), *Regulating Artificial Intelligence* (Cham, Springer International Publishing, 2020) 3 (hereafter Hoffmann-Riem, 'Artificial Intelligence').

[14] Surden, 'Machine Learning' (n 13) 93.

[15] Hoffmann-Riem, 'Verhaltenssteuerung' (n 13) 30.

[16] Hoffmann-Riem, 'Artificial Intelligence' (n 13) 17; Hoffmann-Riem, 'Verhaltenssteuerung' (n 13) 29; N Marsch, 'Artificial Intelligence and the Fundamental Right to Data Protection' in T Wischmeyer and T Rademacher (eds), *Regulating Artificial Intelligence* (Cham, Springer International Publishing, 2020) 36 (hereafter Marsch, 'Artificial Intelligence'); T Wischmeyer, 'Artificial Intelligence and Transparency: Opening the Black Box' in T Wischmeyer and T Rademacher (eds), *Regulating Artificial Intelligence* (Cham, Springer International Publishing, 2020) 81 (hereafter Wischmeyer, 'Artificial Intelligence').

[17] Hoffmann-Riem, 'Verhaltenssteuerung' (n 13) 29; Marsch, 'Artificial Intelligence' (n 16) 36; Wischmeyer, 'Artificial Intelligence' (n 16) 80.

[18] *Cf* Albers, 'Complexity' (n 3) 221: 'The entire approach is guided by the idea that courses of action and decision-making processes could be almost completely foreseen, planned and steered by legal means'; Marsch, 'Artificial Intelligence' (n 16) 39.

[19] Marsch, 'Artificial Intelligence' (n 16) 36.

[20] On the specifics of the transparency requirements set out in art 5(1)(a) alt 3 GDPR and the issues this causes for the use of AI technologies, B Paal, 'Artificial Intelligence as a Challenge for Data Protection Law – and Vice Versa' in S Vöneky, P Kellymeyer, O Mueller and W Burgards (eds), *The Cambridge Handbook of Responsible Artificial Intelligence* (Cambridge, Cambridge University Press, 2022).

Act,[21] the GDPR is to apply to AI systems as well,[22] without any explanation on how this is supposed to work in practice.

# III. The Resubstantivation

These conceptual and practical issues in connection with the hollow formalist right to data protection at a minimum contribute to the political struggles in finding international common ground on data protection rules. Against this backdrop, it seems worthwhile to consider an alternative approach to data protection that injects new substance into the corresponding right by re-establishing the substantive interests it serves and is designed to protect.

## A. Data Protection as a Preemptive Right

The general idea behind such a new approach is to free data protection from the pressure of having to be an independent substantive right. Instead, a resubstantivation of the right to data protection can take its cue from the conceptual basis of the discussion, namely a distinction between data and information. Data as such is inert; it does no harm. Data can only do harm in specific circumstances, ie, where it becomes information[23] – or, to use Gregory Bateson's phrase, where data becomes 'a difference that makes a difference'.[24] These contextual characteristics of data and information pave the way for contemplating the various contexts where data transforms into information and thus the array of fundamental rights relevant to these varying contexts. Take the cases of data collection in the context of public assemblies and protests. What is affected by this type of data collection is not some formal right to data protection but the substantive freedom of assembly. This is due to the chilling effects the collection of data on protesters can have on potential participants; for example, they may have to fear repercussions if their participation were to become known in a work or security context, or be used by foreign agents to sanction their families if they have previously fled another country.

[21] European Commission, harmonised rules on artificial intelligence (artificial intelligence act) and amending certain union legislative acts [2021] COM (2021) 206.

[22] P Voigt and N Hullen, *The EU AI Act* (Heidelberg, Springer Berlin Heidelberg, 2024) 189 ff; R Schwartmann and T Keber and K Zenner and S Kurth, 'The EU AI Act: A Practice-Oriented Interpretation' (2024) 4 *Cri* 145, 146.

[23] Albers, 'Complexity' (n 3) 225; M Albers, 'Zur Neukonzeption des grundrechtlichen "Daten" schutzes' in A Haratsch and others (eds), *Herausforderungen an das Recht der Informationsgesellschaft* (Stuttgart, Boorberg, 1996) 121–23, 131–33; Albers, 'Information' (n 6) 75; M Albers, *Informationelle Selbstbestimmung* (Baden-Baden, Nomos, 2005) 87–148; M Albers, 'Umgang mit Personenbezogenen Informationen und Daten' in W Hoffmann-Riem, E Schmidt-Aßmann and A Voßkuhle (eds) *Grundlagen des Verwaltungsrechts*, 2nd edn (Tübingen, Mohr Siebeck, 2012) 7–28; G Britz, 'Informationelle Selbstbestimmung zwischen rechtswissenschaftlicher Grundsatzkritik und Beharren des Bundesverfassungsgerichts' in W Hoffmann-Riem (ed), *Offene Rechtswissenschaft* (Tübingen, Mohr Siebeck, 2010) 566–568 (hereafter Britz, 'Informationelle Selbstbestimmung'); Albers, 'Complexity' (n 3) 222–224.

[24] G Bateson, 'Steps to an Ecology of Mind: Collected Essays in Anthropology, Psychiatry, Evolution and Epistemology' (Northvale, London, Jason Aronson Inc., 1987) 386.

In his illuminating article 'Nothing to Hide', Daniel Solove developed an entire taxonomy of possible harms that can be caused by data collection.[25] They include the loss of life and liberty, infringements on property interests and the freedom of expression, violations of privacy, and denials of due process guarantees. Solove's taxonomy makes it obvious how the collection and processing of personal data can affect the whole spectrum of liberty and equality interests. Looking at it this way, personal finance information can lead to the loss of property. He even cites a tragic case, which resulted in a loss of life, where a stalker was handed the address of his victim by public authorities – data he used to locate and kill her.[26] Solove's list shows that the essence of data protection cannot be narrowed down to merely a single liberty or equality interest; rather, it potentially relates to every fundamental right. Understood correctly, the right to data protection consists in the protection that all fundamental rights afford to all the liberty and equality interests that might be affected by the collection, storage, processing, and dissemination of personal data.

The way in which fundamental rights prevent the misuse of personal data hinges on doctrinally broadening the concept of rights infringement. Fundamental rights usually protect against *actual* infringements. For example, the state encroaches upon your right to personal freedom when you are incarcerated; your right to freedom of assembly is infringed when your meeting is prohibited or dispersed by the police; and your freedom of expression is violated when you are kept from expressing your political views. That said, as a rule, fundamental rights do not protect against the purely abstract danger of the police incarcerating you, dispersing your assembly, or censoring your views. You cannot go to court claiming that certain behavioural patterns of the police increase the danger of them violating your right to assembly. The court response would generally be that you cannot bring action until these patterns have actually affected you in a concrete instance or until this is in the process of unfolding. In certain scenarios, your fundamental rights might *already* offer protection if there is a *tangible* threat of such an infringement occurring. This way, rights infringements can be prevented before they transpire.[27] However, instances where threats to fundamental rights already constitute a violation are more the exception than the rule.

The right to data protection operates differently. What is unique about data protection is its generally preemptive character. It safeguards against even the abstract dangers associated with collecting, storing, and processing personal data.[28] Data protection

[25] DJ Solove, 'A Taxonomy Of Privacy' (2006) 154 *U Pennsylvania Law Review* 477; see also DJ Solove, '"I've Got Nothing to Hide" and Other Misunderstandings of Privacy' (2007) 44 *San Diego Law Review* 745, 764–772 (hereafter Solove, 'Misunderstandings of Privacy').

[26] Solove, 'Misunderstandings of Privacy' (n 25) 768.

[27] See BVerfGE 51, 324 [1979] – *Verhandlungsfähigkeit des Angeklagten* in which the Court saw it as an infringement of the right to physical integrity to proceed with a criminal trial if the defendant runs the risk of suffering a heart attack during the trial; *cf* also BVerfGE 17, 108 [1963] – *Hirnkammerluftfüllung* (high-risk medical procedure – lumbar puncture – with the aim of determining criminal accountability for a misdemeanor); BVerfGE 52, 214 (220) [1979] – *Zwangsvollstreckung* (eviction of a suicidal tenant) and R Poscher, *Grundrechte als Abwehrrechte* (Tübingen, Mohr Siebeck, 2003) 388–390 (hereafter Poscher, 'Abwehrrechte').

[28] *Cf* N Marsch, 'Das europäische Datenschutzgrundrecht. Grundlagen – Dimensionen – Verflechtungen' (Tübingen, Mohr-Siebeck, 2018), with a focus on the internal peace of mind of deciding on one's exercise of fundamental rights.

thus preemptively protects against violations of liberty or equality interests that are potentially connected to *using* personal data in contexts that affect fundamental rights interests.[29] It is only this use of data in certain contexts that might involve a violation of liberty or equality interests. For example, the collection of personal data on political affiliations or religious beliefs of citizens by the state is generally prohibited because of potential misuse to discriminate against political or religious groups. Data protection demands a justification for the collection of personal data, even if such misuse poses only an abstract danger.[30] It does not require concrete evidence that such misuse took place or even that such misuse is about to take place. Consequently, the right to data protection systematically enhances every other fundamental right already in place to protect against the abstract dangers that accompany collecting and processing personal data.[31] Thus, the right to data protection is resubstantivised by relying on the substantive liberty and equality interests protected by each fundamental right in the catalogue of fundamental rights. The substantive fundamental rights interests behind the right to data protection depend on the type of data and the context in which it is collected, stored, and processed. In turn, the right depends on which kind of abstract danger is created by the collection, storage, or processing of personal data. In this way, the substantive liberty interest may and will often be the right to privacy, but just as well the right to assembly, freedom of speech, the protection of property or against religious or racial discrimination, or any other interest protected by a fundamental right.

## B. The Right to Data Protection in Court

A closer look at court practices regarding the right to data protection reveals that, despite appearances, courts have already embraced the multifaceted character of the right to data protection. They do not treat this right as an independent right but associate it with different fundamental rights, depending on the context and the interest affected.[32] From the very instigation of the right to data protection in Germany, marked by the famous Census Decision (Volkszählungs-Urteil), the court utilised a variety of fundamental rights to underline the need for a new fundamental right to 'informational self-determination'. This included rights such as the right to assembly.[33] In an unusual act of constitutional migration, the court pointed to the 'chilling effects' the collection

[29] Eg, the collection of comprehensive data in the course of a nationwide census is not in itself an imminent threat, but it is dangerous because of the potential (mis)use of the gathered mass data, *cf* BVerfG 65, 1; the collection of data for an anti-terrorism or anti-Nazi database is problematic because of 'potential' negative impacts for those mentioned in it, *cf* BVerfGE 133, 277 (331–332) [2013] – *Antiterrordateigesetz.*

[30] *Cf* the examples mentioned in the previous note. This preemptive protection against state action is not to be confused with the duties to protect against unlawful infringements of liberty interests by 'third parties', *cf* Poscher, 'Abwehrrechte' (n 27) 380–387 on the duty to protect under the German Basic Law. As far as such duties to protect are accepted, data protection would also address pre-emptive dimensions of these duties.

[31] *Cf* J Masing, 'Datenschutz – ein unterentwickeltes oder überzogenes Grundrecht?' [2014] *RDV* 3 (4); Marsch, 'Datenschutzgrundrecht' (n 19) 109–110; T Rademacher, 'Predictive Policing im Deutschen Polizeirecht' (2017) 142 *AöR* 366 (402); Marsch, 'Artificial Intelligence' (n 19) 40.

[32] *Cf* Britz, 'Informationelle Selbstbestimmung' (n 23) 571, 573, who first characterised the German right to informational self-determination as an 'accessory' right.

[33] BVerfGE 65, 1 (43).

of data on assembly participation could have for bearers of that right[34] – an idea first discussed by the US Supreme Court.[35] So even in its 'constitutional birth certificate', data protection is not put forth as a single right on its own but is associated with various substantive fundamental rights, such as the right to assembly.

Further evidence that personal data is not the object of a substantive, independent right is provided by the fact that data protection does not seem to stand alone, even in a jurisdiction in which it is explicitly guaranteed as a fundamental right that ostensibly aligns alongside other substantive fundamental rights. Article 8 CFR *explicitly* guarantees a right to data protection. In the jurisprudence of the Court of Justice of the European Union, however, it is always cited together with another right.[36] Hence, the right to data protection needs another right in order to provide for a substantive interest. In the jurisprudence of the Court of Justice of the European Union, this is usually the right to privacy,[37] but sometimes also other rights, such as free speech.[38] Thus, even when data protection is codified as an explicit, independent fundamental right, as it is in the Charter of Fundamental Rights of the European Union, it is nevertheless regarded as an accessory to other, more substantive fundamental rights.[39] This seems peculiar if the right to data protection is taken at face value as a substantive right on its own. However, it becomes only logical if considered as a general enhancement of other fundamental rights, which provide for the substantive interests protected by it.

## C. The Implications of the Resubstantivation

Interpreting the right to data protection as a general enhancement of, potentially, any fundamental right in order to already address abstract dangers to the liberty and equality interests these rights protect makes it clear how personal data processing systems must be assessed. The critical question in evaluating these systems is, to what extent does a certain type of data collection and processing system pose an abstract danger for the exercise of which substantive fundamental right? Looking at data collection issues through this lens has important implications.

[34] BVerfGE 65, 1 (43).

[35] *Wieman v Updegraff* 344 US 183 (1952) para 195.

[36] CJEU, Joined Cases C-92/09 and C-93/09 *Schecke and Eifert v Hesse* ECLI:EU:C:2010:662, [2010] ECR I-11063, para 47; CJEU, Joined Cases C-293/12 and C-594/*12 Digital Rights Ireland Ltd v Minister for Communications, Marine and Natural Resources, Minister for Justice, Equality and Law Reform, The Commissioner of the Garda Siochana, Ireland and the Attorney General and Kärntner Landesregierung, Michael Seitlinger, Christof Tschohl and Others* ECLI:EU:C:2014:238, [2014] para 53 (hereafter CJEU, *Digital Rights Ireland*); CJEU, Case C-362/14 *Maximillian Schrems v Data Protection Commissioner* ECLI:EU:C:2015:650, [2015] para 78; CJEU, Case C-311/18 *Data Protection Commissioner v Facebook Ireland Limited and Maximilian Schrems* ECLI:EU:C:2020:559, [2020] para 168. There are only a few chamber decisions, in which art 8 CFR plays a marginal role, that cite it without reference to art 7 CFR or another substantive fundamental right, eg, CJEU (third chamber), Case C-458/22 P *Roos and Others v Parliament* ECLI:EU:C:2023:871, [2023].

[37] CJEU, *Digital Rights Ireland* (n 36) para 37; CJEU, *La Quadrature du Net* (n 9) para 115.

[38] CJEU, *Digital Rights Ireland* (n 36) para 28; CJEU, *La Quadrature du Net* (n 9) para 118; CJEU, Case C-623/17 *Privacy International v Secretary of State for Foreign and Commonwealth Affairs and Others* ECLI:EU:C:2020:790, [2020] para 72.

[39] Marsch, 'Datenschutzgrundrecht' (n 19) 132–133.

## *i. Refocusing on Substantive Liberty and Equality Interests*

First, the proposed resubstantivised conception allows us to rid ourselves of a formalistic and hollow understanding of data protection. It helps to refocus on the substantive issues at stake. For many people, the strictly formal idea that some data protection right is always infringed when a piece of personal information is processed, meaning that they have to sign a consent agreement or click a button, has become formalistic in the context of data protection regulation. 'Consent spam' delivers a disservice to data protection rights. The connection to the actual issues that are connected with data processing has been lost.

For example: during my time as vice dean of the Freiburg law faculty, I attempted to obtain the addresses of our faculty alumni from the university's alumni network. The request was denied because it would constitute an infringement of the data protection right of the alumni. The alumni network had not obtained the written consent of its members to justify this infringement. As absurd as it might seem, this line of argument is the only correct one for the traditional, formal approach to data protection. Addresses are personal data, and any transfer of this personal data is an infringement of the formal right to data protection, which has to be justified either by consent or by a specific statute – both of which were lacking. Yet this represents a strictly formal perspective. Our alumni would probably be surprised to learn that the faculty at which they studied for years, which handed them their law degrees, and which paved the road to their legal careers does not know that it is their alma mater. There is no risk involved for any of their fundamental rights when the faculty receives their address information from the alumni network of the very same university. Conversely, an approach that discards the notion that there is a formal right to data protection but asks which substantive fundamental rights positions are at stake can eliminate such absurdities that do not only come at considerable bureaucratic cost but also alienate people from data protection regulation.

## *ii. The Threshold of Everyday Digital Life Risks*

Second, refocusing on the abstract danger for concrete, substantive interests protected by fundamental rights enables a discussion on thresholds. In the analogue world, the law does not respond to each and every risk that is associated with modern society either.[40] Not every abstract risk exceeds the threshold of a fundamental rights infringement. There are general life risks that are legally moot. In extreme weather, even healthy trees in a city park carry the abstract risk of toppling over, falling, and causing considerable damage to property or even to life and limb. Courts, however, have consistently held that this abstract danger is not a sufficient basis for public security measures or civil claims to chop down healthy trees.[41] They consider it part of everyday life risks that we all have to live with if we stroll in public parks or use public footpaths.

[40] On the threshold of everday risks in German police law, LL Wallenfels, *Gefahr und allgemeines Lebensrisiko* (Tübingen, Mohr Siebeck, 2023).

[41] VG Minden (11 K 1662/05) [2005] para 32.

The threshold for everyday life risks is accepted in the analogue world and should hold in the digital world as well. In our digital society, we have to come to grips with a – probably dynamic – threshold of everyday digital life risks that do not constitute an infringement of a fundamental right, even though personal data was stored or processed. During a visit to a doctor shortly after the introduction of the GDPR, I was asked to sign a form that would allow his assistants to use my name, which is stored in their digital patient records, in order to call me from the waiting room when the doctor is ready to see me. The form cited the proper articles of the GDPR (articles 6(1)(a) and 9(2)(a)). There might be occasions where there is some risk involved in letting other patients know my name. If the doctor in question were an oncologist, it might lead to people spreading the rumour that I have a terminal illness. This might find its way to my employer at a time when my contract is up for an extension. So, there may indeed be some risk. We have, however, always accepted this risk – also back in a purely analogue world – as one that comes with a doctor's visit, just as we have accepted the risk of healthy trees being uprooted by a storm and damaging our houses or cars, or even hurting us. And in the same way we have accepted everyday life risks in an analogue world, we need to accept everyday digital life risks in a digital world.

From a design standpoint this means that some IT technologies, including ones that use AI, could be built and implemented in a way that they remain below the everyday digital life risks threshold.[42] For example, when they use anonymised personal data, there is always a risk that the data will be deanonymised. But if sufficient safeguards against deanonymisation are installed in a system, they may lower this risk to such a degree that it does not exceed the level of our everyday digital life risk. This may be the case if the system uses data aggregation for planning purposes or resource management, which does not threaten substantive individual rights positions. An example of a non-AI application is the German COVID-19 alert app, which was designed in such a way as to avoid centralised storage of personal data and thus posed almost no risk of abuse.

### *iii. A Systemic Perspective*

Third, the alternative approach implies a more systemic perspective on data collection and data processing measures. It allows us to step back from the idea that each and every instance of personal data processing constitutes an infringement of a fundamental right. If data protection is understood as protection against abstract dangers, then we do not have to look at the individual instances of data processing. Instead, we can concentrate on the data processing system and its context in order to evaluate the abstract danger it poses. It is also here, at the level of the socio-technical system, that

[42] See also the suggestion by E Orrù, 'Are Publicly Available (Personal) Data "up for grabs"? Three Privacy Arguments' in H Matsumi and P De Hert et al (ed), *Data Protection and Privacy, Volume 16: Ideas That Drive Our Digital World* (London, Bloomsbury Publishing, 2024) 105–123, between data being processed by an AI system and the information it provides.

measures such as privacy by design, data and data usage tracking, and automated oversight can be employed to mitigate the abstract dangers connected with a system.

A focus on the abstract dangers connected with a socio-technical system also has implications for the legal evaluation of AI technologies. Unlike under the traditional approach, AI systems need not be fully transparent. The alternative approach does not require exact knowledge of when and how what kind of data are processed. What is needed, however, is a risk analysis and an evaluation of the risk reduction, management, correction, and compensation measures in line with the specific context of use.[43] This requires regulation on how false positives and negatives are managed in the interaction between AI and human decision-makers. *The New York Times* reported on the first AI-based arrest generated by a false positive of facial recognition software.[44] As discussed in the report, to rely solely on AI-based facial recognition software for arrests seems unacceptable given the failure rate of such systems. Legal regulation therefore has to counterbalance the risks stemming from AI by forcing the police to corroborate AI results with additional evidence. A fundamental rights analysis of facial recognition software should include an evaluation of the technology as well as the entire socio-technological arrangement in light of *habeas corpus* rights and the abstract dangers for the right to personal liberty that come with it. The actual cases, however, are not about some formal right to data protection but about substantive rights, such as the right to liberty or the right to be protected against racial discrimination and the dangers AI technologies pose for these rights.

For AI technologies, the differences between the traditional approach and the proposed approach regarding the right to data protection are similar to differences in the description of the systems as such. Whereas traditionally, the approach to and the description of computational systems have been very much dominated by computer sciences, there is a developing trend to address AI systems – especially given their lack of informational transparency – with a more holistic intradisciplinary methodology. AI systems are studied in their deployment context with behavioural methodologies that are not so much focused on the inner informational workings of the systems but on their output and their effects in a concrete environment.[45] The traditional approach to data protection tends towards a more technical, informational analysis of AI systems – an approach that becomes notably obstructed by the black box phenomenon. Conversely, the shift to the substantive rights perspective would lean towards a more behavioural approach to AI. The law would then not have to delve into the computational intricacies of when and how what type of personal data are processed. It could take a step back and assess how an AI system 'behaves' in the concrete socio-technological setting it is deployed in and what types of risks it generates for which substantive fundamental rights.

[43] *Cf* Albers, 'Complexity' (n 3) 232, who draws a parallel to risk management in environmental law.

[44] K Hill, 'Wrongfully Accused by an Algorithm' (*New York Times*, 24 June 2020), www.nytimes.com/2020/06/24/technology/facial-recognition-arrest.html.

[45] An overview on this emerging field in I Rahwan and others, 'Machine Behaviour' (2019) 568 *Nature* 477 (481–482).

## IV. Chilling Effects Coming Full Circle?

It is not for a European legal scholar to lecture his transatlantic colleagues on how to handle their legal system's data protection challenges. Nevertheless, an outside perspective suggests that these problems are partly due to the constricted conceptual scope that forces them to discuss any data protection issues as a matter of privacy. The notion that data protection is not an independent substantive right, as proposed in this chapter, but a data-specific enhancement of potentially any other fundamental right directed at abstract dangers, connected with a specific socio-technical IT system, might equally have a liberating effect in this conceptually tight space.

It could also build on the curious fact that the idea of 'chilling effects' was first developed in American free speech cases[46] and was not picked up in German constitutional law until much later to establish the right to data protection.[47] This gives chilling effects a broader systematic importance.[48] Indeed, chilling effects are a showcase example of protection against an abstract danger. People are not chilled because they are already targeted with sanctions for exercising their right to free speech, but because of an abstract danger that the state will at some point in the future take action against them for expressing their viewpoint. The collection and storage of data follows the same logic. As with the chilling effect on free speech, chilling effects in a data context do not have to be focused on privacy interests.[49] In this sense, the doctrine of chilling effects might be an entry point to a conception of data protection rights along the lines suggested above. It would bring mutual constitutional reception full circle: The US-American doctrine of chilling effects, at the very least, fostered the evolution of constitutional data protection rights on the continent. Consequently, a resubstantivation of data protection rights on the continent that builds on the general idea behind the chilling effects doctrine to include abstract dangers connected with data collection and processing and, potentially, any fundamental right, would circle back to the US-American context. By incorporating this shift, it could extricate the data protection debate in the US from its conceptual confinement to an increasingly disputed version of privacy rights.[50]

Yet even if this comparative constitutional legal scholar's dream were not to come true, the outlined resubstantivised conception of data protection might prove more productive than other alternatives for facilitating transatlantic dialogue and fostering cooperation on data exchange, considering the issues mentioned in the introduction to

[46] For the origins of the US Supreme Court's argumentative use of 'chilling effects', see *Wieman v Updegraff*, 344 U.S. 183, 195 (1952) (Frankfurter, J., concurring); *Walker v City of Birmingham*, 388 U.S. 307, 345 (1967) (Brennan, J., dissenting). In *Lamont v Postmaster General*, 381 U.S. 301, 307 (1965), the Court relies on the same idea when it invokes the notion of 'deterring effects'.

[47] BVerfG65, 1-71 1 BvR 209, 43, www.servat.unibe.ch/dfr/bv065001.html; 3.

[48] See, eg, BVerfGE 73, 1184, www.servat.unibe.ch/dfr/bv073118.html; BVerfG, 1 BvR 2378/98, 354, www.servat.unibe.ch/dfr/bv109279.html, and the denial of standing in *Laird v Tatum*, 408 U.S. 1, 13 (1972).

[49] On the relevance of chilling effects beyond free speech cases Note, 'The Establishment Clause and the Chilling Effect' (2020) 133 *Harvard Law Review* 1338 (1342); U Ekman Ault, 'The FBI's Library Awareness Program: Is Big Brother Reading Over Your Shoulder?' (1990) 65 *New York University Law Review* 1532 (1547); 6. B Canes-Wrone and MC Dorf, 'Measuring the Chilling Effect' (2015) 90 *New York University Law Review* 1095 (1114).

[50] See in this volume the dissenting vote of Justice Gorsuch, ch 7.

this volume.[51] Recognising that the right to data protection relates to abstract dangers to diverse liberty and equality interests would advocate for an incremental approach for a transatlantic agreement on data protection. This approach would initially identify the specific liberty and equality interests at risk in a particular data exchange area in order to specify what interests are really at stake. The exchange of passenger data, for example, might raise concerns with regard to no-fly lists. These concerns could potentially be mitigated by more transparency, improved oversight, and the incorporation of dependable correction procedures as part of data exchange agreements.[52]

Such a more systemic approach to data protection implies developing systemic risk reduction strategies tailored to the material interests involved in a specific area, selecting from a wide array of instruments: implementation of privacy-enhancing technologies,[53] automated monitoring mechanisms making reflexive use of AI to monitor AI, independent oversight, the minimisation of data collection and data storage only for specific aims, and serious material thresholds for the use of data. Assessments of the abstract dangers involved could also take into account the fact that, at least in some areas, the potential for harm has to be evaluated differently if data are collected by a foreign government with less legal and factual power over the individuals involved. Besides implementing strategies to reduce risks associated with the design of data collection systems, enhancing system transparency could also lower the objective dangers involved. Moreover, it could help distinguish between subjective fears and objective dangers, which is crucial for fundamental rights analysis. Additionally, an added advantage of transparency is that it contributes to building mutual trust. Following an approach along these lines should make it possible to find a compromise, at least in some of the areas concerned, that reduces the abstract dangers of data collection, storage, and processing to a level acceptable to both sides.

[51] R Poscher and E Orrù, introductory chapter to this volume.

[52] Agreement Between the United States of America and the European Union on the Use and Transfer of Passenger Name Records to the United States Department of Homeland Security [2012] OJ L215/5.

[53] See Fairfield and Engel, 'Privacy as a Public Good' (n 7).

PART II

# Data Protection and Privacy in German, European and US-American Constitutional Law and Jurisprudence

# 5

# Data Protection in German Constitutional Law: Overview of Basic Concepts and Mechanisms in the Case Law of the Federal Constitutional Court

GABRIELE BRITZ*

## I. Introduction

Reading the German Basic Law literally, one will find neither a right to data protection nor a right to informational self-determination nor a general right to privacy. But one will find article 2(1) of the Basic Law: 'Every person shall have the right to free development of his personality insofar as he does not violate the rights of others or offend against the constitutional order or the moral law.' In the history of the Basic Law, this guarantee has developed into a particularly powerful fundamental right. On the one hand, the 'general freedom of action' is derived from this fundamental right (*allgemeine Handlungsfreiheit*). This essentially means that, in principle, everyone is free to do as they wish, though the freedom of one person must, of course, be balanced with the freedom of another. On the other hand, the general right of personality is derived from article 2(1) of the Basic Law (*allgemeines Persönlichkeitsrecht*). In its various specifications, this legal guarantee of personality is much more complex than the general freedom of action. In German constitutional law, much of what is explicitly protected in other constitutions by a right to privacy, the protection of private spheres of life, the protection of intimacy, or a right to private life is protected by the general right of personality derived from article 2(1) of the Basic Law.[1] Data protection has been derived from said general right of personality as well. However, upon closer examination of the origins of constitutional data protection and of how the Federal Constitutional Court has established this unwritten fundamental right from

* I would like to thank Paul Herling, Neala Patterson and David Stanzick for helpful assistance.

[1] See on the general right of personality eg, M Eifert, '§ 18 Personal Freedom' in M Herdegen, J Masing, R Poscher and KF Gärditz (eds), *Constitutional Law in Germany* (München, C.H. Beck, 2024) paras 921ff.

article 2(1) of the Basic Law, one realises that the court primarily focused on the protection of freedom of action. Freedom of action and communication, particularly in their roles within the political sphere, are the primary substantive interests protected by the constitutional right to informational self-determination. In German constitutional practice, however, it is well established and almost unchallenged to understand data protection as an expression of the general right of personality.

Ironically, German constitutional law adopted data protection at a very early stage, but unlike more recent constitutions, the Basic Law still does not contain an explicit guarantee of data protection. Over the decades, the German Constitution has proven to be peculiarly open to development. Although the wording of the written Constitution remains unchanged, it alters its content and adapts to the present. In addition to legal scholarship, it is above all the Federal Constitutional Court that drives these developments forward. It continuously develops the guarantees of the Basic Law in view of the real practical changes in the areas regulated by the fundamental rights. The right to informational self-determination is considered a prime example of this in German constitutional science.[2] The Federal Constitutional Court has made it particularly clear that it considers a new interpretation of article 2(1) of the Basic Law to be necessary because the world has changed technically in such a fundamental way that the Constitution must adapt to it. Of course, every time the Federal Constitutional Court makes a major innovation to the Constitution, there is a great deal of discussion as to where the limits of the Court's powers lie. In the end, however, there is broad consensus that the Federal Constitutional Court's 'invention' of the right to informational self-determination was legitimate, even though controversy rightly remains over whether the Court's concept of the protected interests in informational self-determination and certain mechanisms of data protection is convincing.

## II. Decision on the 1983 Census Act as the Starting Point of Constitutional Data Protection (*Volkszählungsurteil*)

The Federal Constitutional Court derived the unwritten 'right to informational self-determination' from the (also unwritten) general right of personality protected under article 2(1) in conjunction with article 1(1)[3] of the Basic Law in 1983 in its *Volkszählungsurteil*,[4] that declared parts of the 1983 Census Act unconstitutional and void. Prior to the census ruling, the legislator himself had already enacted rules on data protection in ordinary law, which could not bind the subsequent federal legislator of

[2] See, eg, BO Bryde, 'Tatsachenfeststellung und soziale Wirklichkeit in der Rechtsprechung des Bundesverfassungsgerichts' in P Badura and H Dreier (eds), *50 Jahre Bundesverfassungsgericht* (Tübingen, Mohr Siebeck, 2001) 533, 558.

[3] Art 1(1) of the Basic Law: Human dignity shall be inviolable. To respect and protect it shall be the duty of all state authority.

[4] BVerfGE 65, 1 [1983] – *Volkszählungsgesetz*.

the 1983 Census Act due to the German hierarchy of norms: the State of Hesse had introduced data protection legislation in 1970 with the world's first data protection law. The first federal data protection law was enacted in 1977. However, it was not until this constitutional Court's ruling from 1983 that the constitutional foundation for data protection law was clarified:

> The value and dignity of the person, acting in free self-determination as a member of a free society, are at the centre of the Basic Law. In addition to the constitutional guarantees laid down in specific freedoms, the general right of personality, guaranteed in Art 2(1) in conjunction with Art 1(1) of the Basic Law, serves to protect these interests.' Based 'on the notion of self-determination, the general right of personality confers upon the individual the authority to, in principle, decide themselves whether and to what extent to disclose aspects of their personal life'.[5] This 'protection may gain even more significance in light of modern developments that pose new risks to one's personality':[6] 'Given the present and future realities of automatic data processing, this authority conferred upon the individual merits special protection.'[7] As a result of automatic data processing 'specific information concerning the personal or material circumstances of an identified or identifiable individual can be stored indefinitely, from a technical perspective, and retrieved at any time within seconds, without distance being an issue. In addition, the data in question can be compared with data collected from other sources, especially by creating integrated information systems, and can be compiled into partial or practically complete personality profiles, leaving the person concerned without sufficient control over the accuracy or use of the data stored on them. This has expanded possibilities of gaining and influencing information to unprecedented levels.[8]

But the strongest concern, according to the court, was 'that even the mere psychological pressure created by public perception may potentially impact individual behaviour'.[9] The Court concluded:

> In the context of modern data processing, the free development of one's personality therefore requires that the individual be protected against the unlimited collection, storage, use and sharing of their personal data. Consequently, the fundamental right of Art. 2(1) in conjunction with Art. 1(1) of the Basic Law encompasses such protection. In this regard, the fundamental right confers upon the individual the authority to, in principle, decide themselves on the disclosure and use of their personal data.[10]

Only recently, in 'Recht auf Vergessen I' (Right to be Forgotten I),[11] has the Court expressly clarified that the right to informational self-determination is also relevant to private law relationships:

> The right to informational self-determination has a bearing on the relationships between private actors by way of indirect horizontal effects.'[12] However, the 'right to informational

[5] ibid para 144.
[6] ibid.
[7] ibid para 145.
[8] ibid.
[9] ibid.
[10] ibid para 147.
[11] BVerfGE 152, 152 [2019] – *Recht auf Vergessen I.*
[12] ibid para 86.

self-determination does not confer upon the individual a general, let alone an unconditional, right to self-determination regarding the use of their data. It does, however, allow the individual the possibility of influencing, in a differentiated manner, the context and manner in which their data is accessible to and can be used by others. Thus, it guarantees the individual substantial influence in deciding what information is attributed to their person.[13]

# III. The Meaning of Informational Self-Determination

One may ask what the purpose of this right is. Is it simply about having decisive power over one's own data? Is that a purpose in itself? At first glance, a right to informational self-determination, which guarantees the right to decide for oneself what the state or private individuals may know about a person, seems to be a simple and plausible construction. However, legal scholars have struggled with it. On closer inspection, the Federal Constitutional Court itself has pursued a much more sophisticated approach from the outset than is immediately apparent within the rather simple notion of 'informational self-determination'.[14]

## A. No Absolute Right to Control Every Disposal of Personal Data or Information

The Federal Constitutional Court's assumption, which has been constantly repeated since the census ruling, that the 'fundamental right confers upon the individual the authority to, in principle, decide themselves on the disclosure and use of their personal data'[15] has been criticised by legal scholars. It is argued that the Federal Constitutional Court has constructed a property-like individual power.[16] The concept

[13] ibid para 87.

[14] Some parts of the following are translated from another text, G Britz, 'Informationelle Selbstbestimmung zwischen rechtswissenschaftlicher Grundsatzkritik und Beharren des Bundesverfassungsgerichts' in W Hoffmann-Riem (ed), *Offene Rechtswissenschaft* (Tübingen, Mohr Siebeck, 2010) 561ff.

[15] BVerfGE 65, 1 para 147.

[16] The discussion in German jurisprudence has been shaped eg, by, HP Bull, *Datenschutz oder die Angst vor dem Computer* (München, Piper, 1984); S Simitis, 'Programmierter Gedächtnisverlust oder reflektiertes Bewahren' in W Fürst, R Herzog and DC Umbach (eds), *Festschrift für Wolfgang Zeidler* (Berlin, De Gruyter, 1987) 1475, 1491; M Albers, 'Zur Neukonzeption des grundrechtlichen "Daten" schutzes' in A Haratsch, D Kugelmann and U Repkewitz (eds), *Herausforderungen an das Recht der Informationsgesellschaft* (Stuttgart, Boorberg, 1996) 113; M Albers, 'Information als neue Dimension im Recht' (2002) 33 *Rechtstheorie* 61ff; M Albers, *Informationelle Selbstbestimmung* (Baden-Baden, Nomos, 2005); M Albers, 'Umgang mit personenbezogenen Informationen und Daten' in W Hoffmann-Riem, E Schmidt-Aßmann and A Voßkuhle (eds), *Grundlagen des Verwaltungsrechts: Band 2*, 1st edn (München, C.H. Beck, 2012); W Hoffmann-Riem, 'Informationelle Selbstbestimmung in der Informationsgesellschaft' (1998) 123 *Archiv des öffentlichen Rechts* 513; HH Trute, 'Der Schutz personenbezogener Information in der Informationsgesellschaft' (1998) 53 *JuristenZeitung* 822; HH Trute, 'Verfassungsrechtliche Grundlagen' in A Roßnagel (ed), *Handbuch Datenschutzrecht* (München, C.H.Beck, 2003) 156; HP Bull, 'Zweifelsfragen um die informationelle Selbstbestimmung – Datenschutz als Datenaskese' (2006) 23 *Neue Juristische Wochenschrift* 1617. About this in recent times eg, S Behrendt, *Entzauberung des Rechts auf informationelle Selbstbestimmung* (Tübingen, Mohr Siebeck, 2023).

of an individual's absolute power to control every usage of personal data or information comparable to that of a proprietor would be inappropriate because what is aimed to be regulated in this case are essentially social processes. In fact, the concept of an absolute right to control – in the way of a proprietor – does not correctly capture the protected interests at hand. Nor does it accurately capture the dangers posed by data processing operations.

### *i. Distinction between Data and Information*

A decisive analytical step taken by critics of the property-analogous concept of fundamental rights was the distinction between data and information.[17] While data is understood as signs recorded on a data carrier and functions as the basis for information, information is understood as meaningful elements that are generated from observations, messages, or data in a specific social context and which then can be used. Information is linked to communicated data but is only created through the meaningful interpretation by the observer.[18] The distinction between data and information is, on the one hand, a condition for an appropriate description of the protected goods of 'informational self-determination'. On the other hand, it is a prerequisite for precisely identifying the sources of data- and information-related threats to fundamental rights. Considering this, as we will see below, a construction of the fundamental right to data protection conceived as an individual power and right of disposal makes no sense, neither in relation to data nor in relation to information.

### *ii. No Right to Control the Disposal of Information*

If the right to informational self-determination were understood as the right to control the collection and use of information, it would be aimed at something unattainable. In general, information is a social phenomenon in which meaning is constructed through data. Accordingly, personal information is the construction of a person by other people based on their personal data. Thus, there can be no right to control information associated with personal data. A right to control information would guarantee the impossible since the subjective observations and constructions of meaning of others simply cannot be controlled.[19] Essentially, the Federal Constitutional Court has already taken up the social dimension of information processes in the census ruling. It states:

> The right to 'informational self-determination' is not, however, guaranteed without limitation. It does not afford the individual absolute or unlimited control over 'their' personal data; rather, the individual develops their personality within the social community, and is

[17] See, eg, Albers, 'Neukonzeption des Datenschutzes' (n 16) 121ff.

[18] See, eg, with additional supporting references Albers, 'Umgang mit personenebezogenen Informationen' (n 16) paras 11f.

[19] Albers, 'Information als neue Dimension' (n 16) 61, 81; Trute, 'Verfassungsrechtliche Grundlagen' (n 16) para 19.

> dependent on communication with others. Any information, including personal data, mirrors social reality and thus cannot be attributed exclusively to the person concerned. … The individual must therefore accept that the right to informational self-determination is, in principle, subject to restrictions serving overriding public interests.[20]

### *iii. No Right to Control Every Disposal of Personal Data*

In contrast, a right to control personal data could be a possible guarantee because data can be thought of as an interaction-free phenomenon.[21] However, a right to control every disposal of personal data would not adequately capture the feared impairment of freedom to which the right to informational self-determination is intended to respond. The single date and its disclosure per se are irrelevant to the freedom of the individual.[22] Impairments only result from the observation and subjective interpretation of personal data by others and their subsequent expectations and measures, or from the anticipation of observation and adverse consequences: the threats or impairments arise in contexts of usages in which information about individuals is being generated.[23] In its essence, the protection of fundamental rights can only relate to these subjectively generated contexts of data usage, not to the disclosure of data per se.

## B. Protection of Freedom of Individual Behaviour from Chilling Effects

Anchoring data protection in the idea of self-determination is therefore misleading. The right to informational self-determination is not an original component of substantively understood self-determination. Nor does it protect data and the right of control for their own sake. However, the Federal Constitutional Court's concept of a data control right can be understood as an instrument that protects against dangers and violations of personal freedom resulting from the unregulated handling of personal data. The right to control one's own data is then a legal instrument for regulating the creation and use of information. It aims to indirectly promote self-determination in the sense of personal freedom of behaviour. Despite the terminologically misleading reference to the idea of self-determination, this accurate connection to the use of freedom can already be found in the census judgment. Informational self-determination is understood there as a means of securing freedom of behaviour, because 'even the mere psychological pressure created by public perception may potentially impact individual behaviour'.[24]

[20] BVerfGE 65, 1 para 148.
[21] Trute, 'Verfassungsrechtliche Grundlagen' (n 16) para 19.
[22] ibid para 23.
[23] ibid para 20.
[24] BVerfGE 65, 1 para 145.

The core of this data protection concept is the assumption that informational uncertainty inhibits the use of freedom.[25] This idea, which the Federal Constitutional Court calls 'intimidating effects',[26] can be found in the Census Decision from 1983 as well:[27]

> If individuals cannot, with sufficient certainty, determine what kind of personal information is known to certain parts of their social environment, and if it is difficult to ascertain what kind of information potential communication partners are privy to, this could greatly impede their freedom to make self-determined plans or decisions. A societal order, and its underlying legal order, would not be compatible with the right to informational self-determination if citizens were no longer able to tell who knows what kind of personal information about them, at what time and on which occasion. Individuals who worry that non-conformist behaviour could be recorded at any time and that such information could permanently be stored, used or shared will try not to draw attention to themselves by not engaging in such behaviour. If individuals anticipate that participation in an assembly or a citizens' initiative, for instance, was going to be recorded by the authorities and could thus expose them to certain risks, they might decide to forgo the exercise of their respective fundamental rights (Arts 8 and 9 of the Basic Law[28]).

It is noteworthy and important that the Federal Constitutional Court places the safeguarding of the uninhibited use of freedom in a wider democratic context: 'Not only would this impair opportunities of personal development for the individual, it would also affect the common good because self-determination is a fundamental prerequisite for the functioning of a free and democratic society which relies on the agency and participation of its citizens.'[29]

## C. Protection from Harmful Consequences of Data Processing

However, it is not just about preventing intimidation and psychologically mediated restrictions on freedom. Rather, the right to informational self-determination is also intended to prevent data processing operations from causing unjustified disadvantages for those affected. The Federal Constitutional Court has described these dangers distinctly and clearly when it comes to data processing by private individuals:

> In all aspects of life, basic services for the general public are increasingly provided by private companies – often with a strong market position – on the basis of comprehensive personal data collection and data processing measures; these companies play a decisive role in forming

[25] This was emphasised early on by W Schmidt, 'Die bedrohte Entscheidungsfreiheit' (1974) 29 *JuristenZeitung* 241; see also S Simitis, 'Die informationelle Selbstbestimmung' (1984) 37 *Neue Jurstische Wochenschrift* 398, 400; S Simitis, 'Anwendung und Zweck des Gesetzes' in S Simitis (ed), *NomosKommentar Bundesdatenschutzgesetz*, 6th edn (Baden-Baden, Nomos, 2006) paras 36 ff; Hoffmann-Riem, 'Informationelle Selbstbestimmung' 519ff.

[26] BVerfGE 113, 29 paras 83f, 87 [2005] – *Strafprozessual veranlassten Zugriff auf den elektronischen Datenbestand*; BVerfGE 115, 166, para 86 [2006] – *Durchsuchung zum Zweck der Ermittlung von Kommunikationsverbindungsdaten*; BVerfGE 120, 378 para 78 [2008] – *Automatisierte Erfassung der amtlichen Kennzeichnung von Kraftfahrzeugen*.

[27] BVerfGE 65, 1 para 43.

[28] Freedom of assembly and Freedom of association.

[29] BVerfGE 65, 1 para 43.

> public opinion, providing or denying opportunities, allowing participation in social life and basic activities of daily life. It is hard for individuals to avoid disclosing personal data to companies on a large scale if they do not want to be excluded from these basic services. Given that the data can be manipulated, reproduced and disseminated virtually without limit in terms of place and time and that the data can be recombined in unforeseen ways through opaque processing measures by means of incomprehensible algorithms, *individuals may become caught in extensive dependencies or severe contractual obligations.*[30] Thus, these developments can give rise to major risks to the development of one's personality, which the right to informational self-determination serves to counteract.[31]

Credit scoring could be another example of this: the processing of personal data, the accuracy of which is difficult for the data subject to verify, can determine credit unworthiness – resulting in obvious harmful consequences.[32] This example shows that regulating data flows can also protect against discrimination:[33] The processing of data whose use often has discriminatory effects can be prohibited. At least data protection law can ensure that those affected can check that such data is only used if it is faultless.

## IV. Distinction from Related Dimensions of Protection of the General Right of Personality

The right to informational self-determination was developed as one manifestation among others within the general right of personality. The protection that the right to informational self-determination guarantees is distinct from those of other manifestations of the general right of personality.[34]

### A. Protection of Personality within the Regulation of Rights of Expression (*äußerungsrechtlicher Persönlichkeitsschutz*)

First and foremost, it is to be distinguished from the protection of personality within the regulation of expression, which regulates which information about a person others may disclose to the public, especially in private legal relationships.

The right to informational self-determination is protected against third parties acquiring and instrumentalising data on individuals in opaque ways:

> Given that the right to informational self-determination aims to afford protection against the risks arising from novel possibilities of data processing, it must primarily be understood as

[30] Emphasis added.

[31] BVerfGE 152, 152 para 85.

[32] See, eg, K Langenbucher, 'Diskriminierung bei der Vergabe von Verbraucherkrediten?' (2023) 2023 *BKR* 205ff.

[33] See G Britz, *Freie Entfaltung durch Selbstdarstellung – Eine Rekonstruktion des allgemeinen Persönlichkeitsrechts aus Art. 2 I GG* (Tübingen, Mohr Siebeck, 2007) 51ff; G Britz, *Einzelfallgerechtigkeit versus Generalisierung* (Tübingen, Mohr Siebeck, 2008).

[34] BVerfGE 152, 152 para 89.

> a guarantee that – besides affording protection against the unintended disclosure of data in private law relationships – particularly protects against opaque data processing and use by private actors. It affords protection against third parties appropriating certain data on individuals and instrumentalising it in opaque ways in order to attribute to those individuals personal characteristics, types or profiles over which they have no control but which significantly bear on the free development of their personality and equal participation in society. The contents of this right are receptive to new developments, allowing it to potentially extend to further developments in information processing that pose risks to one's personality.[35]

This is to be distinguished from the protection against the dissemination of information relating to one's person as a result of communication processes, which is the task of the general right of personality:

> In such cases, the need for protection does not arise from third parties making opaque use of an individual's personal data to attribute personal characteristics or personality profiles, but from the tangible dissemination of certain information in the public sphere. In this context, risks to the free development of one's personality primarily result from the type and contents of the publication itself. The general right of personality in its manifestation as a right protecting against statements affecting one's person affords protection against such risks, whereas the right to informational self-determination is not relevant here. While the way in which information was obtained can be decisive for the protection afforded by the right protecting against statements affecting one's person, it is only relevant as a preliminary question in the assessment of how a certain statement is subsequently handled and thus how a person's image is conveyed to the public.[36]

## B. Protection of Privacy and Intimacy (*Privatsphäre*)

Furthermore, the right to informational self-determination is to be distinguished from the protection of privacy and intimacy. 'Privacy' or the protection of 'intimacy' is not expressly included in the Basic Law as well. But the protection of privacy in a sense of intimacy also derives from the general right of personality protected under article 2(1) in conjunction with article 1(1) of the Basic Law.

In this respect, too, the focus is not on the problem of the intransparency of unmanageable data processing procedures. Rather, the individual should be protected from the disclosure of certain personal information:

> The general right of personality following from Art. 2(1) in conjunction with Art. 1(1) of the Basic Law protects a person's private and intimate spheres … and the right to keep these private. The protection of the private and intimate spheres covers matters that, due to the information they convey, are typically regarded as private in particular because their discussion or display in public is regarded as unseemly, because they are regarded as embarrassing if they become known, or because they provoke negative reactions from one's social environment, which is particularly true when it comes to sexuality. Without any protection against others obtaining knowledge thereof, one's sexual development would be severely impaired even though it is protected by fundamental rights. The right to respect of one's private and

[35] ibid para 90.
[36] ibid para 91.

intimate spheres specifically protects the right not to have to disclose sexual relations with a partner, but to decide oneself whether, how and to whom to disclose information relating to one's intimate sphere and sex life.[37]

## C. Protection of the Confidentiality and Integrity of Information Technology Systems

In 2008, the Federal Constitutional Court identified a fundamental right to protection of the confidentiality and integrity of information technology systems as a further manifestation of the general right of personality.[38] In the decision, this further moulding of the general right of personality fundamentally remained entirely within the logic of informational self-determination, so that it was difficult to comprehend why a further manifestation of the general right of personality was necessary at all.[39] The Court argued that monitoring the use of information technology systems creates new risks to one's personality because monitoring such a system and analysing the data on the system's storage media allows for far-reaching conclusions regarding the personality of the users in question and may even make it possible to compile personality profiles. This spurred a considerable need for protection from a fundamental rights perspective. Later, in 2021, it became clearer that the right to protection of the *integrity* of information technology systems has an additional effect of its own: the state also has a 'duty to protect' arising from the fundamental right to protection of the confidentiality and integrity of information technology systems. To protect this fundamental right, the state bears a responsibility for the security of IT systems. In a case where the authorities are aware of security vulnerabilities in IT systems that are unknown to the developer, the state has a specific duty to contribute towards protecting the users of IT systems against third-party attacks within those systems.[40]

## D. Art 10, Art 13 of the Basic Law

Article 10 GG protects the privacy of telecommunications, while article 13 of the Basic Law protects the inviolability of the home. Both rights establish and protect legitimate expectations of confidentiality for specific contexts. Both are special manifestations of the right to informational self-determination. Like the right to informational self-determination, they serve the uninhibited exercise of freedom: unrestricted telecommunications (article 10 of the Basic Law) and unrestricted actions in one's own home (article 13 of the Basic Law). Furthermore, the inviolability of the home is also a special form of the protection of privacy and intimacy.

[37] BVerfGE 138, 377 para 29 [2015] – *Auskunft über den mutmaßlichen leiblichen Vater.*

[38] BVerfGE 120, 274 [2008] – *Online-Durchsuchungen.*

[39] See, eg, G Britz, 'Vertraulichkeit und Integrität informationstechnischer Systeme – Einige Fragen zu einem "neuen Grundrecht"' (2008) 61 *Die Öffentliche Verwaltung* 411; M Eifert, 'Informationelle Selbstbestimmung im Internet – Das BVerfG und die Online-Durchsuchungen' (2008) 27 *Neue Zeitschrift für Verwaltungsrecht* 521.

[40] BVerfGE 158, 170 [2021] – *IT-Sicherheitslücken.*

# V. Mechanisms and Instruments of Data Protection in the Case Law of the Federal Constitutional Court

The most important mechanisms and instruments of data protection have already been mentioned in the census ruling from 1983. The ruling established the fundamental connection between individual informational security ('knowledge about what others know about you') and freedom (see above). And it derived certain protection mechanisms and instruments from this connection. Mechanisms and instruments that still characterise European data protection today[41] can be found here. The census ruling was a 'general' data protection case, which means that it was not characterised by serious state surveillance measures that occur in a national security context. In the last decades, the case law of the Federal Constitutional Court has increasingly developed regarding secret surveillance measures that deeply encroach upon fundamental rights. However, the mechanisms and instruments of data protection against secret surveillance measures in national security are also based on the techniques developed in general data protection law.

## A. Data Protection in Cases of General Data Processing

The general constitutional principles for the protection of personal data can already be found in the census judgment.

First of all, it is important to note that the protection does not only apply to the use of data. Rather, the individual is protected against the unlimited collection, storage, use and sharing of their personal data.[42] As the fundamental right already protects against the collection and storage of data, the protection includes the stage before fundamental rights are violated. This is because the extensive storage of data increases the risk that the data could be used to the disadvantage of the user in the foreseeable future. In addition, the general risk of misuse remains. If large amounts of data about a person can be collected and stored, there may be uncertainty regarding who knows what about that person, whether legally or illegally. This alone would impair the unrestricted use of freedom.[43]

The census judgment also sets out the mechanisms by which data processing must be regulated to be compatible with the fundamental right to informational self-determination:

> Imposing an obligation to provide personal data requires that the legislator specify precisely, for each subject matter, the purposes for which the data may be used; furthermore, the information obtained must be suitable and necessary for achieving these purposes. The gathering and retention of data that has not been rendered anonymous for undefined or

[41] See Charter of Fundamental Rights of the European Union [2000] OJ C364/01, art 8 (II).

[42] BVerfGE 65, 1 para 147.

[43] See G Britz, 'Informationelle Selbstbestimmung zwischen rechtswissenschaftlicher Grundsatzkritik und Beharren des Bundesverfassungsgerichts' in W Hoffmann-Riem (ed), *Offene Rechtswissenschaft* (Tübingen, Mohr Siebeck, 2010) 575ff.

> yet to be defined purposes would not be compatible with these principles. In addition, it is imperative that data collected by public bodies for the purpose of exercising their functions be limited to what is necessary for achieving the objective pursued. Data may only be used for statutory purposes. Not least in light of risks arising from automatic data processing, it is necessary to provide protection against use of the data for other purposes, by way of statutory prohibitions regarding data sharing and further use, including protection against use of the data in the context of inter-agency administrative assistance (Amtshilfe). Other essential procedural safeguards include notification, information and deletion requirements. Due to the lack of transparency regarding data storage and use from a citizen's perspective in the context of automatic data processing, it is particularly important to involve independent data protection officers in order to ensure effective protection of the right to informational self-determination; this also serves to ensure preventive legal protection by means of timely precautions.[44]

Today, this is similarly provided for in article 8(II) of the Charter of Fundamental Rights of the European Union: according to this article, personal data must be processed fairly for specified purposes and on the basis of the consent provided by the person concerned or some other legitimate basis laid down by law. Everyone has the right of access to data which has been collected from them, and the right to have it rectified. Compliance with these rules shall be subject to control by an independent authority.

## B. Covert State Measures in Security Law

One focus of the Federal Constitutional Court's case law on data protection is the protection against secret surveillance measures carried out by security authorities (police, intelligence services).[45] In this respect, the Federal Constitutional Court assumes that the fundamental rights of the Basic Law are not superseded by the EU Charter of Fundamental Rights.[46] Covert surveillance measures by the security authorities can jeopardise the freedom of the individual, precisely because they are secret. This is the case when the unperceived powers of security authorities intrude deeply into the private sphere. 'The deeper the surveillance measures invade privacy, the more they frustrate legitimate expectations of confidentiality.'[47] Again, it is also the deterrent effect that is irritating from a constitutional point of view: if we are afraid that security authorities can easily carry out surveillance measures that intrude deeply into privacy,

[44] BVerfGE 1, 65 para 46.

[45] BVerfGE 120, 274; BVerfGE 113, 348 [2005] – *Ermächtigung der Polizei zur Erhebung personenbezogener Daten*; BVerfGE 115, 320 [2006] – *Präventive polizeilichen Rasterfahndung*; BVerfGE 125, 260 [2010] – *Vorsorgliche Speicherung von Telekommunikationsverkehrsdaten*; BVerfGE 130, 1 [2011] – *Personenbezogene Informationen im Strafprozess*; BVerfGE 133, 277 [2013] – *Antiterrordateigesetz*; BVerfGE 141, 220 [2016] – *Bundeskriminalamtsgesetz*; BVerfGE 154, 152 [2020] – *BND-Ausland-Ausland-Fernmeldeaufklärung*; BVerfGE 150, 244 [2018] – *Kfz-Kennzeichenkontrollen Bayern*; BVerfGE 155, 119 [2020] – *Bestandsdatenauskunft II*; BVerfGE 156, 11 [2020] – *Antiterrordateigesetz II*; BVerfGE 162, 1 [2022] – *Bayerisches Verfassungsschutzgesetz*; BVerfGE 165, 1 [2022] – *Polizeiliche Befugnisse nach SOG MV*; BVerfGE 165, 363 [2023] – *Automatisierte Datenanalyse*. An overview can be found, eg, in M Eichberger, 'Art. 2 Allgemeines Persönlichkeitsrecht' in: Huber and Voßkuhle (eds), *Grundgesetz: Band I*, 8th edn (München, C.H. Beck, 2024) paras 318ff.

[46] BVerfGE 115, 119 paras 83ff; BVerfGE 156, 11 paras 63ff; BVerfGE 162, 1 paras 142ff.

[47] BVerfGE 141, 220 para 105.

this could intimidate us in the exercise of freedom in our private lives. The same applies to wide-ranging measures with many persons being affected[48] (eg, data retention or grid searches). Such measures can lead to great uncertainty about what the security authorities might know and therefore could also have an intimidating effect.

Data protection operates here with the same methods as those applied to general data processing operations. However, more stringent conditions are placed on the permissibility of data processing. This concerns both the requirements for the initial collection of data and the requirements for the further use of this data. In particular, the powers must be limited to the protection of *sufficiently weighty legal interests* and are constitutional only if there is a *sufficiently specific and foreseeable danger* to these legal interests. The requirements for the actions of police authorities on the one hand and intelligence services on the other differ.

## i. *Police*

The Court formulated central standards that shape all recent case law in its 2016 ruling on the Federal Criminal Police Office Act. Consolidating former case law, the decision addresses the preconditions for carrying out covert surveillance measures and the permissibility of sharing data with other authorities for other purposes.

### a. Authorisation of Police Officers to Carry Out Covert Surveillance Measures

First, the Federal Constitutional Court decided on the statutory authorisation of the Federal Criminal Police Office (*Bundeskriminalamt*) to carry out covert surveillance measures in order to avert dangers posed by international terrorism.[49] The Court summarised that, in particular, the investigation powers would have to be limited to the protection of sufficiently weighty legal interests and are constitutional only if there is a sufficiently specific and foreseeable danger to these legal interests. Expressly strict standards would apply when the investigatory powers affect persons who belong to the target person's contacts but are not themselves legally responsible for the danger. Regarding powers which typically lead to intrusions upon the strictly protected core of private life, specific safeguards are required (see below). Moreover, privileged information from persons bound by professional confidentiality would have to be sufficiently protected. The investigatory powers at issue would also need to satisfy constitutional requirements regarding transparency, individual legal protection, and administrative oversight. These would include notification requirements vis-à-vis affected persons after the measures have been carried out, judicial review powers, and regular administrative oversight, as well as reporting obligations vis-à-vis Parliament and the public. Finally, the investigatory powers would have to be supplemented by statutory requirements regarding the deletion of collected data.[50]

[48] BVerfGE 115, 320 para 94.
[49] BVerfGE 141, 220.
[50] Bundesverfassungsgericht, 'Press release No. 19/2016 of 20 April 2016', www.bundesverfassungsgericht.de/SharedDocs/Pressemitteilungen/EN/2016/bvg16-019.html.

### b. Authorisation of Police Offices to Share Data from Covert Surveillance Measures with Other Authorities for Other Purposes

Second, the decision develops distinctions for requirements regarding data use that goes beyond the specific investigation that prompted the data collection. Such further data use is governed by the principles of purpose limitation and change in purpose. A distinction must be made between further use of data for the purpose for which it was originally collected, which is generally permissible,[51] and a change in purpose, which is only permissible within certain limits.[52] The Court summarised the main considerations as follows:

> The legislator could allow the use of data beyond the specific investigation that prompted the data collection where this further use serves the same purpose as the original data collection (further use), provided that the authority that is authorised to collect data uses this data while acting within the same remit for the protection of the same legal interests and the prosecution or prevention of the same criminal acts as specified in the statutory provision authorising the data collection. Allowing the authority in question to consider the data as mere evidentiary traces used for further investigations does not run counter to the principle of purpose limitation. However, the same would not apply for data stemming from the surveillance of private homes or from remote searches of information technology systems. Due to the severity of the interferences resulting from these measures, any further use of such data must additionally satisfy the prerequisites for establishing sufficient indications of danger that were applicable to the original data collection.
>
> Moreover, the legislator could also allow further data use for purposes other than those for which the data was originally collected (change in purpose). The proportionality requirements applicable to such a change in purpose derive from the principle of a hypothetical recollection of data (*hypothetische Datenneuerhebung*). According to this principle, the new use of the data must serve to protect legal interests or to detect criminal acts of such weight that would, by constitutional standards, justify a new collection of the data with comparably weighty means. However, there would generally be no need to establish, for a second time, the existence of an identifiable danger (*konkretisierte Gefahrenlage*), as was required for the original data collection; it would be necessary but generally also sufficient to require that there be a specific basis for further investigations. By contrast, with regard to surveillance of private homes and remote searches of information technology systems, which result in particularly serious interferences, a change in purpose is subject to the same requirements regarding the danger categories as the data collection itself. By specifying these standards, the Court's decision consolidates a long line of case-law and carefully delimits it.[53]

The decision also contains general statements on the requirements for the sharing of data with foreign security authorities.[54] Insofar as the Court summarised, fundamental rights set limits to data sharing, which serve to uphold data protection guarantees. These limits set by the Basic Law for the domestic collection and processing of data must not be undermined, in terms of their substance, by data sharing with foreign security authorities. Thus, the legislator would have to ensure that this fundamental rights

[51] BVerfGE 141, 220 paras 278ff.
[52] ibid paras 284ff.
[53] Bundesverfassungsgericht, 'Press release No 19/2016 of 20 April 2016', www.bundesverfassungsgericht.de/SharedDocs/Pressemitteilungen/EN/2016/bvg16-019.html.
[54] BVerfGE 141, 220 paras 327, 328.

protection is not eroded, neither by the sharing of data collected by German authorities with other states and international organisations nor by the receipt and use of data from foreign authorities that was obtained in violation of human rights. Moreover, limits to data sharing arise regarding the use of the data by the receiving state if there are concerns about human rights violations. Sharing data with other states is ruled out if there is reason to fear that its use could lead to violations of fundamental principles of the rule of law. Under no circumstances could the state be complicit in violations of human dignity.[55]

### *ii. Intelligence Services*

Those requirements have been a basis for similar demands as to actions of intelligence services. Still, in some respects, informational self-determination gives rise to different requirements as to the actions of domestic intelligence services than as to corresponding actions by police authorities. The Court characterised this to mean that, on the one hand, the surveillance powers of domestic intelligence services are not generally required to be linked to the existence of a danger in the same sense as for police action. On the other hand, the sharing of personal data and information by a domestic intelligence service with other bodies – at least when the data was collected by specific surveillance instruments of the intelligence service – requires that the data sharing both serve to protect a particularly weighty legal interest and that there be a sufficient specific and foreseeable danger to that legal interest. This 'principle of separation of police and intelligence data' (*informationelles Trennungsprinzip*)[56] is a consequence of the fact that under German law intelligence services – unlike the police – have very broad surveillance powers that are not subject to any strict thresholds for intervention.

### *iii. Protection of the Core of Private Life*

In the case of intrusive surveillance powers, additional requirements apply regarding the protection of the core of private life. These requirements apply just as much to domestic intelligence services as they do to police authorities.[57] The free development of one's personality within the core of private life must include the possibility of expressing internal processes such as emotions and feelings, as well as reflections, views, and experiences of a highly personal nature. Protection is afforded to non-public communication with persons enjoying the highest level of personal trust, conducted with the reasonable expectation that no surveillance is taking place.[58] This does not mean that every instance in which highly personal information is collected amounts to a breach of constitutional law or even a violation of human dignity. However, it does require that the protection of the core of private life must be considered on two different levels when

[55] Bundesverfassungsgericht, 'Press release No 19/2016 of 20 April 2016', www.bundesverfassungsgericht.de/SharedDocs/Pressemitteilungen/EN/2016/bvg16-019.html.

[56] BVerfGE 162, 1; Bundesverfassungsgericht, 'Press release No 33/2022 of 26 April 2022', www.bundesverfassungsgericht.de/SharedDocs/Pressemitteilungen/EN/2022/bvg22-033.html.

[57] BVerfGE 162, 1 para 275.

[58] ibid para 276.

carrying out surveillance measures. First, at the data collection stage, safeguards must be put in place to prevent the unintended collection of information relating to the core wherever possible. Second, at the stage of subsequent data analysis and use, the consequences of an intrusion upon the core of private life that could not be prevented despite the presence of such safeguards must be strictly minimised.[59]

## VI. Critique

The case law of the Federal Constitutional Court on informational self-determination has strongly influenced German data protection law. The basic ideas set out in the case law are widely accepted, even if uncertainties repeatedly arise with regard to the conceptual question of what all of this should ultimately be about; this was shown in more detail above. Meanwhile, some more specific developments in the case law of the Federal Constitutional Court on data protection are also subject to persistent criticism. The decisions of the Federal Constitutional Court on data protection are often criticised as intervening too far in the political competences of the legislator. This criticism mainly concerns the decisions on secret surveillance measures in security law. In fact, the Court exercises a relatively strict control over the legislator here. It develops detailed requirements from the constitution against which it measures security laws and regularly declares certain provisions in these laws as unconstitutional. These constitutional requirements are developed from the principle of proportionality. For critics, this reaches too far. They demand more leeway for the legislator.

One reason for stricter control of secret surveillance measures in security law is the secrecy of the measures.[60] If police measures are carried out in secret, affected persons rarely become aware of them. As a result, they can hardly take legal action against specific measures before the administrative courts. Therefore, these measures are hardly ever reviewed by the administrative courts. This also means that the administrative courts have very few options to control how police officers understand and apply laws that authorise them to carry out covert surveillance measures. Therefore, the administrative courts are not able to guarantee from case to case that these statutory authorisations will be interpreted in a way that meets the requirements of data protection, while police and other security offices have a natural interest in using their authorisations in a broad way. This is a special feature of secret surveillance measures. Legal protection is weaker here than for other measures that interfere with fundamental rights. This is partially compensated for by the fact that the Federal Constitutional Court places high demands on the constitutionality of the laws and thus counteracts the danger that the police authorities – without control by the administrative courts – interpret their authorisations to carry out covert surveillance measures too broadly: the legislator must strictly regulate the requirements for secret surveillance measures. And it must formulate these regulations very precisely

[59] ibid para 277.
[60] See BVerfGE 141, 220 para 94.

('specific and clear'[61]). However, the critics are not only concerned with the relationship between the Court and Parliament in terms of democratic theory. Many critics are probably driven less by concerns about the separation of powers but rather by direct scepticism about the strict material requirements imposed by the Federal Constitutional Court. How important data regulation is for the freedom of behaviour and communication of the individual and for a democratic society is currently a very controversial issue.

However, there is also some criticism concerning the general constitutional principles of data protection. Precisely, the principle of purpose limitation and the prohibition of any data processing that is not permitted by a legal provision or covered by the consent of the data subject (see above) has been questioned by legal scholars: it has been criticised that this led to an almost unmanageable abundance of legal regulations on the automation, change of purpose, or transfer of data. This was said to have the paradoxical effect that, although the principle was initiated for the purpose of protection and a high level of transparency for citizens, it could achieve less and less due to its formal perfection.[62] The constitutional requirement of a narrow purpose limitation of data was identified as the trigger for the almost inflationary data protection legislation, which had contributed significantly to the complexity of the regulations and the obvious dissatisfaction with the current situation in science and practice.[63] Therefore, it has been suggested to loosen the principle of purpose *limitation* and to demand only purpose *compatibility* as an overarching requirement.[64] Compatibility of purpose is intended to replace a strict limitation of all use of data only to the original purpose.[65] The Federal Constitutional Court has taken a similar stance with the principle of hypothetical data recollection (see above). Remarkably, this principle modified the principle of purpose limitation for the particularly serious encroachments on fundamental rights caused by secret data processing by security authorities, whereas the German Constitutional Court has not modified the purpose limitation in the general data-protection doctrine.[66] However, this is not surprising: data protection in *security law* is still largely shaped by national fundamental rights and thus by the Federal Constitutional Court. But this does not apply to the *general data protection* doctrine. In view of the primacy of European Union data protection law over general national data protection law (including constitutional law), key developments in data protection will rather tend to take place at the level of European law in the future. Questions of purpose limitation in data protection law are therefore now also being discussed at this level.[67]

[61] BVerfGE 156, 11 paras 85ff.

[62] M Eifert, 'Zweckvereinbarkeit statt Zweckbindung' in W Gropp, M Lipp and H Steiger (eds), *Rechtwissenschaft im Wandel* (Tübingen, Mohr Siebeck, 2007) 139, 140f.

[63] ibid 142.

[64] ibid 146.

[65] See also art 5 I lit b GDPR: 'Personal data shall be … collected for specified, explicit and legitimate purposes and not further processed in a manner that is incompatible with those purposes ….'

[66] At this point, however, it is important to note that the Federal Constitutional Court does not act on its own initiative, but only if someone files an admissible complaint.

[67] See N Marsch, *Das europäische Datenschutzgrundrecht: Grundlagen Dimensionen – Verflechtungen* (Tübingen, Mohr Siebeck, 2018) 157 ff, 160 ff.

# 6

# European Data Protection Law: Don't Let it be (Forever) Misunderstood

GLORIA GONZÁLEZ FUSTER

## I. Introduction

European data protection law is often misunderstood, both in Europe and beyond. A major source of misconception, haunting numerous others, concerns data protection's relationship with privacy. This chapter goes back to the early stages of data protection in Europe to explore the origins of the persistent – and, as it will be demonstrated, not fully accidental – confusion around data protection and its relationship with privacy. By doing so, it will illuminate important aspects of data protection that are typically obscured by the misreading of its history.

A first assumption of this chapter is that data protection is a distinct notion, different from privacy. In the European Union (EU), this has been patently visible at the highest policy level since 2000, when the EU's Charter of Fundamental Rights, recognising the fundamental right to personal data protection as a distinct right, was solemnly proclaimed.[1] Almost a quarter of a century later, however, the news seems to still not have reached everyone in the EU, and certainly also not beyond. It is a fact, nevertheless. A fact that was eventually inscribed at the highest level of the EU's legal framework in 2009, when the Lisbon Treaty entered into force, and granted to the EU Charter legally binding force of the highest order, just like the EU's constitutive treaties.

A second assumption is that explaining data protection by comparing it to, or contrasting it with, privacy is bound to end up mischaracterising both. Very much like trying to describe a fish in reference to a giraffe, it can only inevitably lead to partial understandings, trigger oversimplifications, and result in caricatural portraits. Data protection is, in Europe, a fundamental right, exactly like the right to privacy, but the truth is that they are also, put simply, different kinds of animals.

[1] On this right, see G González Fuster, *The Emergence of Personal Data Protection as a Fundamental Right of the EU* (Cham, Springer, 2014) and G González Fuster, *Study on the Essence of the Fundamental Rights to Privacy and to Protection of Personal Data* (Brussels, European Data Protection Supervisor (EDPS), 2023).

In search of accuracy and nuance, the chapter revisits seminal developments in the 1970s. It focuses on discussions that eventually led to the adoption in 1980 by the Organisation for Economic Co-operation and Development (OECD) of the Guidelines on the Protection of Privacy and Transborder Flows of Personal Data, and on those at the Council of Europe resulting in 'Convention 108' of 1981. To do so, it relies inter alia on cables sent to or from the United States (US) Department of State. In a second section, it explores the issues at stake, placing them in the broader context of European data protection law and thinking, mobilising a variety of national perspectives and thinkers.

## II. Erasing Emerging Data Protection

The OECD Guidelines on the Protection of Privacy and Transborder Flows of Personal Data, adopted as a Recommendation of the OECD Council, came into effect on 23 September 1980. They constituted the first major international instrument in this field.[2] The first sentence of the Guideline's Preamble states that OECD Member countries 'have a common interest in protecting privacy and individual liberties, and in reconciling fundamental but competing values such as privacy and the free flow of information'. The sentence encapsulates the instrument's core message: a framing of the development of any laws regulating the processing of personal data as a need to balance something named 'privacy' (occasionally referred to as 'privacy and individual liberties') with 'the free flow of information'. In such balancing, presented as inescapable, the Guidelines put forward as a key recommendation that 'Member countries endeavour to remove or avoid creating, in the name of privacy protection, unjustified obstacles to transborder flows of personal data.'

This specific framing would eventually spread to the major instruments of European data protection, reverberating across them. The Council of Europe's Convention for the Protection of Individuals with regard to Automatic Processing of Personal Data (CETS No. 108) (generally known as 'Convention 108'), which opened for signature on 28 January 1981, proclaimed in its Preamble that 'it is necessary to reconcile the fundamental values of the respect for privacy and the free flow of information between peoples'. In 1995, the European Union (EU)'s Directive 95/46/EC, prohibited EU Member States' restrictions of the 'free flow of personal data' for reasons connected to the protection of the fundamental rights and freedoms of individuals, 'and in particular their right to privacy with respect to the processing of personal data'.[3] Since 2009,

[2] Council of Europe's Committee of Ministers, *Resolution on the Protection of Privacy of Individuals vis-à-vis Electronic Date Banks in the Private Sector*, Res (73) 22 (1973) and *Resolution on Protection of Privacy of Individuals vis-à-vis Electronic Date Banks in the Private Sector*, Res (74) 29 (1974) – but these were only recommendations addressed to Council of Europe's members.

[3] Directive 95/46/EC of the European Parliament and of the Council of 24 October 1995 on the protection of individuals with regard to the processing of personal data and on the free movement of such data [1995] OJ L281/31–50, *cf* art 1.

article 16 of the Treaty on the Functioning of the EU obliges the EU legislator to lay down rules on the free movement of personal data[4] and the right to personal data protection.[5] In 2016, the General Data Protection Regulation (GDPR), stated that the free movement of personal data within the EU 'shall be neither restricted nor prohibited for reasons connected with the protection of natural persons with regard to the processing of personal data'.[6] The basic parameters of the framing, thus, would persist in time, even if eventually, in the EU, they moved from a need to reconcile the free flow of data and privacy, to the need to reconcile the free flow of data and personal data protection.

The singling out of 'privacy' as what had to be balanced against the free flow of personal data in the 1980 OECD Guidelines was the result of a deliberate effort emanating primarily from the US. The US were, as a matter of fact, the main driving force pushing for the adoption of such text, which presented, in their view, the key advantage of not constituting a legally binding instrument. The US pushed with particular vigour towards the adoption of the OECD Guidelines once they realised the finalisation of Convention 108 at the Council of Europe was imminent. Convention 108 had for them the main disadvantage of constituting a legally binding instrument. Not being a member of the Council of Europe, the US influence on that text was inevitably more limited.

Convention 108 presents itself as a 'data protection' instrument, referring openly to 'data protection' in its first provision, which describes the instrument's object and purpose.[7] The text of the OECD Guidelines does not mention 'data protection' once, despite significant explicit allusions to this notion in the Explanatory Memorandum. Referring to the fact that numerous OECD Member countries have enacted laws 'intended to protect individuals against abuse of data relating to them and to give them the right of access to data with a view to checking their accuracy and appropriateness', the Explanatory Memorandum conceded that 'it is common practice in continental Europe to talk about "data laws" or "data protection laws" (lois sur la protection des données), whereas in English speaking countries they are usually known as "privacy protection laws"'.[8] This explanation might be read as implying that whether to use the term 'privacy' or 'data protection' was a mere formal choice and that somehow both refer to the same legal notion. This is, however, not the correct reading. Already by then, it was clear to many that to data protection could not be reduced to privacy, and vice versa. Thus, to decide to pretend they were synonymous was not a neutral choice, but rather a choice that mirrored tensions during the negotiation procedure and, in the end, the weight of US interests.

[4] Art 16(2) TFEU.

[5] Art 16(1) TFEU.

[6] Regulation (EU) 2016/679 of the European Parliament and of the Council of 27 April 2016 on the protection of natural persons with regard to the processing of personal data and on the free movement of such data, and repealing Directive 95/46/EC (General Data Protection Regulation) [2016] OJ L119/1.

[7] Art 1 of Convention 108 establishes: 'The purpose of this Convention is to secure in the territory of each Party for every individual, whatever his nationality or residence, respect for his rights and fundamental freedoms, and in particular his right to privacy, with regard to automatic processing of personal data relating to him ("data protection")'.

[8] *Cf* para 4 of Explanatory Memorandum.

## A. From Paris to Vienna and Back

Work on what were to become the 1980 OECD Guidelines formally kicked off in 1978, following a highly influential Symposium celebrated in Vienna in 1977. To situate these developments, it might be worth recalling that the OECD, headquartered in Paris, comprises among its members both European and non-European countries. By the mid-1970s, members included 19 European states (Austria, Belgium, Denmark, Finland, France, the Federal Republic of Germany, Greece, Iceland, Ireland, Italy, Luxembourg, the Netherlands, Norway, Portugal, Spain, Sweden, Switzerland, Turkey and the United Kingdom (UK)), but also Canada, the US, Japan and Australia.[9]

In the 1970s it was primarily an expert group named the Data Bank Panel that carried out work around these issues, after some exploratory work by a Group of Experts on Computer Utilisation.[10] The US were paying careful attention to the activities of the Data Bank Panel relatively early.[11]

Work at the Data Bank Panel culminated in the celebration of the 1977 Vienna Symposium. A notable intervention at that Symposium was the contribution by the Frenchman Louis Joinet, a prominent actor in French developments but also, that year, simultaneously the Vice-Chair of the Data Bank Panel of the OECD, and the president of the Committee of Experts on Data Protection at the Council of Europe. For context, the Council of Europe comprised, in 1977, a total of 19 states: 9 that were also Member States of the European Communities (that would later become the EU), plus others such as Sweden, Austria or Switzerland.[12]

In Vienna, Joinet contended that there had been a shift away from an early phase, called 'computers and privacy', during which reigned 'privacy' as an approach focused on the defence of the human being and human rights, protecting the individual against the computer.[13] Afterwards, he argued, a second phase had come, starting in 1974 and marked by the realisation that privacy was perhaps the tree that did not allow to see the forest and that the problem to be tackled was more general, concerning, beyond individual freedoms, democracy itself and the sharing of information among people; starting from privacy, discussions had moved to the question of democracy.[14]

[9] Yugoslavia and New Zealand had a special status (FW Hondius, *Emerging Data Protection in Europe* (Amsterdam, North-Holland Publishing Company, 1975) 57).

[10] A 1970 survey led to answers including for instance information on the 1969 Act on Hesse's data processing centre and local district computer centres (OECD, Directorate for Scientific Affairs, Group of Experts on Computer Utilisation, *Computer Utilisation and the Privacy Problem: German reply to the questionnaire* DAS/SPR/70.10/01 (Paris, 25 September 1970), 8); see also OECD, Directorate for Scientific Affairs, Group of Experts on Computer Utilisation, *Computer Utilisation and the Privacy Problem: Sweden's reply to the questionnaire* DAS/SPR/70.10/18 (Paris, 6 August 1970), which mentioned that in Sweden, in May 1969, two Governmental Commissions had been appointed to deal *inter alia* with problems concerning computerised information systems.

[11] See, for instance CST/CUG *Seminar on data protection and data bank panel meeting June 24–27* 1974STATE120169 (Paris, 6 June 1974), signed by Kissinger.

[12] Spain, Finland, and the Holy See participated as observers (FW Hondius, 'The Action of the Council of Europe with Regard to International Data Protection' in *Transborder Data Flows and the Protection of Privacy, Proceedings of a Symposium held in Vienna, Austria 20–23 September 1977* (Paris, OECD, 1979) 258.

[13] L Joinet, 'Les aspects juridiques, économiques et sociaux des flux transfrontières de données personnelles' in *Transborder Data Flows and the Protection of Privacy, Proceedings of a Symposium held in Vienna, Austria 20– 23 September 1977* (Paris, OECD, 1979) 209.

[14] ibid 210.

After the Vienna Symposium, the US realised some international instrument on these matters was going to be adopted and started to do the necessary to try to make sure the first one on the table was an OECD initiative. For this purpose, the Data Bank Panel was replaced with a new intergovernmental expert group, the Expert Group on Transborder Data Barriers and the Protection of Privacy. This new Expert Group was instructed to carry out its activities in '"close co-operation and consultation" with the Council of Europe and the European Community', and thus had been ordered to be attentive to European views. It did end up, however, presenting what would be described as a '"hard core" of privacy protection rules in domestic legislation' that reflected 'the influence of the language and presentation of the United States Privacy Study Protection Commission rather than that of the Council of Europe resolutions'.[15] The Chair of the Expert Group, the Australian Michael Kirby, observed that 'the intellectual debt of the Expert Group to the United States Commission can be clearly seen in the language of the titles chosen' to describe the main data processing principles.[16] The choice was not the initial preference of European delegations, which, according to Kirby, favoured 'language very similar to that of the Council of Europe Convention'.[17] It was the result of a move by US representatives 'preparing the basis of acceptable Guidelines' by 'adopting as their "conceptual framework" the eight principles identified in the Privacy Act of 1974'.[18]

Such developments contrasted with earlier approaches. When the OECD's Data Bank Panel started discussing the possibility of an 'international agreement on trans-border data flow'[19] in December 1976, it discussed 'principles and guidelines for transborder data flow and data protection'[20] and referred to the different 'country status on data protection'.[21]

## B. Confusion and Glitter in Stockholm

The first working meeting of the OECD Expert Group on Trans-border Data Barriers and Protection of Privacy, tasked with the drafting of the Guidelines, took place in Stockholm between 10 and 12 July 1978.[22] On the first day, the Expert Group started by discussing a draft prepared for the OECD Secretariat by the Swede Peter Seipel. The Chairman, Kirby, criticised the draft 'for confusing preambular material, principles, and machinery'.[23] The US delegation 'stated forcefully that the Seipel document as a whole' presented 'fundamental problems for the U.S.', arguing that the document failed to strike a middle ground 'between approaches to privacy protection on each

[15] M Kirby, 'Transborder Data Flows and the Basic Rules of Data Privacy' (1980) 16 *Stanford Journal of International Law* 16, 27, 43.

[16] ibid 44.

[17] Idem.

[18] Idem.

[19] OECD/CSTP, *Meeting of Data Bank Panel* 12/2–3/76, 1976OECDP36381 (8 December 1976), para 1.

[20] ibid para 2.

[21] ibid para 3.

[22] OECD *Meeting of drafting party of OECD Expert Group on Trans-Border Data Barriers and Protection of Privacy* 1978STOCKH02704 (Stockholm, 3 July 1978).

[23] ibid (summary).

side of the Atlantic but instead takes almost totally a European view, and that it confuses means and ends'.[24] In light of these comments, Kirby requested from the US delegation an outline paper with an alternative text. The text was eventually drafted by members of the US delegation 'between 10 p.m. and 1 a.m. amidst the glittering and resplendent surroundings of the foyer of the Grand Hotel'.[25] Seipel was later asked to produce a second draft trying 'to "marry" the two divergent approaches toward privacy protection'.[26] The US delegation made clear that if drafts continued 'to reflect so totally the European model, U.S. might not be able to adhere to final draft'.[27]

These tensions reflect a clear lack of immediate convergence between the views of different delegations, and in particular the US and European representatives. An interesting subtlety surfacing already by then, and endorsed by the Chairman, was the idea that what had to be protected could be split between a substance – some 'principles' – and a procedure, the 'machinery' of protection.[28] This construction was particularly suited to, in due course, situate under the realm of mere (optional) 'machinery' the adoption of actual legislation (in line with European views, but not US interests),[29] as well as setting up independent authorities to monitor compliance with the law (already a recurrent element in European legislation at the time).

Kirby later described the coexisting viewpoints as centred around two 'major political combatants': on the one hand, 'France, which favoured the strong data protection model that had been copied from the Nordics and embraced by the Council of Europe (based in Strasbourg and in some ways reflective of French values)', and on the other hand, the US, 'with its constitutional and political commitments to free flows of information and with its economic attachment to avoiding restrictions on the already burgeoning US informatics industry arising in Silicon Valley in California'.[30] He situated '(s)omewhere between the positions adopted by the French and American delegations' the 'wise voices from Scandinavia'.[31]

Regarding what exactly had to be regulated and protected by the text being drafted, the very name of the Expert Group appeared to set the tone: 'OECD Expert Group on

[24] ibid para 3.

[25] ibid para 4. On a side note: Stockholm is probably the city where 1970s discussions on these matters reached a peak in terms of glamour. In 1974, for instance, the opening night of the IFIP Congress, chaired by Per Svenonious, Chair of the OECD Computer Utilisation Group, featured the King of Sweden and computer music (produced at Stockholm's reputed Electronic Music Studio) played by the members of the Swedish Royal Orchestra.

[26] ibid para 5.

[27] ibid para 7.

[28] Hans Peter Gassmann, Head of OECD Informatics Studies Unit in the 1970s, had a similar view: he later wrote that 'general principles of privacy protection in the United States, Canada, and the European countries' were 'largely similar', although 'there were, at the beginning of 1979, significant differences in their implementation' (HP Gassmann, 'Privacy Implications of Transborder Data Flows: Outlook for the 1980s' in LJ Hoffman (ed) *Computers and Privacy in the Next Decade: Proceedings of a Workshop Held in Pacific Grove, California, 25–28 February 1979* (New York, Academic Press, 1980) 109.

[29] The idea of legislating on data processing was not a natural choice for the US: 'The notion of regulating the data processing industry is anathema to American policymakers', wrote LW Fishman, Senior Policy Advisor to the Assistant Secretary of Commerce for Communication and Information, in 1980 (WL Fishman, 'Introduction to Transborder Data Flows' (1980) 16 *Stanford Journal of International Law* 1, 6).

[30] M Kirby, 'Privacy Today: Something Old, Something New, Something Borrowed, Something Blue' (2017) 25 *Journal of Law, Information and Science* 1, 5.

[31] ibid 10.

Trans-border Data Barriers and Protection of Privacy'. At the Stockholm drafting meeting, however, there was presumably 'general agreement' that account had to be taken of the 'French translation of name of the Expert Group, which involves protection of "individual liberties"'. This was 'thought to be a concept going beyond "privacy", which also involves fair information practices and embraces the idea of the relationship of the individual to the State and Society'.[32] The account of these discussions as provided by Kennedy-Minott, who reported via cable from Stockholm to Paris and Washington, DC, does not mention anything about that 'concept going beyond "privacy"' being, in practice, closely related to the concept of 'data protection'.

## C. Americans (also) in Strasbourg

The US were actively involved in the OECD developments while keeping a close eye on the activities at the Council of Europe.

In November 1976, a cable sent from Strasbourg to Washington, DC, communicated that the Council of Europe had 'invited U.S. Government to send observer to first meeting of Committee of Experts on Data Protection',[33] expected to 'have as terms of reference problems relating to the protection of privacy vis-à-vis data processing abroad and trans-frontier data processing'.[34] The announcement highlighted US 'interest in this subject', and put forward that if no expert could be sent, the cable's author himself, Consul General Woodward Romine, could be nominated as observer,[35] which was what eventually happened.[36]

In December 1976, Romine reported that at the announced first meeting of the Committee of Experts, where Joinet was elected as President,[37] 'it was immediately apparent that the Council of Europe Secretariat viewed the meeting as the first of a series to draft a convention on international data protection', before adding: 'and that with the carefully worked out support of the French'.[38] A draft had actually already been prepared by the Secretariat.[39] Despite 'the sometimes vigorous but uncoordinated efforts by the British, Italians, Canadians and others' to consider approaches different from the

[32] 1978STOCKH02704 (n 22) para 9(c).

[33] Council of Europe, *Meeting of Committee of Experts on Data Protection, Strasbourg, Nov. 29 – Dec. 1, 1976*, 1976STRASB00196 (Strasbourg, 3 November 1976) para 1.

[34] ibid para 2.

[35] ibid para 3.

[36] Council of Europe, *Meeting of Experts on Data Protection, Strasbourg, Nov. 29 – Dec. 1, 1976*, 1976STATE277597 (Strasbourg, 11 November 1976). A lawyer from Washington, DC, also joined the meeting, attending 'in private capacity, solely for the purpose of monitoring the discussions', bearing all expenses connected to his travel (Council of Europe, *Meeting of Committee of Experts on Data Protection, Strasbourg, Nov. 29 – Dec. 1, 1976*, 1976STATE287097 (Strasbourg, 23 November 1976)). The same lawyer tried attending during the same trip a meeting at the OECD (OECD, *Data Panel Meeting at OECD*, 1976STRASB00215 (Strasbourg, 30 November 1976)), but his presence there was considered inappropriate (OECD, *Data Panel Meeting at OECD*, 1976STATE292023_b (Paris, 30 November 1976)).

[37] Romine's cable refers to Soignet, but this appears to be a misspelling of (Louis) Joinet (*cf* para 3).

[38] Council of Europe, *Meeting of Committee of Experts on Data Protection, Strasbourg Nov. 29 – Dec. 1, 1976*, 1976STRASB00231 (Strasbourg, 17 December 1976) para 3.

[39] ibid para 4.

drafting of a treaty, discussions continued in such direction.[40] A working group was set up to focus on transborder data flows. Considering the effect that a data protection convention 'could have on data banks located within the United States which serve European customers', the Consul General urged 'adequate professional U.S. representation' in the working group, noting that to be effective US observers should participate in the work from the earliest stages.[41]

The Dutchman Frits W Hondius played a key role in the organisation of discussions at the Council of Europe. He apparently appreciated particularly the contributions of Carl Wait, an American working for the US Mission at the OECD. In May 1977, Hondius contacted the US consulate to specifically request Wait's participation in a June 1977 meeting on data protection.[42] Hondius even decided that Wait would be exceptionally welcome also at 'restricted' drafting meetings.[43] Eventually, however, it emerged that Wait's participation would be 'inappropriate'.[44] The US Department of State accepted this fact but noted it would appreciate receiving any documentary information that Hondius would be able to provide.[45] Hondius dramatically surprised US observers, but, according to them, also everyone else, by announcing in October 1977 that the Committee on Experts on Data Protection had formally, as of September 1977, an 'enlarged mandate to prepare draft convention on protection of privacy'.[46] In reality, work on the preparation of a Convention – that Council of Europe's document regularly referred to as a Convention on Data Protection – in November 1976,[47] and a Working Party was then set up to focus on the drafting.[48]

The Council of Europe had been active in this field for years. In 1973 and 1974 had been adopted two important Resolutions.[49] Discussions about the possible elaboration of an international Convention can be traced back to the early 1970s,[50] and since then all national developments started to be followed very closely. In 1974, for instance, an interim version of a report commissioned by the Dutch government on 'the protection

[40] ibid para 4.

[41] ibid para 6.

[42] Council of Europe, *Working Group Meeting on Data Protection, June 1 – 3, 1977* 1977STRASB00102 (Strasbourg, 13 May 1977).

[43] Council of Europe, *Meeting on Data Protection, January 17 – 19, 1978*, 1977STRASB00268 (Strasbourg, 22 December 1977).

[44] Council of Europe, *Meeting on Data Protection, January 17 – 19, 1978*, 1978STATE003959 (Strasbourg, 6 January 1978).

[45] ibid.

[46] Transborder Data Flow and Privacy Protection, Council of Europe, *Second Meeting of Committee of* [sic], 1977PARIS29938 (Paris, 13 October 1977) para 1. 'Not even Chairman, was aware of this development', reported Salzman (idem).

[47] Council of Europe, European Committee on Legal Co-operation (CDCJ), 33rd meeting (Seventh meeting as a Steering Committee), *Meeting report, Addendum I, Protection of individuals with regard to automatic processing of personal data*, 65.431, CDCJ (80) 28, 3 (Strasbourg 24 July 1980).

[48] With experts from Austria, Belgium, France, Germany, Italy, the Netherlands, Spain, Sweden, Switzerland and the UK.

[49] Resolution (73) 22 of the Council of Europe, Committee of Experts on *the Protection of Privacy on the Protection of Privacy vis-à-vis Electronic Data Banks* (Strasbourg, 10 December 1973) and Resolution (74) 29, mentioned above.

[50] See, eg, Seventh Conference of European Ministers of Justice of the Council of Europe, *Meeting in Basle, 15 – 18 May 1972, Conclusions of the Conference*, CMJ/Concl. 72(1) (Basle, 5 June 1972) 25.

of privacy in personal data registration'[51] was shared with them which argued that although until then discussions regarded principally 'strictly private life', emerging new ideas also concerned 'the protection of the individual as a participant in society generally'.[52] The final years of work on the drafting were years of intense activity all over Europe: when experts formally started working on the drafting, only one member of the Council of Europe (Sweden) had a law on the matter in force; only three years later, six additional Council of Europe countries had adopted 'similar laws' (Germany, France, Norway, Denmark, Austria and Luxembourg).[53]

By the second half of 1978, the US strategy regarding Council of Europe developments focused on encouraging delays, which provided extra time for the OECD to come first with an international agreement. This does not mean that at the OECD there were no more frictions: by May 1979, for instance, work on the text of the OECD Guidelines was regarded as completed, but the discussions started to focus on the Explanatory Memorandum, a text with which the US delegation had 'many problems'.[54] The concerns, according to the US Ambassador to the OECD, 'went beyond mere inaccuracies of some statements or ambiguities as to their meaning', and 'primarily went to what we perceived as a fundamental imbalance in the discussions of the issues that stressed the European model of privacy and data protection'.[55]

Regarding progress at the Council of Europe, a US observer openly questioned, at a meeting of the Committee of Experts on Data Protection, whether the Convention being discussed was 'directed at privacy protection or data processing regulations', implying that the latter could be beyond the Committee's mandate.[56] The Committee's Chairman, Joinet, replied that it would be 'policy-level bodies at Council of Europe, not the experts', who would 'decide whether Committee has exceeded its mandate is regulating data processing rather than assuring privacy'.[57] Tensions also surfaced notably in relation to the possibility of referring to a 'regulatory or inspection agency in each country'.[58] According to the US observer, a 'strong national authority might weaken human rights'.[59] This idea was rejected by Joinet, who contrasted the 'European consideration of freedom and its defense with U.S. preoccupation with privacy.'[60]

In August of 1979, the Council of Europe's Committee of Experts on Data Protection discussed a draft for the Convention that, in its introduction, described

[51] Council of Europe, Committee of Experts on the Protection of Privacy, *Interim Report of the Netherlands Government Committee on the Protection of Privacy in Personal Data Registration, published on 29 January 1974*, 35.867, EXP/Prot. Priv. (74) 3 (Strasbourg, 27 June 1974).

[52] ibid 6.

[53] Council of Europe, CDCJ, Committee of Experts on Data Protection (CJ-PD), *Second Interim Report submitted to the CDCJ, Draft Convention for the protection of individuals with regard to automatic processing of personal data*, CDCJ (79) 34, 3 (Strasbourg, 19 June 1979).

[54] OECD, *Meeting of Expert Group on Transborder Data Barriers and the Protection of Privacy, May 28–31, 1979*, 1979PARIS17913, (Paris 5 June 1979) para 11.

[55] Idem.

[56] Council of Europe, *Committee of Experts on Data Protection Meeting of Oct. 16–19*, 1978PARIS34793, (Paris, 20 October 1978) para 1.

[57] ibid para 2.

[58] Idem.

[59] Idem.

[60] Idem.

its object as 'to strengthen data protection, i.e. [sic] the legal protection of individuals with regard to automatic processing of personal data relating to them'.[61] The draft's introduction also referred to 'information power' and noted that, although some countries had some laws 'on privacy, tort, secrecy or confidentiality of sensitive information, etc.', there was a lack of general rules on the use of personal information and on how individuals could exercise control over information.[62] The document described data protection as 'a new legal discipline'.[63] This latter idea did not make it to the final Explanatory Report accompanying Convention 108, although the others did.

## III. (Re-)situating Data Protection

It would be an oversimplification to state that Convention 108 established data protection as a notion completely disconnected from privacy. Its text refers to privacy three times,[64] and there is also an implicit connection through article 8 of the European Convention on Human Rights (ECtHR), on the right to respect for privacy life – often referred to as 'right to privacy' – which is quoted in the Explanatory Report as a particularly relevant right. It would also be a caricature to summarise the described developments as opposing the supporters of a clearly defined notion of privacy against advocates of data protection as a distinct concept. The accounted frictions, nevertheless, illustrate that these two terms had specific connotations at least for some of the involved actors, that they were generally not regarded as synonyms, and that they tended to be assimilated with narrower or broader visions of what was at stake.

The dawn of data protection in Europe, as 'a new corpus of law', was famously heralded by Hondius in his 1975 volume on the matter, pertinently titled 'Emerging data protection in Europe'.[65] It is certainly not a coincidence that Hondius worked at the Council of Europe and had witnessed, from such a privileged position, the progressive advent of numerous laws concerned with data. In 1981, the Norwegian Jon Bing noted that the term 'data protection legislation' was used 'according to the established terminology' for a new body of law regulating the use of personal data, for which 'the traditional term' of 'privacy' was inappropriate.[66] For Bing, data protection law was 'more closely related to the law of public administration than to the law of individual liberties'.[67]

[61] Council of Europe, CDCJ, CJ-PD, *Draft Explanatory Report on the Draft Convention for the Protection of Individuals with Regard to Automatic Processing of Personal Data*, Secretariat Memorandum prepared by the Directorate of Legal Affairs, 60.699, 05.3, 1 CDCJ (79) 34, Addendum (Strasbourg, 18 August 1979).

[62] Idem.

[63] ibid 8.

[64] *Cf* arts 1, 9(3) and 13(3)(b).

[65] Hondius, *Emerging Data Protection in Europe* (New York, Elsevier, 1975) 1; See also, noting data protection had been recognised 'as a new branch of law': JA Zimmerman, 'Transborder Data Flow: Problems with the Council of Europe Convention, or Protecting States from Protectionism' (1982) 4 *Northwestern Journal of International Law & Business* 601, 602.

[66] J Bing, 'Information Law' (1981) 2 *Journal of Media Law and Practice* 219, 232.

[67] Idem.

On the other side of the Atlantic, the term 'data protection' was not unknown but was often used at the time in a dismissive manner to evoke negative policy and legislative developments. In 1978, John Eger referred to European laws as 'privacy or other so-called "data protection" laws',[68] accusing them of presenting 'an imminent threat to the world economy and to all nations'.[69] In 1980, Hogrebe commented that '(i)n the international debate, data protection licensing systems like the Swedish are regarded (especially from American comments) as unwieldy, over-bureaucratic and (for the private organisations concerned) as unnecessarily expensive', and this despite the fact that '(i)n reality the Data Inspection Board (…) is certainly, on the contrary, quite unbureaucratic and efficient'.[70] According to Kirby, there was in some quarters a genuine 'fear of "data protectionism"';[71] in particular, it was the case among US 'business leaders'.[72] Data protection law was since its inception regularly given a bad name in some circles.

## A. The Many Faces of an Emerging Notion

At the very early stages, not all laws that might, in retrospect, be regarded as 'data protection' laws – many of which were indicted for 'data protectionism' – bared such term. Nor did they typically include the word 'privacy'.[73]

A striking feature of pioneering laws in this field is indeed that they surfaced relying on heterogeneous terminology. Whereas the 1970 Datenschutzgesetz of the German Land of Hesse[74] was definitely about 'Datenschutz', that is, 'data protection', the 1973 Swedish Data Act,[75] commonly regarded as the first ever national data protection law and a major reference for all data protection laws to follow,[76] does not mention the term 'data protection'. The Swedish Data Act does refer to 'personal integrity',[77] a term that some translators would translate as 'privacy',[78] but not all. 'Privacy' was also read between the lines of early German data protection.[79]

[68] J Eger, 'Transborder Data Flow: The International Industry' (1978) 24 *Datamation* 50, 52.

[69] Idem.

[70] EFM Hogrebe, *Volume 4. Section 4: International economic aspects of data protection. A Study on data security and confidentiality* (Working Document), Commission of the European Communities, (1980) 113; Hogrebe also reported that the Swedish Federation of Industries had a positive view of data protection, perceived 'as means of avoiding social conflict' (ibid 115).

[71] Kirby, 'Transborder Data Flows' 28.

[72] MB Feldman and DR Garcia, 'National Regulation of Transborder Data Flows' (1982) 7 *North Carolina Journal of International Law and Commercial Regulation* 1, 14.

[73] D Yarn, 'The Development of Canadian Law on Trans-Border Data Flow' (1983) 13 *Georgia Journal of International and Comparative Law* 825, 842.

[74] Datenschutzgesetz (7 October 1970) §6, 1 Gesetz- und Verordnungsblatt für das Land Hessen 625.

[75] The Swedish Data Bank Statute and regulation (11 May 1973).

[76] Hondius (n 65) 4.

[77] See, for instance K Lenk, 'Automated Information Management in Public Administration – Present Developments and Impact' in *Automated Information Management in Public Administration: Present Developments and Impacts*, OECD Informatics Studies 4 (Paris, OECD, 1973) 25.

[78] Including F Henriksen, author of an influential 1973 translation for the Library of Congress.

[79] Drafts made available to the data protection experts at the Council of Europe did not refer to privacy, but described data protection (as matter of fact, 'data protecting') as comprising 'all measures which serve to prevent prejudice to any personal interests that warrant protection during the processing of personal data

In France, in 1974, the President of the Republic tasked a Commission to propose measures to ensure that computers would evolve respecting privacy as well as individual and public freedoms. The Commission's Report, published in 1975 and commonly known as 'Tricot's Report',[80] noted that the Commission did not even attempt to define the contours of 'privacy', because it knew its work was not delimited by this notion.[81] Bernard Tricot, the main rapporteur, evoked in his memoir that the Commission became progressively convinced that they had to be concerned with the protection of all freedoms and not only with the protection of privacy.[82] This was particularly important for the representatives of trade unions, explained Tricot, who were worried about the power of companies over staff, clients, and providers, and 'transborder data flows' in favour of multinationals.[83]

In 1981 was published André Vitalis' *Informatique, pouvoir et libertés*,[84] which argued that the right to privacy had been overrated[85] and stressed that Tricot's report heralded moving beyond privacy and the surpassing of individualistic approaches.[86] As a direct follow-up to that report, the 1978 *Loi informatique et libértés* (France's 'data protection law') was adopted which, according to Vitalis, did not, however, embrace all the collective potential of the report's suggestions.[87] In 1988, the French Data Protection Authority (the Commission nationale de l'informatique et des libértés (CNIL)), reflecting on its first 10 years of activities, noted proudly that it had applied and interpreted the law, showing it was not merely there to protect privacy.[88] In this sense, the CNIL notably underlined its work in the defence of the rights of workers in general and trade union representatives in particular.[89]

A progressive shift from 'privacy' towards 'data protection' was particularly visible in the UK. In 1975, the UK government published a White Paper, Computers

stored in data banks' (Council of Europe, *Committee on the Protection of Privacy vis-à-vis Electronic Data Banks*, Draft Act submitted by the Government of the Federal Republic of Germany on protection against the misuse of personal data in data processing (Data Protection Act) (Bundes-Datenschutzgesetz – BDSG), Draft submitted to Parliament on 21 September 1973, Information Document, EXP/Prot.Priv./EDB(73)2 rev 1, 34.096, 05.2 (Strasbourg, 10 December 1973); See also Council of Europe, *Committee on the Protection of Privacy vis-à-vis Electronic Data Banks*, Preliminary Draft (Referententwurf) Bill on the protection against the misuse of personal data in data processing (Data Protection Act) (BDSG)), 15 August 1972, Federal Republic of Germany, Information Document, EXP/Prot.Priv./EDB(73)2, 1, 28.117 (Strasbourg, 26 January 1973); Early English-speaking commentators, nevertheless, saw references to 'privacy': eg, JL Riccardi, 'The German Federal Data Protection Act of 1977: Protecting the Right to Privacy?' (1983) 6 *Boston College International & Comparative Law Review* 243, 248.

[80] Commission Informatique et libertés, *Rapport de la Commission informatique et libertés* (Paris, La Documentation française, 1975).

[81] ibid 19.

[82] B Tricot, *Mémoires* (Paris, Quai Voltaire, 1994) 400.

[83] Idem.

[84] Republished in 1988 with a preface by Jacques Ellul: *A Vitalis Informatique, pouvoir et libertés*, 2nd edn (Paris, Economica, 1988).

[85] ibid 146.

[86] ibid 159.

[87] Idem.

[88] Commission nationale de l'informatique et des libértés (CNIL), *Dix ans d'informatique et libertés*, (Paris, Economica, 1988) 24.

[89] Idem.

and Privacy,[90] as a follow-up to the Report of the Committee on Privacy of 1972.[91] As further follow-up, in 1976 the Home Department set up a Data Protection Committee, which in turn produced another report.[92]

Portugal, in 1976, and Spain, in 1978, incorporated provisions about the right of access to information stored in data banks (Portugal) and limiting the use of computers in their Constitutions (Spain) – provisions that already in 1979 Council of Europe experts described as incorporating data protection as a fundamental right at the constitutional level.[93] This terminology was also used later at the Council of Europe to refer to developments in Austria and in the Land North Rhine-Westphalia, also described as having incorporated data protection into their Constitutions as a fundamental right.[94] In light of these developments, the Parliamentary Assembly of the Council of Europe considered it was appropriate:

> [T]o examine, as part of the extension of the rights in the European Convention on Human Rights, the desirability of including in the convention a provision on the protection of personal data, by amending art 8 or 10, or by adding a new article to the convention.[95]

For the Italian Mario G Losano, national idiosyncrasies marked different approaches in the field: he saw the Anglo-American concept of 'privacy' as linked to privileged classes and their will not to have to give account of their actions; the Scandinavian one as a response against the suffocating embrace of the state; the German as concerned with political discrimination; and the Italian as closely connected to the rights of workers.[96]

## B. The Heart of Data Protection

What brought all these laws together, in terms of substance, was that they converged on three main elements:[97] a series of rights granted to those about whom data are processed, obligations imposed on those who decide to process personal data, and the existence of an independent supervisory authority. These three elements have been present since 2000 in article 8 of the EU Charter of Fundamental Rights and, now, also in the GDPR and other EU secondary law.

[90] Cmnd 6353.

[91] Known as the 'Younger report' (Cmnd 5012).

[92] Known as the 'Lindop report' (Cmnd 7341).

[93] Council of Europe, CDCJ, CJ-PD, 60.699 (n 61) 05.3, 2.

[94] Counsil of Europe, *Opinion on data processing and the protection of human rights' presented by the Legal Affairs Committee* (Rapporteur: Mr Lewis), Parliamentary Assembly of the Council of Europe, Doc. 4484, 629 (Strasbourg, January 1980).

[95] *Cf* Recommendation 890 (1980) on the Protection of personal data; See also Opinion, Doc. 4484, ibid 3.

[96] MG Losano, *Per una storia dell'informatica giuridica*, Vol. 2 (Milano, Memesis, 2022) 522.

[97] In 1974, Hans Corell broke down 'the elements of what may be described as data protection' as a demand for data quality and data security, and the demand for participation of the individual concerned (H Corell 'Technological Development and its Consequences for Data Protection' in *Policy Issues in Data Protection and Privacy: Concepts and Perspectives, Proceedings of the OECD Seminar 24th – 26th June 1974* (Paris, OECD, 1976) 43).

Beyond this, a constant trend in early policy and legislative developments, but also in early data protection thinking, was the perception that what was at stake is more than the protection of individuals as separate persons wishing to be 'let alone'.

### *i. The Individual/Society Spectrum*

At the 1977 Vienna Symposium, the Austrian Gerhard Stadler, at that moment Chairman of the OECD Data Bank Panel, observed that there were 'many definitions of data protection', and that an essential difference between them was the question of whether data protection 'should only mean protection of the privacy of every individual or whether it should apply to the information resources of society or of single social institutions'.[98] In 1974, Spiros Simitis had described data protection as 'part of a larger system of rules governing the allocation of information within a democratic society'.[99]

The individual has traditionally featured prominently in data protection thinking, even where data protection has been separated from privacy. In 1979, Kirby argued that 'data protection', in his view 'unfortunately' being referred to as 'the protection of privacy' in English-speaking countries,[100] should in reality be read as 'individual liberty' and was primarily concerned with upholding 'the importance of the individual human being'.[101]

The importance of the individual, however, does not automatically invalidate the idea that data protection should also be about protecting something else – envisaged as groups, collectives, communities, or society at large. Hondius contended in 1975 that no one would quarrel with the German Wilhelm Steinmüller's point according to which 'group data protection' was 'an essential part of any data protection regime in a Western democracy'.[102] For Hondius, the question was not whether group data protection was part of data protection, but how to implement it, and whether, in addition to allowing individuals to contest data protection that negatively impacted their group, there should be an obligation for supervisory authorities to act in this regard, or whether groups or associations should have a right to act.[103]

The understanding of data protection as something different than the mere protection of individuals, but rather including also attempts to influence the distribution of power, was very present in early German data protection debates.[104] For Steinmüller, the automation of information resulted at the social level in 'the (wrongly so-called) "privacy" problem, and the issue of the (wrongly so-called) "equality of information"'.[105]

[98] G Stadler, 'From National to International Legislation on Information Flow and Data Protection' in *Transborder Data Flows and the Protection of Privacy, Proceedings of a Symposium held in Vienna, Austria 20th – 23rd September 1977* (Paris, OECD, 1979) 42.

[99] S Simitis, 'General Report' in OECD (n 97) 115.

[100] M Kirby, 'Data Protection and Law Reform' (1979) 3 *Computer Networks* 149, 150.

[101] ibid 151.

[102] Hondius (n 65) 99.

[103] ibid.

[104] See, for instance U Dammann, M Karhausen, P Müller and W Steinmüller, *Datenbanken und Datenschutz* (Frankfurt am Main, Herder & Herder, 1974) 176.

[105] W Steinmüller, 'Legal Problems of Computer Networks: A Methodological Survey' (1979) 3 *Computer Networks* 187, 194.

For him, organising the necessary '*rights of co-determination and control of citizens and state institutions*' required the setting up of 'an international control authority, which must of course not restrict itself to the protection of privacy'.[106]

In 1973, the Italian Stefano Rodotà put forward that centring the whole issue around privacy was misleading.[107] In 1974, discussing the term 'privacy', he argued that conceptions of privacy that put the accent on the idea of controlling information were heralding a move beyond individualistic approaches towards 'the possibility of individuals and groups controlling the exercise of information power, thus contributing to the establishment of more suitable socio-political balances'.[108] For Rodotà, in parallel to privacy's genealogy linking back to Samuel Warren (in his words, 'a conservative traditionalist')[109] and Louis Brandeis ('a liberal'), there existed another genealogy, which had been nurtured 'by progressive groups and left-wing parties', and was a reaction 'against authoritarianism and against a policy of discrimination based on political opinions (or religious, trade-union, racial, etc.)'. Through this different path, privacy had become, Rodotà claimed, 'a means of enabling all citizens to be treated alike, of promoting equality and not of protecting privileges, thus breaking down the identifying link with the bourgeois class'.[110]

A decade later, in 1984, Rodotà argued there had been a transformation in the discourse and that privacy, a concept in the meantime 'redefined', was increasingly leaving room for 'the much more comprehensive notion of "data protection"', which in his view went 'far beyond the problems of protection of private life'.[111] Despite this shift, he argued, 'the problem of privacy' still occupied the centre of attention,[112] partially due to 'a certain intellectual laziness or inability to glance beyond the logic of property rights',[113] but also because a legislative response based in 'an atomised control granted solely to individuals' appeared to be the 'least expensive (politically, socially, economically) for those who keep large masses of data'.[114] Rodotà explicitly linked data protection to 'a greater control over those who hold power'[115] and 'the birth of new collective identities'.[116]

### *ii. About Power*

Again, it must be underlined that the tensions being described cannot be systematically mapped along a solid line demarcating 'privacy' and 'data protection'. These

[106] ibid 197.

[107] S Rodotà, *Elaboratori elettronici e controllo sociale (1973): Ristampa anastatica a cura di Guido Alpa* (Napoli, Jovene Editore, 2018) 39.

[108] S Rodotà, 'Privacy and Data Surveillance Growing Public Concern' in OECD (n 97) 130.

[109] ibid 134.

[110] ibid 135.

[111] S Rodotà 'Policies and Perspectives for Data Protection' in *Proceedings of the Fourteenth Colloquy on European Law, Beyond 1984: The law and information technology in tomorrow's society, Lisbon, 26 – 28 September 1984* (Council of Europe, 1985) 15.

[112] ibid 16.

[113] ibid 17.

[114] Idem.

[115] ibid 20.

[116] ibid 21.

terms are not always used in the same sense, and historically – and still today – both experts, commentators and translators sometimes regard them as interchangeable,[117] partially based on the fact that this is how they have been treated before.[118]

An important European policymaker and intellectual who referred often to 'privacy', but to defend her own conception of it, close to what others eventually called 'data protection', was the Swede Kerstin Anér.[119] Anér has been described as 'the single most influential voice in the debate' that led to the adoption of the Swedish Data Act,[120] that is, to the adoption of the most influential data (protection) law ever. In 1979, she wrote that what was at stake in this field was to put in place a 'control from below' of 'information capitalism', in need of such control like 'any other kind of concentrated power'.[121] The same year she also published 'The political aspect of privacy', a paper where she portrays privacy as 'a question of defending your power, or your powerlessness',[122] and highlights how in Italy this idea of privacy, understood as including the right to express a political will and trade union loyalty without fear, has surfaced as 'a condition for survival, not a luxury for the upper classes'.[123] Privacy, she argued, is about working out 'a living and dangerous and ever shifting balance of power, and try to make it as fair as possible'.[124]

In 1969, the Federal Chancellor of Austria, Josef Klaus, addressed the Consultative Assembly of the Council of Europe, proclaiming that 'one of the noblest and most pressing responsibilities of the Council of Europe in the future' would be to prevent that individuals would lose their freedom of decision 'under the domination of computers'.[125] International organisations such as the Council of Europe were brought

[117] But see arguing that 'data protection' is 'a European term containing several elements of the American concept of "privacy"', but not all (EG Michael, 'Contracts for Transnational Information Services: Securing Equivalency of Data Protection' (1981) 22(1) *Harvard International Law Journal* 157–176, 160).

[118] See for instance, using 'privacy' for what is now most regarded as data protection ACM Nugter and CM Adriana, *Transborder Flow of Personal Data Within the EC: A Comparative Analysis of the Privacy Statutes of the Federal Republic of Germany, France, the United Kingdom, and The Netherlands and their Impact on the Private Sector* (Deventer, Kluwer Law and Taxation, 1990); see also, as example of using both terms as synonyms: 'All but the most cynical of American critics concede that the European concern about privacy – the European term is "data protection" – is genuine' (J Walsh, 'There's Trouble in the Air Over Transborder Data Flow' (1978) 202(4363) *Science* 29–32, 29).

[119] On Anér, see M Arvidsson, G González Fuster and J Pohle, 'Kerstin Anér, Pioneering Thinker of Data Power – Towards A Critical Reimagining the History of Data Law and Policy' [2024] *Critical Legal Thinking: Law and the Political.*

[120] P Lundin 'Computers and Welfare: The Swedish Debate on the Politics of Computerization in the 1970s and the 1980s' (2015) *History of Nordic Computing 4: 4th IFIP WG 9.7 Conference, HiNC 4, Copenhagen, Denmark, August 13 – 15, 2014, Revised Selected Papers 4*, 5.

[121] K Anér, 'Contribution to Theme No. 1 (What requirements for Protection of Individual Data are Reasonable?)' in T Dalenius and A Klevmarken (eds), *Proceedings of a Symposium on Personal Integrity and the Need for Data in the Social Sciences. Hässelby slott, Stockholm, March 15–17, 1976*, (Stockholm, Swedish Council for Social Science Research, 1976) 23.

[122] K Anér, 'The Political Aspect of Privacy' (1979) 7 *TC9: Relationship Between Computers and Society Newsletter* (International Federation for Information Processing (IFIP)) 5, 5.

[123] ibid 6.

[124] ibid 10.

[125] Council of Europe, Consultative Assembly, *Address by Dr. Josef Klaus, Federal Chancellor of Austria, to the Consultative Assembly of the Council of Europe in Strasbourg on 2 October 1969 (14th sitting): The 1970s – A fateful decade for Europe*, 15.411, AS/Inf (69) 15 (Strasbourg 7 October 1969).

to this field not merely driven by pragmatic geopolitical or economic considerations, but also by a genuine will to tackle fundamental threats to individual rights and democracy.

This applies also to the EU and its involvement in data protection. It is not a secret that the EU did not start as a human-rights-focused project, and this may be construed as its original sin:[126] because it was not, originally, (primarily) concerned with fundamental rights, its fundamental rights – including the EU fundamental to data protection – lack, in the eyes of some, the same credibility as other rights, be they those established by the ECHR or by national constitutions. This reading, however, obliterates decades of history, whereby the EU progressively transformed itself into a fundamental rights actor, partially precisely driven by privacy and data protection.[127] In this sense, in 1975 Hondius commented on the eagerness of the European Communities to enter international data protection debates relatively early,[128] attributing such an attitude to a certain will to demonstrate they were 'doing something to defend the fundamental freedoms of the individual Community citizen'.[129]

The Frenchman Guy Braibant noted in 1998 a distinction between two 'compatible' but 'different' perspectives: on the one hand, the French, German or Swedish approaches, for which protecting individuals from the dangers of computers was 'an end in itself', and the approach of international and European law, for which such protection is the counterpart of the principle of free data flows.[130] EU data protection found itself at the crossroads of these two approaches. It did integrate into both its primary and secondary law that the framing according to which data protection is connected to the free flow of data. It did also, however, embrace the significance of data protection as a concern of the highest level, resulting in its recognition as a fundamental right – the outcome of what Stefano Rodotà had described as 'the unrelenting constitutionalisation of the right to personal data protection'.[131]

To fully comprehend European data protection, it is necessary, thus, to avoid reducing it to a single viewpoint and perceive it as simultaneously connected to a history of international negotiations and the multiple intertwined histories of national developments. In this regard, it is not only about power but also marked in many ways by evolving (global and European) power relations.

[126] In the same sense as Warren and Brandeis' background being sometimes perceived and portrayed as elitists views that have 'contaminated' all ensuing privacy discussions (F Rigaux, *La protection de la vie privée et des autres biens de la personnalité* (Bruxelles, Bruylant, 1990) 697).

[127] A history the start of which can be symbolically dated back to Case 29 – 69 *Stauder v City of Ulm – Sozialamt* ECLI:EU:T:1996:38 [1969].

[128] And this despite the fact that 'three States where data protection legislation was of great importance, Sweden, Austria and Norway, were outside of the EEC orbit' (Hondius (n 65) 73).

[129] ibid 72. He also evoked the awareness at the Commission of the European Communities about the need to approach the matter with caution in light of implications in terms of division of powers and the process towards European unity (ibid 252).

[130] G Braibant, *Données Personnelles et société de l'information: Rapport au Premier ministre sur la transposition en droit français de la Directive no 95/46* (1998), 15.

[131] S Rodotà, 'Foreword' in Article 29 Working Party on the Protection of Individuals with regard to the Processing of Personal Data, *Seventh report on the situation regarding the protection of individuals with regard to the processing of personal data and privacy in the European Union and in third countries covering the years 2002 and 2003*, adopted on 21 June 2004, European Commission, European Communities (2004) 7.

## IV. Concluding Remarks

Data protection might be one of the most important legal notions to have emerged in the last century. Probably precisely because of its political significance, it has been regularly dismissed. Partially, at least, due to a spiral of simplifications, mistranslations, and complicated encounters with the notion of 'privacy', its content and potential have been often misunderstood – when it was not just obliterated. If, as Julie Cohen stated, 'Privacy has an image problem',[132] data protection has, over the decades, been amalgamated with all the problems of privacy and managed to develop its own image problems too. In addition, data protection has historically been sidelined in international fora and put under heavy pressure – notably by the US – not to appear as such.

This chapter is far from being the first exploration of data protection's past in the quest for better data protection.[133] It has focused on reviewing the important tensions between divergent approaches coexisting during the negotiations leading to the OECD Guidelines and Convention 108. Getting European data protection right requires being open to acknowledge simultaneously that it is indebted to both the peculiar power relations of historic international negotiations and to advanced reflections centred on the future of democracy.

The revisited unfolding confirms the observation of Fishman in 1980, according to which 'the fundamental intellectual and philosophical premises on which the Council of Europe effort was built' were 'quite disparate from the correlative premises in the U.S.'.[134] The fundamental intellectual and philosophical premises on which European data protection was built came in different shapes, under a variety of names, but converged in terms of substance and shared an uneasiness with reductionist approaches that would downgrade the concerns to anything less than a core element of democratic societies. It is charged with this particular strength that it found its path towards its recognition as an EU fundamental right.

European data protection law regularly finds itself the victim of superficial historical readings, cornered to a side track in partial argumentative constructions. Scholars from all over the world frequently feel the need to rethink it, to reimagine it, and to move beyond it. Take, for example, this grand statement of Timo Harakka: 'Data protection is a false concern, or at least it distracts us from what is important', he writes, adding that 'We speak of individual rights, when we should be talking about societal power.'[135] The data protection experts who helped devise this notion and insisted again and again on the fact that data protection is about power might be sighing in their graves. Of course, it might be a very good idea to rethink, to reimagine, or to move beyond data protection. Any of this, however, is best done after trying to understand data protection a little bit better.

[132] JE Cohen, 'What Privacy is For' (2012) 126 *Harvard Law Review* 1904, 1904.

[133] See, eg, the notable works of J Pöhle, *Datenschutz und Technikgestaltung: Geschichte und Theorie des Datenschutzes aus informatischer Sicht und Folgerungen für die Technikgestaltung* (Berlin, Humboldt-Universität zu Berlin, 2018); F Bieker, *The Right to Data Protection: Individual and Structural Dimensions of Data Protection in EU Law* (The Hague, TM Asser Press, 2022); R Zanatta, *A proteção coletiva dos dados pessoais no Brasil: vetores de interpretação* (Belo Horizonte, Letramento, 2023).

[134] Fishman (n 29) 18.

[135] T Harakka, *Data Capitalism in a World of Crises* (Helsinki, Siltala, 2023) 55.

# 7

# Carpenter v United States

## *Syllabus and Justice Gorsuch, Dissenting*

NEIL GORSUCH

**Syllabus**

No. 16–402. Argued November 29, 2017 – Decided June 22, 2018

Cell phones perform their wide and growing variety of functions by continuously connecting to a set of radio antennas called "cell sites." Each time a phone connects to a cell site, it generates a time-stamped record known as cell-site location information (CSLI). Wireless carriers collect and store this information for their own business purposes. Here, after the FBI identified the cell phone numbers of several robbery suspects, prosecutors were granted court orders to obtain the suspects' cell phone records under the Stored Communications Act. Wireless carriers produced CSLI for petitioner Timothy Carpenter's phone, and the Government was able to obtain 12,898 location points cataloging Carpenter's movements over 127 days – an average of 101 data points per day. Carpenter moved to suppress the data, arguing that the Government's seizure of the records without obtaining a warrant supported by probable cause violated the Fourth Amendment. The District Court denied the motion, and prosecutors used the records at trial to show that Carpenter's phone was near four of the robbery locations at the time those robberies occurred. Carpenter was convicted. The Sixth Circuit affirmed, holding that Carpenter lacked a reasonable expectation of privacy in the location information collected by the FBI because he had shared that information with his wireless carriers.

*Held:*

1. The Government's acquisition of Carpenter's cell-site records was a Fourth Amendment search. Pp. 303–316.

(a) The Fourth Amendment protects not only property interests but certain expectations of privacy as well. *Katz* v. *United States*, 389 U.S. 347, 351. Thus, when an individual "seeks to preserve something as private," and his expectation of privacy is "one that society is prepared to recognize as reasonable," official intrusion into that sphere generally qualifies as a search and requires a warrant supported by probable cause. *Smith* v.

*Maryland*, 442 U.S. 735, 740 (internal quotation marks and alterations omitted). The analysis regarding which expectations of privacy are entitled to protection is informed by historical understandings "of what was deemed an unreasonable search and seizure when [the Fourth Amendment] was adopted." *Carroll* v. *United States*, 267 U.S. 132, 149. These Founding-era understandings continue to inform this Court when applying the Fourth Amendment to innovations in surveillance tools. See, *e.g.*, *Kyllo* v. *United States*, 533 U.S. 27. Pp. 303–305.

(b) The digital data at issue – personal location information maintained by a third party – does not fit neatly under existing precedents but lies at the intersection of two lines of cases. One set addresses a person's expectation of privacy in his physical location and movements. See, *e.g.*, *United States* v. *Jones*, 565 U.S. 400 (five Justices concluding that privacy concerns would be raised by GPS tracking). The other addresses a person's expectation of privacy in information voluntarily turned over to third parties. See *United States* v. *Miller*, 425 U.S. 435 (no expectation of privacy in financial records held by a bank), and *Smith*, 442 U.S. 735 (no expectation of privacy in records of dialed telephone numbers conveyed to telephone company). Pp. 306–309.

(c) Tracking a person's past movements through CSLI partakes of many of the qualities of GPS monitoring considered in *Jones* – it is detailed, encyclopedic, and effortlessly compiled. At the same time, however, the fact that the individual continuously reveals his location to his wireless carrier implicates the third-party principle of *Smith* and *Miller*. Given the unique nature of cell-site records, this Court declines to extend *Smith* and *Miller* to cover them. Pp. 309–316.

(1) A majority of the Court has already recognized that individuals have a reasonable expectation of privacy in the whole of their physical movements. Allowing government access to cell-site records – which "hold for many Americans the 'privacies of life,'" *Riley* v. *California*, 573 U.S. 373, 403 – contravenes that expectation. In fact, historical cell-site records present even greater privacy concerns than the GPS monitoring considered in *Jones*: They give the Government near perfect surveillance and allow it to travel back in time to retrace a person's whereabouts, subject only to the five-year retention policies of most wireless carriers. The Government contends that CSLI data is less precise than GPS information, but it thought the data accurate enough here to highlight it during closing argument in Carpenter's trial. At any rate, the rule the Court adopts "must take account of more sophisticated systems that are already in use or in development," *Kyllo*, 533 U.S., at 36, and the accuracy of CSLI is rapidly approaching GPS-level precision. Pp. 310–313.

(2) The Government contends that the third-party doctrine governs this case, because cell-site records, like the records in *Smith* and *Miller*, are "business records," created and maintained by wireless carriers. But there is a world of difference between the limited types of personal information addressed in *Smith* and *Miller* and the exhaustive chronicle of location information casually collected by wireless carriers.

The third-party doctrine partly stems from the notion that an individual has a reduced expectation of privacy in information knowingly shared with another. *Smith* and *Miller*, however, did not rely solely on the act of sharing. They also considered "the nature of the particular documents sought" and limitations on any "legitimate 'expectation of privacy' concerning their contents." *Miller*, 425 U.S., at 442. In mechanically applying the third-party doctrine to this case the Government fails to appreciate the lack of comparable limitations on the revealing nature of CSLI.

Nor does the second rationale for the third-party doctrine – voluntary exposure – hold up when it comes to CSLI. Cell phone location information is not truly "shared" as the term is normally understood. First, cell phones and the services they provide are "such a pervasive and insistent part of daily life" that carrying one is indispensable to participation in modern society. *Riley*, 573 U.S., at 385. Second, a cell phone logs a cell-site record by dint of its operation, without any affirmative act on the user's part beyond powering up. Pp. 313–316.

(d) This decision is narrow. It does not express a view on matters not before the Court; does not disturb the application of *Smith* and *Miller* or call into question conventional surveillance techniques and tools, such as security cameras; does not address other business records that might incidentally reveal location information; and does not consider other collection techniques involving foreign affairs or national security. P. 316.

2. The Government did not obtain a warrant supported by probable cause before acquiring Carpenter's cell-site records. It acquired those records pursuant to a court order under the Stored Communications Act, which required the Government to show "reasonable grounds" for believing that the records were "relevant and material to an ongoing investigation." 18 U.S.C. § 2703(d). That showing falls well short of the probable cause required for a warrant. Consequently, an order issued under § 2703(d) is not a permissible mechanism for accessing historical cell-site records. Not all orders compelling the production of documents will require a showing of probable cause. A warrant is required only in the rare case where the suspect has a legitimate privacy interest in records held by a third party. And even though the Government will generally need a warrant to access CSLI, case-specific exceptions – *e.g.*, exigent circumstances – may support a warrantless search. Pp. 316–321.

819 F. 3d 880, reversed and remanded.

Roberts, C. J., delivered the opinion of the Court, in which Ginsburg, Breyer, Sotomayor, and Kagan, JJ., joined. Kennedy, J., filed a dissenting opinion, in which Thomas and Alito, JJ., joined, *post*, p. 321. Thomas, J., filed a dissenting opinion, *post*, p. 342. Alito, J., filed a dissenting opinion, in which Thomas, J., joined, *post*, p. 361. Gorsuch, J., filed a dissenting opinion, *post*, p. 386.

**Justice Gorsuch, dissenting.**

In the late 1960s this Court suggested for the first time that a search triggering the Fourth Amendment occurs when the government violates an "expectation of privacy" that "society is prepared to recognize as 'reasonable.'" *Katz* v. *United States*, 389 U.S. 347, 361 (1967) (Harlan, J., concurring). Then, in a pair of decisions in the 1970s applying the *Katz* test, the Court held that a "reasonable expectation of privacy" *doesn't* attach to information shared with "third parties." See *Smith* v. *Maryland*, 442 U.S. 735, 743–744 (1979); *United States* v. *Miller*, 425 U.S. 435, 443 (1976). By these steps, the Court came to conclude, the Constitution does nothing to limit investigators from searching records you've entrusted to your bank, accountant, and maybe even your doctor.

What's left of the Fourth Amendment? Today we use the Internet to do most everything. Smartphones make it easy to keep a calendar, correspond with friends, make calls, conduct banking, and even watch the game. Countless Internet companies maintain records about us and, increasingly, *for* us. Even our most private documents – those that, in other eras, we would have locked safely in a desk drawer or destroyed – now reside on third party servers. *Smith* and *Miller* teach that the police can review all of this material, on the theory that no one reasonably expects any of it will be kept private. But no one believes that, if they ever did.

What to do? It seems to me we could respond in at least three ways. The first is to ignore the problem, maintain *Smith* and *Miller*, and live with the consequences. If the confluence of these decisions and modern technology means our Fourth Amendment rights are reduced to nearly nothing, so be it. The second choice is to set *Smith* and *Miller* aside and try again using the *Katz* "reasonable expectation of privacy" jurisprudence that produced them. The third is to look for answers elsewhere.

Start with the first option. *Smith* held that the government's use of a pen register to record the numbers people dial on their phones doesn't infringe a reasonable expectation of privacy because that information is freely disclosed to the third party phone company. 442 U.S., at 743–744. *Miller* held that a bank account holder enjoys no reasonable expectation of privacy in the bank's records of his account activity. That's true, the Court reasoned, "even if the information is revealed on the assumption that it will be used only for a limited purpose and the confidence placed in the third party will not be betrayed." 425 U.S., at 443. Today the Court suggests that *Smith* and *Miller* distinguish between *kinds* of information disclosed to third parties and require courts to decide whether to "extend" those decisions to particular classes of information, depending on their sensitivity. See *ante*, at 309–316. But as the Sixth Circuit recognized and Justice Kennedy explains, no balancing test of this kind can be found in *Smith* and *Miller*. See *ante*, at 335–336 (dissenting opinion). Those cases announced a categorical rule: Once you disclose information to third parties, you forfeit any reasonable expectation of privacy you might have had in it. And even if *Smith* and *Miller* did permit courts to conduct a balancing contest of the kind the Court now suggests, it's still hard to see how that would help the petitioner in this case. Why is someone's location when using a phone so much more sensitive than who he was talking to (*Smith*) or what financial transactions he engaged in (*Miller*)? I do not know and the Court does not say.

The problem isn't with the Sixth Circuit's application of *Smith* and *Miller* but with the cases themselves. Can the government demand a copy of all your e-mails from Google or Microsoft without implicating your Fourth Amendment rights? Can it secure your DNA from 23andMe without a warrant or probable cause? *Smith* and *Miller* say yes it can – at least without running afoul of *Katz*. But that result strikes most lawyers and judges today – me included – as pretty unlikely. In the years since its adoption, countless scholars, too, have come to conclude that the "third-party doctrine is not only wrong, but horribly wrong." Kerr, The Case for the Third-Party Doctrine, 107 Mich. L. Rev. 561, 563, n. 5, 564 (2009) (collecting criticisms but defending the doctrine (footnotes omitted)). The reasons are obvious. "As an empirical statement about subjective expectations of privacy," the doctrine is "quite dubious." Baude & Stern, The Positive Law Model of the Fourth Amendment, 129 Harv. L. Rev. 1821, 1872 (2016). People often *do* reasonably expect that information they entrust to third parties, especially information subject to confidentiality agreements, will be kept private. Meanwhile, if the third party doctrine is supposed to represent a normative assessment of when a person should expect privacy, the notion that the answer might be "never" seems a pretty unattractive societal prescription. *Ibid.*

What, then, is the explanation for our third party doctrine? The truth is, the Court has never offered a persuasive justification. The Court has said that by conveying information to a third party you "'assum[e] the risk'" it will be revealed to the police and therefore lack a reasonable expectation of privacy in it. *Smith*, *supra*, at 744. But assumption of risk doctrine developed in tort law. It generally applies when "by contract or otherwise [one] expressly agrees to accept a risk of harm" or impliedly does so by "manifest[ing] his willingness to accept" that risk and thereby "take[s] his chances as to harm which may result from it." Restatement (Second) of Torts §§ 496B, 496C(1), and Comment *b*, pp. 565, 570 (1964); see also 1 D. Dobbs, P. Hayden, & E. Bublick, Law of Torts §§ 235–236, pp. 841–850 (2d ed. 2017). That rationale has little play in this context. Suppose I entrust a friend with a letter and he promises to keep it secret until he delivers it to an intended recipient. In what sense have I agreed to bear the risk that he will turn around, break his promise, and spill its contents to someone else? More confusing still, what have I done to "manifest my willingness to accept" the risk that the government will pry the document from my friend and read it *without* his consent?

One possible answer concerns knowledge. I know that my friend *might* break his promise, or that the government *might* have some reason to search the papers in his possession. But knowing about a risk doesn't mean you assume responsibility for it. Whenever you walk down the sidewalk you know a car may negligently or recklessly veer off and hit you, but that hardly means you accept the consequences and absolve the driver of any damage he may do to you. Epstein, Privacy and the Third Hand: Lessons From the Common Law of Reasonable Expectations, 24 Berkeley Tech. L. J. 1199, 1204 (2009); see W. Keeton, D. Dobbs, R. Keeton, & D. Owen, Prosser & Keeton on Law of Torts 490 (5th ed. 1984).

Some have suggested the third party doctrine is better understood to rest on consent than assumption of risk. "So long as a person knows that they are disclosing information to a third party," the argument goes, "their choice to do so is voluntary and the consent valid." Kerr, *supra*, at 588. I confess I still don't see it. Consenting to give a third party access to private papers that remain my property is not the same thing as consenting to a *search of those papers by the government*. Perhaps there are exceptions, like when the third party is an undercover government agent. See Murphy, The Case Against the Case for Third-Party Doctrine: A Response to Epstein and Kerr, 24 Berkeley Tech. L. J. 1239, 1252 (2009); cf. *Hoffa* v. *United States*, 385 U.S. 293 (1966). But otherwise this conception of consent appears to be just assumption of risk relabeled – you've "consented" to whatever risks are foreseeable.

Another justification sometimes offered for third party doctrine is clarity. You (and the police) know exactly how much protection you have in information confided to others: none. As rules go, "the king always wins" is admirably clear. But the opposite rule would be clear too: Third party disclosures *never* diminish Fourth Amendment protection (call it "the king always loses"). So clarity alone cannot justify the third party doctrine.

In the end, what do *Smith* and *Miller* add up to? A doubtful application of *Katz* that lets the government search almost whatever it wants whenever it wants. The Sixth Circuit had to follow that rule and faithfully did just that, but it's not clear why we should.

There's a second option. What if we dropped *Smith* and *Miller*'s third party doctrine and retreated to the root *Katz* question whether there is a "reasonable expectation of privacy" in data held by third parties? Rather than solve the problem with the third party doctrine, I worry this option only risks returning us to its source: After all, it was *Katz* that produced *Smith* and *Miller* in the first place.

*Katz*'s problems start with the text and original understanding of the Fourth Amendment, as Justice Thomas thoughtfully explains today. *Ante*, at 346–357 (dissenting opinion). The Amendment's protections do not depend on the breach of some abstract "expectation of privacy" whose contours are left to the judicial imagination. Much more concretely, it protects your "person," and your "houses, papers, and effects." Nor does your right to bring a Fourth Amendment claim depend on whether a judge happens to agree that your subjective expectation to privacy is a "reasonable" one. Under its plain terms, the Amendment grants you the right to invoke its guarantees whenever one of your protected things (your person, your house, your papers, or your effects) is unreasonably searched or seized. Period.

History too holds problems for *Katz*. Little like it can be found in the law that led to the adoption of the Fourth Amendment or in this Court's jurisprudence until the late 1960s. The Fourth Amendment came about in response to a trio of 18th-century cases "well known to the men who wrote and ratified the Bill of Rights, [and] famous throughout the colonial population." Stuntz, The Substantive Origins of Criminal Procedure, 105 Yale L. J. 393, 397 (1995). The first two were English cases invalidating the Crown's use of general warrants to enter homes and search papers. *Entick* v. *Carrington*, 19 How. St. Tr. 1029 (K. B. 1765); *Wilkes* v. *Wood*, 19 How. St. Tr. 1153 (K. B. 1763); see W. Cuddihy, The Fourth Amendment: Origins and Original Meaning 439–487 (2009); *Boyd* v. *United States*, 116 U.S. 616, 625–630 (1886). The third was American: the Boston Writs of Assistance Case, which sparked colonial outrage at the use of writs permitting government agents to enter houses and businesses, breaking open doors and chests along the way, to conduct searches and seizures – and to force third parties to help them. Stuntz, *supra*, at 404–409; M. Smith, The Writs of Assistance Case (1978). No doubt the colonial outrage engendered by these cases rested in part on the government's intrusion upon privacy. But the framers chose not to protect privacy in some ethereal way dependent on judicial intuitions. They chose instead to protect privacy in particular places and things – "persons, houses, papers, and effects" – and against particular threats – "unreasonable" governmental "searches and seizures." See *Entick*, *supra*, at 1066 ("Papers are the owner's goods and chattels: they are his dearest property; and so far from enduring a seizure, that they will hardly bear an inspection"); see also *ante*, p. 342 (Thomas, J., dissenting).

Even taken on its own terms, *Katz* has never been sufficiently justified. In fact, we still don't even know what its "reasonable expectation of privacy" test *is*. Is it supposed to pose an empirical question (what privacy expectations do people *actually* have) or a normative one (what expectations *should* they have)? Either way brings problems. If the test is supposed to be an empirical one, it's unclear why judges rather than legislators should conduct it. Legislators are responsive to their constituents and have institutional resources designed to help them discern and enact majoritarian preferences. Politically insulated judges come armed with only the attorneys' briefs, a few law clerks, and their own idiosyncratic experiences. They are hardly the representative group you'd expect (or want) to be making empirical judgments for hundreds of millions of people. Unsurprisingly, too, judicial judgments often fail to reflect public views. See Slobogin & Schumacher, Reasonable Expectations of Privacy and Autonomy in Fourth Amendment Cases: An Empirical Look at "Understandings Recognized and Permitted by Society," 42 Duke L. J. 727, 732, 740–742 (1993). Consider just one example. Our cases insist that the seriousness of the offence being investigated does *not* reduce Fourth Amendment protection. *Mincey* v. *Arizona*, 437 U.S. 385, 393–394 (1978). Yet scholars suggest that most people *are* more tolerant of police intrusions when they investigate more serious crimes. See Blumenthal, Adya, & Mogle, The Multiple Dimensions of Privacy: Testing Lay "Expectations of Privacy," 11 U. Pa. J. Const. L. 331, 352–353 (2009). And I very much doubt that this Court would be willing to adjust its *Katz* cases to reflect these findings even if it believed them.

Maybe, then, the *Katz* test should be conceived as a normative question. But if that's the case, why (again) do judges, rather than legislators, get to determine whether society *should be* prepared to recognize an expectation of privacy as legitimate? Deciding what privacy interests *should be* recognized often calls for a pure policy choice, many times between incommensurable goods – between the value of privacy in a particular setting and society's interest in combating crime. Answering questions like that calls for the exercise of raw political will belonging to legislatures, not the legal judgment proper to courts. See The Federalist No. 78, p. 465 (C. Rossiter ed. 1961) (A. Hamilton). When judges abandon legal judgment for political will we not only risk decisions where "reasonable expectations of privacy" come to bear "an uncanny resemblance to those expectations of privacy" shared by Members of this Court. *Minnesota* v. *Carter*, 525 U.S. 83, 97 (1998) (Scalia, J., concurring). We also risk undermining public confidence in the courts themselves.

My concerns about *Katz* come with a caveat. *Sometimes*, I accept, judges may be able to discern and describe existing societal norms. See, *e. g.*, *Florida* v. *Jardines*, 569 U.S. 1, 8 (2013) (inferring a licence to enter on private property from the "'habits of the country'" (quoting *McKee* v. *Gratz*, 260 U.S. 127, 136 (1922))); Sachs, Finding Law, 107 Cal. L. Rev. 527 (2019). That is particularly true when the judge looks to positive law rather than intuition for guidance on social norms. See *Byrd* v. *United States*, 584 U.S. 395, 405 (2018) ("general property-based concept[s] guid[e the] resolution of this case"). So there may be *some* occasions where *Katz* is capable of principled application – though it may simply wind up approximating the more traditional option I will discuss in a moment. Sometimes it may also be possible to apply *Katz* by analogizing from precedent when the line between an existing case and a new fact pattern is short and direct. But so far this Court has declined to tie itself to any significant restraints like these. See *ante*, at 304, n. 1 ("[W]hile property rights are often informative, our cases by no means suggest that such an interest is 'fundamental' or 'dispositive' in determining which expectations of privacy are legitimate").

As a result, *Katz* has yielded an often unpredictable – and sometimes unbelievable – jurisprudence. *Smith* and *Miller* are only two examples; there are many others. Take *Florida* v. *Riley*, 488 U.S. 445 (1989), which says that a police helicopter hovering 400 feet above a person's property invades no reasonable expectation of privacy. Try that one out on your neighbors. Or *California* v. *Greenwood*, 486 U.S. 35 (1988), which holds that a person has no reasonable expectation of privacy in the garbage he puts out for collection. In that case, the Court said that the homeowners forfeited their privacy interests because "[i]t is common knowledge that plastic garbage bags left on or at the side of a public street are readily accessible to animals, children, scavengers, snoops, and other members of the public." *Id.*, at 40 (footnotes omitted). But the habits of raccoons don't prove much about the habits of the country. I doubt, too, that most people spotting a neighbour rummaging through their garbage would think they lacked reasonable grounds to confront the rummager. Making the decision all the stranger, California state law expressly *protected* a homeowner's property rights in discarded trash. *Id.*, at 43. Yet rather than defer to that as evidence of the people's habits and reasonable expectations of privacy, the Court substituted its own curious judgment.

Resorting to *Katz* in data privacy cases threatens more of the same. Just consider. The Court today says that judges should use *Katz*'s reasonable expectation of privacy test to decide what Fourth Amendment rights people have in cell-site location information, explaining that "no single rubric definitively resolves which expectations of privacy are entitled to protection." *Ante*, at 304. But then it offers a twist. Lower courts should be sure to add two special principles to their *Katz* calculus: the need to avoid "arbitrary power" and the importance of "plac[ing] obstacles in the way of a too permeating police surveillance." *Ante*, at 305 (internal quotation marks omitted). While surely laudable, these principles don't offer lower courts much guidance. The Court does not tell us, for example, how far to carry either principle or how to weigh them against the legitimate needs of law enforcement. At what point does access to electronic data amount to "arbitrary" authority? When does police surveillance become "too permeating"? And what sort of "obstacles" should judges "place" in law enforcement's path when it does? We simply do not know.

The Court's application of these principles supplies little more direction. The Court declines to say whether there is any sufficiently limited period of time "for which the Government may obtain an individual's historical [location information] free from Fourth Amendment scrutiny." *Ante*, at 310, n. 3; see *ante*, at 309–313. But then it tells us that access to seven days' worth of information *does* trigger Fourth Amendment scrutiny – even though here the carrier "produced only two days of records." *Ante*, at 310, n. 3. Why is the relevant fact the seven days of information the government *asked for* instead of the two days of information the government *actually saw*? Why seven days instead of ten or three or one? And in what possible sense did the government "search" five days' worth of location information it was never even sent? We do not know.

Later still, the Court adds that it can't say whether the Fourth Amendment is triggered when the government collects "real-time CSLI or 'tower dumps' (a download of information on all the devices that connected to a particular cell site during a particular interval)." *Ante*, at 316. But what distinguishes historical data from real-time data, or seven days of a single person's data from a download of *everyone's* data over some indefinite period of time? Why isn't a tower dump the *paradigmatic* example of "too permeating police surveillance" and a dangerous tool of "arbitrary" authority – the touchstones of the majority's modified *Katz* analysis? On what possible basis could such mass data collection survive the Court's test while collecting a single person's data does not? Here again we are left to guess. At the same time, though, the Court offers some firm assurances. It tells us its decision does *not* "call into question conventional surveillance techniques and tools, such as security cameras." *Ante*, at 316. That, however, just raises more questions for lower courts to sort out about what techniques qualify as "conventional" and why those techniques would be okay *even if* they lead to "permeating police surveillance" or "arbitrary police power."

Nor is this the end of it. After finding a reasonable expectation of privacy, the Court says there's still more work to do. Courts must determine whether to "extend" *Smith* and *Miller* to the circumstances before them. *Ante*, at 309–310, 313–316. So apparently *Smith* and *Miller* aren't quite left for dead; they just no longer have the clear reach they once did. How do we measure their new reach? The Court says courts now must conduct a *second Katz*-like balancing inquiry, asking whether the fact of disclosure to a third party outweighs privacy interests in the "category of information" so disclosed. *Ante*, at 312, 313–316. But how are lower courts supposed to weigh these radically different interests? Or assign values to different categories of information? All we know is that historical cell-site location information (for seven days, anyway) escapes *Smith*'s and *Miller*'s shorn grasp, while a lifetime of bank or phone records does not. As to any other kind of information, lower courts will have to stay tuned.

In the end, our lower court colleagues are left with two amorphous balancing tests, a series of weighty and incommensurable principles to consider in them, and a few illustrative examples that seem little more than the product of judicial intuition. In the Court's defence though, we have arrived at this strange place not because the Court has misunderstood *Katz*. Far from it. We have arrived here because this is where *Katz* inevitably leads.

There is another way. From the founding until the 1960s, the right to assert a Fourth Amendment claim didn't depend on your ability to appeal to a judge's personal sensibilities about the "reasonableness" of your expectations or privacy. It was tied to the law. *Jardines*, 569 U.S., at 11; *United States* v. *Jones*, 565 U.S. 400, 405 (2012). The Fourth Amendment protects "the right of the people to be secure in their persons, houses, papers, and effects, against unreasonable searches and seizures." True to those words and their original understanding, the traditional approach asked if a house, paper, or effect was *yours* under law. No more was needed to trigger the Fourth Amendment. Though now often lost in *Katz*'s shadow, this traditional understanding persists. *Katz* only "supplements, rather than displaces, the traditional property-based understanding of the Fourth Amendment." *Byrd*, 584 U.S., at 403–404 (internal quotation marks omitted); *Jardines, supra*, at 11 (same); *Soldal* v. *Cook County*, 506 U.S. 56, 64 (1992)

(*Katz* did not "snuf[f] out the previously recognized protection for property under the Fourth Amendment").

Beyond its provenance in the text and original understanding of the Amendment, this traditional approach comes with other advantages. Judges are supposed to decide cases based on "democratically legitimate sources of law" – like positive law or analogies to items protected by the enacted Constitution – rather than "their own biases or personal policy preferences." Pettys, Judicial Discretion in Constitutional Cases, 26 J. L. & Pol. 123, 127 (2011). A Fourth Amendment model based on positive legal rights "carves out significant room for legislative participation in the Fourth Amendment context," too, by asking judges to consult what the people's representatives have to say about their rights. Baude & Stern, 129 Harv. L. Rev., at 1852. Nor is this approach hobbled by *Smith* and *Miller*, for those cases are just *limitations* on *Katz*, addressing only the question whether individuals have a reasonable expectation of privacy in materials they share with third parties. Under this more traditional approach, Fourth Amendment protections for your papers and effects do not automatically disappear just because you share them with third parties.

Given the prominence *Katz* has claimed in our doctrine, American courts are pretty rusty at applying the traditional approach to the Fourth Amendment. We know that if a house, paper, or effect is yours, you have a Fourth Amendment interest in its protection. But what kind of legal interest is sufficient to make something *yours*? And what source of law determines that? Current positive law? The common law at 1791, extended by analogy to modern times? Both? See *Byrd*, *supra*, at 412–413 (Thomas, J., concurring); cf. Re, The Positive Law Floor, 129 Harv. L. Rev. Forum 313 (2016). Much work is needed to revitalize this area and answer these questions. I do not begin to claim all the answers today, but (unlike with *Katz*) at least I have a pretty good idea what the questions *are*. And it seems to me a few things can be said.

*First*, the fact that a third party has access to or possession of your papers and effects does not necessarily eliminate your interest in them. Ever hand a private document to a friend to be returned? Toss your keys to a valet at a restaurant? Ask your neighbour to look after your dog while you travel? You would not expect the friend to share the document with others; the valet to lend your car to his buddy; or the neighbour to put Fido up for adoption. Entrusting your stuff to others is a *bailment*. A bailment is the "delivery of personal property by one person (the *bailor*) to another (the *bailee*) who holds the property for a certain purpose." Black's Law Dictionary 169 (10th ed. 2014); J. Story, Commentaries on the Law of Bailments § 2, p. 2 (1832) ("[A] bailment is a delivery of a thing in trust for some special object or purpose, and upon a contract, expressed or implied, to conform to the object or purpose of the trust"). A bailee normally owes a legal duty to keep the item safe, according to the terms of the parties' contract if they have one, and according to the "implication[s] from their conduct" if they don't. 8 C. J. S., Bailments § 36, pp. 468–469 (2017). A bailee who uses the item in a different way than he's supposed to, or against the bailor's instructions, is liable for conversion. *Id.*, § 43, at 481; see *Goad* v. *Harris*, 207 Ala. 357, 92 So. 546 (1922); *Knight* v. *Seney*, 290 Ill. 11, 17, 124 N. E. 813, 815–816 (1919); *Baxter* v. *Woodward*, 191 Mich. 379, 385, 158 N. W. 137, 139 (1916). This approach is quite different from *Smith*'s and *Miller*'s (counter)-intuitive approach to reasonable expectations of privacy; where those cases extinguish Fourth Amendment interests once records are given to a third party, property law may preserve them.

Our Fourth Amendment jurisprudence already reflects this truth. In *Ex parte Jackson*, 96 U.S. 727 (1878), this Court held that sealed letters placed in the mail are "as fully guarded from examination and inspection, except as to their outward form and weight, as if they were retained by the parties forwarding them in their own domiciles." *Id.*, at 733. The reason, drawn from the Fourth Amendment's text, was that "[t]he constitutional guaranty of the right of the people to be secure in their papers against unreasonable searches and seizures extends to *their papers*, thus closed against inspection, *wherever they may be*." *Ibid.* (emphasis added). It did not matter that letters were bailed to a third party (the government, no less). The sender enjoyed the same Fourth Amendment protection as he does "when papers are subjected to search in one's own household." *Ibid.*

These ancient principles may help us address modern data cases too. Just because you entrust your data – in some cases, your modern-day papers and effects – to a third party may not mean you lose any Fourth Amendment interest in its contents. Whatever may be left of *Smith* and *Miller*, few doubt that e-mail should be treated much like the traditional mail it has largely supplanted – as a bailment in which the owner retains a vital and protected legal interest. See *ante*, at 332 (Kennedy, J., dissenting) (noting that enhanced Fourth Amendment protection may apply when the "modern-day equivalents of an individual's own 'papers' or 'effects' … are held by a third party" through "bailment"); *ante*, at 383, n. 6 (Alito, J., dissenting) (reserving the question whether Fourth Amendment protection may apply in the case of "bailment" or when "someone has entrusted papers that he or she owns to the safekeeping of another"); *United States* v. *Warshak*, 631 F. 3d 266, 285–286 (CA6 2010) (relying on an analogy to *Jackson* to extend Fourth Amendment protection to e-mail held by a third party service provider).

*Second*, I doubt that complete ownership or exclusive control of property is always a necessary condition to the assertion of a Fourth Amendment right. Where houses are concerned, for example, individuals can enjoy Fourth Amendment protection without fee simple title. Both the text of the Amendment and the common-law rule support that conclusion. "People call a house 'their' home when legal title is in the bank, when they rent it, and even when they merely occupy it rent free." *Carter*, 525 U.S., at 95–96 (Scalia, J., concurring). That rule derives from the common law. *Oystead* v. *Shed*, 13 Mass. 520, 523 (1816) (explaining, citing "[t]he very learned judges, *Foster*, *Hale*, and *Coke*," that the law "would be as much disturbed by a forcible entry to arrest a boarder or a servant, who had acquired, by contract, express or implied, a right to enter the house at all times, and to remain in it as long as they please, as if the object were to arrest the master of the house or his children"). That is why tenants and resident family members – though they have no legal title – have standing to complain about searches of the houses in which they live. *Chapman* v. *United States*, 365 U.S. 610, 616–617 (1961); *Bumper* v. *North Carolina*, 391 U.S. 543, 548, n. 11 (1968).

Another point seems equally true: Just because you *have* to entrust a third party with your data doesn't necessarily mean you should lose all Fourth Amendment protections in it. Not infrequently one person comes into possession of someone else's property without the owner's consent. Think of the finder of lost goods or the policeman who impounds a car. The law recognizes that the goods and the car still belong to their true owners, for "where a person comes into lawful possession of the personal property of another, even though there is no formal agreement between the property's owner and its possessor, the possessor will become a constructive bailee when justice so requires." *Christensen* v. *Hoover*, 643 P. 2d 525, 529 (Colo. 1982); Laidlaw, Principles of Bailment, 16 Cornell L. Q. 286 (1931). At least some of this Court's decisions have already suggested that use of technology is functionally compelled by the demands of modern life, and in that way the fact that we store data with third parties may amount to a sort of involuntary bailment too. See *ante*, at 311–312 (majority opinion); *Riley* v. *California*, 573 U.S. 373, 385 (2014).

*Third*, positive law may help provide detailed guidance on evolving technologies without resort to judicial intuition. State (or sometimes federal) law often creates rights in both tangible and intangible things. See *Ruckelshaus* v. *Monsanto Co.*, 467 U.S. 986, 1001 (1984). In the context of the Takings Clause we often ask whether those state-created rights are sufficient to make something someone's property for constitutional purposes. See *id.*, at 1001–1003; *Louisville Joint Stock Land Bank* v. *Radford*, 295 U.S. 555, 590–595 (1935). A similar inquiry may be appropriate for the Fourth Amendment. Both the States and federal government are actively legislating in the area of third party data storage and the rights users enjoy. See, *e.g.*, Stored Communications Act, 18 U.S.C. § 2701 *et seq.*; Tex. Prop. Code Ann. § 111.004(12) (West 2014) (defining "[p]roperty" to include "property held in any digital or electronic medium"). State courts are busy expounding common-law property principles in this area as well. *E. g.*, *Ajemian* v. *Yahoo!, Inc.*, 478 Mass. 169, 170, 84 N. E. 3d 766, 768 (2017) (e-mail account is a "form of property often referred to as a 'digital asset'"); *Eysoldt* v. *ProScan Imaging*, 194 Ohio App. 3d 630, 638, 2011-Ohio-2359, 957 N. E. 2d 780, 786 (permitting action for conversion of web account as intangible property). If state legislators or state courts say that a digital record has the attributes that normally make something property, that may supply a sounder basis for judicial decisionmaking than judicial guesswork about societal expectations.

*Fourth*, while positive law may help establish a person's Fourth Amendment interest there may be some circumstances where positive law cannot be used to defeat it. *Ex parte Jackson* reflects that understanding. There this Court said that "[n]o law of Congress" could authorize letter carriers "to invade the secrecy of letters." 96 U.S., at 733. So the post office couldn't impose a regulation dictating that those mailing letters surrender all legal interests in them once they're deposited in a mailbox. If that is right, *Jackson* suggests the existence of a constitutional floor below which Fourth Amendment rights may not descend. Legislatures cannot pass laws declaring your house or papers to be your property except to the extent the police wish to search them without cause. As the Court has previously explained, "we must 'assur[e] preservation of that degree of privacy against government that existed when the Fourth Amendment was adopted.'" *Jones*, 565 U.S., at 406 (quoting *Kyllo* v. *United States*, 533 U.S. 27, 34 (2001)). Nor does this mean protecting only the specific rights known at the founding; it means protecting their modern analogues too. So, for example, while thermal imaging was unknown in 1791, this Court has recognized that using that technology to look inside a home constitutes a Fourth Amendment "search" of that "home" no less than a physical inspection might. *Id.*, at 40.

*Fifth*, this constitutional floor may, in some instances, bar efforts to circumvent the Fourth Amendment's protection through the use of subpoenas. No one thinks the government can evade *Jackson*'s prohibition on opening sealed letters without a warrant simply by issuing a subpoena to a postmaster for "all letters sent by John Smith" or, worse, "all letters sent by John Smith concerning a particular transaction." So the question courts will confront will be this: What other kinds of records are sufficiently similar to letters in the mail that the same rule should apply?

It may be that, as an original matter, a subpoena requiring the recipient to produce records wasn't thought of as a "search or seizure" by the government implicating the Fourth Amendment, see *ante*, at 362–371 (opinion of Alito, J.), but instead as an act of compelled self-incrimination implicating the Fifth Amendment, see *United States* v. *Hubbell*, 530 U.S. 27, 49–55 (2000) (Thomas, J., concurring); Nagareda, Compulsion "To Be a Witness" and the Resurrection of *Boyd*, 74 N. Y. U. L. Rev. 1575, 1619, and n. 172 (1999). But the common law of searches and seizures does not appear to have confronted a case where private documents equivalent to a mailed letter were entrusted to a bailee and then subpoenaed. As a result, "[t]he common-law rule regarding subpoenas for documents held by third parties entrusted with information from the target is … unknown and perhaps unknowable." Dripps, Perspectives on the Fourth Amendment Forty Years Later: Toward the Realization of an Inclusive Regulatory Model, 100 Minn. L. Rev. 1885, 1922 (2016). Given that (perhaps insoluble) uncertainty, I am content to adhere to *Jackson* and its implications for now.

To be sure, we must be wary of returning to the doctrine of *Boyd* v. *United States*, 116 U.S. 616. *Boyd* invoked the Fourth Amendment to restrict the use of subpoenas even for ordinary business records and, as Justice Alito notes, eventually proved unworkable. See *ante*, at 373 (dissenting opinion); 3 W. LaFave, J. Israel, N. King, & O. Kerr, Criminal Procedure § 8.7(a), pp. 185–187 (4th ed. 2015). But if we were to overthrow *Jackson* too and deny Fourth Amendment protection to *any* subpoenaed materials, we would do well to reconsider the scope of the Fifth Amendment while we're at it. Our precedents treat the right against self-incrimination as applicable only to testimony, not the production of incriminating evidence. See *Fisher* v. *United States*, 425 U.S. 391, 401 (1976). But there is substantial evidence that the privilege against self-incrimination was also originally understood to protect a person from being forced to turn over potentially incriminating evidence. Nagareda, *supra*, at 1605–1623; *Rex* v. *Purnell*, 96 Eng. Rep. 20 (K. B. 1748); C. Slobogin, Privacy at Risk 145 (2007).

What does all this mean for the case before us? To start, I cannot fault the Sixth Circuit for holding that *Smith* and *Miller* extinguish any *Katz*-based Fourth Amendment interest in third party cell-site data. That is the plain effect of their categorical holdings. Nor can I fault the Court today for its implicit but unmistakable conclusion that the rationale of *Smith* and *Miller* is wrong; indeed, I agree with that. The Sixth Circuit was powerless to say so, but this Court can and should. At the same time, I do not agree with the Court's decision today to keep *Smith* and *Miller* on life support and supplement them with a new and multilayered inquiry that seems to be only *Katz*-squared. Returning there, I worry, promises more trouble than help. Instead, I would look to a more traditional Fourth Amendment approach. Even if *Katz* may still supply one way to prove a Fourth Amendment interest, it has never been the only way. Neglecting more traditional approaches may mean failing to vindicate the full protections of the Fourth Amendment.

Our case offers a cautionary example. It seems to me entirely possible a person's cell-site data could qualify as *his* papers or effects under existing law. Yes, the telephone carrier holds the information. But 47 U.S.C. § 222 designates a customer's cell-site location information as "customer proprietary network information" (CPNI), § 222(h)(1)(A), and gives customers certain rights to control use of and access to CPNI about themselves. The statute generally forbids a carrier to "use, disclose, or permit access to individually identifiable" CPNI without the customer's consent, except as needed to provide the customer's telecommunications services. § 222(c)(1). It also requires the carrier to disclose CPNI "upon affirmative written request by the customer, to any person designated by the customer." § 222(c)(2). Congress even afforded customers a private cause of action for damages against carriers who violate the Act's terms. § 207. Plainly, customers have substantial legal interests in this information, including at least some right to include, exclude, and control its use. Those interests might even rise to the level of a property right.

The problem is that we do not know anything more. Before the district court and court of appeals, Mr. Carpenter pursued only a *Katz* "reasonable expectations" argument. He did not invoke the law of property or any analogies to the common law, either there or in his petition for certiorari. Even in his merits brief before this Court, Mr. Carpenter's discussion of his positive law rights in cell-site data was cursory. He offered no analysis, for example, of what rights state law might provide him in addition to those supplied by § 222. In these circumstances, I cannot help but conclude – reluctantly – that Mr. Carpenter forfeited perhaps his most promising line of argument.

Unfortunately, too, this case marks the second time this Term that individuals have forfeited Fourth Amendment arguments based on positive law by failing to preserve them. See *Byrd*, 584 U.S., at 404. Litigants have had fair notice since at least *United States* v. *Jones* (2012) and *Florida* v. *Jardines* (2013) that arguments like these may vindicate Fourth Amendment interests even where *Katz* arguments do not. Yet the arguments have gone unmade, leaving courts to the usual *Katz* hand waving. These omissions do not serve the development of a sound or fully protective Fourth Amendment jurisprudence.

# 8

# Property Rights in the Movable and Immovable: A New Constitutional Framework for Privacy in the Internet Age

TIMOTHY M TYMKOVICH AND THEODORE R FURCHTGOTT

Several years ago, the FBI was building a case against Timothy Carpenter for his alleged participation in the robbery of a Detroit, Michigan-area electronics store. Like most Americans, Carpenter had a cell phone, which he carried with him regularly. And like all cell phones, Carpenter's constantly communicated with local cell sites. So, the FBI, equipped with an order from a magistrate judge, compelled Carpenter's two cell service providers to disclose his cell site location information, which in turn enabled the FBI to track his whereabouts for a six-month period. This evidence was crucial to prove Carpenter's guilt in the robberies. Carpenter's innocent cell phone became, in the eyes of law enforcement, a tracking device implicating him in his crimes.

*L'affaire* Carpenter revealed a controversy in the American justice system. The Fourth Amendment of the US Constitution guarantees that

> [t]he right of the people to be secure in their persons, houses, papers, and effects, against unreasonable searches and seizures, shall not be violated, and no Warrants shall issue, but upon probable cause, supported by Oath or affirmation, and particularly describing the place to be searched, and the persons or things to be seized.[1]

The FBI did not access Carpenter's cell site location information pursuant to a warrant supported by probable cause. Instead, it acted pursuant to the Stored Communications Act, which requires telecommunications companies to disclose records of electronic communications if a 'governmental entity offers specific and articulable facts' to a court showing that the communications 'are relevant and material to an ongoing criminal investigation'.[2] Carpenter argued that the absence of a warrant violated his Fourth Amendment rights. The Supreme Court agreed.

In concluding that the FBI's review of Carpenter's cell site location information violated the Fourth Amendment, the Supreme Court articulated a novel statement of

[1] Constitution of the United States Bill of Rights.
[2] United States Code: Titel 18 [2013] § 2703(d).

law. Ever since the 1960s, the Supreme Court has required use of a warrant when a police search would violate a 'reasonable expectation of privacy'. For example, the government generally requires a warrant to search a house, where one has a reasonable expectation of privacy. But the government never needs a warrant to follow a suspect in public, since there is no reasonable expectation of privacy in public spaces. In concluding that the Fourth Amendment required a warrant to search Carpenter's cell site location information, the Supreme Court announced that 'individuals have a reasonable expectation of privacy in the whole of their physical movements'.[3]

Until *Carpenter*, the Supreme Court had defined the Fourth Amendment's scope in terms of forbidden *strategies*, rather than forbidden *outcomes*. For example, the Supreme Court held that police officers required a warrant to bring a drug-sniffing dog to a suspect's porch, and they could not attach a GPS tracking device to a car without a warrant.[4] But as long as the police steered clear of forbidden investigative methods, the Supreme Court was agnostic as to the investigative outcome. The police remained free to discover the same information through constitutional investigative methods.

*Carpenter* changed the calculus. According to the Supreme Court's *Carpenter* decision, the Fourth Amendment forbids not just an investigative method – such as bringing a drug-sniffing dog to a porch or installing a tracking device in a car – but an investigative outcome: knowledge of the whole of an individual's physical movements. Any mundane investigative method, such as surreptitious tailing or witness interviews, is constitutionally suspect if it reveals six months of a defendant's movements.[5]

*Carpenter*'s paradigm shift in Fourth Amendment jurisprudence occurred against the backdrop of dramatic technological changes that transformed the government's law enforcement toolbox. The Fourth Amendment, as contemplated by its drafters and most jurists, protected US citizens against investigations by government agents. The US government cannot install a tracking device in everyone's pocket and affix a camera to every front door. It cannot log everyone's payments, nor record every intimate conversation, nor register every cab ride, nor track romantic preferences. Putting aside the sheer cost of that enterprise, citizens would never comply. Yet, citizens turn over this information voluntarily and even cheerfully to major technology companies every day.

These technology companies, in turn, must disclose any relevant information to law enforcement. As the *Carpenter* court acknowledged, 'a person has no legitimate expectation of privacy in information he voluntarily turns over to third parties … even

[3] *Carpenter v United States*, 585 US 296, 310 (2018).

[4] *Florida v Jardines*, 569 US 1 (2013); *United States v Jones*, 565 US 400 (2012).

[5] At first glance, this might seem like a strawman characterisation of the Supreme Court's holding. But Justice Alito's concurrence in *Jones* suggests sympathy for this interpretation. 565 US 400, 425 (Alito, J., concurring). In that case, the Supreme Court held that inserting a GPS tracking device in a car violated the Fourth Amendment, since the police department, in doing so, intruded into the defendant's car without a warrant. Concurring in judgment alongside three of his colleagues, Justice Alito argued that the Fourth Amendment violation was due to the police department's long-term tracking of the car, rather than its trespass into the car: 'If the police attach a GPS device to a car and use the device to follow the car for even a brief time, under the Court's theory, the Fourth Amendment applies. But if the police follow the same car for a much longer period using unmarked cars and aerial assistance, this tracking is not subject to any Fourth Amendment constraints.' ibid. The implication of Justice Alito's conclusion – one endorsed by four members of the Court – is that constitutionally anodyne investigative methods might violate the Fourth Amendment if they are too effective.

if the information is revealed on the assumption that it will be used only for a limited purpose'.[6] Voluntary surrender of private information to technology companies is a fixture of modern existence. Almost everyone has a cell phone, uses credit cards, and shops online. Major technology companies are co-opted, when needed, to be law enforcement's antennae.

The Supreme Court in *Carpenter* confronted a dilemma. Under the logic of its precedents, the reasonable expectation of privacy trends towards zero. With each new life-changing technology, consumers deliver a new category of data to technology companies, thereby eliminating their expectation of privacy in that information. The Supreme Court's solution was to declare a category of information, the whole of an individual's physical movements, to fall under Fourth Amendment protection.

This solution is deeply unsatisfying. The US Constitution says nothing about location information. And what of the countless other areas of sensitive information that define modern life, such as health records, school transcripts, and dating app histories? Perhaps the Supreme Court will discover another categorical exception in those areas. Citizens will have to wait and see.

Neither the Supreme Court's reasonable expectation of privacy doctrine nor its *Carpenter* alternative is convincing in the Internet Age. The former, paired with the third-party doctrine, lends itself to a vanishing sphere of privacy, one that shrinks with each innovation. The latter contemplates a laundry list of categorical exceptions, which is equally troubling if the exceptions have no basis in the Constitution. Supreme Court justices and academics alike have floated alternative frameworks that avoid the reasonable expectation of privacy and third-party doctrine's implications without resorting to categorical exceptions.[7] This chapter joins the conversation by offering an alternative model rooted in the text of the Fourth Amendment. The Fourth Amendment applies to 'persons, houses, *papers*, and effects'. Warrantless searches for papers motivated the drafting of the amendment, and the Supreme Court, in its early Fourth Amendment cases, repeatedly vindicated Fourth Amendment protections for papers. The Fourth Amendment's guarantee against unreasonable searches of papers has never been more relevant.

The first section of this chapter makes the case that the Supreme Court's modern Fourth Amendment doctrine is untenable in the Internet Age. Its two approaches lend themselves either to near erasure of Fourth Amendment protections or to a laundry list of categorical exceptions. The second section offers a Fourth Amendment framework for online records rooted in the Fourth Amendment's text and history. Pre-ratification cases on government searches and the Supreme Court's early Fourth Amendment cases displayed a sensitivity to property rights and self-incrimination. Early courts frowned on the government's warrantless intrusions into private property not because of the inherent importance of property rights, but because the confiscation of movable property – usually, but not always, papers – led to self-incrimination. To determine whether

[6] 585 US 296, 308 (quoting *Smith v Maryland*, 442 US 735, 743–4 (2018); *United States v Miller*, 425 US 435, 443 (1976)).

[7] See, eg, *Carpenter*, 585 US 296, 342–61 (Thomas, J., dissenting) and 386–406 (Gorsuch, J., dissenting); W Baude and JY Stern, 'The Positive Law Model of the Fourth Amendment' (2016) 129 *Harvard Law Review* 1821; J Bellin, 'Fourth Amendment Textualism' (2019) 118 *Michigan Law Review* 233.

online records are covered by the Fourth Amendment, courts should consider whether they are movable property under the Supreme Court's early precedents.

# I. The Inadequacy of the Supreme Court's Fourth Amendment Doctrine in the Internet Age

## A. The 'Precarious Circularity' of Reasonable Expectations of Privacy

The Fourth Amendment of the US Constitution prohibits unreasonable searches. The Supreme Court interprets this protection as a requirement that the government obtain a warrant before conducting a search, unless specific exceptions apply.[8] The central issue in many Supreme Court cases is determining whether a government activity constituted a search.[9] If an action is considered to be a search, the government must either obtain a warrant, which can then be challenged for its sufficiency, or show one of the narrow exceptions to the warrant requirement. If an action is not considered to be a search, the government does not need a warrant, and the defendant faces more limited avenues to challenge the action.[10] The Supreme Court has adopted multiple tests to determine whether government action constitutes a search. In its early cases, it considered whether the government violated an individual's property rights.[11] In the postwar period, the Supreme Court replaced its property-based test with one rooted in privacy, holding that the government violated the Fourth Amendment when it infringed upon an individual's reasonable expectation of privacy.[12] The new reasonable expectation of privacy framework supplemented without replacing the previous property-based framework.[13]

Although the Supreme Court eventually articulated its reasonable expectation of privacy test as a replacement for (or supplement to) its prior property-based test, it initially conceived of 'reasonable expectation of privacy' as a framework for assessing

[8] See, eg, *Arizona v Grant*, 556 US 332, 338 (2009) ('[S]earches conducted outside the judicial process, without prior approval by judge or magistrate, are per se unreasonable under the Fourth Amendment – subject only to a few specifically established and well-delineated exceptions.').

[9] See, eg, *Carpenter*, 585 US 296, 309–10 (holding that government retrieval of cell site location information constituted a search); *Jones*, 565 US 400, 404 (holding that the government's installation of a GPS device on an individual's vehicle constituted a search).

[10] M Tokson, 'The *Carpenter* Test as a Transformation of Fourth Amendment Law' [2023] *University of Illinois Law Review* 507, 508.

[11] See, eg, *Boyd v United States*, 116 US 616, 624 (1886) (finding that the government's subpoena for glass invoices constituted a search because the invoices belonged to the defendant); *Weeks v United States*, 232 US 383, 390 (1914) (finding that the government violated the defendant's Fourth Amendment rights by entering his house in his absence and taking papers).

[12] See *Katz v United States*, 389 US 347 (1967) (holding that the Fourth Amendment protects what the individual seeks to protect as private); *Warden v Hayden*, 387 US 294, 304 (1967) (repudiating the Supreme Court's Fourth Amendment property rights framework).

[13] *Byrd v United States*, 584 US 395, 403–4 (2018) (citing *Katz*, 389 US 347, 347; *Jardines*, 569 US 1, 8–9). See also *Jones*, 565 US 400, 404 (holding that the government's intrusion into a defendant's car to install a GPS tracking device violated the Fourth Amendment).

property violations.[14] The Fourth Amendment protected property, and property rights guaranteed privacy. As the Supreme Court reasoned in *McDonald v United States*, the Fourth Amendment 'marks the right of privacy as one of the unique values of our civilization'.[15] In *McDonald*, the Supreme Court found a Fourth Amendment violation in the search of a house – hardly new ground – but it articulated the Fourth Amendment's importance in that context due to its privacy-preserving function, a novel and influential rationale.[16] In *Jones*, another forced entry case, the Supreme Court went further and concluded that 'the essential purpose of the Fourth Amendment [was] to shield the citizen from unwarranted intrusions into his privacy'.[17]

The Supreme Court seemingly abandoned its property-based logic in 1967, but the doctrine remained de rigueur in subsequent cases. First, in *Warden*, it announced that 'the premise that property interests control the right of the Government to search and seize has been discredited', observing that 'the principal object of the Fourth Amendment is the protection of privacy rather than property, and [it had] increasingly discarded fictional and procedural barriers rested on property concepts'.[18] Later that year, in *Katz*, it declared that 'the Fourth Amendment protects people, not places', so '[w]hat a person knowingly exposes to the public, even in his own home or office, is not a subject of Fourth Amendment protection', '[b]ut what he seeks to preserve as private, even in an area accessible to the public, may be constitutionally protected'.[19] Justice Harlan's brief concurrence supplied the language that would become canonical: government action constitutes a search when it contravenes a 'reasonable expectation of privacy'.[20] In subsequent cases, however, the Supreme Court resurrected its property-based framework for Fourth Amendment violations.[21]

The reasonable expectation of privacy test sets (perhaps deliberately) shifting goalposts to determine whether the government's use of a technology violates the Fourth Amendment. The test turns on the extent and legality of a technology's deployment, as opposed to any fixed principles. For example, government surveillance of private property from a plane did not constitute a search because '[a]ny member of the public flying in this airspace who glanced down could have seen everything that the … officers observed'.[22] Similarly, viewing private property from a low-flying helicopter did not violate a 'reasonable expectation of privacy' because the helicopter's flight was consistent with flight regulations: 'Any member of the public could legally have been flying over Riley's property in a helicopter at the altitude of 400 feet and could have

[14] *Hayden*, 387 US at 304 (holding that the Supreme Court's property-based Fourth Amendment test had been discredited and replaced by one emphasising privacy violations).

[15] *McDonald v United States*, 335 US 451, 453 (1948).

[16] ibid.

[17] *Jones v United States*, 357 US 493, 498 (1958).

[18] 387 US 294, 304.

[19] 389 US 347, 351.

[20] ibid 360, 362 (Harlan, J., concurring).

[21] See, eg, *Byrd*, 584 US 395, 403–4 (citing *Katz*, 389 US 347, 347; *Jardines*, 569 US 1, 8–9). See also *Jones*, 565 US 400, 404 (holding that the government's intrusion into a defendant's car to install a GPS tracking device violated the Fourth Amendment).

[22] *California v Ciraolo*, 476 US 207, 213–4 (1986); see also *Dow Chemical Co. v United States*, 476 US 227, 238–9 (1986) (holding that aerial view of an industrial plant did not violate the Fourth Amendment, even if 'human vision is enhanced somewhat').

observed Riley's greenhouse.'[23] On the other hand, warrantless use of thermal imaging devices violated the Fourth Amendment since when the government uses '[1] a device that is not in general public use, [2] to explore details of the home that would previously have been unknowable without physical intrusion, the surveillance is a "search"'.[24] Use of aerial photography at a given altitude could flit in and out of constitutionality depending on FAA regulations. But would the once suspect thermal imaging cameras become constitutional if a store decided to stock them on its shelves?

The Seventh Circuit has recently raised the alarm over the Fourth Amendment's 'precarious circularity': cutting edge technologies will eventually and inevitably permeate society. In turn, society's expectations of privacy will change as citizens increasingly rely on and expect these technologies'.[25] The Supreme Court acknowledged the weakness of its test decades ago in *Smith*, noting that 'if the Government were suddenly to announce on nationwide television that all homes henceforth would be subject to warrantless entry, individuals thereafter might not in fact entertain any actual expectation of privacy regarding their homes, papers, and effects'.[26] Instead of defining a right that is constant amid changing societal expectations, the Supreme Court instead ensured that Fourth Amendment rights are downstream of those changes. As technology improves and proliferates, the Fourth Amendment could become a dead letter.

## B. The Supreme Court's Third-Party Doctrine in the Internet Age

Further undermining the Fourth Amendment's reach, the Supreme Court has long held that individuals do not have a reasonable expectation of privacy in information disclosed to third parties.[27] Modern life requires turning over copious amounts of information to third parties. Telecommunications companies collect data on who people talk to and where they go. Search engines track the searches that people make – and therefore the topics that interest them. Credit card companies record transactions. E-commerce companies can claim, and therefore record, a growing share of retail business. Even romance has become the domain of technology companies, with dating apps recording users' romantic preferences and intimate conversations. Each of these activities – calling, texting, buying, ordering, and dating – requires the disclosure of information to third-party technology companies.

Under Supreme Court precedent, voluntary disclosure of information to a third party undermines a reasonable expectation of privacy. In the 1970s, Mitchell Miller was charged with running a bootleg distillery. The Bureau of Alcohol, Tobacco, and Firearms subpoenaed copies of his checks and other records from his bank. Miller challenged his conviction under the theory that this was a warrantless search. The Supreme Court disagreed. It reasoned that '[t]he depositor takes the risk, in revealing his affairs

[23] *Florida v Riley*, 488 US 445, 451 (1989).
[24] *Kyllo v United States*, 433 US 27, 40 (2001) (brackets added).
[25] *United States v Tuggle*, 4 F.4th 505, 527 (7th Cir 2021).
[26] 442 US 735, 740.
[27] See *Miller*, 425 US 435, 443; *Smith*, 442 US 735, 743.

to another, that the information will be conveyed by that person to the Government'.[28] Under *Miller*,

> the Fourth Amendment does not prohibit the obtaining of information revealed to a third party and conveyed by him to Government authorities, even if the information is revealed on the assumption that it will be used only for a limited purpose and the confidence placed in the third party will not be betrayed.[29]

Three years later, the Supreme Court went further. In *Smith*, a phone company, at the police's direction, installed a pen register to record the numbers dialled from a defendant's phone. The Supreme Court concluded that the defendant had no legitimate expectation of privacy in his phone records because he had 'voluntarily turn[ed them] over to third parties'.[30] Under *Smith*, the third-party doctrine applies not only to data collected by counterparties in the course of business but also to information collected by the third party at law enforcement's express instigation.[31]

An obvious reaction to this might be to simply contract out of government disclosures. Terms and conditions are a staple of modern life. Surely, an individual might retain a reasonable expectation of privacy in information that their counterparty is *contractually prohibited* from disclosing to the government. The Supreme Court has yet to address whether terms of service affect a user's Fourth Amendment rights, and lower courts have reached opposite conclusions.[32]

Under the logic of the Supreme Court's past decisions, it is unclear that individuals can establish zones of Fourth Amendment protection through contractual provisions. On the one hand, one cannot reduce Fourth Amendment rights through contract. The archetypal example here is renters, who have Fourth Amendment rights even when the property owner consents to a search.[33] Third parties may only consent to a search if they 'possessed common authority over or other sufficient relationship to the premises or effects sought to be inspected'.[34] Mere contractual entitlement to enter a home, absent common authority, is insufficient.[35]

On the other hand, contracts inform an individual's background assumptions, which in turn inform reasonable expectations of privacy. Dicta in *Chapman v United States* suggests that the existence of an express covenant permitting a landlord to enter an apartment without permission is relevant to the existence of a Fourth Amendment right.[36] Earlier, the Supreme Court found no Fourth Amendment violation where a business owner's contract with the US government specifically permitted a search of

[28] 425 US 435, 443.

[29] ibid.

[30] 442 US 735, 743.

[31] ibid.

[32] Compare *United States v Warshak*, 631 F.3d 266 (6th Cir 2010) (holding that terms of service did not diminish subscriber's Fourth Amendment rights); *United States v Adkinson*, 916 F.3d 605 (7th Cir 2019) (holding that the defendant consented to his cell service provider sharing his data with the government).

[33] See *Minnesota v Olson*, 495 US 91, 98 (1990) (holding that overnight guests have a reasonable expectation of privacy). See also *Stoner v California*, 376 US 483, 489 (1964) (holding that a hotel clerk could not provide consent to search a guest's room). See generally OS Kerr, 'Terms of Service and Fourth Amendment Rights' (2024) 172 *University of Pennsylvania Law Review* 287 (arguing that terms of service do not affect Fourth Amendment rights).

[34] *United States v Matlock*, 415 US 164, 171 (1974).

[35] ibid.

[36] *Chapman v United States*, 365 US 610, 616 (1961).

his accounts and records.[37] The Supreme Court has never addressed whether materials that otherwise would be subject to the third-party doctrine – and therefore subject to warrantless searches – can be shielded from such searches by contractual provisions.

Professor Kerr argues for a middle ground. According to his interpretation, contracts permitting access to data cannot impair a Fourth Amendment right, but contracts permitting common use might be sufficient. Citing the DC Circuit, Professor Kerr argues that a 'legal right' to access does not show a 'sufficient relationship' to waive an individual's Fourth Amendment right.[38] Instead, a contractual counterparty must show 'a common experience or understanding that data is effectively shared, not just that the provider is allowed to look at it'.[39] This stems from the principle that while landlords cannot consent to a search of their renters' property, since they are not effectively sharing the space, 'the voluntary consent of any joint occupant of a residence to search the premises jointly occupied is valid against the co-occupant'.[40] The challenge is determining whether an individual's use of an online service is more akin to leasing a platform from a technology company or sharing data with it for joint use.[41] Since almost every major technology company 'share[s] a common understanding' with its users that it will use the data on its own end – at a minimum, to improve user experience – these companies cannot, consistent with Professor Kerr's theory, create zones of Fourth Amendment protection through contract.[42]

The third-party doctrine is weaker, however, in the *legislative* context. While the Supreme Court has been reluctant to recognise contractually created zones of Fourth Amendment protection, it implied in *Olmstead v United States* that Congress may do so through legislation.[43] In *Olmstead*, the Supreme Court distinguished the postal service from the telephone service, since Congress had made it a crime for 'any postmaster or other person to open any letter not addressed to himself', but had drafted no comparable legislation on telephones.[44] Accordingly, government agents violated the Fourth Amendment – in addition to the relevant criminal statute – by opening the mail but not by tapping a phone call.[45] Under *Olmstead*, Congress could potentially bring electronic records under the Fourth Amendment's ambit by passing a law prohibiting intermediaries from accessing these records. If it did so, the records might have two layers of Fourth Amendment protection, both from the statute penalising third parties from reading them and because the third party could not possibly claim joint use of the records.

The third-party doctrine is the most important application of the reasonable expectation of privacy doctrine in the Internet Age. Almost all Supreme Court cases involve searches by government agents. In the twenty-first century, private companies' investigative abilities dwarf those of the government. The US government has robust

[37] *Zap v United States*, 328 US 624, 627 (1946).
[38] Kerr (n 33) 323 (citing *United States v Whitfield*, 939 US 1071, 1074 (DC Cir 1991)).
[39] ibid.
[40] 415 US 164, 169.
[41] See Kerr (n 33) 324.
[42] See ibid 323.
[43] *Olmstead v United States*, 277 US 438, 464 (1928), overruled by *Smith*, 389 US 347.
[44] ibid.
[45] ibid.

surveillance capabilities and substantial manpower to conduct searches. But the potential data to be gleaned from the government's surveillance capabilities pales in comparison to what the modern private sector can do. Private sector data collection has a key advantage over the government. Its users provide consent for the private sector to collect troves of information. Since companies store this information, the government can access data that predates their investigation into a suspect, and 'the retrospective quality of the data … gives police access to a category of information otherwise unknowable'.[46] An expansive third-party doctrine makes companies arms of the state.

## C. Supreme Court Justices' Proposed Frameworks for the Fourth Amendment in the Internet Age

*Carpenter* revealed the Supreme Court's unease with its post-*Katz* reasonable expectation of privacy doctrine. The reasonable expectation of privacy and third-party doctrines could have provided an easy basis for finding that Carpenter had no Fourth Amendment rights to his cell site location information.[47] Carpenter delivered this information to his cell phone providers voluntarily. And he certainly had no expectation, in the 2010s, that such information would remain secret. Nevertheless, the Supreme Court did not treat *Carpenter* as a straightforward application of its doctrine, and several justices voiced concern about the implication of the Court's Fourth Amendment doctrine. Their solutions are not satisfactory.

Writing for the majority, Chief Justice Roberts decreed that '[a] majority of this Court has already recognized that individuals have a reasonable expectation of privacy in the whole of their physical movements'.[48] In a marked departure from Fourth Amendment jurisprudence, the Chief Justice concluded that an investigative outcome – ie, knowledge of the totality of an individual's movements – violated the Fourth Amendment.

[46] *Carpenter*, 585 US 296, 312.

[47] See ibid 321–41 (Kennedy, J., dissenting).

[48] ibid 310 (citing *Jones*, 565 US 400, 430 (Alito, J., concurring), and 415 (Sotomayor, J., concurring)). The Chief Justice was mistaken. *Jones* was decided on other grounds. The opinion of the Court stated that the District of Columbia police department violated the Fourth Amendment by intruding into Antoine Jones's car to insert a tracking device. Joined by Justices Ginsburg, Breyer, and Kagan, Justice Alito wrote in a concurrence that 'the use of longer term GPS monitoring in investigations of most offenses impinges on expectations of privacy'. ibid 430 (Alito, J., concurring). While he did not 'identify with precision the point at which the tracking of this vehicle became a search', he wrote that 'the line was surely crossed before the 4-week mark'. ibid. Justice Sotomayor, writing separately, raised concerns over the ability of GPS tracking devices to 'chill … associational and expressive freedoms' and their susceptibility to abuse. ibid 416. She wrote that she would 'take these attributes of GPS monitoring into account when considering the existence of a reasonable societal expectation of privacy in the sum of one's public movements', but that '[r]esolution of these difficult questions in this case is unnecessary, however, because the Government's physical intrusion on Jones' Jeep supplies a narrower basis for decision'. ibid 416–8. In other words, Justice Sotomayor noted that GPS surveillance could raise Fourth Amendment concerns, but she explicitly reserved judgment on the Fourth Amendment's scope. The Chief Justice's assertion that '[a] majority of this Court has already recognized that individuals have a reasonable expectation of privacy in the whole of their physical movements' is only true if Justice Sotomayor's concurrence is included in the tabulation – but raising concerns about Fourth Amendment violations falls short of 'recognizing' them, and Justice Sotomayor notably did not join Justice Alito's concurrence.

The Chief Justice's opinion was revolutionary because the entirety of the Supreme Court's pre-*Carpenter* Fourth Amendment jurisprudence prohibited investigative methods, rather than investigative outcomes. In the pre-*Katz* cases grounded in property rights, the Supreme Court considered investigative methods that infringed on property rights to be 'searches' under the Fourth Amendment.[49] Post-*Katz*, the Supreme Court considered investigative methods that violated a reasonable expectation of privacy to be 'searches' under the Fourth Amendment.[50] *Kyllo v United States* is illustrative. In that case, the Supreme Court held that use of a thermal imaging device violated the Fourth Amendment, famously noting that such devices 'might disclose … at what hour each night the lady of the house takes her daily sauna and bath – a detail that many would consider intimate'.[51] The thermal imaging device in *Kyllo* had shown nothing of the sort, of course. It merely revealed the presence of high-intensity lamps, which were used to grow marijuana.[52] The Supreme Court was agnostic to the *substantive outcome* of the investigation and cared only for the *potential harm* resulting from problematic investigative methods.

The Chief Justice's opinion provoked four dissents. Justice Kennedy wrote that the majority's conclusion was inconsistent with the Supreme Court's precedents on the reasonable expectation of privacy and third-party doctrines.[53] Justice Alito wrote that the Fourth Amendment right against searches and seizures is inapplicable to compulsory process, a provocative position that is outside the scope of this paper.[54] Justices Thomas and Gorsuch both challenged the Supreme Court's reasonable expectation of privacy framework.

Justice Thomas argued that the reasonable expectation of privacy framework is erroneous and that the Court instead should have considered who owned Carpenter's cell site location records. As he noted, Carpenter

> did not create the records, he does not maintain them, he cannot control them, and he cannot destroy them. Neither the terms of his contracts nor any provision of law makes the records his. The records belong to MetroPCS and Sprint.[55]

While this approach is conceptually coherent, it begs the question in important ways. In the modern age, ownership of records is often unclear. For example, emails might

[49] See, eg, *Weeks*, 232 US 383, 393 (holding that law enforcement officers violated the Fourth Amendment by searching defendant's house in his absence and taking away his papers and correspondence); *Silverthorne Lumber Co. v United States*, 251 US 385, 391–2 (1920) (holding that seizing, copying, and then replacing corporate documents violated the Fourth Amendment since the government retained an advantage from the violation); *Gouled v United States*, 255 US 298, 305–6 (1921) (holding that the Fourth Amendment prohibited an undercover informant from entering the defendant's office in his absence and taking away papers).

[50] See, eg, *United States v Jacobsen*, 466 US 109, 123 (1984) (holding that chemical test of white substance did not violate Fourth Amendment since government conduct that can reveal whether a product is contraband, but nothing else, compromises no legitimate privacy interest); *Bond v United States*, 529 US 334, 337–8 (2000) (holding that law enforcement agent's exploratory manipulation of carry-on luggage infringed upon reasonable expectation of privacy); *Illinois v Caballes*, 543 US 405, 409 (2005) (holding that use of a well-trained narcotics dog during traffic stop does not infringe on reasonable expectation of privacy).

[51] *Kyllo v United States*, 533 US 27, 38 (2001).

[52] ibid 30.

[53] 585 US 296, 321 (Kennedy, J., dissenting).

[54] ibid 361 (Alito, J., dissenting). Even if Justice Alito's position is correct, this chapter's contribution is still necessary since technology companies may disclose data to law enforcement outside of compulsory process.

[55] ibid 342 (Thomas, J., dissenting).

be stored on a company's server, and the company may have the right to use the emails' content for business purposes, but a user might have the exclusive right to delete them. The same data frequently has overlapping ownership interests.

In his dissent, Justice Gorsuch suggested a return to the Supreme Court's pre-*Katz* jurisprudence. He criticised *Katz*'s reasonable expectation of privacy test as unmoored from precedent, noted that property interests lay at the heart of the Supreme Court's pre-*Katz* jurisprudence, and argued for '[a] Fourth Amendment model based on positive legal rights'.[56] The question, according to Justice Gorsuch, was determining which legal authority was sufficient to instil ownership.[57] Justice Gorsuch offered five considerations: *first*, entrusting property to a third party for safekeeping creates a bailment interest, a common law concept that mirrors a modern data disclosure framework;[58] *second*, Fourth Amendment rights may apply even in the context of competing property interests, such as for apartment tenants or owners of impounded cars;[59] *third*, legislatures may deem things to be property for Fourth Amendment purposes;[60] *fourth*, legislatures may not deem things *not* to be property for Fourth Amendment purposes if there is a longstanding tradition that they are;[61] and *fifth*, constitutional protections may prevent the use of compulsory process to require production of papers.[62]

As Professor Kerr notes, the proposed Justice Gorsuch test is simply a reiteration of *Katz*:

> After scoffing at *Katz* as mere judicial invention, Gorsuch introduces a few notions of his own that strongly echo *Katz*. These suggestions are best understood not as replacements for *Katz* but as a reframing of it using more explicitly textual and historical language.[63]

Indeed, whether a defendant had a bailment or property interest in a searched area, whether the legislature had decreed that the item was property for Fourth Amendment purposes, and whether there was a longstanding tradition that it be treated like property are all relevant to whether the defendant had a reasonable expectation of privacy. The Supreme Court might have decided certain cases differently in applying that test – especially with respect to the third-party doctrine – but Justice Gorsuch's framework is simply a new approach to applying *Katz*'s reasonable expectation of privacy test.

## II. The Fourth Amendment's Application to Incriminating Papers

Complaints about the Supreme Court's reasonable expectation of privacy test are not novel, and the test sits uncomfortably with scholars and justices alike.[64] Attempts to

[56] ibid 398 (Gorsuch, J., dissenting).
[57] ibid 398–9.
[58] ibid 399–400.
[59] ibid 401–2.
[60] ibid 402.
[61] ibid 402–3.
[62] ibid 403–4.
[63] OS Kerr, 'Katz as Originalism' (2022) 71 *Duke Law Journal* 1047, 1091.
[64] See, eg, Baude and Stern (n 7); Bellin (n 7).

delineate the amendment by positive law are particularly tempting, since they avoid the reasonable expectation of privacy test's 'ambiguous meaning, its subjective analysis, its unpredictable application, its unsuitability for judicial administration, and its potential circularity'.[65] The following section offers a framework for establishing the Fourth Amendment right to 'papers' grounded in the Fourth Amendment's history. The Fourth Amendment recognises a constitutional protection for *papers* independent from the space in which they are secured. The protection is tied to their incriminating nature rather than to privacy expectations. Many online records could be characterised as 'papers', so a reinvigoration of the Fourth Amendment's protection of 'papers' addresses some of the Supreme Court's pressing challenges.

## A. The Unreasonable Search of Papers Was of Primary Concern to the Fourth Amendment's Framers

Supreme Court case law on unreasonable searches addresses searches of both movable and immovable property. As the following section illustrates, these are different concerns, triggered by distinct government actions, and resulting in distinct harms to the individual. Pre-founding cases on warrantless searches reflected both of these preoccupations.

Three cases had an outsized influence on the Fourth Amendment's framing, and each of these cases concerned protection for movable property.[66] The Supreme Court and academic articles alike recognise that 'the Fourth Amendment came about in response to a trio of 18th century cases "well known to the men who wrote and ratified the Bill of Rights, [and] famous throughout the colonial population"'.[67] The three cases, *Wilkes v Wood*, *Entick v Carrington*, and *Paxton's Case* each concerned government attempts to seize movable goods.

The first of these cases, *Wilkes v Wood*, arose from the 1763 prosecution of John Wilkes, a member of Parliament and publisher of the *North Briton* pamphlet who was critical of George III's government.[68] His 45th edition of the *North Briton* criticised the 1763 Treaty of Paris, which concluded the Seven Years' War between the UK and France, with such venom that Secretary of State Lord Halifax issued a warrant 'to make strict and diligent search for the authors, printers and publishers of a seditious and treasonable paper, intitled, The North Briton', and 'to apprehend and seize [them], together with their papers, and to bring [them] in safe custody before me, to be examined'.[69]

[65] Baude and Stern (n 7) 1825.

[66] Originalist analysis of the Fourth Amendment is challenging since most of modern Fourth Amendment controversies surround the permissibility of warrantless searches, but the debates at the founding were concerned about the breadth of warrants. The extent of police investigations at the founding was narrower, and many in the generation perceived officials with vague warrants to be a threat to liberty. See T Davies, 'Recovering the Original Fourth Amendment' (1999) 98 *Michigan Law Review* 547; and LK Donahue, 'The Original Fourth Amendment' (2016) 83 *University of Chicago Law Review* 1181.

[67] *Carpenter*, 585 US 296, 391 (Thomas, J., dissenting) (citing WJ Stuntz, 'The Substantive Origins of Criminal Procedure' (1995) 105 *Yale Law Journal* 393, 397). See also Baude and Stern (n 7) 255–6; Donahue (n 66) 1196–204, 1250; Kerr (n 63) 1064.

[68] *Wilkes v Wood*, 19 Howell's State Trials 1153 (1763).

[69] *The Case of John Wilkes*, 19 Howell's State Trials 982, 982. See also Stuntz (n 67) 398; Donahue (n 66) 1201.

Wilkes's butler testified that the government agents, acting pursuant to this warrant, 'rummaged through all the papers together they could find', 'fetched a sack, and filled it with papers', and, with the help of a locksmith, 'opened four locks of the lower drawers of a bureau', after which 'they took out all the papers in those drawers, and a pocket-book of Mr. Wilkes's, and put them all into the sack'.[70]

Wilkes sued the agents for trespass. In instructing the jury on whether the warrant was an adequate legal defence, Chief Justice Pratt noted that the question was 'a point of the greatest consequence he had ever met with in his whole practice'.[71] He argued that if the power to issue a 'general warrant, where no inventory is made of the things thus taken away, and where no offenders' names are specified in the warrant' was 'truly invested in the secretary of state … it certainly may affect the person and property of every man in this kingdom, and is totally subversive of the liberty of the subject'.[72] The jury sided with Wilkes and awarded him £1,000 in damages.[73]

The second case, *Entick v Carrington*, occurred two years later after a similar occurrence. John Entick published another anti-government pamphlet, entitled *The Monitor*.[74] Lord Halifax issued a warrant 'to make strict and diligent search for John Entick, the author, or one concerned in writing of several weekly very seditious papers, intitled the Monitor … which contain gross and scandalous reflections and invectives upon his majesty's government, and upon both houses of parliament'.[75] The warrant further instructed the agents 'to seize and apprehend, and to bring, together with his books and papers, in safe custody before me to be examined concerning the premises, and further dealt with according to the law'.[76] Entick sued, alleging two separate trespassory harms. The defendants 'with force and arms broke into the dwelling house of the plaintiff … and continued there four hours without his consent and against his will, and all that time disturbed him the peaceable possession thereof'.[77] They also

> read over, pryed into, and examined all the private papers, books, &c. of the plaintiff there found, whereby the secret affairs, &c. of the plaintiff became wrongfully discovered and made public; and took and carried away 100 printed charts, 100 printed pamphlets, &c. &. of the plaintiff there found.[78]

The violation of Entick's property interest in his papers constituted a harm independent from the intrusion into his home.

Chief Justice Pratt addressed these two property rights violations separately. With respect to the former, he delivered a paean to England's real property protections, noting

[70] 19 Howell's State Trials 1156.

[71] ibid 1167.

[72] ibid.

[73] ibid 1168.

[74] See Donahue (n 66) 1196–7.

[75] *Entick v Carrington*, 19 Howell's State Trials 1034 (1765).

[76] ibid 1034.

[77] ibid. Professors Arvind and Burset have recently published a previously unknown manuscript of *Entick*. TT Arvind and CR Burset, 'A New Report of Entick v Carrington (1765)' (2022) 110 *Kentucky Law Journal* 265. The manuscript was prepared for Attorney General Charles York based on notes taken in court by barrister Edward Moore. ibid 268.

[78] *Entick* ibid. Wilkes's attorney made a similar argument, that 'of all offences that of a seizure of papers was the least capable of reparation'. *John Wilkes, Esq. v Wood*, 98 Eng. Rep. 490 (1763).

that '[t]he great end, for which men entered society, was to secure their property', and that '[b]y the laws of England, every invasion of private property, be it so minute, is a trespass'.[79] With respect to the latter, he added that

> [p]apers … are [the owner's] dearest property; and are so far from enduring a seizure, that they will hardly bear an inspection; and though the eye cannot by the laws of England be guilty of a trespass, yet where private papers are removed and carried away, the secret nature of those goods will be an aggravation of the trespass, and demand more considerable damages in that respect.[80]

According to Chief Justice Pratt, stepping foot onto Entick's property constituted a violation of his rights, and carrying away his secret papers dealt him a new and independent harm.

Entick and Wilkes's contemporaries were more concerned about protections for movable than immovable property. As Professors Arvind and Burset report

> the warrants with which the case was concerned had been issued to suppress criticism of the government. For authors who opposed those warrants, the key danger was not the brief trespass they enabled but the more enduring damage they might inflict by exposing the secrets of the government's critics.[81]

One of Wilkes's supporters referred to papers as

> the depositories of our fortune; the trustees of our credit, character, and reputation; the secretaries of our pleasures. They are our closest confidents; the most intimate companions of our bosom; and, next to the recess of our own breasts, they are the most hidden repository we can have.[82]

Another 'described papers not only as property themselves, but as containing information "of the utmost consequence to private property", whose security might be undermined by the state's disclosure or destruction of business documents.'[83] According to Moore's transcription of *Entick v Carrington*, Chief Justice Pratt 'root[ed] the protection against lawful searches in the right of criminal suspects not to condemn themselves', rather than in a right against trespass.[84]

The third of the influential cases occurred in Massachusetts in 1761. The opinion was not recorded. The Writs of Assistance Case challenged the British government's ability to search ships and buildings for customs violations.[85] James Otis represented a Boston merchant who challenged a writ.[86] According to John Adams's notes, Otis argued that the writs were so open-ended, both in time and subject matter, that

[79] *Entick* ibid 1066.

[80] *Entick* ibid. These two passages are taken from Hargrave's manuscript, reproduced in Howell's State Trials. They do not feature in Moore's manuscript. Arvind and Burset (n 77) 286–7. Moore's transcription contains parallel language: 'Private Papers are the only way of concealing a man's most valuable Secrets either in his Profession or any other Way, & are his dearest property.' ibid 324–5.

[81] Arvind and Burset (n 77) 288.

[82] ibid 289.

[83] ibid.

[84] ibid 293, 331 ('I shou'd be glad to know, whether the Law obliges a Man in any Case to produce Evidence against himself? – No … it is certain, the Law compels no man to condemn himself.').

[85] See Donahue (n 66) 1247–8.

[86] ibid 1250–1.

they permitted abuse by British officials.[87] As in the two British cases, the incriminating items were movable property – in this case, contraband goods.[88] Unlike the two British cases, Otis focused on violations of physical property rights, arguing that '[e]very man prompted by revenge, ill humour or wantonness to inspect the inside of his neighbour's house, may get a writ of assistance'.[89] In Otis's view, the individual's preeminent interest lay in the location where the goods were stored, rather than in the goods themselves.

## B. The Supreme Court's Distinct Treatment of Movable and Immovable Property under the Fourth Amendment

The standard account of the Supreme Court's Fourth Amendment jurisprudence is that '[f]or much of our history, Fourth Amendment search doctrine was "tied to common-law trespass" and focused on whether the Government "obtains information by physically intruding on a constitutionally protected area"', but that the Supreme Court expanded upon that view in the 1960s 'to protect certain expectations of privacy as well'.[90] This account is oversimplified. For decades, the Supreme Court was primarily concerned with individuals' rights in movable property. Trespass violated the Fourth Amendment, but only to the extent that it resulted in the confiscation of movable property.[91] The Supreme Court's self-conscious expansion of Fourth Amendment rights beyond physical trespass occurred only 20 years after it first considered trespass to be grounds for a Fourth Amendment violation.[92]

### i. *The Supreme Court's Opinion in* Boyd

The Supreme Court issued its first Fourth Amendment opinion in 1886 – almost a century after the amendment's ratification. In *Boyd*, the Supreme Court recognised a Fourth Amendment right against unreasonable searches and seizures that was grounded in property. But the Supreme Court did not interpret the Fourth Amendment as preventing physical intrusion into property. Rather, it interpreted the amendment as preventing confiscation of property that was incriminating to the defendant.

EA Boyd imported glass, and the tax collection authorities permitted him to import some of it without paying duties, under the theory that much of the glass shattered in transit.[93] The government believed that Boyd was exaggerating the amount of glass that had shattered in transit, and it subpoenaed him (without producing a warrant)

[87] LK Wroth and HB Zobel (eds), *Legal Papers of John Adams: Volume 2* (Cambridge, Harvard University Press, 1965) 125–9.
[88] See Donahue (n 66) 1247.
[89] ibid 143.
[90] *Carpenter*, 585 US 296, 304 (citing *Jones*, 565 US 400, 405).
[91] See *Hester v United States*, 265 US 57, 58 (1924).
[92] *Hayden*, 387 US 294, 304 (concluding that Fourth Amendment rights are not tied to property rights); *Davis v United States*, 328 US 582, 588 (1946) (concluding that the Fourth Amendment limited government's power to enter Davis's property to inspect certificates that were government property).
[93] See Stuntz (n 67) 422.

to forfeit 35 cases of glass pursuant to an import tax evasion statute.[94] Boyd challenged the subpoena on Fourth Amendment grounds, and the Supreme Court sided with him.

The Supreme Court deemed the search impermissible for two reasons. First, the search was unreasonable since Boyd owned the goods subject to the search, and his ownership was not in doubt. The Supreme Court reasoned that the Fourth and Fifth Amendments permitted '[t]he search for and seizure of stolen or forfeited goods', but not the 'search for and seizure of a man's private books and papers for the purpose of obtaining information therein contained', since '[i]n the one case, the government is entitled to the possession of the property; in the other, it is not'.[95] The constitutional problem with Boyd's subpoena lay not in a hypothetical trespass onto his property – the Court acknowledged the permissibility of trespass to recover stolen goods – but in the notion that the cases of glass were his, not the government's nor a third party's.

Second, a search was unreasonable if its purpose was to find incriminating evidence against its target. The Supreme Court compared the Fourth Amendment to its neighbouring Fifth Amendment, observing that 'the "unreasonable searches and seizures" condemned in the fourth amendment are almost always made for the purpose of compelling a man to give evidence against himself', while 'compelling a man "in a criminal case to be a witness against himself", which is condemned in the fifth amendment, throws light on the question as to what is an "unreasonable search and seizure" within the meaning of the fourth amendment'.[96] Under *Boyd*, Fourth Amendment rights attached at the prospect of self-incrimination, rather than at a broader invasion of property or privacy. An individual could not rely on *Boyd* if he was merely embarrassed by a police officer's stroll through his property, nor if the police's presence diminished his ability to enjoy the property.

*Boyd* informed the Supreme Court's Fourth Amendment jurisprudence until the Supreme Court repudiated its holdings in the 1960s. In *Warden v Hayden*, the Supreme Court announced that ownership was no longer necessary to establish a Fourth Amendment right since 'the premise that property interests control the right of the Government to search and seize has been discredited'.[97] That case also held that a search could be permissible under the Fourth Amendment even if its purpose was to recover incriminating evidence rather than stolen property.[98] Earlier, in *Griswold v Connecticut*, the Supreme Court concluded that the Fourth Amendment extended beyond the prospect of self-incrimination and established a general right to privacy, from which the Court derived the right to contraception.[99] *Boyd* articulated the Fourth Amendment's

[94] ibid.

[95] *Boyd*, 116 US 616, 624. The Fifth Amendment provides that '[n]o person … shall be compelled in any criminal case to be a witness against himself'. US Const. amend. V.

[96] ibid 633.

[97] 387 US 294, 304 (1967).

[98] In *Warden*, the Supreme Court dispensed with the 'mere evidence' rule, which provided that the government may not seize property if it is 'mere evidence' of a crime, but may seize the fruits and instrumentalities of a crime as well as contraband since the defendant has a diminished property interest in those items. 387 US 294, 300–10.

[99] *See Griswold v Connecticut*, 381 US 479, 484–5 (1965) (holding that specific guarantees in the Bill of Rights have penumbras, formed by emanations from those guarantees, and that the Fourth Amendment guaranteed privacy); *Roe v Wade*, 410 US 113, 152 (1973) (finding the roots of the right to privacy in the Fourth Amendment).

reach in terms of property rights and incrimination, but neither of these factors was controlling 80 years later.

### *ii. From Incriminating Papers to Trespass*

The Supreme Court in subsequent decades applied *Boyd* to a more expansive range of property rights, but only in the context of searches of immovable property. In *Weeks*, for example, the Supreme Court announced a principle far stronger than its holding in *Boyd*:

> every man's house is his castle and that therefore 'no man's house can be forcibly opened, or he or his goods be carried away after it has thus been forced, except in cases of felony; and then the sheriff must be furnished with a warrant, and take great care lest he commit a trespass.[100]

The marshal in *Weeks* went to the defendant's house and 'in his absence and without his authority', 'undertook to make a seizure of private papers in direct violation of the constitutional prohibition against such action'.[101] Although the Supreme Court announced a Fourth Amendment protection grounded in real property, the actual violation that occurred in the case was, consistent with *Boyd*, a confiscation of movable property, Weeks's private papers. In a sign of a post-*Boyd* strengthening of defendants' property rights (and of a corresponding erosion of law enforcement powers), the Supreme Court found a Fourth Amendment violation where prohibition agents, having heard complaints about a garage, 'got the odour of whisky' from it and searched it in its owner's absence.[102] That the whiskey was contraband, such that the the garage owner, John Taylor, 'had no entitlement to it' – the operative consideration under *Boyd* – did not figure in the Court's analysis. The key question in *Taylor* centred on the agents' inspection of the whiskey and consequent violation of Taylor's movable property rights, rather than on the agents' intrusion into his garage.[103]

Contrary to its later characterisation in *Carpenter*, the Supreme Court did not consider mere trespass, in the absence of seizure of movables, to violate the Fourth Amendment. In *Hester*, prohibition officers witnessed an alcohol sale from afar as they stood on the defendant's father's property.[104] The defendant moved to suppress the officers' testimony under the theory that the officers had no right to be on the property. The Supreme Court found the possibility of a trespass to be irrelevant to the defendant's

[100] 232 US 383, 390 (quoting TM Cooley, *A Treatise on the Constitutional Limitations Which Rest Upon the Legislative Power of the States of the American Union* (Cambridge, University Press: Welch, Bigelow, & Co., 1868) 299; F Lieber, *On Civil Liberty and Self Government Volume 2* (Philadelphia, Lippincott, Grambo and Co., 1853) 44–5). The concept originates from Sir Francis Coke's opinion in *Semayne's Case*, 77 Eng Rep 194 (1604). See Donahue (n 66) 1208. James Otis cited it in his famous Writs of Assistance Argument. Wroth and Zobel (n 87) 125.

[101] ibid 393.

[102] *Taylor v United States*, 286 US 1, 5–6 (1932).

[103] Crucial to the Supreme Court's worldview was its view that seizure of evidence to prove guilt for a crime was an inadequate basis for a search. 387 US 294, 294 ('The Fourth Amendment ruling in *Gouled* was based upon the dual, related premises that historically the right to search for and seize property depended upon the assertion by the Government of a valid claim of superior interest, and that it was not enough that the purpose of the search and seizure was to obtain evidence to use in apprehending and convicting criminals.').

[104] 265 US 57, 58.

Fourth Amendment rights: 'It is obvious that even if there had been a trespass, the above testimony was not obtained by an illegal search or seizure'.[105] The Fourth Amendment did not apply because

> [t]he defendant's own acts, and those of his associates, disclosed the jug, the jar and the bottle – and there was no seizure in the sense of the law when the officers examined the contents of each after it had been abandoned.[106]

Contrary to the view outlined by the *Carpenter* majority, the Supreme Court did not conceive of the Fourth Amendment as a right against trespass but as a right against confiscation of incriminating evidence.[107]

To be sure, Fourth Amendment rights in movable property stemmed from rights in immovable property. Government agents violated Weeks's, Gouled's, and Amos's Fourth Amendment rights by intruding onto their property without their consent to seize their belongings.[108] The lack of consent to enter their property was crucial to the Supreme Court's analysis. But the harm at issue in those cases was in the seizure of movable property, not in intrusion onto the property. Trespass was not a distinct harm under the Fourth Amendment.

The Supreme Court continued to reject claims based on trespassory harm for 20 years after *Hester*. Advances in technology instigated new Fourth Amendment theories. Prior to electronic communications, the Fourth Amendment's primary effect was to prevent the seizure of physical evidence to be used at trial. As a result, Fourth Amendment jurisprudence focused on defendants' rights in movable property. The proliferation of the telephone in the 1920s offered government agents a new platform for eavesdropping, a harm that did not require confiscation of movable property. In *Olmstead*, the Supreme Court rejected the theory that phone tapping violated the Fourth Amendment:

> The language of the amendment cannot be extended and expanded to include telephone wires, reaching the whole world from the defendant's house or office. The intervening wires are not part of his house or office, any more than are the highways along which they are stretched.[109]

The use of a listening device placed against the partition wall between two offices also didn't violate the Fourth Amendment, even though the defendant 'intended[ed] his conversation to be confined within the four walls of the room' and did not 'intend his

[105] ibid 58.

[106] ibid.

[107] Other early Fourth Amendment cases implicating movable property include *Hale v Henkel*, 201 US 43 (1906) (concluding that corporations have Fourth Amendment rights and that an overbroad subpoena was therefore unconstitutional); *Wilson v United States*, 221 US 361 (1911) (holding that an officer of a corporation could not assert Fourth Amendment rights to avoid responding to a subpoena addressed to the corporation); *Silverthorne Lumber Co. v United States*, 251 US 385 (1920) (holding that government agents could not confiscate documents, copy them, and then return them to the corporate defendant); *Gouled v United States*, 255 US 298 (1921) (holding that government agent committed a search when he entered defendant's offices under false pretenses to take documents); *Amos v United States*, 255 US 313 (1921) (holding that government agents conducted a search under the Fourth Amendment when they obtained consent to search offices under coercion and seized bottles of whiskey); *Carroll v United States*, 267 US 132 (1925) (holding that prohibition officers could, consistent with Fourth Amendment, search cars if they had reasonable suspicion that the cars contained liquor); *Agnello v United States*, 269 US 20 (1925) (finding Fourth Amendment violation when government agents searched defendant's house and seized can of cocaine in his absence).

[108] See 232 US 383; 255 US 298, 298; 255 US 313, 313.

[109] 277 US 438, 465.

voice [to] go beyond those walls and it [was] not assumed he t[ook] the risk of someone's use of a delicate detector in the next room' – ie, he had a reasonable expectation of privacy.[110] And an informant entering a business with its owner's implied consent, but while wearing a wire, did not violate the Fourth Amendment if he surreptitiously recorded the owner.[111] The business owner, by consenting to the informant's entry onto his premises, surrendered any Fourth Amendment right.

The Supreme Court only recognised a Fourth Amendment protection for trespassory harms in 1946. During the Second World War, the US government required both retail and wholesale purchasers of gasoline to produce a coupon.[112] Gas station owners were prohibited from having more coupons than justified by the gallonage of their tanks, and the coupons remained government property, subject at any time to recall.[113] When Jack Davis appealed his conviction of unlawful possession of gasoline coupons, the Supreme Court noted that the coupons were not 'private papers', but 'remained at all times the property of the government and subject to inspection and recall by it'.[114] As a result, the 'permissible limits of persuasion' required to get consent for a government intrusion were 'not so narrow as where private papers are sought'.[115] That Jack Davis did not own the coupons did not eliminate his Fourth Amendment rights. Officers seeking government property could not 'proceed lawlessly and subject to no restraints', nor could they 'subject … a dealer to a general search of his papers for the purpose of learning whether he has any coupons'.[116] But where 'the custodian [of the papers] is persuaded by argument that it is his duty to surrender them and he hands them over, duress and coercion will not be so readily implied as where private papers are involved'.[117] The amount of consent required to inspect government property was not zero, but it was lower due to the government's property interest in the requested documents. Hence, Davis had a right against trespass that was distinct from his property right in papers – which in the case of gasoline coupons, was arguably nonexistent.

## C. Movable Property as a Roadmap for Fourth Amendment Jurisprudence

The distinction between Fourth Amendment rights in real and movable property is not formalistic. A prohibition against trespassing preserves a right to privacy, while the prohibition against confiscation of movable property, such as papers, not only implicates privacy but also self-incrimination. Interests in privacy and in non-self-incrimination diverge in important ways. Unlike an interest against self-incrimination,

[110] *Goldman v United States*, 316 US 135 (1942). Later, the Supreme Court found use of a different model, which 'made conduct with [the defendant's] heating duct', to violate the Fourth Amendment since it constituted a 'physical intrusion'. *Silverman v United States*, 365 US 505 (1961).

[111] *On Lee v United States*, 343 US 747, 751–2 (1952).

[112] *Davis v United States*, 328 US 582, 588.

[113] ibid.

[114] ibid.

[115] ibid 593.

[116] ibid 591.

[117] ibid 593.

a right to privacy can be waived through behaviour that exhibits an indifference towards privacy. For example, an individual who permits the public to use his personal library has no privacy interest in the library's contents but preserves his interest against self-incrimination. And he preserves this interest long after his materials are removed from his library, because the interest is not tied to the books' location.

This distinction is relevant to modern interpretations of the Fourth Amendment. Under the Supreme Court's jurisprudence, individuals have no reasonable expectation of privacy in information that they deliver voluntarily to technology companies.[118] Individuals retain, however, a right against the search or seizure of their movable property, including papers, that is independent of any Fourth Amendment interest in the location in which the movable property is stored.[119] In other words, the Fourth Amendment applies even absent a reasonable expectation of privacy as long as the seized items belong to the defendant.

The Fourth Amendment's application to online records must be cabined carefully. It does not apply to all online activity. Weeks and Gouled could only assert a Fourth Amendment interest in papers that they owned, not in any papers which they had written.[120] Authorship of a paper is irrelevant to a Fourth Amendment analysis. Weeks and Gouled's Fourth Amendment rights extended to all of the papers they owned, irrespective of authorship, and did not apply to papers that they had written, but no longer possessed.[121] And the Fourth Amendment extends to movable property that has no authorship, such as Boyd's cases of glass.[122]

The common theme in early Fourth Amendment cases is not authorship nor expectation of privacy, but control. In early Fourth Amendment cases, the Supreme Court repeatedly recognised a right against the search and seizure of items that the defendant had the authority to move around – in other words, movable property. This right was distinct from modern privacy concerns. Boyd could have transferred his cases of glass to an endless stream of warehouses and even displayed them in a museum without undermining his Fourth Amendment interest.

Proponents of a positive law interpretation of the Fourth Amendment grounded in property rights face a vexing problem: how to define property interests in online data. In his *Carpenter* dissent, Justice Thomas laid out four considerations of ownership, reasoning that since Carpenter 'did not create the records, he does not maintain them, he cannot control them, and he cannot destroy them … [t]he records belong to MetroPCS and Sprint'.[123] Treating online records as movable property, in the vein of early Fourth Amendment cases, provides a solution to this problem. The key consideration is Justice Thomas's third, that of 'control'. The government conducts a search when it appropriates a record that the target could use and move to alternative locations. The clearest example for the doctrine's application is in emails or documents stored on a cloud storage service. A defendant may not have a reasonable expectation of privacy in the document since he has voluntarily disclosed the document to the service provider.

[118] See *Miller*, 425 US 435, 443; *Smith*, 442 US 735, 735.
[119] See *Boyd*, 116 US 424; *Silverthorne Lumber Co.*, 251 US 385, 391–2.
[120] See 232 US 283, 390; 255 US 298, 298.
[121] ibid.
[122] See 116 US 616, 624.
[123] 585 US 296, 342 (Thomas, J., dissenting).

But the document is, in a figurative sense, his movable property, since he can control it and move it to alternative storage locations, such as a hard drive.

The concept of control frequently overlaps with reasonable expectations of privacy. An individual who posts on a social media platform has no reasonable expectation of privacy in the post, and he also does not control it. The post belongs as much to its author as to other users of the social media platform, each of whom has an equal right to copy the post and deliver it to law enforcement. Similarly, an individual has neither a reasonable expectation of privacy nor control over content that is created by a technology company to record the individual's online activities, such as cell site location information, credit card records, and ride-share app trips. No individual can assert control over these records because his corporate counterparty has an equal and independent interest in logging the information.

The hardest case concerns data that is routinely copied and stored by the technology company even after the user deletes the information from his account or deletes the account altogether. Consider, for example, an email service that permits users to delete emails and to delete their account but maintains records of all emails on its servers irrespective of a user's deletion. Applying the Supreme Court's later Fourth Amendment jurisprudence, the individual lost any expectation of privacy as soon as he typed or received the email, since in doing so, he shared it with his corporate counterparty. Applying its earlier cases, the user lost his rights not because he shared his emails with the service, but because the service, in creating its own copies outside of the user's control, developed an independent movable property interest in the emails. But this problem is easily solved: a company can guarantee Fourth Amendment protections by committing not to store records of the user's activity without the user's permission. As long as a user's online records can properly be characterised as his movable property, the Fourth Amendment forbids unreasonable searches and seizures of those records.

## III. Conclusion

Justice Gorsuch observed in his *Carpenter* dissent that the Supreme Court could address data sharing in the Internet Age in one of three ways. First, it could 'ignore the problem, maintain *Smith* and *Miller*, and live with the consequences', even if 'the confluence of these decisions and modern technology mean our Fourth Amendment rights are reduced to nearly nothing'.[124] Second, it could 'set *Smith* and *Miller* aside and try again using the *Katz* "reasonable expectation of privacy" jurisprudence that produced them'.[125] Third, it could 'look for answers elsewhere'.[126] The *Carpenter* majority opinion chose the third avenue by inventing categorical exceptions to the reasonable expectation of privacy doctrine that were not founded in text or precedent. This chapter offers another option: reviving the logic of some of the Supreme Court's earliest Fourth Amendment cases to articulate a vision of the Fourth Amendment that is both relevant to modern times and grounded in objective legal principles.

[124] 585 US 296, 387 (Gorsuch, J., dissenting).
[125] ibid.
[126] ibid.

A potential Fourth Amendment interest against searches of online records that are a user's movable property is far from a panacea. Important doctrinal challenges would remain, including the degree to which a host company could use a record for its own purposes without undermining the user's Fourth Amendment rights, and whether courts would look to contractual language or empirical determinations to chart out the scope of a right. The Supreme Court's early cases, however, provide a workable roadmap for resolution of those challenges that does not rely on subjective social expectations.

# PART III

# European Privacy and Digital Law: The Role of Trust and of the Transatlantic Digital Economy

# 9

# The GDPR as Mid-Atlantic Regulation

MARIA GRAZIA PORCEDDA

## I. Introduction

The global pull exercised by European data protection law has long been known.[1] But what is 'European' data protection law? Far from being a monolithic regulatory regime, European and specifically EU data protection law is a jigsaw puzzle of regulatory traditions from different jurisdictions. This chapter argues that EU data protection law, and its flagship instrument, the General Data Protection Regulation (GDPR),[2] are heavily influenced by the US in a way that metaphorically pulls its axis away from Brussels and towards the north-west shore of the Atlantic, resulting in 'mid-Atlantic' regulation.[3]

This happens, first, because EU data protection law incorporates regulatory traditions and tools devised on the north-western shore of the Atlantic, often via the Organisation for Economic Cooperation and Development (OECD), although the OECD is not the only vehicle for norm diffusion. Second, this also happens because the most common (automated) measures used to process personal data are designed and developed by US companies. Not only do companies located west of the Atlantic enjoy significant market penetration in the EU (and elsewhere), but they also play a preeminent role in the ecosystem that devises technical specifications for information technology development. The metaphorical pulling away from Brussels into the middle of the Atlantic expresses how the US regulatory and market influences affect the workings of EU data protection law and its crown jewel, the GDPR, including with respect to its fundamental rights mandate because, as will be shown, the market plays an important role in the determination of what constitutes the essence of the right.

[1] 'It is also worth noting that the principal exporter of data protection policy has been Europe', C Bennett and C Raab, *The Governance of Privacy. Policy Instruments in Global Perspective* (Cambridge, The MIT Press, 2006) 114. More recently, the export has been celebrated as part of 'the EU's unilateral power to regulate the global marketplace': A Bradford, *The Brussels Effect: How the European Union Rules the World* (New York, Oxford University Press, 2020) 1. For a critique of the Brussels Effect as 'stealth unilateralism': G Capar, 'Global Regulatory Competition on Digital Rights and Data Protection: A Novel and Contractive Form of Eurocentrism?' (2022) 11 *Global Constitutionalism* 465.

[2] Regulation (EU) 2016/679 of the European Parliament and of the Council of 27 April 2016 on the protection of natural persons with regard to the processing of personal data and on the free movement of such data, and repealing Directive 95/46/EC (General Data Protection Regulation) [2016] OJ L119/1.

[3] In the following, 'west' Atlantic will be used as a short-hand for north-west Atlantic and 'regulation' is taken to be synonymous with 'law'.

This research draws from constitutional law, cyberlaw, and data protection scholarship to show that the 'mid-Atlantic' character of EU data protection law is an expression of the law's composite nature that partly results from the diffusion of norms between legal orders. The use of the concepts of 'syncretism' and 'conflictual fusion', drawn from constitutional and interdisciplinary studies, will help show how the amalgam of US and EU norms can affect the functioning of EU data protection law in unintended ways. To set the scene for the substantive analysis, the work reflects on the role played by the OECD in EU digital law as one of the powerful vehicles for the transplanting of US regulatory fashions and devices into the EU and the Organisation's connection to post-WWII US market penetration into Europe that continues to this day. The argument is that market penetration alone is insufficient to understand the impact of West Atlantic companies on EU data protection law, but must be complemented by an analysis of the ecosystem of information technology development at large (section II).

Having set the scene, the work turns to a hermeneutic analysis of chapter I of the GDPR – the Regulation's foundational chapter – which examines West Atlantic regulatory influences with the aid of data protection and cyberlaw scholarship. The interpretation focuses on five articles: 1 on subject matter, 3 on territorial scope, 5 on principles, and 6 and 7 on legal bases. Article 1 effects a compromise between the permissive US approach and the restrictive EU attitude to data flows. Article 5 is the heir to data protection principles first developed in the US, including the crucial accountability principle, the rules giving expression to which facilitate market penetration. Article 6 embodies forms of notice and consent first experimented with in the US, while article 7 tries to remedy the shortcomings caused by the prevalence of wrap contracting practices also originating in the US. Finally, article 3 draws on notions of 'establishment' and 'country of origin principle' instrumental to the one-stop-shop used in the e-commerce framework, which was heavily influenced by the US light-touch regulatory philosophy (section III). Arguably, all IT law is mid-Atlantic in character.

An analysis of the accountability principle and the risk paradigm through the lenses of data protection regulatory theory helps introduce the mechanism by which market forces pull the axis of EU data protection law away from Brussels. The duties of data controllers to adopt technical and organisational measures to process data and demonstrate compliance with the GDPR must be read in light of the ecosystem of digital technology development within which the GDPR is embedded (as discussed in previous work of mine).[4] The pre-eminence of (US) digital companies in the structures that adopt voluntary technical specifications for technology development, and the deliberate absence of rulebooks for technology development, weaken the GDPR's aspirations to influence compliant technology development. What is more, the disconnect between 'hard' and 'soft' law mechanisms prevents European judges from engaging with the technological specifications that so deeply affect the functioning of the GDPR, which carries consequences for the essence of the right to data protection (section IV).

The mid-Atlantic character of EU data protection law could be seen as the understandable outcome of a local system of rules with transnational application, which does not exist in isolation but instead interacts with frameworks of powerful trade

[4] MG Porcedda, *Cybersecurity, Privacy and Data Protection in EU Law. A Law, Policy and Technology Analysis* (Oxford, Hart Publishing, 2023).

partners[5] and global trade. To remedy the distorting effects of such interactions, the analysis points to the crucial need for data regulators and enforcers to re-engage with technology design. While there are measures that can be taken locally, existing trade frameworks may limit the extent to which unilateral actions can be taken. Such frameworks are themselves in flux. On the one hand, there are calls to embed human rights in standardisation processes; on the other hand, the world order which produced such frameworks may be in the process of shifting (conclusions).

## II. EU Data Protection Law: A Syncretic Text Displaying 'Conflictual Fusion'

The global pull exercised by European data protection law has long been known.[6] But what is 'European' data protection law? Far from being a monolithic regulatory regime, European and specifically EU data protection law is a jigsaw puzzle of regulatory traditions from different jurisdictions – and even different branches of the law. To start with, EU law is the composite product of cooperation between states that pool their sovereignty[7] and, by extension, legal traditions and cultures. Well-known examples of influential national contributions in the field are the German concept of *Datenschutz* and 'informational self-determination', the Scandinavian tradition of openness and transparency, the emphasis on rights contained in early French, Austrian, Danish and Norwegian laws, and British proposals for a Data Protection Officer.[8] Moreover, EU data protection law is known to descend from multiple legal initiatives external to (and preceding) the EU. Bennett and Raab remind us that the predecessor of the GDPR, Directive 1995/46/EC, 'was only possible because of prior agreement on data protection principles within the OECD and the Council of Europe'.[9]

Then as today, critical features of EU data protection law originate outside of the Union, adding to its composite nature. Regulatory research on digital law can help make sense of such influences. Emerging work on regulatory theory and EU data protection law is starting to systematise essential attributes of the GDPR and the data protection framework at large, such as risk, technology neutrality, and by-design approaches.[10]

[5] ie the US, where 'the major global information businesses now reshaping the political economic landscape are headquartered' J Cohen, *Between Truth and Power* (Cambridge, Harvard University Press, 2019) 8.

[6] See n 1 above.

[7] Treaty on European Union [2010] OJ C83/17, art 1.

[8] On informational self-determination: S Simits, 'Privacy: an Endless Debate' (2010) 98 *California Law Review* 6; A Rouvroy and Y Poullet, 'The Right to Informational Self-Determination: Reassessing the Importance of Privacy for Democracy' in S Gutwirth, Y Poullet, P de Hert, C Terwagne and S Nowut (eds), *Reinventing Data Protection?* (Cham, Springer, 2009); on European approaches to data protection law, V Mayer-Schonberger, 'Generational Development of Data Protection in Europe' in P Agre and M Rotenberg (eds), *Technology and Privacy: The New Landscape* (Cambridge, The MIT Press, 1997) 227, cited in Bennett and Raab (n 1) 126; proposals for a DPO were first contained in the British Kenneth report: F Hondius, 'Data Law in Europe' (1980) 16 *Stanford Journal of International Law* 87, cited in R Gellert, *The Risk-based Approach to Data Protection* (Oxford, Oxford University Press, 2020) 74.

[9] Bennett and Raab (n 1) 114.

[10] See the seminal work by Gellert (n 8); K Yeung and L Bygrave, 'Demystifying the Modernized European data protection regime: Cross-disciplinary Insights from Legal and Regulatory Governance Scholarship' (2022) 16 *Regulation & Governance* 137–155; Porcedda (n 4).

Work feeding into debates within constitutional law, regulatory policy and cyberlaw[11] lends valuable tools to advance our understanding in this area.

One such tool is that of the diffusion of norms. The composite nature of data protection law is in keeping with the interplay between legal orders, which Capar notes brings about the diffusion of norms, captured by terms such as 'transplant, borrowing, reception, transfer, imposition, transposition, expansion and spread'.[12] A related framework is that of amalgamation and syncretism. Gebeye defines syncretism as 'the process and the result of the adoption, rejection, invention, and transformation of diverse and seemingly opposed legal rules, principles and practices'.[13] The term is borrowed from other disciplines, where it relates to the fusion of religions, cultures and schools of thought.[14] Gebeye applies the term to a 'constitutional state with imperial or colonial legacy',[15] a framing that sparks interesting reflections but is unhelpful for this work.[16] The point is that 'syncretism' has both positive and negative connotations within the disciplines that adopt it, and multidisciplinary input helps bring the legal argument forward. Archaeology scholars Hall and Webster treat syncretism as ambiguous and enmeshed in power structures, insofar as the 'adoption of a dominant … culture' is not coterminous with 'acceptance of an alien world'.[17] Webster cites Hall to remark that 'what appears to be acculturation can, then, be a complex mix of fear and desire, resistance and adaptation', generating 'conceptual fusion'.[18]

The GDPR is a syncretic text that incorporates several imported legal devices.[19] Well-known examples include personal data breach reporting via the e-privacy framework, which was inspired by Californian privacy legislation,[20] and data protection

[11] The literature is too broad to be reported here; by means of example: L Lessig, *Code v 2.0* (New York, Basic Books, 2006); J Reidenberg, 'Lex Informatica: the Formulation of Information Policy Rules Through Technology' (1998) 76 *Texas Law Review* 553; Cohen (n 5); Bradford (n 1); Capar (n 1) 465.

[12] Capar (n 1) 468.

[13] BA Gebeye, *A Theory of African Constitutionalism* (Oxford, Oxford University Press, 2021) 10.

[14] 'Religious Syncretism' (Encyclopedia Britannica Online, 30.08.2019), www.britannica.com/topic/religious-syncretism. For an overview of its use in law, Gebeye (n 13) 28–33.

[15] Gebeye (n 13) 10.

[16] Economic aid such as the Marshall Plan could be characterised as a form of (neo)colonialism; however, the 'Marshall Aid did not save Western Europe from economic collapse.' AS Milward, *The Reconstruction of Western Europe, 1945–51* (Methuen, University Paperbacks, 1986) 465–66 and 469. Equally, the US resistance to EU data protection legislation could be a remnant of colonial resistance. According to Westin, '[the US] deliberately chose to break with European institutions in 1776, and it would be remarkable if we thought that a return to deference without agreement was the right course in 1996'. Westin was referring to adequacy with the EU standard in a testimony to the US House of Representatives on 11 June 1996, cited in Bennett and Raab (n 1) 114. In the mid-Atlantic relationship, it would be difficult to identify on which shore the coloniser lives; Cohen (n 5) 59 remarks that global data processing is post-colonial. As an aside, Capar (n 1) 490–1, interestingly sees both the EU and US data protection approaches as being 'problematic due to their apparent disregard for how their policies impact third parties and deny them a forum for active participation'.

[17] J Webster, 'Necessary Comparisons: A Post-Colonial Approach to Religious Syncretism in the Roman Provinces' (1997) 28 *World Archaeology* 326–7.

[18] ibid 327, citing M Hall, 'Small Things and the Mobile Conflictual Fusion of Power, Fear and Desire' in AE Yentsch and MC Beaudry (eds), *The Art of Mystery of Historical Archeology, Essays in Honor of James Deetz* (Boston, C.R.C. Press, 1992) 373.

[19] And may be open to more. For proposals for collective data protection rights based on Ubuntu: B Mutiro, 'The Future of EU Data Protection Law for Collectives: A Reverse Brussels Effect' (2023) 9 *European Data Protection Law Review* 409.

[20] R Barcelò, 'EU: Revision of the ePrivacy Directive' (2009) 10 *Computer Law Review International* 155–6.

(privacy) by design stemming from a Canadian–Dutch collaboration.[21] Other imports come from Convention 108, so much so that Bygrave speaks of a 'Strasbourg Effect' modelled after Bradford's 'Brussels Effect'.[22] The influence of the Council of Europe over EU data protection law is uncontested. Article 8 of the European Convention of Human Rights[23] and Convention 108[24] are sources of the right to the protection of personal data enshrined in the Charter of Fundamental Rights of the European Union (the Charter).[25] The GDPR maintains a residual connection to Convention 108 in its Recital 105. The connection between the EU and the Council runs deeper than data protection law and is explicitly recognised in the Treaties.[26]

In turn, and in keeping with the diffusion of norms, article 8 ECHR and Convention 108 were respectively influenced by United Nations[27] and OECD processes.[28] The OECD Privacy Guidelines[29] are usually credited for the consolidation of Fair Information (Privacy) Principles (FIPs or FIPPs), the ancestors to data protection principles contained in article 5 GDPR, and for having indirectly influenced EU data protection law through Convention 108. But the role of the OECD in EU data protection law is not as celebrated as the Council of Europe's.[30] This is understandable considering that the OECD has no pride of place in the Treaties and is mentioned neither in the GDPR nor the Charter. However, the OECD is highly influential in many areas of EU policy and eventually law and is an important vehicle for the type of amalgamation that is the focus of this work. In particular, the OECD 'operates as the major international arena through which … especially the United States can influence international information policy'.[31]

This takes us to the main argument of this work. The GDPR is a syncretic text that is mid-Atlantic in (i) origin and (ii) practical application and which bears significant marks of conflictual fusion. This mid-Atlantic character results from the incorporation of regulatory/legislative devices originating from the other side of the (northern)

[21] A Cavoukian, *Privacy by Design … Take the Challenge* (Toronto, Information and Privacy Commissioner of Ontario, 2009).

[22] L Bygrave, 'The "Strasbourg Effect" on Data Protection in Light of the "Brussels Effect": Logic, Mechanics and Prospects' (2021) 40 *Computer Law & Security Review*; Bradford (n 1).

[23] Convention for the Protection of Human Rights and Fundamental Freedoms (Rome, 4 November 1950).

[24] Convention for the Protection of Individuals with regard to Automatic Processing of Personal Data (Strasbourg, 28 January 1981).

[25] Charter of Fundamental Rights of the European Union [2016] OJ C202/2.

[26] Treaty on European Union, art 6.

[27] European Commission of Human Rights, 'Preparatory Work on Article 8 of the European Convention on Human Rights' (Council of Europe, 09.08.1956), www.echr.coe.int/documents/d/echr/echrtravaux-art8-dh-56-12-en1674980.

[28] Committee of Ministers, 'The protection of individuals with regard to automatic processing of personal data in the context of profiling: explanatory memorandum' (Council of Europe, 23.11.2010), rm.coe.int/16807096c3 para 8.

[29] OECD, 'Recommendation of the Council Concerning Guidelines Governing the Protection of Privacy and Transborder Flow of Personal Data' (2024), legalinstruments.oecd.org/public/doc/114/114.en.pdf.

[30] Acknowledging the importance of the OECD in the framework of the development of Convention 108, P Hustinx, 'Data Protection and International Organizations: a Dialogue Between EU Law and International Law' (2021) 11 *International Data Privacy Law* 78. A notable, but understandable, exception: M Kirby, 'The History, Achievement and Future of the 1980 OECD Guidelines on Privacy' (2011) 1 *International Data Privacy Law* 6.

[31] Bennett and Raab (n 1) 88.

Atlantic Ocean and the practical effects caused by the interplay of the jurisdictions involved.

In terms of regulatory influences, the OECD is an important – but not the only – vehicle for the incorporation of regulatory influences from the western side of the Atlantic. Such influence is visible in the Better Regulation framework,[32] which underpins all EU lawmaking, and in discrete policy areas[33] including trade, which encompasses data flows.[34] Mendonca goes so far as to say that 'OECD policies strongly influence European policies to such an extent that it could be argued that the OECD indirectly, or at times directly, shapes EU trade policy.'[35] The EU also influences the OECD, but in a way that does not detract from the argument.[36] While current OECD membership extends to the four corners of the world, enabling the Organisation to act as a vehicle for broader regulatory transfer, at its inception the OECD was solely mid-Atlantic. Its members were European countries, the US and Canada,[37] the latter two having been heavily – if informally – involved in the entity that preceded it, the Organisation for European Economic Cooperation, whose focus was to administer the Marshall Plan. The Marshall Plan supported European post-WWII recovery and included conditionality, such as eliminating discrimination against US imports,[38] thus enabling economic penetration from a country that enjoyed economic superiority through higher productivity and 'high tech' leadership.[39] As Milward's research shows: 'In order to defend America's own

[32] For a list of documents: Directorate-General for Communication, 'Better Regulation: why and how' (European Commission), commission.europa.eu/law/law-making-process/planning-and-proposing-law/better-regulation_en#documents. At its inception: Mandelkern Group on Better Regulation, 'Final Report' (13.11.2001), smartreg.pe/reportes/Mandelkern%20Report%20on%20Better%20Regulation%202001.pdf; Council of the OECD, 'OECD Reference Checklist for Regulatory Decision-making' (09.03.1995), one.oecd.org/document/OCDE/GD(95)95/en/pdf; OECD, The OECD Report on Regulatory Reform: Synthesis (Paris, OECD, 1997).

[33] See for instance J Korving, 'The Influence of the OECD in the Creation of Binding Legislation on Exchange of Information within the EU: Why is the EU Always re-inventing the Wheel?' (Review of European Administrative Law Blog, 11.03.2022), realaw.blog/2022/03/11/the-influence-of-the-oecd-in-the-creation-of-binding-legislation-on-exchange-of-information-within-the-eu-why-is-the-eu-always-re-inventing-the-wheel-by-jasper-korving/.

[34] Kirby recalls that the Expert group that elaborated the OECD Guidelines was initially called 'trans-border data *barriers* and the protection of privacy', where 'barriers' was what drew the attention of the OECD. Kirby (n 30).

[35] S Mendonca, 'Briefing: The Role of the OECD in Shaping EU Trade Policy' (DG for External Policies Policy Department European Parliament, January 2016), www.europarl.europa.eu/RegData/etudes/BRIE/2016/570455/EXPO_BRI(2016)570455_EN.pdf. Since 21 out of 27 EU Member States are also Members of the OECD and since the EU is an observer, the EU also exerts regulatory influence. It is worth remembering that the EU did not exist before the 1990s. It was when it became clear that the lack of a data protection instrument could obstruct the creation of the Internal Market that the Commission heeded the calls of the European Parliament to propose a draft Directive; the reference to the free movement of personal data was added at revised draft stage in 1992, which is 'consistent with the economic motivations that permeated the OECD' Bennett and Raab (n 1) 93–94.

[36] 21 out of 27 EU Member States are also Members of the OECD and the EU participates in the works pursuant to Protocol No 1. Mendonca (n 35). See Supplementary Protocol No. 1 to the Convention on the OECD (Paris, 14 December 1960).

[37] OECD, 'The Organisation for European Economic Co-operation (OEEC): From the ashes of war to the foundations for lasting cooperation' www.oecd.org/en/about/history/the-organisation-for-european-economic-co-operation-oeec.html.

[38] International Monetary Fund, 'Cooperation for Recovery: The Marshall Plan', www.imf.org/external/np/exr/center/mm/eng/mm_dr_03.htm.

[39] RR Nelson, 'Diffusion of Development: Post-World War II Convergence Among Advanced Industrial Nations' (1991) 81 *The American Economic Review* 271.

strategic interests it allowed some Western European governments to continue to pursue by means of an extensive array of trade and payments controls extremely ambitious, expansionist domestic policies' and 'the main economic importance of Marshall Aid ... was the imports, particularly capital goods imports, which it permitted'.[40]

Economic penetration fostered by conditionality and the success of reconstruction generated interdependence across the Atlantic. This has continued to the present day in a way that affects the enforcement of data protection rules in practice.[41] EU data protection rules and its crown jewel, the GDPR, are impacted by the fact that automatic processing is often based on digital technology designed, developed and owned by US corporations.[42] Bradford sees penetration by (US) Big Tech in the EU as the medium for the 'de facto Brussels effect', whereby under certain market conditions, Big Tech corporations find it more cost-effective to apply the most stringent standard across their operations, with the unintended outcome of spreading EU data protection law.[43] The argument has merit but does not account for any counter-effects. When the impact of US big tech penetration is assessed in light of the architecture of (EU) digital law, of which data protection law is part, it becomes clear that such penetration changes how EU data protection law works in a way antithetical to the de facto Brussels effect, and detrimental to the fundamental right to data protection.

The next two sections explain how the GDPR is a syncretic text that is mid-Atlantic in (i) origin and (ii) practical application, and which bears significant marks of conflictual fusion.

## III. West Atlantic Regulatory Influences on the GDPR: A Hermeneutic Analysis

What is crucial to EU data protection law is that it implements a fundamental right.[44] The architecture resulting from the integration of primary and secondary sources pivots around the notion of 'protection', a notion stronger than the duty to 'respect' but weaker than the duty to 'fulfil' in human rights parlance. Protection rests on a combination of the rights of data subjects, the obligations of those who determine the means and purposes of data processing, and the powers of monitoring and sanctioning to safeguard the former and enforce the latter.[45] The right methodological approach to uphold the data protection

[40] Milward (n 16) 465–6 and 469. See also Milward, *The European Rescue of the Nation-state* (London, Routledge, 2000).

[41] I acknowledge that by the 1980s Australia had joined the OECD and it was an Australian, M Kirby, who chaired the OECD Expert Group that adopted the Guidelines. To the best of my knowledge, however, the regulatory imports discussed here were not Australian in origin. For a list of the jurisdictions whose work the OECD expert group drew from while working at the Privacy Guidelines: Kirby (n 30).

[42] Historically 'by 1978, it was already obvious that the largest player in the processing of automated data (including for airlines, hotels, business, insurance, and banking information) was the United States of America'. Kirby (n 30).

[43] These are technology non-divisibility, inelastic targets, regulatory capacity, stringent standards and market size, Bradford (n 1) 94, 142–43.

[44] Argentina, Brazil and Chile also have a constitutionally protected right of habeas data. L Bygrave, 'Privacy Protection in a Global Context' (2004) 47 *Scandinavian Studies in Law* 341.

[45] Porcedda (n 4) 114, reflecting on the link between art 8 Charter, art 5(1) GDPR and Rec 11 GDPR.

architecture requires reading the law in light of the fundamental right to the protection of personal data.

But the goal here is not to interpret the law. Rather, it is to identify key West Atlantic regulatory influences, which ultimately have a bearing on the implementation of the law and, down the line, the protection of the right. The focus is on chapter I of the GDPR, which lays the foundations for the Regulation: Article 1, which embodies a compromise between the prohibitive European approach and the protective US approach; article 3 on territorial scope, which incorporates notions taken from the e-commerce framework that was heavily influenced by the 'light touch' outlook of the Clinton US administration; article 5 on principles, heirs to the Fair Information Principles of US descent; and articles 6 and 7 on consent, which finds their roots in US consumer law and the practice of wrap contracting.

## A. Art 1: A Compromise between Data Embargoes and 'laissez traiter' Imperatives

Chapter I of the GDPR opens by stating the goal of data protection law: making the most of data flows without compromising the protection of individuals to whom data relate, both in the present and with an eye to the future.[46] The complex balance between data flows and the safeguarding of data subjects has old roots. Today's legislative and judicial approach results from the historical compromise between two traditions, which González Fuster and Gutwirth have helpfully labelled 'proscriptive' and 'permissive'.[47] The 'proscriptive' tradition is rooted in the German understanding of protection as a prohibition to process data.[48] This is echoed by the Court's view that the right to the protection of personal data, mentioned in article 1(2) GDPR, is interfered with by any processing that falls within the scope of data protection law.[49] The 'permissive' tradition is rooted in the US understanding of protection as control over one's personal information, actioned through principles overseeing data processing activities.[50] Such control is part of market dynamics, where data are a commodity and privacy holders are consumers.[51] To this should be added 'the strong affirmation of free flows of information expressed in the First Amendment to the United States Constitution'.[52]

The GDPR tries to achieve a happy medium, dodging both data embargoes and the free-for-all of a 'laissez processer' or, more correctly, 'laissez traiter' approach, in line with the EU law imperative of reconciliation, which eschews zero-sum games.[53]

[46] GDPR, art 1(1).

[47] G González Fuster and S Gutwirth, 'Opening up Personal Data Protection: A Conceptual Controversy' (2013) 29 *Computer Law and Security Review* 531–9. Their contribution focuses on art 8 of the Charter of Fundamental Rights of the European Union, which is operationalised by the GDPR.

[48] ibid 533.

[49] ibid 538, noting that the Court does not fully espouse the proscriptive approach.

[50] ibid 534.

[51] Eg, Bradford (n 1) 140 citing T Shaw, 'Privacy Law and History: WWII-Forward' (International Association of Privacy Professionals, 01.03.2013), iapp.org/news/a/2013-03-01-privacy-law-and-history-wwii-forward/. See also W Hartzog, *Privacy's Blueprint. The Battle to Control the Design of New Technologies* (Cambridge, Harvard University Press, 2018) ch 1.

[52] Kirby (n 30).

[53] Porcedda (n 4) ch 1.

The GDPR is an instrument enabling the free movement of personal data as mandated by article 1(3) GDPR. This is echoed by the Court's view that interferences with the right to the protection of personal data are lawful if they comply with the safeguards found in the applicable law and the Charter.[54]

The Court's identification of the two elements of the essence of personal data protection bears an interesting resemblance to the proscriptive and permissive traditions.[55] One element of the essence is the security safeguards found in the legal basis that echo the proscriptive tradition rooted in the strong security safeguards of the German *Datenschutzgesetz*. The other element of the essence, the provision of purpose limitation in the legal basis, echoes the permissive tradition insofar as 'purpose limitation' is one of the bedrock principles of data protection law across the Atlantic (see article 5 below and section IV.B).

The essence appears tied to the two traditions influencing EU data protection law, one of which is the US control framework mediated by principles.[56] Navigating which permissible processing operations are proscribed and which are instead permissible is done through risk management, a crucial component of the data protection regulatory architecture discussed in section IV.

## B. Art 5: Heir to the FIP(P)s

The principles relating to the processing of personal data in the GDPR are the heir to the Fair Information (Practice) Principles, which were developed in the US in a report named after its chairperson, The Rand Corporation's Corporate Research Staff member Willis H Ware.[57] That work recommended the adoption of a Federal 'Code of Fair Information Practice' for all automated personal data systems premised on five basic principles acting as 'safeguard requirements' for automated personal data systems.[58] Those encapsulated the contemporary principles of transparency/openness, access/individual participation, use limitation, accuracy/data quality, and security safeguards later set in stone by the OECD Privacy Guidelines and the Council of Europe's Convention 108.

Article 5 GDPR merges the data protection principles contained in both the Privacy Guidelines and Convention 108. This includes the accountability principle drawn from the Guidelines, whereby the controller as the duty bearer[59] (section IV) is responsible for, and must be able to demonstrate compliance with, the data protection principles listed in article 5(1).[60] The principles in the two instruments operate under different

[54] González Fuster and Gutwirth (n 47) 538–9, with some criticism of the Court's approach pre-GDPR.
[55] Porcedda (n 4) 126.
[56] Hovsha goes further to argue that the control paradigm underpins the GDPR, along legal certainty: J Hovsha, *The Problem of Control in Data Protection Law and AI Regulation* (PhD Thesis, Trinity College Dublin, 2024) ch 5.
[57] WH Ware, 'Computers and the Rights of Citizens. Repot of the Secretary's Advisory Committee on Automated Personal Data Systems' (U.S. Department of Health, Education & Welfare, July 1973), epic.org/documents/hew1973report/.
[58] ibid, 9.
[59] Kirby (n 30).
[60] GDPR, art 5(2).

logics: the Privacy Guidelines are 'based on "risk" as a threshold condition: they only apply where there is a risk for privacy, while the Convention takes a more pro-active human rights approach', reflecting 'differences in legal culture' (where the emphasis is on transatlantic relations).[61] Notions of risk, right-bearing, and duty-bearing have been amalgamated in the GDPR through the focus on averting 'risks to the rights and freedoms of data subjects' incumbent upon the duty-bearer.

The formulation has puzzled scholars and practitioners alike, since rights have a 'dignitarian basis', while risks express 'a numerical assessment of probability and severity of harm'.[62] Gellert finds a conceptual overlap in the proportionality principle, which applies to both the regulation of rights and risk management, although with qualitative differences.[63] The operationalisation of the principles rests on a mix of regulatory tools, which includes outcome-based standards restricting processing in conformity with values or set outcomes,[64] including self-regulatory measures typical of the US approach.[65] Challenges lie in the identification of the appropriate value-based response to risks[66] and the fact that the enforcement of rights is delegated to the duty-bearer, which, in the case of automatic data processing, is mediated by the private sector and thus tends to operate horizontally. To fully articulate this point, it is necessary to discuss the mix of regulatory tools in use, which is the goal of section 3.

Data protection principles usually 'appear either explicitly or implicitly within all national data protection laws',[67] meaning that global and EU data protection law alike owe an intellectual debt of gratitude to the US with respect to the FIP(P)s. The GDPR results from an amalgamation of different understandings and regulatory approaches to the principles, which include hard and soft law mechanisms. As will be shown, the mid-Atlantic compromise generates conflictual fusion insofar as the formulation of 'risks to the rights and freedoms' is concerned.

## C. Arts 6 and 7: Notice and Consent against Wrap Contracting

Consent is seen as the Achilles' heel of the protection of individuals' data by scholars on each side of the Atlantic,[68] but it has not proven possible to do without it yet.[69] Consent features in the original data protection principles – but 'only required where appropriate'[70] in the Privacy Guidelines – and is etched in the definition of the

[61] Hustinx (n 30) 78.

[62] Yeung and Bygrave (n 10) 143.

[63] The regulation of rights follows a preemptive, one-size-fits-all approach, while risk-management is supposed to adapt to the circumstances. Gellert (n 8) conclusions.

[64] Yeung and Bygrave (n 10) 140.

[65] Bennett and Raab (n 1).

[66] Yeung and Bygrave (n 10) s III.A appear to propose an 'Alexian' solution based on rating the intensity of the harm.

[67] Bennett and Raab (n 1) 12.

[68] BJ Koops, 'The Trouble with European Data Protection Law' (2014) 4 *International Data Privacy Law* 250; H Nissenbaum, 'A Contextual Approach to Privacy Online' (2011) 140 *Daedalus, the Journal of the American Academy of Arts & Sciences* 4. Cohen (n 5) 54–8.

[69] 'Control and consent … can be counterproductive if overleveraged. We should stop treating control as the cosmos of privacy' Hartzog (n 51) 278.

[70] Hustinx (n 30) 78.

fundamental right to the protection of personal data: 'Such data must be processed fairly for specified purposes and on the basis of the consent of the person concerned or some other legitimate basis laid down by law.'[71]

Data subjects' consent tops the list of legal bases that can justify the processing of personal data in article 6 GDPR. The notion of 'consent' is the focus of abundant literature, guidance and case law, which will not be summarised here. Rather, the objective is to highlight the 'West Atlantic' influences through origin, lobbying and practice.

The provisions on consent contained in the GDPR seek to redress the weaknesses of Directive 95/46. Gellert recalls that the original Commission proposal of Directive 95/46 based most processing operations on consent, which was framed as a right rather than a legal basis and lacked a provision akin to article 7 GDPR.[72] However, European and North American business interests found the text to be too tight.[73] Citing Regan, Bennett and Raab recount that American businesses supported both financially and politically European lobbying groups,[74] such as efforts by the European Direct Marketing Association to water down 'positive' consent provisions contained in the first draft of the Directive.[75]

At its origin, consent is rooted in private law and especially consumer protection law, which overlaps with data protection law.[76] Gellert relies on Jasanoff to explain that 'informed consent' emerged 'in the 20th century as part of new lot of provisions and mechanisms (ie safeguards) aiming at protecting citizens in the face of new industrial processes',[77] especially in the field of consumer protection. Furthermore, following Burkert, consent as an endorsement to data processing follows the contractual model.[78]

The omission of strong protection of consent in Directive 95/46 and, for what concerns consumer protection, the E-Commerce Directive and contemporary OECD Guidelines,[79] enabled 'wrap' online contracting practices that became prevalent in the US to spread in the EU. Kim explains that wrap contracts are those 'which users accepted through actions such as clicking on an "Accept" icon or tearing off product packaging.'[80] She continues: 'Although these novel contracting forms defied traditional contract law rules, courts enforced them in order to prevent bad actors from engaging in unfair business practices that would have hindered the growth of fledging software and

[71] Charter, art 8(2).

[72] Gellert (n 8) 81.

[73] Bennett and Raab (n 1) 94.

[74] PM Regan, 'American Business and the European Data Protection Directive: Lobbying Strategies and Tactics' in C Bennett and R Grant (eds), *Visions of Privacy* (Toronto, University of Toronto Press, 1999), cited in Bennett and Raab (n 1) 95.

[75] Bennett and Raab (n 1) 95.

[76] Case C-319/20 *Facebook Ireland and Others v Gegevensbeschermingsautoriteit* ECLI:EU:C:2021:483.

[77] Gellert (n 8) 81, citing S Jasanoff, 'Beni Incalcolabili. Reimmaginare il Nostro Futuro Tecnologico' in S Jasanoff, A Benessia and S Funtowicz (eds), *L'Innovazione tra Utopia e Storia* (Codice Edizioni, 2013) 17.

[78] Gellert (n 8) 81, citing H Burkert, 'Data Protection Legislation and the Modernization of Public Administration' (1996) 62 *International Review of Administrative Sciences* 556.

[79] Directive 2000/31/EC of the European Parliament and of the Council of 8 June 2000 on certain legal aspects of information society services, in particular electronic commerce, in the Internal Market (Directive on Electronic Commerce) [2002] OJ L178/1; OECD, 'Guidelines for Consumer Protection in the Context of Electronic Commerce' (09.03.2000), www.oecd.org/en/publications/guidelines-for-consumer-protection-in-the-context-of-electronic-commerce_9789264081109-en-fr.html.

[80] NS Kim, 'Wrap Contracting and the Online Environment: Causes and Cures' in JA Rothchild (ed), *Research Handbook on Electronic Commerce Law* (Cheltenham, Edward Elgar Publishing, 2016).

Internet companies.'[81] Interestingly, US Judge Frank Easterbrook – of *Law of the Horse* fame[82] – was behind some of the early cases that helped entrench wrap contracting.[83] Browsewrap, clickwrap, and shrinkwrap contracts,[84] typically delivered in boilerplate format,[85] have become staple modes of delivery of privacy and data protection terms and conditions online. Such are those enabling pervasive behavioural advertising, now an entrenched practice because of the failure to embed transparency in technical standards for cookies[86] and the regulatory underestimation of the impact of marketing practices when transposed online.[87]

Speaking of cookies, Orrù recognises that the aim of notice and consent policies is to 'nudge users into accepting cookies' but suggests the GDPR acts 'as a positive example of legal norm-making that has been able to partially reshape contextual norms', empowering users with the knowledge that 'the use of cookies should not legally be the default'.[88] With its article 7, the GDPR is trying to tilt the balance away from a conception of consent affected by West Atlantic practices unhindered by 20 years of application of the minimum harmonisation framework of the e-commerce Directive, to a mid-Atlantic compromise. The full significance of this attempt will become apparent as case law and, to a lesser extent, interpretation by the European Data Protection Board unfold.[89]

## D. Art 3: Establishment, Country of Origin and Data Flows

The e-Commerce Directive is of relevance in the context of article 3 GDPR, which defines the instrument's far-reaching territorial scope and underscores the transborder nature of data flows. The international dimension of the GDPR is well-explored in the literature on adequacy and, when it comes to transatlantic relations, the politico-judicial saga that began with the invalidation of the Safe Harbor agreement. That is a well-discussed example of mid-Atlantic compromise that I will not summarise here since the focus is on the concept of establishment instead.

[81] ibid.

[82] In which he challenges the need to develop new law to address the challenges of the information society, comparing information technology to a horse. FH Easterbrook, 'Cyberspace and the Law of the Horse' (1996) 1 *The University of Chicago Legal Forum*, 207.

[83] In cases *ProCD, Inc., v Zeidenberg*, 86 F.3d 1447, 1449 (7th Cir 1996) and *Hill v Gateway 2000, Inc.*, 105 F.3d 1147, 1149 (7th Cir 1997), both cited in Kim (n 80).

[84] These terms refer to modalities of expression of acceptance of the contract, respectively by browsing, clicking on an 'accept' icon and shrinking a webpage. See Kim (n 80).

[85] Cohen (n 5) 27.

[86] Originally invented by Lou Montulli of the Netscape Corporation to enable e-commerce: Cohen (n 5) 54–7.

[87] Gellert (n 8) 81 recalls that at the time of Directive 95/46, marketing was not seen as dangerous processing. Equally, the e-Privacy Directive has been unable to stop the development of real-time bidding. For an evolution of marketing practices in the US, Cohen (n 5) 21–3 and ch 2.

[88] E Orrù, 'Are Publicly Available (Personal) Data "up for grabs"? A Discussion of Three Privacy Arguments' in P de Hert, H Matsumi, D Hallinan, D Dimitrova and E Kosta (eds), *Data Protection and Privacy, Ideas That Drive Our Digital World 16* (Oxford, Hart Publishing, 2024) 120.

[89] Case C-673/17 *Bundesverband der Verbraucherzentralen und Verbraucherverbände v Planet49 GmbH* ECLI:EU:C:2019:801; Case C-252/21 *Meta Platforms* and Others *v Bundeskartellamt* ECLI:EU:C:2023:537; Case 446/21 *Schrems v Facebook* ECLI:EU:2024:834.

The freedom of establishment includes 'the right to take up and pursue activities as self-employed persons and to set up and manage undertakings, in particular companies or firms',[90] and has an autonomous meaning in EU law. Polański explains that, unlike Directive 95/46/EC, the GDPR draws from the concept of establishment found in the e-Commerce Directive, although he argues that the GDPR does not follow the e-Commerce Directive's country of origin principle.[91] The principle allows for a provider to observe the rules, and be subject to controls, in the country of its (main) establishment rather than in all the Member States in which it operates, thus insulating it from the burden of compliance with multiple and often conflicting domestic legal regimes (although with significant exceptions).

Notwithstanding Polański's reservations,[92] the 'one-stop-shop mechanism'[93] overseeing supervisory arrangements of data controllers established in more than one Member State and their cross-border data transfers follows the rationale of the country of origin principle. The mechanism aims to ease the regulatory burden on cross-border establishments and simplify enforcement, insofar as the data protection authority of the country of the main establishment of the cross-border data controller takes the lead in supervisory efforts. The practice has proved more controversial than the theory: the mechanism can be torpedoed by the inaction of the lead supervisory authority, an accusation moved against the Data Protection Commission (DPC) in charge of supervising many multinational corporations, including Big Tech companies, whose main establishment is in Ireland, so much so that cross-border enforcement is under revision.[94] Some made allegations of obstruction by the DPC based on the political inconvenience of exercising too close a supervision of (mostly US) Big Tech companies, which bring in crucial tax revenue.[95]

While the concepts of 'establishment' and the country of origin principle developed outside of data protection law, and investigating their genesis and use in the field of international commerce is beyond the scope of this work,[96] this discussion stands to show how the GDPR is permeable to constructs external to privacy and data protection policy, where West Atlantic influences are at play in different ways. The e-Commerce

[90] Treaty on the Functioning of the European Union (TFEU) [2012] OJ C-326/47 art 49. Art 56 further recognises the freedom to provide services 'in respect of nationals of Member States who are established in a Member State other than that of the person for whom the services are intended'. The e-Commerce Directive is based on arts 53, 62 and 114 TFEU.

[91] PP Polanski, 'Revisiting Country of Origin Principle: Challenges Related to Regulating E-commerce in the European Union' (2018) 34 *Computer Law and Security Review* 566.

[92] The GDPR applies extra-territorially and a country of destination can neither claim exemptions from the principle nor block an uncompliant service provider, although Polanski overlooks that the supervisory authority can impose the suspension of data processing activities; Polanski (n 91) 580.

[93] GDPR Recitals 127–8, arts 56 and 60.

[94] See Houses of the Oireachtas Joint Committee on Justice, 'Report on meeting on 27th April 2021 on the topic of GDPR' (July 2021), data.oireachtas.ie/ie/oireachtas/committee/dail/33/joint_committee_on_justice/reports/2021/2021-07-22_report-on-meeting-on-27th-april-2021-on-the-topic-of-gdpr_en.pdf; Case C-645/19 *Facebook Ireland and Others* ECLI:EU:2021:483; for the latest draft of the enforcement amendment to the GDPR and related literature, see https://oeil.secure.europarl.europa.eu/oeil/en/procedure-file?reference=2023/0202(COD).

[95] S Sinha, 'US Big Tech Companies' Complicated Role in Ireland's Booming Economy' (*Observer*, 15.07.2024), observer.com/2024/07/us-big-tech-companiess-complicated-role-in-irelands-booming-economy/.

[96] On establishment, P Craig and G de Búrca, *EU Law. Text, Cases, and Materials*, 8th edn (Oxford, Oxford University Press, 2024); On Country of origin: US International Trade Commission, 'Country-of-Origin Marking: Review of Laws, Regulations, and Practices' (July 1996), www.usitc.gov/publications/332/pub2975.pdf; Agreement on Rules of Origin Annex 1A Multilateral Agreements on Trade in Goods, Marrakesh Agreement Establishing the World Trade Organization (Marrakesh, 15 April 1994).

Directive was strongly influenced by the light-touch approach to e-trade advocated by then US President Bill Clinton[97] and visible in relevant OECD work,[98] and Sartor discusses how the Directive's rules on intermediary liability were heavily influenced by contemporary US legislation.[99] The rationale for such an approach was to favour digital innovation, which is heavily premised on data flows, and remove barriers to its trade in a field where the uncontested leader was the US. Data protection law does not exist in isolation but converses with other digital law frameworks connected to international obligations of the EU, such as those arising from the World Trade Organisation, which will be discussed in the conclusions.

## IV. West Atlantic Digital Penetration and its Practical Influence on the Workings of the GDPR

Having discussed key regulatory influences drawn from the West coast of the Atlantic, this section shows how the application of the GDPR by the data controller is a vehicle for a different kind of West Atlantic influence, one mediated by technical measures and effected by the digital supremacy of the US.

The section begins by introducing the accountability principle and the risk paradigm that underpins it, for which the OECD was once more influential. To demonstrate how the penetration of digital US companies undermines attempts to embed EU values into digital technology and transform digital companies into the final arbiters of the essence of data subject rights, the section presents a discussion of articles 24, 25 and 32 read in light of the current ecosystem for the development of technical measures.

### A. Accountability and the Risk Paradigm (Arts 5(2) and 24)

The architrave of EU applied data protection law is the data controller, the natural or legal person, public authority, agency, or other body which, alone or jointly with others, determines the purposes and means of the processing of personal data.[100] This 'duty-bearer' role was first established by the OECD Guidelines[101] that marked 'the true onset of the "controller-based responsibility system" which defines the GDPR'.[102]

[97] W Clinton, 'A Framework for Global Electronic Commerce' in B Fitzgerald (ed), *Cyberlaw* (Farnham, Ashgate, 2006).

[98] OECD, 'Guidelines for Consumer Protection in the Context of Electronic Commerce' (09.03.2000), www.oecd.org/en/publications/guidelines-for-consumer-protection-in-the-context-of-electronic-commerce_9789264081109-en-fr.html; see also, MW Thompson, 'U.S. Implementation of the OECD E-Commerce Guidelines' (Federal Trade Commission, 12.02.2020), www.ftc.gov/news-events/news/speeches/us-implementation-oecd-e-commerce-guidelines.

[99] G Sartor, 'Liabilities of Internet Users and Providers' in M Cremona (ed), *New Technologies and EU Law* (Oxford, Oxford University Press, 2017).

[100] GDPR art 4(7).

[101] Kirby (n 30).

[102] Hovsha (n 56), borrowing the 'controller-based responsibility system' from B Wong, 'Problems with Controller-Based Responsibility in EU Data Protection Law' (2021) 11 *International Data Privacy Law* 375.

The Pole Star of data controllers' operations is the principle of accountability introduced earlier. By means of a recap, under the principle the controller is responsible for, and must be able to demonstrate compliance with, the data protection principles listed in article 5(1).[103] This principle is also drawn from the OECD Guidelines, where it was connected to the role of duty-bearer.[104] The concise formulation is 'given expression'[105] by article 24 contained in chapter IV of the GDPR:

1. Taking into account the nature, scope, context and purposes of processing as well as the risks of varying likelihood and severity for the rights and freedoms of natural persons, the controller shall implement appropriate technical and organisational measures to ensure and to be able to demonstrate that processing is performed in accordance with this Regulation. Those measures shall be reviewed and updated where necessary.
2. Where proportionate in relation to processing activities, the measures referred to in paragraph 1 shall include the implementation of appropriate data protection policies by the controller.
3. Adherence to approved codes of conduct as referred to in article 40 or approved certification mechanisms as referred to in article 42 may be used as an element by which to demonstrate compliance with the obligations of the controller.

The controller demonstrates compliance with the GDPR by adopting 'technical and organisational measures' (TOMs) appropriate to the nature, scope, context, and purposes of processing as well as the *risks* of varying likelihood and severity for the rights and freedoms of natural persons. Articles 5(2), 24 and 32 on security 'set out a rule of general application',[106] whereby the controllers, who bear the burden of proof, 'must be encouraged to do everything in their power to prevent the occurrence of processing operations that do not comply with that regulation'.[107] With respect to article 32, 'reference to "a level of security appropriate to the risk" and to an "appropriate level of security" shows that that regulation establishes a risk management system and that in no way purports to eliminate' all risks.[108]

Risk was always inherent in EU data protection law, especially in articles 17 on data security and 20 on prior checking of Directive 95/46/EC, as a 'scalable and proportionate approach to compliance'.[109] The Article 29 Working Party – the predecessor to the European Data Protection Board – released guidance during the negotiations towards the GDPR to clarify that any emphasis on a risk-based approach could not be taken to undermine data subject rights and that *any* processing was to respect the right to data protection. The Article 29 Working Party's concern is justified by the fact that powerful frameworks, such as the OECD Guidelines, 'only apply where there is a risk for privacy'.[110]

[103] GDPR, art 5(2).
[104] Kirby (n 30).
[105] Case C-340/21 *VB v Natsionalna agents za prihodite* ECLI:EU:C:2023:986 para 57.
[106] ibid para 53.
[107] ibid paras 55, 56.
[108] ibid para 29; see also para 34.
[109] Article 29 Data Protection Working Party, 'Statement on the Role of a Risk-based Approach in Data Protection Legal Frameworks', (European Commission, 30.05.2014), ec.europa.eu/justice/article-29/documentation/opinion-recommendation/files/2014/wp218_en.pdf 1.
[110] Hustinx (n 30) 78.

It is also manifest in the danger of conflation of the risk-based approach with risk-based regulation, according to which the evaluation of risk guides enforcement efforts where resources are constrained.[111] This approach was, for instance, explored by the Irish Data Protection Commission in its 2021 regulatory strategy,[112] at the same time as it was under scrutiny for its role as lead supervisory authority (section III.B).[113]

While the notion of 'risk' has old roots,[114] its introduction into EU law was facilitated by the Better Regulation agenda, which took significant inspiration from OECD work.[115] This shift is premised on 'a broad range of new policy tools', such as 'information disclosure, economic incentives, voluntary agreements, and creation of new markets through tradable property rights' that 'can improve policy effectiveness and reduce costs, while promoting innovation' and are to be 'used alone or with regulation', because 'incentives are better than commands'.[116] There is no internationally agreed vocabulary for such tools, which go by different names,[117] but there is some level of common understanding around core regulatory strategies.

The GDPR is a syncretic text that combines traditional regulation with such (now not-so-) new tools. Yeung and Bygrave follow Gellert in stating that the GDPR displays elements of command and control legislation – traditional regulation – but also design-based and principle-based tools[118] that engender a co-regulatory approach falling under the 'meta regulation' umbrella. As Gellert explains,

> this model of regulation is said to be collaborative because it relies upon the delegation of regulatory activities typically falling within the remit of the regulator's competences to the regulatee, ie data controllers … In order to be endowed with these activities, regulatees must be made responsible in the first place. Such responsibilisation occurs through the risk management agenda and the ensuing transformation of the latter's activities as a form of risk-taking.[119]

[111] Yeung and Bygrave (n 10) 147.

[112] 'The DPC will apply a risk-based regulatory approach to its work, so that its resources are always prioritised on the basis of delivering the greatest benefit to the maximum number of people.' Data Protection Commission, 'Regulatory Strategy: Consultation' (April 2021), www.dataprotection.ie/sites/default/files/uploads/2021-04/DPC_Regulatory%20Strategy_APRIL%202021_PUBLIC%20CONSULTATION.pdf 5.

[113] See Houses of the Oireachtas Joint Committee on Justice 'Report on meeting on 27th April 2021 on the topic of GDPR' 26.

[114] Gellert (n 8) 27.

[115] 'The recommended practices come from a variety of sources such as … OECD' Mandelkern Group on Better Regulation, 'Final Report' 11. This refers to the OECD Reference Checklist for Regulatory Decision-making 1995, cited in Annex A of the Report, which embodies forms of risk-management in the guise of cost-benefit analysis to decision-makers and across social groups (points 6 and 7). This reform gave impetus for the standard adoption of regulatory impact assessments; impact assessments are the 'main risk management tool in the GDPR' (Gellert (n 8) 23). See also OECD, *The OECD Report on Regulatory Reform* (n 32) 18: 'Better information on benefits and costs can help governments set more effective priorities for action. Governments can waste considerable resources and permit unnecessary risks by regulating tiny risks while leaving important risks untouched.' And 'Reasonable standards applicable to all producers, based on benefit-cost analysis, scientific criteria, and risk assessment techniques, and underpinned by effective enforcement, are crucial to sound regulation' (ibid). I am grateful to my colleague S Arduin for drawing my attention to this body of work. For a review of some overarching case law, see S Arduin, 'The Precautionary Principle and Impact Assessment: The Case of School Closures during the Pandemic in Ireland' (2024) 15 *European Journal of Risk Regulation* 1017.

[116] OECD, *The OECD Report on Regulatory Reform* (n 32) 28.

[117] Eg, European Commission, *Better Regulation Toolbox 2021* (Brussels, European Commission, 2021) 172ff Tool #22 Research and Innovation, and especially future-proofing, outcome-oriented legislation, test of alternatives and top-runner approach.

[118] Yeung and Bygrave (n 10) 141.

[119] Gellert (n 8) 239.

The key channel for this is the accountability principle, which makes controllers responsible.[120] It is through such mechanisms that the GDPR becomes mid-Atlantic in practice.

## B. TOMs, SoTA, Standards and Design (Arts 24, 25 and 32)

As seen, the controller must adopt TOMs, which can include policies that are appropriate to the nature, scope, context and purposes of processing as well as the risks to the rights and freedoms of data subjects. Recital 74 GDPR clarifies the measures must be effective. Articles 25 and 32 GDPR list additional criteria applying to the selection of TOMs to fulfil data protection principles, especially data minimisation and data security: the *state of the art* and the *cost of implementation* of the measures. The GDPR defines neither term. The 'state of the art' (SoTA), also known as prior art, is a notion used in patent law. It was possibly imported from that cognate legal sector, similarly to the concepts of establishment and country of origin discussed earlier (section III.C). The 'cost of implementation' echoes the notion of BATNEEC, ie, the 'Best Available Technology not Entailing Excessive Cost', mentioned by Gellert among common risk management measures.[121] Advocate General (AG) Pitruzzella commented on these concepts in his opinion on the *Natsionalna agents za prihodite* (hereafter NAP) case as 'the solutions that the state of the art in science, technique, technology and research offers at the time, also taking into account … the implementation costs'.[122]

Article 25 (1) GDPR, the famed 'data protection by design' clause of Canadian–Dutch origin, expects the controller to adopt TOMs *designed* to implement data protection principles when deciding on the means of processing and during processing. Article 32 speaks of ensuring a level of security appropriate to risks, which is an obligation of conduct rather than of result, insofar as the controller cannot be expected to prevent all data breaches.[123] Controllers can demonstrate compliance with both articles 25 and 32 GDPR by leveraging approved *certification mechanisms* (article 42 GDPR) and, for security only, adherence to an approved *code of conduct* (article 40 GDPR), which are informal mechanisms[124] that fulfil a self-regulatory approach to the legislation.

Taken at face value, these provisions may seem to offer robust mechanisms to protect data subjects in a world potentially hostile to their rights. Suffice to say here[125] that the data protection by design clause is at the heart of the de facto Brussels effect, according to which the obligation for controllers to adopt TOMs 'designed' to satisfy data protection principles would force international corporations to embrace EU data

[120] Gellert (n 8) 151.
[121] ibid 34.
[122] Opinion of Advocate General Pitruzzella, Case C-340/21 *VB v Natsionalna agents za prihodite* ECLI:EU:C:2023:353 para 32.
[123] Case C-340/21 para 34.
[124] See I Kamara, 'Misaligned Union Laws? A Comparative Analysis of Certification in the Cybersecurity Act and the General Data Protection Regulation' in D Hallinan, R Leenes and P de Hert (eds), *Data Protection and Privacy* (Oxford, Hart Publishing, 2021). For a criticism of certification as a mechanism to fulfil by design aspirations, see IS Rubinstein and N Good, 'The Trouble with Article 25 (and how to fix it): the Future of Data Protection by Design and Default' (2020) 10 *International Data Privacy Law* 37.
[125] I discuss this in Porcedda (n 4) ch 5.

protection standards.[126] By the same token, Yeung and Bygrave see the hardwiring of norms into systems development as a fulfilment of the aspirations of Reidenberg's 'Lex Informatica' to make the GDPR self-enforcing.[127] But such interpretations overlook the logic of co- or meta-regulation and the interplay between the GDPR, standardisation and technology development in practice.[128]

Articles 24, 25 and 32 GDPR are examples of the meta-regulation discussed by Gellert. They are outcome-based tools that rely on techniques such as technology neutrality, future-proofing, and top-runner approach.[129] The OECD recalls that 'the risks of self-regulation and voluntary approaches – undue influence by private interests, barriers to competition, and lack of transparency and accountability – need to be rigorously managed …'.[130] Yeung and Bygrave recognise that outcome-based standards such as that contained in article 32 GDPR can be gamed and require significant expertise, but that regulatory agencies possess the necessary knowledge to counter the perverse effects.[131] Also, with respect to article 32 GDPR, the ECJ has stated that 'the controller has some discretion in determining the appropriate TOMs' but that 'a national court must be able to evaluate the complex assessment carried out by the controller … and make sure those measures are appropriate'.[132]

These approaches do not account for the ecosystem of digital law and technology development, which can be succinctly described by way of the stairless house metaphor.[133] This house has top, middle, and ground floors, but no stairs connecting them. The top floor is inhabited by primary and secondary public law functioning according to command and control, top-down logics, such as article 8 of the Charter and (parts) of the GDPR. The middle floor is inhabited by standardisation, a private law, and a voluntary mechanism, which lays down the technical specifications for TOMs that data controllers need to adopt. And the ground floor is occupied by technology development as an informal modality of regulation in cyberspace (Reidenberg's *Lex Informatica*[134]), a process which generates the SoTA referred to in articles 25 and 32 GDPR. The lack of a staircase translates into the absence, especially for primary law, of mechanisms to influence[135] standards and technology design, discussed in the following.

[126] Bradford (n 1) 142–43.
[127] Yeung and Bygrave (n 10) 141.
[128] For a critique, see E Orrù, 'Minimium Harm by Design. Reworking Privacy by Design to Mitigate the Risks of Surveillance' in R Leenes, R van Brakel, S Gutwirth and P de Hert (eds), *Data Protection and Privacy: (In)visibilities and Infrastructures* (Cham, Springer, 2017) 107–137; Hartzog (n 51); Rubinstein and Good (n 124)'; Porcedda (n 4) especially ch 5.
[129] European Commission, *Better Regulation Toolbox* Tool #28 and, to an extent, Tool #22.
[130] OECD, *The OECD Report on Regulatory Reform* (n 32) 28.
[131] Yeung and Bygrave (n 10) 140.
[132] Case C-340/21 para 43.
[133] MG Porcedda, 'The Effacement of Information Technology from EU Law: The Need for Collaborative Approaches to Redesign the EU's Regulatory Architecture' in F Bieker, S de Conca, I Schiering, N Gruschka and M Jensen (eds), *Proceedings of the 18th IFIP Summer School 2023, Privacy and Identity Management: Sharing in a Digital World* (Cham, Springer, 2024); MG Porcedda, 'Rights and Technical Standards in EU Law' in M Giuffrida and S Muscella (eds), *Human Rights and ICT Standardisation: examples across diverse SDOs, current challenges and recommendations* (StandICT.eu, 2024).
[134] Reidenberg (n 11).
[135] Although this may not be an afterthought: 'Network-and-standard-based legal-institutional arrangements connect protocol and policy directly to one another and eliminate separation between them … The policy is the standard and vice versa.' Cohen (n 5) ch 7.

Under their mandate, international Standards Development Organisations (SDOs) cannot embrace the values or laws of a given jurisdiction:[136] the EU could achieve alignment with its own values only in the context of European Standards developed by European Standardisation Organisations. The GDPR is not part of the New Legislative Framework (NLF), the mechanism to produce EU harmonised standards against which the presumption of conformity of a product (traditionally excluding software) with a given specification is asserted.[137] Even if the GDPR mimics the logics of the NLF, no TOMs can enjoy presumption of conformity with the GDPR and its values – although, as Kamara recalls, the Better Regulation toolbox contemplates the adoption of standards other than harmonised standards,[138] which the GDPR mentions at Recital 168 and article 43(9).[139] Standards for software and processes are developed by representatives of national governments, academia, and, to a great extent, of technology companies. While the process of standards development is transparent and driven by many well-meaning participants, due to the voluntary – ie unpaid – nature of work at SDOs, Big Tech employees are over-represented, especially employees of companies from the global leader in the production of software: the US.[140] The most powerful regulatees of the GDPR have a significant say in the processes that identify specifications for the development of TOMs.

As discussed, the GDPR requires the controller to adopt the best TOMs available on the market to meet the Regulation's objectives, subject to cost-effectiveness. When it comes to the 'technical' in TOMs, the GDPR cannot force the market to *develop* a new technology, typically software, to meet its objectives. This is because of the 'effacement of technology from the law', whereby the law engages with technological functions but not actual technologies, which are seen as mere 'tools' best left to the technical expertise of private actors (sometimes this concept is substantivized as 'tooling').[141] The mechanism, which rests on the regulatory device of technology neutrality, is presented as a form of future-proofing at the service of innovation.[142] It went hand-in-hand with the depoliticisation of technology in the 1980s, setting the scene for the co- or meta-regulatory approaches discussed here,[143] which were seen as better mechanisms than top-down regulation to support technological advancements.[144]

In dealing with technology development, market players can prioritise their economic objectives: standards are voluntary, and there are no compulsory design manuals for

[136] I am grateful to my colleague D Lewis, member of ISO/IEC JTC1/SC42 and CEN/CENELEC JTC21, for this point. See in particular, D Golpayegani, HJ Pandit and D Lewis, 'To Be High-Risk, or Not To Be – Semantic Specifications and Implications of the AI Act's High-Risk AI Applications and Harmonised Standards' in Association for Computing Machinery (ed), *Proceedings of the 6th ACM Conference on Fairness, Accountability, and Transparency (FAccT 2023)* (New York, Association for Computing Machinery, 2023).

[137] Porcedda (n 4) ch 5 and conclusions.

[138] I Kamara, 'Legal Aspects of Standardisation – Relationship of Standards and Law in the EU' (HSBooster.EU, 2023), hsbooster.eu/sites/default/files/2023-03/B1%2005%20LEGAL%20ASPECTS%20OF%20STANDARDISATION.pdf.

[139] Prior to the GDPR, the Commission requested CEN/CENELEC the adoption of a non-harmonised standard which was published in 2022. For a discussion, see Porcedda (n 4) ch 5.

[140] See, among others, at CompaniesMarketcap, 'Top publicly traded software companies by revenue' (2024), companiesmarketcap.com/software/largest-software-companies-by-revenue/.

[141] Porcedda (n 4) ch 5 and conclusions.

[142] ibid.

[143] ibid.

[144] Reidenberg (n 11).

software development, especially since software has been historically excluded from the scope of product regulations.[145] Comments by AG Pitruzzella in the NAP case are symptomatic of this reality. For him, the SoTA and cost criteria engender 'a balancing exercise between the interests of the data subject, which generally tend towards a higher level of protection, and the economic interests and technological capacity of the controller, which sometimes tend towards a lower level of protection', an exercise that must comply with 'the general principle of proportionality'.[146] His reasoning was not adopted by ECJ – as it arguably favours risk regulation over a risk-based approach – but it exemplifies the conflictual fusion that underpins the GDPR. While controllers are many and varied, the same is not true of developers of technical measures commonly used to process personal data, where US companies retain leadership.[147] The GDPR, on its own, lacks the power to force these players, which are often processors, to develop better technical measures.

West of the Atlantic, regulatory influences and market penetration generate conflictual fusion, with unintended impacts on the fundamental rights mandate of EU data protection law. The effacement of technology from the law creates indeterminacy at the judicial level: if the law does not engage with technology, neither will the EU judge, who cannot intervene to correct overarching perverse effects.[148] This was visible in the NAP case, where the Court delegated the assessment of the appropriateness of TOMs to national courts without entertaining the fragmentation of EU law this may cause.[149] As discussed (section III.A), the Court identified two elements of the 'essence' of data protection, ie, the core, the violation of which is supposed to trigger the automatic impermissibility of a measure: the presence, in the legal basis, of provisions on 'security safeguards' and 'purpose limitation'. By overlooking the fact that security safeguards are determined in practice by the regulatee, the Court has handed the determination of the practical determination of the essence to the market of automated processing and, by extension, US Big Tech.

## V. Conclusion: The GDPR as Mid-Atlantic Regulation

This chapter has claimed that EU data protection law, and its flagship instrument, the GDPR, is heavily influenced by the US in a way that metaphorically pulls its axis away from Brussels towards the north-western shores of the Atlantic Ocean,[150] resulting in

[145] Porcedda (n 4) ch 5 and conclusions.

[146] Opinion of Advocate General Pitruzzella, Case C-340/21 para 36.

[147] See, among others, at CompaniesMarketcap, 'Top publicly traded software companies by revenue' (2024), companiesmarketcap.com/software/largest-software-companies-by-revenue/.

[148] Porcedda (n 4) ch 5.

[149] MG Porcedda, 'The GDPR as a Cyber Risk Management System: the ECJ Cautiously Tackles Data Breaches in the NAP case' (*European Law Blog*, 23.01.2024), europeanlawblog.eu/2024/01/23/the-gdpr-as-a-cyber-risk-management-system-the-ecj-cautiously-tackles-data-breaches-in-the-nap-case/.

[150] While this may be reminiscent of Lessig's 'East-coast' law v 'West-coast' code argument (L Lessig, *Code and Other Laws of Cyberspace* (New York, Basic Books, 1999) 53) insofar as, when we take the Atlantic Ocean as reference, the 'West' (the US) exports digital technology and the 'East' (Brussels) exports data protection law, the focus here is on 'conflictual fusion' caused by west of the Atlantic regulatory and market influences on EU data protection law.

'mid-Atlantic' regulation. The analysis of chapter I of the GDPR shows the mid-Atlantic outcome happens, first, because EU data protection law incorporates regulatory traditions and tools devised on the north-western shore of the Atlantic, often via the Organisation for Economic Cooperation and Development (OECD), although this is not the only vehicle for norm diffusion. The GDPR is premised on a compromise between the permissive US approach and the restrictive EU attitude to data flows (article 1) mediated by data protection principles first developed in the US (article 5 GDPR). The crucial legal basis of consent draws from the heritage of US consumer law and the legacy of 30 years of wrap contracting, which case law is only starting to scratch (articles 6 and 7 GDPR). Finally, the one-stop-shop builds on the notions of establishment and country of origin principles drawn from the e-Commerce framework and reflective of the US light-touch regulatory approach (article 3 GDPR); arguably, all IT law is mid-Atlantic in character.

The mid-Atlantic outcome also happens because the most common measures used to process personal data are designed and developed by Big Tech leaders – mostly US companies. The duties of data controllers to adopt Technical and Organizational Measures (TOMs) to process data in accordance with the principle of accountability (articles 24, 25, and 32 GDPR) must be read in light of the ecosystem of digital technology development which the GDPR espouses. The co- or meta-regulatory approach of the GDPR means that regulatees hold the choice of the most 'appropriate' technology for any given processing operation; this gives the upper hand to companies headquartered west of the Atlantic because of their market dominance. Furthermore, any desire to stir technology development in the GDPR is counterbalanced by the fact that technology (development) is effaced from the law and left instead to mechanisms of standardisation that adopt voluntary technical specifications for the development of information technologies. The same US companies that enjoy market dominance play a preeminent role in the ecosystem that devises such technical specifications. In the absence of any hard rules on technology development, the state of the art of technology is determined more by business models than by data protection and security considerations. The effacement of technology from the law dispossesses the European courts from the ability to correct this state of affairs, with the effect that the market has the final say in the practical determination of what constitutes the essence of the right, insofar as data security measures are concerned.[151]

The mid-Atlantic character of EU data protection law could be seen as the understandable outcome of a local system of rules with transnational application, but it is for economists and political scientists to assess the extent to which this is a desirable equilibrium. It is possible this is the only form of equilibrium in a post-WWII order predicated on free trade under complex WTO rules[152] and regulatory coordination through the OECD. Indeed, the GDPR does not exist in isolation but rather interacts

[151] A similar argument could be developed for the proportionality prong of the essence, which is emptied by the reality of practices of re-use of data. These are liable to cause privacy violations per se, as argued by (Orrù (n 88) 119). The re-use of raw data to produce aggregated profiles nudging consumers into managed consumption deprives individuals of the bargaining power (Cohen (n 5) 71–73) inherent in notions of consent, ultimately displaying the limitations of the individual rights construct of personal data protection (Orrù (n 88) 119) and of its enforcement on a case-by-case basis.

[152] Agreement on Rules of Origin Annex 1A Multilateral Agreements on Trade in Goods, Marrakesh Agreement Establishing the World Trade Organization. Information Technology Agreement (ITA) (Singapore, 13 December 1996).

with other frameworks, including those for global trade, which have a bearing on any unilateral actions that may be taken to address mid-Atlantic consequences.[153] Following Cohen,

> … the European Union has worked to institutionalize stronger data protection norms around the world but has been stymied by the policy hegemony of the United States and by the rising economic influence of Asian nations. Faced with increasingly aggressive demands for data protection emanating from the European Union, parties seeking liberalization have shifted their emphasis toward inserting strengthened mandates for cross-border flow in trade agreements.[154]

The analysis points to the crucial need for (EU) data regulators and enforcers to re-engage with technology design to remedy the impact of mid-Atlantic conflictual fusion. There are multiple calls in this direction, and the EU has adopted the first instrument capable of influencing software design, the Cyber Resilience Act,[155] which will come into effect from late 2027. The interaction of such a framework with the GDPR needs to be studied, but the related understanding of software as a product is likely to have a positive impact on data protection mechanisms and particularly on the quality of security measures.

So, how to go forward? Hartzog, who cautions that 'design is everywhere … is power … is political',[156] notes that FIPs are still necessary but need to be complemented by a 'design agenda' enforced by regulators, which he calls 'Privacy's Blueprint' as 'the right place to start' because without sustainable design any system can become 'dangerous and untrustworthy'.[157] Under Orrù's 'Minimum Harm by Design', the design of surveillance functionalities must be theoretically assessed against all their possible harms and only enabled if proven safe and with the benefit of strong regulatory frameworks providing the necessary enforcement powers.[158] In previous work of mine, I proposed a mechanism to align data protection principles and attributes of the right to data protection with privacy engineering principles.[159] Rubinstein and Good suggest enforcers should get involved by mandating the adoption of certain PETs.[160] Another option is the creation of rankings of TOMs by their potential appropriateness to use cases. Yet another is the attempt by EU

[153] Indeed, the 'mid-Atlantic' character applies to early (EU) digital or IT law, of which data protection is part. It will be for separate work to discuss this point.

[154] Cohen (n 5) ch 7.

[155] Regulation (EU) 2024/2847 of the European Parliament and of the Council of 23 October 2024 on horizontal cybersecurity requirements for products with digital elements and amending Regulations (EU) No 168/2013 and (EU) No 2019/1020 and Directive (EU) 2020/1828 (Cyber Resilience Act) [2024] OJ L2024/2847.

[156] Hartzog (n 51) 279.

[157] ibid 277.

[158] E Orrù, 'Minimum Harm by Design: Reworking Privacy by Design to Mitigate the Risks of Surveillance' in R Leenes, R van Brakel, S Gutwirth and P de Hert (eds), *Data Protection and Privacy: (In)visibilities and Infrastructures* (Cham, Springer, 2017) 126–133, which challenges the 'Privacy by Design' win-win, business-friendly approach.

[159] MG Porcedda, 'Privacy by Design in EU law. Matching Privacy Protection Goals with the Essence of the Rights to Private Life and Data Protection' in M Medina, A Mitrakas, K Rannenberg, E Schweighofer and N Tsouroulas (eds), *Lecture Notes in Computer Science* (Barcelona, Springer Nature, 2018) 183–204; MG Porcedda, 'On Boundaries. In Search for the Essence of the Right to the Protection of Personal Data' in R Leenes, R van Brakel, P de Hert and S Gutwirth (eds), *Data Protection and Privacy: The Internet of Bodies* (Oxford, Hart Publishing, 2018).

[160] Rubinstein and Good (n 124)'.

actors to get more involved in standardisation processes,[161] a late response to Reidenberg's call in his *Lex Informatica* article,[162] although such involvement would not be the appropriate avenue to secure the alignment of technologies with EU values, for reasons discussed earlier.

Current standardisation mechanisms and trade frameworks are themselves in flux. At present, there are United Nations-backed calls to embed human rights in standards, a tricky proposition in light of international disagreement over the meaning of human rights and the role of courts in interpreting them.[163] As for trade frameworks, the EU and US have, up to 2024, jointly committed to such rules as close trading partners.[164] It remains to be seen whether that will remain the case under shifting geopolitical forces, and what constraints they will bring to bear on unilateral attempts to engage with technology design. Perhaps the axis of EU data protection law may then tilt back towards Brussels.

[161] Eg, European Commission and High Representative of the European Union for Foreign Affairs and Security Policy, 'Joint Communication: The EU's Cybersecurity Strategy for the Digital Decade' (16.12.2020), digital-strategy.ec.europa.eu/en/library/eus-cybersecurity-strategy-digital-decade-0 18.

[162] Reidenberg (n 11).

[163] Porcedda, 'Rights and Technical Standards in EU Law' (n 133).

[164] 'In 2023, the United States was the largest partner for EU exports of goods (19.7 %) and the second largest partner for EU imports of goods (13.7 %)' Eurostat, 'USA-EU – international trade in goods statistics' (Feb 2024) ec.europa.eu/eurostat/statistics-explained/index.php?title=USA-EU_-_international_trade_in_goods_statistics. Office of the United States Trade Representative, 'European Union', ustr.gov/countries-regions/europe-middle-east/europe/european-union (note that US trade statistics tend to disaggregate EU countries, so that no EU Member State ever tops the trading charts).

# 10

# Trust in Privacy Law

JOHANNES EICHENHOFER

## I. Theoretical Foundations

### A. Functions and Values of Privacy

Privacy is best understood as a social institution[1] – ie, a set of rules that is generally recognised and practised and therefore a solid basis to stabilise expectations in the behaviour of others.[2] This institution can be found all over the world, even in the earliest history of humanity.[3] Accordingly, every society seemed and seems to generally appreciate 'the value of privacy'[4] – although the conflict with other rights and interests naturally leads to varying degrees of effective privacy protection from society to society. This general appreciation may surprise, since privacy does not have an intrinsic value.[5] Much more, it aims to serve other values such as individual freedom or autonomy, (mental) health, or, in some cases, the individuals' property or other financial interests.[6] Among the privacy scholars, it was primarily Alan Westin who examined these interrelations between privacy and other values by distinguishing between four functions that privacy had to fulfil: according to him, privacy aims to grant the individual's 'personal autonomy', 'emotional release', 'self-evaluation' and 'limited and protected communication'.[7] While these *purposes* of privacy are comparatively undisputed and apparently refer to historically constant needs, the *instruments* of privacy protection are constantly changing in the face of new social, cultural, economic, and technological developments.

[1] See, eg, F Schoeman, 'Privacy and Intimate Information' in F Schoeman (ed), *Philosophical Dimensions of Privacy* (Cambridge, Cambridge University Press, 1984) 403, 415.

[2] N Luhmann, *Grundrechte als Institution. Ein Beitrag zur politischen Soziologie* (Berlin, Duncker & Humblot, 1974).

[3] See on this A Westin, *Privacy and Freedom* (New York, Atheneum, 1967).

[4] B Rössler, *The value of privacy* (Hoboken, Wiley & Sons, 2004).

[5] On the values of privacy see, eg, J Rachels, 'Why Privacy is Important' in F Schoeman (ed), *Philosophical Dimensions of Privacy* (Cambridge, Cambridge University Press, 1984) 290.

[6] A similar observation on the purposes of data protection has been made by R Poscher, 'The Right to Data protection – A No-Rights thesis' in R Miller (ed), *Privacy and Power* (Cambridge, Cambridge University Press, 2017).

[7] See Westin (n 3) 32ff.

## B. Classical Approaches to Privacy

### i. *Sphere Models*

A classical conception of (informational[8]) privacy, at least in German Constitutional law, is the so-called 'sphere theory', as established by the German Federal Constitutional Court in its early jurisdiction of the 1960s and 1970s.[9] Herein, the Court derived a 'right to privacy' from the general right of personality (article 2(1) in combination with article 1 I GG), which in turn can be differentiated into three 'spheres' of an individual's personal life: the 'social' or 'public sphere', the 'private sphere', and the 'intimate sphere' as the 'core' of all three spheres. Because this 'core' is protected by the constitutional guarantee of human dignity (article 1 of the German Constitution), interferences in the intimate sphere can under no circumstances be justified, while the slightly more 'external' (viewed from the core) sphere, the 'private' sphere, may be infringed, even though only under high requirements. Interferences in the 'social' or 'public sphere', as the even more 'external' sphere, are possible under even lower standards. The 'sphere theory' hence constitutes an attempt to assess to which extent an aspect of an individual's personal life is private and therefore worthy of protection by *objective* criteria (ie, its 'proximity' to the guarantee of human dignity), while the subjective views and the will of the individual concerned are irrelevant in this regard.

### ii. *Privacy as an Individual Right to Determination or Control*

The next step in the evolution of (information) privacy theories responds to this problem as it perceives privacy as an individual right to (informational) self-determination[10] or control[11] over personal information. It is now up to the individual if and to which extent she or he allows others access to her or his personal information. Any access without the consent of the authorised person must therefore be seen as an infringement. And this infringement requires a justification, ie, a legal basis and further justification standards, in particular adherence to the requirements of proportionality and legal certainty. In sum: by conceptualising privacy as an individual (fundamental) right, which in its scope aims to protect the individual's autonomous decision of if and to which extent she or he grants others access to her or his personal life, this attempt can

[8] This chapter will only focus on the 'informational' dimension of privacy, which of course is, to some extent, overlapping with the so-called 'decisional' dimension, which also will be covered. The 'spatial' dimension however, will not be considered in the following. See on the distinction between these three dimensions: B Rössler, *The Value of Privacy* (Cambridge, Polity Publishing, 2004).

[9] See, eg, BVerfGE 27, 1 (6) [1969] – *Mikrozensus*; BVerfGE 27, 344 (351) [1979] – *Ehescheidungsakten*; BVerfGE 32, 373 (379) [1972] – *Ärztliche Schweigepflicht*. For a detailed analysis see the contribution of G Britz, ch 5 in this volume.

[10] This right has been invented in the famous 'public census' decision of the German Federal Constitution – BVerfGE 65, 1 (41ff) [1983] – *Volkszählungsgesetz*. See, eg, the famous definition by Westin (n 3) 7: 'Privacy' is 'the claim of individuals, groups, or institutions to determine for themselves when, how, and to what extent information about them is communicated to others.'

[11] See, eg, C Fried, 'Privacy' (1968) 77 *The Yale Law Journal* 475, 482: 'Privacy […] is the control we have about information about ourselves.' According to R Gavison, 'Privacy and the Limits of Law' (1980) 89 *The Yale Law Journal* 421, 425, privacy protects a 'concern for limited accessibility', which the individual should be able to exercise.

easily apply the legal doctrine that has been developed for fundamental rights. However, this concept presupposes that individuals are (factually) able to make self-determined decisions about how their data is handled at all. This may have been possible at the time of the census ruling (1983), in which the German Constitutional Court established the right to informational self-determination, but it seems more and more doubtful under the given circumstances of digitalisation.

## C. Challenges of Digitalisation: The New Dependency and Vulnerability

Digitalisation offers individuals new opportunities to access information, to communicate with others and hereby solve a multitude of problems in their everyday lives, as we all know from our own practical experiences. This problem-solving capacity of digital tools tends to improve the more it is being used (as the impressive development of artificial intelligence in the last years shows). However, there is a flipside to the coin: every use of digital information and communication technology places individuals in a position of dependency; in order to realise the desired benefits, they are initially dependent on the technologies and services that private companies provide them. Since every use of the Internet necessarily involves the dissemination of data (at least to providers whose services and technologies have been used) – which under the aforementioned classical approaches should be perceived as 'private' – this sort of exposure of users (at least to their providers) puts them (in relation to the providers) in a state of *vulnerability*. At least from a technical point of view, providers have the possibility of generating information and knowledge about their customers from the data traces they have left behind, which the providers can then use to their disadvantage. However, it has always been the concern of privacy protection to reduce precisely these risks.

Still, this finding makes it necessary to rethink privacy as a social institution: what does it mean for individuals' private lives if they are constantly dependent on others (ie the developers and providers of information technology) and exposed to their 'good will' and their will to comply with the current law? Can the 'traditional' concepts of privacy, and in particular the self-determination and control approach (I.B.ii.), still be upheld in a meaningful way? Or is it not rather necessary to substitute the very fundamental premise that the self-determination and control paradigm is built on, ie, the individual's actual competence to determine and control the individual data flow through the aforementioned (I.B.ii.) dependencies in the digital age? These dependencies must not lead to the assumption that privacy in the online world no longer exists.[12] Much more, they can also be taken as a starting point for a new way of construing privacy in legal terms. This approach requires us to have a closer look at the (social and legal) relation[13] between users and providers. Some important terms, which characterise these relations, have already been mentioned: dependency and vulnerability of the users on the one hand,

[12] In this context, the statement by the CEO of Sun Microsystem, S McNealy, is notorious: 'You have zero privacy anyway. Get over it' (*Wired*, 1999), www.wired.com/1999/01/sun-on-privacy-get-over-it/.

[13] See on this view of law in general J Nedelsky, *Law's Relations: A Relational Theory of Self, Autonomy and Law* (Oxford, Oxford University Press, 2011).

and power of the providers on the other hand. Yet, there is still one important element missing, as in particular Neil Richards, Woodrow Hartzog and Ari Ezra Waldman[14] have impressively shown: the element of trust.

## D. 'Trust' as a New Paradigm of Privacy Law?

Trust is a fundamental psychological mechanism that is not only ubiquitous in all societies. In fact, it is a fundamental prerequisite for social coexistence in the first place.[15] It is necessary whenever people find themselves in uncertain situations and dependent relationships, and it helps them to remain capable of acting.[16] In the words of the German sociologist and philosopher Georg Simmel (1858–1918), trust can be described 'as the hypothesis of future behavior that is certain enough to base practical action on' and therefore 'as a hypothesis, a middle state between knowing and not knowing'.[17] This is exactly the situation in which most (if not all) individuals find themselves whenever they are using the Internet. It therefore seems both close at hand and attractive to view privacy from the 'lens' of the 'trust paradigm'. This change of perspective requires us to focus not only on the 'atomised' individual and her or his rights and interests, but rather on the social relationships in which he or she is involved when using the Internet. Privacy thus necessarily becomes a *relational* concept.

But trust is not only ubiquitous and necessary in concrete (typically personal, familiar, or intimate) relations between single individuals. As philosophy and political and legal science have taught us, there is also a form of 'general trust' that is based on the expectation and the behaviour of a large number of people, namely all members of a society or, in the language of political philosophy, a political community – which leads us to the importance of trust for the social, political and legal realm. This point was already made by Thomas Hobbes.[18] According to him, trust is a sort of sentiment that arises from the belief in someone from whom we expect or hope for good and which is so free of doubt that we do not pursue any other way to achieve it. Distrust, however,

[14] N Richards and W Hartzog, 'Taking Trust seriously in Privacy Law' (2016) 19 *Stanford Technology Law Review* 431; AE Waldman, *Privacy as Trust. Information Privacy for an Information Age* (Cambridge, Cambridge University Press, 2018). See also with a focus on EU Data Privacy Law J Eichenhofer, 'Privatheit im Internet als Vertrauensschutz. Eine Neukonstruktion der Europäischen Grundrechte auf Privatleben und Datenschutz' (2016) 55 *Der Staat* 41; J Eichenhofer, *e-Privacy. Theorie und Dogmatik eines europäischen Privatheitsschutzes im Internet-Zeitalter* (Tübingen, Mohr Siebeck, 2021).

[15] See, eg, JR Blöcher, *Regulierung trotz Nichtwissen: Epistemisches Vertrauen als Handlungsressource im Recht* (Tübingen, Mohr Siebeck, 2023) 10, who justifies this finding mainly by stating that under the conditions of modern life, it is de facto no longer possible to act with conclusive knowledge.

[16] This insight has in particular been articulated by N Luhmann, *Trust and Power* (Hoboken, Wiley & Sons, 2017) 27ff. According to Blöcher (n 15) 9 trust is a social heuristic that continuously bridges knowledge gaps. AB Seligman, *The Problem of Trust* (Princeton, Princeton University Press, 1997) 13 makes a similar statement: 'On the most general and abstract level it can be stated that the need for perduring, stable, and universally recognized structures of trust is rooted in the fundamental indeterminacy of social interaction.'

[17] Translation of the author. The original quote goes: 'Vertrauen, als die Hypothese künftigen Verhaltens, die sicher genug ist, um praktisches Handeln darauf zu gründen, ist als Hypothese ein mittlerer Zustand zwischen Wissen und Nichtwissen' – see: G Simmel, *Soziologie. Gesamtausgabe*, vol 11 (Frankfurt am Main, Suhrkamp, 1992) (edited by O Rammstedt) 393 (First released in 1908).

[18] See on this in particular D Baumgold, '"Trust" in Hobbes' Political Thought' (2013) 41 *Political Theory* 838.

is the doubt that causes us to look for other means.[19] Hobbes was very aware that this (psychological) state could never be achieved in the so-called 'state of nature', ie, the lack of any political order. For Hobbes, this 'state of nature' is characterised by 'competition, diffidence and the desire for glory'[20] (*homo homini lupus*). In the absence of any social rules, individuals would have to expect to be subjected to violence by others at any time. This situation could only be ended by a social contract (the installation of a 'Leviathan'), with which the individuals promise each other peaceful coexistence. And this promise can be enforced by the 'Leviathan' by force if necessary. Ultimately, therefore, it is the existence of legal regulations in combination with an effective sanctions system[21] that creates trust.[22]

This concept was later challenged by John Locke in his major work, 'Two Treatises of Government'.[23] In contrast to Hobbes, Locke assumed that subjective rights such as freedom and equality already existed in the 'state of nature'. However, these had to be defended by the individuals themselves. With the assignment of the social contract, the individuals, however, transferred this right to 'self-justice' to the sovereign (for Locke: a king). By doing so, they established a 'vertical' relationship of trust towards the king (in contrast to the 'horizontal' trust relationships between individuals).[24] This 'fiduciary trust' demanded the king supervise the legislature. The distinction between horizontal and vertical trust, which can be traced back to Locke, continued to occupy political science research decades later. Ernst Fraenkel,[25] for example, assumed that the horizontal relation was based on the 'egalitarian nature'[26] of all people, while the question of horizontal trust ultimately referred to a form of legitimisation of existing rule. And Robert D Putnam[27] has shown that individuals primarily trust those institutions that are most likely to represent their values.

It seems that trust (in both the horizontal and vertical dimensions) is particularly connected to the law.[28] A reason for this interconnectedness might be seen in the fact that the law is often seen as a social mechanism that should generate and preserve trust by stabilising the individual's expectations of the behaviour of others.[29] However, trust and law have also been contrasted to each other. In particular, representatives of the Enlightenment emphasised that trust was based on moral duties (Kant) or a

[19] See T Hobbes, *The Elements of Natural Law and Politic* (public-library, 1640), www.public-library.uk/ebooks/31/91.pdf ch. I.9.

[20] See T Hobbes, *Leviathan* (1651), edited by R Tuck (Cambridge, Cambridge University Press, 1996) ch I.13. 88.

[21] R Hardin, *Trust and Trustworthiness*, RSF Series on Trust 4 (New York, Russell Sage Foundation, 2002) 69.

[22] See also Seligman (n 16) 14 et seq who notes that '[f]rom the writings of Pufendorf and Grotius to those of John Locke, David Hume, and Immanuel Kant, the duty of "promise keeping" … becomes a central component of political theory.'

[23] J Locke, *Two Treatises of Government* (1689), in particular ch II.7.

[24] On this J Dunn, 'The Concept of 'Trust' in the Politics of John Locke' in R Rorty and JB Schneewind and Q Skinners (eds), *Philosophy in History, Ideas in Context* (Cambridge, Cambridge University Press, 1984) 279.

[25] E Fraenkel, *Deutschland und die westlichen Demokratien* (Frankfurt am Main, Suhrkamp, 1991) 334.

[26] EM Uslaner, *The Moral Foundations of Trust* (Cambridge, Cambridge University Press, 2002) 3, 79ff.

[27] R Putnam, *Making Democracy Work: Civic Traditions in Modern Italy* (Princeton, Princeton University Press, 1993) 167.

[28] See, eg, JR Blöcher, *Regulierung trotz Nichtwissen* (2023) 61 ff.

[29] See, eg, KF Röhl, *Rechtssoziologie* (Köln, Carl Heymanns, 1987) 262.

kind of natural law (Grotius).[30] For Emile Durkheim, too, trust is a precondition of legal relationships ('precontractual'); in other words, trust comes first, then the legal relationship. The systems theorist Niklas Luhmann uses the term 'trust' only for personal relationships (the horizontal dimension), while an expectation regarding the functionality of entire systems (so-called system trust) should be described as 'confidence'.[31] However, this does not mean that *institutions* cannot also be trusted, as they are, in fact, 'nothing but patterned, internalized, normative role expectation'.[32] In the following, the term 'trust' will be used for both personal relationships[33] and those with law-making and law-enforcing (state, supra-, or international) institutions. The aim of the following part is to examine the extent to which the current EU (and US) Privacy Law (see section II.) and AI Regulation (see section III.) can be reconstructed under the 'trust paradigm'.

## II. Trust and Privacy Law

Trust is not just a 'lens' through which the law can be observed. Moreover, the law is also considered to have the general function of controlling the behaviour of individuals and making it predictable, thereby stabilising the trust of others.[34] The concept of trust is therefore one of the most fundamental principles of any legal system[35] – whether in the form of judicial law, such as the 'reasonable expectation of privacy' doctrine of the US Supreme Court (II.A.), or in the form of statutory rules (such as, for example, in EU law).

Regardless of whether it is judge-made or statutory law, these rules are always intended to solve the same problem: an individual finds itself in a situation in which it must trust another legal subject (eg, because it has to use a service that it cannot provide itself – such as flying an aeroplane or providing access to the Internet) but knows nothing or not much about this other legal subject ('information asymmetry'), which is now in a position to infringe the legal interests of its counterpart due to legal obligations (eg, a contract) and/or certain factual circumstances (eg, the factual possibility of accessing a user's data). At this point, law comes into play. Legal rules can actually serve to protect the 'trust giving party' (who shall be called 'trustor' in the following), at least in two ways: They can either impose certain a priori obligations on the 'trust taking party' (who

[30] Seligman (n 16) 15.

[31] Luhmann (n 16) 48.

[32] AB Seligman (n 16) 19 ff, who in the following links the concept of trust with theories of the social role of George Herbert Mead and Charles Cooley. See, eg, 24 (with further references): 'Trust is something that enters into social relations when there is role negotiability.'

[33] In contrast, it is controversial whether trust in technology or entire systems is possible. The former is disputed by Fried (n 11) 475, 486: 'One does not trust machines [...] one takes the fullest economically feasible precautions against their going wrong.' The latter is denied by Luhmann (n 16) 48, who speaks of 'confidence' in this regard.

[34] See again eg, Röhl (n 29) 232.

[35] CW Canaris, *Die Vertrauenshaftung im Deutschen Privatrecht* (München, Beck, 1971) 3: 'Der Vertrauensgedanke gehört zweifellos zu den fundamentalsten Prinzipien einer jeden Rechtsordnung' (in English: 'The concept of trust is undoubtedly one of the most fundamental principles of any legal system.' Translation by the author of this article).

can be called 'trustee' or 'entrustee'[36]) in order to disclose the trustees' identity to the trustor[37] or to demonstrate to the trustor which rights they have vis-à-vis the trustee (eg, the 'notice and consent' principle). Another way in which legal rules can protect trust is as they impose liability on the trustee in the event that he or she claims special trust for her- or himself vis-à-vis the trustor and disappoints this trust by behaving differently than he had previously explicitly or implicitly promised.[38] Now what has all of this to do with privacy law?

## A. Why Speak of 'Trust' in Privacy Law?

In fact, regarding privacy law through the 'lens' of trust is still quite unusual – at least in Europe.[39] In the US, however, the 'reasonable expectation' doctrine[40] and its later variations, such as the 'third party' doctrine,[41] are at least very closely related to the concept of trust:[42] also, according to this conception, an individual's eligibility for protection under US constitutional law ultimately depends on his or her individual 'expectations', insofar as they are 'legitimate', because they are generally recognised by the society or even protected by the law. What the 'trust approach' adds to this conception is, above all, its strictly *relational* approach. Trust, by definition, presupposes a *relationship* between trustor and trustee. And this relationship is characterised by the information (and often power) asymmetry just described, and this is a social dependence of the trustor on the abilities or resources of the trustee, which is what makes the trustor put his trust in the trustee in the first place.[43] Trust is thus 'most required exactly when we least know whether a person will or will not do an action'.[44] This insight in turn results in a specific *vulnerability*[45]

[36] This term is used by Richards and Hartzog (n 14) 431, 450, who make the argument that 'trustee' was reserved for trust law.

[37] This is the task of the so called 'trust services' in EU law, as they are regulated in the so-called eiDAS-Regulation (Regulation (EU) No 910/2014 of the European Parliament and of the Council of 23 July 2014 on electronic identification and trust services for electronic transactions in the internal market and repealing Directive 1999/93/EC).

[38] This approach is fundamental in particular in German law – both in civil law as in public law. See on the first eg, CW Canaris, *Die Vertrauenshaftung im Deutschen Privatrecht*, on the latter eg, KA Schwarz, *Vertrauensschutz als Verfassungsprinzip* (Baden-Baden, Nomos, 2002).

[39] See, however, J Eichenhofer, 'Privatheit im Internet als Vertrauensschutz. Eine Neukonstruktion der Europäischen Grundrechte auf Privatleben und Datenschutz' (2016) 55 *Der Staat*, 41; J Eichenhofer, *e-Privacy* (n 14).

[40] This doctrine was established by the famous '*Katz*' decision of the US Supreme Court – *cf Charles Katz v United States*, 389 U.S. 347 (1967).

[41] *United States v Miller*, 425 U.S. 435, 443 (1976): '[T]he Fourth Amendment does not prohibit the obtaining of information revealed to a third party and conveyed by him to Government authorities, even if the information is revealed on the assumption that it will be used only for a limited purpose and the confidence placed in the third party will not be betrayed.'

[42] On the importance of these two doctrines in the digital world eg, K Brennan-Marquez 'Fourth Amendment Fiduciaries' (2015) 84 *Fordham Law Review* 611.

[43] See, eg, Seligman (n 16) 21: 'For central to the definition of trust (as opposed to confidence) is that it involves one in a relation where the acts, character, or intentions of the other cannot be confirmed. In this reading one trusts or is forced to trust – perhaps led to trust would be better – when one cannot know, when one has the capacities to apprehend or check on the other so has no choice but trust.'

[44] V Held, 'On the Meaning of Trust' (1968) 78 *Ethics* 156 (157).

[45] See, eg, Richards and Hartzog (n 14) 431, 449: 'In the context of information relationships, trust means the willingness to become vulnerable to a person or organization by disclosing personal information.'

of the trustor vis-à-vis a trustee, which requires legal protection. And this protection already exists – in the form of the current Privacy Law. But why then should the current privacy law be analysed in the 'trust paradigm' at all? There are two reasons for this: first, this approach helps to better understand the problem of privacy protection on the Internet (II.B.). And second, a need for further regulation can be derived on this basis (II.C.).

## B. How does 'Trust' Help to *Understand* the Privacy Problem?

The 'trust paradigm' initially has a *descriptive* value: it describes the situation of what happens when we use the Internet far better than the traditional 'control paradigm' (I.B.) and in particular the 'notice and consent' principle, as the latter requires individuals to be in a position to have a complete overview of their actions and to be in a position in which they can autonomously make their decision. In the case of privacy online, this would mean Internet users would need to fully comprehend who is processing 'their' data, to what extent, and for which purposes. And they would need to have the power to eventually restrict this data procession executed by an ISP (and potential third parties). In reality, however, individuals can at least not do the latter – they can only decide to abstain from using certain Internet services or the Internet at all.[46] Alternatively, and this is what the 'trust paradigm' calls for, they can *trust* ISPs to provide their services within the framework of the applicable privacy law. It was justifiably remarked that this process of forming and disposing of trust is highly individual and therefore difficult to generalise.[47] Nonetheless, it is perfectly possible to reconstruct privacy protection as trust protection. A key role is played here by privacy norms,[48] such as those laid down in privacy law. As will be shown now, these norms can at least help to protect *generalised* trust.

And this is where the *analytical* value of the trust approach becomes apparent: it shows that privacy protection on the Internet is dependent on the existence of legal norms.[49] These norms have the task of making the ISP respect the privacy of its users. Since any legal norm can be enforced compulsorily if necessary, legal privacy norms take over the control that users still had under the 'control paradigm' to a certain extent. The purpose of this legal regulation can either be seen in the (re-)establishment of a position of control for users – but this goal can only be achieved to a very limited extent. On the basis of the 'notice and consent' model, users can improve their information base about how ISPs and any third-party providers process 'their' data. However, users have no influence whatsoever on

[46] Richards and Hartzog (n 14) 431 speak in this respect correctly of a 'control illusion' (444), which leaves consumers 'exposed and bewildered' (434).

[47] See, eg, E Schmidt-Aßmann and G Dimitropoulos, 'Vertrauen in und durch Recht. Überlegungen zum Verhältnis von Vertrauen und Recht als Beitrag zu einer Phänomenologie des Vertrauens' in MA Weingardt, *Vertrauen in der Krise* (Baden-Baden, Nomos, 2011) 129, 131 f, who point to the need for interdisciplinary work, in particular the inclusion of findings from (social) psychology.

[48] See Waldman (n 14) 67: 'information privacy is a social norm of information flow based on trust'.

[49] Richards and Hartzog (n 14) 431, 452: '[…] privacy rules – rules governing the uses of personal information – are essential requirements for the existence of these trust-dependent relationships in the first place.'

how the ISPs and data processors actually process their data or, to give an example, protect their servers (and the user data stored on them) against hacking attacks by third parties.

It therefore seems unrealistic and thus inappropriate to claim a comprehensive right of self-determination or control as an overarching goal of privacy law insofar as it regulates the relationships between users and ISPs.[50] Rather, it seems reasonable to rethink the relationship between users, ISPs and the state and the varying 'roles' that privacy law assigns to them.[51] Users are no longer expected to control data processing by ISPs. This is the task of the state by setting statutory privacy laws. Of course, users can deviate from these laws and thus exercise their right to self-determination again (eg, by giving their 'consent', or through a very permissive approval of cookies, or by dispensing with voluntary protective measures such as ad blockers or encryption techniques). Apart from that, they can *trust* that privacy laws, which regulate the aspects of data processing that users cannot determine (such as measures of data security or the principle of purpose limitation), will be respected and carried out by the ISPs (and other data processors). The protection of user trust, in this regard, becomes the actual objective of Privacy Law. And this change of perspective is well-founded: trust is not only a necessary strategy for individuals to overcome situations of information asymmetries and dependencies (I.D.), as they are characteristic of the relationship between users and ISPs. Much more, the psychological and social mechanism of trust ultimately fulfils for the individual users the same functions as the execution of self-determination, since both social mechanisms provide users with autonomy and all the other benefits, which are usually related to the social institution of privacy (I.A.).[52]

'Without trust', as Neil Richards and Woodrow Hartzog argue, 'people share less information, bad information, or no information at all. They become anxious, bewildered, and suspicious.'[53] But the user's trust can be built – through strong legal safeguards in privacy law.[54] In this regard, it is true that 'modern privacy law is incomplete because from its inception it has failed to account for the importance of trust'.[55] And this account has necessarily to focus on the regulation of concrete relationships,[56] eg, between users and ISPs, which are characterised by an information asymmetry and therefore a dependency and vulnerability of users.[57] And this description applies precisely to the

[50] This relationship has, very similar to the aforementioned trust relations, been called 'vertical privacy', which has to be distinguished from the so-called 'horizontal relations' between different users, eg, in social networks – see on this distinction between horizontal and vertical privacy: T Dienlin, 'Das Privacy-Paradox aus psychologischer Perspektive' in L Specht-Riemenschneider and N Werry and S Werry (eds), *Handbuch Datenrecht und Digitalisierung* (Berlin, Erich Schmidt 2019) 305, 313, who in turn attributes this to B Schwartz, 'The Social Psychology of Privacy' (1968) 73 *American Journal of Sociology*, 741.

[51] Like here Waldman (n 14) 77: 'Using trust as a benchmark for privacy would reorient privacy law away from a narrow focus on individual choice to a broader focus on the relationships that give rise to disclosure.'

[52] See on this eg, Eichenhofer, *e-Privacy* (n 14) 171 ff: similar: Waldman (n 14) 61 ff.

[53] Richards and Hartzog (n 14) 431, 435. A similar point is made by Waldman (n 14) 61: 'Trust [...] is at the core of our contextual decisions to share personal information with others.'

[54] Richards and Hartzog (n 14) 431, 447: 'Privacy rules can govern the uses of information in relationships, and these rules can build trust.'

[55] Richards and Hartzog (n 14) 431, 435.

[56] Likewise Richards and Hartzog (n 14) 431, 449: '[...] We offer instead a theory of trust in the context of information relationships that allows us to better understand why legal, technological, and social rules regulating the collection, uses, and flows of information in those relationships can make us all better off.'

[57] Richards and Hartzog (n 14) 431, 451: 'Because disclosure of personal data leaves people vulnerable, trust is the glue that holds together virtually every information relationship.'

aforementioned relationships that are already regulated by current privacy law. From this perspective, current privacy law already fulfils a trust-protecting function,[58] insofar as it regulates the relationship between ISPs and users to protect the latter. If, for example, ISPs are obliged to process users' data only for certain purposes[59] not to pass it on to third parties without any restriction and without reason, or to protect the consumer data stored on their servers from hacking attacks by third parties,[60] all of this has the purpose of protecting users' interests. Even if users cannot influence ISPs to respect their interests, they can at least *trust* that ISPs will do so.

But trust is not only a 'by-product of a functioning privacy regime'.[61] Rather, it can be argued, that preserving the user's trust is the *main goal* of privacy law under the non-transparent conditions of data processing on the Internet.[62] By establishing reliable rules for this processing, which must be made transparent to the user,[63] and by ensuring that a breach of these rules is sanctioned, privacy law can ensure that the purposes of privacy protection (I.A.) can be achieved even in asymmetrical relationships such as that between user and ISP, just as if users had to assert their interests themselves. The relevance of trust in privacy law hence lies in the fact that the breach of privacy norms of privacy law is sanctioned by the law itself. From this perspective, privacy protection cannot only be invoked once the norm has already been violated. Rather, the mere validity of a standard that threatens a sanction[64] already has a 'prior effect' in the sense that it will reasonably induce ISPs to behave in a legally compliant manner. And it does not seem 'unreasonable' for users to rely on this.

Certainly, it is quite difficult for the trustor to predict what risks she or he is exposing her- or himself to when making use of the service provided by an ISP, since this person (the trustee), usually a big tech firm, is completely unknown to him or her. The user (trustor) can neither foresee to which extent nor for which purposes the ISP (trustee) uses the data that the trustor has disclosed in the course of using the service of the trustee. However, the information that the ISP is obliged to communicate to the user under the privacy law already gives the user a certain orientation from which she or he can form her or his expectations. Since ISPs (and other 'trustees') are obliged to comply with the applicable privacy law when processing personal data, and a breach of these rules can, as seen, lead to severe sanctions and other serious consequences for the trustee, it seems very reasonable for the trustee to comply with the law. It is therefore not unlikely that the information provided by the trustee as to how and for what purpose it processes the trustor's data corresponds to reality. And therefore the expectations that the trustor has with regard to the processing of 'his' data by the trustee on the basis of the information provided to him can justifiably be described as 'reasonable'.

[58] See on potentials of the 'trust approach' to further regulate the privacy problem (II.C.).

[59] This principle of purpose limitation is eg, enshrined in art 5(1) lit. b) GDPR.

[60] See, eg, art 32 GDPR, which requires the data processor to 'implement appropriate technical and organisational measures to ensure a level of (data) security appropriate to the risk' of the data procession.

[61] Waldman (n 14) 62. This observation, the privacy has a trust-generating function, has already been made eg, by Fried (n 11) 475, 477 ff.

[62] See on this in particular Eichenhofer, *e-Privacy* (n 14) 171 ff, 299, 429 ff.

[63] See, eg, art 13 ff GDPR.

[64] The GDPR, for example, provides for violations of privacy norms significant sanctions (art 84), fines (art 83) and an obligation to pay damages (art 82), these rules are a considerable incentive for ISPs to comply with privacy norms and thus not to betray the trust of individuals.

All in all, it can therefore be said: the 'privacy as trust' approach has both a descriptive and an analytical value. By adopting a relational perspective, it becomes visible that privacy law takes on a new form in the relationship between users and ISPs, but that it can safeguard the usual functions of privacy protection just as well as the control approach. The main instrument of privacy protection is privacy norms. It is therefore a matter of safeguarding legitimate expectations of compliance with privacy norms. These assign specific roles (data subject, controller, processor, etc) to the legal entities involved, which are associated with certain rights and obligations and expectations.[65] In this respect, adopting the perspective of trust initially serves to view the applicable law in a new light.

## C. How does 'Trust' Help to *Regulate* the Problem?

But can the 'trust perspective' also be used to further develop existing privacy law? There are various conceivable approaches here. One possibility would be to subject ISPs and third parties to even stricter rules. These could then, if they were known to users, help to 'encourage and fortify information relationships'.[66]

A consequent advancement of ISPs' duty program on the one hand and a reinforcement of users' trust on the other hand would be to consistently assign the ISPs the role of 'fiduciaries'.[67] The fiduciary law 'focuses on a few special relationships that are based on trust and confidence. A client puts his trust in a fiduciary, and the fiduciary has an obligation not to betray that trust. She must act in her client's interests, not in a way that harms him.'[68] In this way, fiduciary law refers precisely to the asymmetries and vulnerabilities[69] that we identified above for the relationship between users and ISPs. Accordingly, fiduciaries 'owe duties of loyalty to those that rely on them'.[70] In our case, ISPs would then have to be regarded as fiduciaries for the data that users have entrusted to them.[71]

Consequently, Neil Richards and Woodrow Hartzog have also proposed for US law that the principles of 'Confidentiality', 'Transparency', and 'Security' of the Fair Information Principles should be supplemented by the principles of 'Discretion', 'Honesty', and 'Protection' or an overriding principle of 'Loyalty'.[72] This principle of loyalty is intended to have a gradual effect: 'Where there is greater trust (or greater potential for exposure), entrustees should be held to higher duties of care and loyalty.'[73] Similarly, John Balkin and Jonathan Zittrain suggest 'to adapt old legal ideas to create a new kind of law – one that clearly states the kinds of duties that online firms owe their

[65] Very similar: Waldman (n 14) 67.
[66] Richards and Hartzog (n 14) 431, 434.
[67] K Brennan-Marquez 'Fourth Amendment Fiduciaries' (2015) 84 *Fordham Law Review* 61; JM Balkin, 'Information Fiduciaries and the First Amendment' (2016) 49 *U. C. Davis Law Review* 1183; Richards and Hartzog (n 14) 431, 457, 458; Waldman (n 14) 67, 85 ff.
[68] Waldman (n 14) 85.
[69] Balkin (n 67) 1183, 1215.
[70] Waldman (n 14) 67.
[71] ibid 85.
[72] Richards and Hartzog (n 14) 431, 458.
[73] ibid.

end users and customers'.[74] What fiduciaries instead should never be allowed to do is to act like 'con men', ie, to use the users' data 'in unexpected ways [...] that violate some other important social norm'.[75]

In Europe, on the other hand, an extensive level of data protection already exists in the form of the GDPR and various sector-specific regulations at both the EU and the domestic level. Also to mention in this regard is the EU Digital Services Act[76] (DSA), which intends to regulate 'systematic risks' of digital intermediary systems or 'platforms' (such as social networks) for users and competitors and which, according to its article 1, is intended to help create a 'trustworthy online environment'. Finally, the famous AI Act[77] (AIA), potentially the most advanced regulation on the use of AI worldwide, has been fundamentally founded on a concept called 'trustworthy AI', which shall be observed closer now.

# III. Trust and AI Regulation

## A. Why Speak of 'Trust' in AI Regulation?

As we have seen (I.E., II.A.), trust always becomes relevant when one person (the 'trustor') knows little about another person (the 'trustee') with whom the trustor nevertheless has a social relationship that allows the trustee to influence the trustor's interests or rights. This description applies not only to privacy law, insofar as it regulates the processing of data, but also to the (still relatively unregulated) use of AI. Given the high complexity of this technology, the trust problem becomes even more crucial than in 'traditional' privacy law, ie, the laws on the digital procession of personal data (II.B.), as it enhances the user's knowledge deficit once again. Especially with new AI technologies such as self-learning algorithms, it is often impossible even for experts to predict the outcome of an algorithm-driven decision. Much has been written in legal literature about this 'lack of transparency'.[78] Herein lies a major problem for the law, as it is dependent on identifying causalities and accountabilities in order to impose certain legal consequences (eg, liability or criminal liability). If the state uses an AI, another problem arises: the lack of transparency of the algorithms means that state action becomes as unpredictable as it is inexplicable or unjustifiable – an unacceptable situation for a constitutional state.[79] In other words, the use of AI carries considerable risks – not only for those who are affected by an algorithm-based decision, but also for those who use AI, since they run the risk of violating fundamental legal principles of constitutional and administrative

[74] JM Balkin and J Zittrain, 'Grand Bargain to Make Tech Companies Trustworthy' (2016) *The Atlantic* (3 Oct 2016).

[75] Balkin (n 67) 1183.

[76] Regulation (EU) 2022/2065 of the European Parliament and of the Council of 19 October 2022 on a Single Market For Digital Services and amending Directive 2000/31/EC (Digital Services Act).

[77] Regulation (EU) 2024/1689 of the European Parliament and of the Council of 13 June 2024 laying down harmonised rules on artificial intelligence and amending Regulations (EC) (Artificial Intelligence Act) [2014] OJ L2024/1689.

[78] See only T Wischmeyer, 'Artificial Intelligence and Transparency: Opening the Black Box' in T Wischmeyer and T Rademacher (eds), *Regulating Artificial Intelligence* (Berlin, Springer, 2019) 75.

[79] On this problem again eg, Wischmeyer ibid 75.

law. Nevertheless, the relationships shaped by the use of AI technologies can also be described as asymmetrical, as in the aforementioned relations, as the 'provider'[80] of the AI still has comparatively more knowledge about the functionality and, above all, the specific application scenarios than the affected individual.

On the other hand, AI undoubtedly has the potential to solve numerous problems. Not only can it satisfy numerous individual needs, but it can also help with the execution of public tasks insofar as they require the processing of huge amounts of data. Therefore, there is also a certain need to allow the use of AI systems for certain purposes and to a certain extent. And this is where trust comes into play: 'As digital technology becomes an ever more central part of every aspect of people's lives', the EU Commission denotes in its 2020 White Paper on Artificial Intelligence, 'people should be able to trust it.'[81] And to ensure that this 'trust' the EU Commission refers to is not 'blind' but 'reasonable', the EU Commission has decided to subject the use of AI under a general and comprehensive regulatory regime – which later turned into the AI Act. We can hence observe a new example of the familiar regulatory approach: *trust protection through regulation.*

Remarkably, this approach has decisively shaped the entire legislative process of the AI Act. This begins with its very first origins, which date back to 2018. On 7 December of this year, the EU Commission, Council and Parliament presented a Coordinated Plan[82] to implement the AI Strategy[83] adopted around eight months earlier, which provides, among other things, for the establishment of a High Level Expert Group. This group presented its final report[84] on 8 April 2019. It bears the promising title: 'Ethics Guidelines for Trustworthy AI'. Now what is meant by that expression? 'Trustworthy AI', the Report states,

> is the right way to build a future with AI. A future where democracy, the rule of law and fundamental rights underpin AI systems and where such systems continuously improve and defend democratic culture will also enable an environment where innovation and responsible competitiveness can thrive. (…) We believe in an approach to AI ethics based on the fundamental rights enshrined in the EU Treaties, the EU Charter and international human rights law.[85]

The High Level Expert Group therefore proposes to generate trust through a regulation that takes as its starting point the fundamental values, principles, and rights that have always characterised the legal order of the EU and its Member States. Of course, this is particularly plausible from the perspective of trust, as it is precisely the most fundamental rules that guide action. However, this proposal is of course associated with an enormous 'abstraction gap' which, in the opinion of the High Level Group, has to be established in three subsequent steps: (1) based on the human rights laid down

[80] This expression is defined in art 3(3) AI Act: 'a natural or legal person, public authority, agency or other body that develops an AI system or a general-purpose AI model or that has an AI system or a general-purpose AI model developed and places it on the market or puts the AI system into service under its own name or trademark, whether for payment or free of charge'.

[81] European Commission, White Paper on Artificial Intelligence – A European approach to excellence and trust [2020] COM (2020) 65 final, 1.

[82] European Commission, Coordinated Plan on Artificial Intelligence [2018] COM (2018) 795 final.

[83] European Commission, Artificial Intelligence for Europe [2018] COM 2018 (237) final.

[84] Independent High Level Group of Artificial Intelligence, Ethic Guidelines for Trustworthy AI (European Commission, 2019).

[85] ibid 9.

in the Charter of Fundamental Rights of the European Union (CFR), the High Level Expert Group has (2) developed four ethical principles for the development and use of AI (namely respect for human autonomy, prevention of harm, fairness, and explicability), which (3) are reflected in seven technical and organisational specifications (namely human agency and oversight, technical robustness and safety, privacy and data governance, transparency, diversity, non-discrimination and fairness, environmental and societal well-being and accountability),[86] which should bring the values and rights of the CFR into the AI laboratories. It was precisely this concept of 'Trustworthy AI'[87] that the EU Commission referred to when it presented its proposal for an AI Regulation in 2021, which states, among other things: 'This proposal aims to implement the … objective for the development of an ecosystem of trust by proposing a legal framework for trustworthy AI.'[88] Moreover, the actual text of the AI Act, which finally came into force on 12 July 2024, makes reference to the concept in various places. According to recital 2, the aim of the act consists of 'making the Union a leader in the uptake of "trustworthy AI"'. And Recital 176 points out this conception in more detail:

> Since the objective of this Regulation, namely to improve the functioning of the internal market and to promote the uptake of human centric and trustworthy AI, while ensuring a high level of protection of health, safety, fundamental rights enshrined in the Charter, including democracy, the rule of law and environmental protection against harmful effects of AI systems in the Union and supporting innovation, cannot be sufficiently achieved by the Member States and can rather, by reason of the scale or effects of the action, be better achieved at Union level, the Union may adopt measures in accordance with the principle of subsidiarity as set out in Article 5 TEU.

And ultimately, the conception even made it to the most prominent article 1 of the Act, which describes the goal of the whole Regulation as follows:

> The purpose of this Regulation is to improve the functioning of the internal market and promote the uptake of human-centric and trustworthy artificial intelligence (AI), while ensuring a high level of protection of health, safety, fundamental rights enshrined in the Charter, including democracy, the rule of law and environmental protection, against the harmful effects of AI systems in the Union and supporting innovation.

## B. How does 'Trust' Help to *Understand* the Problem?

The idea of trust does indeed appear to be a well-founded guiding regulatory axiom for European AI regulation. This is because it refers to the basic social problem described

[86] ibid 2: 'Trustworthy AI has *three components*, which should be met throughout the system's entire life cycle: (1) it should be *lawful*, complying with all applicable laws and regulations (2) it should be *ethical*, ensuring adherence to ethical principles and values and (3) it should be *robust*, both from a *technical* and *social perspective* since, even with good intentions, AI systems can cause unintentional harm. Each component in itself is necessary but not sufficient for the achievement of Trustworthy AI. Ideally, all three components work in harmony and overlap in their operation.' (Emphasis added)

[87] See for this conception eg, J Laux and S Wachter and B Mittelstadt, 'Trustworthy Artificial Intelligence and the European Union AI Act: On the Conflation of Trustworthiness and the Acceptability of Risk' in *Regulation & Governance* (Hoboken, Wiley, 2023) (www.doi.org/10.1111/rego.12512); J Eichenhofer, 'Trustworthy AI and Fundamental Rights' (2024) 36 *European Review of Public Law* 147.

[88] European Commission, Proposal for an AI Regulation [2021] COM (2021) 206 final, 1.

above (III.A.), which also characterises the relationship between the AI 'provider' and the individual concerned. The AI Act is intended to protect the fundamental rights and interests of individuals from the risks associated with the (unregulated) use of AI. At the same time, the AI Act assigns central roles to the persons involved in this relationship, especially on the 'user side' (eg, the 'provider' and 'deployer'[89]), which in turn are associated with certain obligations, which will now be discussed.

## C. How does 'Trust' Help to *Regulate* the Problem?

At its core, the regulatory model of the AI Act is based on a 'proportionate risk-based approach', which 'sets harmonised rules for the development, placement on the market and use of AI systems in the Union'.[90] Distinguishing between 'unacceptable', 'high', or 'lower risk', the development and use of AI systems is either banned or permitted under high requirements or under the condition to fulfil specific transparency obligations.[91] This differentiation – which is often outlined in the form of a 'risk pyramid' with the colours of a traffic light[92] – is so catchy and informative that the highly complex regulatory model can be quickly understood even by laypersons. They can be confident that only those AI systems that no longer pose any unacceptable risks are in use. Any lower risk levels must be pointed out to the users by means of appropriate information. The AI Act hence succeeds in pursuing two goals at the same time: on the one hand, it intends to protect the individual's fundamental rights, while at the same time promoting the uptake of the technology.[93]

# IV. Conclusion

The 'trust paradigm' is an attempt, initially inspired by legal theory, to translate privacy into new dogmatic categories. In essence, it involves a shift from an 'individual' perspective focused on the individual and their individual rights to a *relational* perspective,[94] which makes it possible to better identify the interests at stake, as it can take many circumstances of the individual case into account. This approach is particularly recommended in the digital world. It shows that individuals hardly have any opportunities to assert their privacy interests against ISPs. This makes them vulnerable to ISPs' position of power, but not unprotected. Privacy protection is granted to them by legal privacy norms.

[89] This role is defined by art 3(4) AI Act as 'a natural or legal person, public authority, agency or other body using an AI system under its authority except where the AI system is used in the course of a personal non-professional activity'.

[90] European Commission, Proposal for an AI Regulation [2021] COM (2021) 206 final, 3.

[91] See for an overview eg, J Eichenhofer (n 87) 147.

[92] See, eg, 'AI Act' (European Commission, 2024), www.digital-strategy.ec.europa.eu/en/policies/regulatory-framework-ai.

[93] European Commission, p 1 and Recital 81. Laux and Wachter and Mittelstadt (n 87) 1 speak of the 'dual purpose' of the AI Act.

[94] Nedelsky (n 13).

By controlling behaviour and therefore making it predictable, like legal norms in general, privacy norms can help to ensure that individuals, despite their dependence on ISPs and the vulnerability described above, can legitimately exercise the freedoms that the protection of privacy has always been intended to provide them with – namely, in reliance on privacy law. Admittedly, there is no guarantee that ISPs will behave in accordance with the law, just as there is no general guarantee that others will behave in accordance with the law. Nevertheless, trust can be 'reasonable' as long as the constitutional state is under the rule of law[95] and willing and able to enforce the law if necessary. It is therefore fair to say to all users: 'Trust in privacy law'.

[95] On the connection between trust and the rule of law, eg, A von Bogdandy, *Strukturwandel des Öffentlichen Rechts* (Berlin, Suhrkamp, 2022), C. Das Prinzip Rechtsstaatlichkeit, § 31 Vertrauen als Fluchtpunkt.

# 11

# Beyond Digital Pessimism: How a Focus on Trust Can Enhance EU Digital Law

NEIL RICHARDS, WOODROW HARTZOG, CLAIRE BOINE AND LEA DESPOTIS

## I. Introduction

Over the past decade, the European Union (EU) has enacted a series of high-profile regulations and directives aimed at governing the digital environment. From the General Data Protection Regulation (GDPR)[1] in 2016 to the Artificial Intelligence Act (AI Act)[2] in 2024, the EU Commission consistently cites trust as a foundation for consumer uptake of new technologies. In the EU Commission documents, the logic is clear: if the EU adopts laws to prevent harm and negative consequences of new technology, individuals will be more likely to embrace digital services. This, in turn, is expected to foster innovation and growth in the EU's digital market.

On its face, this premise is difficult to dispute. Trust – the willingness to accept vulnerability to the actions of others – matters; it lowers perceived risks and encourages the adoption of new platforms and services. Yet, current EU digital law is premised on avoiding negative events – such as data breaches, unlawful profiling, algorithmic discrimination, or manipulation. By emphasising risk reduction, the Commission seems to assume that trust already exists and merely needs to be protected or maintained. This chapter challenges that assumption. It argues that many consumers do not, in fact, trust companies' digital practices because companies are not honest with them. As a result, consumers (to the extent that they have a meaningful choice) refuse to adopt certain services that feel intuitively scary, and they install blockers and VPNs to prevent tracking. Rather than strengthening trust as it intends, the law's near-exclusive focus on preventing negative consequences overshadows the need to actively build and cultivate trust in the first place.

[1] Regulation (EU) 2016/679 of the European Parliament and of the Council of 27 April 2016 on the protection of natural persons with regard to the processing of personal data and on the free movement of such data, and repealing Directive 95/46/EC (General Data Protection Regulation) [2016] OJ L119/1.

[2] Regulation (EU) 2024/1689 of the European Parliament and of the Council of 13 June 2024 laying down harmonised rules on artificial intelligence and amending Regulations (EC) No 300/2008, (EU) No 167/2013, (EU) No 168/2013, (EU) 2018/858, (EU) 2018/1139 and (EU) 2019/2144 and Directives 2014/90/EU, (EU) 2016/797 and (EU) 2020/1828 (Artificial Intelligence Act) [2024] OJ L2024/1689.

This chapter contends that while EU regulators are correct in identifying trust as the backbone of a flourishing digital market, their reliance on a risk-avoidance paradigm underestimates just how fragile consumer trust really is. To bolster genuine trust, lawmakers and businesses alike must move beyond defensive strategies and adopt affirmative duties of confidentiality, transparency, security, and loyalty. Only then can the EU achieve the sustainable, trust-based digital economy it envisions.

Our argument proceeds in two parts. In Part II, 'The EU's trust preservation strategy', we examine the EU's current approach to maintaining consumer trust in digital products through three key mechanisms. We begin by analysing the EU's data privacy express consent framework, which requires companies to obtain voluntary affirmative consent from users. While this approach improves upon basic notice-and-choice models, we demonstrate how it fails to address fundamental issues of user comprehension and meaningful choice, particularly given the overwhelming volume of policies users encounter. We then examine the EU's risk mitigation framework, showing how its limitations prevent it from fully addressing trust concerns. Finally, we explore the EU's attempts to regulate manipulative practices, revealing how these well-intentioned regulations fall short of their trust-building goals.

In Part III, 'From prevention to production: building trust through a principle-based approach', we argue that merely preventing negative outcomes is insufficient to build meaningful consumer trust. Trust is not simply the absence of harm but a positive expectation of fair and ethical treatment in the face of one's own vulnerabilities. It requires recognising that individuals do not engage with digital services based solely on the elimination of risks or rational actor trade-offs, but also on the presence of affirmatively trustworthy practices. Trust has a normative dimension – it reflects the moral and social expectation that companies will act with integrity, honesty, fairness, and respect for users' interests, rather than merely avoiding regulatory violations. Without this affirmative commitment, trust remains fragile, as consumers may perceive compliance as a legal necessity rather than a genuine commitment to their well-being. To strengthen trust in the EU digital ecosystem, we propose that European data protection law could be strengthened by incorporating additional principles. We examine four key principles: confidentiality reconceptualised as *discretion*, transparency understood as *honesty*, security reframed as *protection*, and the introduction of substantive *loyalty* obligations. For each principle, we analyse current EU legal frameworks, identify their limitations, and demonstrate how these concepts could enhance their effectiveness. We pay particular attention to loyalty, exploring its roots in US law and demonstrating its potential application in European digital regulation. We conclude by offering a roadmap for incorporating these trust-building elements into EU digital law, creating a framework that not only prevents trust erosion but actively cultivates it.

## II. The EU's Trust Preservation Strategy

In the past decade, the EU has embarked on an ambitious regulatory agenda to try to keep pace with the digital transformation. Among the many relevant regulations and directives, the GDPR, the Digital Services Act (DSA),[3] and the AI Act stand out as particularly groundbreaking. The EU's authority to legislate in the digital realm stems from two core responsibilities: safeguarding fundamental rights and ensuring the proper functioning of the internal market. These responsibilities are anchored, respectively, in the European Charter of Fundamental Rights and article 114 of the Treaty on the Functioning of the European Union.

Yet when we examine the official reasoning set forth by the European Commission to justify these measures, a common theme emerges. The Commission consistently argues that if the EU fails to regulate the risks to safety and fundamental rights posed by digital technologies – and those risks subsequently materialise – consumers will lose trust in new technologies. This erosion of trust, the Commission contends, will slow adoption rates and ultimately undermine Europe's economic competitiveness.

For instance, recital 7 of the GDPR explicitly states that '[t]hose developments require a strong and more coherent data protection framework in the Union, backed by strong enforcement, given the importance of creating the trust that will allow the digital economy to develop across the internal market'. Likewise, the impact assessment accompanying the AI Act warns that 'mistrust in AI would slow down AI development in Europe and reduce the global competitiveness of the EU econom[ie]s'.[4] It further suggests that a horizontal legislative instrument (ie, one that regulates the relationships among people and companies) would 'help citizens and companies build trust in the AI technology placed on the Union market'.[5] Similarly, the Digital Services Act declares that its 'obligations should aim in particular to guarantee different public policy objectives such as the safety and trust of the recipients of the service'.[6] It also states that '[t]he misuse of online platforms by frequently providing manifestly illegal content or by frequently submitting manifestly unfounded notices or complaints under the mechanisms and systems, respectively, established under this Regulation undermines trust'.[7]

This same argument was reinforced in the Commission's recent Fitness Check of EU consumer law on digital fairness.[8] Citing a survey of 10,000 consumers across ten different countries, the Commission's report documented consumers' apprehensions about how their data is used or shared, profiling practices, the installation of cookies, and the difficulty in distinguishing between genuine information and advertising.[9] Most importantly, it found that concerns about personal data discouraged online purchases. It is clear that consumers perceived level of trust influences their online behaviour – and thus can have a detrimental effect on businesses.

[3] Regulation (EU) 2022/2065 of the European Parliament and of the Council of 19 October 2022 on a Single Market For Digital Services and amending Directive 2000/31/EC (Digital Services Act) [2022] OJ L277.

[4] Annexes Commission Staff Working Document Impact Assessment Accompanying the Proposal for a Regulation of the European Parliament and of the Council Laying Down Harmonised Rules on Artificial Intelligence (Artificial Intelligence Act) and Amending Certain Union Legislative Acts [2021] SWD/2021/84.

[5] ibid.

[6] Regulation (EU) 2022/2065 of the European Parliament and of the Council of 19 October 2022 on a Single Market For Digital Services and amending Directive 2000/31/EC (Digital Services Act) [2022] OJ L277.

[7] ibid.

[8] European Commission, 'Fitness Check of EU Consumer Law on Digital Fairness' (03.10.2024) ec.europa.eu/info/law/better-regulation/have-your-say/initiatives/13413-Digital-fairness-fitness-check-on-EU-consumer-law.

[9] ibid.

Substantial evidence supports the proposition that distrust is detrimental to business. Without trust, people may be spooked when advertising aligns too closely with their interests or when they are asked to divulge too much or too sensitive information, driving them away from the company behind the product. Even when consumers continue to engage with the product, lack of trust can lead consumers to engage in behaviours that are harmful for businesses. In other work, we have argued that consumer efforts at self-help, such as obfuscation or data sabotage, are often caused by distrust.[10] European scholars echo similar themes. For example, Fox et al. suggest that 'consumers' perception of privacy online can lead to negative outcomes for organisations such as consumers spreading negative word of mouth, falsifying data disclosed, reduced purchasing intentions, reactance to personalised advertising, and negative stock returns.[11] For those companies whose business models rely on data collection, consumers' willingness to provide incomplete or false information when signing up for a service can be particularly detrimental. In a study of online behaviours in Spain, Sáez-Ortuño et al. showed that users frequently lied when asked to disclose personal data for three main reasons: 1) for their personal amusement; 2) because of a lack of trust in the company and how it will use their data; 3) because they felt that their privacy was being violated and they were being asked too much information.[12] A lack of trust potentially introduces a host of issues, showing it is especially important that consumers feel that they can depend on companies to act in a trustworthy way.

In previous work, we argued that the field of data privacy suffers from a counterproductive ailment: privacy pessimism.[13] Data privacy has focused so much on avoiding harm and negative consequences that it has not been built to promote trust and other positive outcomes. In this section, we make the broader point that EU digital law has been framed in a similarly pessimistic way, which, in turn, has led to the exact loss of trust that lawmakers wish to avoid. We will call this broader irony 'digital pessimism'. We show how this pessimism is pervasive through the European express consent framework, through its focus on risk mitigation, and through its concerns about the avoidance of manipulation.

## A. Consent as a Defensive Mechanism

Over the past decade, the EU's shift toward an express consent framework has been widely celebrated as a clear improvement over the traditional US notice-and-choice model.[14] Under the US approach, companies typically notify users about existing data collection practices and then leave them with a binary choice – to either accept

[10] NM Richards and W Hartzog, 'Privacy's Trust Gap' (2017) 126 *Yale Law Journal* 1180.

[11] G Fox, T Lynn and P Rosati, 'Enhancing Consumer Perceptions of Privacy and Trust: A GDPR Label Perspective' (2022) 35 *Information Technology & People* 181.

[12] L Sáez-Ortuño et al, 'Online Cheaters: Profiles and Motivations of Internet Users Who Falsify Their Data Online' (2023) 8 *Journal of Innovation & Knowledge* 100349.

[13] N Richards and W Hartzog, 'Taking Trust Seriously in Privacy Law' (2015) 19 *Stanford Technology Law Review* 431.

[14] DJ Solove, 'Murky Consent: An Approach to the Fictions of Consent in Privacy Law' (2024) 104 *Boston University Law Review* 593.

the terms or forgo access to a service. By contrast, article 4 of the GDPR requires that consent be freely given, specific, informed, and unambiguous, ostensibly ensuring that any agreement to process personal data arises from an active and deliberate choice. Yet, despite its promise, this framework has not resolved the deeper issues inherent in securing genuine consumer consent.

At its core, the problem lies in the assumption that consent, as currently structured, can meaningfully empower individuals in the digital economy and that it can put them meaningfully 'in control' over their data and their digital lives. While the GDPR aims to strengthen user autonomy, the reality is that most consumers face an overwhelming volume of consent requests, leading to habituation, fatigue, and ultimately, disengagement. As a result, consent often becomes a mere formality rather than a genuine exercise of choice. At its worst, given the power of design over the defaults and the options given to consumers, consent-based models can offer a fiction of control that in practice allows designers to control consumers rather than the other way around.[15]

This reflects a broader issue: the EU's consent regime is embedded within a framework of digital pessimism – a regulatory stance that prioritises negative harm prevention over affirmative trust-building. In this view, privacy is narrowly conceived as a shield against potential harms, leading to defensive legal mechanisms that seek to mitigate risks rather than fostering affirmative trust. Two central myths underlie this approach. First, there is the belief that individuals are fully capable of protecting their own privacy through informed decision-making. Second, it is assumed that granting users detailed control over their personal data will, in turn, foster trust in digital companies. These assumptions – that people can manage complex data practices on their own and that control inherently builds trust – are fundamentally flawed in today's intricate digital landscape.

A critical shortcoming of the current model is what we have elsewhere called *unwitting consent*.[16] In many instances, consumers agree to terms without truly understanding what they are consenting to, including failing to understand the technologies they are using, the legal terms they are submitting to, or the risks they are assuming. The legal agreements underpinning digital services are frequently excessively lengthy, couched in confusing or overly technical language, or rendered so vague that the precise implications of data processing remain unclear. One recent study, for example, found that more than half of the participants misunderstood privacy policies.[17] Other research has found that the mere presence of a privacy policy consumers did not read caused consumers to share more data based upon a misplaced belief in its protection.[18] This failure to grasp the full scope of the agreement strips the 'informed' from 'informed consent', leaving consumers to consent by default rather than through a fully intentional decision-making process. Moreover, consumers are often unaware of the technological complexities that underlie these agreements – from the inherent insecurities of modern

[15] See N Richards, *Why Privacy Matters* (New York, Oxford University Press, 2021).

[16] N Richards and W Hartzog, 'The Pathologies of Digital Consent' (2018) 96 *Washington University Law Review* 1461.

[17] D Ibdah et al., '"Why Should I Read the Privacy Policy, I Just Need the Service": A Study on Attitudes and Perceptions Toward Privacy Policies' (2021) 9 *IEEE Access* 166465.

[18] A Acquisiti, L Brandimarte and G Loewenstein, 'Privacy and Human Behavior in the Age of Information' (2015) 347 *Science* 509, 512.

telecommunications systems to the opaque data flows generated by layered applications. Without a clear understanding of these factors, users are ill-equipped to assess the potential risks and harms that might result from their consent.[19]

The problem is compounded by the coercive context in which consent is often obtained. Rather than presenting a genuine choice, companies frequently offer 'take-it-or-leave-it' options that force consumers into a dilemma: consent to intrusive data practices or face significant service or lifestyle limitations. In fact, scholars like D'Amico have argued that consent can never be freely given to a dominant company.[20] When consumers are faced with either accepting the terms of companies like Meta or Google or social isolation and ostracisation, they have little choice but to 'consent'. Digital platforms can also leverage design features to nudge users toward consenting through manipulative interfaces and disloyal so-called 'dark patterns'.[21] For instance, in the case of cookie consent, they might emphasise a specific choice or preselect an option for the users.[22] In such environments, what appears to be an act of free choice is, in reality, a product of coercion – whether overt or subtle – that undermines the very notion of voluntary consent.

Furthermore, consent fatigue has become an endemic issue in today's digital landscape.[23] With consumers bombarded by incessant requests to agree to various terms and conditions, the act of consenting has increasingly become a routine, almost reflexive gesture rather than a considered decision. For instance, a study showed that 87 per cent of people accept privacy policies without reading them.[24] As Solove has explained, the expectation that users will carefully read and evaluate each consent request is a fiction that many companies proffer, but that does not mean it is any less of a fiction.[25] While the EU's express consent framework was designed to empower consumers and foster trust in the digital marketplace, it fails to do so. Ironically, Griffiths has shown that the pre-existing level of trust a consumer has in a company is a factor in their decision to consent or not.[26] The other important factor is a heuristic judgment about whether a consent request appears justified.[27]

Taken together, these shortcomings reveal how the express consent model not only reflects but also reinforces digital pessimism. By relying on the two myths – that individuals can safeguard their own privacy and that such 'control' naturally engenders trust – the current regime frames privacy solely as a defensive mechanism. Worse, it places consumers in a situation where they have to protect themselves against more powerful

[19] See Richards and Hartzog (n 16).

[20] AS D'Amico, 'Market Power and the GDPR: Can Consent Given to Dominant Companies Ever Be Freely Given?' (2023) 8 *European Papers* 611.

[21] See J Gunawan et al., *Dark Patterns as Disloyal Design* (2025) 100 *Indiana Law Journal* 1389.

[22] C Utz et al., '(Un)Informed Consent: Studying GDPR Consent Notices in the Field' (2019) *Proceedings of the 2019 ACM SIGSAC Conference on Computer and Communications Security* 973.

[23] ibid.

[24] 'Many people accept privacy policies without reading them, study reveals' (*The Papers*, 25.11.2020) thepaypers.com/payments-general/many-people-accept-privacy-policies-without-reading-them-study-reveals--1245901.

[25] Solove (n 14).

[26] M Griffiths, 'Consumer Acquiescence to Informed Consent: The Influence of Vulnerability, Motive, Trust and Suspicion' (2014) 13 *Journal of Customer Behaviour* 207.

[27] ibid.

entities, creating an environment of mistrust. This approach neglects the broader potential of privacy regulation to foster positive, sustainable information relationships. In an era in which digital technologies, including artificial intelligence, are increasingly pervasive and opaque, the limitations of a consent-centric model become ever more apparent. Rather than assuming that granular control will empower consumers, we must recognise that genuine trust emerges from affirmative, transparent, and accountable practices that extend far beyond a series of opt-in checkboxes and an invisible sign reading *caveat emptor*.

## B. Risk Mitigation

In modern American privacy law, the concept of harm has largely dominated how privacy has been conceptualised – tort privacy and the Fair Information Practices (FIPs) focus on preventing and remedying individual harm from invasions of privacy. While the US and EU offer vastly different regulatory approaches to data protection, the EU's GDPR also fundamentally relies on a risk-mitigation approach to processing personal data.

The definition of risk adopted by the EU Commission is 'the combination of the probability of occurrence of a hazard generating harm in a given scenario and the severity of that harm'.[28] The GDPR focuses on the risk of certain data practices negatively affecting data subjects' rights. While risk is framed exclusively in terms of fundamental rights, which is the legal basis for the GDPR, recital 75 provides insight into the nature of the harm the GDPR seeks to prevent. The GDPR is concerned with processing activities that result in 'physical, material, or non material damage'. A non-exhaustive list of these damages includes 'discrimination, identity theft or fraud, financial loss, damage to the reputation, loss of confidentiality of personal data protected by professional secrecy … unauthorised reversal of pseudonimisation or any other significant economic or social disadvantage'.

This risk-based structure is ubiquitous throughout the provisions of the GDPR; risk is mentioned over 75 times throughout the text. In articles 22 and 24, controllers must assess risk to fundamental rights in implementing appropriate technical and organisational measures. In article 25, risk evaluation is a key component of an overarching principle of the GDPR – data protection by design and default. In article 35, situations posing 'high risk' to the rights and freedoms of individuals trigger a data protection impact assessment. Processing sensitive data is one category that receives this heightened protection, justified by the possibility of distinctive harms like discrimination. Thus, a core feature of GDPR compliance rests in requiring controllers to account for risk and adopt risk-measured responses. Influenced by US tort law concepts, the GDPR also strengthens enforcement by providing a victim's right to compensation from law-breaking data processors (article 82).

[28] European Commission, 'EU General Risk Assessment Methodology: Action 5 of Multi-Annual Action Plan for the Surveillance of Products in the EU (COM(2013)76)' (16.10.2015) ec.europa.eu/docsroom/documents/17107/attachments/1/translations/en/renditions/pdf.

The GDPR's fixation on risk is mirrored in the AI Act. The first comprehensive regulation of AI, the AI Act is rooted in EU product safety law, which is exactly about preventing harm and risk mitigation. Article 1 of the EU AI Act reads:

> [T]he purpose of this Regulation is to improve the functioning of the internal market and promote the uptake of human-centric and trustworthy artificial intelligence (AI), while ensuring a high level of protection of health, safety, fundamental rights enshrined in the Charter, including democracy, the rule of law and environmental protection, against the harmful effects of AI systems in the Union and supporting innovation.

The Act then creates a tiered approach in which different safety requirements are imposed onto the different stakeholders of the AI value chain based on the estimated level of risk of the system. The entire regulatory edifice thus relies on defensive strategies against estimated risks.

While the EU offers a notably stronger data protection regime, the GDPR is too focused on types of data and how to process them, ignoring the broader issue of power disparities in information relationships. Similarly, instead of merely accounting for risk and deterring harm, AI law should promote a concept of trust as a guiding principle. Trust as an alternative framework for digital law would allow the digital economy to flourish and enable the development of long-term, sustainable information relationships that benefit all parties.

## C. Avoiding Manipulation

The EU's approach to digital manipulation further exemplifies the problems of digital pessimism and reveals a deeper tension in how European law conceptualises the agency of digital consumers. Rather than building a coherent framework for sustainable trust relationships, EU law oscillates between two extremes: treating users as fully autonomous rational actors while simultaneously viewing them as vulnerable subjects needing protection from manipulation.

Traditionally, the EU has viewed individuals as rational actors.[29] In EU consumer protection law, the 'average consumer' test is meant to determine what reasonable expectations a non-vulnerable consumer would have. Vulnerability is a characteristic that has traditionally been limited to groups such as minors and individuals with a disability. This view has been reinforced by the consent model of the GDPR and further reaffirmed in the AI Act that initially focused on 'subliminal techniques' that would escape reason by bypassing rational cognition.

At the same time, the EU has increasingly recognised the manipulative nature of certain digital technologies. At first, the definition of advertising was expanded to recognise that in the digital era, advertising has become diffuse and pervasive and has taken on new forms in new media. Early EU jurisprudence defined advertising purely in informational terms – the Court of Justice held in 1993 that 'advertising consists in the dissemination of a message intended to inform consumers of the existence and qualities of a product or service'.[30] Yet by 2006, the definition had shifted dramatically

[29] C Boine, 'The AI Manipulation Gap' (2025) 39 *Emory International Law Review*.
[30] Case 68/92 *Commission of the European Communities v French Republic* ECLI:EU:C:1993:888.

to encompass any 'representation in any form' made to promote goods or services.[31] This shift acknowledges the reality that digital commercial practices involve more than just rational information exchange but are acts of persuasion that frequently involve dimensions of vulnerability and risks of manipulation.

Recent European regulation directly addresses manipulative practices. Article 25 of the Digital Services Act (DSA) directly addresses dark patterns and prohibits providers of online platforms from

> design[ing], organis[ing] or operat[ing] their online interfaces in a way that deceives or manipulates the recipients of their service or in a way that otherwise materially distorts or impairs the ability of the recipients of their service to make free and informed decisions.

Along the same lines, the AI Act prohibits

> the placing on the market, the putting into service or the use of an AI system that deploys subliminal techniques beyond a person's consciousness or purposefully manipulative or deceptive techniques, with the objective, or the effect of materially distorting the behaviour of a person or a group of persons by appreciably impairing their ability to make an informed decision, thereby causing them to take a decision that they would not have otherwise taken in a manner that causes or is reasonably likely to cause that person, another person or group of persons significant harm.

While these provisions appear comprehensive at first glance, they reveal the limitations of digital pessimism's defensive posture. The Act's requirements that manipulation 'appreciably impair' informed decision-making and cause 'significant harm' reflect an underlying assumption that users are generally rational actors whose autonomy is only compromised in extreme cases. This harm-based, defensive approach fails to recognise how manipulation can operate more subtly through information asymmetries, power imbalances, and the power of design and default-setting.

The Commission Staff Working Document Accompanying the Artificial Intelligence Act illustrates the flawed reasoning behind informed consent and transparency requirements. It states:

> Other manipulative and exploitative practices enabled by algorithms that are usually identified as harmful (e.g., exploitative profiling and micro-targeting of voters and consumers) were considered as potential candidates for prohibition but discarded, since these problems have been specifically examined and targeted by the recent proposal for the Digital Services Act. To a large extent, they are also already addressed by existing Union legislation on data protection and consumer protection that impose obligations for transparency, informed consent/opt out and prohibit unfair commercial practices, thus guaranteeing the free will and choice of people when AI systems are used.

As this reasoning reveals, the Commission treats consent and transparency as sufficient safeguards against manipulation, assuming that individuals – when provided with the right disclosures and opt-out mechanisms – can freely exercise their will and avoid manipulative influences. However, this perspective overlooks the reality that consent is often a formalistic exercise rather than a meaningful choice, especially in environments

[31] Directive 2006/114/EC of the European Parliament and of the Council of 12 December 2006 concerning misleading and comparative advertising [2006] OJ L376 21–27, art 2.

where users lack real alternatives, face cognitive overload, or are subject to the very algorithmic persuasion that regulations claim to mitigate.[32]

While the EU seems to assume that users have free will and can meaningfully consent, its evolving concept of vulnerability creates a contradiction. On the one hand, EU law assumes that individuals are generally rational actors whose autonomy is only compromised in extreme cases. On the other hand, the Commission acknowledges that consumers can be highly susceptible to digital manipulation. While the AI Act treats vulnerability as an inherent characteristic of certain groups, more recent guidance on how to interpret the Unfair Commercial Practices Directive recognises that vulnerability can be situational – that any consumer might be 'particularly susceptible to personalised persuasion practices in the digital environment'.[33] This more nuanced understanding acknowledges that manipulation cannot be addressed simply by protecting specific vulnerable populations while leaving rational actors to fend for themselves. Though while it is more nuanced and grounded in actual practice, this guidance is not legally binding as a technical matter.

Taken together, these measures show that the EU framework persists in leaving people to fend for themselves through consent mechanisms and an expectation of rational choice, while recognising that they can be manipulated by deceptive digital design. These regulatory tensions ultimately undermine the EU's ability to foster genuine trust in digital systems. EU law creates uncertainty about when and how users will be protected from manipulation. The focus on harm and vulnerability reflects the broader problem of digital pessimism – assuming that trust can be maintained simply by preventing worst-case scenarios rather than actively cultivating it. When consumers cannot predict whether they will be treated as rational actors or vulnerable humans, they are less likely to develop the stable expectations necessary for genuine trust relationships.

A more effective approach would move beyond this defensive posture toward a framework built around active trust-building. Rather than focusing narrowly on subliminal techniques or specific vulnerable groups, EU law should recognise that all users require protection through flexible principles that are suitable to relationships with significant imbalances of power. Put another way, we are all vulnerable to the vast power wielded by the designers and deployers of digital technologies. As we demonstrate in Part III, principles of discretion, honesty, protection, and loyalty offer a path toward building the kind of sustainable trust that digital relationships require.

## III. From Prevention to Protection: Building Trust Through a Principle-Based Approach

In the late 1990s, as e-commerce began to emerge, many consumers refused to make online purchases because they were afraid of giving away their credit card information.[34]

[32] See Richards and Hartzog (n 16).

[33] Commission Notice – Guidance on the Interpretation and Application of Directive 2005/29/EC of the European Parliament and of the Council Concerning Unfair Business-to-Consumer Commercial Practices in the Internal Market [2021] OJ C526/01.

[34] 'Many Still Fear Using Their Credit Cards on Web' (*Chicago Tribune*, 08.12.1996) www.chicagotribune.com/1996/12/08/many-still-fear-using-their-credit-cards-on-web/.

A 2004 survey by Forrester Research found that 61 per cent of online consumers were still hesitant to provide their credit card information online due to concerns over privacy and security.[35] These fears were, in many ways, rational – why should anyone trust sending their financial details into the digital void? Yet today, global e-commerce sales exceed $6 trillion annually, with billions of people routinely making online purchases from their mobile devices.[36] This transformation did not happen by accident or by the mere passage of time – it required the active construction of trust with online shoppers.

Today's digital ecosystem faces a similar crisis of trust, but on a far grander scale. Companies engage in an endless game of whack-a-mole with regulators, seeking ways to extract maximum data while maintaining minimal compliance. Policymakers respond by framing digital law primarily as a shield against corporate misconduct – a litany of 'thou shalt nots' that might seem to treat every 'innovation' as a potential threat. This dynamic creates an atmosphere of mutual suspicion that undermines the very trust necessary for digital relationships to flourish. In fact, evidence shows that the GDPR failed to increase consumer trust as the European Commission was hoping.[37] Just as trust in human relationships is built over time through shared positive experiences, so is trust between companies and consumers.

The FIPS, which have profoundly influenced EU data protection law, including the GDPR, attempted to address these challenges through the establishment of binding principles of ethical data processing. The FIPs emerged in the 1970s as a framework for managing the collection and use of personal data, establishing principles like notice, choice, access, and security that remain foundational to privacy law worldwide. Yet while the FIPs provide important procedural protections, they have often been reduced to a compliance checklist that has failed to build meaningful trust.

We propose reimagining three core elements of the FIPs – confidentiality, transparency, and security – as the more robust, trust-building principles of *discretion*, *honesty*, and *protection*. To these three, we add a fourth principle drawn from fiduciary law: *loyalty*. While fiduciary obligations are most developed in common law jurisdictions, their underlying logic of managing asymmetric power relationships through trust-building duties offers valuable lessons for EU digital law. These four principles should be implemented flexibly, following the model of principle-based regulation seen in frameworks like the Unfair Commercial Practices Directive (UCPD). Unlike highly prescriptive approaches that detail exact compliance requirements, principle-based regulation provides judges and regulators room to adapt standards to changing circumstances while maintaining consistent underlying values. While the GDPR includes what it terms 'principles', these function more as specific rules with detailed compliance obligations rather than true guiding principles that can evolve through interpretation.

A more flexible, principle-based approach built around discretion, honesty, protection, and loyalty would enable EU digital law to move beyond mere harm prevention toward actively fostering the trust necessary for sustainable digital relationships.

[35] 'Survey Information: Americans Care Deeply About Their Privacy' (*Center for Democracy and Technology*, 22.10.2009) cdt.org/insights/survey-information-americans-care-deeply-about-their-privacy/.

[36] Y Lin, 'Global Ecommerce Sales Growth Report' (*Shopify*, 20.10.2024) www.shopify.com/blog/global-ecommerce-sales.

[37] PC Bauer et al., 'Did the GDPR Increase Trust in Data Collectors? Evidence from Observational and Experimental Data' (2022) 25 *Information, Communication & Society* 2101.

Rather than treating every interaction as a potential threat to be controlled, this framework recognises that trust must be actively constructed through institutions and practices that show all participants in the digital economy that their interests are in fact aligned.

In the sections that follow, we examine how each of these principles can be understood and implemented to build, rather than simply defend, trust in digital relationships. While drawn partially from US legal concepts, these principles offer valuable guidance for evolving EU digital law beyond its current defensive posture toward a more constructive vision of trust-building governance.

## A. Confidentiality as Discretion

Having identified the limitations of the EU's defensive approach to digital regulation, we now turn to how principles drawn from information relationships and fiduciary law can provide a more constructive framework. These principles move beyond merely preventing harm to actively fostering the conditions necessary for trust. While the EU assumes that trust can be preserved through defensive measures, trust is not merely the absence of harm – at its best it can also be a positive expectation of ethical treatment such that the trusting party knows that their interests are being put first. Just as trust in personal and professional relationships is built through consistent, responsible behaviour, digital trust must be actively cultivated through affirmative obligations that align the interests of all parties in digital interactions and protect against vulnerabilities. A useful analogy comes from the financial sector: individuals trust banks not just because fraud is illegal, but because banks take proactive steps to safeguard assets, provide insurance protections, and implement security measures that go beyond regulatory requirements. Similarly, trust in digital services requires more than compliance – it requires visible, meaningful commitments to discretion, honesty, protection, and loyalty.

While EU law does not provide a single definition of confidentiality, it is generally understood to consist in the protection of information against unauthorised access or disclosure. Among the principles relating to the processing of personal data expressed in article 5 of the GDPR, one is called 'integrity and confidentiality'. It mandates that data be 'processed in a manner that ensures appropriate security of the personal data, including protection against unauthorised or unlawful processing and against accidental loss, destruction or damage, using appropriate technical or organisational measures'. Confidentiality in the GDPR is almost reduced to cybersecurity – focusing on preventing breaches rather than fostering responsible stewardship of information.

This framing misses an important dimension of trust. Trust is not just about securing data from unauthorised access but also about avoiding lawful but undesirable practices. For example, under the GDPR's current framework, the sale of user data to third parties – including advertisers and data brokers – is permitted if it complies with disclosure and consent requirements. Yet, many users perceive this practice as a fundamental betrayal of trust, even when it adheres to legal standards. As a result, companies that rely on data-driven business models often find themselves in a paradox: they comply with transparency and consent rules, yet still face widespread consumer scepticism.

This limited view of confidentiality as nondisclosure has constrained what could otherwise be a more nuanced and effective concept. When confidentiality is viewed solely as nondisclosure, most people in information relationships are not confidants at all – they are free to share information with whomever they wish. The law is rightfully reluctant to make most recipients of information bound by a legal obligation of complete confidentiality. People need to be able to share most of the information they receive, whether they are businesses, intermediaries, or friends and acquaintances. Yet people still trust recipients of personal information who are not formal confidants not to harm them with that personal information.

This assumption is flawed in the current digital landscape. First, there are countless companies that trade 'free access' to their service against the collection and sale of user data. In fact, the data broker industry is now valued at over $294 billion.[38] This issue is compounded by the emergence of chatbots and other systems that lead people to disclose more to companies because they have the illusion of a trusted one-to-one relationship.[39] What's more, companies can now infer information that users have not disclosed, aggregate it with other data, and sell it.[40] Yet, companies that adopt affirmative policies to protect consumer data are building trust with their users, which is good for their business. For instance, as users became increasingly concerned with WhatsApp's integration with Meta and its data practices, millions of users switched to Signal, attracted by its end-to-end encryption and a strict no-data-collection policy.[41]

We propose that there is a middle ground between strict confidentiality and complete freedom to share – the obligation of *discretion*. There are ways other than rigid nondisclosure that entrustees can protect trusters. They can limit to whom they disclose information, they can limit what they share with others, and they can control how they share information to preserve the trust placed in them.

Perhaps the most basic assumption people make when disclosing personal information is that the recipient will be discreet. Discretion, defined as 'the quality of behaving or speaking in such a way as to avoid causing offense or revealing private information', is an implicit part of most information relationships.[42] In informational relationships, the quickest way to betray trust is indiscretion: revealing personal information to the wrong person or in the wrong way.

[38] Mordor Intelligence, 'Data Broker Market Size & Share Analysis – Growth Trends & Forecasts (2025–2030)' (2024) www.mordorintelligence.com/industry-reports/data-broker-market.

[39] R Calo, 'Digital Market Manipulation' (2014) 82 *The George Washington International Law Review* 995; C Boine et al., 'In Love with a Corporation Without Knowing It: An Asymmetrical Relationship' in M Nørskov, J Seibt and OS Quick (eds), *Culturally Sustainable Social Robotics-Proceedings of Robophilosophy, Frontiers in Artificial Intelligence and Applications 335* (Amsterdam, IOS Press, 2020).

[40] A Solow-Niederman, 'Information Privacy and the Inference Economy' (2022) 117 *Northwestern University Law Review* 357.

[41] K O'Flaherty, 'Is It Time to Leave WhatsApp – and Is Signal the Answer?' (*The Observer*, 24.01.2021) www.theguardian.com/technology/2021/jan/24/is-it-time-to-leave-whatsapp-and-is-signal-the-answer.

[42] 'Discretion' (Oxford English Dictionaries, 2013) www.oxforddictionaries.com/us/definition/american_english/discretion.

The GDPR today already contains elements that are consonant with what we are calling discretion: its principles of purpose limitation and data minimisation. According to purpose limitation, data shall be 'collected for specified, explicit and legitimate purposes and not further processed in a manner that is incompatible with those purposes'. According to purpose minimisation, data shall be 'adequate, relevant and limited to what is necessary in relation to the purposes for which they are processed'. Our goal is not to argue that these crucial principles be eliminated. We propose discretion to ensure data processors exercise more care in what they disclose and to whom, and to offer a principle that shows the important, trust-building ways in which these otherwise isolated principles are related.

The limited view of confidentiality as mere nondisclosure has constrained what could otherwise be a more nuanced and effective concept. While the GDPR's principles of purpose limitation and data minimisation provide important procedural safeguards, they function primarily as restrictions rather than affirmative obligations. A more effective approach would reframe confidentiality as discretion – the careful judgment of how, when, and with whom information is shared.

Trust is not built through rigid prohibitions alone but through responsible decision-making. This means digital service providers should be expected not just to avoid breaches but to actively ensure that their data-sharing practices align with users' reasonable expectations and interests. Companies that adopt discretion as a guiding principle – minimising data collection, restricting third-party sharing even when consent is obtained, and ensuring that disclosures serve legitimate user interests – can foster sustainable consumer trust in ways that compliance checklists cannot. By striking a balance between necessary information flows and meaningful privacy protections, discretion provides a more effective middle ground for maintaining trust in digital relationships.

## B. Transparency as Honesty

EU digital regulations like the GDPR, DSA, and the AI Act place heavy emphasis on transparency as a tool for trust. In theory, transparency should empower consumers with information about how their data is used, how platforms operate, or how AI systems make decisions. The GDPR enshrines this in its very text – recital 58 declares that 'any information addressed to the public or to the data subject be concise, easily accessible and easy to understand, and that clear and plain language and, additionally, where appropriate, visualisation be used'. Article 12(1) of the GDPR further requires controllers to communicate with data subjects 'in a concise, transparent, intelligible and easily accessible form, using clear and plain language, in particular for any information addressed specifically to a child'. The DSA follows suit: article 14 mandates that online intermediaries include any content moderation policies in their terms of service 'clear, plain, intelligible, user-friendly and unambiguous language', and even requires very large platforms to provide a concise, easy-to-read summary of their terms. Similarly, the proposed AI Act imposes transparency duties – for example, any AI system interacting with humans, such as chatbots, must disclose that it is artificial (article 50), and users of emotion recognition or deep fake AI must inform people exposed to such systems that AI is in operation (articles 50). On paper, these provisions aim to arm users with knowledge, ostensibly to build trust in digital services.

In practice, however, these transparency obligations often fall prey to digital pessimism and an excess of formalism: long privacy policies, dense terms of service, and technical reports that satisfy legal requirements but do little to foster genuine understanding.[43] Under the GDPR's notice requirements, many companies still present users with voluminous privacy notices or cookie banners that few actually read or comprehend. Even though EU law demands clear language, the reality is that much disclosure remains inscrutable. The proliferation of information – exacerbated by fear of liability – often leads controllers to err on the side of exhaustive detail and legalese. Users are inundated with data use descriptions, tracking every conceivable processing activity, but with so much complexity that effectively no information is conveyed to the average person. Empirical critiques have long noted that mandated disclosures (particularly in large volumes) rarely achieve informed consent or understanding.[44] Transparency as practised can devolve into a box-ticking exercise, one that technically fulfils the law while practically undermining trust.

The Digital Services Act amplifies this trend on digital platforms. It requires extensive transparency reporting by intermediaries and platforms (articles 15, 24, and 42 DSA), including statistics on content removals, details on content moderation algorithms, and the resources devoted to reviewing illegal or harmful content. Article 27 of the DSA even mandates that platforms disclose 'the main parameters' of their recommender systems in 'plain and intelligible language', including why certain content is suggested and how users can influence recommendation criteria. These are laudable requirements aimed at opening up the black boxes of platform curation – ones that can certainly provide important information that NGOs, researchers, and regulators can use. However, if their goal is to inform and empower consumers, they are doomed to failure.

Indeed, the implementation of the DSA so far illustrates such limits of a purely transparency-driven approach. The first wave of DSA transparency reports from major technology companies, rather than delivering easy accountability, mostly produced massive troves of data. Ironically, instead of being consulted by users of online platform, this data has been used primarily by academic researchers to show the limits of the DSA's approach. Kosters and Gstrein note that the information published by

[43] See Richards and Hartzog (n 13).

[44] Eg, AM McDonald and LF Cranor, 'The Cost of Reading Privacy Policies' (2008) 4 *I/S: A Journal of Law and Policy for the Information Society* 543, 565; JA Obar and A Oeldorf-Hirsch, 'The Biggest Lie on the Internet: Ignoring the Privacy Policies and Terms of Service Policies of Social Networking Services' (2018) 23 *Information, Communication & Society* 1; O Ben-Shahar and CE Schneider, 'The Failure Of Mandated Disclosure' (2014) 159 *University of Pennsylvania Law Review* 647; OH Kaldestad, '250,000 Words of App Terms and Conditions' (Norwegian Consumer Council, 24.05.2016) www.forbrukerradet.no/side/250000-words-of-app-terms-and-conditions.

TikTok is often incomprehensible to users.[45] They also report issues surrounding malicious flagging, discriminatory practices, and suppression of marginalised groups in the platform's moderation practices. After analysing 353.12 million records submitted by the eight largest social media platforms in the EU during the first 100 days of the database, Trujillo et al. state that although 'submission and transparency reporting are mandatory under the DSA, so far the reliability of the data lies on the willingness and the resources of the platforms to be comprehensive and accurate in their mapping of existing moderation processes to the novel and complex norms. As we have shown this is not yet the case'.[46] Based on a similar analysis, Drolsbach and Pröllochs revealed that there exist significant differences in how large social media platforms implement their obligations under the DSA.[47] In addition, initial DSA-mandated reports led some platforms to actually contract the breadth of information in key areas – reporting fewer categories of government takedown requests than before, or grouping content removals under vague labels that obscure important details.[48] The language of these reports often remains highly technical or self-serving, reducing their value to the public. Crucially, an ordinary user would struggle to find, let alone understand, these transparency reports buried in corporate websites. The DSA also requires platforms to explain their content rules in clear terms and notify users of changes, which is a step toward clarity. But if those terms are still lengthy documents that users seldom read, the trust benefits are minimal. The pattern is familiar: formal transparency is achieved, yet substantive transparency – users honestly understanding how platforms impact them – is lacking. This continues the familiar regulatory pathology of the digital age that transparency requirements can encourage mere forms of protection at the expense of actual substance.

Continuing this trend, the EU's draft AI Act leans heavily on transparency as a safeguard for AI systems. It creates obligations for both high-risk AI providers and deployers to document and disclose information. For instance, high-risk AI systems must come with extensive instructions for use, including information about the system's capabilities, limitations, and how to interpret its outputs. The idea is that those deploying AI (eg, a hospital using an AI diagnostic tool) will know its proper context and risks, which in turn should protect end-users. For sophisticated entities, such an approach could work, but for ordinary consumers it would seem doomed to failure, yet this is precisely the strategy taken by the AI Act. For AI systems that directly interact with the public, the Act also takes a disclosure approach: a chatbot or virtual assistant must ensure that natural persons are aware that they are interacting with an AI system unless it should be obvious, and any AI-generated deepfake content must be clearly labelled as such. Such thin transparency rules do not guarantee trust. Telling someone that a video was 'AI-generated' or that a decision was made by an algorithm is only a first step. It does

[45] L Kosters and OJ Gstrein, 'TikTok and Transparency Obligations in the EU Digital Services Act (DSA) – A Scoping Review' (2024) 27 *Zeitschrift für Europarechtliche Studien* 110.

[46] A Trujillo, T Fagni and S Cresci, 'The DSA Transparency Database: Auditing Self-Reported Moderation Actions by Social Media' (2025) 9 *Proceedings of the ACM on Human-Computer Interaction*.

[47] CP Drolsbach and N Pröllochs, 'Content Moderation on Social Media in the EU: Insights From the DSA Transparency Database' (2024) *Companion Proceedings of the ACM Web Conference 2024* 939.

[48] A Zornetta, 'Is The Digital Services Act Truly A Transparency Machine?' (*Tech Policy Press*, 11.07.2024) techpolicy.press/is-the-digital-services-act-truly-a-transparency-machine.

not give meaningful information to users about whether they can trust the content of the video or the outcome of the decision. Users also need to grasp what that means for them – for example, why the AI made a certain decision, whether they can challenge it, and whether the provider has their best interests at heart. Here we encounter the same naïveté: regulators assume that if companies notify users about AI involvement, the job is done. In truth, information asymmetries and comprehension gaps persist. A loan applicant informed that an algorithm denied their application might still be left in the dark about the reasons, especially if the explanation is technical. Even in the context of a right to an explanation of individual AI decisions by high-risk systems (article 86), the explanation will not help if it consists of a complex algorithmic description or if it is buried in paperwork. Simply put, disclosure is different from understanding because it places the onus on the vulnerable consumer rather than the sophisticated and powerful processor. Transparency as currently conceived can thus devolve into a one-way data dump on the user, where companies flood users with information to avoid liability, rather than to genuinely inform them.

In the context of certain AI systems, transparency might not even be achievable. Deep learning models remain paradigmatic 'black boxes'.[49] To this day, it is not possible to know exactly why and how a deep learning model produced a certain output. In fact, foundation models still exhibit behaviours that their developers did not expect.[50] Worse, they can also exhibit deceptive and manipulative behaviours.[51]

What is missing across these regimes is an affirmative orientation toward the user's understanding and interests – honesty. If we want to build trust, being merely open or transparent in a procedural sense is insufficient; true trust requires an affirmative obligation of honesty on the part of companies. Honesty, in this sense, means not just making information available, but communicating in good faith so that users are not misled or overwhelmed. It means actively correcting misconceptions and dispelling false confidence that users might have. And it means taking on the substantive obligation of ensuring understanding over and above the mere procedural obligation of disclosure. Under a duty of honesty, the burden shifts back to the service or product provider to ensure the user actually knows what they need to know – as opposed to the current model, which places the burden on consumers to wade through complex disclosures and *caveat emptor*. In the EU context, this calls for a reconceptualisation of transparency obligations away from pessimistic, check-the-box disclosures and toward relational transparency. Rather than treating transparency as a mere compliance task ('publish x information and you're done'), regulators and companies should treat it as a communication ethic centred on honesty and trustworthiness.

The table below presents examples of transparency requirements mandated by European law and how they could be enhanced by an honesty approach.

[49] F Pasquale, *The Black Box Society: The Secret Algorithms That Control Money and Information* (Cambridge, Harvard University Press, 2016).

[50] D Ganguli et al., 'Predictability and Surprise in Large Generative Models' (2022) *Proceedings of the 2022 ACM Conference on Fairness, Accountability, and Transparency* 1747.

[51] A Meinke et al., 'Frontier Models Are Capable of In-Context Scheming' (Apollo Research, 05.12.2024) arxiv.org/abs/2412.04984; R Greenblatt et al., 'Alignment Faking in Large Language Models' (20.12.2024) arxiv.org/abs/2412.14093.

| Legal text | Article | Transparency requirements | Reference | Issue | Honesty-inspired improvement |
|---|---|---|---|---|---|
| AI Act | 49 | Registration of high-risk systems in the EU database | Before placing on the market or putting into service a high-risk AI system listed in Annex III, with the exception of high-risk AI systems referred to in point 2 of Annex III, the provider or, where applicable, the authorised representative shall register themselves and their system in the EU database referred to in article 71. | End users will probably not consult the database. | Informing users each time they encounter a high-risk system. |
| AI Act | 50(1) | Disclosing that a system is artificial | Providers shall ensure that AI systems intended to interact directly with natural persons are designed and developed in such a way that the natural persons concerned are informed that they are interacting with an AI system, unless this is obvious from the point of view of a natural person who is reasonably well-informed, observant and circumspect, taking into account the circumstances and the context of use. | Assuming that people are reasonably 'well-informed, observant and circumspect'. | Always informing users they are interacting with an AI system (in part covered by article 26(11) for high-risk systems used for decision-making). |
| AI Act | 50(4) | Labelling AI-generated content | Deployers of an AI system that generates or manipulates image, audio or video content constituting a deepfake, shall disclose that the content has been artificially generated or manipulated. | This does not necessarily say anything about whether the content is accurate or not. | Warning users if content is misleading or deceptive. |
| Digital Services Act | 26 | Disclosure of reason for specific targeting in advertising on online platforms. | Providers of online platforms that present advertisements on their online interfaces shall ensure that, for each specific advertisement presented to each individual recipient, the recipients of the service are able to identify, in a clear, concise and unambiguous manner and in real time, the following: (a) that the information is an advertisement, including through prominent markings, which might follow standards pursuant to article 44; (b) the natural or legal person on whose behalf the advertisement is presented; (c) the natural or legal person who paid for the advertisement if that person is different from the natural or legal person referred to in point (b); (d) meaningful information directly and easily accessible from the advertisement about the main parameters used to determine the recipient to whom the advertisement is presented and, where applicable, about how to change those parameters. | The criteria disclosed might serve as proxies for other individual characteristics. | Disclosure of honest reason behind algorithmic choices. |

| | | | | | |
|---|---|---|---|---|---|
| Digital Services Act | 27(1) and 27(2) | Disclosure of parameters. | Providers of online platforms that use recommender systems shall set out in their terms and conditions, in plain and intelligible language, the main parameters used in their recommender systems, as well as any options for the recipients of the service to modify or influence those main parameters. The main parameters referred to in paragraph 1 shall explain why certain information is suggested to the recipient of the service. They shall include, at least: (a) the criteria which are most significant in determining the information suggested to the recipient of the service; (b) the reasons for the relative importance of those parameters. | Users do not read terms of service. | Such information should be on the main interface (eg, 'why am I seeing this' below each post). |
| Digital Market Act | 5(9) | Disclosure of real cost of advertising and potential surcharges. | The gatekeeper shall provide each advertiser to which it supplies online advertising services, or third parties authorised by advertisers, upon the advertiser's request, with information on a daily basis free of charge, concerning each advertisement placed by the advertiser, regarding: (a) the price and fees paid by that advertiser, including any deductions and surcharges, for each of the relevant online advertising services provided by the gatekeeper, (b) the remuneration received by the publisher, including any deductions and surcharges, subject to the publisher's consent; and (c) the metrics on which each of the prices, fees and remunerations are calculated. | Transparency alone may not fully eliminate the imbalance in bargaining power or information asymmetry. Even if advertisers learn that a gatekeeper's platform is charging high fees or that only a small portion of ad spend reaches publishers, they might have no practical alternative if the gatekeeper's platform is still the only effective way to reach certain audiences. | Fair pricing scheme. |

*(continued)*

*(Continued)*

| Legal text | Article | Transparency requirements | Reference | Issue | Honesty-inspired improvement |
|---|---|---|---|---|---|
| General Data Protection Regulation | 12(1) | Disclosure of information to the data subject. | The controller shall take appropriate measures to provide any information referred to in articles 13 and 14 and any communication under articles 15 to 22 and 34 relating to processing to the data subject in a concise, transparent, intelligible and easily accessible form, using clear and plain language, in particular for any information addressed specifically to a child. The information shall be provided in writing, or by other means, including, where appropriate, by electronic means. When requested by the data subject, the information may be provided orally, provided that the identity of the data subject is proven by other means. | Users do not read terms of service. | Finding effective ways to inform users. |
| Regulation on the transparency and targeting of political advertising | 11 | Disclosure of information related to each political ad. | Political advertising publishers shall ensure that each political advertisement is made available together with the following information in a clear, salient and unambiguous way: (a) a statement that it is a political advertisement; (b) the identity of the sponsor of the political advertisement and, where applicable, the entity ultimately controlling the sponsor; (c) where applicable, the entity ultimately controlling the sponsor; applicable, the election, referendum, legislative or regulatory process to which the political advertisement is linked; (d) where applicable, a statement to the effect that the political advertisement has been subject to targeting or ad-delivery techniques; (e) a transparency notice containing the information referred to in article 12(1), or a clear indication of where it can be easily and directly retrieved. | Transparency alone is insufficient to stop deception – at best, it flags who is behind the ad but does not correct the message's honesty. | Flagging demonstrably false factual claims in political ads or empowering an independent body to fact-check and label false content. |
| Regulation on the transparency and targeting of political advertising | 11(d) | Disclosure of targeting. | (d) where applicable, a statement to the effect that the political advertisement has been subject to targeting or ad-delivery techniques | This does not tell users the meaningful reason why they are targeted with specific ads. | Disclosure of honest reason behind algorithmic choices. |

## C. Security as Protection

The EU's approach to digital security exemplifies the limitations of digital pessimism. While crucial security requirements exist across multiple regulations, they tend to be fragmented and focused primarily on preventing specific harms rather than building comprehensive protection that fosters trust. The GDPR's security requirements, the AI Act's safety provisions, and various sector-specific regulations create a patchwork of defensive measures that may prevent worst-case scenarios but fail to create the kind of robust, holistic protection necessary for sustainable trust relationships.

Article 32 of the GDPR illustrates this defensive approach. It requires controllers and processors to 'implement appropriate technical and organisational measures to ensure a level of security appropriate to the risk', including features like pseudonymisation, encryption, and regular testing. While these measures are important, they reflect a narrow view of security focused primarily on preventing unauthorised access or data breaches. This risk-based approach assumes that security can be achieved through a checklist of technical safeguards rather than through a broader commitment to protection.[52]

The AI Act similarly adopts a defensive posture toward safety, categorising AI systems based on their risk level and imposing very specific requirements. The problem with this approach is its lack of flexibility. Instead of having to achieve the goal (safety), AI operators simply must demonstrate compliance.

The EU's defensive posture is further evident in how the proposed AI Liability Directive interacts with the AI Act's safety requirements. Under article 4 of the Liability Directive, providers of high-risk AI systems can effectively shield themselves from fault-based liability by demonstrating compliance with the AI Act's requirements around data quality, transparency, and human oversight. While this creates strong incentives for compliance, it reflects the broader pattern of digital pessimism – focusing on meeting minimum safety requirements to avoid liability rather than building genuinely trustworthy systems. Companies are incentivised to treat safety as a compliance exercise rather than an opportunity to develop the kind of robust protection that builds sustainable trust. This approach assumes that trust will naturally follow from the absence of harm, rather than requiring active cultivation through positive obligations that go beyond mere compliance.

Attackers have always sought unauthorised access to personal information, from file cabinets with locks to the earliest password-protected databases. Such stores of information were traditionally maintained by 'secretaries', a profession dating to medieval times defined as 'one who is entrusted with private or secret matters; a confidant; one privy to a secret'.[53] This historical perspective reminds us that protection of sensitive information has always been about more than just technical safeguards – it requires a holistic commitment to safeguarding the interests of those who have entrusted us with their data.

[52] See DJ Solove and W Hartzog, *Breached!: Why Data Security Law Fails and How to Improve It* (New York, Oxford University Press, 2022).

[53] Richards and Hartzog (n 10).

The AI Act and the GDPR treat security as processes to adopt rather than burdens to assume. A more comprehensive approach would reconceptualise security as protection, encompassing not just technical measures but a broader duty to safeguard the interests of those who share their data or use AI systems. This means going beyond firewalls and encryption to consider how information is collected, used, shared, and protected throughout its lifecycle. This also means a higher standard of risk mitigation than that contemplated by the AI Act.

This broader concept of protection would help bridge the current gap between security and safety requirements. Rather than treating them as separate domains – with security focused on data protection and safety focused on preventing physical harm – protection provides a unified framework for safeguarding both informational and physical interests. This is particularly important as AI systems increasingly blur the line between digital and physical risks.

Protection also means more than just data security. It involves protecting the identity and sensitive attributes of individuals in stored and released data sets. For instance, when organisations release data sets, protection requires proper deidentification techniques to minimise the risk of reidentification. This is particularly important as data science advances make it increasingly possible to reidentify allegedly 'anonymised' data.[54]

Just as physical security combines technologies like door locks with legal prohibitions on burglary and assault, data protection must rely on both technical and legal safeguards. This can include contracts prohibiting reidentification attempts and requiring downstream data recipients to maintain protective measures.[55] For example, recent guidance from data protection authorities suggests that those who receive anonymised data should be contractually bound not to attempt reidentification.[56]

This more robust conception of protection acknowledges that building trust requires more than just preventing security breaches or safety incidents and is more than a checklist approach to avoiding specified harms. Instead, it requires demonstrating an ongoing commitment to safeguarding the interests of those who have entrusted us with their data and safety. By moving beyond a purely defensive approach focused on risk mitigation, protection provides a foundation for the kind of sustainable trust relationships necessary in our digital society.

## D. A Duty of Loyalty

In US and English common law, fiduciary duties arise in relationships marked by significant asymmetries in knowledge, power, and ability, where one party (the fiduciary) is entrusted to act in the best interests of another (the beneficiary). Traditional fiduciaries

[54] L Rocher and J Hendrickx, 'Estimating the Success of Re-Identifications in Incomplete Datasets Using Generative Models' (2019) 10 *Nature Communications* 1; P Ohm, 'Broken Promises of Privacy: Responding to the Surprising Failure of Anonymization' (2010) 57 *UCLA Law Review* 1701. We note that this notion of protection is also resonant with our principles of both discretion and loyalty.

[55] Richards and Hartzog (n 10).

[56] Information Commissioner's Office, *Anonymisation: Managing Data Protection Risk Code of Practice* (2012).

include professionals such as doctors, lawyers, and financial advisors. The cornerstone of fiduciary obligations is the duty of loyalty, which requires fiduciaries to act selflessly and prioritise their beneficiaries' interests over their own. The duty of loyalty encompasses several key elements: the prohibition against conflicts of interest, the requirement to avoid conflicts between different beneficiaries' interests, the obligation to not profit from the relationship without explicit consent, and the duty to act in good faith and in the beneficiary's best interests.[57]

The relationship between digital service providers and their human customers exhibits many of the characteristics that traditionally give rise to fiduciary duties. Digital platforms and AI assistants collect vast amounts of personal data and often possess significant power to influence the behaviour and decisions of data subjects. In turn, those data subjects must trust these services while having limited ability to monitor or understand their operations. Several factors make this power asymmetry particularly acute in the digital context. Many digital services have become essential for daily life, making it difficult for people to meaningfully withdraw their participation.[58] Social networks, for instance, often serve as crucial infrastructure for professional and social connections. The technical complexity of AI systems and data processing creates an unprecedented knowledge gap between service providers and users.[59] People often cannot understand how their data is being used or how algorithmic systems make decisions affecting them. Moreover, the anthropomorphising of chatbots, AI assistants, and companions can create a false sense of intimacy, leading users to share sensitive information without fully appreciating the commercial nature of these interactions.[60]

Consequently, we propose that loyalty be embedded in the design of certain digital services that collect critical data or have significant power or influence over people. The degree of loyalty required should vary based on the nature and intensity of the information relationship.[61] While not every digital service requires the stringent loyalty obligations of a doctor or lawyer, even routine commercial relationships require some baseline loyalty protections. The key is matching loyalty obligations to the level of vulnerability and trust in each relationship. Loyalty is especially critical in the context of AI systems, where traditional concepts of loyalty must evolve to encompass both company intentions and algorithmic behaviour. Companies must ensure not only that they intend to be loyal but also that that their AI systems behave in trustworthy ways aligned with the interests of the people using or being significantly affected by their systems. This requires going beyond superficial compliance to build systems that actively promote and protect human interests and human values. This is even more the case when AI systems are used in the place of a traditional human fiduciary (eg, digital mental wellness applications substituting for a therapist, financial applications substituting for a financial advisor, AI will-drafting applications, etc).

[57] PB Miller, 'A Theory of Fiduciary Liability' (2010) 56 *McGill Law Journal* 235; AS Gold, 'The Fiduciary Duty of Loyalty' in EJ Criddle, PB Miller and RH Sitkoff (eds), *The Oxford Handbook of Fiduciary Law* (New York, Oxford University Press, 2019) 383.

[58] Y Hou et al., 'Social Media Addiction: Its Impact, Mediation, and Intervention' (2019) 13 *Cyberpsychology*.

[59] R Calo, 'Digital Market Manipulation' (2014) 82 *George Washington Law Review* 995.

[60] C Boine et al. (n 39).

[61] Richards and Hartzog (n 10).

The implementation of loyalty obligations requires moving beyond risk prevention to actively promoting trust. Loyalty is about affirmative measures to build and maintain trust. This might include enhanced transparency about data practices, meaningful human control over personal information, and regular auditing of AI systems behaviour to ensure continued alignment with human interests.

Regulatory oversight must focus on substantive loyalty rather than mere procedural compliance.[62] While transparency and disclosure requirements play important roles, they must be coupled with meaningful restrictions on disloyal behaviour. This means examining whether information practices genuinely serve human interests rather than simply extracting value while maintaining technical compliance.

Even if digital law does not evolve to incorporate a principle of loyalty, organisations can voluntarily adopt loyalty-enhancing practices that build sustainable trust relationships and will be good for their business.[63] Rather than viewing loyalty obligations as constraints, companies should recognise them as opportunities to develop deeper, more valuable relationships with the people who use their services.

## IV. Conclusion

The EU's digital regulatory framework suffers from a fundamental misalignment between its goals and its methods. While the EU Commission correctly identifies trust as essential for a flourishing digital economy, its regulatory approach remains trapped in a paradigm of digital pessimism that undermines the very trust it seeks to preserve. The GDPR, DSA, and AI Act share a common flaw: they assume trust can be maintained purely through defensive measures aimed at preventing worst-case scenarios. This defensive posture manifests in three key ways: an over-reliance on express consent mechanisms that place unrealistic burdens on consumers, a narrow focus on risk mitigation that neglects the positive dimensions of trust-building, and an inconsistent approach to manipulation that leaves consumers uncertain about when and how they will be protected.

The limitations of this approach are increasingly evident. Express consent has become a reflexive and disempowering ritual rather than a meaningful choice or actual control. Risk mitigation frameworks encourage compliance rather than genuine safety. And attempts to prevent manipulation flounder because they fail to address the underlying power imbalances in digital relationships. Most troublingly, the EU's defensive strategy may actually erode trust by treating every digital interaction as a potential threat to be controlled rather than an opportunity to build sustainable relationships.

We propose reframing EU digital law around four trust-building principles drawn from information relationships and fiduciary law: discretion, honesty, protection, and loyalty. This shift from harm prevention to trust production recognises that trust requires more than just avoiding harm – it demands affirmative commitments that align the interests of all participants in the digital economy. Discretion moves beyond rigid

[62] ibid.
[63] ibid.

confidentiality requirements to embrace contextual judgment about information sharing. Honesty replaces procedural transparency with substantive candour about digital practices. Protection expands security requirements into comprehensive safeguards for consumer interests. And loyalty provides a flexible and robust framework for managing the power imbalances inherent in digital relationships.

This principle-based approach offers several advantages over the current regulatory regime. It provides flexibility to address evolving technologies while maintaining consistent values. It acknowledges that trust must be actively constructed rather than merely defended. And it creates incentives for companies to develop sustainable business models built on genuine user trust rather than data extraction and manipulation.

The stakes could not be higher. As artificial intelligence and other emerging technologies reshape the digital landscape, the EU faces a choice: double down on digital pessimism or chart a new course toward sustainable trust relationships. The current framework's focus on harm prevention, while important, is insufficient for building the kind of trust necessary for a flourishing digital society. By embracing principles of discretion, honesty, protection, and loyalty, EU digital law can move beyond defensive postures to actively cultivate the trust relationships that will define our digital future.

This transformation will not be easy. It requires reimagining fundamental concepts in privacy and digital regulation. It demands that companies reshape their business models around genuine user interests rather than mere compliance. And it calls on regulators to develop more sophisticated approaches to oversight and enforcement. But the alternative – continuing down the path of digital pessimism – risks creating an environment of perpetual suspicion that undermines both innovation and human flourishing. The time has come to move beyond simply preserving trust to actively building it through principle-based regulation that aligns the interests of all participants in our shared digital future.

# PART IV

# Data Protection as a Procedural Limitation of Public Power, and the Power to Delimit the Public and the Private

# 12

# Ominous Progression of European Constitutionalism. A Political Account of the Fundamental Right to Privacy and Data Protection

PAUL DE HERT*

## I. Introduction

Classical constitutional principles of the past, such as constitutional and legal supremacy, division of powers, checks and balances, and the integrity of the rule of law, tend to embody hierarchical and purely linear visions about the legitimacy and legality of power in constitutionalism.[1] The legitimacy of states has prominently been accounted for upon dichotomic narratives between the constitutional vs. the unconstitutional.[2] Powers in the constitutions given to a branch were 'constitutional' and ready to use as if it were crystal clear what power is and where it can be located.[3] As core doctrines underpinning contemporary constitutions – classical constitutional principles focused on power establishment rather than power management – fall short of providing a faithful account of the functioning of state power in modern societies.[4]

* The author thanks Giovanni De Gregorio (for his encouragement), Cristina Cocito (with whom earlier, a shorter piece on constitutionalism was produced), Anja Dekhuijzen, Pawel Hajduk and the editors of the book for their patience. Of course, this contribution would not have seen the light without my ongoing collaboration with Serge Gutwirth whose path of freedom has led him away from the classical rule-of-law project approaches towards a more radical understanding of power and resistance.

[1] M Cohn, *A theory of the Executive branch: Tension & Legality* (Oxford, Oxford University Press, 2021) 352. See also M Cohn, 'Tensions and Legality: Towards a Theory of the Executive Branch' (2016) 29 *Canadian Journal of Law & Jurisprudence* 321–350.

[2] The supremacy of law also embodies a vision of law as fixed, predictable, and accessible (Cohn, *A theory of the Executive branch* (n 1) 57).

[3] D Levinson. 'Looking for Power in Public Law' (2016) *Harvard Law Review* 130, 33–40. With several examples of disagreements or confusion about how power is distributed.

[4] ibid 112–128.

The 2006 paper 'Privacy, Data Protection and Law Enforcement. Opacity of the Individual and Transparency' presented a 'program' to understand new constitutional developments in Europe with regard to power management within the democratic constitutional state. The separateness of the right to privacy and the right to data protection in the EU Charter on Fundamental Rights (2000) was used as a case study of this development.

This chapter goes back to that program. It examines in more detail the differences in constitutional logic behind privacy and data protection and the distinct contributions of both rights to contemporary thinking about constitutionalism. The right to have personal data protected is a quintessential analogue of a due process safeguard that looks at how accepted power is exerted in the digital world and ensures accountability. Drawing on the distinction between privacy and data protection and between constitutional tools of opacity and transparency,[5] this contribution illustrates how privacy as a tool of opacity worked well within old constitutionalism insofar as it focused on setting the legal limits of governmental power and promoted input legitimacy. The right to data protection is more directly associated with throughput legitimacy, as it places greater focus on how to process data rather than on the question of who can process data. In principle, every actor, be it public or not, can process data, and data protection will explain how to do it. The importance of its applicability to private actor processing of data – and the power that comes with this activity – is worth stressing in a constitutional context.

This chapter is structured as follows. It incepts by briefly discussing the pillars of the old or classical constitutionalism. It looks at its limits and 'grey holes', the impact of developments such as the advent of the welfare and surveillance states, and the process of fuzzy reality. The chapter then illustrates how constitutionalism has evolved to respond to those challenges, particularly with the emergence of a new constitutionalism logic that has found primary codification in the European Charter of Fundamental Rights. Drawing on the distinction between constitutional tools of opacity and transparency, the constitutional roles of privacy (old constitutionalism) and data protection (new constitutionalism) are presented. The last sections defend a combined approach of the two legal rights and explain with van der Sloot, Nasir, and Arendt why our take on these rights and on the underlying value of freedom is political. Arendt argues that we ought to think of freedom as primarily political, as the human capacity to interrupt old, quasi-automatic processes and begin new ones. Ideally, this is what privacy and data protection should allow humans to do.

[5] P De Hert and S Gurtwirth, 'Privacy, Data Protection Law Enforcement. Opacity of the Individual & Transparency of Power' in E Claes, A Duff and S Gutwirth (eds), *Privacy and the Criminal Law* (Antwerp/Oxford, Intersentia, 2006) 61–104. The chapter was re-published as P De Hert and S Gutwirth, 'Privacy, Data Protection and Law Enforcement. Opacity of the Individual and Transparency of Power' (2021) 18 *Direito Público* 500–549.

## II. The Project of Old Constitutionalism: Balance of Powers and the Rule of Law

The project of modern constitutionalism in delineating and limiting the state's power[6] has been realised through fundamental imperatives such as the principles of separation and balance of powers and the rule of law.[7]

The first principle of separation and balance of powers sets up a system of harmonious institutional separation and balancing between the three powers of the state through mutual checks and balances.[8] Classic constitutionalism sees the executive submitting to lawmakers, the legislature deciding and exerting indirect but meaningful control over the executive, and courts ultimately controlling powers' legitimacy pursuant to the idea of law as supreme authority.[9] This tripartite system of power is often thought to translate into clear, linear, and reciprocal accountability relationships between the state's pillars (the idea of separation of powers), but from the start, constitutionalism has added a degree of overlap between the powers of the branches, forcing them to collaborate and control each other (the idea of balancing of powers).

The second principle of the rule of law complements the first and has developed over time.[10] It brings all state organs, including the legislator, under the scrutiny of the judiciary and thus opposes all attempts to rule by the arbitrary will of states (rule by law). The rule of law implies that the use of public power, including the use of the power of lawmaking, needs to be justified by law (legalism) and controlled by courts.[11] All conflicts of law can, therefore, be brought and solved before a judge. In Madisonian terms, the rule of law itself is preserved by the division and mutual monitoring of powers.

[6] Levison defines constitutionalism as 'the project of creating, allocating, and constraining state power' (Levinson (n 3) 33).

[7] These are only two out of many elements of constitutionalism. For Geer and Vildhaber, the 'constitution refers to how any entity, for example, the human body, is constructed and how it functions. In the narrowest sense, it is confined only to the fundamental laws of the modern sovereign nation-state as expressed in a single formal document.' There are, however, various meanings that lie in between. S Greer and L Wildhaber, 'Revisiting the Debate about 'constitutionalising' the European Court of Human Rights' (2013) 12 *Human Rights Law Review*. For a longer discussion of these principles, see my work with Gutwirth.

[8] Additional features of constitutionalism can be included under this principle of separation and balance of powers are rules of the federalist structure (if there is any), describing the rights and responsibilities of state governments, and rules on constitutional amendment.

[9] According to most analysis on constitutionalism, the judiciary is the ultimate protector of the law. See CH McIlwain, *Constitutionalism: Ancient and Modern*, revised edn (Ithaca, Cornell University Press, 1947).

[10] On the contested role of the rule of law, on the rule of law as a set of formal standards and the rule of law as constitutionalism, see SH Stimson, 'Constitutionalism and the Rule of Law' in J Dryzek, B Honig and A Phillips (eds), *The Oxford Handbook of Political Theory* (Oxford, OUP, 2006) 317–332; on its role in Europe, opposing the continental tradition with the Anglo-American tradition, J Meierhenrich, 'Rechtsstaat versus the Rule of Law' in J Meierhenrich and M Loughlin (eds), *The Cambridge Companion to the Rule of Law* (Cambridge, Cambridge University Press, 2021) 39–67.

[11] The rule of law also provides that everyone should be equally subjected to law and human rights must be protected. AV Dicey, *Introduction to the Study of the Law of the Constitution*, 8th edn (London, Macmillan, 1915) 110.

These principles served the primary function of past constitutionalism with its constitutions, written or unwritten: justifying and legitimising a state's authority by designing standards and conditions for legal and illegal power and decision-making procedures within a state.

Constitutionalism's primary concern in the past has been to constrain a state's power mainly by delineating and regulating its branches (and not by regulating its use).[12] The result is constitutions that teach us what the powers of each branch are, without really adding detail about how they should use these powers. Most constitutions partly remedy this by recognising rights as disabling constraints on power.[13] When these rights apply, constitutionalism as a system of power establishments merges with constitutionalism as a system of power management. But again, the remedy is of a partial nature. Power is not fully managed: it is established and only when it affects recognised rights further checked.

## III. The Limits of Old Constitutionalism: Legal Grey Holes and Fuzzy Legality

There is a large body of literature on the limits of traditional constitutionalism. Constitutionalism and its core dogmas (for instance, 'why only three Montesquieuan branches?'; 'why only addressing state power?') fail to reflect and contain an array of power dynamics operating in modern society. It leaves out not only new normative conditions but also new powers 'competing' with traditional ones and their agenda.[14] It also mistakenly promises full coverage of power in a given system. David Dyzenhaus' idea of legal grey holes illustrates, however, that no existing system within the rule of law tradition is perfect.[15] All have (empty) spaces where power autonomously proliferates. Legal grey holes are, for instance, created by the legislature's open-ended statutes – in the absence of specific regimes regulating specific agendas – that give discretionary authority to the executive. Open-ended statutes only establish a semblance of legality

[12] Levinson (n 3) 46. The core function of constitutionalism, in its broadest sense, is to identify how a state is constructed (aspect 1) and how it functions (aspect 2). Especially in the case of written canonical documents, such as constitutions, the focus is most often on the first aspect of constitutionalism (how the state is constructed) and thus on input legitimacy. A typical grievance in the Declaration of Independence on 4 July 1776 is this about 'quartering large bodies of armed troops among us' (Grievance 14). The matter addressed in this grievance is about how a legitimate army should be used, not whether there should be a government-controlled army. The 1789 US Constitution, classic constitutionalism of early modernity (delineating the new federal state frame and constraining the state powers), identifies procedures for setting up a federal army but is silent about details on the use of the army.

[13] Constitutional rights imply normative assessments and decisions about the limits of constitutional and unconstitutional state's power and establish off-limit private areas removed from the reach of state's power to protect individuals' liberty. Through their limiting function, rights add a layer to the systematisation of legitimacy of governmental power and thus inform constitutionalism, permitting and forbidding state's actions on the basis of society's will and giving them means to exert control.

[14] The foregoing issues are not meant to provide an exhaustive critique of constitutionalism. Tully, for instance, sets out eight paradoxes of the modern arrangement of constituent powers and constitutional democracy (J Tully 'The Imperialism of Modern Constitutional Democracy' in *The Paradox of Constitutionalism: Constituent Power and Constitutional Form* (Oxford, OUP, 2008)).

[15] D Dyzenhaus, *The Constitution of Law. Legality in Times of Emergency* (Cambridge, CUP, 2006) 250.

that ends up being discretionarily filled in by other actors, particularly the executive.[16] They are said to be typical of today's administrative or bureaucratic states.[17] It is in these normative voids or vague lawmaking that space is created for new powers and agendas to emerge and consolidate uncontained by old constitutionalism. Still, grey holes, like black holes, are an affront to core liberal values,[18] and they make a mockery of the legality principle that is central to the rule-of-law project in which each state institution and all institutional actors should engage.[19] Margit Cohn equally paints a rather drastic vision of legality and constitutionalism at large. Similarly to Dyzenhaus' legal grey holes, to which she refers, Cohn uses the picture of 'fuzzy law' to illustrate how public law inherently leads the executive branch to act 'in the shadow of law', ie, between legality and illegality.[20] Because fuzzy law is endemic to rule-of-law systems,[21] Cohn suggests that both fuzzy legalities must be accepted as an unavoidable feature of state governance[22] but need to be addressed directly since this façade only benefits certain state institutions but does not respect the rule-of-law project: drawing power from 'grey holes', executive action can remain 'perfectly legal', that is, would not be found contrary to law, but, simultaneously, would not derive any substantive direction from it.[23] In Cohn's view classical constitutionalism has surprisingly under-researched the executive branch and wrongly approaches the institutional landscape in terms of hierarchy (submission of the executive to the legislative) in a concern to avoid having to discuss the internal tensions of constitutionalism. One of these tensions relates to the virtually impossible task in the practice of the executive to be both an executor of law and an executive (CEO) entrusted with steering the state. The reality of these tasks creates a tension between constraining power and granting power. Neither complete submission to the legislature nor

[16] For Dyzenhaus, legal grey holes are typical of a state's emergencies, but its analysis well extends beyond situations of emergency and has become applicable also to 'normal times'. See about the blurring of the normal and exceptional F Ost, 'L' État de droit, une notion paradoxale à l'épreuve de la pandémie' in S Parsa and F Tulkens (eds), *État de droit, état d'exception et libertés publiques* (Limal, Anthemis, 2022) 11–46; F Saint-Bonnet, 'Métamorphose de l'état d'exception' in S Parsa and F Tulkens (eds), *État de droit, état d'exception et libertés publiques* (Limal, Anthemis, 2022) 47–58.

[17] Legal grey holes undermine the traditional accountability role of both legislature and courts, especially in times of crisis. Because extraordinary times often raise extraordinary questions and powers (of a political nature), and legal grey holes are brought about and contained in law, this thin cloak of legality is mostly endorsed by judges that conduct lenient or fully deferential judicial review of the executive.

[18] Unlike black holes, grey holes preserve a façade of legality, but this façade only serves to conceal rather than constrain government arbitrariness (Dyzenhaus (n 15) 3).

[19] Dyzenhaus (n 15) 139.

[20] She points to 'practices under which an authorizing rule may present a façade of legality that derives from its binding formal status, while its content or application offer broad options for action (and possible abuse) which conceals a reality of a-legality'. Her vision of problematic legality does not differ from Dyzenhaus', but she more drastically sees internal tensions as a constant in ordinary times and, in fact, endemic to constitutionalism. Cohn, *A theory of the Executive branch* (n 1) 352.

[21] Fuzzy law is generated by multiple sources of authority in constitutions or legislation: it is created both by inherent characteristics of these norms, such as vagueness and open-endness, and the presence of multiple sources of legality across 'complex hyper-legislated policy areas'. Cohn, in her book, classifies and analyses 13 forms of fuzziness, ranging from open-ended or semi-written constitutions to unapplied legislation. Useful is her distinction between legislation-generated fuzziness (through patchwork legislation) and executive-generated fuzziness (playing with (non-)implementation). She is, however, attentive to other creators of grey holes, namely constitutions, administrative bodies and the judiciary.

[22] For Cohn governance is the result of consistent political interaction between numerous players in the social and political spheres.

[23] SM Cohn, 'Tensions and Legality (n 1) 346.

imperialism fully characterises the executive. Current power mechanisms, because of fuzzy legality and simplifying or binary constitutional templates, remain masked, benefitting the executive that formally acts under the law without being substantively limited by it.[24]

The systemic presence in the law of legal grey holes with their fuzzy legality illustrates what was said before: by placing primary focus on input legitimacy, constitutionalism has given marginal or no account to throughput legitimacy of power, namely the legitimacy of processes of power implementation by the powers properly mandated and recognised in the Constitution to hold these powers.[25] Constitutionalism *classical style* seems primarily concerned with the basics of the institutional structure, less with how power is de facto exerted by the different powers of the state. *Who* plays the cards is defined, but *how* hardly is.

The rise of the welfare state in western politics in the twentieth century is emblematic of the development of new state agendas, competences, and powers unforeseen in the templates of old constitutionalism. Normative voids on welfare favoured consolidation of the power of the executive and delegation of new powers in the policy arena, particularly administrative agencies entrusted with rulemaking, enforcement, and adjudicative functions.[26] Traditional accountability became fragmented and layered while formally removed from the executive and parliaments. The term 'fourth branch of government' in this context is used to bundle a string of new actors exercising power in one way or another (jury and press, for example). The same term is also used to label the factual power of regular administrative agencies of government and the intelligence agencies that were able to centralise powers in ways never envisioned in the constitutions.[27]

[24] The way ahead for constitutionalism, in Cohn's view, is to recognise and celebrate ingrained tensions and to come up with better templates to understand ongoing games of power that are now unseen because of incomplete theories. Both Dyzenhaus and Cohn count on the role of the judiciary to unmask fuzziness and uphold rule-of-law values, but both go further and seek for new actors to step in Dyzenhaus turns to new institutional experiments with administrative bodies, designed to meet novel situations to take over part of the role of courts (Dyzenhaus (n 15) 129–149). Cohn suggests new mechanisms for review (complementing the supremacy roles of judiciaries in traditional constitutionalism) that operate as an additional forum and intermediator between individuals and decision-makers can help solve tensions with legality by promoting deliberation and participation (Cohn, *A Theory of the Executive Branch* (n 1) 310–330). I will return to this point when discussing European data protection's insistence on supervisory administrative authorities.

[25] Throughput legitimacy refers to the quality of the governance process, including their 'efficacy, accountability, transparency, inclusiveness and openness to interest consultation'. V Schmidt, 'Is There a Deficit of Throughput Legitimacy in the EU?' in S Garben, I Govaere and P Nemitz (eds), *Critical Reflections on Constitutional Democracy in the European Union* (Oxford, Hart Publishing, 2019), first author draft via www.open.bu.edu/server/api/core/bitstreams/8ca8034a-aaf2-4811-94dc-845a4330796d/content; V Schmidt and M Wood, 'Conceptualizing Throughput Legitimacy: Procedural Mechanisms of Accountability, Transparency, Inclusiveness and Openness in EU Governance' (2019) 97 *Public Administration* 727–740.

[26] Administrative agencies in welfare are, to a varying degree, separated but controlled by the executive. PL Strauss, 'The Place of Agencies in Government: Separation of Powers and the Fourth Branch' (1984) 84 *Columbia Law Review* 573. These agencies blurred the separation between the legislative, executive, and judicial powers. See also K Verhoest, 'Agencification in Europe' in E Ongaro and S Van Thiel (eds), *The Palgrave Handbook of Public Administration and Management in Europe* (London, Palgrave Macmillan, 2018) 327–347; LM McCarthy-Cotter and M Flinders, 'Accountability in Liberal Democratic, Parliamentary Systems' in E Ongaro and S Van Thiel (eds), *The Palgrave Handbook of Public Administration and Management in Europe* (London, Palgrave Macmillan, 2018) 187–206.

[27] They legislate through delegated rulemaking authority; they investigate, execute, and enforce such rules (via the executive power these agencies are typically organised under); and apply, interpret, and enforce compliance with such rules (a power separately vested in the judicial branch. See KB Smith and MJ Licari, *Public*

The welfare state also marked the dismantling of the centralised Leviathan while consolidating the power of non-state entities and groups of interest.[28] These *many hands of the state*[29] were never properly included in the constitutionalist project.[30]

But there are other societal developments hardly covered by these power-managing principles. Today's surveillance states naturally grew out of welfare and national security states due to the development of bulk data collection and processing technologies. The new powers made possible by these technologies and their roll-out against strengthened the executive and its agencies,[31] as well as forces outside constitutions, ie, private companies. Again, classical constitutionalism was confronted by a seeming lack of relevance. Neither the turn to preemptive policing nor the growing role of private parties was adequately conceptualised in the constitution. Digital technologies have thus led to a scenario of power hybridisation and polarisation, where public power is exercised in new preemptive ways or is used by private companies. Rulemaking became either fluid, as flexible as possible,[32] or increasingly decentralised to private parties under the banner of 'standardisation'.[33]

Similar developments in terms of changing powers have also occurred at the EU institutional level. As a regulatory organisation, the EU has progressively relied on agencies entrusted with policymaking and expert knowledge provision.[34] The expanding scope of EU competences has not led to more regulatory detail. Since the 1980s, traditional EU lawmaking has been kept more and more general, open-textured, and vague while leaving harder issues outside the formal institutional dimension. In this approach,

*Administrations: Power and Politics in the Fourth Branch of Government* (Oxford, OUP, 2006); T Engelhardt, *Shadow Government: Surveillance, Secret Wars, and a Global Security State in a Single Superpower World* (Chicago, Haymarket Books, 2014).

[28] Think of political parties (key contributors to the structure and expansion of welfare state) and private and no-profit organisations (increasingly responsible for administrating, funding, or distributing services). The latter include 'non-profit organizations, churches, mutual aid societies, cooperatives, volunteer groups, foundations, and trade unions' (D Beland, K Morgan, H Obinger and C Pierson, *The Oxford Handbook of the Welfare State* (Oxford, OUP, 2021).

[29] The welfare state has been said to 'contain […] many hands that operate through varying relationships with private entities and territorial levels of government' (J Morgan and A Orloff, *The Many Hands of the State* (Cambridge, CUP, 2017)).

[30] E Posner and A Vermeule, *The Executive Unbound: After the Madisonian Republic* (Oxford, OUP, 2010) These authors provide more explanations reasons why constitutionalism 'does not even approximate the political terrain it purports to cover'. The considerable power of these non-state actors in daily affairs challenges the principles of separation and balance of powers and of the rule of law, and the accountability mechanism made possible by them. Their considerable power in daily affairs challenges the principles of separation and balance of powers and the rule of law, and the accountability mechanism made possible by them.

[31] JM Balkin, 'The Constitution in the National Surveillance State' (2008) 93 *Minnesota Law Review* 1–25. This includes preventative law enforcement through data-driven technology removed from the scrutiny of legislature and judicial bodies. Data expediency has allowed the executive to institute 'parallel' tracks for exerting power routing around constitutional guarantees such as human rights and oversight mechanisms, while leading private entities 'to amass and analyze more and more information about people' (Balkin 17).

[32] P De Hert, 'La répression liquide des infractions COVID à travers le droit penal et les SAC' in D Tatti, C Guillain, A Jonckheere and E Schils (eds), *Le droit à l'épreuve de la crise sanitaire: retour sur les sanctions administratives communales et les poursuites pénales des infractions Covid* (Brussels, La Charte, Les dossier de la Revue de Droit Pénal et de Criminologie, 2023) 75–94.

[33] G De Gregorio and G Radu, 'Digital Constitutionalism in the New era of Internet Governance' (2022) 30 *International Journal of Law and Information Technology* 68–87.

[34] P De Hert, 'Post-GDPR Lawmaking in the Digital Data Society: Mimesis without Integration. Topological Understandings of Twisted Boundary Setting in EU Data Protection Law' in D Curtin and M Catanzariti (eds), *Data at the Boundaries of European Law* (Oxford, OUP, 2023) 95–132.

'more concrete norm building work and the more controversial or complex work is left over to less democratic decision making, either by the agencies acting together or by the CJEU'.[35] Agencies have filled the normative gaps of broad EU lawmaking.[36] In sectors with agencies without enforcement powers, business interest groups are less visible than other actors, and their presence is less formalised, but in some sectors, like energy, they can be very influential on decision-making processes within European networks and agencies.[37]

With the EU we touch upon the next driver away from the classical constitutionalist state. The Union and its forerunners are clear products of technocratic thought introduced by Claude Henri de Saint-Simon (1760–1825), propagating a normative theory about the need to entrust state leadership to elites drawn from the public and private sectors.[38] In the technocratic domination view, the ordinary citizen is not capable of coping with many of today's complex policy challenges 'because she lacks the requisite cognitive capacities and public orientation'.[39] Technocracy, Bruce Gilley observes, is the other face of western governance up until today, but unlike democracy, it is less dominant in the constitutional architecture that, at face value, seems to prioritise democratic principles in the sense that the power to amend the constitution resides with the people. The reality is, however, that democracy and technocracy are both usually at work and that in some areas, like central banking or national security, more explicit weight is given to expert control, with a significant amount of public policymaking in these areas taken out of the hands of legislative control. Technocrats and democrats tussle for control, Gilley holds, but this messy reality is hardly theorised in classical constitutionalist literature.[40]

## IV. The Project of New Constitutionalism in the Twentieth Century: Incorporating Real Powers

While powers in modern societies have changed, constitutionalist sensitivities have not stopped evolving. With the growing competences of the welfare and surveillance state, its focus has been enlarged beyond traditional power restraint. In terms of the state's capacity-building, for instance, the twentieth-century expansion of human rights to include social and economic aspects and the interpretation of human rights as entailing positive duties served as normative backgrounds for a more proactive and positive state function (as opposed to simply refraining from actions in the case of civil rights).

[35] This has also led to 'prohibiting states to clarify European data protection via national laws and creating a guidance monopoly for the European Court and data protection agencies. De Hert (n 34).

[36] Courts, instead, have been seen as gaining an active role within administrative states.

[37] M Maggetti, 'Interest Groups and the (Non-)Enforcement Powers of EU Agencies: The Case of Energy Regulation' (2019) 10 *European Journal of Risk Regulation* 458–484.

[38] See on the international reach and importance of Saint-Simonian ideas J Eijking, 'A Priesthood of Knowledge: The International Thought of Henri de Saint-Simon' (2022) 66 *International Studies Quarterly* 11.

[39] B Gilley, 'Technocracy and Democracy as Spheres of Justice in Public Policy' (2017) 5 *Policy Sci* 14.

[40] ibid 18.

Rights as disabling constraints of old constitutionalism have been paralleled with forms of power-enhancing constraints.[41]

With the new welfare state came the need for better coverage of power mechanisms by constitutionalism. Legal systems approached evolving state powers by extending the idea of due process to welfare systems. Introducing due process in welfare matters allowed to contain these new forms of governance. It also served as a starting point for designing new legal procedures to counteract discretionary use or abuse of power by administrative agencies while ensuring that individuals are treated fairly and equally through the law's control and transparent decision-making.

Levinson argues that constitutionalism should no longer be exclusively devoted to arranging traditional institutional powers ('the superstructural power' of the state lying in the executive, judiciary, and legislative) but also look at and analyse the power of interest groups to influence policymaking, such as political parties, social groups, and powerful economic 'elites'.[42] Constitutionalism in the twenty-first century, Levinson holds, needs to include new power holders in modern society and to go beyond a distribution of power at the structural level that has no systematic relation to how power is actually distributed at the democratic level.[43]

In 'The National Surveillance State' (2008), Balkin studies the constitutional consequences of the transition from western welfare states towards security states. For the constitution to remain relevant, due process constitutional guarantees should be updated to contain the increasing power of the executive and private parties with the growing surveillance power of states.[44] What distinguishes a surveillance non-democratic state from a surveillance democratic state is not whether they use data technologies or not but how the power derived from data is managed by those states.[45] For Balkin, democratic constitutional states in times of surveillance should be 'information gourmets' and 'information philanthropists'.[46] As gourmets, democratic states ought to collect and collate only the information they need to ensure efficient government and national security. These gourmet surveillance states ought to create regular systems of checks and procedures to avoid abuse and to strictly regulate the use of information by all actors involved. They should also be philanthropic in the sense that they provide access to

[41] Levinson (n 3) 62–65. We observe, however, that the doctrine of human rights as entailing not only negative, but also positive duties is a creation of European courts, unanticipated by traditional constitutionalist logic and by the states; see A Backé, 'The Positive Obligations Doctrine: A Means of Effective Fundamental Rights Protection in EU Member States?' (2024) 31 *Maastricht Journal of European and Comparative Law* 147–170.

[42] Levinson (n 3) 40.

[43] ibid.

[44] Dyzenhaus already noted that any realistic conception of the rule of law and constitutionalism needs to link 'procedural constraints to substantive values' in controlling power so that procedural principles 'constrain the decisions of those who wield public power in a way that protects the interests of the individuals subject to those decisions' (Dyzenhaus (n 15) 14).

[45] Paraphrasing Balkin, Miller notes that 'whatever a democratic state does with data is legitimate – and that, in fact, a state's illegitimate use of data is an excellent indicator that it is not democratic. There is not a great deal that lawmakers can do in Balkin's analysis to manage or regulate the work of data or the operation of information systems – but analyzing this work and operation can help lawmakers to identify those aspects of governance that may not reflect the democratic ideals of whatever state is benefiting from them' (RA Miller, *Flourishing Thoughts: Democracy in the age of Data Hoards* (Ann Arbor, University of Michigan Press, 2016) 176).

[46] Balkin (n 31) 17–18.

information to the public and distribute much valuable information they create to the public to ensure the accountability of surveillance actors.[47]

## V. New Logic in Constitutionalism and the European Charter of Fundamental Rights

Concepts such as 'information gourmets' and 'information philanthropists' did not make it as such in European constitutionalism, but the developments that took place in Europe to face the governance challenges created by new power dynamics are related to this development of expanded due process. Data protection is (only) a part of it, as will be demonstrated, but it is there that Balkin's concepts for a new constitutional design are most likely to be found in one way or another.

Contemporary use of power requires more than the conventional 'gatekeeping' function of constitutionalism in determining what power should be justified and declared legitimate. The old constitution did not adequately control disproportionate power accumulation of the executive gained by drivers such as IT, political parties, and the welfare system, nor did it formalise the role of new actors in constitutions.[48]

Towards the end of the twentieth century, a new logic in constitutionalist design developed. The classical interrogations ('What are legitimate powers?') were complemented with equally classical but less prominently treated questions like 'How can actors identified in the constitutional landscape use their legitimate powers?' to make sure that justified state power – legally accepted state powers – are equally being controlled or disciplined. The project of constitutionalism evolved in a way that it was no longer only about rejecting the 'unconstitutional' but also about channelling the 'constitutional'.

This new logic has found an echo in a set of legal tools aimed at channelling, rather than merely limiting, legitimate power by focusing the constitutional attention on procedures of power implementation and decision-making.[49] A range of new rights grounded upon the idea of due process and the need for third parties enforcing due process have started being codified in the constitution and recognised as general applicable.[50] An example of this is given by the progressive introduction, either within constitutions or legislation, by the end of the twentieth century of the Ombudsman's figure.[51]

[47] Balkin (n 31) 17–18.

[48] With the growing power of the state, constitutional guarantees were needed to 'keep governments devoted to the public good' (Balkin (n 31) 17).

[49] This idea resonates with Dyzenhaus' need for a renewed procedural value of constitutionalism.

[50] Criminal law has acted as a consistent driver for constitutionalism. The principle of legality was first formulated with regard to crimes and then expanded. Due process equally evolved from criminal law-related rights to more general rights. The principle of due process had a solid constitutional impact not only in terms of controlling the government's power but also in interpreting constitutional rights, making sure that these are upheld in legal proceedings and acts of administration through procedural guarantees such as providing individuals notice and chance to a hearing before any adverse decision taken.

[51] The ombudsman investigates complaints against public officials, ensures that government agencies act lawfully and fairly, and protects individuals from abuses of power by the government. This actor first saw the light in Nordic Europe, but other countries followed. European constitutional recognition of the role of the ombudsman followed with the enactment of the European Charter of Fundamental Rights around the turn of the century. See *Charter of Fundamental Rights of the European Union* C 364/1 (2000) art 43.

The transformative nature of the Charter must be understood in this light. It gave constitutional recognition and significant relevance to several rights of a due process nature, such as the expanded right to a fair trial and presumption of innocence,[52] the right to good administration and to access to governmental documents,[53] and the right to collective bargaining (article 27).

This injection of due process logic – other speak of procedural justice – facilitates controlling how state powers that are, in principle, legitimate function in practice. Due process rights submit and link governmental exercise of power and administrative decision-making to requirements of a qualitative character, ie, procedural conditions of legality, transparency, fairness, and accountability. Simona Demková and Herwig Hofmann explicitly situate the rise of these new rights, their inclusion in the Charter, and subsequent success in case law in the context of the previous analysis of increasing delegation of powers towards the executive and other new actors at the European level.[54]

In other words, this new constitutionalist part of the Charter has placed a burgeoning focus on ensuring procedural legitimacy, or so-called throughput legitimacy, of governmental power and governance process.[55] Data protection elevated to the rank of an autonomous fundamental right in article 8 Charter is another clear example of this constitutionalist reform agenda. It is part of the chapter in the Charter on 'Freedoms', and it does protect them, but, as we will see, in another way compared to the classical freedoms.

## VI. Opacity in 'Old' Constitutionalism: The Constitutional Role of the Right to Privacy

Our previous work underlined the specific nature of privacy by contrasting it to data protection in terms of opacity of power (privacy) vs. transparency of power (data protection). Speaking in terms of opacity and transparency is a way of defining things by saying what they do or should do.[56]

Meant to conceal (opacity) a set of individual liberties from public scrutiny and control, opacity tools – in unwritten law and written law (constitutional provisions, civil and political rights …) – serve to delineate allowed (constitutional) and prohibited (unconstitutional) state authority in relationship with individuals. Being directly

[52] The right to a fair trial is a direct expression of the principle of due process. Whereas its scope was kept limited in the 1950 European Convention on Human Rights, its scope in the Charter is, in principle, of a general nature (ibid art 47–49).

[53] ibid art 41–42. For the constitutional value of informational transparency, see TF De Freitas, 'Administrative Transparency in Portugal' (2016) 22 *European Public Law* 667–688.

[54] S Demková and H Hofmann, 'General Principles of Procedural Justice' in KS Ziegler, PJ Neuvonen and V Moreno-Lax (eds), *Research Handbook on General Principles in EU Law: Constructing Legal Orders in Europe* (Cheltenham, Edward Elgar, 2022) 209–226.

[55] V Schmidt, *Is There a Deficit of Throughput Legitimacy in the EU?* (Oxford, Hart Publishing, 2019).

[56] Behind the different concepts lurks the difference in focus between old and newer constitutionalism and the distinction between constitutional disabling power constraints and empowering constraints (Levinson (n 3) 62–65).

associated with the primary power-building and power-limiting function of constitutionalism, opacity tools are a strong dimension of input legitimacy.[57]

Unlike opacity tools, transparency tools such as due process do not aim to delineate and identify acceptable constitutional power but rather to control and channel it when it is set in motion. These tools are not rooted in normative questions about *what* power should be permitted (before legitimisation) but rather in questions about *how* normatively 'greenlighted' power is exercised and how decisions derived from such power are taken (after legitimisation).[58] This qualitative spotlight on power is canvassed with procedural requisites of transparency and accountability that explain how accepted power should be exercised.

Privacy is a legal concept that translates the political endeavour to ensure opacity in individual affairs.[59] Privacy implies decisions of a normative character about what governmental power a society is willing or unwilling to accept considering the constitutional spirit of the state: it justifies and provides legitimacy to power. Privacy focuses weightily on the 'what' dimension of power, namely on questions about what society wants from the state and other powers and what power should not be wanted but blocked.[60] A strong privacy right acknowledged in law reduces power and is primarily negative towards governmental and other unwanted intrusions.[61]

However, the privacy right, as it is shaped in Europe, does not abolish or make impossible any intrusion. The affirmation of the right in the leading European documents should be read together with the rights-limitation possibilities elaborated in article 8 ECHR, second paragraph, and article 52 Charter. Together, they explain the shape that the

[57] 'Through these tools, the (constitutional) legislator takes the place of the individual as the prime arbiter of desirable or undesirable acts that infringe on liberty and legitimze power.' De Hert and Gutwirth (n 5) 71' Examples of opacity tools are strong moral commands that are perceived as self-evident in a given polis (the Europeans never had any new Holocaust), clear uncontested political mandates (the powers and inviolability of the *tribuni plebis* (tribunes of the plebs, or lower classes)) in Ancient Rome, clear enforced choices in criminal law and other enforceable areas of law, and strong rights shielding against utilitarian policies (Dworkin's trumps; Habermas' firewall) that are uphold and affirmed (never subjected to balancing tests) by courts. See R Dworkin, *Taking Rights Seriously* (Cambridge (MA), Harvard University Press, 1977); J Habermas, *Between Facts and Norms* (Cambridge (MA), MIT Press, 1996). On the tendency of European courts to water down the deontological European framework (eg, 'do not torture', 'do not enact retroactive legislation', 'do not discriminate against minority groups') with a balancing or proportionality approach treating principled normative questions as (vulgar) conflicts of two equal rights by to equal parties, see B van der Sloot, 'The Practical and Theoretical Problems with 'Balancing': Delfi, Coty and the Redundancy of the Human Rights Framework' (2016) 23 *Maastricht Journal of European and Comparative Law* 439–459.

[58] We take the example of nudging. Opacity tools will answer the question of whether a government should be allowed to nudge or not. If the answer is yes, transparency tools will answer the question of how this power to nudge citizen needs to be framed and subjected to legal norms. For similar assessments of practices such as profiling and CCTV, see S Gutwirth and P De Hert, 'Regulating Profiling in a Democratic Constitutional State' in M Hildebrandt and S Gutwirth (eds), *Profiling the European Citizen. Cross-Disciplinary Perspectives* (Berlin, Springer, 2008) 271–292.

[59] De Hert and Gurtwirth (n 5) 71.

[60] ibid 91. This role of privacy in informing input legitimacy has also been interpreted through requirements in the court's case law, ie, the exercise of invasive powers must be necessary to meet a 'pressing social need' and 'relevant and sufficient' to a legitimate aim.

[61] On the other hand, privacy is pivotal to the self-development of individuals as socio-political entities, safeguarding their capacity of free expression and decision-making. Privacy thus contributes to preserving input legitimacy by promoting citizens' participation, inclusive decision-making, and responsiveness to the legislative mandate. On how privacy functions positively, see De Hert and Gurtwirth (n 5) 73–74.

privacy understanding takes in a certain context.[62] Although quintessential for a democratic constitutional state because it refers to liberty, privacy is a relational, contextual, and per se social notion that only acquires substance when it clashes with other private or public interests.[63] In these cases, it will be up to the legislator or the judge to determine how heavily privacy weighs against other rights and legitimate interests. But if privacy is found to prevail in a case, this will lead to a prohibition of interference.[64]

Van der Sloot insists on the essential binary outcome of shaping privacy and testing limitations to privacy: 'Either an infringement is prescribed for by law or it is not, either it is aimed at one of the legitimate interests or it is not, either it is necessary in a democratic society, or it is not.'[65] Our past work insisted on the importance of the last test, the most political of the three.[66] The first test – is the interference based on foreseeable, detailed laws that provide for effective guarantees – has resulted in case law addressing legislators and the work they need to do to make compliant laws. Also, the requirement of foreseeability has allowed the courts to fuse due process requirements regarding fair trial and effective remedies into the privacy requirements of the legislature, strengthening the accountability and transparency of state powers.[67]

It is, however, 'sinister' to understand rights as a question of laws and organisation of power since laws cannot establish for themselves the very conditions of their own legitimacy.[68] The transformation of the European privacy right into a source of procedural rights and conditions takes it away from the job it was designed for, viz., to prohibit unreasonable exercises of power and to create zones of opacity.[69] Only the test

[62] M Nasir, 'Oikopolitics, Regulation and Privacy: An Essay on the Governmental Nature of the Right to Private Life' (2018) 45 *Philosophy & Social Criticism* 347.

[63] On the non-absolute nature of privacy, see De Hert and Gurtwirth (n 5) 74–75.

[64] The privacy right offers a fine example of a disempowering constitutional right typical of old constitutionalism. States and their institutions eager for policymaking and power accept these and other disempowering constitutional tools because self-restraint and openness for being checked in practice can lead to more acceptance of decisions and mandates and thus create empowering effects. On the potentially empowering effects of constitutional restraints on constitutional actors, see Levinson (n 3) 65–67, who calls for further research. Comp. 'Viewing constitutional rules and arrangements that limit the choices of officials and institutional actors myopically or in isolation risks seeing only the disempowering constraint and missing the power that constraint might simultaneously create. At the same time, while it is almost always possible to concoct a story about how an apparent legal or political constraint could be empowering on the net, sometimes a constraint is just a constraint. Distinguishing empowering from disempowering constraints is yet another challenge for constitutional assessments of structural power' (67–68).

[65] 'Take the sanctity of one's home, as protected under art 8 ECHR. If the police enter a person's house for a legitimate reason – if it has reason to believe that this person committed a murder, and it wanted to search the premises for a murder weapon – this might be considered as necessary for the protection of public order. If the police enter a person's home without a legitimate reason – because the person is a famous football player and police officers were curious to know the living conditions of that person, it is not. Note that no balancing of interests takes place; the test is simply whether an infringement is necessary or not. The same holds true with reference to whether such infringement is prescribed by law: it is a binary test' (van der Sloot (n 57) 441).

[66] De Hert and S Gurtwirth (n 5) 86–91.

[67] P De Hert and G Malgieri, 'One European Legal Framework for Surveillance: The ECtHR's Expanded Legality Testing Copied by the CJEU' in V Mitsilegas and N Vavoula (eds), *Surveillance and Privacy in the Digital Age. European, Transatlantic and Global Perspectives* (Oxford, Hart Publishing, 2021) 255–295.

[68] M Nasir, 'Negative Governmentality Through Fundamental Rights: The Far Side of the European Convention on Human Rights' (2018) 24 *European Law Journal* 300–301.

[69] The notion of zones of opacity must not necessarily be understood in a spatial sense. In '*Glukhin*' the Court reiterates that the concept of 'private life' is a broad term not susceptible to exhaustive definition. 'It can embrace multiple aspects of the person's physical and social identity. It is not limited to an "inner circle" in which the individual may live his or her own personal life without outside interference but also encompasses

of necessity deals with the political questions of whether power should be accepted, limited, stopped, or prohibited; in other words, whether opacity must be protected.[70] In its facial recognition judgment, *Glukhin v Russia* (2023), the ECtHR rightly reduced the threefold test of article 8 ECHR to only one test (the test of necessity) because 'questions of lawfulness and of the existence of a legitimate aim cannot be dissociated from the question whether the interference was "necessary" in a democratic society'.[71]

Are fundamental rights in Europe blocking power when needed? In the line of Habermas, van der Sloot regrets the tendency of the European courts to disregard the original purpose of European human rights law, identifying fundamental duties and restrictions. In return, we do not get a proper assessment of the binary questions about the lawfulness and necessity of certain actions by the state but a case-by-case approach with little to no legal certainty and therefore only ask and add to the caseload of these courts.[72] The power-relevant questions are not asked, and the fundamental answers about what counts in a society are not given.[73] Legal privacy functions as an opacity tool only under certain circumstances. It is as strong as the hands of men make it in a certain

the right to lead a "private social life", that is, the possibility of establishing and developing relationships with others and the outside world. It does not exclude activities taking place in a public context. There is thus a zone of interaction of a person with others, even in a public context, which may fall within the scope of "private life"' (ECtHR, *Glukhin v Russia*, 4 July 2023, application no. 11519/20, §64 with ref. to ECtHR, *López Ribalda and Others v Spain* [GC], 17 October 2019, application nos. 1874/13 and 8567/13, §§87-88).

[70] De Hert and Gurtwirth (n 67) 91.

[71] *Glukhin v Russia* (Application no. 11519/20) (ECtHR, 4 July 2023) § 78.

[72] Van der Sloot (n 57) 448. See on the tendency of the ECtHR to resort to loose balancing, also E Brems and L Lavrysen, 'Don't Use a Sledgehammer to Crack a Nut: Less Restrictive Means in the Case Law of the European Court of Human Rights' (2015) 15 *Human Rights Law Review* 1–30. See A Ashworth, 'Eroding the Structure of the Convention? The Public Interest in Prosecutions for Serious Crime' in KS Ziegler and PM Huber (eds), *Current Problems in the Protection of Human Rights* (Oxford, Hart Publishing, 2013) 31–44. The result is anecdotical balancing of all interests involved (protected by rights or not), such as the general interest in national security and the particular interest of a claimant to privacy. Every possible interest in a privacy dispute is considered as relative or as important as fundamental rights interests (van der Sloot (n 57) 442). The analysis of B van der Sloot is subtle. Case dependency and casuistry are inherent elements of the work of courts, and, in the case of the CJEU, one could argue that art 51(1) Charter leaves no other option. I understand van der Sloot's observation as one that correctly senses that the role of these Courts should be more ambitious in interpreting the societal context in which a given dispute should be situated. An important part of the task is to rightly understand the disputed intrusion of rights-limitation: what interest protected by a recognised right is at stake for the claimant and how much weight should be given to it. A discussion of access by a private person to data held by another person who needs to respect professional secrecy should start with a reflection of the weight of professional secrecy and then turn to the government's role in allowing such access by assessing the three binary questions. These methods prevent gliding into a horizontal presentation of the dispute, where the decisive role of the government and its institutions is ignored. On the tendency to handle all sorts of interests, including state interests, as equally important, regardless of their status as protected human rights interest, see P De Hert, 'Proportionality in Modern Regulatory States Confused about Priorities. Judges Like, but do not Comply with Academic Doctrines' in J Czarnocki and P Przemyslaw (eds), *Proportionality in EU Digital Law: Balancing Conflicting Rights and Interests* (Oxford, Hart Publishing, 2024) ch 3, 33–97.

[73] To bring down all questions to the specificities of a case and to turn to balancing of all interests involved considered equal is to dodge the questions which have a wider and broader significance, like can a person invoke a given right? How important is the sanctity of one's home or a system of bank secrecy for a given society? Are limitations of a given right in a Member State necessary in a democratic society, and do they serve a pressing need? If bank secrecy protects more than individual interest but also protects general interests and is a precondition for the functioning of the banking sector as such, when and under what circumstances can this secrecy of banks be curtailed?

context of social practices and norms. A string of cases that accepts privacy limitations is not necessarily a failure of legal privacy's overall normative role.[74]

The previous paragraphs tried to understand the strengths and limits of privacy's normative role. Privacy can be good in giving clear, binary answers to essential questions of the limits of power, but it does not have the suitable legal capacity to question how justified power is exercised. Elements of legality and legal certainty have been embedded into privacy analysis through European case law. The European courts' insistence on detailed, foreseeable rules with judicial guarantees allows them to control whether certain organised privacy-invasive practices are not only legitimate but also lawfully exercised through procedural safeguards. But privacy's essential function remains normative in nature. It focuses on what normative choices about power should be taken in the first place.[75] Conversely, the constitutional dimension of data protection relies on questioning how normatively accepted power derived from data is implemented and thus channelling and bounding the implementation of power to accountability and transparency conditions.[76]

## VII. Four Profound Innovative Constitutionalist Dimensions of Data Protection

Data protection laws were initially implemented in the second half of last century at the domestic level. However, as with many other rights mentioned above, a right to data protection, including the right to have access to personal data, has received constitutional codification with the entry into force of the Charter. A stand-alone right to data protection was not only included in article 8 Charter but also in article 16 Treaty on the Functioning of the European Union (TFEU), placing this right straight at the core of the European constitutional axis. The GDPR and its stepbrother (the LED), flagships of

[74] Nasir (n 62) 347. Comp. 'The idea of an autonomous life becomes meaningless without governmental discipline. The latter is a necessary condition for freedom to be both socially established and individually exercised in a satisfactory manner. Thus, limits and exceptions to rights are Janus-faced. On the one hand, such limits and exceptions restrain individual freedom and empower the state; at the same time, it is such limits and restrictions that render freedom possible and limit the power of public institutions by setting their legitimate scope. What emerges is the very principle of the rule of law, to the extent that the latter wards off not only arbitrary exercises of legal and political power but also reproachable patterns of action and conduct from legal subjects. The former constitutes a necessary guarantee of freedom. The latter ensures the regulation of subjects through freedom. Both go hand in hand' (M Nasir, 'Negative Governmentality Through Fundamental Tights: The Far Sside of the European Convention on Human Rights' (2018)' 24(4-5) *European Law Journal* 300).

[75] As such, 'informational privacy cannot be accomplished by declaring it a fundamental right and outlawing all processing of personal information. To legally realize and enforce a privacy right in personal information, incremental, graduated, and practical legislation better achieve the goal than sweeping proclamations that have applications to actions unrelated to the harms associated with the absence of the right' (M Cunningham. 'Next Generation Privacy: The Internet of Things, Data Exhaust, and Reforming Regulation by Risk of Harm' (2014) 2 *Groningen Journal of International Law* 115).

[76] Due process requirements have hence been updated to the demands of the digital and are now an essential component of the constitutional approach adopted by Europe in the digital, namely digital constitutionalism (De Gregorio).

European digital constitutionalism,[77] have further increased data protection's constitutional value (see below) while at the same time calibrating the right with the necessities of free flow of data (GDPR) and of law enforcement (LED).

The right to access personal data is evidently linked to the right to privacy and shares with it a certain degree of opacity capacity.[78] However, going beyond privacy, data protection is also a quintessential analogue of a due process safeguard. Westin and Baker underline how this right is a direct extension of the doctrine of (procedural) due process 'towards all situations in which decisions are (or can be) made based on the processing of personal data.'[79] It has been created to define *how* legitimate power should be exercised and close the loop to avoid or stop the opaque, unaccountable, or unconstitutional exercise of power through data processing activities,[80] a prerogative it shares with all other due process requirements.[81]

The more recent codification of a right to data protection in constitutional texts thus goes beyond privacy to ensure respect for individuals' autonomy in the context of emerging new powers. While privacy sets the legitimacy of (data-driven) power, data protection starts from the presumption that personal data can be legitimately (in the sense of lawfully) collected and processed by governments.[82] It thus also has an empowering rather than disempowering rationale as privacy.[83] It stems from the knowledge that 'in all administrative systems there is an urge to collect, store and use data, an urge which must be curtailed by legal regulation.'[84] Given equivalent patterns between welfare and surveillance, this function of administrative law in welfare has been extended

[77] De Gregorio, 'The Rise of European Digital Constitutionalism' (2020) 19(1) *International Journal of Constitutional Law* 64.

[78] Data protection is meant to safeguard individuals' information privacy. Moreover, certain types of data processing are prohibited by data protection. GDPR art 9; De Hert and Gurtwirth (n 5) 78.

[79] AF Westin and MA Baker, *Databanks in a Free Society* (New York City, Quadrangle Books, 1972).

[80] G De Gregorio, *Digital Constitutionalism in Europe. Reframing Rights and Powers in the Algorithmic Society* (Cambridge, CUP, 2022) 224. This right does in Europe what Balkin's advocates for constitutions to do ahead of increasing amass of power of the state: 'taming new forms of governance within constitutional boundaries'. It hence meets his vision of constitutionalism.

[81] This due process nature of data protection has been made clear in '*Schrems*', where the CJEU has directly linked the right to have access to personal data not only to classical privacy but also to art 47 Charter, which is the right emblematic of transparency. The right to data protection is seen as falling in the essence of this right. Likewise, other issues regarding data subject rights, such as data rectification, are often considered as concerned with art 47 rather than art 8. See Case C-362/14, *Schrems I*, judgment of 6 October 2015, ECLI:EU:C:2015:650 par 95. 'Legislation not providing for any possibility for an individual to pursue legal remedies in order to have access to personal data relating to him, or to obtain the rectification or erasure of such data, does not respect the essence of the fundamental right to effective judicial protection, as enshrined in art 47 Charter. The first paragraph of art 47 Charter requires everyone whose rights and freedoms guaranteed by the law of the European Union are violated to have the right to an effective remedy before a tribunal in compliance with the conditions laid down in that Article. The very existence of effective judicial review designed to ensure compliance with provisions of EU law is inherent in the existence of the rule of law.'

[82] De Hert and Gurtwirth (n 5) 93–96. See also V Mitsilegas, 'The Transformation of Privacy in an Era of Pre-Emptive Surveillance' (2015) 20 *Tilburg Law. Review* 52. Their moment of 'constitutional intervention' differs, and data protection is less concerned with input legitimacy as much as privacy is. As much as due process recognises the legitimacy of state prerogatives to perform tasks in welfare and national security contexts, data protection also recognises that governments need to process data for performing public tasks provided in the constitution. With some exceptions, therefore, data protection is not prohibitive as privacy is as an opacity tool. The right to data protection is not only channelling but also prohibitive, for instance, in relation to certain categories of data processing.

[83] It is in fact often considered the 'positive side of the right to privacy' (De Gregorio (n 77) 225).

[84] De Hert and Gurtwirth (n 5) 78–81.

to data protection law.[85] Data protection codifies the idea that data provide immense power to digital players, hence purporting to balance asymmetries of power.[86]

In this light, data protection lays down rules that govern, channel, and check power exercised through potentially privacy-invasive modalities, ie, data processing. In exerting its function, data protection does not simply control but also asks very specific questions about how power is exercised, including what the purpose is, how much data is collected, how securely these data are processed, etc, by subjecting data processing to a series of principles of a due process matrix.[87] These principles attach to legitimate data processing powers strict procedural conditions based on legality, transparency, fairness, and accountability.[88]

*First innovation (adding a new logic).* Data protection fits the new constitutionalist agenda because it asks questions that focus on the 'how' dimension of power. By overseeing and disciplining the process of data protection law implementation (between input and output governance) through procedural requisites, the ultimate constitutional value of data protection is inherently linked to ensuring the throughput legitimacy of exercised power (above).[89] Through this procedural lens on governance, data protection is relevant where input politics or governance is at many levels taken away from policy-making and thus distributed or diffused. As such, in addition to rights of opacity such as privacy, data protection frames *all* use by *all that use it* of digital power, hence coping with more complex power mechanisms and dynamics at a broader level. It is not a classic civil right of the first generation but functions according to the logic of a due process right (section V, above), because it links governmental and other exercises of power and decision-making to requirements of a qualitative character, ie, procedural conditions of legality, transparency, fairness, proportionality and accountability. To achieve its purpose, it sets a very low threshold to be triggered (*all* processing of data, including the most vulgar or banal processing and including low-risk processing) permanently monitored through a double governance system (the individual citizen and specialised supervisory bodies[90]).

*Second innovation (addressing private power).* Data protection law recognises the great power of the private sector in using data with its consequent direct application to private companies. The GDPR, in particular, bends the conventional vertical character of fundamental rights' application,[91] including privacy rights, and imposes

[85] ibid.

[86] ibid 78–81. For Rodota, the right of access serves as a procedural counterbalance to place power in the hands of citizens. S Rodotà, *Elaboratori Elettronici E Controllo Sociale* [Computers and Social Control] (Bologna, Il Mulino, 1973).

[87] GDPR art 5. 'The sheer wordings of the data protection principles(…) already suggest heavy reliance on notions of procedural justice rather than normative (or substantive) justice.'

[88] Principles in the GDPR inherently aim at counteracting interferences with data subjects' rights, including privacy, and thus also perform a constitutional role of a substantive nature.

[89] Thus, it is linked to the 'efficacy, accountability, transparency, inclusiveness and openness to interest consultation' of power exercised through technologies. Schmidt (n 25).

[90] Data protection sets up more collective or polycentric systems of rights protection and enforcement that include many actors. Bennett and Raab note that data protection underlines a system of co-production comprising many actors: supervisory authorities and data protection officers but also media, academics and social movements. J Bennett and CD Raab, *The Governance of Privacy: Policy Instruments in Global Perspective* (Cambridge (MA), MIT Press, 2006) 272.

[91] De Gregorio (n 77) 254.

transparency and accountability norms on the processing of both public and private actors in the EU.[92] With its recognition of the hybridity of power, data protection does not only limit the further consolidation of power in the hands of private companies and online platforms but also aims to subject this power to constitutional control (in line with Levinson's constitutionalism of interests). It also sets in place an additional internal system of transparency tools in the form of procedural rights to remedy the asymmetry of power between individuals and in the form of new powers, such as the right to access information or the right to data portability.

*Third innovation (the integration of most of the data protection package at the constitutional level).* The EU version of the right to protection of personal data, however, is not only anchored in article 8 Charter but also, more importantly, in article 16 TFEU.[93] Its first paragraph echoes the article 8 Charter by recognising a right to the protection of personal data for everyone. The second paragraph mandates the EU to make secondary laws that 'lay down the rules relating to the protection of individuals with regard to the processing of personal data subject'. The 'data protection package' consisting of the GDPR and the Law Enforcement Data Protection Directive (LED) is therefore given special constitutional status in that they spell out the scope and reach of the EU right to data protection.[94]

The substance of data protection law is not set in stone.[95] Other data protection regimes do not follow the EU approach[96] for reasons like the sheer length and detail of the GDPR (99 provisions), its administrative burden, and its encyclopedic ambition to regulate *all* processing by *all* once and for all through a combination of principles and concrete rules. Data protection in Europe has become what the GDPR says it is. This comprises much more in terms of ideas, principles and detail than what is proclaimed in article 8 Charter, but through article 16 TFEU's second paragraph, an essential

[92] This excludes law enforcement authorities. It is true that privacy may also embed positive obligations leading states to ensure that privacy is respected not only by public but also private actors, privacy is conventionally a right with vertical application to public power thus only binding public actors to individuals.

[93] This primary law continues to foster surprises. See P De Hert, 'The Right to Protection of Personal Data. Incapable of Autonomous Standing in the Basic EU Constituting Documents?' (2015) 3 *Utrecht Journal of International and European Law* 1–4. For more surprising expansions of Charter rights, see A Słowik, 'Multiple Sources of Right to an Effective Remedy in EU Migration and Asylum Law: Towards Common Standards on Judicial Protection?' (2024) 31 *Maastricht Journal of European and Comparative Law* 31 (discussing the relation between art 47 Charter and art 19 TFEU both on the right to an effective remedy).

[94] W van Ballegooij, 'Data Protection and General Principles of EU Law' in KS Ziegler, PJ Neuvonen and V Moreno-Lax (eds), *Research Handbook on General Principles in EU Law: Constructing Legal Orders in Europe* (Cheltenham, Edward Elgar, 2022) 549. On the question of whether all GDPR-data subject rights (including those not mentioned in art 8 Charter, are fundamental rights themselves, see nuanced: L Drechsler, 'Data Subject Rights in International Personal Data Transfers' (2023) 16(1) *Review of European Administrative Law* 69–76 (ch 1). See also 35–56.

[95] There are different models around, and seemingly crucial ingredients, such as the establishment of data protection authorities, are not present everywhere. Many non-European countries, with the US as the most striking example, have no independent supervision as an essential component of data protection. Europe's secondary laws, like the GDPR and the LED, follow a 'binary governance' approach. They combine individual due process rights with a collaborative governance approach to follow and protect personal data to ensure it is always processed fairly See ME Kaminski, 'Binary Governance: Lessons from the GDPR's Approach to Algorithmic Accountability' (2019) 92 *Southern California Law Review* 1552–1553.

[96] See W Hartzog and N Richards, 'Privacy's Constitutional Moment and the Limits of Data Protection' (2020) 6 *Boston College Law Review* 1687–1762.

part of the GDPR surplus is taken on board in constitutional discussions about data protection.[97]

*Fourth innovation (adding proxy advocates).* Article 8 Charter and article 16 TFEU attach to the right to data protection an obligation to establish an independent authority overseeing compliance with data protection law. The right to data protection has thus also an institutional component provided by primary law, which directly anchors it to EU constitutional law. Both provisions insist on the independence of these authorities. Article 52(1) GDPR adds that such independence must be 'complete', a requirement broadly interpreted both by the CJEU and by the EU Commission.[98] This way, a real new watchdog with a direct constitutional foundation was added to the three traditional Montesquieuian branches to provide additional layers of accountability in the digital.[99]

There are other new branches in Europe, but the data protection authorities stand out since they do not only regulate and enforce law in the public sector but also in the private sector, where private companies operate. Their constitutional mandate is

[97] It suffices to read the CJEU's case law on art 5 GDPR principles (mainly lawfulness, purpose limitation, data minimisation, and storage limitation) and art 6 GDPR (clarifying the legal grounds for processing) to understand the enormous transfer of secondary law material into the realm of primary constitutional law. Take, for instance, the data minimisation principle – the closest European data protection comes to Balkin's concepts of 'information gourmets' or 'information philanthropists'. The data minimisation principle is mentioned in the GDPR, not in the text of art 8 Charter, but as part of the human rights testing of data protection questions by the CJEU. In his Opinion in *Direktor na Glavna direktsia 'Natsionalna politsia' pri MVR – Sofia*, AG Pikamäe writes that '[…] the principle of 'data minimisation' […] gives expression to the principle of proportionality. The same applies to the principle of storage limitation […] which involves assessing the proportionality of the treatment in relation to its purpose' (Opinion of AG Pikamäe in *Direktor na Glavna direktsia 'Natsionalna politsia' pri MVR – Sofia*, C-118/22, 15 June 2023, ECLI:EU:C:2023:483, §27). In her Opinion in *Norra Stockholm Bygg*, AG Ćapeta states that both art 6 and art 5 of the GDPR '[…] require not only a legitimate aim but also that the specific processing is necessary for achieving that aim. The GDPR, therefore, requires that the court undertake a proportionality analysis when determining whether the disclosure of personal data in a concrete situation is necessary […]'. (Opinion of AG Ćapeta in *Norra Stockholm Bygg*, C-268/21, 6 Oct. 2022, ECLI:EU:C:2022:755, §55–56). On the expansive fundamental rights status of data protection, see LD Corte, 'On Proportionality in the Data Protection Jurisprudence of the CJEU' (2022) 12 *International Data Privacy Law* 259–275; M Brkan, 'Privacy, Data Protection and the Role of European Courts: Towards Judicialisation and Constitutionalisation of European Privacy and Data Protection Framework' in G González Fuster, R Van Brakel, and P De Hert (eds), *Research Handbook on Privacy and Data Protection Law* (Cheltenham, Edward Elgar Publishing, 2022) 273–301.

[98] More in detail on this profound innovative dimension of anchoring data protection authorities in the primary texts, see P De Hert and C Cocito, 'The Added Value of Data Protection within the Framework of Digital Constitutionalism in Europe' in G De Gregorio, O Pollicino and P Valcke (eds), *The Oxford Handbook of Digital Constitutionalism* (online edn Oxford Academic, 2024) section 5 and also section 6 on the possible role of data protection authorities with regard to Dyzenhaus's grey holes and Cohn's fuzzy reality.

[99] See M Tushnet, *The New Fourth Branch: Institutions for Protecting Constitutional Democracy* (Cambridge, CUP, 2021) 186, 25–41. Tushnet defends adding new branches to the constitutional pallet. *The New Fourth Branch: Institutions for Protecting Constitutional Democracy* offers theoretical and functional arguments for this development in today's constitutional world. How can you preserve the Constitution and uphold the laws if new actors and power assemblages surface that the traditional branches cannot control, such as in party-political systems (nineteenth century) and in the global economy with its global IT firms (twentieth century)? Tushnet focuses on the eroding impact of the party-political system: neither the legislature nor the executive can be trusted to safeguard respect for constitutional and legal provisions since legislatures controlled by one party would not investigate threats to the constitution posed by an executive of their own party, and would exaggerate the threats posed by an executive of the opposition party – and conversely, with executive oversight of threats posed by the legislature. Hence, there is a need for constitutional courts and new branches that, by concentrating within themselves distinctive forms of expertise, deploy that expertise more effectively than the traditional branches can do. On the question of whether agency independence restricts state power (the intuitive view) or empowers it (the pragmatic understanding of constitutionalism), see Levinson (n 3) 67.

explicit: *all* compliance or non-compliance is subject to their control. The processing power of public and private parties might be legitimate in many cases, but even in these cases, its concrete deployment and compliance need to be systematically watched over by individual rights holders and official agencies, acting as 'proxy advocates' or 'offices of goodness'.[100]

## VIII. The Vitality of European Constitutionalism after Lisbon

Rights such as data protection and offering a tool to assess the legality of powers derived by data expediency and technology ubiquity, both in formal and substantive terms, have made constitutions ready for the twenty-first century. They bring new powers, such as that of economic elites, within constitutionalism.

Some authors seem to believe that a proportionality-based review of all state actions is a sufficient basis for constitutional rights protection insofar as proportionality looks at and asks questions about how states justify their actions.[101] If this view is shared broadly, it might be an option to take the principle *out* of human rights law and transfer it into the chapter on the judiciary in the regular constitutional texts. Such a transfer would testify to the vitality of human rights law as one of the main testing grounds of constitutionalism in the past decades.[102]

But there are good reasons to avoid blind trust in a principle that often tends to be no more than state-friendly loose balancing. Undeniably, proportionality review enhances and ensures accountability of public power and can contribute to restricting this power. Data protection law recognises proportionality as one of its foundational principles, but it is also about much more. Through recognising data subject rights, duties for those that process data, and, most importantly, the elaboration on a broad range of principles,[103] data protection goes beyond a proportionality test and offers a broad(er) range of tools to oblige states to explain state actions and justify them.

[100] Levinson (n 3) 117. Both terms refer to government officials who are charged with representing disempowered interests in administrative decision-making processes.

[101] K Moller, 'Dworkin's Theory of Rights in the Age of Proportionality' (2018) 12 *Law & Ethics of Human Rights* 288.

[102] On the impact of human rights and its impulses as part of a process of constitutionalising of legal areas, see the chapters of A Davies, AL Young, C Herresthal, PM Huber and A Bradley who address the process of constitutionalisation in the area of labour law, private law and administrative law from different perspectives in KS Ziegler and PM Huber (eds), *Current Problems in the Protection of Human Rights* (Oxford, Hart Publishing, 2013).

[103] Art 5 GDPR sets out the seven fundamental principles for the lawful processing of data. They are the principles of: 'lawfulness, fairness and transparency' of processing; the principle of 'purpose limitation' (only collect and process data for clearly articulated purposes, and not for just 'anything'); the principle 'data minimisation' (no data collection than necessary); the principle of 'accuracy' (data must be accurate, relevant and up to date); the principle of 'storage limitation' (data stored must be necessary or deleted); the principle of 'integrity and confidentiality' and the principle of 'accountability' (those that process data are responsible and must obey rules on document keeping). These principles should lie at the heart of an approach to processing personal data.

If fuzzy legality (Cohn) is a permanent grey hole (Dyzenhaus) of the contemporary administrative state (be it the welfare state or surveillance state), there is more need than ever for understanding power mechanisms that operate in the shadow of the law without being substantively framed by it. Although not 'illegal' under conventional legal standards, fuzzy legality sweeps away laws' advantages, weakens accountability, and limits participation. Law, in its statutory form, is still visible and operates as a protective shield for the true nature of actions that cannot be judged or reviewed in light of the statute.[104] Both Dyzenhaus and Cohn offer new directions of constitutional innovation, one of them being that of augmenting all forms of review of executive action. As seen above, data protection can play a role in balancing fuzzy legality. Its long list of rules, principles, and duties to respect individual data subject rights enriches the palette of judges that within human rights law is now narrowly focused on whether a restriction on the right is proportionate or not. More questions can be asked to powerful administrations that operate in the shadow but are now forced to undergo both proportionality *and* data protection review. The template is not only superior in terms of granularity of question asking but also in terms of operationality: the enforcement hugely benefits from the work (advisory, policing, and regulatory) of permanent administrations (the supervisory authorities) that take over the role of the courts without making these redundant (courts still have the last word after administrative enforcement of data protection rules). These authorities or proxy advocates hold great potential in the context of additional or extended mechanisms of accountability that supplement traditional accountability mechanisms.[105] We recall Margit Cohn's proposal for new review mechanisms (complementing the role of judiciaries in traditional constitutionalism) that operate as an additional forum and intermediator between individuals and decision-makers. For these additional mechanisms to be successful, any idea of the supremacy of the supervisor based on hierarchical thinking (central in classical but non-performing constitutionalism) must be left aside in favour of a review that promotes deliberation and participation.[106] Data protection authorities can play such a role when supervising compliance and reacting to complaints about data protection violations by individuals. The discretion left to them by European data protection law has led to practices of arbitrage, with these authorities moving back and forth between the complaining individual and the respective actor (public or private) processing their data before reaching an opinion about the matter that eventually could lead to an administrative sanction. Data protection thus offers important means to keep legality tensions under control.

The distinction made in our contribution in relation to privacy and data protection within old and new constitutionalism should not be seen as creating a point of friction between these legal instruments. Privacy is an important dimension of data protection, and data protection adds important dimensions to privacy enforcement. 'A mixed approach between two instruments should be favored, but that also chooses

[104] M Cohn, 'Fuzzy Legality in Regulation. The Legislative Mandate Revisited' (2001) 23 *Law & Policy* 490.
[105] C Scott, 'Accountability in the Regulatory State' (2000) 27 *Journal of Law and Society* 38–60. More in detail, see P De Hert and P Hajduk, 'EU Cross-regime Enforcement, Redundancy and Interdependence. Addressing Overlap of Enforcement Structures in the Digital Sphere after Meta' (2024) *Technology and Regulation* 291–308.
[106] Cohn, *A Theory of the Executive Branch* (n 1) 310–330.

the right policy and regulatory option at time.'[107] A good way to see this is to look at whether certain issues raised by technologies bring to the fore either the question about the kind of powers that we need in society or the subsequent question about how to regulate powers that we find compatible with our society. The first question is about input legitimacy, and the subsequent or second question is about legitimacy or procedural legality. The first question stands central in the privacy provisions like article 8 ECHR and article 7 Charter ('What kind of interference is necessary in a democratic society?'); the second question is answered in Charter provisions like article 8 Charter (data protection), article 47 (effective remedy), article 41 (right to a good administration), article 42 (right of access to documents) and article 43 (ombudsman).

Due process rights such as data protection, like other due process rights such as access to information, are very much needed in current constitutions. While being no replacement for input and output legitimacy, they close the loop of the rule of law by focusing on distinctive normative criteria such as transparency and accountability and distinctive elements for institutional reform and regulation of new developments. The empirical reality of power with its ability for abuse in the course of action is complex, and due process rights help interrogate it.[108]

Legitimacy is not a matter of solely delineating powers but of guaranteeing legitimacy in the full circle of power use (input, throughput, and output). All these rights make power more transparent and give a voice to every citizen. Hence our choice in our 2006 writings to speak about *transparency rights* as opposed to *opacity rights*. Most of the transparency rights provisions in the Charter open with the reassuring opening words 'Every person has the right to.' Although present amongst the general principles of law or as rights in the 1950 European Convention on Human Rights, all the transparency rights mentioned above received an expansive makeover when incorporated in the Charter,[109] testifying to the transformative constitutional relevance of this document. With the Lisbon Treaty solidifying the Charter's binding character, this relevance was understood by the CJEU through its case law, which fundamentally changed the EU legal argumentation on rights limitations and the goal of effective judicial protection. With its updated list of fundamental rights, the Charter (with its explicit mentioning of data protection as a new autonomous fundamental right) became the standard in the whole of Europe, the reference document to face the challenges of the twenty-first century, and allowed better putting into terms of fundamental rights and fundamental rights principles arguments that were previously latent.[110]

[107] De Hert and Gutwirth (n 5) 93–95. Comparing the 'superficial conflation of the fundamental right to privacy and data protection' is risky, indeed doubly risky: on the one hand, if data protection is subsumed under privacy, it might weaken the former; but, on the other hand, if data protection subsumes privacy, this might weaken the latter (R Brownsword, *Law, Technology and Society. Reimagining the Regulatory Environment* (Milton, Routledge, 2019) 304).

[108] Schmidt and Wood (n 25) 727.

[109] On the Charter as a transformative, rather than codifying constitution, see P De Hert and S Gutwirth, 'Data Protection in the Case Law of Strasbourg and Luxemburg: Constitutionalisation in Action' in S Gutwirth, Y Poullet, P De Hert, S Nouwt and C de Terwange (eds), *Reinventing Data Protection?* (Berlin, Springer, 2009) 3–45.

[110] 'It has also fostered the consolidation of some fundamental rights that were formerly considered to be components or derivations of other fundamental rights' (S Iglesias Sánchez, 'The Court and the Charter: The impact of the entry into force of the Lisbon Treaty on the ECJ's approach to fundamental rights' (2012) 49

## IX. Why a Political Account? The Democratic Role of Legality and Rights

The title of the contribution promises a *political* account of privacy and data protection as opposed to a pre-political or natural law account or any other philosophical or definitional account of privacy and data protection. Of course, we have intuitions and personal views on the nature of both concepts. In previous work, a liberty-, freedom-, or autonomy-based understanding of privacy was defended (we used the terms interchangeably).[111] Rights like privacy, data protection, freedom of thought, and others protect liberty interests. In law, there is no raw or pure understanding of freedom. Our system of rights (including its exceptions and limitation clauses) functions as a filter that allows (or not) all sorts of liberty to be brought into the constitutional realm, with, at least in Europe, privacy being the most frequently used filter and gateway.[112]

*Glukhin v Russia* (2023) is about Russian authorities using facial-recognition technology against a citizen (Glukhin) while he was holding a solo demonstration in the Moscow underground.[113] A formal, narrow understanding of the human rights at stake was avoided in the judgment. The European Court of Human Rights used the language of data protection and of classical human rights like privacy and freedom of expression. It found a violation of article 8 (right to respect for private life)[114] *and* a violation of article 10 (freedom of expression)[115] of the European Convention on Human Rights. The judgment testifies to the vitality of European privacy law capable of incorporating modern threats in the public space,[116] but the section on article 10 ECHR shows that this is more than just another privacy case.

*Common Market Law Review* 1578). On the effects of the updated list of rights in the Charter, see: Iglesias Sánchez 1599–1600. See also A Torres Pérez, 'The Federalizing Force of the EU Charter of Fundamental Rights' (2017) 15 *International Journal of Constitutional Law* 1080–1097.

[111] S Gutwirth, *Privacy and the Information Age* (Lanham, Rowman & Littlefield Publishing, 2002) 158; P De Hert, *Article 8 ECHR and the Law in Belgium. Protection of Privacy, House, Family and Correspondence* (Ghent, Mys en Breesch Uitgeverij, 1998) 367. See also F Rigaux, *La protection de la vie privée et des autres biens de la personnalité* (Brussel/Paris, Bruylant/L.GDJ, 1990) 849.

[112] 'There is no "raw" or "pure" understanding of freedom, and consequently, no "raw" or "pure" understanding of rights. Praxis constitutes (and rationalises) autonomy. Rights are interwoven with collective goods, institutional structures, rationalities of government, and with law as a means of social integration. Not only do the subjective rights of individuals enter into conflict, but also there are obvious tensions between the protection of the collective goods on which the effectiveness of the system of rights rests, and the protection of specific and concrete subjective rights' (Nasir (n 74) 299).

[113] ECtHR, *Glukhin v Russia*, 4 July 2023, application no. 11519/20.

[114] The Court concluded that the processing of Glukhin's personal data in the context of his peaceful demonstration, which had not caused any danger to public order or safety, had been particularly intrusive. The use of facial-recognition technology in his case had been incompatible with the ideals and values of a democratic society governed by the rule of law.

[115] The solo demonstration had not caused any danger to public order or safety and no 'relevant or sufficient reasons' were given to justify escorting Glukhin to the police station, arresting and convicting him.

[116] Privacy violations have been a key yellow card through which poorly regulated technology has been identified as problematic and challenged. The ECtHR applied a broad understanding of the concept of 'private life', which included '(…) multiple aspects of the person's physical and social identity (and) is not limited to an "inner circle (…), but also encompasses the right to lead a "private social life", meaning the right to develop a relationship with others and the outside world without outside interference' (§64). Participation in public activities, such as the demonstration in question, implies an awareness that one may be observed and recorded, limiting an individual's reasonable expectation of privacy (Comp. V Aston, 'State Surveillance

In the past, our focus was on the political function of human rights and their contribution to the other tenets of constitutionalism.[117] That contribution is rich, sometimes too rich. Is it not time to transfer entire human rights chapters, like the one on the quality of law and the requirement that laws need to be foreseeable to the classical constitutional texts and be woven into the chapters on the tasks, duties, and prerogatives of the legislator?

(All) European rights are about curtailing the conduct of states and the use of abusive stratagems by states and rights-holders that might undermine democratic constitutionalism.[118] The objective of European human rights law is to keep *all* state institutions in check, including the legislator, by imposing on them a series of duties.[119] These duties, together with the limitation clauses, exceptions, and anti-abuse provisions in human rights (case)law, inform about what can be done and, as importantly, about what cannot be done (hence Muhammad Nasir's term 'negative governmentality'). The limitation clauses and exceptions set the respective rights and freedoms in their socio-economic context and allow rights (formulated in a general way) to be calibrated, taking into account specific relationships between the individual and public authorities.[120]

of Protest and the Rights to Privacy and Freedom of Assembly: A Comparison of Judicial and Protester Perspectives' (2017) 8 *European Journal of Law and Technology* 19, 13 (via www.ejlt.org/index.php/ejlt/article/view/548) Still, the ECtHR recognised the application of the privacy right in this case: systematic recording of certain public activities could still constitute an interference with an individual's private life (§66). In this instance, the expansion of the scope of 'private life' to include public activities was a warranted approach to the pervasive nature of mass surveillance technologies in public spaces.

[117] De Hert and Gurtwirth (n 5) 91. Van der Sloot rightly recalls that this political objective of human rights law is the original and still valid focus of the Convention (more so than protecting individual rights): 'the Convention first and foremost provides minimum rules for the conduct of state parties to the Convention (referred to in this contribution simply as "states"). The focus is on duties (of care) for states, rather than individual and subjective rights' (B van der Sloot (n 57) 441). This constitutional focus on power and the duties of states to respect minimum conditions is also clear form the text of the more absolute provisions in the Convention with state duties, that cannot be violated by states, not even in the state of emergency (art 15 ECHR), to respect life (art 2 ECHR), not to torture or to apply inhuman or degrading treatment or punishment (art 3 ECHR), not to hold in slavery or servitude (art 4), not to use retrospective legislation (art 7 ECHR), not to abuse its powers (art 17 ECHR) or abuse prescribed restrictions of rights (art 18 ECHR). Even with the four qualified rights in art 8–11 ECHR (right to privacy, freedom of religion, freedom of speech and freedom of association) the primary focus of the Convention authors seemed to be on curtailing the conduct of states. See B van der Sloot (n 57) 441.

[118] Nasir (n 62) 229.

[119] When drafting the Convention there was considerable discussion over the question of to what extent the ECtHR should scrutinise the legislative branch of Member States, van der Sloot observes, 'the hope of the "constitutionalists" was that the Court would focus especially on questions over whether laws and the legal regime as such were in conformity with the rule of law and whether they served the general interest' but 'the Convention turned out to be a system providing relief to individuals who are harmed specifically by an action or inaction of the executive or judicial branch, such as when the police unlawfully enters a person's home' (B van der Sloot, 'The Quality of Law: How the European Court of Human Rights Gradually Became a European Constitutional Court for Privacy Cases' (2020) 11 *Journal of Intellectual Property, Information Technology and E-Commerce Law* 163). The constitutionalists' hope for a court scrutinising laws and policies as such and remedying structural and societal problems only started to materialise around the 1980s with judgments, in particular in the area of privacy, that focused on the role of the domestic legislator, assessed the quality of laws in detail and even instructed the legislator on how to revise or amend its legal regime (van der Sloot 163). See also section VI, above.

[120] Nasir (n 74) 297–320.

European human rights law is legal or political. Its rights cannot be understood in a pre-political or natural (law) sense but in a political or constructivist sense.[121]

Concepts such as *opacity* and *transparency* with their complementary role might help to understand the human rights framework but go beyond. They were formulated to understand how constitutionalism works or should work. The human rights framework only adds tools to the existing opacity and transparency tools in (un)written constitutions.[122] If the notion of opacity has a meaning in the area of human rights, it must combine both the negative and positive sides of rights: not only what can be done with and through rights, but also what cannot be done with and through rights, and this not on paper but in the reality of a legal system. A formal proclamation of rights is not enough,[123] and continued analysis is needed to find out whether powers are constrained by fundamental rights.

The case law of the European courts on privacy and data protection might be too fuzzy to please philosophical understandings of privacy averse to plural grounding,[124] but politically, it is delivering *sometimes* when it finds a deontological tone and clarifies our understanding of hierarchies of principles and interests.[125] Without any hierarchy, it is difficult to conceive any order.

[121] Yes, these rights affirm certain normative standards, but in a general way that does not inform a given society without context. Rights like art 8 are not to be construed as 'natural' rights or privileges, where we see freedom as an individual property or as a capacity subsequently protected by law. See Nasir (n 62) 334–355. Limitations and exception-clauses are constructivist tools that allow to flesh out the value of freedom and connect the said rights with the other constitutional principles, written or unwritten, in a given society. The Convention message is that, as a rights-holder, we are free to the extent that laws respect our private and family life. 'This includes legitimate legal interferences into our privacies, structuration of conduct and enabling certain conduct through social practices backed by laws. Consequently, art 8 does not allow legal rules to evaluate the wills and preferences of rights-holders with reference to a fixed normative lens' (Nasir (n 62) 349). About the two rights and their definitions, Kirsty Hughes can be followed when she notes that there is not much 'unique' about individual privacy. In legal settings, it is difficult to weight privacy against other rights and interests because, for instance, many rights and interests, not just privacy, are fundamental to autonomy and dignity (K Hughes, 'The Absence of Privacy in the Right to Privacy'(2018) *PLSC paper* 47–48). In a similar way, this contribution treats data protection as (only) a new branch on the due process tree, that is one of the pillars of the rule-of-law project. The definition is (about) what it does and when. Data protection law is everywhere there is processing, even a very banal one. The legal right to privacy should guide us when important questions are raised about power implications for private life and our legal intuition tells us that the privacy right and not any other rights (like the legal right to protection of family life, of communication, of the house, etc) should be the filter or starting point for the normative exercise about the amount of discipline of those with power.

[122] Provisions in a constitution on the power of the legislature (or the lack of power) to have or not a standing army in peace time is an example of an opacity provision. The 1776 US Constitution without a Bill of Rights was perfectly capable of addressing some important issues of (abuse of) power.

[123] Nasir (n 74) 299.

[124] Rössler asserts, for instance, that the concept of privacy is 'far too heterogeneous for there to be a single consistent and meaningful right to it' (B Rössler, 'Privacy as a Human Right' (2017) 117 *Proc Aristot Soc* 193–194). Pragmatic belief in plural grounding of judicial reasoning explains why I do not see that much of a problem with the ECtHR including data protection in the scope of the right to privacy and with the CJEU that often chooses a combined approach in its judgments that does not allow the scholarly community to understand in a precise manner where one right stops and another one starts. Critical about the lack of full exploitation of the possibilities of the right to data protection, see W van Ballegooij (n 94) 551–552 with a discussion of the work of Maria Tzanou. More in general on this issue, GG Fuster, *The Emergence of Personal Data Protection as a Fundamental Right of the EU* (Berlin, Springer, 2014).

[125] Case C-470/21, *La Quadrature du Net and Others v Premier ministre and Ministère de la Culture*, CJEU, 30 April 2024.

Let us return to some of the strong points in *Glukhin*. *First*, the holistic method of problem assessment. The language of data protection ('facial recognition is processing of personal power') and its specific sources[126] are used to build up a privacy and freedom of expression case and to identify the duties of the state when applying surveillance methods. Mixing of these three tools (data protection, privacy, and freedom of expression) allows for a better, more holistic human rights understanding of novel problems and power practices like the one applied in *Glukhin*.[127] *Second*, the normative guidance. The judgment contains a clear freedom of expression veto to blind punishment of unlawful conduct in the context of demonstrations.[128] Equally, there is a privacy veto to the use of highly intrusive facial recognition technology by police for investigating a minor administrative offence that did not pose a threat to public order. The added value of these vetoes is considerable. It is not too difficult to draft far-reaching police laws using abundant data protection language; as a matter of fact, it is part of the common tactics used in the expansion of surveillance around the globe.[129] If you want police forces to use drones, just avoid the term and amend your basic laws on the use of CCTV. Technology neutrality is inspired by data protection law, and the power differences that matter are gone.[130] After *Glukhin*, it should be inconceivable that states pass facial recognition laws that do not explicitly address the bright-line rules contained in both vetoes.

*Third*, the judgment connects in a refreshing way with the constitutional rule-of-law project and its principles of legality and legal certainty by attacking the fuzzy legality of the Russian legal system regarding demonstrations and facial recognition.[131] There

[126] The ECtHR cites the GDPR (European Union) and Guidelines of the European Data Protection Board, on the one hand, and the Guidelines on Facial Recognition (2021) by the Consultative Committee of the Convention for the Protection of Individuals with regard to Automatic Processing of Personal Data (ETS 108), on the other hand. Neither this Council of Europe Convention nor its Consultative Committee nor the European Data Protection Board have been discussed in this contribution, but their existence only proves the richness of the data protection apparatus setting up more collective or polycentric systems of rights protection and enforcement that include many actors. See our discussion of Bennett and Raab above.

[127] C Cocito, P De Hert and T Marquenie, 'Do Human Rights Frameworks Identify AI's Problems? The Limits of a Burgeoning Methodology for AI Problem Assessment' (2025) *The International Journal of Human Rights* 1–24.

[128] The right to freedom of expression and the limitation grounds in art 10 ECHR demand for governmental discipline: 'The only relevant consideration was the need to punish unlawful conduct. This is not a sufficient consideration in this context, in terms of Art 10 of the Convention, in the absence of any aggravating elements' (§57).

[129] See MH Murphy, *Surveillance and the Law Language, Power and Privacy* (Milton Park, Routledge, 2019) 106. This book by Maria Helen Murphy is a very valuable addition to the work on grey holes by Dyzenhous and fuzzy legality by Margit Cohn.

[130] P De Hert, 'The Future of Privacy. Addressing Singularities to Identify Bright-Line Rules That Speak to Us' (2016) 2 *European Data Protection Law Review* 461–466.

[131] The ECtHR found that the Russian prohibition on 'quickly (de)assembled objects' contained no criteria allowing a person to foresee what kind of objects could be covered by that provision (§54). It also found that domestic law did not contain specific limitations on the nature of situations that triggered the use of facial recognition technology, nor its intended purposes, the potential targets, and the categories of personal data to be collected (§83). The absence of clear standards failed to ensure data processing was confined to what was strictly necessary, granting the police authorities an unacceptable degree of discretion in determining what constitutes a justifiable interference to the right of private life. Moreover, the ECtHR also considered that the legal provision permitting the processing of biometric personal data 'in connection with the administration of justice' was too vague (§83). Such ambiguity, coupled with the absence of authoritative, restrictive interpretative Russian case law (§83), allowed for its application to an overtly broad range of offences – encompassing criminal, administrative, and civil matters – in an unreasonable undifferentiated manner. Lastly, the Court

is no doubt in the eyes of the Court that the domestic laws on both topics did not meet the quality requirement. However, these findings on the legality requirement were given *in passing*. Seemingly, the European Court was driven by the need to express itself on the necessity requirements to produce normative knowledge by clarifying the meaning of both rights so that the homework to be done by the Russian legislator to amend the fuzziness of its laws would guarantee not only formal but also substantive compliance. Freedoms are explained in their normative context, and the political or constitutional function of human rights is at its peak.

A concern for freedom in the light of possible abuses by powerful public and private actors and a concern for democracy explain why, on the one hand, our writings do not really care about privacy and data protection per se and question their uniqueness in the broader constitutional landscape, but, on the other hand, there is in these writings enchantment if both of them combine forces in human rights disputes like *Glukhin*: 1) the legal privacy right with its binary outcomes and its focus on the normative necessity principle clarifying fundamental go's and no's and with a material scope that keeps up with contemporary developments in society and its technology,[132] and 2) data protection law with the work of the proxy advocates and their impact on concrete disputes, state discipline and caselaw, with its focus on complementary principles such as transparency, accountability and its low threshold to be applicable: a simple processing of data, however banal, triggers data protection, and through this broad material scope, sets the wheel of law in motion with possible legal crowbars to put a crack in the walls of power.[133]

## X. Why a Political Account? Freedom to Question Brutal or Creepy Power in the Realm of Action

There is literature offering political accounts more directly connected with privacy and data protection.[134] The account presented here is limited to privacy and data protection *qualitate qua* human rights to confront power. In my view, the disciplining of power

found that the government also did not provide any safeguards accompanying the use of facial recognition technology, that would have lessened the effects of the interference (§83).

[132] From a human rights perspective, a proliferation of privacy understandings has its positives. This proliferation, not only in literature but also in judicial settings, has had a manifest benefit in clarifying, providing concreteness, and refining more tailored interpretations of the interests encompassed by an abstract human right. The European courts, such as the European Court of Human Rights, have played a leading role in multiplying the facets of privacy in Europe and thus in expanding the contours of what comes to be conceived as a privacy violation. Privacy in Europe has become a fairly inclusive legal right, whereby all kinds of issues that do not easily fit in existing rights are fit by the Court into privacy rights. For instance, harm to health or environmental interests may be assessed as a privacy violation. In section VI, above, we commented on the broad, pragmatic handling in *Glukhin* of the concept of 'private life', a broad term not susceptible to exhaustive definition and including the right to lead a 'private social life' with others and the outside world. It does not exclude activities taking place in a public context.

[133] S Gutwirth and P De Hert, 'Human Rights: A Secular Religion with Legal Crowbars. From Europe with Hesitations' (2021) 33 *National Law School of India Review* 420–462.

[134] See, eg, C Véliz, *Privacy is Power* (London, Penguin (Bantam Press) 2020). For Carissa Véliz, privacy is not a personal preference; it is a political concern and a kind of power. If people give too much of their data to corporations, the wealthy will rule. If people give too much personal data to governments, there is a risk of

constitutes a necessary guarantee of freedom. Like most of the notions employed in this contribution, *freedom* too is not used in a pre-political or philosophical sense as the philosophical idea of free will, but in its political sense: freedom as a matter of action. It was Hannah Arendt who reminded us of this original meaning of the term.[135] Freedom as an inner human disposition, as an attribute or property of free will of thought of individuals, is a relatively recent invention, having been created by Christians for theological and strategical reasons[136] and picked up by liberalism to further divorce freedom from politics.[137] Freedom as a matter of action in the world is the original sense of the term, stemming from the Greek and Roman experience of public life. Arendt has a relational concept of freedom, very similar to the ideas defended above. Freedom does not come to the fore in isolation but is enjoyed or hampered in intercourse with others and not in the intercourse with oneself. Mankind can only *be* free, she argues, with reference to one another, only, that is, in the fields of politics and of the things they do; it is only in these spheres that they come to realise that freedom is something positive and not merely a negation of compulsion. Arendt's relational concept is not naïve: not every human relation involves freedom. Freedom only becomes possible in the political sphere – the realm of action.[138]

With Augustine's political work, she elaborates on the idea of freedom as *qua* beginning that starts from human existence in the world: man is free because he is a beginning and a beginner.[139] With every newborn, this initial beginning is reaffirmed. 'God', Arendt states, based on her reading of Augustine, 'created man in order to introduce into the world the faculty of beginning: freedom'.[140] Freedom is the sheer capacity to begin; it remains present even when political life has become petrified, and political action has become important to interrupt automatic processes.[141] We are surrounded by cosmic and natural processes and are part of organic nature. All these processes are automatic, and even processes started by men (in political life) tend to become as automatic as these natural or cosmic processes. History seems to be a determined, automatic

sliding into authoritarianism. For democracy to be strong, the bulk of power needs to be with the citizenry, and whoever has the data will have the power.

[135] H Arendt, 'What is Freedom' in *Between Past and Future. Eight Exercises in Political Thought* (New York, The Viking Press, 1968) 143–171.

[136] One of the more strategic reasons for the inner self-freedom concept of the early Christians is their suspicion of and hostility against the public realm as such, from whose concerns they demanded to be absolved in order to be free (Arendt (n 135) 150–151).

[137] Part of this typical liberal approach is to narrow politics to security, maintenance of life and to safeguard the interests the interests of society and its individuals. 'Here freedom is not even the nonpolitical aim of politics, but a marginal phenomenon – which somehow forms the boundary government should not overstep unless life itself and its immediate interests and necessities are at stake' (Arendt (n 135) 150). Government is now identified with the total domain of politics and is no longer the protector of freedom, but of the life process, the interests of society and its individual (Arendt 150). Under this sway of necessity and the priority to take care of life necessities, the administration of social and economic life in modern states will overshadow the political realm. Everything is ultimately springing from economic factors and interests with only one exception: foreign affairs because of its relationship between nations harbours hostilities and sympathy that cannot be reduced to economic factors and is left as a purely political domain (Arendt (n 135)).

[138] 'Freedom as a demonstrable fact and politics coincide and are related to each other like two sides of the same matter' (Arendt (n 135), 149).

[139] Augustine laid some of the foundations of the Christian concept of individual free will, but Arendt finds in his political work *The City of Gods* an account of political freedom as the capacity for beginnings.

[140] Arendt (n 135) 167.

[141] ibid 169.

process like the other processes, but it is full of unpredictability that we usually forget to see. Freedom, then, is a capacity to do miracles, to do the unexpected. It is no less than the human capacity to interrupt old processes and begin new ones.[142] Thriving constitutionalism does not come into being naturally, but grey holes and fuzzy legality do. If privacy and data protection, with their complementary gifts, help block abusive power mechanisms, either brutal or insidious, and lift the sway of self-interest or necessity so that democratic and constitutional action and discussion can take place, they perform miracles.

[142] ibid 169–170. For a more democratic conception of European data protection law, with a role for national states, see P De Hert, 'Data Protection's Future without Democratic Bright Line Rules. Co-existing with Technologies in Europe after Breyer' (2017) 3 *European Data Protection Law Review* 20–35.

# 13

# A Fundamental Right to Data Protection – Or Rather a Rule of Law for the Digital Age? A Search for Clues in Judicial Procedural Law

NIKOLAUS MARSCH*

## I. Introduction: Thesis, Structure … and Jimmy

For the past three years, we have had a Parson Russell terrier called Jimmy. I never wanted a dog because I'm not particularly fond of dogs. But my wife and children outvoted me – and now I love Jimmy, too. In Germany, dog owners are required to pay a tax. To do so, you must register your dog with the local authority, which will then send you an annual tax bill. Therefore, the city of Saarbrücken, where we live, has stored the information that my wife owns a dog (she did not have to communicate the name of Jimmy). This information is neither particularly sensitive nor does it reveal much about our private life. After all, my wife or my children leave the house with Jimmy several times a day – and when we are not at home, Jimmy usually lies on the window-sill and watches the passers-by (and often they watch him). Nevertheless, according to the case law of the German Federal Constitutional Court, the storage of this trivial and publicly known information by the city of Saarbrücken constitutes an infringement (not necessarily a violation!) of a fundamental right, namely the right to informational self-determination. This is not entirely intuitive, so: why does the Federal Constitutional Court rule this way? And why does the ECJ today also have the same understanding of article 8 of the EU Charter of Fundamental Rights (CFR)?

To explore these questions, I will begin this contribution by briefly recalling two interrelated questions that are also discussed in several articles in this book. First, how is the right to informational self-determination, as developed by the Federal Constitutional Court, constructed – in other words: what is the content of the right? Second (following on from this, but not to be confused with it), what do the right to informational self-determination of the German Basic Law and the fundamental right to data protection

* The author would like to thank Sven Braun and Timo Rademacher for their valuable comments and advice.

of the EU Charter of Fundamental Rights actually protect against, or: why is such a fundamental right needed? (II).

My thesis is that the answer (or at least part of it) can be found in German constitutional *procedural* law. This stipulates that constitutional complaints by citizens are only admissible if they can claim a violation of fundamental rights. The Federal Constitutional Court, which in 1983 had to decide on the constitutionality of the census, therefore had to 'develop' a fundamental right in order to be able to control the underlying law at all. Keeping this in mind, the question of what the fundamental right is supposed to protect against can be discussed much more openly, because it is no longer consistently necessary to link every aspect of the fundamental right to the specific interests of the citizen concerned. Especially the comparison to the famous *Elfes* decision of the Federal Constitutional Court, which is fundamental to public law in Germany, shows that the right to informational self-determination can also (or even better?) be understood as an anchor for a rule of law for the digital age (III).

Such an understanding of the right to informational self-determination as a fundamental right, which owes its existence to procedural law and through which a digital rule of law is subjectivised, also helps to better understand the case law of the German Federal Constitutional Court, the ECtHR and the ECJ. Therefore, I will try to substantiate and explain my thesis with the help of a few examples (IV). This leads to a brief presentation of my considerations, as set out in detail elsewhere,[1] that the fundamental right to data protection in article 8 CFR should not be understood as a right to informational self-determination in the German sense, but rather as an obligation on the legislator to enact data protection legislation that is adequate to protect (other) fundamental rights (V).

## II. Construction and Concept of the Fundamental Right to Informational Self-Determination

Let us therefore first consider the right to informational self-determination as it has been derived from the Basic Law by the Federal Constitutional Court. In this regard it is important to distinguish between the technical construction (ie, the content) of the fundamental right (A) and its underlying theoretical concept (B).

### A. Construction: The Requirement of a Legal Basis for Data Processing by Public Authorities as the Core of the Fundamental Right

What exactly does the right to informational self-determination entail? The Federal Constitutional Court ruled in the census judgment, and has maintained ever since,

[1] See (in German) my book N Marsch, *Das europäische Datenschutzgrundrecht. Grundlagen – Dimensionen – Verflechtungen*, Jus Publicum 270 (Tübingen, Mohr Siebeck, 2018); for a summary (in English) see my contribution N Marsch, 'Artificial Intelligence and the Fundamental Right to Data Protection: Opening the Door for Technological Innovation and Innovative Protection' in T Wischmeyer and T Rademacher (eds), *Regulating Artificial Intelligence* (Cham, Springer, 2020) 33, 43–6.

that this fundamental right 'confers upon the individual the authority to, in principle, decide themselves on the disclosure and use of their personal data'.[2] Therefore, any data processing by state authorities constitutes an infringement of fundamental rights. This means that the Federal Constitutional Court goes one step further than the ECtHR, which always asks whether data is related to private life or whether it has been stored in a systematic way (especially by security agencies).[3] As early as 1983, the Federal Constitutional Court stated that, in view of the possibilities created by information technology for processing and linking data, no data can now be considered insignificant.[4]

The basic assumption that everyone should be able to freely determine how all their data is processed (because there is no longer any insignificant data) hardly seems realistic today. Especially during the Covid pandemic, the fight against which required the processing of personal data, its plausibility was also called into question. However, this criticism is essentially due to the excessive interpretation and application of the fundamental right, which in turn is based on two misunderstandings that the Federal Constitutional Court itself had addressed in the decision. *First*, the description of the content of the right to informational self-determination must not be misunderstood to mean that the fundamental right gives individuals a kind of right of control over their personal data, similar to a property right.[5] In the words of the Court, the right to informational self-determination 'does not afford the individual absolute or unlimited control over "their" personal data ... Any information, including personal data, mirrors social reality and thus cannot be attributed exclusively to the person concerned'.[6] *Second*, it does not follow from the decision (and especially not from the finding that there is no insignificant data) that the processing of personal data by state agencies is in some way axiomatically problematic or even to be avoided. Instead, the Federal Constitutional Court states that 'in the context of modern data processing, the free development of one's personality ... requires that the individual be protected against the *unlimited* [emphasis added] collection, storage, use and sharing of their personal data'.[7]

The Federal Constitutional Court does not consider data processing to be problematic when it is limited but rather when it is unlimited. The difficulty, however, is that unlimited data processing can only be prevented by addressing individual data processing operations. The example of video surveillance illustrates this problem well: it can be argued that individual video surveillance measures in public spaces, indicated by signs, do not infringe upon fundamental rights, as individuals have the option to avoid such surveillance. Besides, it is only their behaviour in public that is filmed, and they may adapt their behaviour in response to the surveillance. However, anyone who takes this

[2] BVerfGE 65, 1 [1983] – *Volkszählungsgesetz* para 147; the decision is also discussed in detail by Albers, ch 2 in this volume.

[3] In the decision ECtHR, *Magyar Helsinki Bizottság*, 8 November 2016, Case 18030/11, para 194, the Court, sitting as Grand Chamber, explicitly stated, that not every disclosure of personal data by a public authority constitutes an infringement of art 8 ECHR; regarding the previous case law of the ECtHR, see Marsch, *Datenschutzgrundrecht* (n 1) 8–17.

[4] BVerfGE 65, 1 para 150.

[5] See Masing, ch 3 this volume; R Poscher, 'The Right to Data Protection – A No-Right Thesis' in R Miller (ed), *Privacy and Power – A Transatlantic Dialogue in the Shadow of the NSA-Affair* (Cambridge, Cambridge University Press, 2017) 132–3.

[6] BVerfGE 65, 1 para 150.

[7] ibid.

view is going to run into a problem if not only one but hundreds or thousands of video cameras are installed in a city. This is because a quantitative determination of when behaviour that is neutral in terms of fundamental rights turns into an infringement of fundamental rights raises considerable difficulties.

For this reason, the core of the right to informational self-determination is, first and foremost, a very formal one, namely the requirement of a legal basis that also defines the purpose of the data processing (more or less specific, depending on the significance of the data processing[8]). This prevents the state from collecting and processing personal data for any conceivable purpose without limitation. The requirement of a legal basis with regard to the right to informational self-determination thus has an independent status that goes beyond the usual function of the general requirement of a legal basis for encroachment on fundamental rights. It is not without reason that the fundamental right to data protection under article 8 CFR explicitly reiterates the requirement of a legal basis (article 8(2)), although this is already stipulated in article 52(1) CFR for all fundamental rights – including the fundamental right to data protection.

## B. Concept: An Instrumental and Supra-Individualistic Fundamental Right

While the requirement of a legal basis forms the substantive core of the construction of the right to informational self-determination, this does not yet answer the question of the theoretical concept, the 'why'. What is the protected interest of the fundamental right – which individual interest is at the centre of the right to informational self-determination? There are a multitude of answers to this question, which has long preoccupied not only German legal scholars but is also at the heart of this book. I will summarise some of these answers here only very briefly and selectively.

Ralf Poscher's provocative 'no-right thesis' serves as a starting point.[9] In a first step, just as in the well-known fairy tale 'The Emperor's New Clothes', Poscher describes the fundamental right as naked in a first step, since it does not protect any particular liberty interest and is therefore not really a fundamental right at all. However, Ralf Poscher does not leave it at that finding.[10] In a second step, he goes on to turn the right to informational self-determination into a positive right – one could say in the sense of an 'all-rights thesis'. In his view, the purpose of the right to informational self-determination, or data protection, is to enhance all other fundamental rights by protecting not only against encroachment and specific risks, as in the case of classic fundamental rights, but also against abstract dangers associated with data processing. Gabriele Britz takes a similarly constructive approach, although she chooses a different

[8] See generally N Marsch and T Rademacher, 'Generalklauseln im Datenschutzrecht – Zur Rehabilitierung eines zentralen Bausteins des allgemeinen Informationsverwaltungsrechts' (2021) 54 *Die Verwaltung* 1.

[9] Poscher (n 5). In his contribution to this book (ch 4), Ralf Poscher speaks – somewhat less provocatively – of a 'hollow shell of a right', but in my understanding, he is describing the same characteristic of the fundamental right to data protection.

[10] S Behrendt, *Entzauberung des Rechts auf informationelle Selbstbestimmung. Eine Untersuchung zu den Grundlagen der Grundrechte* (Tübingen, Mohr Siebeck, 2023), takes a different view and therefore rejects the justifiability in legal theory of a right to informational self-determination.

starting point (namely that of the Federal Constitutional Court) by deriving a protection of freedom of individual behaviour from chilling effects from the general right of personality.[11] What both approaches have in common is the understanding of the right to informational self-determination as an instrumental fundamental right. The constitutional prohibition on processing personal data without a legal basis does not represent an end in itself but serves to protect other fundamental rights, whereby this protection intervenes well in advance of any specific impairment of fundamental rights.

Marion Albers goes one step further, rejecting a purely individualistic conception.[12] She argues that the many risks associated with the processing of personal data by public bodies for a wide range of different interests make it necessary to structure the handling of information through regulations at a first level. Only at a second level could data processing be identified in terms of fundamental rights that pose a specific threat to specific freedoms.

Like Johannes Masing, I think that the different conceptual explanations of the right to informational self-determination very often lead to the same results.[13] And despite their different theoretical starting points, to me the concepts do not seem to be so far apart at their core as well. However, in my opinion, each of them emphasises different aspects, which, on the one hand, offer different explanatory approaches for certain court decisions and therefore allow for different reactions to the decisions or to criticism of them. At this point, I do not want to conceal the fact that, in my view, a stronger (not only!) supra-individualistic understanding offers the more convincing explanatory approaches in many cases and immunises data protection both against unjustified criticism and against libertarian misconceptions.

My plea for a perspective that is more abstracted from individual interests follows, on the one hand, from the fact that even an instrumental conception is, at least rhetorically, excessive in its starting point and, on the other hand, that it sometimes fails to capture this rhetorical excess in the application of the law. Let me illustrate this with two simple examples. First: what is the specific interest worthy of protection that leads to the state's knowledge of Jimmy's existence and my wife's ownership being understood as an infringement of fundamental rights? Data protection lawyers regularly answer this question with more or less absurd scenarios, which they use to construct a threat to individual interests in very rare and often very specific individual cases. Apart from the fact that the risks are regularly completely overemphasised here, this line of argument often leads to the burden of justification imposed on the state in specific processing situations being set far too high by many participants in the data protection discussion. The second example is about guest lists that restaurants had to keep for contact tracing purposes during the Covid pandemic. While in the pre-pandemic period no one was concerned about providing personal data when making a reservation, guest lists have been seriously compared to an unfounded and broad-based data retention of

[11] See Britz, ch 5 in this volume; see also Masing, ch 3 in this volume. A Rouvroy and Y Poulet, 'The Right to Informational Self-Determination and the Value of Self-Development: Reassessing the Importance of Privacy for Democracy' in S Gutwirth et al (eds), *Reinventing Data Protection?* (Dordrecht, Springer, 2009) also speak of a more 'intermediate' or 'instrumental' value of data protection.

[12] M Albers, *Informationelle Selbstbestimmung* (Baden-Baden, Nomos, 2005).

[13] See Masing, ch 3 in this volume.

telecommunications metadata. One might object that this is an example of poor legal interpretation, but I think that the strong individual foundation of the right to informational self-determination is partly responsible for the bias in many data protection discussions.

However, in view of the debates at the European level, it seems more important to me that, at least here, this instrumental understanding leads to gaps in protection. As I will explain in a moment (III), the German Basic Law contains two fundamental rights, the general freedom of action and the general right of personality, which offer comprehensive protection of the internal and external freedom of development of a person. An instrumental right to informational self-determination based on this far-reaching protection of fundamental rights ultimately offers 360-degree protection against the risks of data processing by public bodies. However, where there is no comprehensive subsidiary protection of freedoms, as in the EU Charter of Fundamental Rights and the constitutions of many states, it is difficult to uphold comprehensive protection against data processing by public bodies by means of an instrumental conception. I will return to this at the end of my concluding remarks (VI).

## III. The Right to Informational Self-Determination as a Fundamental Rights Anchor for a Rule of Law for the Digital Age

### A. Background: The Subjectivation of the Rule of Law Through the *Elfes* Decision

Before I begin to outline an approach to explaining why the Federal Constitutional Court had to construct the right to informational self-determination as an individual right, although in terms of its content it is aimed more at providing an objective legal framework for data processing by public bodies, we must briefly go back to the *Elfes* decision of the Federal Constitutional Court in 1957, which is central to the protection of fundamental rights in Germany. In this decision, the Court first interpreted article 2(1) of the German Basic Law broadly and ruled that, despite its rather narrow wording,[14] it places *every* human activity under the protection of fundamental rights.[15] In subsequent cases, the Court has also considered the feeding of pigeons or riding in the forest to be covered by this general freedom of action.[16] There is a second aspect of the decision that is at least as important, and it is this aspect that I will focus on in the current context. The Court also ruled that state measures that restrict the general freedom of action are only justified if they are fully compatible with the legal system as a whole, in particular the constitution.

[14] 'Every person shall have the right to free development of his personality insofar as he does not violate the rights of others or offend against the constitutional order or the moral law.'

[15] BVerfGE 6, 32 [1957] – *Elfes*.

[16] BVerfGE 54, 143 [1980] – *Taubenfütterungsverbot*; BVerfGE 80, 137 [1989] – *Reiten im Walde*.

Why is this so significant? To answer this question, we need to take a look at constitutional procedural law. The central procedure by which citizens can defend themselves against encroachments on their fundamental rights is the constitutional complaint. It serves to enforce fundamental rights and, as a subjective legal protection procedure, consistently provides that only a citizen whose own fundamental rights have been affected can defend themselves against the state measures in question. As a consequence of the '*Elfes*' decision and the establishment of a general freedom of action, citizens can now not only defend themselves against any state measure that requires them to act or refrain from acting by invoking, eg, the disproportionate nature of a measure with regard to a fundamental right. Since the measure itself must also be entirely legal, ie, must be in accordance with the entire constitutional law, the citizen affected by a measure can, in principle, also invoke the violation of the provisions concerning legislative competences or the legislative procedure.[17] The Federal Constitutional Court has thus not only created a fundamental right to freedom from unlawful constraint but has also made it possible for itself to control the violation of norms of objective constitutional law within the framework of subjective legal protection proceedings. In this way, not only the Federal Constitutional Court but also the administrative courts can ensure compliance with norms that are part of the rule of law as elements of a separation of powers.

## B. Data Protection Law as an Expression of the Separation of Powers

The fact that the Federal Constitutional Court has empowered itself, through the '*Elfes*' decision, to control violations of objective constitutional law (such as the separation of powers) within the framework of subjective legal protection proceedings (the constitutional complaint) is interesting for the present considerations because data protection law in its early phase is often also referred to as an element of an informational separation of powers. This notion of an 'informational separation of powers' was coined by the first Federal Data Protection Commissioner, Hans Peter Bull, even before the Federal Constitutional Court's census judgement.[18] The question of the separation of powers also plays a decisive role in the writings of Adalbert Podlech, who can be considered one of the intellectual fathers of the right to informational self-determination,[19] for example, when he calls for the separation of political, technical, and professional responsibility for information systems.[20] And it is probably no coincidence that at the same time, Bernhard Schlink was further developing the (controversial) doctrine of the separation

[17] See generally R Poscher and T Kingreen, *Grundrechte Staatsrecht II*, 40th edn (Heidelberg, CF Müller, 2024) paras 366–7.

[18] HP Bull, 'Datenschutz contra Amtshilfe – Von der "Einheit der Staatsgewalt" zur "informationellen Gewaltenteilung"' (1979) 32 *Die Öffentliche Verwaltung* 689.

[19] See AB Kaiser, *Die Kommunikation der Verwaltung – Diskurse zu den Kommunikationsbeziehungen zwischen staatlicher Verwaltung und Privaten in der Verwaltungsrechtswissenschaft der Bundesrepublik Deutschland*, Neue Schriften zur Verwaltungsrechtswissenschaft 8 (Baden-Baden, Nomos, 2009) 184–185.

[20] See inter alia A Podlech, 'Aufgaben und Problematik des Datenschutzes' (1976) 5 *Datenverarbeitung im Recht* 23.

of powers *within* the administration, underpinning it in terms of constitutional theory and linking it to the issues of data protection law.[21]

The Federal Constitutional Court already addresses the separation of powers in the census judgment by emphasising that for statistical data 'an effective regime on shielding data against external access is of particular importance'.[22] In this context, the Court does refer to access by private third parties, but by state entities that have not been permitted to access the data by law. It can be seen here and in other decisions (in particular on information sharing systems) that the constitutional requirements derived by the Federal Constitutional Court from the right to informational self-determination, on the one hand, stabilise the distribution of responsibilities within the administration under statutory law and, on the other hand, require the demarcation of responsibilities.[23] When considered in the context of the fact that the core content of the fundamental right (primarily) consists of demanding a legal basis for every data processing, it becomes clear why the former judge of the Federal Constitutional Court *Dieter Grimm* says that the protection provided by the right to informational self-determination is less about the behaviour of citizens and more about the way they are treated by the state.[24]

## C. The Right to Informational Self-Determination as a (Mere) Fundamental Rights Anchor

All in all, the central tenets of the right to informational self-determination and the data protection rules on the handling of information by public authorities could be understood as part of a set of general rules on information that prevents unlimited data processing by public authorities. As a rule of law for the digital age, this would be seen as an expression of an informational principle of the separation of powers, which can be derived from objective constitutional law. This would be, in a way, an update of the traditional jurisprudence on the principle of the separation of powers, which is considered part of the rule of law and which, according to the jurisprudence of the Federal Constitutional Court, aims at 'moderation of state power as a whole'.[25]

Why has the Federal Constitutional Court now taken a different approach and derived an individual fundamental right to informational self-determination from the general right of personality, although the Court itself repeatedly relies on more objective (ie, supra-individualistic) considerations in the census judgment? A possible explanation lies in constitutional *procedural* law, namely in the character of the constitutional complaint as a procedure for the protection of individuals and the resulting requirement of standing as a condition for admissibility. In order to be able to enforce a principle of objective law, such as the informational separation of powers, by means of a

[21] B Schlink, *Die Amtshilfe – Ein Beitrag zu einer Lehre von der Gewaltenteilung in der Verwaltung*, Schriften zum Öffentlichen Recht 424 (Berlin, Duncker & Humblot, 1982).

[22] BVerfGE 65, 1 para 161.

[23] T Wischmeyer, '§ 24 Informationsbeziehungen in der Verwaltung' in A Voßkuhle, M Eifert and C Möllers (eds), *Grundlagen des Verwaltungsrechts – Band I*, 3rd edn (München, CH Beck, 2022) para 63.

[24] D Grimm, 'Der Datenschutz vor einer Neuorientierung' (2013) 68 *JuristenZeitung* 585.

[25] BVerfGE 68, 1 [1984] – *Aufstellung nuklearbestückter Mittelstreckenraketen* para 144.

constitutional complaint, modelled on the '*Elfes*' construction, a new fundamental right was first required on the basis of which the complainants could bring action against the census. The general freedom of action, even in the broad interpretation applied by the Federal Constitutional Court, was not that right, since it could hardly be argued that the idea that not only the disclosure but also the further processing of personal data prescribed or prohibited a particular behaviour for the individual citizen. Consequently, the Federal Constitutional Court had no other choice but to develop a new fundamental right if it wanted to bind the legislature and the administration to the requirements of the rule of law for the census.

In light of this finding, the right to informational self-determination can be understood as a fundamental right that makes it possible to enforce a constitutional handling of information by state authorities through the courts. Just as the '*Elfes*' construction subjectivises the rules on competences, the right to informational self-determination subjectivises the informational separation of powers. In its essence, the fundamental right can thus also be understood as a mere fundamental rights anchor that has enabled the Federal Constitutional Court to derive and enforce a rule of law for the digital age from the constitution.

## IV. Four Spotlights on the Case Law of the Federal Constitutional Court, the ECtHR and the ECJ

In the following, drawing on relevant court decisions I will discuss why I believe that an understanding of the right to informational self-determination as a subjectivisation of a rule of law for the digital age is more convincing than a purely individualistic conception. My aim here is not to negate individualistic aspects or the corresponding dimension of the fundamental right. Like Johannes Masing, I also believe that the results of the different conceptions do not differ that much; in fact, I see many similarities among them. Nevertheless, I argue that a stronger focus on the supra-individualistic dimension of the right to informational self-determination and a corresponding interpretation of article 8 ECHR and article 8 CFR would allow some judgments to be better explained and further developments to be suggested.

### A. The Scope of Protection – Too Broad or Too Narrow?

I will start with two judgments by the Federal Constitutional Court concerning a technology that involves scanning the number plates of passing cars with a camera to automatically compare the registration number with a database of wanted vehicles. In an initial decision in 2008, the Federal Constitutional Court had distinguished between cases in which a match was found and those in which no match was found.[26] Since in the latter cases the registration number is immediately deleted again and the filming

[26] BVerfGE 120, 378 [2008] – *Automatisierte Kennzeichenerfassung*.

and automated matching take place in less than a second, the Court only deemed the right to informational self-determination to be violated in the cases in which a match was found. This is plausible because, among other things, if there is no match, only the numbers and letters of a vehicle number plate are processed. As such, they do not contain any personal reference if the short processing time ensures that no link can be established with data relating to the owner. However, the decision has been criticised not so much for limiting the scope of protection, but rather for an (alleged) inconsistency. This inconsistency is said to lie in the fact that, as part of the proportionality test, the Court speaks of a measure with a high degree of variance due to the large number of drivers being recorded (for a very short period of time). In doing so, the Court is using precisely those drivers as an argument to make the intervention more difficult for whom it has ruled out the scope of protection of the fundamental right. If we leave aside for a moment these difficulties in the legal construction, then the reliance on cases where there is no match is convincing in the proportionality test, since a chilling effect cannot be ruled out for all drivers who pass a corresponding checkpoint.

In 2018, the Federal Constitutional Court explicitly abandoned this distinction between match and non-match cases and now also recognises an infringement of the right to informational self-determination in cases of no match. While this decision can now better explain the wide range of the measure, it must rely on the chilling effect with regard to the expansion of the scope of application. Specifically, the Court, with reference to its established case law, states: 'It is integral to a free society that anyone may in principle move freely, without having their movements arbitrarily registered by the state, without having to prove their integrity as law-abiding citizens, and without the feeling of constantly being under surveillance.'[27] By relying on a 'free society' (*die Freiheitlichkeit des Gemeinwesens*), the Court reveals to some extent that the right to informational self-determination can hardly be explained in purely individualistic terms. The proximity to the above-developed thesis of a rule of law for the digital age is obvious. Such an understanding would also immunise the Court more strongly against the criticism that a chilling effect is weakly or not at all proven (and presumably cannot be proven). After all, as long as no specific fundamental rights are affected (such as freedom of assembly by filming the assembly), this argument is more of a normative assumption than a sociological fact. But such an assumption, which is also at a high level of abstraction, can be better located in a rule of law for the digital age than in a fundamental right.

Timo Rademacher goes one step further in his book on the algorithmic realisation of the law and the significance of chance in a liberal and innovative democracy.[28] Using the example of new technologies that enable surveillance without the need to process personal data, he shows that the right to informational self-determination ultimately refers to the wrong element, even in its construction.[29] The more such technologies become established in the future, the clearer it will become that data processing is only a proxy, which, with regard to the census, had a high intuitive plausibility, but which

[27] BVerfGE 150, 309 [2018] – *Kfz-Kennzeichenkontrollen.*

[28] T Rademacher, *Recht ohne Zufall? Algorithmische Rechtsverwirklichung in der freiheitlichen Demokratie*, Habilitationsschriften Recht 1 (Baden-Baden, Nomos, 2025).

[29] ibid ch 1 § 2 I. 6. d.

does not precisely address the core of the problem of state surveillance. Even today, the example of camera dummies, which are not particularly innovative in technological terms, shows how difficult it is for the legal system and the courts to deal with the mere simulation of surveillance with the aim of steering behaviour.

## B. Judicial Review of Surveillance Measures

The above serves as an introduction to the next two examples, which also come from the area of (mass) surveillance and which, on the one hand, concern the legal standing and, on the other hand, the central standard of review of the ECtHR.

### *i. No (Real) Need for Legal Standing*

First, the fundamental weakness of a purely individualistic concept becomes clear when one considers that the Federal Constitutional Court almost completely refrains from examining the specific plaintiffs' legal standing when it comes to complaints against the legal basis for mass surveillance measures.[30] In this specific area, to some extent an *actio popularis* is therefore admissible in order to ensure judicial review at least of the legal basis for secret service activities.

This peculiarity of constitutional procedural law also explains the change in case law with regard to automated number plate recognition. This is because the first of the two judgments concerned a constitutional complaint directly against the legal basis, which is why it did not matter whether the complainant had already been the subject of a match, ie, whether his number plate was part of the search. The second decision, however, was based on a case in which the complainant had initially turned to the administrative courts to defend himself against the short-term registration of his number plate. Since there was no positive match with the search database in this case, the Federal Constitutional Court had no choice but to regard even the non-match as an infringement of the right to informational self-determination. The opposite decision would have led to the absurd result that the complainant could have taken direct action against the legal basis, but not against a specific surveillance measure, which would have meant that the legal basis would have had to be reviewed for its constitutionality.

This seems to me to be a fundamental difference between European and US case law. While the US Supreme Court tends to take a narrow view of the legal standing in mass surveillance cases, requiring plaintiffs to demonstrate a reasonable probability that they have been the subject of surveillance,[31] the ECtHR, with its rather liberal case law, is in line with the German Federal Constitutional Court. The ECtHR allows direct complaints against the legal basis for mass surveillance measures where the measure potentially affects all citizens and there is no possibility of ex post legal protection; even

[30] *Cf* Marsch, *Datenschutzgrundrecht* (n 1) 121 on the example of a case.
[31] *Clapper v Amnesty International*, 568 US 398 (2013).

when there is such a possibility, complaints should be admissible where the complainant is particularly exposed to the risk of surveillance.[32]

One possible explanation for this liberal jurisprudence of the Federal Constitutional Court and the ECtHR is that mass surveillance measures potentially affect the entirety of citizens, or that a chilling effect cannot be ruled out even for those individuals who are not (yet) the subject of surveillance measures. However, it seems more convincing to me that the requirements for mass surveillance measures that the Federal Constitutional Court and the ECtHR derive from human rights are not so much rules that protect the specific interests of individuals, but rather supra-individualistic rules that – to use the words of the Federal Constitutional Court – protect 'the free society' (*die Freiheitlichkeit des Gemeinwesens*). This is also reflected in the examination of the merits of the case, in particular by the ECtHR.

### *ii. The Quality of Law Test as a Central Standard of Review*

The finding that this examination of the merits by the ECtHR is also rather supra-individual in nature is particularly illustrated by the fact that the quality of law test is at the heart of the Court's review of the legal basis for surveillance measures. This quality of law test is based on article 8(2) ECHR, which requires that the interference be in accordance with the law. In its general case law, the Court has given this requirement a substantive content, requiring that the legal basis for interference be compatible with the rule of law, which means, inter alia, that interference must be foreseeable for citizens.[33] Since this is, of course, not a meaningful requirement for secret surveillance measures, especially mass surveillance measures, the Court does not require foreseeability for the individual, but rather that a sufficiently specific legal basis offers protection against abusive and arbitrary action by not leaving too much leeway to the authorities and the courts.[34] As a result, the Court has developed specific substantive requirements for various forms of surveillance, which are part of the quality of law test as elements of protection against abuse.[35] One important example is the obligation to provide for independent supervision at all stages of data collection, use and disclosure.

With regard to the location of these requirements, it is particularly interesting that the ECtHR very early on established the link with the principle of democracy, emphasising that secret surveillance measures 'may undermine or even destroy democracy under the cloak of defending it'.[36] At the same time, the ECtHR itself notes that the quality of law test and the necessity test (ie, the proportionality test) are closely related and overlap to some extent.[37] It is therefore not surprising that the Federal Constitutional Court examines comparable requirements as the ECtHR does at the last stage of proportionality,

[32] *Roman Zakharov v Russia*, 4 December 2015, Case 47143/06 (2016) 63 EHRR 17 para 171.

[33] See WA Schabas, *The European Convention on Human Rights – A Commentary* (Oxford, Oxford University Press, 2015) 402–3.

[34] *Zakharov* (n 32) paras 229–30.

[35] See for bulk interception of communications *Big Brother and Others v the United Kingdom*, 25 May 2021, Case 58170/13, Case 62322/14 and Case 24960/15 (2022) 74 EHRR 17 paras 332–64.

[36] *Case of Klass and Others v Germany* Series A no 28 (1978) 2 EHRR 2014 para 49; *Zakharov* (n 32) para 232.

[37] *Zakharov* (n 32) para 236; *Big Brother and Others* (n 35) paras 334, 361.

namely as a question of appropriateness (also referred to as proportionality in the narrower sense).[38] In German legal literature, however, it has certainly raised eyebrows that the Federal Constitutional Court has developed extensive guidelines at this level (at which a weighing of the conflicting fundamental rights is actually carried out), particularly with regard to ensuring data security and legal protection, which it requires the legislature to observe when drafting laws.[39]

One might take the view that it ultimately does not matter under which heading the courts develop human rights requirements for surveillance measures. However, as already indicated, I find it more convincing to view these requirements at least in part as components of a rule of law. On the one hand, this makes it easier to counter criticism that has touched on a sore point in this respect, since the chilling effect of surveillance measures has so far been, and is likely to remain, difficult to prove. For example, Horst Dreier criticises the Federal Constitutional Court for assuming that even publicly conducted surveillance measures such as the automated checking of vehicle number plates may lead to a chilling effect, which he considers to be 'a blatant case of armchair psychology'.[40] If, however, the chilling effect is to some extent detached from the individual and understood rather as a normative assumption, then it contains a useful premise that makes it possible and necessary to limit surveillance measures and to surround them with substantive requirements. This idea can easily be applied to any form of data processing by public bodies (and thus beyond the narrow area of surveillance measures), since the common feature is that citizens do not immediately perceive data processing (as opposed to interference with other fundamental freedoms) as a restriction of their freedom. On the other hand, anchoring the constitutional requirements in the rule of law also makes it possible to abstract from the individual in the opposite direction of the argument. If the legislature takes the necessary measures to protect against abusive or arbitrary data processing, it no longer matters whether individual citizens feel intimidated. For example, if the state ensures that data collected through video surveillance will only be stored for a few hours or days and can only be analysed by a few people under strict conditions, then it is no longer important that particularly paranoid people continue to be suspicious of state authorities. In my opinion, integrating the requirements into a rule of law for the digital age can help ensure that the chilling effect does not become an argumentative wild card that trumps everything.

## C. The Publication of Data – Not a Data Protection, but a Privacy Issue

The basic premise that the right to informational self-determination and the fundamental right to data protection, as instrumental fundamental rights, contain an inherent gap becomes even more apparent when considering a specific and particularly intensive

[38] BVerfGE 125, 260 [2010] – *Vorsorgliche Speicherung von Telekommunikationsverkehrsdaten*.

[39] M Cornils, 'Der grundrechtliche Rahmen für ein (trans-)nationales Datenschutzrecht im digitalen Zeitalter' in KE Hain and KN Peifer (eds), *Datenschutz im digitalen Zeitalter – global, europäisch, national* (München, CH Beck, 2015) 11, 41.

[40] H Dreier, 'Art 2(1)' in H Dreier (ed), *Grundgesetz*, 3rd edn (Tübingen, Mohr Siebeck, 2013) para 87.

type of processing, namely the publication of data. In its famous *Schecke* ruling, which concerned the obligation to publish the recipients of agricultural subsidies, the ECJ did not base its decision solely on the fundamental right to data protection under article 8 CFR. Instead, it applied article 7, the right to protection of private life, in conjunction with article 8 as the standard of review.[41] Similarly, the Federal Constitutional Court has ruled that in the case of press publications, it is not the right to informational self-determination that is affected, but the general right of personality.[42] Finally, the ECJ ruled – not on the publication of data, but on a particularly serious encroachment, namely data retention – that the obligation of telecommunications companies to store telecommunications metadata without cause primarily concerns the right to privacy and communication, ie, article 7 CFR.[43] The fundamental right to data protection (as a right in itself) is used in this decision only as a supplementary argument to provide normative support for the requirements of data security and independent supervision.[44] In all these cases, the distinction between classical human rights that protect individuals and instrumental human rights, that provide a supra-individualistic protection, which can rather be assigned to the rule of law, once again comes to the fore.

The significance of this distinction between the general right of personality (in Germany) or the right to protection of privacy (in the ECHR and the CFR) on the one hand and the right to informational self-determination/the fundamental right to data protection on the other can be well illustrated by two examples. In the *Huber* case, which concerned a state database (the German Central Register of Foreigners), the ECJ relied solely on data protection law as the standard of review under EU law. Whether the establishment of this database is 'necessary for the performance of a task carried out in the public interest' within the meaning of the current article 6(1)(e) GDPR depends (only) on whether it 'contributes to the more effective application of that legislation as regards the right of residence of Union citizens who wish to reside in a Member State of which they are not nationals'. The data protection concept of necessity is therefore based solely on whether the data processing supports the fulfilment of the task. In other words, the state should only carry out data processing that contributes to the fulfilment of the task. It is therefore sufficient for the data processing to contribute to the effectiveness or efficiency of the fulfilment of the task. In cases involving the publication of data or particularly far-reaching encroachments on the right to protection of privacy, the ECJ has tightened this standard of review and considers such encroachments to be justified only if they are limited to what is 'strictly necessary'. This is convincing because in these cases the right at stake is a weighty individual interest (as opposed to the creation of a database for the purpose of administrative efficiency). It is unfortunate that this stricter standard has been increasingly generalised in the case law of the ECJ and applied even

[41] Case 92/09 and Case 93/09 *Volker und Markus Schecke GbR and Hartmut Eifert v Land Hessen* ECLI:EU:C:2010:662 paras 52, 65, 85–7: 'The right to respect for private life with regard to the processing of personal data, recognised by Articles 7 and 8 of the Charter'.

[42] BVerfGE 152, 152 [2019] – *Recht auf Vergessen I*.

[43] Case 293/12 and Case 594/12 *Digital Rights Ireland Ltd v Minister for Communications, Marine and Natural Resources and Others and Kärntner Landesregierung and Others* ECLI:EU:C:2014:238 paras 27–8, 33–5, 39, 53–65.

[44] ibid 66–8.

in cases involving data processing by private individuals,[45] as this stricter standard is ill-suited to such contexts, for reasons that will be explained below.

## D. Horizontal Effect: Data Processing by Private Actors

The question of the horizontal effect of the right to informational self-determination/ the fundamental right to data protection is another reason why I consider a supra-individualistic approach to be more convincing. This is because it initially prevents a profound misunderstanding that is not uncommon in data protection literature. Quite a few legal scholars assume that the prohibition arising from the fundamental right against processing data without a legal basis applies directly to private individuals.[46] However, this would effectively create a fundamental right of individuals to control their personal data, which is incompatible with the realities of a society based on communication and social interaction. Furthermore, the one-to-one transfer of the right to informational self-determination to private data processors also fails because, unlike the state, private data processors cannot create a legal basis for data processing themselves. The Federal Constitutional Court also pointed this out.[47] At the same time, it emphasised the importance of protecting against non-transparent data processing and informational power asymmetries, including those of some private data processors and their practices, and stressed the responsibility of the legislator to establish an adequate protection regime.[48]

The European legislator has now established such a comprehensive data protection regime. The fact that the GDPR in article 6(1) regulates a prohibition principle is therefore, as far as private data processors are concerned, not a direct and compelling expression of the fundamental right to data protection, but one (possible) decision of the legislator (among many others). In this sense, the GDPR also provides for a household exemption for those data processing operations that the legislator considers to be less dangerous.[49] From the above, it can also be deduced that the rules for private data processors are primarily a highly abstract regulatory regime that can be better understood as a general information regime that also contains (instrumental) subjective rights, especially for the purpose of enforcement. As far as companies that process data are concerned, it is also a matter of binding them to certain requirements that structure the handling of information and limit the processing of data, without it being possible to conclude from this fact that each data processing operation actually affects the data subject in their specific interests.

[45] Case 136/17 *GC and others v Commission nationale de l'informatique et des libertés* ECLI:EU:C:2019:773 para 68; Case 621/22 *Koninklijke Nederlandse Lawn Tennisbond v Autoriteit Persoonsgegevens* ECLI:EU:C:2024:858 para 57.

[46] See as an example A Roßnagel, 'Kein "Verbotsprinzip" und kein "Verbot mit Erlaubnisvorbehalt" im Datenschutzrecht – Zur Dogmatik der Datenverarbeitung als Grundrechtseingriff' (2019) 72 *Neue Juristische Wochenschrift* 1.

[47] BVerfGE 152, 152 paras 86–7.

[48] ibid para 88.

[49] See art 2(2)(c), which excludes data processing by a natural person in the course of a purely personal or household activity from the material scope of the GDPR.

## V. The Fundamental Right to Data Protection in Article 8 CFR: An Obligation of the Legislator to Regulate the Processing of Personal Data

In light of the above, according to which the right to informational self-determination also owes its existence to constitutional procedural law and, due to its character as a right without its own core, can be better understood as a subjectivised rule of law for the digital age, I would like to conclude with a brief comment on the interpretation of article 8 CFR.

The interpretation, which I can only outline below, but which has been explained and developed in detail elsewhere, starts from the premise that both the wording and the history of the norm's emergence argue against regarding article 8 CFR as a European right to informational self-determination.[50] During the deliberations of the European Convention on Fundamental Rights, chaired by the former German head of state and former president of the Federal Constitutional Court, Roman Herzog, a wording was discussed for a while that would have corresponded literally to the Federal Constitutional Court's census decision ('Everyone has the right to determine for himself whether his personal data may be disclosed and how they may be used'). However, this proposal was rejected by the Convention, as several members feared that the administration and its effectiveness would be unduly compromised. The Convention therefore returned to the original draft, which was then adopted: 'Everyone has the right to the protection of personal data concerning him or her.'

The structure of article 8 CFR also suggests that it was not intended to create a right to informational self-determination in the German sense. This is because the first paragraph just quoted is followed by a second paragraph that states: 'Such data must be processed fairly for specified purposes and on the basis of the consent of the person concerned or some other legitimate basis laid down by law.' What is surprising here is that the requirement of a legal basis, which is enshrined in the horizontal clause of article 52(1) for all fundamental rights, is repeated. This and the fact that there is no interference with fundamental rights in the case of consent under the general rules suggest that article 8(2) CFR does not contain a specific limitation clause but rather a provision governing the conditions under which data processing is generally permissible.[51]

This distinction seems very subtle, but it is crucial for understanding article 8 CFR. In light of the wording and its history, and taking into account the structure of the article and in particular the provision in its second paragraph, there is much to suggest that the fundamental right to protection of personal data should be understood as a mandate to the legislator.[52] According to article 8(1) CFR, the legislator is obliged to regulate the handling of personal data by public authorities in a way that effectively

[50] See for more details Marsch, *Datenschutzgrundrecht* (n 1) 74–5; Marsch 'Artificial Intelligence' (n 1) para 21.

[51] In their extremely lucid article G González Fuster and S Gutwirth, 'Opening up Personal Data Protection: A Conceptual Controversy' (2013) 29 *Computer Law & Security Review* 531–3, distinguish between a 'prohibitive concept' and a 'permissive or regulatory concept'.

[52] This interpretation is discussed in detail in Marsch, *Datenschutzgrundrecht* (n 1) 128–203; more succinct Marsch 'Artificial Intelligence' (n 1) paras 25–8.

protects fundamental rights. In doing so, he shall observe the requirements of the second paragraph, from which he may only deviate if such deviation is proportionate in accordance with article 52(1) CFR. Only in cases where data has a particular bearing on private life, or the processing method is particularly sensitive in terms of fundamental rights, should article 8 be invoked in conjunction with article 7 to strengthen the protection of fundamental rights of the data subjects in these specific cases.

This understanding of article 8 CFR has three advantages over the interpretation as a right to informational self-determination that unfortunately seems to be favoured by the ECJ.[53] *First*, the democratically legitimised legislator is primarily entrusted with the creation of a data protection regime that is adequate for a fundamental right, so that a rule of law for the digital age is created in the *interplay* between fundamental rights regulation and legislative activity. *Second*, this leads in principle to a greater openness to innovation and a dynamic flexibility of the regulations, since they can be adapted relatively easily by the legislator to technical and social developments, in contrast to court rulings on fundamental rights. This should not result in a weaker protection of fundamental rights overall. Rather, it is a question of giving the legislator the possibility to choose innovative protection concepts in certain areas, which, for example, can ideally offer even more effective protection. The right to informational self-determination and the idea that each step in the data processing chain requires a legal basis represent a constitutionalisation of the data protection concept of the 1970s, when data processing took place in mainframe computer systems and was not ubiquitous. Looking at AI and large language models, it is clear that traditional concepts, such as strict purpose limitation, are proving to be both an obstacle to innovation and no longer able to provide effective protection. In this respect, the interpretation of article 8(1) CFR as an obligation of the legislator to create a data protection regime offers the necessary openness to development in the face of technical progress and at the same time enables the ECJ to review the legislative provisions to determine whether they ensure adequate protection of fundamental rights. *Third*, the horizontal effect of the fundamental right interpreted in this way can also be more easily determined. Data processing by private actors must also be regulated by the legislator, who must, however, take into account at the horizontal level that private data processors (unlike public bodies) can also invoke fundamental rights.

## VI. Conclusion: It's about the Administration … not about Jimmy

Data protection law largely only protects natural persons, but not legal entities[54] and certainly not animals. With the animal rights movement, one could now raise the question of whether animals should also have a right to informational self-determination, in

[53] See Opinion 1/15 *Opinion of the Court (Grand Chamber) of 26 July 2017* ECLI:EU:C:2016:656 para 126; for an analysis of the jurisprudence see Marsch 'Artificial Intelligence' (n 1) paras 29–31.

[54] See art 4(1) GDPR; slightly deviating from this with regard to the interpretation of art 8, Case 92/09 and Case 93/09 para 53.

other words, whether our dog Jimmy should also be protected by data protection law. This question does not need to be pursued here, since the aim was to show, by way of contrast, that the right to informational self-determination and the fundamental right to data protection are fundamental rights that are less concerned with the person (or animal) concerned, ie. Jimmy or my wife as his owner, but that the main issue is to provide the public administration with rules on how it has to process data. In order to effectively claim the enactment of such rules from the legislature, and to then be able to have these rules reviewed by the constitutional courts and enforced against the administration, it was necessary to create a fundamental right. One can therefore go one step further than Dieter Grimm and say that this fundamental right is neither about the behaviour of individuals nor about how they are treated by the state, but rather about information-related behaviour of public officials *within* the administration, which is to be regulated. The idea of the separation of powers within the administration can be used as a basis,[55] since it is precisely the link between the data processing and the task of a specific authority that constitutes an important limitation of data processing.[56] An understanding of the fundamental rights as a subjectivised rule of law for the digital age may also have its weaknesses, but it is suited not only to better explain controversial points, but above all it is to be more open to development and thus better suited to guarantee meaningful protection. At the same time, it also makes it clear once again who is primarily responsible for the creation of an effective data protection legal regime: not the courts, but the democratically legitimised legislator.

[55] The idea of a separation of powers within the administration, as further developed by B Schlink, is not isolated in comparative law; in other countries, such as Italy, for example, an extension of the idea of the rule of law to the administrative organisation can be observed, which aims to ensure that tasks are performed efficiently and impartially, see G Napolitano, 'Chapter 21: The Rule of Law' in P Cane, HCH Hofmann and PL Lindseth (eds), *Comparative Administrative Law* (Oxford, Oxford University Press, 2021) 421, 429.

[56] Marsch and Rademacher (n 8).

# 14

# Obscurity and the Fallacy of No Privacy in Public Information

WOODROW HARTZOG*

## I. Introduction

Sometimes the way we discuss and regulate privacy feels a little delusional. We 'agree' to privacy policies. We are promised 'control' over our personal information. Unless our identities or money are stolen, computer hacks do not seem to register as 'harmful' to us. But one of the most overlooked misconceptions lawmakers and society often labour under is that 'public' information is an established and objective concept.[1] One of the most reliable permission slips for surveillance and data practices in the US is successfully claiming that the information at issue was 'public' or that the person being surveilled was 'in public.'[2]

Judges considering privacy tort claims have said for years that 'there can be no privacy in that which is already public.'[3] Their opinions are littered with statements like '[u]sers would logically lack a legitimate expectation of privacy in the materials intended for publication or public posting.'[4] The FBI alleges it does not need permission to conduct surveillance using powerful technologies like cell-site simulators (often called Stingrays), so long as they are doing so in public places.[5] Judges have refused to

* This chapter was adapted from *The Public Information Fallacy*, 98 Boston University Law Review 459 (2019).

[1] See, eg, JL Hill, 'The Constitutional Status of Morals Legislation' (2009) 98 *Kentucky Law Journal* 1 (2009).

[2] See *Gill v Hearst Publishing* Co, 253 P2d 441, 444–45 (Cal. 1953); *Moreno v Hanford Sentinel Inc*, 91 Cal Rptr 3d 858, 862–63 (Cal Ct App 2009).

[3] See, eg, *Gill v Hearst Publishing* (n 2) 253 P.2d at 444.

[4] *Guest v Leis*, 255 F3d 325, 333 (6th Cir 2001); see also *United States v Maxwell*, 45 M.J. 406, 419 (CAAF 1996); *Dexter v Dexter*, No. 2006-P-0051, 2007 WL 1532084, at *6 n.4 (Ohio Ct. App. May 25, 2007).

[5] D Kravets, 'FBI Says Search Warrants Not Needed To Use 'Stingrays' in Public Places', (*Ars Technica*, 5 January 2015), www.arstechnica.com/tech-policy/2015/01/fbi-says-search-warrants-not-needed-to-use-stingrays-in-public-places/ [www.perma.cc/J5JE-U29B]; D Kravets, 'Feds: Privacy Does Not Exist in 'Public Places', (*Wired*, 21 September 2010), www.wired.com/2010/09/public-privacy/; Press Release, 'Leahy & Grassley Press Administration on Use of Cell Phone Tracking Program' (*Chuck Grassley*, 31 December 2014), www.grassley.senate.gov/news/news-releases/leahy-grassley-press-administration-use-cell-phone-tracking-program [www.perma.cc/4PQL-H2GD].

punish people for taking 'upskirt' photos because the women photographed have no reasonable expectation of privacy 'in public', no matter how fleeting their exposure.[6]

And those are just a few examples. The concept of public information and acts is entrenched in US law and policy. Tort law, statutes, and interpretations of constitutional amendments regularly deploy the concept of public information to justify surveillance or data practices.[7] The Securities and Exchange Commission ('SEC') does not consider buying or selling securities on the basis of public information insider trading.[8] The US Department of Health and Human Services ('HHS') even briefly considered excluding 'public' data sets from research oversight because, in its view, doing so presents a low risk of harm.[9] Law and society regularly endow the concept of public information with great power while at the same time uncritically accepting the concept as a tenet of faith. It is as though the concept is invoked assuming that surely someone, somewhere, must know what 'public' actually means.[10]

This justification for surveillance and data practices is so common it has become a trope. For example, in 2016 a group of Danish researchers released a data set on nearly 70,000 users of the popular dating website OK Cupid.[11] The researchers used an automated tool called a 'scraper' that captures parts of a webpage – a possible violation of the website's terms of use.[12] These users had answered questions on intimate topics like drug use and sexual preferences.[13] The researchers took no steps to de-identify the data set when they released it, despite it being possible to re-identify many of the profiles.[14] When the researchers were called out about this lapse on Twitter, one of them shrugged it off with the flip statement '[d]ata is already public.'[15]

This idea that the 'public' nature of information and people justifies information collection, use, and dissemination is rooted in our collective consciousness. Whenever

[6] Order to Suppress Physical Evidence and Statements at 2–3, *United States v Cleveland*, No. 10-DVM 1341 (DC Super Ct Sept 4, 2014), www.pdfserver.amlaw.com/nlj/Cleveland%20motion%20to%20suppress%20order.pdf.

[7] See, eg, *Florida v Jardines*, 133 S Ct 1409, 1414 (2013); *Illinois v Caballes*, 543 US 405, 409–10 (2005); *California v Ciraolo*, 476 US 207, 212–14 (1986); *United States v Jacobsen*, 466 US 109, 118–22 (1984); *United States v Place*, 462 US 696, 706–07 (1983); *Smith v Maryland*, 442 US 735, 744–46 (1979); *United States v Miller*, 425 US 435, 442–43 (1976).

[8] More accurately, the SEC prohibits buying or selling securities on the basis of material 'nonpublic' information where there is a duty to disclose or refrain from trading. But this concept's inverse implication is that trading on public information is otherwise permissible. 17 CFR § 240.10b5-1 (2018); Selective Disclosure and Insider Trading, Securities Act Release No. 33-7881, Exchange Act Release No. 34-43154, Investment Company Act Release No. IC-24599, 65 Fed. Reg. 51716-01 (15 Aug. 2000).

[9] Federal Policy for the Protection of Human Subjects, 80 Fed. Reg. 53933, 53944–45 (proposed 8 September 2015).

[10] Spoiler alert: no one does.

[11] B Resnick, 'Researchers Just Released Profile Data on 70,000 OkCupid Users Without Permission' (*Vox*, 12 May 2016), www.vox.com/2016/5/12/11666116/70000-okcupid-users-data-release [www.perma.cc/2KG2-SQE5].

[12] J Cox, '70,000 OkCupid Users Just Had Their Data Published' (*Vice Motherboard*, 12 May 2016), www.motherboard.vice.com/en_us/article/70000-okcupid-users-just-had-their-data-published [perma.cc/H63N-AK3W].

[13] ibid.

[14] Resnick, (n 11).

[15] When pushed on the possible privacy problems from this practice, one of the researchers said 'If you don't want other people to see things, don't post them publicly on the Internet' and "Public is public." Emil OW Kirkegaard (@KirkegaardEmil, Twitter, 13 March 2016).

someone's social media posts go viral, people often take great zeal in shooting down any privacy concerns with statements like '[t]witter is public.'[16] Photographers create advice blog posts with sentiments like '[i]n the United States, public space photography of pretty much anything is legal.'[17] Lawyers create advice blog posts that lead off with statements like '[y]ou have no expectation of privacy in anything you do or say in public.'[18] It is even encoded in the design of our technologies; social media platforms like Facebook categorise information that is not protected by some sort of authentication protocol as 'public'.[19] This belief is used to justify all kinds of research practices and information flows.[20] The idea is so entrenched that the phrase 'there is no privacy in public' has become an almost reflexive defence of certain surveillance and information practices.[21]

Sometimes this argument is justified. What is 'public' is often obvious. The half-time performance at the Super Bowl is easy to classify as public under most definitions. But there is trouble at the margins. While privacy scholars for years have argued that people should be able to expect a reasonable amount of privacy in public,[22] few inroads have been made. This is partly because the argument itself gives the concept of public information far too much deference. This deference is understandable – the concept of public information is powerful and compelling. But it has come to play a deterministic, linchpin-like role in both law and society that can excuse a host of dubious information practices. This deference to public information is made worse by the fact that the concept in practice is usually best described as 'just a hunch'.[23]

In this chapter, I argue that the 'no privacy in public' justification is misguided because nobody knows what 'public' means, since it has no set definition in law or policy. Appeals to the public nature of information in order to justify surveillance and data practices are often just guesswork. At worst, appeals to the 'public' nature of information and acts provide cover for unscrupulous and dangerous data practices and surveillance by making it seem as though there is some objective and established criteria for what constitutes public information. There is no such consensus.[24] The related concept of

[16] N Hamilton, 'Twitter Is Public' (*Gawker*, 13 March 2014), www.gawker.com/twitter-is-public-1543016594 [perma.cc/5AAG-KN7H].

[17] J Corral, 'Don't Take My Picture: Street Photography and Public Privacy' (*PetaPixel*, 29 July 2016), www.petapixel.com/2016/07/29/dont-take-picture-street-photography-public-privacy/ [perma.cc/Y5PX-E7JH].

[18] R Carter, 'No Expectation of Privacy in Public' (Carter Law Firm, 6 June 2013), www.carterlawaz.com/no-expectation-of-privacy-in-public/ [perma.cc/AZQ4-96M8].

[19] M Zimmer, '"But the Data Is Already Public": On the Ethics of Research in Facebook' (2010) 12 *Ethics and Information Technology* 313, 318–19.

[20] See ibid.

[21] See, eg, 'Expect No Privacy In Public Spaces' (*The Gleaner*, 12 May 2013), www.jamaica-gleaner.com/gleaner/20130512/lead/lead6.html [perma.cc/3VL9-4WYZ] ('Once you are in a public space, you have no privacy …').

[22] See, eg, C Slobogin, *Privacy at Risk: The New Government Surveillance and the Fourth Amendment* (Chicago, University of Chicago Press, 2007) 81; D Solove, *The Digital Person* (New York, New York University Press, 2004) 97–100; PS Abril, 'Recasting Privacy Torts in a Spaceless World' (2007) 21 *Harvard Journal of Law & Technology* 1, 6; JB Mintz, 'The Remains of Privacy's Disclosure Tort: An Exploration of the Private Domain' (1996) 55 *Maryland Law Review* 425, 440–41; H Nissenbaum, 'Toward an Approach to Privacy in Public: Challenges of Information Technology' (1997) 7 *Ethics & Behavior* 207, 208; JR Reidenberg, 'Privacy in Public' (2014) 69 *University of Miami Law Review* 141, 157–59; Zimmer (n 19) at 323.

[23] Or, in the words of the great Inigo Montoya, 'You keep using that word. I do not think it means what you think it means.' *The Princess Bride* (Act III Communications 1987).

[24] See n 22 above (detailing disagreement).

privacy has been rightfully criticised as too vague or protean.[25] What is meant by terms like 'privacy' must be clarified to be useful in law or policy. But in the US, the concept of public information has been given a free pass.

We must put to rest the misguided notion of a value-neutral and objective criterion of 'public' information for justifying surveillance and data practices. There are several different ways to conceptualise the concept of 'public', and they are all value-laden and ideological. This chapter highlights the under-theorised and often tautological meanings of 'public' and makes the case for clarifying the concept in privacy law to embrace its normative nature.

The concept of public information seems intuitive. If it is 'out there', it is public, right? But digging deeper, it becomes clear that public could mean anything from fleeting exposure to collectively shared knowledge and more. Is the criteria for determining publicness whether it was hypothetically accessible to anyone?[26] Or is public anything that is controlled, designated, or released by state actors?[27] Or maybe what's public is simply everything that's 'not private'?[28]

The main thesis of this chapter is that because there are so many different possible interpretations of 'public information', the concept cannot be used to justify data practices and surveillance without first articulating a more precise meaning that recognises what is at stake. By disposing of the myth that there is an objective and dispassionate concept of public information, judges and lawmakers can clear the way for information rules based on overt value choices. In short, if the concept of 'public' is going to shape people's social and legal obligations, its meaning and neutrality should not be assumed.

My argument is based on a fundamental ambiguity: courts and lawmakers have failed to clarify the concept of public information. This ambiguity has resulted in a confused body of doctrine and frustrated attempts at clear, cogent policy surrounding the collection, use, and disclosure of information. The time has come to end this confusion.

My argument proceeds in two parts. First, I survey the law and literature to propose three different ways in which 'public information' is currently conceptualised: as a description, as a designation, or as the inverse of 'private information'. These three notions all work differently, serve different values, and cause different problems.

Second, I make the case for clarity. Law and society should treat the notion of 'public information' as a value-laden construct that is not self-defining. Thus, whenever the concept of 'public information' is invoked to justify surveillance and data practices, it should be scrutinised and clarified. Regardless of whether policymakers and society think of public as a description, designation, or the inverse of privacy, our analytical frameworks for making that determination are out of whack. There must be some workable way to determine what information should be broadly available to all in the data commons and what sorts of practices are generally acceptable. If everything is private, then nothing is. And if nothing is private, we all suffer.

[25] See, eg. DJ Solove, *Understanding Privacy* (Cambridge (MA), Harvard University Press, 2008) 1; DJ Solove, 'Fourth Amendment Pragmatism' (2010) 51 *Boston College Law Review* 1511, 1512–13.

[26] See, eg, *Sandler v Calcagni*, 565 F Supp 2d 184, 197 (D Me 2008).

[27] See section II.C. (discussing public records doctrine and privacy right to those documents).

[28] See, eg, DRC Pongrace, 'Stereotypification of the Fourth Amendment's Public/Private Distinction: An Opportunity for Clarity' (1985) 34 *American University Law Review* 1191, 1196.

To that end, I propose that two concepts should be incorporated into the calculus that determines whether information is public: obscurity and trust. These two concepts play a key role in shaping people's decisions about when, where, how, and with whom to share information or interact with others.

## II. There are Three Ways to Conceptualise Public Information

Labelling information or contexts as 'public' has important consequences, so we should be intentional and careful about what we choose to label as public. The publicness of data or acts is too often waived like a talisman to justify a host of information practices like mass surveillance, big data analytics, and shaming. It is too rarely scrutinised. Often, the surveillance and disclosure practices at issue are desirable. For example, quality journalism and research for the public good are invaluable to society. But other types of surveillance and data practices can be quite harmful.[29]

This places privacy policy in a confused and untenable state. How can public information be given such incredible exculpatory power when it has yet to even be adequately defined? Designating information as public is not a clinical, empirical judgment, but a political, instrumental move. Law and policy should treat it as such. And if the law is going to give the category of public information the power to excuse surveillance and data collection practices, it should be based on something more than 'just a hunch'.

The problem with public information in the law is that it can be defined a few different ways, and in many contexts, it is not clear which definition is meant. If public information is defined too broadly, it will include many different kinds of acts and information in which people might have some legitimate privacy interest. If the concept of public information is left ambiguous, those who seek to validate surveillance and data practices can use the normative and legal appeal of publicness without having to meaningfully defend the categorisation.

The standard dictionary definition for 'public' is deceptively simple. Black's Law Dictionary defines the adjective as '1. Of, relating to, or involving an entire community, state, or country. 2. Open or available for all to use, share, or enjoy.'[30] A closer look of this definition shows why public is a complex construct.

Even if information is observable or accessible, that does not necessarily mean that it is socially acceptable for all to share, use, or enjoy. Also, what does 'open or available' mean? Structurally exposed? Normatively inclusive? Legally permissible physical presence? And who are the 'all' in 'open and available for all'? A few passers-by might be able to catch a fleeting glimpse of an exposed undergarment or compromising position, yet that same piece of information would hardly seem to extend to 'all to share, use, or enjoy' both as a practical and normative matter. But if 'all' is an entire community, does that mean only what is actually or hypothetically visible to anyone in a community?

[29] See J Cohen, 'The Biopolitical Public Domain: The Legal Construction of the Surveillance Economy' (2017) 31 *Philosophy and Technology* 213, 230–31.

[30] 'Public' in BA Garners (ed), *Black's Law Dictionary*, 10th edn (Minnesota, West, 2014).

I should be careful to point out that I am not taking issue with the term 'public' to the extent it is used to mean government or quasi-government entities or activities, such as 'public sector' or 'public law' or 'public school'. There might be grey areas within these notions,[31] but it is relatively clear in most instances who government actors are. Nor am I concerned with the term 'public' when it is used to generally modify terms like 'public policy' or the specific meaning of 'public utility'. General, umbrella terms that act as shorthand for complex concepts can be quite useful in certain contexts. Terms like 'privacy' and 'big data' work in similar ways. But we should be more specific when it comes to defining rights and obligations.[32] My critique lies with treating public information as though it were part of an objectively measured map capable of being easily divided up by metes and bounds that can justify the abridgement of privacy rights.

The concept of public information is deployed in various legal regimes, often with little clarification.[33] However, the different concepts of 'public information' can be broadly categorised into three overlapping, yet generally discernible, conceptualisations. These conceptualisation respectively define 'public information' as (1) descriptive of content and context; (2) anything that is 'not private'; and (3) that which is designated for collection, use, and disclosure.

Importantly, these conceptualisations can have significantly different effects when implemented. Thinking of public as a description reduces determinations of people's privacy down to an empirical appeal. To determine one's privacy rights, you need only check to see if you are 'in public' or if the data was 'publicly available'. Thinking of public as 'not private' means you simply have to answer a different question – what is private? And thinking of public as a designation for information to collect, share, and use means a process must be established by the relevant authority to determine which pieces of information should be made public and under what circumstances.

In many legal regimes, it is unclear which conceptualisation governs or should govern. The result is inconsistent and conflicting rules about when information becomes public. At their worst, legal regimes sacrifice nuance and even policy goals by drawing easy descriptive lines at the disclosure of information. Often, the rationale is that once information is shared with others, it is public. As I argue in section III, we need better, more nuanced notions of public information that recognise it as an exercise of power, not an overly simplified, purportedly objective description of shared information.[34]

## A. Descriptive of Context or Content

The default notion of public information in law and society seems to be descriptive of the context in which the information was shared. When people say there is no privacy 'in public' or that data is 'already public', they most plausibly seem to be describing an

[31] See, eg, *Marsh v Alabama*, 326 US 501, 502 (1946).

[32] The notion of 'reasonable expectation of privacy' suffers from a similar problem. See Solove, *Understanding Privacy* (n 25) 1512–13.

[33] See text at section II.A (describing different legal concepts in which privacy is material issue).

[34] N Richards, *Intellectual Privacy: Rethinking Civil Liberties in the Digital Age* (Oxford, Oxford University Press, 2015) 166.

attribute or context of the act or information.[35] Descriptive factors such as who the information was shared with, how many people were actually exposed to certain acts, how many people actually saw and internalised information, where the acts occurred, where the information was located, and any particular barriers to access or dissemination are all relevant to articulating what is public.[36] These descriptive concepts have basically served as proxies for the dividing line between public and private.[37] A review of the law and literature reveals there are at least three different popular descriptive accounts of 'public' used in legal regimes: accessible, known, and 'of interest to society'.

### i. *Freely Accessible*

The most common descriptive conceptualisation of public information within the law seems to be any information that is hypothetically or 'freely' accessible. It is the way the dictionary describes 'public'.[38] It is often the colloquial use.[39] And most importantly for law and policy, it is the way that notions of public are described in statutes, case law, and other doctrinal sources.[40] The freely accessible conceptualisation of public also creates the most problems for privacy.

The most important trait of public as 'freely accessible' is that it is not contingent upon how many people have *actually* accessed or were cognisant of information, but rather either how hypothetically difficult it would be for people or just one person to access information or for others to be geographically close enough to be exposed to a person's acts.[41] Cognition of information is irrelevant. It is an exercise in conjecture.

The idea of hypothetical accessibility explicitly underlies the 'plain view' doctrine, which exempts objects that are immediately apparent to officers lawfully present in a place where evidence can be plainly viewed from the warrant requirements of the Fourth Amendment.[42] In order to determine if something can be 'plainly viewed', courts often ask whether any hypothetical member of the public could have seen an object or act without trespass or hardship. For example, the US Supreme Court in *California v Ciraolo*[43] focused on the fact that 'any member of the public flying in this airspace who cared to glance down could have seen everything that the officers observed' in holding that the Fourth Amendment did not apply to the search.[44] In *California v Greenwood*,[45] the Supreme Court concluded that

[35] The word 'in' here is likely being used as a preposition describing information or acts surrounded by or enclosed in 'public' and the word 'is' is likely being used to describe a state of being.

[36] See, eg, RG Wilkins, 'Defining the 'Reasonable Expectation of Privacy': An Emerging Tripartite Analysis' (1987) 40 *Vanderbilt Law Review* 1077, 1122.

[37] ibid at 6–18; *Creel v ICE & Assocs, Inc*, 771 NE2d 1276 (Ind Ct App 2002); *Daily Times Democrat v Graham*, 162 So 2d 474, 476 (Ala 1964)).

[38] See below section III.

[39] See below section II.A.ii.

[40] See below section II.A.i.

[41] 'Publication of Private Facts' (Digital Media Law Project, 2012), www.dmlp.org/legal-guide/publication-private-facts; see JE Cohen, 'Privacy, Visibility, Transparency, and Exposure' (2008) 75 *The University of Chicago Law Review* 190.

[42] *Horton v California*, 496 US 128, 134–37 (1990); *United States v Legg*, 18 F3d 240, 242 (4th Cir 1994).

[43] *California v Ciraclo*, 476 US 207 (1986).

[44] ibid at 208.

[45] *California v Greenwood*, 486 US 35 (1988).

> respondents exposed their garbage to the public sufficiently to defeat their claim to Fourth Amendment protection. It is common knowledge that plastic garbage bags left on or at the side of a public street are readily accessible to animals, children, scavengers, snoops, and other members of the public[,]

equating making something freely accessible with the waiver of privacy rights.[46] Similarly, in *United States v Knotts*,[47] the US Supreme Court held that '[a] person travelling in an automobile on public thoroughfares has no reasonable expectation of privacy in his movements from one place to another' because he voluntarily conveys 'to anyone who wanted to look the fact that he was traveling over particular roads in a particular direction[.]'[48]

The intrusion upon seclusion tort also largely exempts 'public places' or things that are in 'plain view' from its reach mainly because they are freely accessible.[49] Electronic surveillance law also embraces the notion of public as freely accessible – sometimes quite explicitly. The Wiretap Act, which regulates the interception of electronic communication while in transit, explicitly exempts (and thus permits) the interception of communications that are 'readily accessible to the general public'.[50]

The freely accessible conceptualisation of public information is also implicit in claims where exposure to others invalidates a privacy interest because 'anyone could have seen you'. This colloquial reference to hypothetical accessibility has been common in society since the turn of the nineteenth century and persists today.[51] In *Daly v Viacom, Inc.*,[52] the plaintiff brought a tort claim for public disclosure of private facts based on the defendants publicising her kissing a man in a bathroom stall.[53] In rejecting the plaintiff's claim, the court noted that the plaintiff had already kissed the man in public and in plain view, both in a bar and on a city sidewalk.[54] As a result, the fact that she had kissed this man was not private.[55]

The freely accessible view of public as a waiver of privacy rights was encapsulated bluntly by Judge Sciarrino in his decision rejecting any privacy interest in posts made on Twitter.[56] The judge wrote 'if you post a tweet, just like if you scream it out the window,

[46] ibid at 40 (citing *Smith v State*, 510 P.2d 793, 795–95 (Ala 1973); *State v Fassler*, 503 P2d 807, 813–14 (Ariz 1972); *State v Schultz*, 388 So2d 1326, 1329 (Fla Dist Ct App 1980); *People v Huddleston*, 347 NE2d 76, 80–81 (Ill App Ct 1976); *Commonwealth v Chappee*, 492 NE2d 719, 721–22 (Mass 1986); *People v Whotte*, 317 NW2d 266, 268–69 (Mich Ct App 1982); *State v Oquist*, 327 NW2d 587, 591 (Minn 1982); *State v Ronngren*, 361 NW2d 224, 228–30 (ND 1985); *State v Brown*, 484 NE2d 215, 217–18 (Ohio Ct App 1984); *Cooks v State*, 699 P2d 653, 656 (Okla Crim 1985); *State v Purvis*, 438 P2d 1002, 1005 (Or 1968); *Commonwealth v Minton*, 432 A2d 212, 217 (Pa Super Ct 1981); *Willis v State*, 518 SW2d 247, 249 (Tex Crim App 1975); *State v Stevens*, 794–97 (Wisc 1985); *Croker v State*, 477 P2d 122, 125–26 (Wyo 1970)). But see *People v Krivda*, 486 P2d 1262, 1268–69 (Cal 1971); *State v Tanaka*, 701 P2d 1274, 1276–77 (Haw 1985).

[47] *United States v Knotts*, 460 US 276 (1983).

[48] ibid at 281–82.

[49] See, eg, *Shulman v Grp W Prods, Inc*, 955 P2d 469, 490 (Cal 1998).

[50] Wiretap Act, 18 U.S.C. § 2511(g) (2018); see *Joffe v Google, Inc*, 746 F3d 920, 925 (9th Cir 2013).

[51] See S Barbas, 'Saving Privacy from History' (2012) 61 *DePaul Law Review* 973, 1002–03; HS Hadley, 'The Right to Privacy' (1894) 3 *Northwestern Law Review* 1, 11–12.

[52] *Daly v Viacom*, 238 F. Supp. 2d 1118 (N.D. Cal. 2002).

[53] ibid at 1124.

[54] ibid.

[55] ibid.

[56] *People v Harris*, 949 N.Y.S.2d 590, 593 (N.Y. Crim. Ct. 2012).

there is no reasonable expectation of privacy. There is no proprietary interest in your tweets, which you have now gifted to the world'.[57]

In fact, the Internet has proven to be a poor fit for this notion of public information. Courts tend to treat information on the World Wide Web that is accessed via a URL and does not require authentication credentials (like a username and password) as freely accessible.[58] This assumption applies whether the website in question is massively popular, like ESPN.com, or a random family blog or website dedicated to an extremely niche or obscure interest. That is because a hypothetical Internet user armed with the right web address or search terms could find the information. For example, in *United States v Gines-Perez*,[59] the US District Court for the District of Puerto Rico considered whether government accessing and downloading information from a website violated the defendant's right of privacy.[60] The Court found that merely 'placing information on the information superhighway' of the Internet inherently makes that information accessible to the public and thus 'public information'.[61]

Similarly, in the case of *Sandler v Calcagni*,[62] the court found the fact that the plaintiff 'revealed her decision to seek psychological help during college on her publicly accessible myspace.com webpage' prevented her from bringing a claim for disclosure of that decision as 'a private fact'.[63] This argument seems to boil down to the fact that passwords make things private, but absent that, everything on the World Wide Web is public because it is hypothetically available to anyone with an Internet connection.

The notions of 'accessibility' and 'exposure' are used interchangeably to define 'public' here and throughout the doctrine. But it is not clear that they are synonymous. The literal definition of exposure – 'the condition of being presented to view or made known' – conflates hypothetical availability and cognition.[64] In other words, it fails to recognise the difference between information that could conceivably be processed by other people and information that is at all likely to be processed.

In *United States Department of Justice v Reporters Committee for Freedom of the Press*, the Supreme Court seemed to acknowledge such a distinction when asked whether there was a privacy interest in a criminal 'rap sheet' containing aggregated public records.[65] The Court found that there was indeed a privacy interest in this information even though it was technically available as a public record.[66] This sort of semantic ambiguity is at the heart of the public information fallacy, and it matters because hypothetical realities are constructed through conjecture. This conjecture requires a host of assumptions about the pre-existing knowledge base, resources, motivations, and abilities of people who make up 'the public'. It requires assumptions about social norms and architectural

[57] ibid. Though for those that study modern electronic surveillance, the notion of emails and direct messages as 'private' might be so dubious as to elicit a snicker.

[58] *Ashcroft v ACLU*, 535 U.S. 564, 605 (2002).

[59] *United States v Gines-Perez*, 214 F. Supp. 2d 205 (D.P.R. 2002).

[60] ibid at 224.

[61] ibid at 225 (emphasis omitted).

[62] *Sandler v Calcagni*, 565 F. Supp. 2d 184 (D. Me. 2008).

[63] ibid at 197.

[64] 'Exposure', *Merriam-Webster's Collegiate Dictionary*, 11th edn (Springfield (MA) 2012).

[65] *United States Department of Justice v Reporters Committee for Freedom of the Press*, 489 US 749, 751 (1989).

[66] ibid.

restraints surrounding the environment of exposure. And it requires assumptions about the timing and the relative visibility, audibility, and comprehensibility of the acts to be surveilled or the data to be collected. There are no rules about how to arrive at these assumptions, which means that determining that something is 'freely accessible' can be wildly inconsistent and is often no better than a guess.

## *ii. Widely Known*

Sometimes it is not availability or observability that defines what is public, but rather a significant threshold of peoples' actual cognition of information or acts. I call this the 'widely known' conceptualisation of public information. This is sometimes referred to as 'broadly known', 'effective dissemination', 'publicised', or simply 'famous'.[67] The focus of this definition is on what people actually found, saw, or understood.[68]

Things that are shared or common knowledge among a group of people can be said to be public information. Most people in the US probably know that the Cubs finally won the World Series.[69] Many people know that Beyoncé and Jay-Z are married and have three children.[70] Many people probably know that Taylor Swift just completed her highly successful 'Eras' tour. While it can be incredibly difficult to consistently determine the boundaries of what is widely known, it is an ascertainable concept. The hard part is understanding the threshold quantity of people in the know or the boundaries of the relevant community.

An interesting example of conceptualising public as 'broadly known' is the case of *Sipple v Chronicle Publishing Company*.[71] Oliver Sipple was near Sara Jane Moore on 22 September 1975 when she attempted to assassinate President Ford.[72] Sipple interfered with Moore's assassination attempt and was credited as a hero.[73] Some of the publications that covered Sipple's story revealed the fact that he was gay, which was unknown to many close to him, including his parents, brothers, and sisters.[74] Sipple brought a tort claim against these publications for public disclosure of private facts.[75]

The California Court of Appeal upheld the dismissal of the claim on the grounds that Sipple's sexual orientation was not a private fact because he had made the information public by marching in gay parades, frequenting gay bars, and being named in gay magazines.[76] There, the Court did not focus on hypothetical accessibility. Rather, it focused on the fact that Sipple's sexual orientation 'had been known by hundreds of people in a variety of cities' and was thus 'already in public domain'.[77] While there is

[67] See, eg, *Sipple v Chronicle Publ'g Co.*, 201 Cal. Rptr. 665, 669 (Cal. Ct. App. 1984).
[68] ibid.
[69] See C Muskat, 'Holy Now! 108 Years Later, Cubs Best in World' (*MLB*, 3 November 2016), www.mlb.com/news/cubs-win-world-series-after-108-years-waiting/c-207995060.
[70] See J Juneau, 'How Beyoncé and JAY-Z Took All Three Kids – Even Their Year-Old Twins – on Tour' (*People*, 22 June 2018), www.people.com/parents/beyonce-jay-z-twins-daughter-blue-ivy-on-tour/.
[71] *Sipple v Chronicle Publishing Company* 201 Cal. Rptr. 665, 669 (Ct. App. 1984).
[72] See ibid at 666.
[73] ibid.
[74] ibid at 667.
[75] ibid.
[76] ibid at 671.
[77] ibid at 669.

some ambiguity caused by referring to information that 'had been known' by hundreds and 'left open to the eye of the public' – the accessibility/knowledge distinction – it appears that the Court was largely persuaded by the fact that people actually knew Sipple was gay in determining that this information was in the 'public domain'.[78]

Some laws that turn on whether information is 'nonpublic' also often seem to adopt the 'widely known' conceptualisation of public. For example, in *Dirks v SEC*,[79] the Supreme Court stated that parties with inside information cannot trade based on such information unless they disclose it to the public.[80] For this sort of 'public disclosure', the SEC requires more than mere disclosure to purchasers or sellers. It has indicated:

> [p]roper and adequate disclosure of significant corporate developments can only be effected by a public release through the appropriate public media, designed to achieve a broad dissemination to the investing public generally and without favoring any special person or group.[81]

However, the Court did not provide examples of things that met this standard, and further, the term 'public' as applied in this definition is left undefined by the SEC and the US Supreme Court.

Some conceptualisations of public combine 'accessible' and 'well-known' in a sort of 'either-or' test. For example, the guidance provided by the Office of Information Policy in the US Department of Justice provides that '[u]nless the information has become "practically obscure" ... there is generally no expectation of privacy regarding information that is particularly *well known* or is *widely available* within the public domain.'[82] Trade secret law has a developed body of law around the 'known' concept as well, whereby some information would not be protected as a trade secret if it is either 'generally known', either to the public or specific groups, or 'readily ascertainable' without much time, trouble, or expense.

The 'widely known' conceptualisation of privacy seems more defensible than 'freely accessible' as a descriptive account of public information because it generally requires less speculation and fewer assumptions. And while the general concept of privacy includes more than just secrets, to the extent the law does turn on secrecy, doing so based on what people actually know rather than hypothetical access seems more likely to match the expectations of those disclosing information and lead to a more consistent line in the sand to cut off privacy interests.

### iii. Of Interest to Society

A final, significant way to describe public information is that which is 'of interest to society'. The focus of this conceptualisation is not whether people can access information or whether they actually know it, but rather whether it is the kind of information that a significant part of society *would be* interested in accessing and knowing. Another

[78] ibid.
[79] *Dirks v SEC*, 463 U.S. 646 (1983).
[80] ibid at 678.
[81] Certain Trading in the Common Stock of Faberge, Inc., 45 S.E.C. 249, 256 (1973).
[82] DOJ, DOJ Guide to the Freedom of Information Act Office of Information Policy Guidance: Exemption 6, at 435 (2014) (emphasis added).

version of this notion of public information adds a normative component, which defines the concept as that which is of 'legitimate' interest to society, or what society *should* be concerned about. Sometimes this information is referred to as 'newsworthy' or matters of 'public concern'.

This conceptualisation of public information describes a feature of the subject matter of information rather than the context within which it was disclosed. The rationale behind endowing this conceptualisation of public information with exculpatory power is that in many contexts peoples' privacy interests will be overridden by benefits of a more public disclosure or society's 'right to know'.

For example, the disclosure tort requires a plaintiff to show that the information in issue is not a 'matter of legitimate public concern' before relief can be granted.[83] In determining whether former child prodigy William James Sidis has a privacy interest in certain aspects about his current life, the Second Circuit Court of Appeals recognised 'that at some point the public interest in obtaining information becomes dominant over the individual's desire for privacy'.[84] The Court refused to grant Sidis relief based largely on the fact that his personal information was of interest to society and, thus, made him a 'public' figure.

Joel Reidenberg has suggested applying a 'public significance filter' to questions of privacy in public in order to avoid the problems associated with focusing solely on the observability of information or acts.[85] Jonathan Mintz has noted that the formidable protection afforded to publishing things of legitimate interest to society 'is greatly enhanced by the relatively amorphous, and thus far-reaching, definitions of "in the public interest", "news-worthy", and "news"'.[86] Mintz asked:

> [i]s the term "newsworthy" a descriptive predicate, intended to refer to the fact that there is widespread public interest? Or is it a value predicate, intended to indicate that the publication in question is a meritorious contribution and that the public's interest is praiseworthy?[87]

I do not intend to take up the question of what is newsworthy in this chapter, but I reference its ambiguity to point out that, like the concept of privacy, even nuanced articulations of what is public are contested.

## B. Anything that is 'Not Private'

Every year near the beginning of my Information Privacy Law course, before we dive into doctrine, I call on each student and ask them to define the concept of privacy to the class. As you might expect, I usually get a variety of answers, ranging from 'control over information' to 'secrets' to 'dignity' and everything in between. Almost every year at least one student defines privacy as 'everything that isn't public'. I also ask the students at some point in the semester to define the concept of 'public' for me. Again, I get many

[83] *Green v Chi. Tribune Co.*, 675 N.E.2d 249, 255 (Ill. App. Ct. 1996).
[84] *Sidis v F-R Pub. Corp.*, 113 F.2d 806, 809 (2d Cir. 1940).
[85] Reidenberg (n 22) 155.
[86] Mintz (n 22) 442.
[87] ibid.

different answers. And nearly every year, at least one student says 'everything that isn't private'.

I call this the 'negative' conceptualisation of public. We define the concept by what it is not, referring to the notion of privacy, instead of what it is. The upside to this approach is that it simplifies the number of complex constructs at play and channels our questions straight to what constitutes privacy. The downside is that it can sometimes force us to think of privacy in terms of an overly simplistic dichotomy between public and private.

One way in which this 'negative' view of public information is represented is within the construct of public and private spheres. Nissenbaum wrote 'that theories of privacy should . . . recognize the systemic relationship between privacy and information that is neither intimate nor sensitive and is drawn from public spheres'.[88] Under some conceptualisations, however, in public spheres our autonomy is more justly curtailed, whereas the private spheres should remain free from interference.[89] Other scholars inversely use the term 'public' to define the concept of privacy. Professor Milton Konvitz referred to privacy as 'a sphere of space that has not been dedicated to public use or control'.[90] Harry Kalven also viewed privacy as a non-delimiting 'residual' interest: '[W]hat is left after the state or society has made its demand'.[91] But again, this leads us to the as-of-yet unanswered question as to what 'public' means.

Most of the sources of law I reviewed for this chapter did not explicitly adopt negative conceptualisations of public information. Instead, courts, lawmakers, and regulators usually deployed the term 'public' without much clarification. This substantial ambiguity is what makes reliance on public information a problem.

The negative conceptualisation of public information is more often seen in discussions about the 'public domain' in intellectual property regimes. In intellectual property, some conceptualisations describe the public domain as the common pool of knowledge and information not protected by intellectual property laws, though this is a contested concept.[92] The idea of public as 'negative space' or as the 'body of common resources' defined by what is *not* a common resource is popular among some. This notion treats public information as sort of the 'residual existence' or 'regulatory leftovers' and operates under a sort of implied waiver theory.[93] If it is not protected by law, then it is fair game.

Using 'public information' as shorthand for 'that which is not protected by privacy law' might not be inherently problematic. It might actually help reduce definitional ambiguity by being deferential to other concepts, such as privacy, that should be the focus of clarification efforts. This way, courts and lawmakers can cut down on duelling ambiguity and inconsistency.

[88] H Nissenbaum, 'Protecting Privacy in an Information Age: The Problem of Privacy in Public' (1998) 17 *Law & Philosophy* 559, 559.

[89] Pongrace (n 28) 1196.

[90] MR Konvitz, 'Privacy and the Law: A Philosophical Prelude' (1966) 31 *Law & Contemporary Problems* 272, 280.

[91] H Kalven, Jr., 'The Right of Privacy in Tort Law – Were Warren and Brandeis Wrong?' (1966) 31 *Law and Contemporary Problems* 327.

[92] E Samuels, 'The Public Domain in Copyright Law' (1993) 41 *Journal of the Copyright Society of the USA* 137, 141.

[93] See Mintz (n 22) 456–57.

The problem with the negative conceptualisation of public information comes when it is used consequentially in privacy law and policy. Used this way, the negative conceptualisation deflects a substantive determination regarding the status of information by bootstrapping and perpetuates a tautology. Those who subscribe to and deploy the negative conceptualisation of public information to justify surveillance and data practices are assuming the publicness of information in their argument that information is public. In other words, it makes no sense to say 'this information is not private because it's public' when what's meant is 'this information is not private because it's not private.'

## C. Designated as Public

The final way to conceptualise public information is as an official designation or category by a relevant authority that indicates the information is for general use by anyone or that the surveillance of certain people or acts that are exposed to others is explicitly permitted. The most common example of something that is designated as public is a 'public record', sometimes referred to in law as 'open records'. These records, when released, have been designated as 'public' through legislation and a deliberative process that weighed any possible exemptions. Their designation as a public record carries with it the imprimatur of government authorisation as well as a signal to society that these documents are intended to be collected, used, and shared. Another example of legal regimes designating acts as public is open meetings laws, which are sometimes called 'sunshine laws'.[94] These laws prohibit denying access to the general public and are meant to encourage transparency through reporting. When meetings are subject to sunshine laws, they are sometimes said to be 'public meetings'.[95]

While the purpose of designating information held by the government as public is usually motivated by a desire for transparency and accountability, many other values can be served by designating information as public. For example, 'open data', meaning generally 'data that can be freely used, re-used and redistributed by anyone', is also colloquially a form of designated public information.[96] The goal of open data initiatives is to increase transparency, improve reproducibility, and create a quicker path to new knowledge and discovery.[97] Open data can include personal information, though it is regularly protected through concepts like deidentification and controlled access.[98]

[94] See CN Davis et al, 'Sunshine Laws and Judicial Discretion: A Proposal for Reform of State Sunshine Law Enforcement Provisions' (1996) 28 *The Urban Lawyer* 41, 41; DR Stewart, 'Let the Sunshine in, or Else: An Examination of the 'Teeth' of State and Federal Open Meetings and Open Records Laws' (2010) 15 *Communication Law & Policy* 265, 265–66.

[95] See Utah Open and Public Meetings Act, Utah Code Ann. § 52-4-303 (West 2006).

[96] What Is Open Data?', (Open Data Handbook, 17 May 2016), www.opendatahandbook.org/guide/en/what-is-open-data [perma.cc/48ZA-YGFS]. Open data has also been defined as 'information that is accessible to everyone, machine readable, offered online at zero cost, and has no limits on reuse and redistribution'. E Tran and G Scholtes, 'Open Data Literature Review' in *19th Annual BCLT/BTLJ Symposium: Open Data: Addressing Privacy, Security, and Civil Rights Challenges* (2015) 1, www.law.berkeley.edu/wp-content/uploads/2015/04/Final_OpenDataLitReview_2015-04-14_1.1.pdf [perma.cc/UL5X-P5SS]; see also Budapest Open Access Initiative, www.budapestopenaccessinitiative.org [perma.cc/KMH3-ERX6].

[97] KE Emam and B Malin, 'Sharing Clinical Trial Data: Maximizing Benefits, Minimizing Risk' (Institute of Medicine edn 2015) 203, 214 (emphasising importance of de-identification).

[98] See IS Rubinstein and W Hartzog, 'Anonymization and Risk' (2016) 91 *Washington Law Review* 703, 720.

Open data is commonly described as 'public' both colloquially and officially.[99] In their document, 'The 8 Principles of Open Government Data', a group of open government advocates wrote that, '[p]ublic data is data that is not subject to valid privacy, security or privilege limitations.'[100]

The designation of information as public is legally significant, not just because it makes it more accessible, but also because it signals to those who wish to collect and use it for some kind of legal validation. For example, the Restatement of Torts defers to the notion of matters of public record in determining what is private, claiming that giving publicity to things like one's date of birth, marriage, military records, or professional licensures cannot give rise to liability.[101]

It is not clear if 'matter of public record' referred to here is information that is available, widely known, or designated public by the government. However, given the items listed by the Restatement, it would seem to be records designated as public and made available by the government. Courts often give deference to the fact that public records are 'lawfully obtained' when determining what information is private and what information is in the 'public domain' (and thus not private).[102] In a series of privacy tort cases that denied the plaintiff's recovery, the defendants divulged information that they lawfully obtained from what the court referred to as the 'public domain'.[103]

The Supreme Court in *Smith v Daily Mail Publishing*[104] also referenced notions of information that was 'lawfully obtained', 'publicly revealed', and in the 'public domain' in stating that those concepts 'suggest strongly' that the Constitution prohibited punishing speakers for publishing matters of public significance that were obtained lawfully.[105] And in *Florida Star v B.J.F.*,[106] the Supreme Court looked to whether information was 'lawfully obtained' because it was 'furnished by the government' in determining contested disclosures involving information in the 'public domain' and, thus, could not be lawfully constrained.[107]

The justification behind validating information that has been designated as public is based upon more than just a description of the information's context or failing to find a privacy interest. It is value-driven. Many reasons can justify designating information as public, including government accountability, research, industry and market support, facilitation of government services, civic participation, and much more. Privacy is part of the calculus in determining what is to be collected, sorted, and released. But this notion of public includes goals and procedures that are about more than personal information.

[99] See, eg, M Kress, 'By the Numbers: Port Statistics for Some of the Largest U.S. Ports' (*Data.gov*, 1 March 2017), www.data.gov/maritime/p24529331/ [perma.cc/QMZ4-M42M].

[100] 'The Annotated 8 Principles of Open Government Data', (*Data.gov*), www.opengovdata.org [perma.cc/W7VC-VWSY] (including complete, primary, timely, accessible, machine processable, non-discriminatory, non-proprietary, and licence-free).

[101] *Restatement (Second) of Torts* § 652D (Philadelphia, American Law Institute, 1977).

[102] See Mintz (n 22) 456–57 (citation omitted).

[103] See *Fla. Star v B.J.F.*, 491 U.S. 524, 536 (1989); *Smith v Daily Mail Publ'g Co.*, 443 US 97, 99 (1979); *Cox Broad Corp. v Cohn*, 420 U.S. 469, 495 (1975).

[104] *Smith v Daily Mail Publishing* 443 U.S. 97 (1979).

[105] See Mintz (n 22) at 456.

[106] *Florida Star v B.J.F.* 491 U.S. 524 (1989).

[107] ibid at 535.

# III. What is 'Public' must be Clarified

In this chapter I hope to make one point very clear: we should be sceptical and deliberate when deploying the concept of public information in a legally significant way because it can be conceptualised in several different and value-laden ways. It is a mistake to validate the 'no privacy in public' argument without being clear about what public even means. In this part, I propose a path to precision.

First, regardless of which conceptualisation is adopted, privacy law and policy should recognise labelling information as public as a value-laden exercise of power. The normative choices made in law are most evident in the 'designation' conceptualisation of public information. For example, sometimes privacy concerns about information in public records are overridden because releasing information is in the 'public interest'. The 'not private' conceptualisation also compels us to ask the normatively fraught question of 'what is privacy?' Even descriptive accounts of public information necessarily require value judgements, even if those judgements are repackaged as neutral, objective observations.

To the extent descriptive factors are an important part of determining what constitutes public information, some of the common frameworks are out of whack. In particular, notions of hypothetical accessibility and exposure regularly fail to properly account for what shapes peoples' perceptions and behaviour. I argue the concepts of obscurity and trust should be better considered in the descriptive calculus about what constitutes public information.

Obscurity and trust play a key role in shaping people's decisions about when, where, how, and with whom to share information or interact with others. Ignoring these factors renders accessibility-based notions of public information harsh and repressive. Virtually everything we do is, in theory, accessible to someone, somewhere. And this mistake is at the heart of our approach to many modern privacy quandaries.

## A. 'Public' is a Value Judgment

In this chapter I have catalogued the various ways in which courts and lawmakers treat the concept of public as though it is an objective, pre-existing state that need only be ascertained by looking to degrees of accessibility and exposure, which then determine people's privacy interests in their information and acts. But this is a misguided approach to public information. To say something is 'public' is to make a value-laden conclusion about what information should be protected and what kinds of surveillance and data practices should be permissible. It is an exercise of power.[108]

The semantic ambiguity of public information means that implementation of the concept requires many different assumptions about the resources, motivations, abilities, and pre-existing knowledge of people who make up 'the public'. It also requires assumptions about norms, architectural restraints, traffic density and timing, and the relative visibility, audibility, and comprehensibility of the acts to be surveilled or the data to be

[108] See Cohen (n 29) 213–14.

collected. By the time all of these assumptions are made, the idea of public becomes a construct further removed from empirical observation, with the conclusion of what is 'public' determined by the thresholds and boundaries set by these assumptions.

Those who set the assumptions used to determine what is public can predetermine the winner before the questions are even asked. For example, those seeking to justify broad and pervasive surveillance would be best off conceptualising public information as all that is 'freely accessible', since it allows for the most conjecture about who *could* see or access information, rather than who actually did. Meanwhile, the designated and 'widely known' conceptualisations of public information are narrower. Public records are only a small part of the world's data ecosystem, and hardly anyone except you actually knows your exact daily routine or everything you share online.[109]

The UK's Information Commissioner's Office's ('ICO') approach to determining what falls into the public domain is an example of how to treat the concept of public information as a prescriptive, not descriptive, concept. The ICO has a relatively nuanced approach to what constitutes falling within the public domain. Critically, it determined that '[e]ven if the information itself is already in the public domain, this is not decisive and is not an automatic argument either for or against disclosure.'[110] Rather, several different considerations must be weighed before the decision to make information freely available is made.

The benefit of explicitly treating 'public' as a prescriptive, value-laden concept is that it helps facilitate the debate when values such as free speech, privacy, and security conflict. There are often good reasons to favour free speech over privacy in certain contexts, but by cloaking the concept of public information entirely in descriptive terms, we obscure the value choices at stake and disadvantage privacy by creating presumptions of the public nature of information using questionable assumptions about behavioural norms and societal expectations.

## B. Trust and Obscurity: A More Accurate Notion of the Public Sphere

While determining the public nature of information is not exclusively a descriptive question, descriptive factors such as the degree of exposure and internalised knowledge are relevant. But, as Julie Cohen has written, 'interpreting self-exposure either as a blanket waiver of privacy or as an exercise in personal empowerment would be far too simple.'[111] The problem is that too often the framework for assessing the degree of exposure or accessibility gives short shrift to two of the most important factors that shape peoples' behaviour and perceptions of risk in any given environment – the obscurity of people and data and the existence of relationships of trust. People feel relatively safe when their acts and data exist in zones of obscurity and are disclosed within

[109] Except, perhaps, your internet service provider ('ISP'). But that is a different fight altogether.
[110] Information Commissioner's Office, *Information in the Public Domain* (2013) 11, www.ico.org.uk/media/for-organisations/documents/1204/information-in-the-public-domain-foi-eir-guidance.pdf [perma.cc/J3HW-ZHRV].
[111] Cohen (n 41) 198.

relationships of trust. If disclosing information in 'public' is going to act as a waiver of sorts to justify surveillance and data practices, then the concept should at least rest on a more accurate assessment of social behaviour and risk.

### *i. Zones of Obscurity*

Obscurity as a privacy value is the notion that when our activities or information are unlikely to be found, seen, or remembered, they are, to some degree, safe. People calculate risk every day based upon how obscure they are or are likely to be. For example, you probably feel comfortable discussing relatively sensitive topics (or perhaps just gossiping) over dinner in a public restaurant because the likelihood of that disclosure being more publicly disseminated or coming back to harm you is pretty low. You are in a room full of strangers. They are probably not eavesdropping.

In work with Evan Selinger and Fred Stutzman, I have explored the concept of obscurity as an essential component of modern notions of privacy.[112] Every day we make decisions about where we go, what we do, and what we share based upon how obscure we think we are. Most of our information online is obscure as well. For example, just because information is hypothetically available does not mean most (or even a few) people have the knowledge and ability to access information. Without the right search terms, URL, access credentials, or pre-existing knowledge to make sense of data, information will remain obscure. We are all at least subconsciously aware of this reality and adjust our risk calculus accordingly. I have argued that obscurity is heavily relied upon as a form of privacy in the modern age.[113] Yet these societal expectations of obscurity are regularly overlooked when public information is conceived of as freely accessible and endowed with the power to defeat privacy claims.[114]

Some pockets of privacy law recognise the importance of obscurity with respect to public information better than others. Recall the Reporter's Committee decision by the Supreme Court that recognised a privacy interest in the 'practical obscurity' of disaggregated public records. This privacy interest is grounded in the notion of how transaction costs can make certain bits of information hard or unlikely to be found and that these costs can shift over time. The Court wrote that 'the extent of the protection

[112] See W Hartzog and E Selinger, 'Surveillance As Loss of Obscurity' (2015) 72 *Washington & Lee Law Review* 1343, 1356; W Hartzog and F Stutzman, 'The Case for Online Obscurity' (2013) 101 *California Law Review* 1, 24; W Hartzog and F Stutzman, 'Obscurity by Design' (2013) 88 *Washington Law Review* 385, 387; E Selinger and W Hartzog, 'Obscurity and Privacy' in J Pitt and A Shew (eds), *Routledge Companion to Philosophy of Technology* 119, 119 (New Jersey, Blackwell Publishing, 2014); W Hartzog and E Selinger, 'Obscurity: A Better Way to Think About Your Data Than "Privacy"' (*The Atlantic*, 17 January 2013), www.theatlantic.com/technology/archive/2013/01/obscurity-a-better-way-to-think-about-your-data-than-privacy/267283/ [perma.cc/4ZHQ-5VM8]; E Selinger and W Hartzog, 'Why You Have the Right to Obscurity' (*Chirstian Science Monitor*, 15 April 2015), www.csmonitor.com/World/Passcode/Passcode-Voices/2015/0415/Why-you-have-the-right-to-obscurity [perma.cc/JC57-8DEW]; E Selinger and W Hartzog, 'Google Can't Forget You, But It Should Make You Hard to Find' (*Wired*, 20 May 2014), www.wired.com/2014/05/google-cant-forget-you-but-it-should-make-you-hard-to-find/ [perma.cc/VTR2-TE9U].

[113] ibid; see also MJ Blitz, 'The Fourth Amendment Future of Public Surveillance' (2013) 63 *American University Law Review* 27–28; DJ Solove, 'Access and Aggregation: Privacy, Public Records, and the Constitution' (2002) 86 *Minnesota Law Review* 1178; H Surden, 'Structural Rights in Privacy' (2007) 60 *Southern Methodist University Law Review* 1605, 1607.

[114] Hartzog and Stutzman, 'The Case for Online Obscurity' (n 112) 24.

accorded a privacy right at common law rested in part on the degree of dissemination of the allegedly private fact and the extent to which the passage of time rendered it private'.[115] The passage of time makes information harder to recall because people forget things, records get lost, databases get deleted, and links rot. Information has a natural way of becoming obscure. Even at the micro-level, social applications like Snapchat that build in a sort of ephemerality are seeking to encourage disclosure by manufacturing some sense of obscurity for users. Assuming they are not saved by a screenshot, 'Snap' photos become practically obscure after a few seconds because they are only retrievable through a considerable expense of resources.

Another example of attempts to integrate obscurity into public information doctrine comes from the UK's ICO's guidance on public records regarding what information is in the 'public domain'.[116] The ICO has determined that '[i]nformation is only in the public domain if it is realistically accessible to a member of the general public at the time of the request. It must be available in practice, not just in theory.'[117] That is, under the ICO's approach, information only falls within the public domain 'a hypothetical average member of the general public who is interested enough to conduct some searches for the information' could access the information without 'unrealistic persistence or specialised knowledge … even if it is theoretically available somewhere in a library or on the internet'.[118] This is in direct contrast to cases in the US that assume that a website is public information because it is *theoretically* available to someone who happens to know the right URL or search terms, regardless of its obscurity.[119]

The transaction costs for accessing information also change over time. Information thus becomes more or less obscure, which alters people's risk calculus and privacy expectations. The impermanence of exposure should be better reflected in US privacy law. For example, the ICO said in regard to whether something is in the 'public domain', information must be 'available at the time of the request'.[120] This conceptualisation gets closer to capturing the role of transaction costs in finding and understanding information and the natural obscurity produced by the mere passage of time.

In summary, the question of what is public is often just the threshold line that is drawn somewhere on the spectrum of things that range from completely obscure to totally obvious or known. People value their obscurity and build their disclosures and acts in reliance upon it. The calculus for what makes things obscure is complex and includes many different factors like searchability, permanence, comprehensibility, identifiability, and the resources, motivation, and pre-existing knowledge of those who seek to surveil or make use of data. These factors should be better valued when formulating accounts of public information.

[115] *U.S. D.O.J. v Reporter's Comm. for Freedom of the Press*, 489 U.S. 749, 763 (1989).

[116] See generally Information Commissioner's Office (n 110).

[117] ibid.

[118] ibid at 6.

[119] W Hartzog and Stutzman, 'The Case for Online Obscurity' (n 112) 24; *Sandler v Calcagni*, 565 F. Supp. 2d 184 (D Me 2008); *United States v D'Andrea*, 497 F Supp 2d 117 (D. Mass. 2007); *Four Navy Seals v Associated Press*, 413 F. Supp. 2d 1136 (S.D. Cal. 2005); *United States v Gines-Perez*, 214 F Supp 2d 205 (DPR. 2002); *Moreno v Hanford Sentinel, Inc.*, 91 Cal. Rptr. 3d 858, 862–63 (Ct App 2009); *Yath v Fairview Clinics*, 767 NW2d 34 (Minn Ct App 2009); *State v Birchfield*, No. 04-08-00132, 2007 WL 1437235 (NJ Super Ct App Div May 17, 2007)).

[120] See Information Commissioner's Office (n 110) 8–9.

### *ii. Relationships of Trust*

The other most important factor relevant to how people perceive risk, choose to expose themselves, and share information that too often gets glossed over in descriptive accounts of public information is the role of relationships of trust. In previous work with Professor Neil Richards, we have argued that trust – the willingness to accept vulnerability to the actions of others – is necessary for a safe and sustainable digital world.[121] We wrote,

> In the privacy context, trust allows us to develop long-term, sustainable information relationships by sharing meaningful but often sensitive information and having sincere exchanges with the confidence that what we share will be used for our benefit and not come back to haunt or harm us.[122]

Ari Ezra Waldman has conceptualised privacy itself as 'a behavioral exchange of trust and discretion'.[123] If we cannot trust others with our personal information, society will suffer.

Trust is everywhere. Our modern networked world is mediated by what Richards and I referred to as 'information relationships', in which 'professionals, private institutions, or the government hold information about us as part of providing a service'.[124] These relationships surround us.

> We see them when we share sensitive personal information with [internet service providers] …, doctors, banks, search engines, credit card companies, and countless other information recipients and intermediaries. We also see them as we get information via large and small computers to access apps, social media, and the Internet at large.[125]

Even traditional merchants that people interacted anonymously with, like grocery stores, have gotten into the game.[126]

This is to say nothing of our interpersonal relationships, where we gossip, share secrets, and expose our feelings and weaknesses. Trust isn't just a fundamental component of privacy. It is the glue that holds society together.

But relationships of trust are often seemingly glossed over in determining what information is public. Concepts like the 'third party doctrine' treat disclosures to anyone, no matter how trusted, as a waiver of privacy rights.[127] The privacy torts are maddeningly inconsistent in their recognition of trusted confidants.[128] Privacy law, it seems, is

[121] See N Richards and W Hartzog, 'Taking Trust Seriously in Privacy Law' (2016) 19 *Stanford Technology Law Review* 431, 435.

[122] N Richards and W Hartzog, 'Privacy's Trust Gap' (2017) 126 *Yale Law Journal* 1180, 1213.

[123] AE Waldman, 'Privacy As Trust: Sharing Personal Information in a Networked World' (2015) 69 *University of Miami Law Review* 559, 630.

[124] Richards and Hartzog (n 122).

[125] ibid.

[126] ibid.

[127] See, eg, JM Balkin, 'Information Fiduciaries and the First Amendment' (2016) 49 *University of California Davis Law Review* 1183, 1230; K Brennan-Marquez, 'Fourth Amendment Fiduciaries' (2015) 84 *Fordham Law Review* 611, 611, 616.

[128] See *Fisher v Ohio Dep't of Rehab. & Corr.*, 578 N.E.2d 901, 903 (Ohio Ct. Cl. 1988); L Strahilevitz, 'A Social Networks Theory of Privacy' (2005) 72 *University of Chicago Law Review* 919, 920–21.

often content to treat disclosures to anyone outside of narrowly prescribed, formalised confidential relationships as 'public'.[129] This is a problem.

Modern accounts of public information should better consider relationships of trust in their decision-making framework. If obscurity is concerned with who *might* see us or find our information, trust is the relevant factor for evaluating whether the *actual* recipients of information render certain disclosures public. These recipients need not be fully-fledged 'confidants' in the formal sense of the word. People trust others to be discreet, loyal, honest, and protective all the time without demanding a formal obligation of confidentiality. They adjust their risk calculus on this trust and the likelihood that information will not travel too far or be used against them.[130] If we want this kind of trust to continue (and we should), our law and policy should accommodate it when labelling and evaluating what is public.

We can see bits of respect for trust at the margins of privacy law and policy, particularly the law of public records. Formal promises of confidentiality are 'generally given weight with regard to an individual's expectation of privacy' and the privacy exception of FOIA.[131] The ICO holds that 'Information disclosed only to a limited audience will not generally be in the public domain, as it is unlikely to be available to a member of the general public.'[132] This is an implicit recognition that limited disclosures generally carry with them expectations of discretion and loyalty – two hallmarks of trust in relationships.

One way to better account for trust in the law and policy of public information would be to seek to develop and identify common indicators of trust. This might include looking to such factors as custom, the kind of relationships between the discloser and the recipients, the purpose of a disclosure, whether a disclosure was solicited, the relative sophistication and power between the parties, and any communication through words or design that trust would be kept.[133] Helen Nissenbaum has proposed that conditions of trust include the recipient's history and reputation, inferences about the recipient's trustworthiness based on personal characteristics, mutuality and reciprocity within relationships, reliance on the recipient filling a role (such as doctor, merchant, or ISP), and other contextual factors.[134] The literature and empirical evidence for what might indicate a relationship of trust is vast and should not be ignored in privacy law.[135]

[129] See W Hartzog, 'Reviving Implied Confidentiality' (2014) 89 *Indiana Law Journal* 763, 764.

[130] Strahilevitz (n 128) 930 (discussing the way that trust builds intimacy and willingness to reveal certain information).

[131] 37A Am. Jur. 2d Freedom of Information Act § 239 (citing *U.S. Dept. of State v Ray*, 502 U.S. 164 (1991)); *District of Columbia v Fraternal Order of Police*, Metro. Police Dep't Labor Comm., 75 A.3d 259 (D.C. 2013); *Wash. Post Co. v U.S. Dept. of Health and Human Serv.*, 690 F.2d 252 (D.C. Cir. 1982); *Ray v U.S. DOJ*, 908 F.2d 1549 (11th Cir. 1990), judgment rev'd on other grounds, 502 U.S. 164 (1991)).

[132] Information Commissioner's Office (n 110) 6.

[133] For a more complete list of the factors courts look at in determining whether a trust in the form of implied confidences exist, see Hartzog (n 129) 774–800.

[134] H Nissenbaum 'Securing Trust Online: Wisdom or Oxymoron?' (2001) 81 *Boston University Law Review* 635, 643.

[135] See, eg, Reidenberg, 'Privacy in Public' (n 22) 155–56; *Katz v United States*, 389 US 347 (1967); *Whalen v Roe*, 429 US 589 (1977); Strahilevitz (n 128) 921.

# IV. Conclusion

The debate over privacy in public information has tied us into knots. Recognising restrictions on public information conflicts with many traditional notions of privacy as secrecy. Yet abandoning privacy in public can feel counterintuitive, unfulfilling, and dangerous. To untie the knot, we must change the terms of the debate.

The 'no privacy in public' argument has, thus far, put the cart before the horse. Before lawmakers and society can answer the question of whether privacy can exist in public, we must first understand what the concept of public means. As I have tried to demonstrate in this chapter, 'public' can be conceptualised several different ways, from descriptive to designated. These conceptualisations are at best under-theorised and at worst tautological. This means that the term must be given a more articulated meaning to be useful in law and policy.

Most importantly, law and society must recognise that to label something as public is both consequential and value-laden. We must reject a neutral, empirical notion of 'public' that is separate from legal and social construction. There is no such thing. How we define public information sets the rules for surveillance and data practices, so we should proceed intentionally and with caution. We should be more critical of claims like 'data is public' to justify surveillance and data practices. To move forward, we should focus on the values we want to serve, the relationships and outcomes we want to foster, and the problems we want to avoid.

# 15

# What's Private and What's Public? On Defining a Contested Line

BEATE RÖSSLER*

## I. Introduction

When homosexuality was still a crime in many countries, homosexuals, or queer people more generally, were confined to secrecy. This meant they were forced to stay in some private homes or in the secrecy of clubs or other meeting points. Only in these public but secret spaces, or in the privacy of their dwellings, could queer people live how they wanted given their gender identity.[1] This form of repressive privacy has changed over the last 30 years – has mostly changed, we should say. To be queer is no longer forbidden in the EU and in the US, to name but two legislations. This change of what should be private and what can be public, this new line between the spheres or dimensions of lives, is clearly an emancipatory change, although it does remain contested even in some ideologies in liberal democracies. And of course, to be queer still is – or is again – rejected in Russia, in Georgia, and in many other countries.[2]

In this chapter, I am interested not so much in the questions concerning analyses of the legal right to privacy but rather in the question of *how our idea of what should be private and what should be public has changed over the last decades*. In one sense, this is obvious because of the enormous amount of data and surveillance, which was unheard of and simply impossible 20 years ago. In another sense the question is not so obvious: what does it mean to have privacy, who are the people who claim

* With many thanks to Ralf Poscher and Elisa Orrù for inviting me to the original workshop at the MPI in Freiburg, and especially to Elisa for her patience waiting for my final manuscript. I also owe many thanks to Lukas Hjulmann Seidler and Anna Beerends who helped enormously to finish the manuscript.

[1] See S Brady and M Seymour, 'From Sodomy Laws to Same-Sex Marriage: Historical Transformations' in S Brady and M Seymour (eds), *From Sodomy Laws to Same-Sex Marriage: International Perspectives since 1789* (London, Bloomsbury Academic, 2019).

[2] See Euronews, 'Georgian Parliament Approves Anti-LGBTQ+ Law in Lockstep With Russia' (*Euronews*, 2024), available at www.euronews.com/my-europe/2024/09/17/georgian-parliament-approves-anti-lgbtq-law-in-lockstep-with-russia.

privacy, and how do they want to live in their intimate relations? In which way have our self-conception and our sense of identity with respect to our privacy changed?

The issue I want to pursue revolves around these shifts in the separation of privacy and the public sphere: I will tie in with the discussions about the protection of privacy on the internet but also with the debates in the 1990s, in which feminists – centrally Anita Hill, as well as philosophers such as Nancy Fraser – in the context of Clarence Thomas's nomination to the Supreme Court have shown that what is considered private is not naturally or necessarily so but is subject to the powers of definition that prevail in the public sphere.

The thesis I want to argue for is that attempts at emancipation and experiences of liberation should often be seen as shifting the boundary between private and public: the boundary must always be conceived of as one that is produced by power structures. Hence, my questions are the following: what does it mean to say that the separation of the spheres has changed or shifted? How do we reconcile the legitimate protection of the private sphere with the public's legitimate interest in avoiding misuse or violation of privacy of the domestic sphere? These are not only empirical questions; they are also conceptual and normative, and my thesis is that the perspective of the private can help to better understand the inherent ambivalences in judging social transformations but also to understand the discourses of power and liberation. We will see later that the conservative framing of 'woke' as a cancel culture is also a setback against the emancipatory attempt to make public what previously was perceived as a private issue, such as homosexuality or transgender identities.[3]

I want to proceed in the following steps: I will first remind you of the debates surrounding the nomination of Clarence Thomas and the accusations raised against him by Anita Hill. Nancy Fraser wrote a very helpful article on this, which I will present briefly. In a second step, I want to take on a different perspective: that of one of the first European Court of Human Rights (ECHR) decisions on homosexuality. I will examine this decision and the ensuing debates.

In a third step, I want to have a brief look at the idea of a public sphere, which is necessary to provide the scene for (heated, maybe even polarised) debates about what's private and what's public. Only against this background will I then come to the question of the more recent shifts between the private and public, and I'll focus, on the one hand, on the #MeToo debates, and, on the other hand, on the public presence of trans people negotiated under the title 'culture wars'. At the end I will tie the threads together and argue why the emancipatory aspects of these social and political transformations are best analysed and framed as changes in the politically drawn line between the private and the public.

However, before taking these steps, let me first explain the concept of privacy and the public. which stands in the background of the following thoughts and arguments, in more detail, to clarify some of the conceptual issues which will be discussed later.

[3] For the following see B Rössler, 'Privacy as a Human Right' (2017) 117 *Proceedings of the Aristotelian Society* 187 and B Rössler, 'Where Lies the Power to Define What's Private? Some Recent Shifts of the Boundary Between the Private and the Public' in SO Søe, T Wiehn, RF Jørgensen and B Valtýsson (eds), *Beyond Privacy: People, Practices, Politics* (Bristol, Bristol University Press, 2025).

## II. Privacy: Three Dimensions

When discussing the concept of privacy, it's first helpful to focus on the link between privacy and freedom or autonomy: Conceptions of privacy based upon a concept of autonomy or individual freedom provide the most interesting and forward-looking possibilities for a conceptualisation of the term. Three such dimensions of privacy should be distinguished. These dimensions – not realms, not spaces – of individual privacy serve to protect, facilitate and effectuate individual liberties in a variety of respects. Freedom-orientated theories of privacy are to be found within the whole range of theories of privacy, from those that deal with the privacy of (intimate) actions to those concerned with informational privacy or the privacy of the household. It makes sense, therefore, to discuss these different aspects of freedom and privacy individually.[4]

The first dimension of privacy is the *decisional* dimension: the privacy of decisions we make, mostly but not exclusively with respect to our bodies. It is only in recent years that decisional privacy, or the privacy of actions, has been a specialist term in the literature. A decisive factor here was the ruling of the US Supreme Court in the *Roe v Wade* case, where for the first time in US legal history women were granted a right to physical and sexual self-determination and to terminate a pregnancy, this being grounded upon an appeal to a *right to privacy*.[5] This verdict and the discussions that preceded and followed it were hugely influential upon the conceptualisation of privacy not only in the US. As a result, feminist theory has treated sexual freedom of action, the privacy of intimate and sexual acts, and the woman's right of sexual self-determination as central elements in the theory of privacy. Decisive significance is given to the *privacy of the body*.[6] This includes the woman's then newly won right to conceive of her body as private to the extent that she can decide for herself whether to bear a child and thus enjoys rights of reproductive freedom.

As we know, this landmark ruling of the US Supreme Court from 1973 was overruled and fundamentally revised by the same institution, the US Supreme Court, in 2022: the Dobbs ruling leaves it up to the individual states in the US to enact their own abortion rights legislation. Since then, abortion has been banned in most states. Decisional privacy no longer covers the right a woman has over her own body when this right concerns the right to abortion.[7]

But let me widen the perspective on decisional privacy a little in order to focus on the idea of physical privacy as the privacy of actions that concern the intimate sphere of women and men and which lies at the heart of decisional privacy. Two further central aspects of this form of privacy, therefore, are decisive for the societal coding and meaning of decisional privacy: these relate to the issues of sexual harassment and sexual

[4] See B Rössler, and J DeCew, 'Privacy' (2023) *The Stanford Encyclopaedia of Philosophy*.

[5] *Roe v Wade*, 410 U.S. 113 (1973).

[6] M Gatens, *Imaginary Bodies: Ethics, Power and Corporeality* (New York, Routledge Taylor & Francis Group, 1995) and M Gatens, 'Can Human Rights Accommodate Women's Rights? Towards an Embodied Account of Social Norms, Social Meaning, and Cultural Change' (2004) 3 *Contemporary Political Theory* 275.

[7] See J Waldron, 'Denouncing Dobbs and Opposing Judicial Review' (2022) *NYU School of Law, Public Law Research Paper* 1.

orientation. Both protection from sexual harassment and the respect for diverse sexual orientations form *aspects of decisional privacy* because and to the extent that it is the privacy of the body that is here vulnerable to infringement. The reason that privacy with respect to intimate, sexual decisions is considered so vital is that these decisions form the core of very general decisions that may have far-reaching consequences in terms of who one wants to be and how one wants to live: the core, in other words, of one's freedom to develop and to live one's own authentic identity. This will also play a role later in this contribution.

When decisional privacy is placed within such a context and understood as serving to secure the possibility of a self-determined, authentic life, and an individual practical identity, it becomes clear that it is a dimension of privacy which is relevant to securing *private behaviour* in *public contexts*, too. It emerges that the protection of decisional privacy is necessary so that freedom in social space and with respect to other individuals in society can be enjoyed in such a way that modes of action, ways of life, and projects can be pursued without undesired interference from others. Restraint, inattention, reserve, and indifference – as forms of respect for this decisional privacy – are expected from others when it comes to the private aspects of the life a person leads in public. Within very different social contexts the person can demand that her decisions and actions should be respected (in the sense that they are 'none of your business'). The limits to such privacy are regulated by laws and by conventions, which are, of course, subject to constant renegotiation. Yet, this sort of respect for a person's 'privacy' in public contexts is especially relevant for women. The spectrum of decisional privacy thus extends from reproductive rights to freedom of conduct in public space.[8]

Let me now turn – more briefly – to the *second* dimension of privacy, which demonstrates the close connection between privacy and freedom, *informational privacy*: this dimension also goes back to the interpretation of the US Constitution, in this case beginning with an essay written by Justices Warren and Brandeis after what they felt was an invasion of privacy by intrusive paparazzi at the wedding of Warren's daughter (in 1890). It was here for the first time that the *right to be left alone* was described as a constitutional right to privacy in the sense that information about a person is worthy of protection even when it involves something that occurs in public. This is grounded in an appeal to the protection of individual freedom and thus known as the *right to be left alone*.[9]

Of course, there have been enormous technological advances that have radically transformed not only the possibilities for keeping people under surveillance but have also transformed our concepts of privacy as well as freedom and autonomy. Especially in the age of Big Data, the surveillance of people as consumers by companies and social platforms, as well as the surveillance by the state, is a permanent threat to or violation of informational privacy.[10] The idea of informational privacy, however, also

[8] On decisional privacy and religious freedom see Rössler, 'Privacy as a Human Right' (n 3).

[9] See S Warren, and L Brandeis, 'The Right to Privacy' (1890) 4 *Harvard Law Review* 193.

[10] V Mayer-Schönberger, and K Cukier, *Big Data: A Revolution That Will Transform How We Live, Work, and Think* (New York, Houghton Mifflin Harcourt, 2013) and E Morozov, *To Save Everything, Click Here: The Folly of Technological Solutionism* (New York, Public Affairs, 2013).

incorporates a further framework. At issue here is not only the question of not wanting to have one's smartphone or other devices tapped, but also the more general point that people like to keep the knowledge that others have of them under control and within limits they can expect. This brings to light the deep-seated connection between informational privacy and autonomy: as far as possible, people want to have control over their own self-presentation and thus over the roles they play in their various social spaces. If everyone knew everything about everyone else, differentiated relations and self-presentations would no longer be possible, nor would autonomy and the freedom to determine one's own life. As the German Federal Constitutional Court argued as early as 1983:

> A person who cannot tell with sufficient certainty what information concerning him in certain areas is known to his social environment, or who is unable to assess in some measure the knowledge of his communication partners, may be substantially restricted in his freedom to make plans or take decisions in a self-determined way.[11]

Of central importance nowadays, however, is the fact that we now live in the digital society. Overwhelming evidence suggests that new information and communication technologies (ICTs) are radically transforming our social and political relations: Twitter (X), Facebook and other social media are changing the ways the public sphere functions; 'Big Data' is accumulating ever more personal information. Mobile and wearable computing and reconfigurable sensor networks are used ubiquitously and are converging in an Internet of Things. This new confluence of socio-technical practices will lead to amassing ever-larger quantities of data, large parts of which relate to traceable persons, a development which has been described as a revolution in the history of information technologies.[12]

With the *third* dimension of privacy, *local privacy*, we now reach the classic, traditional place of privacy, its most genuine locus: one's own home, which for many people still intuitively represents the heart of privacy. It is within our own four walls that we can do just what we want, unobserved and uncontrolled.[13] Yet it should be made clear from the outset that this form of local privacy is not derived from a 'natural' separation of spheres but from the idea that one of the vital conditions for protecting individual freedoms in modern western liberal democracies is to be able to withdraw to one's own four walls. This has nothing to do with 'nature', but a great deal to do with the notion that (culturally or conventionally constructed) opportunities for withdrawal are a constitutive element of a person's freedom to live her life the way she wants to. Two different aspects of privacy are of relevance here: solitude and *being-for-oneself* on the one hand, and the protection of family communities or other intimate relationships on the other. The privacy of the household provides the opportunity for people to deal with one another in a different manner, and to take a break from roles in a way that is often not possible nor desirable when dealing with one another in public. As is known, however, this dimension or sphere of privacy is especially prone to generate

[11] BVerfGE 65, 1 (43) [1985] – *Volkszählungsgesetz.*

[12] See L Floridi, *The Fourth Revolution: How the Infosphere is Reshaping Human Reality* (Oxford, Oxford University Press, 2014).

[13] Rössler and DeCew (n 4).

potentials for conflict. This means that in debates about this local form of privacy, it is especially important to recall the meaning and function of privacy, which is to protect and facilitate freedom and autonomy, and more specifically to protect and facilitate equal freedoms and equal opportunities to lead a rewarding life for women and men alike. Traditional conceptions of the gender-specific division of labour have nothing to do with a protection of privacy that is orientated towards the protection of equal individual freedom.[14]

## III. The Power of Definition: Anita Hill and Clarence Thomas

On the background of this clarification of the conception of privacy, let me come back to the steps announced above, the debate in the American public sphere accompanying the hearing of Clarence Thomas before his nomination to the Supreme Court in 1991. Even before starting to discuss this, one can see that very often the conventions governing the boundary between private and public are typically directed against women's interest in equality. A right to privacy as a right to be left alone, as a right to the protection of one's personality, is *gendered*. The different coding for men and women works in such a way that in cases of conflict men are granted a far more generous protection of their private lives than women. A paradigm case of this conflict is Nancy Fraser's analysis of the hearing of Clarence Thomas: she demonstrated the fact of the gendered coding in a now classic study on the case of the allegations of sexual harassment made against him by Anita Hill.

Anita Hill was a professor of law at Oklahoma University and had worked as an attorney adviser to Clarence Thomas in 1982–83, when Thomas was the Chairman of the Equal Employment Opportunity Commission (EEOC). President Bush nominated Clarence Thomas to succeed Thurgood Marshall as a Supreme Court judge, although Thomas had only served for one year as a judge in the federal circuit. It is during this time at the EEOC that Thomas, as Hill's supervisor, sexually harassed her. She claimed this in the 11 October 1991 televised hearing for the Senate.

Fraser precisely analyses the hearing as well as the ensuing fights in the press about Hill's accusations and Thomas's defence strategy (I will summarise only briefly). She makes out three axes of power: sex or gender, race, and class. Fraser first shows that Thomas was much better able and much more efficient in defending his privacy than Hill because of the gendered power relations. On the one hand, he fought against being associated with privacy because this would effeminate him. On the other hand, he claimed that watching pornography had nothing to do with his public persona, that it was his private business.

Thomas's insistence that his behaviour with respect to a woman was private and had nothing whatever to do with the question of his trustworthiness was protected at the expense of Anita Hill's attempting to keep her private life out of the public discussion.

[14] SM Okin, *Justice, Gender, and the Family* (New York, Basic Books, 1989).

These gendered conventions governing the protection of privacy blatantly exposed, Fraser argued, the reproduction of power relations and inequalities in the freedoms available to women and to men.

On the second axis, the axis of race, Fraser demonstrates another way in which Thomas successfully downsized Hill's accusations with the help of public discourse and conventions and stereotypes, in this case racist: Thomas played with his blackness and succeeded in 'owning' it in an ambiguous way, both positively by referencing black men's sexual prowess and negatively by arguing he was turned into being the victim of racial stereotypes, claiming that the hearings were a lynching. The result was, as Fraser points out, that Hill became 'in effect, functionally white'.[15]

This was supported by the third axis constituting the public discourse, the axis of class. Thomas and his defence managed to construct Hill as bourgeois (and implicitly white), implying that he in fact was the poor working-class black victim, thereby insinuating that Hill, as the educated, ambitious, successful career woman, belonged to the white elite and was therefore not someone with whom one must show any solidarity.

Fraser's article is a showpiece of feminist social criticism, and it is exceedingly helpful if one wants to understand the connection between the conventions governing privacy and the public sphere and the underlying patriarchal structures. The role of gendered privacy conventions is still very much visible and lively in contemporary societies. Therefore, this criticism keeps being essential, for nothing is private in itself: privacy has to be understood as a function of convention, not of nature. These gendered conventions explain the fact that women symbolically, even nowadays, belong to the bourgeois private sphere and are still supposed to have their fallback position always in the home and in the privacy of the house.

Consequently, it is not only the actual different role assignments in different social spaces (private or public) that contribute to these gendered, patriarchal conventions, but also the gender-specific coded definitions of what can be considered private and worthy of protection for individuals. This coding is essentially a power game, since it is used by men (and also women), maybe not everywhere and always any longer, to keep women out of the public sphere, but to show them their place and, if need be, push them back into the private sphere.

Although we can see that social media can be used to help women, especially young women, to free themselves from stereotypes and mandated forms of life, this stereotyping and form of repression has not changed fundamentally in the age of social media.[16]

## IV. Homosexuality and the ECHR

It is almost a truism nowadays to state that the history of homosexuality is also a history of the demarcation of what is public and what is private. Since homosexuality was, in

[15] N Fraser, 'Sex, Lies, and the Public Sphere: Some Reflections on the Confirmation of Clarence Thomas' (1992) 18 *Critical Inquiry* 595.

[16] See AE Marwick, *The Private is Political: Networked Privacy and Social Media* (New Haven, CT, Yale University Press, 2023).

most liberal democracies (to speak only of them), illegal until late in the twentieth century, there was always the hidden and dangerous playing with it in public places. Marcel Proust narrates these games – although he is also completely clear about the fact that the playfulness has its cruel limits (see Proust, 1993).[17] In order to understand the specific legalisation that is pertinent in Europe, I want to have a look at especially those cases where the privacy of a person's sexual identity is at issue.

Several prominent cases brought before the ECHR concerned domestic legislation by which homosexual conduct was prohibited or otherwise suppressed.[18] One of the best known and most discussed cases is *Dudgeon v United Kingdom*, which resulted in a ruling that has occupied many legal scholars. The question to be settled by the Court was

> whether the existence of criminal offences relating to homosexual conduct in private between consenting males over the age of 21, or some lesser age, constituted an interference with a person's right to respect for his private life in contravention of art 8 of the European Convention on Human Rights.[19]

The Court ruled that such legislation did indeed constitute an interference in the private life of homosexuals. But the reasoning given for this ruling – that is, the normative principle on which it relied – came in for criticism. To quote the court:

> There can be no denial that some degree of regulation of male homosexual conduct, as indeed of other forms of sexual conduct, by means of the criminal law can be justified as "necessary in a democratic society". The overall function served by the criminal law in this field is, … "to preserve public order and decency [and] to protect the citizen from what is offensive or injurious". Furthermore, this necessity for some degree of control may even extend to consensual acts committed in private, notably where there is call … to provide sufficient safeguards against exploitation and corruption of others, particularly those who are especially vulnerable because they are young, weak in body or mind, inexperienced, or in a state of special physical, official or economic dependence.[20]

Why was this decision so controversial (and has remained so)? On the one hand, the Court's argument is quite unambiguous, since it clearly held that the concept of private life is 'a concept which covers the physical and moral integrity of the person, including his or her sexual life'. Thus, the Court decided, on the one hand, that homosexual acts among consenting adults in private should be free from any interference, and also that the freedom to do so constituted a matter of human rights.[21]

Yet, on the other hand, in defending a right to homosexual conduct, the Court was relying on a traditional, purely spatial distinction between private and public and was

[17] See Proust (1993), here especially the introductory passages, and Proust (2005), see also Brady and Seymour (n 1).

[18] See Rössler, 'Privacy as a Human Right' (n 3).

[19] *Dudgeon v United Kingdom* Series A no 45 (1981) 4 EHRR 149 available at: www.chr.up.ac.za/images/database/sexual_minority_database/cases/SOGIESC-Dudgeon-v.-United-Kingdom-1981.

[20] *Dudgeon v United Kingdom* (1981) 4 EHRR 149.

[21] See E Heinze, *Sexual Orientation: A Human Right. An Essay on International Human Rights Law* (Dordrecht; Boston, MA; London, Martinus Nijhoff Publishers, 1995) and P Johnson, 'An Essentially Private Manifestation of Human Personality': Constructions of Homosexuality in the European Court of Human Rights' (2010) 10 *Human Rights Law Review* 67.

relegating homosexual life to the secrecy of a private space. By endorsing particularly this spatial division in the interest of having control over public social practices, the Court also remained committed to the very idea that public homosexuality is incompatible with public morality and that it can be kept coercively from public view. The relevant discourse here is one which views gay men as corrupting public morality due to their 'deviant' behaviour, which should therefore be confined to private spaces.[22]

To fully understand the issue, we must see that a *spatial concept of privacy* is not sufficiently explanatory and that one therefore needs a different, a *dimensional* concept of privacy. That is exactly the reason why I introduced the *three dimensions* of privacy above. It is only this way that we have the conceptual resources to understand homosexuality as both a private matter and one that people are entitled to bring into public space. And this way, we are in a position to criticise the Court's reasoning in a different and more plausible way. The right to privacy protects people within relationships, independently of whether those relationships are being lived in the private sphere or in public. Since choices concerning one's sexual identity should be seen as private choices, it is normatively most adequate to conceptualise homosexuality as being protected by decisional privacy and not a local, domestic idea of privacy. The Court – and the discourse relating to it – does not realise that the critique of a hitherto wrong understanding of privacy shifts the boundaries between private and public in a different way than a purely spatial concept of privacy can comprehend. However, this is precisely the central insight that we need to see the emancipatory force of the struggle of homosexuals who insist on not being reduced to a 'private affair'.[23]

## V. Struggles in the Public Sphere

Where does the struggle for power and about the meaning of a concept take place? In both cases of Fraser and Hill and in the case of the ECHR, we have seen that what is crucial is the question of *where* and *how* the dividing lines between the private and the public are debated and negotiated.

This struggle takes place in an always contested public sphere, contested because there are always issues that should not be discussed in public since they affect people's private, personal lives. But that is what it is all about: where exactly is the boundary between private and public? And to what extent are we dependent on a democratic, critical public discourse? Let me briefly discuss some important points about the function and challenge of the public sphere.

Empirically, the public sphere has never been neutral: there are no good old days we could refer to.[24] Especially the feminist critique has shown that public disputes and exchanges of arguments are very much a struggle for democratic power. *What* we debate and *who* is allowed to take part in these debates is nothing neutral, as can

[22] Johnson (n 21).
[23] Rössler, 'Privacy as a Human Right' (n 3).
[24] See for instance the criticism in U Baer, *What Snowflakes Get Right: Free Speech, Truth, and Equality on Campus* (New York, Oxford University Press, 2019).

be seen, for instance, in the last 30 years in movements such as LGBTQ and *Black Lives Matter*: their striving for democratic participation and freedom from oppression and for their concerns to be heard in public in the first place proves that the public is not a neutral area. The very question of *who* has a voice in public is a question of power.[25]

Normatively, too, the public sphere has never been 'neutral': if we understand as one of the tasks of the public sphere to debate issues which are of concern to everyone, then neutrality would pretend that people could exclude their different standpoints, interests, beliefs, and aims. Since some of those voices come with more power, and therefore some of the voices are louder than others, this pretension would only cover up but not eliminate the power structures. In the age of social media, this has changed slightly, because everyone can raise their voice. But raising the voice and having followers is not immediately the same as having political power.[26]

The public sphere is the site of controversies about practical identities, self-understandings, and self-descriptions, which are always and necessarily co-constituted through public recognition in the public sphere. This public sphere is never 'neutral' precisely for this reason, too. When it comes to the seemingly private question of what projects I want to pursue in my life, which relationships and self-descriptions, and which options are available to me, I rely upon the public provision of meaningful options and of public recognition, without which I would not be able to describe myself as the person I am or want to be, of *becoming who I am*. To see this, we can refer to the centuries of public refusal to recognise homosexuality and queer forms of life. This social and political refusal evidently proved a decisive and restrictive influence upon the *public* and *private* lives of homosexuals. The private search for a meaningful life is dependent upon publicly possible, socially, and politically recognised life-options.

Furthermore, the controversies in the public sphere concern not only topics but also people: their public presence, their representation as agents, and their perspectives in public discourses. Therefore, the well-functioning of the public sphere also concerns the democratic structures of our society. To represent a perspective has, as we know, a social as well as a semantic side. And here we can even better understand that we are talking about power structures. *Who* is being heard, and *how many voices* are taking part in the struggles is of essential relevance when we talk about the *meaning* and the *reach* of concepts. As many have pointed out before, semantic criticism is always social criticism (Luise Pusch (1984) was the first German linguist who wrote about this). As Fraser argues, 'arrangements that accommodate contestation among a plurality of competing publics better promote the ideal of participatory parity than does a single, comprehensive, overarching public'. An overarching 'neutral' public

[25] To reference just one among the many feminist critiques, see N Fraser, 'Rethinking the Public Sphere: A Contribution to the Critique of Actually Existing Democracy' (1990) 25/26 *Social Text* 56 and J Habermas, *Strukturwandel der Öffentlichkeit: Untersuchungen zu einer Kategorie der bürgerlichen Gesellschaft* (Frankfurt am Main, Suhrkamp Verlag, 1990).

[26] A Marwick, *The Private Is Political: Networked Privacy and Social Media* (New Haven, Yale University Press, 2023).

sphere, Fraser claims, would 'mask domination by absorbing the less powerful into a false "we" that reflects the more powerful' and are less egalitarian and democratic than a variety of publics, which she calls 'subaltern counter-publics'.[27]

This way, the public sphere, following Fraser, is conceptualised as the site or the sites where power is exercised in and over language, over social boundaries, and over meaningful options for ethical, practical identities. It is the site where social transformations take place and are being made visible.[28] And it is here that we must place and analyse the migration of issues from the private into the public space.

These different sites, as well as this migration, can be explored from different perspectives: the perspective of hermeneutic injustice and the 'way in which relations of power can constrain women's ability to understand their own [only seemingly private] experience';[29] the perspective of social media and how they have changed our conceptions of private and public in very different and significant ways (for young women, for instance, exploring their bodies or having their bodies shamed); and the perspective of sexual harassment in all areas and social milieus of our contemporary societies.[30]

## VI. MeToo, Transgender, and Privacy in Public

> The MeToo movement is many things, but perhaps most powerfully, it is a frame. It transformed how sexual assault is perceived, not as something to be kept private but something that could be made public. The declarations on Twitter became a source of empowerment and liberation. MeToo reversed the stigma: women need not be ashamed, and could bring shame upon the men who assaulted them.[31]

In a way, I agree with Cukier, Mayer-Schönberger, and Véricourt, although I think they got it the wrong way round: the separation between the private and the public is the *frame*, and sexual harassment is *being framed* in a new way. The MeToo movement led to a shift in the boundary between the private and the public, and this way it became clear that Weinstein was, in fact, not doing something 'private' which no one else needed to be concerned with. Weinstein, of course, is used here as a symbol for the widespread male idea that they are entitled to use women in this way, in the privacy of their hotel room or even office and do here something which is nothing of public concern or business. Actually, Weinstein did not even worry about whether or

[27] Fraser (n 25).

[28] ibid; C Taylor, *Sources of the Self: The Making of the Modern Identity* (Cambridge, Cambridge University Press, 1992); C Mouffe, 'Deliberative Democracy or Agonistic Pluralism?' (1999) 66 *Social Research* 745; M Fricker, *Epistemic Injustice: Power and the Ethics of Knowing* (Oxford, Oxford University Press, 2007) and H Rosa, *Alienation and Acceleration: Towards a Critical Theory of Late-Modern Temporality* (Malmö, NSU Press, 2010).

[29] Fricker (n 28).

[30] B Rössler, *Autonomy. An Essay on the Life Well-Lived* (Cambridge, Polity Press, 2021).

[31] K Cukier, V Mayer-Schönberger, and F Véricourt, *Framers: Human Advantage in an Age of Technology and Turmoil* (New York, Ebury Publishing, 2021).

not his behaviour was private or secret (everyone seemed to know anyway) precisely because of men's belief in being entitled to have sex with women who are dependent on them.

Whereas Catharine MacKinnon argued in the 1980s that what for men was sex, for women was the perception that they 'are violated every day by men'. I think Amia Srinivasan is right here in her criticism: sexual harassment and the MeToo movement are not about sex having a different meaning for men than for women.[32] If one maintained this difference, one would try to exculpate men to a certain extent ('they think it's only sex, after all'), and I agree with Srinivasan that this is both psychologically wrong (they know what they are doing) and politically wrong.[33] The difference between sex and harassment or rape is, among other things, that sex should be, can be, and usually is private, whereas rape must be a public matter: it is a criminal act.

Let me remind you of another, shockingly recent example of the shifting of the boundaries between the private and the public: the fact that rape within marriage was only made illegal in the 1990s in many European legislations – before that, marriage and the behaviour of the partners was a private matter and still is in many non-European countries, like India. A woman had no possibility to take legal action against her husband when he raped her. Here, as well, it has only been a development of the last 30 or so years that the separation between private and public domains or dimensions has shifted in fundamental and liberating ways. As I'm finalising this chapter, Gisèle Pelicot's husband, Dominique Pelicot, has been sentenced to 20 years after having raped and invited at least 50 other men to rape his drugged wife for more than a dozen years.

We should understand Gisèle Pelicot's lawsuit as well as the legal changes over the last 30 years as fundamental changes in the boundary between the private and the public, changes that are both emancipatory and liberating for women. The language as well as the social and legal practices and structures are being transformed: it is, at least legally, no longer evident that men have the power to do what they want when it comes to sex with women. Going public, as in MeToo, or as in the case of Gisèle Pelicot's decision to allow her trial to be conducted publicly, is often a first step towards shifting the balance of power and giving emancipation a nudge.

I therefore want to suggest that the dispute about the presence of *transgender people* in the public sphere must also be seen in this tradition. Already the development in the terminology – transsexuals, transgender – is and was always associated with struggles for one's own identity, and it is a development of the last decades that trans people are programmatically stepping out into the public eye. Again, the framing is central here: being trans is no longer about private corners of society or about sporadic, isolated people, but being trans must be publicly recognised; again, this is about fundamental equalities and freedoms in liberal democracies.

The response of some powerful people in what they saw as 'their' public sphere was to announce that trans women were not real women since one simply could not change one's biological sex. Therefore, there should be no public or institutional recognition of

[32] A Srinivasan, *The Right to Sex* (London; New York; New Delhi, Bloomsbury Publishing, 2021) 20.
[33] ibid 20f, 28f.

trans women *as women*.[34] Instead of accepting that trans women simply want to move in public without constant discrimination and a constant flow of comments, powerful participants in social media (most famously JK Rowling) mocked and insulted trans women because of their gender identity. This position was exemplified in the 'bathroom question': no trans women should enter the women's bathroom, because, as former men, 'normal' women could feel intimidated by them. However, this seems to be a particularly weak move and is rejected, for instance, by Celikates et al (my translation):

> The aim [of referring to particular cases] is to spread the fear that violent men will break into women's spaces under the guise of transsexuality – toilets are often mentioned alongside prisons. But this argument is absurd: nowhere else do we hold an entire group liable to prevent the possibility of a violent attack. Sexualized violence is predominantly perpetrated by men in families and on the street – but men are still allowed to have families and go outside.[35]

Since it's wrong that someone can change their gender, so they would argue, it should not be allowed to show oneself in public when one has the self-identity of being trans. The anti-trans faction was in fact trying to push trans people back into the private sphere: in private, they could do what they wanted to, if no one had to publicly deal with it. However, as everyone taking part in the debates knows, the liberal-democratic society stipulates in its constitution that everyone should be able to live their life in public places with whichever gender identity they choose.

This new challenge to the boundary between private and public is obviously a challenge to the power of definition and a struggle for public recognition. Therefore, it is no surprise that many people react fearfully, uncomprehendingly, and aggressively. Such border shifts are unfailingly a loss of power over who is allowed to define and determine the meaning of terms and of social practices: this is no different with the affairs of Clinton and Weinstein than with the de-privatisation of queer identities. And as we have seen, it is precisely here that the public spheres are essential for someone to be able to invent and explore their own identity, how they should live, and who they are.

In the debate following JK Rowling's tweets, Bonnie Wright, better known as Ginnie Weasley, tweeted:

> I do know that my dear transgender friends and colleagues are tired of this constant questioning of their identities, which all too often results in violence and abuse. They simply want to live their lives peacefully, and it's time to let them do so.[36]

Bonnie Wright/Ginnie Weasley is, of course, right: critics like Rowling not only do not want to acknowledge that trans women are women, but they also do not want to call them that, and they certainly do not want to change their own social (or legal) practices. The question of how trans people can live their lives peacefully is, on the one hand, an issue of rights and legal freedoms that are constitutive if one wants to take part in public

[34] On the debate around JK Rowling, see A Gardner, 'A Complete Breakdown of the J.K. Rowling Transgender-comments Controversy' *Celebrity News* (2024) available at: www.glamour.com/story/a-complete-breakdown-of-the-jk-rowling-transgender-comments-controversy.

[35] R Celikates, K Hoppe, D Loick, M Nonhoff, E von Redecker, and F Vogelmann, 'Machtverhältnisse statt Mythen. Für ein emanzipatorisches Verständnis von Wissenschaftsfreiheit. Geschichte der Gegenwart' (Geschichte der Gegenwart, 2021) available at: www.geschichtedergegenwart.ch/machtverhaeltnisse-statt-mythen-fuer-ein-emanzipatorisches-verstaendnis-von-wissenschaftsfreiheit/.

[36] Gardner (n 34).

space. But on the other hand, the issue is about how you live your rights in the public sphere; what is the value or worth (as Rawls put it) of these rights and freedoms?

This brings me to the end: we need privacy, and we need a pluralist, diversified public sphere, each for different reasons. Both sorts of reasons are linked to our freedom to live our own lives. Especially when individual or collective attempts to liberate from patriarchal and sex-essentialising structures, public discourses, and spaces are both difficult to reach and crucial for the development of an emancipated identity. And the subtext of the struggles around the meaning of concepts or the possibility of practices ('transgender', or 'trans woman'; or 'my culture', 'your culture') remains: who has the power to define what is private and what is public? Debating concepts, behaviour, or attitudes in public always has an emancipatory potential. Who draws the line, therefore, comes down to the question: How can we ensure that the lines can be debated and redrawn in an emancipatory, solidary, egalitarian way?

# PART V

# Privacy in Society: Technology Challenges, Individuals' Autonomy and Freedom

# 16

# Countering Privacy Nihilism

SEVERIN ENGELMANN AND HELEN NISSENBAUM*

## I. Introduction

Remarkable capacities of artificial intelligence (AI) inferring novel information from information at hand have fuelled its growing influence on nearly every aspect of society. The dramatic advancements in inferential analysis based on massive collection, storage, and processing of data have provoked enthusiasm and excitement among AI practitioners and designers.[1] Popular narratives frame AI models as being able to extract nearly any information of interest from nearly any data available.[2] It's not difficult, however, to see how these ascendant inferential powers may evoke their opposite among privacy advocates and regulators. Indeed, regulatory resignation grows

* For their editorial guidance and support, we would like to extend a special thanks to Elisa Orrù and Ralf Poscher at the Max Planck Institute for the Study of Crime, Security, and Law. The authors gratefully acknowledge the valuable feedback on draft versions of this article from participants at the 2024 'Privacy and Public Policy Conference' at Georgetown University, the xD Team at the US Census Bureau, the 2024 'eLaw Conference Law and/versus Technology: Trends for the New Decade' at Leiden University, the 2024 'Conference on Conceptions of Data Protection and Privacy' at the Max Planck Institute for the Study of Crime, Security, and Law, and the 'Digital Life Initiative Reading Group' at Cornell Tech. We also extend our sincere gratitude to Daniel Susser, Francien Dechesne, Margot Hanley, Ben Sobel, Kat Geddes, David Widder, and Ben Laufer for their insightful comments on this work.



Against a backdrop of increasing intolerance of diverse life choices, amounting to the repression of human autonomy, the authors wish to note their ongoing commitment to principles of diversity, equity, and inclusion (DEI), to a woman's right to reproductive freedoms, and to equal consideration for historically oppressed minorities. In supporting these values, privacy is fundamental to human flourishing and social integrity. As mentioned in the editors' introduction, contributors to this volume hold divergent and often strongly conflicting views on human rights – a reality we acknowledge as part of our own participation in this collection.

[1] C Anderson, 'The End of Theory: The Data Deluge Makes the Scientific Method Obsolete' (2008) 16(7) *Wired Magazine* 16–07; N Maslej et al, 'The AI Index 2023 Annual Report' (AI Index Steering Committee, Institute for Human-Centered AI, Stanford University, April 2023), aiindex.stanford.edu.

[2] V Mayer-Schönberger and K Cukier, *Big Data: A Revolution That Will Transform How We Live, Work, and Think* (Boston, Houghton Mifflin Harcourt, 2013).

in the shadow of AI excitement.[3] Along with AI enthusiasm, there is a sentiment of hopelessness in privacy scholarship that AI has become an all-encompassing technology of discovery, so powerful that it may even be capable of inferring 'everything from everything' (EfE).[4] Accepting this premise would have profound implications for the role of information in privacy and data protection. In the United States (US), the European Union (EU), Canada, and China, privacy and data protection regulations mandate data processing restrictions based on a classification of information into categories, for example, personal information, financial information, and, in particular, sensitive information.[5] Each data type can be subject to varying levels of protection and legal oversight. However, these bedrock privacy regulations are, prima facie, vulnerable to the alleged inferential superpowers of AI, developed to transcend semantic categories and effectively nullify information types as a normative parameter in privacy and data protection law.[6]

Different intellectual traditions and disciplines evaluate the legitimacy of inferences through distinct epistemic standards. Across disciplines, standards for inference are shaped by distinct rules and procedures that govern how conclusions are drawn and validated. A simplified account might suggest that logical inference prioritises formal validity and consistency; empirical sciences emphasise falsifiability and experimental verification; statistical inference focuses on probabilistic generalisation from samples; causal inference relies on counterfactual reasoning to substantiate causal claims; and computational modelling often privileges predictive accuracy as its primary benchmark. In practice, however, each discipline integrates multiple epistemic norms rather than adhering strictly to a single standard. The crucial point is that inference-making, as an epistemic practice – and AI inferences, conceptualised as a technology of discovery – are fundamentally about interrogating their justification. Whether producing an interpretation, drawing a conclusion, or even generating knowledge, inference demands a valid pathway between old and new information. Consequently,

[3] NA Draper, CP Hoffmann, C Lutz, G Ranzini and J Turow, 'Privacy Resignation, Apathy, and Cynicism: Introduction to a Special Theme' (2024) 11(3) *Big Data & Society*; NA Draper and J Turow, 'The Corporate Cultivation of Digital Resignation' (2019) 21(8) *New Media & Society* 1824–1839; M Fong and Z Arsel, 'Protecting Privacy Online Begins with Tackling Digital Resignation' (*The Conversation*, 11 April 2023), www.theconversation.com/protecting-privacy-online-begins-with-tackling-digital-resignation-198979.

[4] DJ Solove, 'Data Is What Data Does: Regulating Based on Harm and Risk Instead of Sensitive Data' (2023) 118 *Northwestern University Law Review* 1081; P Ohm and S Peppet, 'What If Everything Reveals Everything?' in B Frischmann, M Madison, and K Strandburg (eds), *Governing Knowledge Commons* (Cambridge (MA), MIT Press, 2016).

[5] See, eg, in the General Data Protection Regulation (GDPR) in Europe: commission.europa.eu/law/law-topic/data-protection/reform/rules-business-and-organisations/legal-grounds-processing-data/sensitive-data/what-personal-data-considered-sensitive_en; In the US' sectoral privacy landscape, for example, the Health Insurance Portability and Accountability Act (HIPAA) of 1996 specifies 'protected sensitive' data, see US Department of Health and Human Services, 'Privacy' (HHS.gov), www.hhs.gov/hipaa/for-professionals/privacy/index.html; Canada's Personal Information Protection and Electronic Documents Act (PIPEDA) protects information according to their sensitivity, as well as the amount, distribution, format, and method of storage, see Office of the Privacy Commissioner of Canada, 'Privacy' (Office of the Privacy Commissioner of Canada), www.priv.gc.ca/en/.

[6] Solove (n 4); P Quinn and G Malgieri, 'The Difficulty of Defining Sensitive Data – The Concept of Sensitive Data in the EU Data Protection Framework' (2021) 22(8) *German Law Journal* 1583; M Fazlioglu, 'Beyond the Nature of Data: Obstacles to Protecting Sensitive Information in the European Union and the United States' (2019) 46 *Fordham Urban Law Journal* 271.

AI inferences raise fundamental questions of legitimacy: What standards govern AI inferences and, critically, who determines their standards? Whose interests do these standards reflect, and what justifies their authority?

Establishing privacy norms in the context of AI inferences requires careful consideration of the epistemic standards we choose to adopt. Historically, arriving at novel insights or new information through data aggregation, disaggregation, combination, or repurposing – driven by advancements in information technology (eg, database linking) – could have challenged the normative role of information categories in privacy and data protection. Yet, neither the privacy fears of a 'dossier society',[7] voiced as a response to the computerisation of records in taxation, health, and education in the 1970s and 1980s, nor concerns around the construction of comprehensive 'mosaics'[8] due to Big Brother-like digital state surveillance in the 2000s resulted in a discontinuation of data categories in data protection law. Unlike these historic vignettes, the current wave of resignatory concerns frames AI as a powerful technology of discovery that moves far beyond a Sherlock Holmesian piecing together of disconnected information to arrive at novel insights. Behind EfE rests a worldview that assumes AI can infer anything of interest about us from anything we reveal, whether intentionally or unintentionally, explicitly or implicitly. *Privacy nihilism*, as we use the term, refers to the abandoning of data categorisation in privacy theory and regulation as a consequence of embracing an EfE position.

In this chapter we raise objections against privacy nihilism. Across data collection, ground truth manufacturing, and model evaluation, EfE follows a process of epistemic convenience that we anchor on the notion of *conceptual overfitting*. Conceptual overfitting captures the epistemic shortcutting involved in fitting complex constructs of interest to conceptually under-representative or irrelevant data using AI. We question whether this convenient 'anything goes' justification for AI inferences warrants abandoning data types as a focal parameter in privacy theory and law. At the same time, we highlight that privacy cannot serve its fundamental values to society by sole reliance on the types of data (or information) involved. Theories like contextual integrity assess the normative value of privacy across several parameters, making them better equipped to address the challenges posed by powerful inferential models.

## II. Defining Privacy Nihilism

The rapid proliferation of powerful AI technologies – including predictive and generative models – has intensified challenges in managing their inferential capabilities. Current enthusiasm surrounding AI as an epistemic tool highlights its promise for uncovering hidden insights and complex patterns from vast datasets. Such optimism is widespread among AI practitioners, scientists, and broader societal discourse.

[7] 'Dossier Society', see, eg, KC Laudon, *Dossier Society: Value Choices in the Design of National Information Systems* (New York, Columbia University Press 1986).

[8] 'Mosaic Theory', see, eg, DE Pozen, 'The Mosaic Theory, National Security, and the Freedom of Information Act' (2005) 115 *Yale Law Journal* 628.

Pausing for a moment to reflect on AI's advancements and realising the significant political and economic influence its creators have already gained and are poised to expand further inspires both amazement and unease. The 2024 Nobel Prize underscored AI's 'techno-epistemic momentum'.[9] For the first time, the award in chemistry was given to AI developers of a major tech company. The AI model, called AlphaFold, built on a mature theoretical understanding of protein synthesis,[10] is capable of predictively inferring the structure of the human proteome.[11] Recently, researchers have employed generative AI to infer models of research participants using data snippets of real participants, suggesting that such methods could replace traditional approaches involving costly human participants.[12] Early research even suggests that large language models could automate the entire scientific process – from generating novel research ideas and writing code to conducting experiments, visualising results, drafting complete scientific papers, and simulating peer-review evaluations.[13]

Politically, a powerful tech-centric oligarchy heavily funded the 2024 US election campaign, paving the way for a government demonstrably committed to advancing its techno-libertarian agenda. The fate of society and democracy is increasingly shaped by a techno-utopian ethos – one that sees humanity transacting through unregulated decentralised crypto services, thriving in metaverses, interacting with LLM-driven 'agents', and perhaps, one day, even 'colonising' Mars.[14] It is evident that these developments have fostered a pervasive sense of regulatory resignation, as existing frameworks struggle to keep pace with the rapid evolution of sophisticated AI technologies that shape and mediate our participation in social, political, and cultural life.

An illustrative example of the current resignation is the widespread attribution of virtually limitless epistemic power to AI *inferences* across different research disciplines, in political narratives, and in the popular imagination.[15] AI inferences – the epistemic practice of producing new information from old using AI – play a foundational role in modern digital systems. Inferential models are integral to data mining, data analytics, and data science. A central paradigm in AI mandates datasets to be divided into three parts: a training set $D$, a validation set $V$, and a testing set $T$.

[9] HJ Rheinberger, 'Infra-experimentality: From Traces to Data, from Data to Patterning Facts' (2011) 49 *History of Science* 337; E Callaway, 'Chemistry Nobel goes to developers of AlphaFold AI that predicts protein structures', (*Nature*, 9 October 2024), www.nature.com/articles/d41586-024-03214-7.

[10] K Tunyasuvunakool and others, 'Highly Accurate Protein Structure Prediction for the Human Proteome' (2021) 596 *Nature* 590.

[11] Note that this remarkable breakthrough was deeply informed by existing theoretical understanding and empirical knowledge of protein structures developed by scientists over the last century. For commentary, see also M Andrews, 'The Immortal Science of ML: Machine Learning & the Theory-Free Ideal' (*Research Gate*, 2023), preprint rgdoi.net/10.13140/RG2.28311.75685.

[12] JS Park, et al, 'Generative Agent Simulations of 1,000 People' (2024) *arXiv preprint* arXiv:2411.10109; LP Argyle, et al, 'Out of One, Many: Using Language Models to Simulate Human Samples' (2023) 31(3) *Political Analysis* 337.

[13] C Lu, et al, 'The AI Scientist: Towards Fully Automated Open-Ended Scientific Discovery' (2024) *arXiv preprint* arXiv:2408.06292.

[14] See, eg, M Andreessen, 'The Techno-Optimist Manifesto Andreessen' (*Horowitz*, 16 October 2023), www.a16z.com/the-techno-optimist-manifesto/; see also E Luce, 'Beware Elon Musk's Warped Libertarianism' (*Financial Times*, 24 May 2023), www.ft.com/content/7ca8e38d-8ecf-4de2-870d-9bd0a2476147.

[15] H Peters and SC Matz, 'Large Language Models Can Infer Psychological Dispositions of Social Media Users' (2024) 3(6) *PNAS Nexus* 231; JW Hall, 'What Machines Can Tell from Your Face' (*The Economist*, 9 September 2017), www.economist.com/leaders/2017/09/09/what-machines-can-tell-from-your-face.

An AI model is trained on *D*, its performance assessed on *V*, and its final evaluation conducted on *T*, taken as an unbiased estimate of how well the model's inferences perform in real-world applications. Generally, inductive reasoning governs model development, while a developed model serves as a deductive lens for interpreting novel data.[16] Search engines and social media platforms use AI to infer thousands of user attributes for profiling – interests, behaviours, relationships, and moral or political views – which they sell to advertisers for targeted marketing.[17] In computer vision, AI models 'make sense' of visual data[18] by drawing inferences about them: vision models in robotics,[19] self-driving vehicles,[20] emotion recognition systems,[21] cancer prediction software,[22] and beauty apps[23] analyse the semantics of images and videos – billions of which are generated daily across the internet.[24] Every few milliseconds, smart TVs take visual and auditory screenshots to infer viewing habits.[25] On lending platforms AI models infer credit loaners' creditworthiness from both traditional and non-traditional variables.[26] Each year, millions of job applicants undergo video interviews analysed by AI models inferring employability.[27] Fitness and health trackers gather physiological signals (eg, heart rate, body temperature)

[16] A Narayanan and S Kapoor, *AI Snake Oil: What Artificial Intelligence Can Do, What It Can't, and How to Tell the Difference* (Princeton, Princeton University Press, 2024); S Engelmann and O Papakyriakopoulos, 'Social Media as Classification Systems: Procedural Normative Choices in User Profiling' in S Lindgrens (ed), *Handbook of Critical Studies of Artificial Intelligence* (Cheltenham, Edward Elgar Publishing, 2023) 619–630.

[17] A Andreou and others, 'Investigating Ad Transparency Mechanisms in Social Media: A Case Study of Facebook's Explanations' in *NDSS 2018 – Network and Distributed System Security Symposium* (2018); S Engelmann et al, 'Social Media Profiling Continues to Partake in the Development of Formalistic Self-Concepts. Social Media Users Think So, Too' (2022) *Proceedings of the AAAI/ACM Conference on AI, Ethics, and Society.*

[18] D Bhatt and others, 'CNN Variants for Computer Vision: History, Architecture, Application, Challenges and Future Scope' (2021) 10 *Electronics* 2470.

[19] F Cavallo and others, 'Emotion Modelling for Social Robotics Applications: A Review' (2018) 15 *Journal of Bionic Engineering* 185.

[20] J Janai and others, 'Computer Vision for Autonomous Vehicles: Problems, Datasets and State of the Art' (2020) 12 *Foundations and Trends in Computer Graphics and Vision* 1.

[21] A Hassouneh, AM Mutawa and M Murugappan, 'Development of a Real-Time Emotion Recognition System Using Facial Expressions and EEG Based on Machine Learning and Deep Neural Network Methods' (2020) 20 *Informatics in Medicine Unlocked* 100372.

[22] H Lee and YP Chen, 'Image Based Computer Aided Diagnosis System for Cancer Detection' (2015) 42 *Expert Systems with Applications* 5356.

[23] Visage Technologies, 'Visage Technologies', www.visagetechnologies.com/.

[24] P Dootson, '3.2 Billion Images and 720,000 Hours of Video Are Shared Online Daily. Can You Sort Real from Fake?' (Queensland University of Technology, 2021), www.qut.edu.au/insights/business/3.2-billion-images-and-720000-hours-of-video-are-shared-online-daily.-can-you-sort-real-from-fake#:~:text=QUT%20%2D%203.2%20billion%20images%20and%20720%2C000,daily.%20Can%20you%20sort%20real%20from%20fake.

[25] G Anselmi, Y Vekaria, AD'Souza, P Callejo, AM Mandalari and Z Shafiq, 'Watching TV with the Second-Party: A First Look at Automatic Content Recognition Tracking in Smart TVs' in *Proceedings of the 2024 ACM on Internet Measurement Conference* (November 2024) 622–634.

[26] For example, Upstart, 'Upstart', www.upstart.com; See also M Chen, S Engelmann and J Grossklags, 'Social Credit System and Privacy' in S Treptes and P Masurs (eds), *The Routledge Handbook of Privacy and Social Media* (Milton Park, Taylor & Francis, 2023).

[27] SA Woods and others, 'Personnel Selection in the Digital Age: A Review of Validity and Applicant Reactions, and Future Research Challenges' (2020) 29 *European Journal of Work and Organizational Psychology* 64.

to infer sleep quality and physical activity.[28] Devices such as augmented reality (AR) glasses, virtual reality (VR) headsets, and mixed reality (MR) leverage biometric and neural data to infer their cognitive-emotional content, such as stress and intentions.[29] Large language models (LLMs) are 'inference machines', with LLM-based chatbots inferring user preferences, intentions, and goals to act as intimate companions, friends, romantic partners, or mentors.[30]

In a digital economy driven by a data imperative,[31] organisations must use AI for inferential techniques to extract value from data through models that infer something new from the data collected. Inferences make data useful; they are the primary value proposition of today's digital economy, more aptly called an 'inference economy'.[32] One would expect academic scholarship in privacy and data protection to be on high alert, taking a leading role behind the regulatory and policy wheel, steering towards proposals grounded in a careful evaluation of AI inferences.

## A. 'Everything from Everything' (EfE)

What we observe, however, is a sense of awe tempered by a sense of resignation and hopelessness. In light of grandiose inferential claims published by parts of the AI community, the allure of attributing conclusive epistemic authority to AI inferences is perhaps understandable. Well-known examples include deep learning models that discover depressive markers in the colour profile of social media images,[33] sexual preferences in people's facial morphology,[34] and political orientation in aggregated location data.[35] In these cases, mundane data, easy to amass in today's data economy, are presumed sufficient for AI models to discover sensitive data constructs (eg, health, sexual, and political orientation) from non-sensitive data types. The promise of AI inference-making suggests that nearly *any data can* serve as a potential source of meaning in the process of inferring any construct of interest.[36] This perspective often

[28] AN Balaji, A Narayanan and L Peh, 'AI-On-Skin: Towards Enabling Fast and Scalable On-body AI Inference for Wearable On-Skin Interfaces' (2023) 7(EICS) *Proceedings of the ACM on Human-Computer Interaction* 1–34.

[29] P Magee, M Ienca and N Farahany, 'Beyond Neural Data: Cognitive Biometrics and Mental Privacy' (2024) 112 *Neuron* 3017.

[30] I Gabriel and others, 'The Ethics of Advanced AI Assistants' (Ithaca, arXiv, 2024) arXiv preprint arXiv:2404.16244.

[31] M Fourcade and K Healy, 'Seeing Like a Market' (2017) 15 *Socio-economic Review* 9.

[32] A Solow-Niederman, 'Information Privacy and the Inference Economy' (2022) 117 *Northwestern University Law Review* 357.

[33] AG Reece and CM Danforth, 'Instagram Photos Reveal Predictive Markers of Depression' (2017) 6(1) *EPJ Data Science* 15.

[34] Y Wang and M Kosinski, 'Deep Neural Networks Are More Accurate than Humans at Detecting Sexual Orientation from Facial Images' (2018) 114(2) *Journal of Personality and Social Psychology* 246.

[35] I Liccardi, A Abdul-Rahman and M Chen, 'I Know Where You Live: Inferring Details of People's Lives by Visualizing Publicly Shared Location Data' in *Proceedings of the 2016 CHI Conference on Human Factors in Computing Systems* (2016).

[36] J Hinds and AN Joinson, 'What Demographic Attributes Do Our Digital Footprints Reveal? A Systematic Review' (2018) 13(11) *PLoS One* e0207112; Privacy International, *Data Points Used in Tracking* (Privacy International, 2018), www.privacyinternational.org/sites/default/files/2018-04/data%20points%20

represents a broader epistemic shift toward seemingly meaningful semantics produced solely based on statistical evidence. The presumed revelatory potential of credit in the US offers a compelling case. Insurance companies often predictively correlate a person's financial credit score with their insurance premiums.[37] The underlying rationale is that a person's financial behaviour reliably predicts how well they will maintain their home or drive safely. Such inferences are primarily actuarial, where the correlation itself serves as the basis for guiding decision-making procedures. Treating purely statistical evidence as authoritative sidelines reflection on domain assumptions and the conceptual justification linking collected data to the constructs inferred. Extending this idea further, one might come to believe that ever-increasing datasets and powerful models are able to demonstrate that, after all, 'every fact about an individual reveals every other fact about that individual'.[38] Data attributes considered sensitive, such as sexual orientation, ethnicity, mental health conditions, or religious beliefs, can be inferred from (nearly) any non-sensitive data proxy, such as household electricity patterns, images and videos, mouse clicks, location data, or purchasing habits, privacy scholarship concludes.[39] After all, traces of sensitivity may be embedded in any of these data, ready to be conveniently unearthed by AI's inferential prowess.

If these beliefs were true, traditional regulatory approaches to privacy based on distinctions between sensitive and non-sensitive data would be severely challenged.[40] In the US, EU, Canada, China, and many other countries, information types represent a central normative parameter in privacy and data protection. Regulatory schemes typically specify a set of attributes that fall into the category of sensitive data, such as sexual orientation, ethnicity, or religious beliefs. In the US, provisions protecting special information categories include sectoral privacy regulations such as the Health Insurance Portability and Accountability Act (HIPAA)[41] as well as omnibus state laws such as the California Consumer Privacy Act (CCPA)[42] and the Colorado Privacy Act (CPA).[43] In the EU, the General Data Protection Regulation (GDPR) mandates enhanced protections and legal obligations regarding the processing of sensitive data in article 9.[44] Processing sensitive data requires data processors to conduct a data protection impact

used%20in%20tracking_0.pdf; M Kosinski, D Stillwell and T Graepel, 'Private Traits and Attributes Are Predictable from Digital Records of Human Behavior' (2013) 110(15) *Proceedings of the National Academy of Sciences* 5802–5805.

[37] K Hill, 'Carmakers Want to Track Your Driving Habits to Cut Insurance Rates' (*New York Times*, 11 March 2024), www.nytimes.com/2024/03/11/technology/carmakers-driver-tracking-insurance.html: 'Insurance companies commonly ask for access to a consumer's credit or risk reports, though they are barred from doing so in California, Massachusetts, Michigan and Hawaii'.

[38] Ohm and Peppet (n 4).

[39] Solove (n 4).

[40] Fazlioglu (n 6); Quinn and Malgieri (n 6).

[41] Health Insurance Portability and Accountability Act of 1996, Pub L No 104–191, 110 Stat 1936 (1996), www.govinfo.gov/content/pkg/PLAW-104publ191/pdf/PLAW-104publ191.pdf.

[42] California Office of the Attorney General, California Consumer Privacy Act (CCPA) (OAG California) (2018), www.oag.ca.gov/privacy/ccpa.

[43] Colorado Attorney General, Colorado Privacy Act (Colorado Attorney General) (2021), www.coag.gov/resources/colorado-privacy-act/.

[44] European Commission, 'What Personal Data is Considered Sensitive?' (European Commission) www.commission.europa.eu/law/law-topic/data-protection/reform/rules-business-and-organisations/legal-grounds-processing-data/sensitive-data/what-personal-data-considered-sensitive_en.

assessment (article 35) and the appointment of a data protection officer (article 37).[45] Canada's Personal Information Protection and Electronic Documents Act (PIPEDA) employs a tiered approach to data protection, with heightened safeguards in place for sensitive information categories such as health data, financial records, and sexual orientation.[46] China's Personal Information Protection Law (PIPL), implemented in 2021, categorises certain data types as sensitive, including biometric information, religious beliefs, medical records, location data, and any information pertaining to individuals under the age of 14.[47]

These regulatory approaches construct a categorical framework in which certain types of information, classified as sensitive, for example, warrant special and restrictive treatment.[48] However, the acceptance of the EfE thesis – the belief that 'everything can be inferred from everything' using AI – fundamentally challenges this approach. In summary, there is a prevailing sense of resignation in privacy and data protection, epitomised by EfE, that AI's seemingly boundless inferential capabilities make it impossible to maintain robust privacy norms in theory and regulation.

## III. Conceptual Overfitting

We contend that privacy nihilism is untenable, as its premise, here defined as EfE, lacks sufficient justification to abandon data types (sensitive, financial, etc) as a normative parameter in privacy and data protection. Nonetheless, we are not oblivious to the many eye-catching illustrations that purportedly claim AI can infer sensitive from non-sensitive data types. The underlying logic of privacy nihilism, as we have defined it, starts with the premise that AI has virtually limitless capacities to derive new information from information at hand. This position risks being more of a caricature than a defensible stance. To argue this point, we develop the notion of *conceptual overfitting*. Conceptual overfitting documents norms of convenience in producing inferences that seemingly allow fitting complex constructs to conceptually under-representative or irrelevant data. Conceptual overfitting exposes forms of epistemic shortcutting whereby EfE models offer seemingly conclusive statistical evidence but sidestep any meaningful commitment to meet conceptual expectations of contested inference constructs – including political affiliation, sexual orientation, or mental health conditions. Specifying *conceptual* commitments prior to model development would disrupt the frictionless

[45] Regulation (EU) 2016/679 of the European Parliament and of the Council of 27 April 2016 on the Protection of Natural Persons with Regard to the Processing of Personal Data and on the Free Movement of Such Data (General Data Protection Regulation) [2016] OJ L119/1, www.eur-lex.europa.eu/legal-content/EN/TXT/PDF/?uri=CELEX:32016R0679.

[46] www.priv.gc.ca/en/.

[47] Q Li, T Jiang and X Fan, 'Examining Sensitive Personal Information Protection in China: Framework, Obstacles, and Solutions' (2023) 58(3) *Information & Culture* 247–273; China Briefing, 'The PRC Personal Information Protection Law: Final A Full Translation' (*China Briefing*, 2021), www.china-briefing.com/news/the-prc-personal-information-protection-law-final-a-full-translation/.

[48] The GDPR justifies sensitive data types also as an 'end in itself' in the recognition of their protection as fundamental rights (Quinn and Malgeri (n 6)).

design of models that claim to infer everything from everything. This tendency toward inferential model design reflects broader norms of epistemic convenience, which we examine across three key stages of AI model development: data collection, ground truth manufacturing, and model evaluation.

## A. Data Collection

Contemporary organisations are situated within a data economy that prioritises data-centric business models and a technological infrastructure engineered to minimise resistance in data collection. Data is abundant, on tap, lying around on easily accessible large public datasets such as ImageNet, LAION-5B, LibriSpeech, or CommonCrawl, a publicly available crawl of the web.[49] Even when organisations do not know exactly for what purposes they should collect data, they believe they will lose their place in the data economy if they stop gathering data or delete their data repositories.[50] Powerful and easily accessible, open-source data collection tools such as scraping and crawling software require little technical competence to extract troves of data from public and semi-public websites. Organisations that need to fill up their own data repositories pay for data at specialised data gathering companies, data brokers, such as Acxiom or LexisNexis that pull together data from different channels and sources, including digital traces, exhaust, or data dumps. In the prevailing culture of datafication and inference-making, AI-producing organisations are driven by incentives to exploit readily available datasets, extracting value by developing models that generate inferences of interest. This focus on value extraction, underpinned by a 'more data is always better'[51] directive, has fostered norms of indiscriminate data amassing to find valuable insights in 'data kitchen sinks'. A tale known as the Drunkard's Search might serve as an illustration of this phenomenon:

While on duty, a police officer encounters a drunk individual rummaging around under a streetlight. The officer asks what the person is searching for, and the individual mentions that they have lost their keys. Together, they search beneath the light for a few minutes. Eventually, the officer questions the person's certainty about losing the keys there, prompting the individual to admit they were actually lost in the park. Puzzled, the

[49] OpenAI's large language models are trained on diverse datasets, including publicly available resources such as The Common Crawl, a comprehensive web crawl dataset, see W Knight, 'The Fight Against AI Comes to a Foundational Data Set' (*Wired*, 13 November 2023), www.wired.com/story/the-fight-against-ai-comes-to-a-foundational-data-set/.

[50] J Sadowski, 'When Data is Capital: Datafication, Accumulation, and Extraction' (2019) 6.1 *Big Data & Society* 2053951718820549.

[51] Such and similar convictions seem widespread in the field of AI. A recent analysis of introductory AI courses highlighted a concerning trend: most courses overemphasised the role of large datasets while neglecting the critical importance of data quality, guided by conceptual assumptions, see: S Engelmann, MZ Choksi, A Wang and C Fiesler, 'Visions of a Discipline: Analyzing Introductory AI Courses on YouTube' in *The 2024 ACM Conference on Fairness, Accountability, and Transparency* (New York, ACM, June 2024) 2400–2420.

officer enquires why they are searching in that spot, to which the individual responds: 'Because it's illuminated here'.[52]

Organisations are motivated to look for value in the data that they happen to have at their disposal or that they can access with ease. A prominent example of such a data comfort zone has been social media. Offering semi-public access to the profiles, behaviours, and interactions of billions of individuals globally, social media platforms run on the promise to provide actionable insights on specific, granular audiences to marketers. Data on social media have been a playground for developing and testing inferential AI models. Take for instance the numerous example cases that purportedly infer contested, dynamic constructs such as *political orientation* from social media kitchen sink data.[53] In research, the typical approach involves collecting all accessible profile data – such as likes, number of friends, and other attributes – from users who explicitly disclose their political affiliation. During training, an AI model learns to identify patterns in this kitchen sink dataset and associates them with political affiliations (eg, 'Democrat' or 'Republican'). In testing and validation, the model predicts political orientation based solely on the accessible profile data. When deployed, the AI model predictively infers the political orientation of users who have not explicitly disclosed it, relying only on their kitchen sink profile data. Eventually, a model appears to discover a dynamic, fluid, contested, and sensitive data type – political orientation – in mundane, conceptually unrelated pieces of information[54] based on the correlation of similarity to users that did reveal this construct (perhaps by accident). AI models are powerful at picking up regularities and patterns in data. Patterns should not be treated as conceptually accountable semantics when they cannot be evaluated against prior conceptual claims about the phenomenon of interest (eg, political orientation). The ease of amassing data encourages organisations to bypass data collection norms grounded in explicit assumptions about a construct, along with the accountability that comes from committing to them. Tempted by the convenience of data amassing, inferential models fit constructs onto conceptually under-representative and irrelevant data. By sifting through vast quantities of data, it is presumed that contested constructs, such as political or sexual orientation, simply emerge from the data and are ultimately 'discovered' by AI models: '[d]ata speak for themselves', so the adage goes, they can be harvested as intrinsic bearers of semantic meaning. Data are, in fact, not factual, fixed representations; they are not gateways to an objective reality. Even if datasets expand to gigantic Internet-sized repositories, their representational scope does not necessarily broaden to the point where AI models can simply pick up nearly any construct of interest, as suggested by privacy nihilism. Conceptual assumptions about

[52] N Belludi, 'Drunkard Search and the Streetlight Effect' (*Right Attitudes*, 26 February 2016), www.rightattitudes.com/2016/02/26/drunkard-search-streetlight-effect/.

[53] A Boutet, H Kim and E Yoneki, 'What's in Twitter, I Know What Parties Are Popular and Who You Are Supporting Now!' (2013) 3 *Social Network Analysis and Mining* 1379; M Kosinski, D Stillwell and T Graepel, 'Private Traits and Attributes Are Predictable from Digital Records of Human Behavior' (2013) 110(15) *Proceedings of the National Academy of Sciences* 5802; Y Wang, I Weber and P Mitra, 'Quantified Self Meets Social Media: Sharing of Weight Updates on Twitter' in *Proceedings of the 6th International Conference on Digital Health Conference* (New York, ACM, 2016).

[54] H Nissenbaum, 'Contextual Integrity Up and Down the Data Food Chain' (2019) 20(1) *Theoretical Inquiries in Law* 221–256.

the construct of interest guide the search for construct-relevant data in inferential AI models. The notion 'accurate data' is meaningless if devoid of a conceptual reference. Against what else should we evaluate the accuracy of our data, if not conceptual claims and assumptions about the constructs we aim to infer? A commitment to accurate data necessitates conceptual commitments prior to data collection. This, in turn, requires discipline-specific expertise and with it a willingness to step outside of data comfort zones – challenging the convenience of data collection driven by a Drunkard Search principle.

Besides, fitting sensitive constructs to data without accountability to any conceptual relevance while hoping all noise will come out in the wash of ML algorithms increases the likelihood of measurement errors and well-documented downstream harms, such as discrimination and disparate treatment – issues that a significant part of the data science community has identified and warned against.[55] It would be puzzling if privacy and data protection norms should promote epistemic standards that reinforce such established risks.

## B. Ground Truth Manufacturing

All supervised AI models require a ground truth – an epistemic reference from which models interpret new data. In the previous example on self-revealed political orientation on social media, the ground truth was conveniently embedded in the collected data as an incidental byproduct. However, in other cases, developers first need to add their construct of interest to the data so that a model can learn the association between data and inference construct. In other words, developers need to *manufacture* a ground truth. Manufacturing a conceptually justified ground truth can be the foundation for the development of breakthrough inferential AI models such as AlphaFold, the 2024 Nobel Prize-winning AI model for proteome prediction. AlphaFold was trained on high-quality, labelled protein structure data[56] donated to the open-source Protein Data Bank (PDB)[57] by over 50,000 structural biologists worldwide starting in 1971.[58] Clearly, such a highly conceptualised, structured, and systematised dataset, built over decades, fundamentally contradicts the notion of convenient inferential model development promoted by EfE.

[55] N Sambasivan and others, '"Everyone Wants to Do the Model Work, Not the Data Work": Data Cascades in High-Stakes AI' in *Proceedings of the 2021 CHI Conference on Human Factors in Computing Systems* (New York, ACM, 2021); A Wang and others, 'Measuring Representational Harms in Image Captioning' in *Proceedings of the 2022 ACM Conference on Fairness, Accountability, and Transparency* (New York, ACM, 2022); AZ Jacobs and H Wallach, 'Measurement and Fairness' in *Proceedings of the 2021 ACM Conference on Fairness, Accountability, and Transparency* (New York, ACM, 2021); C Ullstein, S Engelmann, O Papakyriakopoulos, Y Ikkata, NP Arnez-Jordan, R Caleno, … and J Grossklags, 'Attitudes Toward Facial Analysis AI: A Cross-National Study Comparing Argentina, Kenya, Japan, and the USA' in *The 2024 ACM Conference on Fairness, Accountability, and Transparency* (New York, ACM, 2024) 2273–2301.

[56] Tunyasuvunakool et al (n 11). We note that AlphaFold not only trained on labelled data in the PBD: 'The AlphaFold architecture is able to train to high accuracy using only supervised learning on PDB data, but we are able to enhance accuracy (Fig. 4a) using an approach similar to noisy student self-distillation.'

[57] RCSB Protein Data Bank, www.rcsb.org/.

[58] D Markowitz (F Noé), 'How AlphaFold Works' (*Dale on AI*, 2024), www.daleonai.com/how-alphafold-works.

### *i. Data Labelling and Annotation*

The PBD demonstrates that the assumption that AI models infer constructs by simply 'letting the data speak' collapses since human annotators – whether volunteers, crowd-sourced workers, or domain experts – carry out the interpretative task of assigning a target construct, the intended inference concept, to individual data records for model training. Model training crucially relies on the inherently commercial, social, and collaborative process of assigning semantics to data. Organisations typically provide their data either to in-house labellers or to a data processing company to facilitate dataset labelling.[59] Data processing companies supply the necessary infrastructure, including project supervisors, human labellers, and quality control systems, making the process convenient for the requesting organisation. Human labellers, however, must navigate the inherent semantic ambiguity, fluidity, procedurality, and contextuality that mediate the relationship between data and inference. Labelling and annotation practices prioritise the pragmatic interests of requester organisations, smoothing over epistemic complexities for convenience.[60] Take, for example, cases where data requesters ask human labellers to assign race and ethnicity categories to people depicted in visual images. Annotation companies provide human labellers with a *predefined* set of race categories, such as – 'White', 'Hispanic', 'African American', 'Asian', 'Indian', or 'Ambiguous' – and instruct them to map these constructs onto clients' image data.[61] Race and ethnicity are complex constructs not receptive to self-evident, intuitive identification, unlike distinctions between, say, a tennis ball and a basketball. With no conceptual interpretation in hand, annotators' cultural backgrounds and subjective experiences with people of different races and ethnicities influence how they perceive and classify each image into predefined race categories. As a result, disagreement among labellers is a common occurrence. To identify this disagreement, data processing companies invest in 'consistency monitoring,' reviewing labelling patterns and re-training labellers for specific tasks.[62] The most prevalent method for resolving annotator disagreements is majority voting, which creates a ground truth that implies a single correct interpretation for every data record.[63] Each semantic unit of a data record (eg, a specific part of an image) is labelled by several annotators but can only receive a single semantic labelling. Labelling does not allow for a plurality of semantic annotation. Not only does such 'annotation bias' generate misclassifications that harm data subjects for whom the model incorrectly assigns the majority interpretation,

[59] M Muller and others, 'Designing Ground Truth and the Social Life of Labels' in *Proceedings of the 2021 CHI Conference on Human Factors in Computing Systems* (New York, ACM, 2021) 1–16.

[60] S Engelmann and others, 'What People Think AI Should Infer from Faces' in *Proceedings of the 2022 ACM Conference on Fairness, Accountability, and Transparency* (New York, ACM, 2022); M Miceli, J Posada and T Yang, 'Studying Up Machine Learning Data: Why Talk About Bias When We Mean Power?' in *Proceedings of the ACM on Human-Computer Interaction GROUP 1* (New York, ACM, 2022) 6.

[61] Miceli et al (n 61).

[62] D Melchior, K Mistry and K Proskudin, *Accuracy Upfront: Methods and Process for Measuring and Improving Accuracy in AI through Human Supervision* (CloudFactory Whitepaper, 2023).

[63] E Fleisig et al, 'When the Majority is Wrong: Modeling Annotator Disagreement for Subjective Tasks' in H Bouamor, J Pino and K Balis (eds), *Proceedings of the 2023 Conference on Empirical Methods in Natural Language Processing* (Singapore, Association for Computational Linguistics (ACL), 2023).

but it also risks oversimplifying nuanced and contested constructs, including race and ethnicity.[64]

When we hear AI slogans of inferential mastery, we should remind ourselves that such epistemic performativity may rest on the meaning that human labellers ascribe to data during socio-commercial negotiations.[65] Privacy nihilism ignores that AI models infer complex constructs such as racial or ethnic categories, emotional profiles, or gender types only because, in a largely invisible infrastructure, a human labeller fits a computationally digestible and readable representation of an infinitely more complex construct to each training data record.

## *ii. Survey Questionnaires*

Conceptual overfitting arises when models treat correlations between survey questionnaire results and kitchen sink datasets as evidence of complex constructs such as medical conditions. Mental health illustrates the point: diagnosis depends on clinicians' holistic interpretation of survey responses together with other diagnostic evidence, not on correlation alone.[66] Because conditions like depression, anxiety, or schizophrenia each present distinct symptom profiles, mental health survey questionnaires play a *supportive* role – for screening, guiding diagnosis, and gauging symptom intensity – rather than serving as a stand-alone basis for inference.[67] Yet their epistemic convenience encourages substituting them for the richer evidentiary standards such inferences require. Numerous clinically approved mental health questionnaires are available online, and can be accessed conveniently, many as free downloads. These questionnaires often include a scoring system that seemingly facilitates straightforward interpretation of results into definite diagnostic categories. Given their availability and apparent ease of interpretation, mental health questionnaires are common tools of ground truth manufacturing for AI models that purportedly infer mental health conditions by correlating questionnaire results with easily available but conceptually unrelated data.[68] A typical AI project might recruit online crowdworkers and request them to complete a clinically certified survey questionnaire focused on a specific health condition. After completing the task, crowdworkers consent to share unrelated data, such as their social media information. This social media data is then

[64] J Muldoon, M Graham and C Cant, *Feeding the Machine The Hidden Human Labour Powering AI* (London, Bloomsbury Publishing, 2024).

[65] M Muller, et al, 'Designing Ground Truth and the Social Life of Labels' in *Proceedings of the 2021 CHI Conference on Human Factors in Computing Systems* (New York, ACM, 2021); similar to human labelling in these supervised learning procedures, note that in reinforcement learning from human feedback (RLHF), collecting human preferences over pairs of outputs has become the standard approach for aligning large language models (LLMs).

[66] ABR Shatte, DM Hutchinson and SJ Teague, 'Machine Learning in Mental Health: A Scoping Review of Methods and Applications' (2019) 49 *Psychological Medicine* 1426.

[67] ibid.

[68] S Chancellor and M De Choudhury, 'Methods in Predictive Techniques for Mental Health Status on Social Media: A Critical Review' (2020) 3(1) *NPJ Digital Medicine* 43; ibid Reece and Danforth (n 34); M De Choudhury and others, 'Predicting Depression via Social Media' in *Proceedings of the International AAAI Conference on Web and Social Media* (Washington, AAAI Press, 2013) 7(1).

correlated with participants' questionnaire responses to train a model that allegedly infers medical conditions from social media activity.

To give one example, a well-cited study paid online crowdworkers to complete the clinically validated Center for Epidemiologic Studies Depression Scale.[69] Based on their questionnaire responses, researchers classified crowdworkers as either depressed or healthy. Using an AI model, they then analysed how these classifications correlated with the colour hues of crowdworkers' social media images.[70] The authors claim that their random forest classifier identified markers of depression by detecting variations in colour hues within social media images of individuals classified as either 'depressed' or 'healthy'. The authors concluded that 'markers of depression' could be predictively inferred from social media images. When diagnosing depression, clinicians combine multiple diagnostic methods, including various physical examinations, medical history, and patient interviews to explore symptoms and potential causes (eg, family history), *as well as* administer depression scales[71] for diagnostic evaluation.[72] Given the complexity of mental health conditions – recognised as sensitive data under most data protection laws worldwide – doctors rely on evidence from a combination of these practices to arrive at a diagnosis. Are we to accept that an AI model inferring depression markers from image colour hues captures the constitutive dimensions of depression as comprehensively as trained clinicians who conduct and interpret a range of diagnostic assessments?

When AI projects claim to achieve the same diagnostic value as trained clinicians while relying on conveniently produced ground truths, they engage in conceptual overfitting – reducing a multifaceted construct to conceptually unrelated, surface-level correlations, such as colour hues in images, while disregarding its nuanced psychological, social, and biological dimensions. By prioritising proxies over underlying causes, these AI models risk producing contextually fragile predictions that lack the robustness[73] required for reliable diagnostic applications.[74]

### *iii. Proxy Hopping*

In some cases, the inferential leap from data to inferred construct is so large, conceptually, that the construct of interest is first inferred from another construct, itself an

[69] Reece and Danforth (n 34).

[70] Crowdworkers had consented to sharing their social media images as part of the study.

[71] Examples include the Hamilton Depression Rating Scale, the Montgomery-Åsberg Depression Rating Scale, or the Center for Epidemiologic Studies Depression Scale.

[72] The process of diagnosing depression at a hospital is much more complex than outlined here. For the purpose of the argument, I have drawn information from: www.nyulangone.org/conditions/depression/diagnosis.

[73] For example, in S Mullainathan and Z Obermeyer, 'Does Machine Learning Automate Moral Hazard and Error?' (2017) 107(5) *American Economic Review* 476: 'Machine learning algorithms excel at predicting outcomes (y) based on inputs (x). In automation tasks, measuring y – such as the majority opinion of ophthalmologists – is straightforward. However, in health policy applications, y and x are often derived from electronic health records or claims data, where the very construction of these datasets introduces large and systematic mismeasurement. These inaccuracies, in turn, can bias algorithmic predictions and, in some cases, automate policies that amplify existing clinical errors and moral hazard.'

[74] For example in Reece and Danforth (n 34), the authors state: 'These results suggest new avenues for early screening and detection of mental illness.'

inference. For example, AI models take as input signal streams from data primitives such as accelerometer or gyroscope sensors in smart devices and output constructs such as emotions,[75] health conditions,[76] stress,[77] or gender[78] as inferences. We call this *proxy hopping*, as it requires 'hopping' from data proxy to data proxy to arrive, finally, at the construct of interest. This recursive cycle of leaping between data and inference necessitates producing a corresponding ground truth for each data-inference pair. In Olsen and Torresen,[79] for example, accelerometer[80] data streams serve as the first proxy $P_1$ to infer a specific type of movement (eg, walking) $I_1$. $I_1$ is then considered a proxy ($P_2$) for the final inference, emotion ($I_{final}$). To manufacture the ground truth for $P_1 \rightarrow I_1$ participants install a smartphone application that collects accelerometer data while they perform the desired movement (walking, running, jumping etc). This results in a ground truth of accelerometer data that signifies a particular movement profile. The same participants then complete a survey questionnaire to capture their emotional state[81] in relation to the type of movement ($P_2 \rightarrow I_{final}$). Hence, an AI model makes inferential leaps from sensor streams to emotional states. Since each inference can be mapped onto conceptually irrelevant data, proxy hopping is particularly susceptible to conceptual overfitting. In turn, models that engage in proxy hopping are especially prone to generating downstream harm through misclassification, as measurement errors may compound across inferential leaps, with each error undermining the validity of all subsequent inferences.

Following the easy collection of data, model development often relies on ground truth manufacturing practices that operationalise conceptual overfitting. This occurs when data are assigned the meaning of complex constructs through convenient labelling processes or are merely correlated with questionnaire results or a combination thereof, as is the case with proxy hopping. In fact, human discretionary work infuses model development even before ground truth production: data cannot be labelled, annotated, or otherwise humanly interpreted without prior data preparation efforts that require an organisational infrastructure to enable human decision-making on data processing and cleaning.[82] Before a single data record can be semantised by human interpretation for ground truth manufacturing, data must first be made intelligible for interpretative

[75] AF Olsen and J Torresen, 'Smartphone Accelerometer Data Used for Detecting Human Emotions' in *3rd International Conference on Systems and Informatics (ICSAI)* (Shanghai, IEEE, 2016).

[76] A Jalal et al, 'A Study of Accelerometer and Gyroscope Measurements in Physical Life-Log Activities Detection Systems' (2020) 20 *Sensors* 6670.

[77] E Garcia-Ceja, V Osmani and O Mayora, 'Automatic Stress Detection in Working Environments from Smartphones Accelerometer Data: A First Step' (2015) 20 *IEEE Journal of Biomedical and Health Informatics* 1053.

[78] A Jain and V Kanhangad, 'Investigating Gender Recognition in Smartphones Using Accelerometer and Gyroscope Sensor Readings' in *International Conference on Computational Techniques in Information and Communication Technologies* (ICCTICT) (New Delhi, IEEE, 2016).

[79] Olsen and Torresen (n 75).

[80] A smartphone's accelerometer is a sensor that detects movement and orientation by measuring acceleration along three axes. This allows the device to interpret motion, adjust screen orientation, and enable various interactive features.

[81] Olsen and Torresen (n 75). The emotion questionnaire administered in this study was based on the Circumplex Model of Affect.

[82] For an in-depth account on the epistemological significance of data cleaning in contemporary data science, see M Boumans and S Leonelli, *From Dirty Data to Tidy Facts: Clustering Practices in Plant Phenomics and Business Cycle Analysis* (Cham, Springer International Publishing 2020).

work through filtering (excluding outliers, eg), sorting, ordering, and a plethora of other human-led practices crucial for ground truth manufacturing. AI models do not uncover constructs of interest from the intrinsic structures and patterns of data. Instead, their representational value is assigned through human modularisation, collaboration, and interpretation.[83] When this assignment of meaning prioritises pragmatic convenience over conceptual rigour, models can conceptually overfit a complex construct onto conceptually under-related or irrelevant data.

## C. Model Evaluation

AI models and the inferences they produce are conceptualised, developed, and validated through the dominant train-test paradigm in supervised machine learning. This paradigm mandates that accuracy metrics serve as standard evaluation and validation devices of AI model performance. Privacy nihilism assumes that high accuracy scores are sufficient to declare a model is able to infer one thing from another. However, accuracy rates are empty validators when they are disconnected from any meaningful interpretation about the relationship between the inferred construct and the statistical results. This is the case in models that conceptually overfit, where data is collected without a meaningful commitment to conceptual assumptions, enabling the manufacturing of ground truth based on oversimplified constructs. Now, at the model evaluation stage, all we have are accuracy metrics that appear convenient to interpret: the higher, the better.[84] But how high is high enough? 55? 78? 95 or 99 per cent? The reigning heuristic remains: the higher the accuracy score, the better the performance. But no one really seems to be able to tell (including us) when accuracy scores are high enough. Should we deem an AI model to work when it predicts a person's political orientation (Democrat or Republican) with 72 per cent accuracy on a validation set, based solely on facial morphology?[85] Probability scores or percentages lend model evaluation an appearance of scientific objectivity.[86] In the end, however, human designers and practitioners choose an accuracy cut-off threshold that turns a probabilistic expression into a deterministic declaration of classification. For example, if a model predictively infers an 80 per cent probability that an individual should be assigned an inference construct, a cut-off value of 79 per cent would indicate that a relationship between the individual and the inference construct exists. In contrast, a cut-off value of 81 per cent would denote no existing relationship. Accuracy cut-off choices are essentially arbitrary in models that conceptually overfit. Accuracy rates may be persuasive devices of performativity and indicate whether inferential models are 'hitting or missing' target

[83] F Jaton, 'Assessing Biases, Relaxing Morality: On Ground-Truthing Practices in Machine Learning Design and Application' (2021) 8 *Big Data & Society* 20539517211013569.

[84] Alternatively, the lower the better when assessing error rates.

[85] M Kosinski, P Khambatta and Y Wang, 'Facial Recognition Technology and Human Raters Can Predict Political Orientation from Images of Expressionless Faces Even When Controlling for Demographics and Self-Presentation' (2024) 79(7) *American Psychologist* 942–955.

[86] G Grill, *Constructing Certainty in Machine Learning: On the Performativity of Testing and Its Hold on the Future* (2022).

constructs.[87] When models conceptually overfit, they cannot be interpreted in relation to any meaningful theoretical claims or assumptions about the target construct. As a result, there is no conceptual accountability for the accuracy they produce.

Moreover, since accuracy metrics are often produced by the same actors who stand to benefit from their positive presentation, privacy scholarship should exercise caution in relying on them to inform normative claims for governance proposals. For example, Birhane et al show that tests of generalisability usually occur on datasets and tasks that researchers select and have access to.[88] In their analysis of 100 highly cited machine learning papers, they underline the convenience that performance metrics rarely extend beyond curated datasets. Reporting AI accuracy rates under conditions comparable to a laboratory setting is akin to evaluating performance in an overly controlled environment. This practice risks creating an illusion of performance, obscuring the documented challenges and limitations of deploying AI in real-world contexts.[89] Indeed, we observe a growing 'how did we get here?' sense of self-reflection among data scientists, which goes hand in hand with the realisation that the persistent clinging to accuracy measures might lead the field into a dead end.[90] Current evaluation practices centre on accuracy optimisation competitions separating winners from losers on leaderboards. For models that conceptually overfit, benchmark-driven assessments are particularly convenient. Model validation focuses primarily on achieving equal or higher scores than previous models on the same datasets, tasks, and settings, effectively sidelining other important epistemic norms, such as conceptual accountability. Privacy nihilism wrongly equates high accuracy rates with model functionality, ignoring their lack of meaningful interpretation in conceptually overfitted models.

In summary, conceptual overfitting refers to the adoption of norms of convenience that simplify the development of AI models by forcing complex constructs to fit data that are conceptually under-representative or irrelevant. Models built on an EfE approach conceptually overfit, conveniently inferring this from that at the expense of producing any meaningful conceptual accountability. Such processes typically fail to explicate why the collected data are relevant to the inference construct *in conceptual terms*. Consequently, practitioners circumvent a deliberate commitment to robust assumptions or claims, which would add friction to approaches that mandate looking for constructs of interest in data that one happens to have easy access to. A lack of conceptual accountability allows ground truth manufacturing to instantiate oversimplified

[87] A standard set of metrics – for regressions, mean absolute error (MAE) or root mean squared error (RMSE), for example, or, for classification, accuracy, recall, specificity, and others – typically serves to demonstrate that an AI model performs a task as expected. This terminology owes its origin from AI development in the military, see L McGuigan, *Selling the American People: Advertising, Optimization, and the Origins of Adtech* (Cambridge (MA), MIT Press, 2023).

[88] A Birhane, P Kalluri, D Card, W Agnew, R Dotan and M Bao, 'The Values Encoded in Machine Learning Research' in *Proceedings of the 2022 ACM Conference on Fairness, Accountability, and Transparency* (New York, AMC, 2022) 173.

[89] ID Raji, EM Bender, A Paullada, E Denton and A Hanna, 'AI and the Everything in the Whole Wide World Benchmark' (Ithaca, arXiv, 2021), *arXiv preprint* www.arxiv.org/abs/2111.15366; ID Raji, IE Kumar, A Horowitz and A Selbst, 'The Fallacy of AI Functionality' *Proceedings of the 2022 ACM Conference on Fairness, Accountability, and Transparency* (New York, AMC, 2022) 959, www.doi.org/10.1145/3531146.3533150; KW Church and V Kordoni, 'Emerging Trends: SOTA-Chasing' (2022) 28(2) *Natural Language Engineering* 249, www.doi.org/10.1017/S1351324921000374; Grill (n 86).

[90] Church and Kordoni (n 89) 249.

constructs that can be easily attached to available data. Subsequently, model evaluation relies on accuracy scores as a heuristic, where 'higher is better' becomes a rubber stamp for performance – disconnected from any meaningful sensemaking about the relationship between the inferred construct and the produced statistical results. Conceptual overfitting is not the absence of underlying concepts in EfE models; rather, it's the reluctance of developers and practitioners to critically evaluate foundational assumptions behind their constructs. Although convenient, this avoidance prevents conceptual accountability, making it impossible to understand and engage with the phenomena AI models truly infer.

## IV. AI Challenges To Privacy: The Persistent Inference Problem

Taking stock of the argument to this point, conceptual overfitting is an antidote insofar as it challenges the underpinnings of privacy nihilism. Instead of substantiating the radical proposition that AI yields the power to infer everything from everything (EfE), many of the most dramatic, rhetorically persuasive displays of AI's boundless capacity are epistemically flawed, potentially verging on epistemic arbitrariness. These flaws are due to what we have called conceptual overfitting, permeating key components of inference-making – data collection (or creation), ground truth manufacturing, and model evaluation. In revealing these flaws, our aim has been not only to undermine the foundations of privacy nihilism but also to stanch a retreat from privacy advocacy through regulation that a nihilistic position would suggest: discarding data categories as a normative anchoring in privacy and data protection as a result of an *unconditional acceptance* of AI's inferential capacities. At the same time, as successful as we may be at achieving this aim, there is no denying that AI's power to amplify inferential capacity poses unprecedented challenges to privacy regulation – even if not to the point of privacy nihilism's EfE.

The most undermined by AI's power to amplify inferential capacity are approaches to privacy regulation that rely only on distinctions among various types of data, traditionally, a dichotomy that marks certain categories of data as sensitive, private, or personal and accords them special consideration. For example, regulation-based privacy, defined as a right to control information about ourselves, might extend only to sensitive information, or, where it is defined as a form of secrecy, may extend only to these special classes of information.[91] On the other side of this dichotomy, either implied or explicitly stated, is its opposite, namely, data that is 'public' – neither sensitive nor private, privacy – to which regulation does not apply or is muted. Such approaches are unquestionably challenged by powerful inferential capacities of AI, to the extent they enable private information to be inferred from its obverse.[92]

[91] This language is common in discussions of differential privacy.

[92] H Nissenbaum, 'Protecting Privacy in an Information Age: The Problem of Privacy in Public' in *The Ethics of Information Technologies* (Milton Park, Routledge, 2020) 141–178: 'Information belies the adage about sewing silk purses out of sow's ears, for out of worthless bits of information we may sew assemblages that are rich in value.'

## A. Introducing Contextual Integrity: A Brief Digression

Developed in response to this and other challenges to privacy posed by digital technology, contextual integrity (CI) addresses gaps in other conceptions by positing contextual factors relevant to privacy that others had not systematically theorised.[93] At first glance, however, it doesn't seem to save CI from the inference attacks to which these alternative approaches are vulnerable. Although, on the one hand, CI demands finer-grained data ontologies rooted in social contexts (ie, not public/private but, for example, symptoms, diagnoses, drugs prescribed, etc) the data flows that preserve contextual integrity (ie, are *appropriate*) still may yield inappropriate data flows due to clever data or model-driven inferences. One may reasonably wonder whether there is a path forward for a meaningful conception of privacy (including those embodied in omnibus privacy regulation noted above) to resist radical inference-making.

The lens of contextual integrity can offer some clarity on the problem space and what is at stake in formulating a response.[94] To begin, CI rests on an assumption about social life drawn from disciplines of social theory and social philosophy, namely, that it is constituted by distinctive social domains, or realms, such as healthcare, education, political governance, and commerce, each defined by respective ends, purposes, and values. These contexts – for this is the term-of-art adopted in CI theory – are further constituted by respective ontologies of roles and data types. Behaviour is governed by contextual norms, which may or may not be rendered as explicit rules or embedded in law and other forms of policy and regulation. A subset, contextual informational norms (abbreviated as, privacy norms), govern information flows by prescribing or proscribing them.[95] Appropriateness of information flows, at the heart of contextual integrity, is a function of privacy norms.

The top-level statement of CI, namely, that privacy is appropriate information flow, draws into play all the elements we have introduced thus far. There are a few more, however, that we need to introduce. First, privacy norms comprise five parameters: subject, sender, recipient, data type (attribute), and transmission principle. When expressing a privacy norm, all five parameters must be specified, and they must be specified in terms of the capacities (roles) in which the actors are acting and, for the data types, in terms of respective contextual ontologies (for this reason, CI is a semantic theory). The transmission principle parameter refers to constraints under which data flows from one party to another, most familiarly 'with consent', but, potentially, innumerably others, such as 'reciprocally', 'with authorisation', 'with notice', and so forth. When evaluating the privacy standing of an existing socio-technical practice, or one that is in development – be it ad targeting, facial recognition, or a myriad other possibilities – a description of any of the associated data flows must include values for all of the parameters. Failing to do so renders it incomplete and ambiguous. Second, privacy norms inherit an ambiguity that is not unusual when characterising social

[93] H Nissenbaum, 'Privacy as Contextual Integrity' (2004) 79 *Washington Law Review* 119.

[94] A few key aspects of CI theory are important to mention here, though interested readers may wish to seek fuller elaboration, explanation, and argument in other publications. For example: H Nissenbaum, *Privacy in Context: Technology, Policy, and the Integrity of Social Life* (Redwood City, Stanford University Press, 2009).

[95] Because it isn't the case that there are norms governing all possible information flows, it is possible that for a given data flow, the question of its appropriateness is indeterminate.

norms, namely, they may serve as descriptions of common or conventional behaviours and expectations, or may be expressed as morally weighty prescriptions, or both, simultaneously. In either case, CI introduces the idea of legitimacy: privacy norms are legitimate, or morally defensible, insofar as they support contextual ends, purposes, and values and illegitimate, or morally indefensible, insofar as they undermine them.[96]

The inference challenge, through the lens of CI, is most acute for conceptions of privacy that rest entirely, or almost entirely, on the single parameter of attribute, or data type, without further qualifying the values of other – ideally, all the other – parameters required for flows to be appropriate. Although this may seem overly pedantic, it is worth noting that failure to do so has allowed data brokers, for decades, to justify their unremitting practices of seeding massive individual dossiers by scraping information from so-called public records. This failure has also served companies, such as OpenAI and Clearview AI, who have defended their data practice by declaring that they collect only 'publicly available' data.[97] Even without incorporating missing parameters, one immediate approach might be to adjust the categories of private and public by switching data attributes to 'private' that previously had been classified as 'public', as occurred with the Social Security Number in the US. At most, however, this can serve as a stopgap, inevitably outpaced by potent advancements in AI-based inference-making.[98]

CI opens up an array of effective alternatives for regulation, allowing all five parameters to be in play as levers of governance. Not as radical as this might initially seem, there is already a law on the books that has done this, HIPAA, for example, which spells out the proper recipients of different types of health information, acting in their respective capacities, including physicians, mental health professionals, business services, and so forth. The HIPAA privacy rules spell out not only the proper recipients but also what the recipients may and may not do with information received and under what conditions. Academic researchers pledge to human subjects that specified restrictions will curtail how the researchers handle data collected from and about them. Regulation curbs not only *how* law enforcement agents (in liberal democracies) may go about gathering information about suspects but also what that information may include. The last illustrates the power of transmission principles to stipulate prior conditions and constraints on data flows, even when the other parameters are non-determinative for many actions. In some cases, when parties in an instance of data flow are acting in historically familiar capacities, for example, teachers or lawyers, their obligations, determined exogenously, may be imported into entrenched norms governing it. In sum, giving regulators (governmental and nongovernmental) the discretion to govern data practices through all of the five parameters, not merely data type, means, at least, that when data is generated in individuals' interactions with others, including businesses, services, platforms, apps, etc, they will be held accountable for the capacities in which they are acting and, like lawyers and teachers, held to specific restrictions.

[96] The same may be said of data flows, even in the absence of entrenched norms, viz. that they are legitimate or illegitimate.

[97] These declarations were made in respective Privacy Policies, slightly more complicated in the case of OpenAI, who admit that they also obtain data through licensing agreements with other data holders.

[98] See discussion in Nissenbaum (n 55).

A fuller account of how the CI parameters could provide critical levers to privacy regulation would require more painstaking detail than this chapter allows. Before concluding this section, however, it is critical to mention that tailoring data flow norms to sensibly limit the application of AI's inferential power is no arbitrary exercise. It is not about simply capping, reducing, and stopping; instead, legitimacy remains the guiding light. Just as carefully crafted rules governing data flows in healthcare are justifiable only if they promote its purposes and values, norms governing data flows in the provision of legal services promote provision by lawyers of individuals rights to representation, and desired norms in education would promote the ends of learning, so must we evaluate restrictions on nontraditional data practices. If societal and contextual values are disserved by existing data flows, any new normative restrictions need to be evaluated against their capacity to turn the tables.

## V. Conclusion

By centring privacy exclusively on data types – only to abandon them by granting AI models unconditional inferential power – privacy nihilism fails to offer any substantive advancement for privacy in a world shaped by ubiquitous AI inference-making. In this chapter, we have shown that while AI may *seem* to transcend any data category and possibly infer 'everything from everything', such claims rest on fragile epistemic foundations. We introduced the notion of conceptual overfitting to describe how AI model development can follow norms of convenience, mapping complex constructs – including sensitive data types – onto readily available data that is often at hand but conceptually under-representative or even irrelevant. A dominant data economy allows for 'anything goes' in acquiring, generating, and capturing data and for utilising it at the arbitrary convenience of the burgeoning array of actors – commercial but not always – who either accrue data and generate data products as their core business or who generate (collect, capture) data as an incidental artefact of their primary service. We documented how conceptual overfitting can arise when requesters instruct labelling of data as if it were adequately capturing rich, nuanced constructs, such as political orientation, mental health status, or religious beliefs. Accuracy metrics can offer a veneer of objectivity that masks the absence of genuine conceptual grounding – leading to a false impression that AI models have attained near-limitless inference capabilities. In summary, we have argued that 'everything from everything' perspectives fail to provide a justified descriptive foundation from which to derive normative conclusions about privacy in both theory and law. Crucially, our findings do not refute the mounting challenges that novel AI systems pose for privacy regulation. Instead of calling for the outright dismissal of data categories, we have underscored the importance of other factors, such as those proffered in contextual integrity, including social norms, key actors, and contextual purposes and values. By factoring in these additional elements, privacy values are not relegated to the back but remain central to privacy protection as AI's inferential capabilities increase. An epistemic 'anything goes' approach to AI inferences disrupts an equilibrium that an adequate theory of privacy would seek to reach. Why should the authority to determine the legitimacy of inferences rest solely with those who produce, develop, and deploy inferential AI models? Who stands to gain, and who stands to lose, when such positions are advanced? These questions lie at the heart of the possibilities and limitations of governing information in the age of AI inferences. Instead of giving in either to privacy dogmatism or to privacy nihilism, defending privacy will mean avoiding hyperbole while taking a clear-eyed approach to the real challenges of AI's dramatic powers of inference-making.

# 17

# On the Nexus between Privacy and Autonomy. A Contextual Integrity Approach

ELISA ORRÙ*

## I. Introduction

Privacy and autonomy are deeply intertwined. In privacy theory and law, there is broad agreement that privacy is a necessary precondition for autonomy.[1] In order to make decisions according to our own preferences and live our lives according to our own goals, we need protected, ie, private, physical and metaphorical spaces.[2] This is all the more true in the digital age, as the collection and analysis of personal information exposes the vulnerabilities of individuals, which can be exploited to influence and manipulate them, thus posing a serious threat to individual autonomy.[3] The German constitutional way of protecting informational privacy, namely the right to informational self-determination, makes this conceptual link explicit in its very name.[4]

If the value of privacy rests (if not exhaustively, then certainly decisively) in enabling autonomy, then a good understanding of privacy requires a robust theory of autonomy.[5] However, it has been noted that legal understandings of privacy often

* Some of the ideas presented here were discussed at the Workshop on Modern Technologies and Self Determination at the Arctic University of Norway in Tromsø in October 2023, during the Public Law Seminar at the Max Planck Institute for the Study of Crime, Security and Law in Freiburg in April 2024, as well as at a two-day conference held at the same Institute in July 2024. I would like to thank all participants for their insightful and stimulating comments and suggestions. My sincere gratitude goes also to James Angove, Daniel Buchmann, Eran Fish and Christian Thönnes, who read an earlier draft of the chapter and provided invaluable feedback. Their incisive criticism and constructive suggestions were instrumental in refining the theses and enhancing the argument. Clearly, the responsibility for any errors remains with me.

[1] JE Cohen, *Configuring the Networked Self: Law, Code, and the Play of Everyday Practice* (New Haven, Yale University Press, 2012) 4.

[2] B Rössler, *Der Wert des Privaten* (Frankfurt, Suhrkamp, 2001) 137.

[3] D Susser, B Rössler and H Nissenbaum, 'Technology, Autonomy, and Manipulation' (2019) 8 *Internet Policy Review* 2.

[4] On the right to informational self-determination see M Albers, *Informationelle Selbstbestimmung*, Studien zu Staat, Recht und Verwaltung (Baden-Baden, Nomos, 2005); G Britz, *Freie Entfaltung durch Selbstdarstellung* (Tübingen, Mohr Siebeck, 2007).

[5] For a different view on this point, which instead opts for decoupling the value of privacy from its ability to support autonomy, see T Matzner, ch 18 in this volume.

rely on an oversimplified account of the autonomous 'self', conceived as an entity with a pre-existing, fixed, autonomous core, detached and independent of interpersonal relations and the socio-cultural environment.[6] This chapter aims to contribute to underpinning existing conceptions of privacy with an understanding of autonomy that is capable of making sense of the interplay between the self-relatedness and sociality of individuals.

To this end, I first elaborate on the nexus between privacy and autonomy and the importance of a robust theory of autonomy for privacy protection (section II). I then present exemplary cases of privacy violations in the digital environment that are considered to also result in autonomy harms and review existing theories of autonomy in search of explanations for these – widely perceived yet under-conceptualised – harms (sections III and IV). I conclude this overview by arguing that existing understandings of autonomy, however sophisticated and helpful, are nevertheless unable to account for the specificity of the challenges to autonomy posed by digital technologies.[7] A contextual approach to autonomy, inspired by Helen Nissenbaum's understanding of privacy,[8] I suggest, seems better suited to grasping the specificity of the current challenges to autonomy posed by digitalisation. I therefore outline the core of Nissenbaum's conception of privacy as contextual integrity (section V). In section VI, I draw a parallel between the issues that motivated the conceptualisation of privacy as contextual integrity and the current challenges to autonomy and outline the main features of the proposed contextual-integrity theory of autonomy. According to this approach, autonomy can best be conceptualised in terms of norms that distinguish between legitimate and illegitimate heteronomous influences in particular social contexts. What is special about the challenges that digitalisation and AI pose to autonomy is that they blur the previous relative separation between the respective contexts. As a result, heteronomous influences that would be considered inadmissible and a violation of autonomy under 'analogue' conditions become increasingly possible and normalised. The current ecosystem of online interaction, indeed, is designed in ways that make it opaque to individuals what roles, contexts, and relationships they interact in. In section VII, I test the empirical validity of this framework by examining examples of digital harms to privacy and autonomy. Finally, in section VIII, I discuss the implications of a contextual understanding of autonomy for privacy theory and law, highlighting limitations and open questions of the proposed approach.

[6] Cohen (n 1) 115–26; JE Cohen, 'What Privacy Is For' (2013) 126 *Harvard Law Review* 1904–33.

[7] In this chapter, I use terms such as 'digital technologies', 'information technologies', 'big data', 'AI', 'digitally mediated practices', etc in a broad meaning, to refer to a wide range of socio-technical systems typical of online interaction, ranging from profiling techniques in the broadest sense (from cookie-based profiling to inferring mental health status from tweets) to newsfeed algorithms and, depending on the context of use, generative AI systems, including large language models and image or video manipulation tools (which may be involved in the production of targeted advertising or disinformation material).

[8] H Nissenbaum, 'Protecting Privacy in an Information Age: The Problem of Privacy in Public' (1998) 17 *Law and Philosophy* 559–96; H Nissenbaum, *Privacy in Context: Technology, Policy, and the Integrity of Social Life* (Stanford, Stanford Law Books, 2010).

## II. The Nexus between Privacy and Autonomy

In privacy scholarship and jurisprudence, the connection between autonomy, on the one hand, and privacy and the associated family of rights, such as data protection and informational self-determination, on the other, is widely acknowledged.

According to Beate Rössler, privacy enables individuals to lead autonomous lives in all three 'dimensions' that she identifies as constitutive of privacy: spatial, informational and decisional.[9] Privacy protects autonomy, because autonomy depends on a person's control over others' access to herself, to her thoughts and decisions, and to information about her. In the case of informational privacy, this control is concretised as control over the way people portray and present themselves to others. By influencing the kind of information about themselves that is shared with others, people are able to regulate the social relationships in which they find themselves.[10] Ultimately, privacy enables individuals to ask themselves who they are and what kind of life they want to live. Being able to ask and answer these questions in a way that is not completely influenced by others is a core aspect of individual autonomy.[11]

This line of argument is also one of the most compelling explanations of the interests protected by the right to informational self-determination in German constitutional law (*Recht auf informationelle Selbstbestimmung*).[12] The right to informational self-determination, like the right to privacy, is an expression of the constitutionally protected general right of personality (*allgemeines Persönlichkeitsrecht*). The German Federal Constitutional Court, in its famous 1983 judgment in which it recognised for the first time the existence of a constitutionally protected right to informational self-determination, explicitly placed the protection of individuals' authority over themselves at the centre of the subject matter of protection:

> The value and dignity of the person, acting in free self-determination as a member of a free society, are at the centre of the Basic Law … this protection may gain even more significance in light of modern developments that pose new risks to one's personality … [B]ased on the notion of self-determination, the general right of personality confers upon the individual the authority to, in principle, decide themselves whether and to what extent to disclose aspects of their personal life.[13]

This core orientation has been further confirmed and elaborated in subsequent decisions and constitutional theory. Martin Eifert, on the basis of a consolidated jurisprudential interpretation, considers the general right of personality to be the 'internal' dimension of the more general right to the free development of personality (*Recht auf freie Entfaltung der Persönlichkeit*), which is flanked on the 'external' side by the general freedom of action (*allgemeine Handlungsfreiheit*). This 'internal' side of the right to free development of personality coincides with the possibility of autonomously defining

[9] Rössler (n 2) 137.
[10] ibid 209.
[11] ibid 138.
[12] For an extensive and in-depth elaboration on the meaning of the right to informational self-determination see Britz, ch 5 in this volume.
[13] BVerfGE 65, 1 [1983] – *Volkszählungsgesetz* para 144.

one's own personality.[14] As Gabriele Britz has insightfully shown, the right to informational self-determination protects the possibility for individuals to influence the image that others have of them. It increases the chances that a person will be perceived by others as she wishes to be perceived. This opportunity is significantly diminished when others have unregulated access to information about a person that is combined and merged to create a comprehensive, pre-defined and fixed personality profile.[15] Within the German constitutional understanding, the connection to autonomy is so strong that it has been suggested that '*informationelle Selbstbestimmung*' should be better translated as 'informational autonomy'.[16]

The aforementioned accounts of the relationship between privacy and autonomy emphasise the need for individuals to gain 'critical distance' from external influences, yet the subject of this right is not to be understood as an isolated, pre-formed, and self-sufficient individual. On the contrary, legal and philosophical interpretations emphasise that the process of defining one's personality is a process involving both self-reflection and sociality.[17] Indeed, the importance of privacy in creating and protecting places of retreat, zones of 'relative insulation'[18] or 'breathing room(s)'[19] that allow individuals not to isolate themselves from society but instead to engage in sociality in an autonomous way, is the core around which the most elaborated explanations of the nexus between privacy and autonomy converge. Moreover, the processes of self-formation and self-presentation to others are not to be understood as chronologically distinct processes, as if the subject first forms himself and then presents himself to others. Rather, the presentation of the self to others also has a constitutive character for one's personality: it is through this interaction and presentation to others that one's personality is formed and developed.[20] As Julie E Cohen effectively summarises: 'Subjectivity is a function of the interplay between emergent selfhood and social shaping; privacy, which inheres in the interstices of social shaping, is what permits that interplay to occur.'[21]

The right to informational self-determination also protects the individuals' ability to change their personality and the image of it that they wish to convey to others: the purpose of informational self-determination is not to preserve fixed images of the self, but to allow it to evolve over time without being fixed by others into previously fabricated profiles.[22]

[14] M Eifert, 'Das Allgemeine Persönlichkeitsrecht des Art. 2 Abs. 1 GG' (2015) 37 *Juristische Ausbildung* 1181. See also G Hornung and C Schnabel, 'Data Protection in Germany I: The Population Census Decision and the Right to Informational Self-determination' (2009) 25 *Computer Law & Security Review* 84–8.

[15] Britz (n 4) 71; G Britz, 'Verfassungsrechtlicher Schutz der freien Persönlichkeitsentfaltung' in C Bumke and A Röthel (eds), *Autonomie im Recht. Gegenwartsdebatten über einen rechtlichen Grundbegriff* (Tübingen, Mohr Siebeck, 2017) 361. The creation of a complete personality profile was classified by the German Federal Constitutional Court as a violation of human dignity, see BVerfGE 65, 1 paras 145, 167ff.

[16] Albers, ch 2 in this volume.

[17] M Eifert, '§ 18 Persönliche Freiheit' in M Herdegen, J Masing, R Poscher and F Gärditz (eds), *Handbuch des Verfassungsrechts* (München, C.H. Beck, 2021) para 49; Britz (n 4); B Rössler, *Autonomie. Ein Versuch über das gelungene Leben* (Berlin, Suhrkamp, 2023) 290–320.

[18] H Nissenbaum, 'Privacy as Contextual Integrity' (2004) 79 *Washington Law Review* 148, quoting JE Cohen, 'Examined Lives: Informational Privacy and the Subject as Object' (2000) 52 *Stanford Law Review* 1424.

[19] Cohen, 'What Privacy Is For' (n 6) 1906.

[20] Britz (n 4) 18.

[21] Cohen, 'What Privacy Is For' (n 6) 1911.

[22] Britz, 'Verfassungsrechtlicher Schutz der freien Persönlichkeitsentfaltung' (n 15) 361; Cohen, 'What Privacy Is For' (n 6) 1911.

In addition to the functional value of privacy for autonomy, some accounts of privacy acknowledge another facet of the relationship between privacy and autonomy. This facet emerges with particular clarity when privacy is conceptualised as control. Controlling access (to private spaces, to oneself, to information about oneself, etc) is a way of exercising autonomy.[23] Privacy is thus not only a precondition of autonomy but also a form of its exercise. In both cases, autonomy is placed higher than privacy in the hierarchy of values. Privacy is not only functional for autonomy, but it can also be limited by autonomous decisions of the individual, as the recognition of consent as a basis for processing personal data that could not otherwise be processed by several legal systems testifies.[24]

The foregoing illustrates that privacy law and theory fully recognise the importance of privacy in protecting personal autonomy. Privacy law and theory are therefore, explicitly or implicitly, based on conceptions of subjectivity and autonomy. But are these underlying conceptions of autonomy up to the task of providing a robust foundation for privacy protection?

Over a decade ago, Cohen lamented that US privacy law had become isolated from the evolving research on subjectivity in the social sciences and humanities, with detrimental consequences for privacy protection.[25] US privacy law, in her view, is based on static views of the self, according to which each subject possesses an autonomous core that emerges after all external influences have been removed. This understanding suggests that the subjects protected by privacy are pre-formed and need to be shielded from the outside in order to preserve their fully formed autonomous core. Understood in this way, privacy is something static, whereas for Cohen, successful privacy protection avoids individuals becoming fixed (and therefore predictable) through data processing and profiling activities.[26] To remedy this, for Cohen 'a robust theory of privacy requires an understanding of the processes by which selfhood comes into being and is negotiated through contexts and over time'.[27]

Whether US privacy law still suffers from this lack of connection to advances in autonomy research is not for me to judge.[28] As far as German constitutional law is concerned, as we have seen above, this shortcoming no longer seems to hold true, although the earlier German constitutional decisions on the right to informational self-determination have also been criticised for suggesting an oversimplified, undertheorised and ultimately counterproductive understanding of privacy and subjectivity.[29]

[23] Nissenbaum (n 18) 149.

[24] See for instance Regulation (EU) 2016/679 of the European Parliament and of the Council of 27 April 2016 on the protection of natural persons with regard to the processing of personal data and on the free movement of such data, and repealing Directive 95/46/EC (General Data Protection Regulation) [2016] OJ L119/1, art 6(I)(a) GDPR. However, the power of the individual to 'give up' privacy by autonomous decision does not equate a general abdication to the right to privacy. Rather it is a punctual restriction of it in specific situations.

[25] Cohen (n 1)107–26.

[26] Cohen, 'What Privacy Is For' (n 6) 1905–7.

[27] Cohen (n 1) 114.

[28] For these and related issues, the reader can refer to the chapters of this book dealing with US privacy law.

[29] R Poscher, 'The Right to Data Protection: A No-Right Thesis' in RA Miller (ed), *Privacy and Power a Transatlantic Dialogue in the Shadow of the NSA-Affair* (Cambridge, Cambridge University Press, 2017) 129–41; Albers (n 4) 174–8.

In what follows, I aim to show that, even in the best case – that is, when privacy law and privacy theory are based on the most elaborate conceptions of autonomy – the latter are unable to provide a reliable theory for capturing the harms to autonomy that result from particular uses of information technologies. This is not to say that autonomy theory is not heuristically helpful. On the contrary, as I will show below, autonomy theories have moved far away from conceptions of the 'isolated' self and have long recognised the constitutive role of interactions with others and the environment. However, they still need to be refined in crucial ways in order to account for the contextual variability of autonomy understandings and the impact of digital practices on autonomy.

## III. Autonomy Challenged: Privacy Breaches Undermining Autonomy in the Digital Environment[30]

Autonomy has always been a contested concept. The idea that human beings are capable of living and acting for reasons that they can recognise as 'their own'[31] is not only contradicted by our everyday experience but has also been philosophically challenged. Metaphysical scepticism about free will,[32] the inescapability of influences of socialisation and relationships of subjugation,[33] and the entanglement of freedom and obligation[34] have been at the centre of long-running controversies about autonomy.

The challenges to autonomy have become even more acute since digital technologies entered everyday life. Phenomena such as online manipulation, hypernudging, personalised advertising, political microtargeting, filter bubbles, and fake news seem to call autonomy into question in particular ways. Big data analytics, for example, can be used to identify the vulnerabilities of particularly fragile groups and exploit them

[30] In the following, because of the thematic focus on privacy, I rely only on examples in which potential autonomy harms result from privacy violations. A further question would be whether autonomy violations, both on- and offline, can also result from actions that do not constitute privacy violations. Examples of such actions and practices online would be non-personalised dark patterns or disinformation campaigns. Preliminarily, I consider such practices to threaten autonomy without constituting a privacy problem, and I think that their specific autonomy harms could be explained by a contextual theory of autonomy such as the one I propose. However, a discussion of these case studies and the theoretical issues they raise is beyond the scope of this chapter.

[31] M Betzler, 'Einleitung: Begriff, Konzeptionen and Kontexte der Autonomie' in M Betzler (ed), *Autonomie der Person*, Map – Mentis Anthologien Philosophie (Münster, Mentis, 2013) 11; Rössler (n 17) 29.

[32] B Libet, 'Do We Have Free Will?' (1999) 6 *Journal of Consciousness Studies* 47–57; B Stockdale, 'The Libet Paradigm and a Dilemma for Epiphenomenalism' (2022) 37 *Philosophical Psychology* 2244–61.

[33] C Mackenzie and N Stoljar, 'Introduction: Autonomy Refigured' in C Mackenzie and N Stoljar (eds), *Relational Autonomy* (New York, Oxford University Press, 2000) 3–31.

[34] J Rebentisch and D Setton, *Willkür,* Freiheit und Gesetz II (Berlin, August-Verlag, 2011); T Khurana and C Menke (eds), *Paradoxien der Autonomie. Freiheit und Gesetz I* (Berlin, August Verlag, 2019); D Setton, *Autonomie und Willkür. Kant und die Zweideutigkeit der Freiheit*, Deutsche Zeitschrift für Philosophie 42 (Berlin, De Gruyter, 2021).

for manipulative purposes. A paradigmatic example is Facebook's ability to determine when teenagers are feeling particularly insecure in order to pass this information on to companies for targeted advertising.[35] These techniques not only selectively influence the behaviour of Facebook users but can also affect the constitution of a 'self' in a very sensitive phase of life.[36]

Big data and AI can have a negative impact not only on the 'private' side of autonomy but also on its political side. A series of reports between 2015 and 2018 revealed that the political consulting firm Cambridge Analytica used big data analytics on 87 million Facebook users to build psychographic profiles. Based on these, users were then targeted with tailored advertising aimed at influencing their political opinions in the run-up to elections. In this and similar cases, the ability to make autonomous choices is not just selectively compromised. Rather, such practices systematically 'reduce people's rational control over the information they generate or receive'.[37]

These two examples can be seen as representative of a ubiquitous 'culture of manipulation in the online environment',[38] which arguably is leading people to behave more and more like 'simple stimulus-response machines': completely predictable and controllable beings – the exact opposite of autonomous individuals.[39] There seems to be a widespread concern, therefore, that information technologies can pose fundamental challenges to human autonomy. But what are the specifics of these challenges, and how do they differ from traditional ones? As I will argue in the next section, notwithstanding their ability to provide important insights, existing theories of autonomy are not able to answer these questions.

## IV. Philosophical Conceptions of Autonomy and their Limitations in Face of Information Technologies

Autonomy is a key concept in practical philosophy and, at least since the modern era, has been one of its guiding principles. Questions about the value and conditions of human autonomy have been central to debates in moral philosophy, applied ethics, political philosophy, and the philosophy of law. Jean-Jacques Rousseau's and Immanuel Kant's view that autonomy consists in self-legislation still provides the common core

[35] D Davidson, 'Facebook Targets "Insecure" Kids' (*The Australian*, 01.05.2017) www.theaustralian.com.au/business/media/digital/facebook-targets-insecure-young-people-to-sell-ads/news-story/a89949ad016eee7d7a61c3c30c909fa6.

[36] S Milano, M Taddeo and L Floridi, 'Recommender Systems and Their Ethical Challenges' (2020) 35 *AI & Society* 957–67.

[37] M Ienca and E Vayena, 'Cambridge Analytica and Online Manipulation' (*Scientific American*, 30.03.2018) www.scientificamerican.com/blog/observations/cambridge-analytica-and-online-manipulation/.

[38] EDPS, 'EDPS Opinion on online manipulation and personal data' (European Data Protection Supervisor, 19.03.2018) www.edps.europa.eu/sites/default/files/publication/18-03-19_online_manipulation_en.pdf 9.

[39] B Frischmann and E Selinger, *Re-Engineering Humanity* (Cambridge, Cambridge University Press, 2018) 67.

of most theories of autonomy.[40] While Rousseau's and Kant's conceptions of autonomy were restricted to the political and moral spheres, respectively, current debates around autonomy share what has been termed a neo-Humean approach: namely, the idea that autonomy is primarily concerned with the relationship a person maintains with her desires and attitudes that are relevant to the way she wants to live.[41]

Against this background, a kaleidoscope of theories of autonomy has developed. Current approaches can be broadly systematised into two main strands: internalist and externalist theories. The former are often referred to as procedural theories, while the latter tend to have a more or less strong substantive component.

## A. Hierarchical Autonomy

Internalist theories of autonomy focus on the processes of will formation and decision-making. They have a particular affinity with Kant's view that humans are autonomous only if the norms that direct their actions are not guided by external empirical influences or purposive rational considerations. Internalist accounts of autonomy have two central features: they are content-neutral and individual-centred. They are content-neutral because they are indifferent to the content of the decisions that subjects make, focusing instead on procedural aspects. They are individual-centred because they concentrate on the individual's internal processes of will formation and decision-making that lead to a particular action.

In contemporary philosophy, Harry Frankfurt's 'hierarchical' conception is probably the most influential instance of procedural appraisals of autonomy.[42] Parallel to Frankfurt, Gerald Dworkin developed a similar, hierarchical-reflexive theory of autonomy.[43] Key to both views is the question of how subjects relate 'to themselves' and to their own desires. In Frankfurt's model, people are autonomous when they act on the basis of desires that are 'their own'. Own desires are those with which subjects can identify because they have a 'second-level' desire (also called a second-order 'volition' by Frankfurt) for the (first-level) desire to become effective. Similarly, Dworkin distinguishes between notions such as wish and desire on the one hand and notions such as intention, will, decision, and choice on the other. The critical factor for autonomy is the agent's attitude towards the wishes and desires that motivate his behaviour. Only when the agent is able to critically reflect on and subsequently identify with the first-order motivations that guide his actions is he autonomous.[44]

[40] I Kant, *Grounding for the Metaphysics of Morals* (Cambridge, Hackett, 1993) [first published 1785]; JJ Rousseau, *The Social Contract* (London, Wordsworth, 2013) [first published 1762].

[41] M Oshana, *Personal Autonomy in Society* (London, Routledge, 2016) vii–xi.

[42] HG Frankfurt, 'Freedom of the Will and the Concept of a Person' (1971) 68 *The Journal of Philosophy* 5; HG Frankfurt, *The Importance of What We Care About: Philosophical Essays* (New York, Cambridge University Press, 1988).

[43] G Dworkin, *The Theory and Practice of Autonomy*, Cambridge Studies in Philosophy (Cambridge, Cambridge University Press, 1988).

[44] G Dworkin, 'Acting Freely' (1970) 4 *Noûs* 367–83; G Dworkin, 'The Concept of Autonomy' (1981) 12/13 *Grazer Philosophische Studien* 203–13.

This condition for autonomy is also referred to in the literature as the 'authenticity' requirement.[45]

This focus on the 'self' and internal decision-making processes has, however, exposed these theories to criticism for not taking sufficient account of external influences that may affect the individual's will formation and decision-making. So-called 'historical' approaches to autonomy, such as that of John Christman, have attempted to incorporate these considerations into procedural accounts. They regard people as autonomous if they are able to take a stance on external influences and, if necessary, reject the desires they cause.[46] Christmas's account shifts the focus to the *process of forming a desire* that becomes the basis for an action or decision. The key requirement for autonomy is then the possibility for the subject to take a stance on this process of desire formation: if the person having the desire was able to resist the formation of the desire and she did not, then the person is autonomous with respect to the given desire. Further specifications of this model of autonomy require that the act of self-reflection necessary for the apprehension and non-rejection of the desire be carried out under conditions of minimal rationality and without self-deception.[47]

At first sight, these three internalist accounts of autonomy offer a way of addressing some of the challenges of digitalisation outlined above. For instance, taking the example of personalised advertising targeted at vulnerable teenagers, we could say that the targeted teenagers are autonomous if, when presented with the advertised products, they are able to resist the desire to click the 'buy' button and act in accordance with their 'volition' (or second-order desire) not to buy the product. In contrast, they are not autonomous if they give in to the impulse (or first-order desire) to buy the advertised product despite their second-order desire not to do so.

The fact that advertising is personalised and exploits individual vulnerabilities is not a crucial problem for interpretations based on strictly internalist and procedural accounts such as those of Frankfurt and Dworkin. These theories offer an explanation of why, in certain circumstances, some decisions and actions can be considered autonomous and others cannot. From the perspective of hierarchical theories of autonomy, phenomena such as personalised advertising can be seen as factors that make autonomous choices more difficult, but their line of explanation remains focused on the deciding and acting subject and does not seek to explain why certain phenomena or practices hinder autonomy. From this perspective, one might say that there are easier and more difficult choices to make autonomously, but in either case it is possible to align one's desires with one's second-order volitions and act autonomously. Situations in which individuals are systematically impaired in their ability to decide and act autonomously are explained in terms of a lack of rationality and the ability to critically reflect on one's own will on the side of the agent, not by focusing on the elements of the situation itself that constitute a problem for autonomy. The unsympathetic portrayal of a 'wanton', ie, an agent lacking the capacity to form second-order volitions, exemplified by Frankfurt in the example of a drug addict who is no longer capable of forming

[45] Betzler (n 31) 14.
[46] J Christman, 'Autonomy and Personal History' (1991) 21 *Canadian Journal of Philosophy* 1–24.
[47] ibid 10–11, 18.

second-order desires – and who, according to Frankfurt, is therefore not to be regarded as a 'person' – is the extreme, but logical, conclusion of this line of discourse.

Moreover, as we have seen above, these theories have been criticised for their inability to account for cases in which the second-order volitions that provide the benchmark for autonomous choices are themselves shaped by a manipulative environment.

Christman's historical account was intended to provide explanations for just such situations. He discusses the example of a person who has joined a religious sect and consequently acts in a way that, according to her own desires and views before joining the sect, she would have judged to be non-autonomous. Christman's question is whether her decisions and actions after joining the group are autonomous simply because they are in accordance with her 'new' second-order desires. According to the requirements for autonomy introduced by Christman and presented above, the answer to the autonomy question depends on the attitude the friend actually took to her second-order desires when they arose (did she resist them?) – or would take if she had the chance to reflect on them under conditions of minimal rationality and without self-deception.

In our microtargeting example, we have a similar situation where teenagers who acquiesce to the advertising prompt to buy a product also have a second-order desire to do so (eg, because they really want to keep up with the latest fashion trends). In Christman's terms, if they consented to the desire to be in line with the latest fashion trends in a (at least minimally) rational and non-deceptive way (or hypothetically would have done so if given the chance), then they are autonomous with respect to the desire and act of buying the advertised product. Thus, we could argue that some adolescents exposed to microtargeted advertising perform their act of purchase autonomously, and others do not, depending on how they judge, or would judge, their desires under rational and non-deceptive conditions.

Again, however, the focus of Christman's argument is on the characteristics of decisions and actions and the internal processes that led to them, rather than on the characteristics of external practices or phenomena that may interfere with autonomy. These enter the discussion as complicating factors that help to refine the criteria that make a decision or act autonomous, but not as something to be explained and investigated in itself. Christman's aim is to build a robust 'test for autonomy'[48] consisting of criteria of minimal rationality and self-awareness. His discussion of various examples allows for binary results of this test: either a choice, decision, or act is autonomous, or it is not.[49] We can, of course, use the test to assess individual choices made by teenagers targeted by personalised advertising. If the result were negative in all cases, then Christman's account would allow us to claim that personalised advertising undermines some conditions of autonomy (eg, self-awareness), and we would then be building an account of why personalised advertising is problematic for autonomy because of its destructive effects on self-awareness. But apart from such very drastic results, Christman's autonomy test would leave us with a set of pass-fail results, the differences in which would be explained by differences in individual decision-making processes.

[48] ibid 18.
[49] ibid 13–18.

These judgements would then be judgements about internal processes of will formation, not about systemic features of the practices being analysed.

## B. Autonomy and Objectivity

Attempts to overcome these and other difficulties posed by internalist-procedural accounts of autonomy have been made by scholars who introduce into the conditions of autonomy elements external to the subjects themselves. As part of these externalist theories, Susan Wolf's account of autonomy rests on the observation that persons with paranoid tendencies, for example, may be perfectly 'consistent' in their will on internalist accounts such as Frankfurt's – and yet hardly appear to be autonomous in any meaningful sense:

> Such people will have problems with the world, no doubt, but not with themselves. They may act wholeheartedly, exercising the will they want to have. But far from being free (or from having a free will), they seem to me to be examples of people who are trapped, constrained, shackled.[50]

Analogous considerations hold for individuals whose personalities have been shaped by an environment that systematically perverts notions of right and wrong and encourages morally wrong behaviour. Such individuals, Wolf argues, are usually not held to bear full responsibility for their actions, such as slave owners in the 1850s and Nazis in the 1930s. In order to overcome these short-circuits of purely procedural accounts, Wolf argues, we need to introduce requirements of objectivity. Central to autonomy is 'connectedness' with the world, ie, the ability to see and understand the world 'as it is', as well as the ability to distinguish right from wrong.[51]

At first glance, this enriched account seems to provide an explanation of the problems raised by manipulative digital practices. If we now refer to Cambridge Analytica's political microtargeting, for example, we could say that these practices interfere with people's ability to connect with the world 'as it is', by influencing them to act in ways they would not have chosen if they had access to 'objective' information.

On closer inspection, however, such considerations do not align with the core of Wolf's conception. Wolf's aim is to add a condition of objectivity to Frankfurt's internalist account of autonomy. For a person to be able to act autonomously, Wolf argues, it is not enough that her internal will-forming and decision-making processes are coherent. Rather, this internal coherence must correspond to 'objective' external facts. Wolf's point is to identify the necessary *minimal* conditions for autonomy, and unless the effects of practices such as political microtargeting, filter bubbles, and disinformation are so pervasive as to destroy these very capacities, the necessary minimal conditions for individual autonomy are still met. Despite disinformation and

[50] S Wolf, 'The True, the Good, and the Lovable: Frankfurt's Avoidance of Objectivity' in S Buss and L Overton (eds), *Contours of Agency. Essays on Themes from Harry Frankfurt* (Cambridge, MIT Press, 2002) 240.

[51] S Wolf, 'Sanity and the Metaphysics of Responsibility' in F Schoeman (ed), *Responsibility, Character, and the Emotions: New Essays in Moral Psychology* (Cambridge, Cambridge University Press, 1988).

microtargeting, people still have the ability to connect with the world by interacting with people offline, reading newspapers, etc. Only all-encompassing filter bubbles or disinformation in a world essentially shaped by digitality could amount to an impairment of individual autonomy, and even then in a way that is not significantly different from the mechanisms of propaganda, indoctrination, and manipulative education in totalitarian or structurally unjust societies. In conclusion, it seems to me that the difficulties of Wolf's externalist account in providing an explanation of autonomy harmed by information technologies and AI lie once again in the fact that, despite its insistence on 'external' factors, it retains a focus on the capacities of individuals as minimal necessary conditions for autonomy.

## C. Personal Autonomy

While the line of debate outlined above was unfolding, Joseph Raz's 'perfectionist' theory introduced a critical shift in autonomy scholarship by moving the focus from autonomy as a capability to autonomy as a characteristic of a person's whole life. Raz calls this 'personal' autonomy to distinguish it from the autonomy of individual choices or the ability to make them. Personal autonomy encompasses the actual ability to shape one's own life, ie, to make free choices about the goals and relationships people want to pursue. According to this conception, autonomy is primarily a quality of life, not a particular capacity of a person, and is therefore also determined by structural factors outside the individual's personality.[52]

Autonomy in this sense requires three conditions: appropriate mental capacities, the existence of an adequate, morally acceptable ('good') range of options from which to choose, and independence. While the first condition roughly corresponds to the requirements of internalist conceptions of autonomy, the other two add to them. The second requirement, namely the existence of a range of good options, is indeed an external factor that depends on an institutional and cultural environment that is autonomy-supportive. Even in such an environment, however, the possibility of choice does not extend to *all* aspects of life. The parent-child relationship is one that typically excludes choice about who enters it and whether to enter it at all, and yet, in Raz's view, is perfectly compatible with an autonomous life.[53] Finally, the third condition, independence, at first sight recalls purely internalist conceptions of autonomy. But in explaining why independence is compromised by coercion and manipulation, Raz introduces a relational element: coercion and manipulative practices distort proper relationships between persons because they subordinate the will of one person to that of another.[54]

By including structural and relational elements, Raz's concept brings us closer to understanding the problem of targeted advertising and political microtargeting. It allows us to shift the focus to structural conditions and ask to what extent such practices contribute to shaping (part of) our environment in ways that are not conducive

[52] J Raz, *The Morality of Freedom* (Oxford, Clarendon Press, 2009) [first published 1986] 369–72.
[53] ibid 391–94.
[54] ibid 378.

to autonomy. We can interpret personalised advertising and political microtargeting as manipulative practices and see the problem in the distortion of a relationship in which the will of one person (the targeted teenager or Facebook user) is subordinated to that of others. This assessment, I would argue, points in the right direction, but it remains fuzzy. Raz's account, indeed, fails to provide a basis to explain what relationship exactly is distorted when the user's will is manipulated by microtargeting and whether some distortions of the will's relationship are specific to digital technologies. On a more general level, Raz's theory also lacks an explanation of why some areas of life can be excluded from the exercise of free choice (such as which parents to have) without compromising autonomy.

## D. Global Autonomy

Like Wolf and Raz, Marina Oshana also seeks to overcome the shortcomings of purely internalist theories of autonomy.[55] Like Wolf, Oshana maintains that purely psychological accounts are inadequate to capture the essence of human autonomy and that external, empirical, and 'objective' aspects contribute significantly to making a person autonomous.[56] Like Raz, Oshana emphasises that autonomy extends beyond internal psychological states that lead to certain decisions, however extended in time these states may be. Autonomy, she argues, is a 'status' in which a person finds herself and a socio-relational phenomenon.[57] But she goes beyond both Wolf's and Raz's accounts in that she makes external factors constitutive elements of autonomy, not just conditions that may facilitate or sustain a person's autonomy:

> Autonomy is a condition of persons constituted in large part by the social relations people find themselves in and by the absence of other social relations. Autonomy is not a phenomenon merely enhanced or lessened by the contingencies of a person's social situation; social relations do not just causally facilitate or impair the exercise of autonomy. Rather, appropriate social relations form an inherent part of what it means to be self-directed.[58]

In a sense, paradoxically, personal autonomy in Oshana's account is partly *heteronomous* because it is also constituted by conditions that are external and beyond the control of the autonomous person.[59] These external aspects contribute both causally and substantively to autonomy. They have a causal influence on the abilities, including epistemic competence, rationality, and self-respect, that constitute a person's capacity for autonomy. Some more refined internalist accounts, such as Christmas's, would partly agree with this. But for Oshana, external elements also *substantially* determine autonomy. In addition to a set of (partly heteronomously induced) capabilities, to be

[55] M Oshana, 'Personal Autonomy and Society' (1998) 29 *Journal of Social Philosophy* 81–102; M Oshana, *Personal Autonomy in Society* (London, Routledge, 2016). Relational theories of autonomy have also been advanced by Catriona Mackenzie, Natalie Stoljar and Beate Rössler: C Mackenzie and N Stoljar (ed), *Relational Autonomy: Feminist Perspectives on Autonomy, Agency, and the Social Self* (New York, Oxford University Press, 2000); Rössler (n 17).

[56] Oshana, '*Personal Autonomy in Society*' (n 55) 50.

[57] ibid 81.

[58] ibid 49.

[59] ibid 96.

autonomous a person must also have access to a set of relevant options, and these must be options of a particular kind, namely those that enable a person's self-government. Finally, the conditions for personal autonomy include socio-relational characteristics of material independence. These include security; freedom from fear of reprisal for making choices different from the ones favoured by those who have authority over one; not being required to provide for the needs of others to an unreasonable extent; financial self-sufficiency; and not being subject to misinformation about what one is capable of doing.[60] When all these aspects combine, a person finds herself in a condition of what Oshana calls 'global' autonomy, ie, a status and quality of life that is distinct from mere 'local' autonomy, understood as the autonomy of desires, preferences, and decisions.

Interestingly, and in clear contrast to internalist approaches to autonomy, authenticity is not a condition for autonomy in Oshana's account. A person can be autonomous even if her life and choices are not in line with her deepest desires and beliefs. Far more important than authenticity, for Oshana, is what she calls 'contrafactual power', the ability to take control of one's life, or significant parts of it, when others attempt to deprive one of that control.[61] A would-be surrendered woman who desires nothing more than to devote her life to obeying her husband and providing for the needs of her family but who is unable to realise this desire because of external impediments is autonomous in the Oshana account as long as the above requirements are met.[62] Autonomy, to sum up with Oshana's words, 'is not a matter of being free to act as one pleases, but a matter of living in a particular way'.[63]

Oshana's shift to socio-relational aspects is, in my view, crucial to achieving a more comprehensive and adequate account of autonomy. I will return to this below when I suggest an account of autonomy as contextual integrity. In my view, however, Oshana's account is too 'global' to explain the challenges to autonomy posed by digitalisation and AI. Take our initial example of Facebook's microtargeting of vulnerable teenagers. If we assume that, prior to microtargeting, the targeted teens were able to enjoy global autonomy, including having the capacities for it, having access to a range of valuable opportunities to manage their lives in a self-governing way, and also enjoying the socio-relational conditions of a safe life, etc, then Facebook's microtargeting does not really change these conditions. Unless Facebook's personalised advertising is so pervasive as to undermine teenagers' capacities for autonomy, it does not really affect users' autonomy in Oshana's sense: they still have options for self-governance, they still have the counterfactual power to act differently, and their empirical socio-relational conditions are not significantly altered, at least not at the macro level. Finally, like Raz, Oshana concedes that there are limitations to self-government that do not amount to impediments to autonomy but fails to provide an explanation why it is so.[64]

[60] ibid 76–90.
[61] ibid 68–71, 75–6.
[62] ibid 68.
[63] ibid 73.
[64] ibid fn 36.

## V. Privacy as Contextual Integrity as Inspiration for Refining Autonomy Theory

Privacy theory, in comparison with autonomy theory, has acknowledged the urgency of the challenges posed by information technologies for a longer time. This is not surprising, since privacy is more directly affected by technologies whose core lies in the exchange of information. The leap to appreciate the impact of digitisation on autonomy is greater: in order to affect autonomy, digital technologies must not only collect and process personal information but also additionally be able to reach individuals and affect their will or behaviour. Nevertheless, autonomy theory can benefit from some of the most recent debates on privacy, and in particular from what I consider to be one of the most significant theories for understanding privacy in the digital age: Helen Nissenbaum's privacy as contextual integrity framework.

My suggestion of drawing on contextual integrity to better understand autonomy does not assume that all digitally mediated inferences about individuals' autonomy are based on privacy violations. There may well be autonomy harms in the digital environment that do not depend on previous privacy violations. Dark patterns and disinformation campaigns are potential examples of online practices that can interfere with the autonomy of individuals without the mediation of privacy violations. Contextual integrity, I think, can also provide an explanation for these autonomy harms, but to elaborate on them is beyond the scope of this chapter. What matters for my argument is that contextual integrity provides useful insights not only, and not primarily, because many autonomy harms are mediated by privacy violations. Much more important is the fact that privacy and privacy research present structural analogies to the issues and challenges facing autonomy and autonomy theory in general and as a result of technological change.

In this section, I therefore provide a brief summary of the contextual integrity framework as developed by Nissenbaum, starting with the core problems and issues in traditional privacy theories that have been brought to light by the emergence of information technologies. These challenges, I argue, are structurally similar to those faced by autonomy theory today, and thus an appraisal along the lines of the contextual integrity framework can provide a path to an adequate conceptualisation of autonomy in the digital age.

In two articles written in the late 1990s, Nissenbaum diagnoses a discrepancy between privacy theories and social practices related to privacy.[65] Practices such as the processing for profiling purposes of personal information that individuals had previously willingly shared for other purposes were not considered to violate privacy norms under the legal and philosophical understandings of privacy that prevailed in the US at the time. However, the same practices were perceived as unacceptable by broad sectors of society. As a result, the dominant legal and philosophical norms were out of

[65] H Nissenbaum, 'Toward an Approach to Privacy in Public: Challenges of Information Technology' (1997) 7 *Ethics & Behavior* 207–19; Nissenbaum, 'Protecting Privacy in an Information Age' (n 8) 199.

step with society's acutely perceived need for privacy protection.[66] This mismatch has been brought about by technological transformation, which has made practices such as data analytics and profiling much faster and cheaper. Similarly, I argue, technological change is affecting human autonomy in ways that are still difficult to conceptualise yet acutely felt, as evidenced by widespread concern about practices such as targeted advertising and political microtargeting.

Nissenbaum attributes the conceptual shortcomings of the then-dominant theories of privacy to two common problematic assumptions. The first problematic assumption posits a rigid separation between the private, personal, and intimate sphere and the public realm and asserts that privacy protection does not apply to information that has left the intimate and personal sphere and is already available in the public realm. The second assumption is that an aggregation of information is not a breach of privacy if its parts, taken in isolation, do not violate privacy.[67]

In order to realign philosophical and legal conceptions of privacy with social practice, Nissenbaum rejects these assumptions and instead proposes a conceptualisation of privacy based on the following three core ideas. First, instead of thinking in terms of a dichotomy between the private and the public, we should acknowledge the existence of multiple contexts. Second, and accordingly, information is never either public or private in absolute terms: information that is considered 'public' in one context may be 'private' in another. As a consequence, privacy deserves protection also when the relevant information has already been shared and is available in what is usually termed the 'public' domain. Finally, individual 'harmless' information, when aggregated, can lead to 'rich portraits of people' and thus lead to privacy violations:[68] privacy norms should therefore also protect information that is neither private nor sensitive.[69] Following her initial reflections on the shortcomings of earlier dominant theories of privacy and her suggestions for overcoming their problematic assumptions, Nissenbaum developed a fully-fledged conception of privacy that she labelled 'privacy as contextual integrity'.[70] Within this theory, the idea that we need to move beyond the private/public dichotomy and recognise the existence of a panoply of realms is further developed in the notion of specific contexts of social interaction. Examples of these contexts are the medical, educational, familial, professional, religious, and commercial spheres. Social contexts are 'structured social spheres' within which we interact not only as human beings but also in specific roles, ie, as patients or doctors, teachers or students, parents or children, and so on.[71] Each context is governed by norms that define context-appropriate information flows. According to this understanding, a right to privacy is neither a right to secrecy or seclusion nor a right to control, but a right to *context-appropriate flows*.[72]

[66] Nissenbaum, 'Toward an Approach to Privacy in Public' (n 65) 212.
[67] ibid 212–17.
[68] ibid 217.
[69] Nissenbaum, 'Protecting Privacy in an Information Age' (n 8) 560.
[70] See in particular Nissenbaum, *Privacy in Context* (n 8); Nissenbaum (n 18).
[71] Nissenbaum, *Privacy in Context* (n 8) 130.
[72] ibid 127. Nissenbaum is surely not alone in acknowledging that privacy is not just an individual value. Many of the contributors to this volume have long argued for moving beyond a strictly individualistic understanding of privacy. In addition to drawing the reader's attention to their contributions to this volume, I will limit myself to referring to the pioneering work of PM Regan, *Legislating Privacy* (London, The University of North Carolina Press, 1995) and to the collected volume by B Rössler and D Mokrosinska (eds), *Social Dimensions of Privacy: Interdisciplinary Perspectives* (Cambridge, Cambridge University Press, 2015).

Contextual norms, in turn, are defined by four parameters: the contexts themselves, the actors involved, the attributes or types of information, and, finally, the principles of transmission. For example, in the medical context, actors are defined by their roles as doctors, patients, nurses, and other medical personnel. In the educational context, actors are defined as teachers and students, and in the friendship context, they are defined as friends. The kind of information that can be legitimately exchanged (attributes) is different in each context: between patients and health professionals, detailed information about physical conditions can be shared without violating privacy, but this is not the case in an educational context. Among friends, in turn, there are virtually no limits to the kind of information that can be legitimately exchanged. Finally, transmission principles define the way in which information flows legitimately. In the healthcare context, asymmetry is the norm: patients' personal information flows from patients to healthcare professionals, but not the other way around. Necessity (for treatment) is another transmission principle that regulates the flow of information in the medical sector: doctors and nurses are entitled to ask for any information necessary for the treatment of the patient. Friendship, on the other hand, is characterised by reciprocity and voluntariness: information is expected to flow equally in both directions and on a voluntary basis.

As these examples show, sources of contextual norms are not always explicit, only relatively stable, and often partial and incomplete. Only in some areas are they codified in legal texts. They can derive from sources as diverse as tradition, law, morality, conventions, etiquette, etc.[73] By virtue of the social entrenchment of contextual norms, they protect not only individuals but ultimately and decisively the very 'fabric of social life'.[74] If they were systematically violated, not only would individuals be deprived of their privacy, but social relationships would be devoid of meaning, and social interaction as we know it would be impossible.

## VI. Autonomy as Contextual Integrity?

Can the framework of contextual integrity provide a suitable background for conceptualising autonomy and understanding the challenges to it posed by digital technologies?

To begin with, we can observe a structural similarity between the problems raised by information technologies for theories of privacy and for conceptualisations of autonomy. First, we can note a disruptive effect on the alignment between autonomy norms and practices similar to that which has occurred on privacy due to the impact of information technologies. Digital technologies make it possible to influence individuals with much less effort than before: it is easier and cheaper to target, approach, and attempt to influence individuals, even in real time and regardless of the physical distance between actors. Coupled with potentially privacy-invasive techniques such as profiling, such influence can also be easily personalised. A second structural analogy concerns the separation of spheres: like earlier dominant understandings of privacy

[73] Nissenbaum (n 18) 137, 157.
[74] Nissenbaum, *Privacy in Context* (n 8) 3.

based on a dichotomy between private and public realms, earlier theories of autonomy postulate a distinction between an internal (to the individual) and an external sphere and consider only the former to be relevant to autonomy. This is the common substrate of internalist theories of autonomy, of the 'inner citadel' paradigm.[75] As we have seen above, externalist theories of autonomy have already challenged this assumption, arguing convincingly that external factors, such as the interpersonal relationships and the social, cultural, and political contexts in which individuals are always immersed, should also be normed and protected if autonomy is to be preserved. Finally, in parallel with Nissenbaum's suggestion that the aggregate processing of information items that are singularly non-private and non-sensitive can lead to privacy harms, authors such as Raz and Oshana have pointed to the necessity of thinking about autonomy not exclusively in 'local' terms, but rather as a quality of life and a 'global' phenomenon.

As mentioned above, I find these intuitions heuristically fruitful, but I think they need to be specified in order to provide a better account of what autonomy is, to get a better grip on everyday experiences, and to better understand the challenges of digital technologies and AI. In what follows, I suggest a theoretical appraisal inspired by the contextual integrity framework, which I believe is better able to achieve these goals.

The existence of distinctive social contexts has long been theorised in various disciplines, most notably by philosophers and sociologists such as Max Weber, Erving Goffman, Niklas Luhmann, Pierre Bourdieu and Michael Walzer.[76] Nissenbaum's theory is a specification of the general assumption that human life unfolds in these separate spheres of interaction and is therefore not specific to conceptualisations of privacy. I propose to consider autonomy in terms of these conceptualisations of social interaction within spheres or contexts and to see the description of social contexts given by Nissenbaum and outlined above as a good approximation for theorising autonomy as well. The examples given above of health care, education, work, family, friendship, etc, I would argue, are valid examples of social contexts in which human beings assume different roles that shape not only expectations and practices about privacy but also about autonomy. The basic idea of a conceptualisation of autonomy as contextual integrity would therefore be that different norms of autonomy apply in different social contexts. When a patient and a doctor interact, some actions are seen as perfectly acceptable that would be a clear violation of autonomy if the two actors were interacting as, say, teacher and student. A doctor can legitimately persuade a patient to take certain medicines or to follow certain dietary rules, whereas the same influence (or attempts at influence) by a teacher on a pupil would be regarded as a clear violation of the pupil's autonomy.

In general terms, different contextual autonomy norms apply in different social contexts, and these norms determine, in each specific context, which heteronomous

[75] Oshana, *Personal Autonomy in Society* (n 55) 21–47; JP Christman (ed), *The Inner Citadel: Essays on Individual Autonomy* (New York, Oxford University Press, 1989).

[76] M Weber, 'The Meaning of "Ethical Neutrality" in Sociology and Economics' in M Weber, *Methodology of Social Sciences* (New York, Routledge, 2011) [first published 1917] 1–48; E Goffman, *The Presentation of Self in Everyday Life* (New York, Anchor, 1959); N Luhmann, *Grundrechte als Institution: ein Beitrag zur politischen Soziologie*, Schriften zum öffentlichen Recht 24 (Berlin, Duncker & Humblot, 1986); P Bourdieu, *La distinction. Critique sociale du jugement* (Paris, Les éditions de minuit, 1979); M Walzer, *Spheres of Justice* (New York, Basic Books, 1983); Nissenbaum, *Privacy in Context* (n 8) 129–32.

influences on one's preferences, decisions and actions are considered legitimate and which are not, and therefore amount to an autonomy violation. In the case of privacy, the purpose of contextual norms is not so much to keep individuals secluded and information secret but to enable appropriate information flows. Similarly, in the case of autonomy, the purpose of contextual norms is not to keep individuals completely autarchic or independent of each other but to allow intersubjective interaction involving *appropriate influences* between subjects. Heteronomous influences, in other words, are not in absolute opposition to autonomy. They are a fundamental part of autonomous lives and crucial to the development of capacities for autonomy. Think of the importance of parents educating their children to take a critical distance from their immediate desires, for example, to eat a whole box of sweets at once. Such interference with the children's will is not seen as a diminution of their autonomy, because it is part of what we understand as appropriate family relationships for parents to monitor and intervene in children's actions to some extent. But even in the family context, not all influences are allowed. In Central European societies, for example, most people would consider it a violation of children's autonomy for parents to insist on directly choosing or vetoing their children's choice of playmates and, later, partners. Seen in this way, it becomes possible to understand why, as Raz and Oshana acknowledge, some non-free choices about very important aspects of life do not amount to a diminution of autonomy. This is because the contextual norms of that context (in Raz's example, the family) frame certain heteronomous influences as legitimate (such as deciding which children and which parents to have).

In line with these considerations, I posit that contextual norms of autonomy, like those of privacy, are defined by four parameters: contexts, actors, attributes, and principles of influence (in place of transmission). Contexts provide the setting, and actors indicate the roles enacted by the interacting persons. Attributes define what, in a given context, can be the subject of legitimate influence on the will or actions of others. Finally, influence principles regulate how and on what basis legitimate influences can take place. Whereas attributes are substantive norms, influence principles are procedural. An example of the former is the idea introduced above that a doctor can legitimately persuade a patient to follow certain dietary rules, but the same subject would be strange if the actors involved were a university professor and her student. Examples of influence principles in health care would be asymmetry – meaning that legitimate influence works in one direction (from the doctor to the patient, but not the other way round) and necessity – meaning that doctors are entitled to influence the will and actions of patients whenever this is necessary for their treatment.

## VII. Contextual Autonomy, Personalised Advertising and Political Microtargeting

Is autonomy as contextual integrity a useful conceptualisation for understanding the issues raised by practices such as targeted advertising and political microtargeting?

Consider the contexts and contextual norms involved in the above examples of problematic practices. Both practices in the aforementioned examples originated in interactions on Facebook. Facebook is presented by its owner and perceived by most of its users as a platform for communication between friends (or at least it was in the mid-2010s). To a first approximation, we can assume that Facebook users understand their interactions on the platform as part of a social interaction context of friendship. Although the norms governing this relatively new digital context may not fully replicate what previously existed as 'analogue' friendship contexts, some core pillars of this type of relationship can be considered typical of digitally mediated friendship contexts as well. For example, actors interacting with each other expect to be interacting as friends, and interactions that amount to influences of each other's will and behaviour are governed by norms such as symmetry, reciprocity, and voluntariness. If this interpretation is correct, then people interacting on Facebook expect to deal with autonomous 'peers', ie, people who, when they seek to influence one's will or behaviour, do so on an equal footing and principally under conditions of reciprocity.

What the practices of personalised targeting of vulnerable teenagers and political microtargeting by Cambridge Analytica imply is that actors with roles 'external' to what we can call the context of digital friendship have entered this context and have been able to influence Facebook users in ways that violate the contextual norms of the context. Advertising companies, whether commercial or political, do not interact with Facebook users on the basis of symmetry, reciprocity, and voluntariness. They thus violate the kind of norms I have proposed to label 'influence norms', which express the procedural principles governing appropriate influence among actors in a given context.

To appreciate the shift, we can draw a parallel with the analogue world. Imagine a private party organised by a group of friends who have told their invitees to feel free to extend the invitation to their friends. At the party, many people will not have met each other before, and because it has turned out to be a very large party, everyone wears name tags. Even though some people will be meeting each other for the first time at the party, everyone will interact on the assumption that they have a common understanding of their roles and goals at the party, namely to be there to have fun, cultivate their friendships, and make new ones. Now imagine that the company that has 'lent' its premises to the party organisers sends representatives of commercial companies and political parties to the party without the knowledge of the invitees and the organisers. These 'intruders' join groups, listen to their conversations, and note the names and characteristics of the people they meet. After the party, they look up the home addresses of the people they met in the telephone directory and use the information gathered at the party to produce targeted advertisements. A partygoer who confesses to having tried for years to lose weight, unsuccessfully, because he cannot resist chocolate, will receive an advertisement for a 50 per cent discount on Swiss chocolate, or a diet programme that promises miracles – or both. Another person, who says he sleeps badly at night for fear of burglars, receives political advertising for a conservative party. The moment the invitees make the connection between their conversations at the party and the advertisement, they retrospectively change their view of the nature of the event and no longer see it as 'a party'. They are likely to feel 'betrayed', taken off guard, and induced to behave in a way they would not have chosen had they fully understood the context in which they were acting.

A possible counter-argument would be that everyone is – or should be – aware that the web is not an advertising-free space and that everyone should expect to encounter commercial attempts to influence their behaviour when they are online. Another way of framing this argument is that commerce is central to the web's purpose. But even if we accept this perspective and consider that interaction on the web is always shaped by the norms of autonomy that are characteristic of the commercial context, we can see a violation of contextual norms of autonomy in the two examples. The attempts to influence Facebook users are only possible because users interact in a context in which they are inclined to expose their preferences, feelings, and emotions to others. The same inferences about the emotional states of teenagers or the psychographic profiles of potential voters would not have been possible by observing their behaviour in a purely commercial context.

Either way, the result is to enable actors to influence subjects in a context in which their role is not foreseen and on the basis of principles that do not pertain to that context. Moreover, the actors playing roles exogenous to the context of reference (advertising companies) or those mediating their inference (Facebook) do not make the presence of the former explicit, thus depriving Facebook users of the possibility of adapting their behaviour to the changing context (ie, from the friendship to the commercial or political one).

Two clarifications are in order at this juncture. First, the blurring of contexts is not the only way in which autonomy can be impaired in online interactions. Violations of specific contextual norms still count as ways in which autonomy can be undermined, both online and offline. For example, even if it were transparent to Facebook users that they were interacting in a commercial context, practices that exploit their vulnerabilities for manipulative purposes would still amount to a violation of autonomy because these practices would also violate contextual autonomy norms typical of commercial contexts. The relevant norms prohibiting such manipulative practices in this case are not only of a moral and societal nature but are also in part legally recognised and sanctioned, as evidenced by the inclusion of these practices among the prohibited AI practices under the EU AI Act.[77] The point I want to make, however, is that the conflation of societal contexts is a specific and additional way in which digital environments and AI techniques typically challenge individual autonomy. As the 'analogous' example above shows, these autonomy impairments due to context blurring or context collapse are conceivable in principle in offline environments as well, but they are particularly characteristic and insidious in online settings and when supported by AI techniques. Second, the fact that digital technologies, and AI in particular, pose such challenges to autonomy is not an inherent characteristic of digitality or AI but is intrinsic to the current architecture, business model, and mindset that characterise today's online environment and AI applications as sociotechnical phenomena.[78]

[77] Regulation (EU) 2024/1689 of the European Parliament and of the Council of 13 June 2024 laying down harmonised rules on artificial intelligence and amending Regulations (EC) No 300/2008, (EU) No 167/2013, (EU) No 168/2013, (EU) 2018/858, (EU) 2018/1139 and (EU) 2019/2144 and Directives 2014/90/EU, (EU) 2016/797 and (EU) 2020/1828 (Artificial Intelligence Act) 2024 OJ L2024/1689, art 5 and European Commission, 'Commission Guidelines on prohibited artificial intelligence practices established by Regulation (EU) 2024/1689 (AI Act)' (04.02.2025) ec.europa.eu/newsroom/dae/redirection/document/112367.

[78] Their characteristics have been acutely described and interpreted among others by Frischmann and Selinger (n 39); S Zuboff, *The Age of Surveillance Capitalism: The Fight for a Human Future at the New Frontier of Power* (New York, PublicAffairs, 2019) and K Crawford, *Atlas of AI – Power, Politics, and the Planetary Costs of Artificial Intelligence* (New Haven, Yale University Press, 2021).

## VIII. Conclusion: The Implications of Contextual Autonomy for Privacy Theory and Law and Limitations of the Suggested Approach

This chapter has focused on the relationship between privacy and autonomy. The core of the value of privacy resides – at least in part, and certainly crucially – in its supportive role for autonomy. A robust theory of privacy, capable of making a strong case for its value, therefore requires a clear understanding of autonomy. In considering the current digital challenges to autonomy, this chapter has reviewed the main conceptualisations of autonomy and argued for building on socio-relational understandings of personal autonomy to develop a contextual conception of autonomy. This approach seems to be best suited to provide an account of digitally-driven harms to autonomy and is therefore better able to explain how privacy protects autonomy in an era of pervasive information technologies and AI.

According to the suggested understanding, autonomy, like privacy, is not an absolute concept that can be defined by binary rules that apply to every place and time. Rather, autonomy depends on social practices and is best defined by the conditions that determine which heteronomous encroachments on self-determination are considered justified or legitimate in particular situations and contexts. What is special about the challenges to autonomy posed by digitalisation and AI is that they blur the hitherto relative separation between contexts of social interaction. At their extreme, digital technologies and AI have the potential to make the very idea of contextual separation obsolete. In order to better protect autonomy in the digital sphere, it is therefore appropriate to focus not only on the individual but also on the integrity of social contexts and the systemic impact of AI and digital technologies on them. The question of whether subjects have autonomy implies a judgement not only about the individuals involved but also about the society in which they live, as constituted by multiple contexts.

What are the implications of this conceptualisation of autonomy for privacy theory and law? Understanding autonomy in a contextual way does not imply a radical revision of the way privacy is conceptualised and protected, at least not as far as current privacy debates and German and EU law are concerned. But contextual autonomy can help to better understand and explain why it is important to protect privacy in certain ways and why certain ways of understanding and legally protecting privacy are preferable to others.

The first and most basic implication of a contextual understanding of autonomy for privacy is that the relative separation of contexts of social interaction is crucial for the protection of autonomy. We can only be autonomous if we can act and interact with others in different roles and are not constantly subject to scrutiny and influence under all – or many – aspects at once. Privacy supports autonomy because it protects the ability to act in a sphere (context) in the role appropriate to that sphere. At a very basic level, in order to be autonomous, we need contexts of social interaction that are separate.

This is in line with the rationale of exemplary decisions on data protection by the German Constitutional Court. The German Constitutional Court, in the landmark

'Census Decision' of 1983 mentioned above, can be read as pointing to the importance of the separation of social spheres of interaction by emphasising the need for individuals to be able to ascertain who knows what about them:

> If individuals cannot, with sufficient certainty, determine what kind of personal information is known to certain parts of their social environment, and if it is difficult to ascertain what kind of information potential communication partners are privy to, this could greatly impede their freedom to make self-determined plans or decisions. A societal order, and its underlying legal order, would not be compatible with the right to informational self-determination if citizens were no longer able to tell who knows what kind of personal information about them, at what time and on which occasion. Individuals who worry that non-conformist behaviour could be recorded at any time and that such information could permanently be stored, used or shared will try not to draw attention to themselves by not engaging in such behaviour. If individuals anticipate that participation in an assembly or a citizens' initiative, for instance, was going to be recorded by the authorities and could thus expose them to certain risks, they might decide to forgo the exercise of their respective fundamental rights (arts 8 and 9 of the Basic Law). Not only would this impair opportunities of personal development for the individual, it would also affect the common good because self-determination is a fundamental prerequisite for the functioning of a free and democratic society which relies on the agency and participation of its citizens.[79]

The preservation of different spheres of interaction seems also to provide the most basic rationale for legal devices of data protection such as purpose limitation and specification: personal data captured in a certain context and for a given purpose cannot simply be used for any other purpose, because that would weaken the relative separation of contexts. One example of legal concretisations of these principles is the provisions of article 6(4)b of the GDPR, according to which the lawfulness of further processing for different purposes depends, among other factors, on 'the context in which the personal data have been collected, in particular … the relationship between data subjects and the controller'.[80] A further example is provided by the principle of hypothetical new collection of data as established by the German Federal Constitutional Court in its decision on the Federal Criminal Police Office Act (*Bundeskriminalamtgesetz*). According to this principle,

> the new use of the data must serve to protect legal interests or to detect criminal acts of such weight that would, by constitutional standards, justify a new collection of the data by means entailing interferences that are comparable in severity [to the original data collection measures].[81]

Purpose limitation and specification are, thus, a way to legally capture and protect the separation of contexts, at least in those areas where contextual norms are formalised by law.

[79] BVerfGE 1, 65 para 146. This understanding has been confirmed and specified in several later key decisions of the German Federal Court, see for instance BVerfGE 152, 152 [2019] – *Recht auf Vergessen I* paras 83–90 and Bundesverfassungsgericht, Judgment of 1 October 2024, 1 BvR 1160/19 – *Bundeskriminalamtgesetz II* para 90.

[80] GDPR, art 6(4)b.

[81] BVerfGE 141, 220 Headnotes 5.

The second, related, important implication is that in order for privacy protection to support autonomy, it must not only prevent harm to individuals but also preserve the integrity of social contexts. This provides a further argument to explain why certain jurisdictions, such as Germany's, consider the mere collection of data to be a potential invasion of privacy, regardless of the uses (if any) that are made of them.[82] If the data are not processed and used to infer information about a person, there is apparently no harm to that person. However, as the Census Decision reads, 'data that by itself appears insignificant may gain new relevance' as a consequence of data processing.[83] Moreover, the indiscriminate collection of personal data also puts pressure on the integrity of a given social context and its separation from others. The importance of focusing not only on individuals but also on the 'infrastructure', including the integrity of social contexts, also resonates with some of the suggestions on the meaning of data protection and the duties of the state and public authorities to promote and maintain the structural conditions for effective data protection, put forth by Marion Albers, Paul de Hert and Nikolaus Marsch in this volume. Autonomy and privacy protect not only individuals but also specific forms of interaction, political systems, and social structures. Accordingly, the role of the state and public authorities cannot be limited to a mere duty of non-interference but also includes positive obligations.

Along with these benefits, the proposed contextual approach has limitations as well. The first is that the relationship between autonomy and digital technologies has been considered only through the lens of harms. There are several reasons for this, some of which are inherited from existing approaches to privacy and data protection that focus on avoiding harms, and some of which depend on methodological assumptions specific to my approach.[84]

Explaining the positive effects of information technologies on autonomy is a task for another day. But in principle, the fact that digitalisation can have restrictive effects on autonomy does not exclude the possibility that digitalisation can have positive, autonomy-promoting effects in other ways. For example, social media can – and has in the past – created new opportunities for socially under-represented groups to network and interact with like-minded people in ways that would have been limited in analogue contexts. They have also been instrumental in bringing supposedly 'private' oppressive relationships into the public eye, and thus, as Beate Rössler reminds us in this book, in liberating individuals from oppressive relationships, thereby enhancing their self-determination.[85] And this can create opportunities for self-development processes in interaction with others that are more autonomy-supportive.

This leads us to two further and related points that deserve attention in future research. First, existing social contexts and their autonomy norms may not be

[82] See Masing, ch 3 in this volume. In a critical vein, see Poscher (n 29) as well as his contribution to this volume, ch 4.

[83] BVerfGE 65, 1 para 150.

[84] It would be out of scope to dwell into methodological issues here, but the interested reader can refer to E Orrù, *Legitimität, Sicherheit, Autonomie. Eine philosophische Analyse der EU-Sicherheitspolitik im Kontext der Digitalisierung* (Baden-Baden, Nomos, 2021) 43–96 and E Orrù, 'The European PNR Directive as an Instance of Pre-Emptive, Risk-Based Algorithmic Security and Its Implications for the Regulatory Framework' (2022) 27 *Information Polity* 131f.

[85] B Rössler, ch 15 in this volume.

particularly supportive of autonomy, at least not for all people interacting in that context to the same extent. Second, social contexts and their norms are dynamic and change over time. All change results – at least prima facie – in a violation of contextual norms, but not all change is for the worse: how then to distinguish positive or even necessary change from negative change? Both objections are exacerbated by the fact that technological change not only challenges existing norms of autonomy but also gives rise to new accepted practices and normative understandings. Digitalisation not only potentially disrupts existing contexts and creates new spheres of interaction, but it also *normatively* influences our understanding of appropriate and inappropriate influences.

With respect to the first objection, namely that not all existing 'intact' contexts are autonomy supportive, it can be said that at least the relative separation of contexts is important for autonomy as such, even if not all existing contexts are autonomy supportive, or not equally so for all people interacting within them. The separation of contexts provides the framework within which adaptations are possible. As for the second objection, this is a problem that the contextual integrity theory of privacy also faces, and for which some ideas about how to overcome it have been put forward.[86] The central question in distinguishing changes 'for the better' from harms to autonomy is what the changes mean for the basic functions of the respective contexts. For example, the principle of the autonomy of citizens in their relations with the state serves, among other things, to protect core principles of the rule of law.[87] In the medical context, so the hypothesis goes, patient autonomy enables a relationship of trust to be maintained between patients and doctors, while in the political context, citizens' autonomy is the precondition for democracy. The crucial question for the evaluation of existing and proposed norms will then be under which conditions and through which autonomy norms these fundamental protective functions can continue to be guaranteed.

[86] Nissenbaum, *Privacy in Context* (n 8) 158–85.
[87] Orrù, 'The European PNR' (n 84).

# 18

# Privacy in Light of Critiques of Autonomy or: Privacy as Freedom to Change

TOBIAS MATZNER

## I. Introduction

The concept of privacy and its value are a regular matter of debate. Certainly this is in part due to recent developments – above all in the field of information technologies – that challenge some established views and preconditions of the way in which privacy has been conceived. However, on a more general level, the concepts 'privacy' and 'private' are applied in a huge variety of cases which are hard to unify in one concept – some even argue this is impossible. Here I focus on normative concepts of privacy – as opposed to descriptive ones – and the arguments for its value for the individual – as opposed to its value for society. Most of these arguments, despite their different forms and scopes, share a common characteristic, that is, linking the value of privacy to some form of autonomy. This is hardly a surprise, given that the development of privacy is inherently tied to liberal political thought.

Concepts of autonomy prevalent in this tradition have been criticised from various quarters – which often extends to a critique of privacy. More recent theories have reconstructed privacy in light of this criticism, often by invoking more relational concepts of autonomy. Here, I propose a different approach. I concede that some of the aforementioned criticism is right and add some points of my own to show that the focus on autonomy leads to ignoring important cases which deserve privacy protection. I propose a new argument for the value of privacy, which is based on the moderation of different forms of heteronomy. Thus privacy essentially is shown to protect the possibility for individual change – even if this does not happen autonomously. That way I show that an argument for the value of privacy does not need the relation to notions of autonomy, and its value can be defended even in light of critiques of autonomy.

## II. Autonomy as Foundation for the Value of Privacy

Normative accounts of privacy can be loosely grouped in reductive and non-reductive versions.[1] Reductive theories argue that privacy is just a name or collection of other liberal rights, like property rights, for example. This view has been defended maybe most prominently by Judith Jarvis Thomson.[2] Non-reductive accounts of privacy (which are the vast majority) see privacy as necessary for an underlying value. Privacy, in this sense, has a functional value, as Rössler calls it.[3] This functional value can be related to the social or political value of privacy, eg, arguing that privacy is necessary for certain social institutions like healthcare[4] or political values like democracy.[5] These theories are not the primary topic of this text, even if the account of privacy developed here has some similarities to them. Other theories concern the individual value. Most of these theories argue that privacy is necessary for, but cannot be reduced to, some version of autonomy. What exactly autonomy amounts to in these theories varies and is closely related to how privacy itself is understood. Warren and Brandeis, in their seminal definition of privacy as the 'right to be let alone',[6] still breathe the spirit of Locke's and Hobbes' liberalism, prominently renewed by Mill's 'On Liberty', published 30 years before 'The Right to Privacy'.[7] In this tradition, the autonomous individual conceived as possessing encompassing negative freedoms is the theoretical starting point. Accordingly, being alone means having a space without infringements by others. In this sense, privacy as the right to be let alone protects autonomy.

Such strong notions of autonomy that also animate many later concepts of privacy[8] have drawn criticism, especially from feminist theory. The objections raised can be loosely grouped into three interrelated issues. First, privacy (at least in its current form) does not achieve equal protection of autonomy. This is especially salient in analyses centred on the family. From the development of western bourgeois societies from the seventeenth century onwards, much of privacy protection concerned private property and housing. Here not only the male adult citizens but also female family members and children, and (often female) household employees live. It has been shown that conceiving this as a private space strengthens the dependence of women and children. More generally, if something is regarded as a private matter in the sense of being left alone, persons are left in the dependent or independent state that they are currently in. While this enhances freedom for some, who have all that is necessary to do whatever they

[1] *Cf* B Rössler, *The Value of Privacy* (Cambridge, Polity Press, 2005) 76; A Moore, 'Defining Privacy' (2008) 39 *Journal of Social Philosophy* 411, 413.

[2] JJ Thomson, 'The Right to Privacy' (1975) 4 *Philosophy & Public Affairs* 295.

[3] Rössler (n 1) 69.

[4] H Nissenbaum, *Privacy in Context: Technology, Policy, and the Integrity of Social Life* (Stanford, Stanford University Press, 2010).

[5] A Lever, 'Feminism, Democracy and the Right to Privacy' (2005) 9 *Minerva: An Internet Journal of Philosophy* 1.

[6] SD Warren and LD Brandeis, 'The Right to Privacy' (1890) 4 *Harvard Law Review* 193.

[7] For a more detailed discussion of Warren and Brandeis' relation to the liberal tradition, see DJ Glancy, 'The Invention of the Right to Privacy' (1979) 21 *Arizona Law Review* 1.

[8] See, eg, the discussions in AL Allen, *Why Privacy Isn't Everything: Feminist Reflections on Personal Accountability* (Lanham, Rowman & Littlefield, 2003) or Rössler (n 1).

desire to do in private, this precludes freedom for others since they are left alone in their private dependence.[9]

This is tied to the second objection: individual autonomy itself should not be the theoretical starting point because it has all kinds of social preconditions. Classical liberal theories disavow these necessities in positing an autonomous individual.[10] This is partly possible because many of these social preconditions are traditionally considered matters of the private sphere – procreation, subsistence, care – and thus disappear from political theories.[11] Most theorists who defend a more socially situated theory of autonomy or the subject in general have used such theories to criticise the adverse effects of privacy. Some, like Julie Cohen, in contrast, argue for reconstructing a theory of privacy based on a more socially situated theory of the subject.[12] However, this second objection does not only concern privacy but also very much engages directly with a critique of the prevailing concept of autonomy in liberal theory. It is based on the problem that the social conditions of subjectivity in general and autonomy in particular are not all available individually. Extending this to normative arguments, some authors hold that even if these conditions could be privately organised, they should not be.[13]

What is more, if autonomy is a social achievement and has social preconditions, then clearly not everyone is autonomous – at least not all the time. How could we justify privacy protection in these situations? Rössler suggests that we should treat subjects in a way that they could eventually attain autonomy or even as if they already were autonomous.[14] This, however, would preclude the reality of the lives of many persons which, in the sense here discussed, cannot attain autonomy: ill persons, persons with disabilities, young children, and persons in need of special care. This is an important problem since all of these groups of persons are in the scope of increased data collections which impinge on their lives – data collected by states, private educational institutions, care providers, insurances, future and current employers, and many more. Thus, they all are confronted with particularly salient of issues of privacy.

The third group of arguments focuses on the consequences of privacy. Even if privacy offers protection for individuals and their acts, this comes with the cost of de-politicisation. A case in point are the debates on forced outing of homosexuals, which split activist communities in the 1970s and 1980s. While the privacy of sexual life protects forms of sexuality that are not fully accepted in society, it renders them invisible at the same time. Thus, chances to address such discriminatory stances and to establish homosexuality as normal diminish. In addition, this way homosexual relations are reduced to sexual acts and other intimate interactions but cannot reach the social recognition and standing that heterosexual partners or spouses have. This has led to the request that homosexuals seek not the protection of the private but

[9] CA MacKinnon, *Feminism Unmodified: Discourses on Life and Law* (Cambridge, Harvard University Press, 1994) 96.

[10] See, eg, the summary and critical discussion of such positions in M Friedman, *Autonomy, Gender, Politics* (New York, Oxford University Press, 2003) ch 4.

[11] H Arendt, *The Human Condition*, 2nd edn (Chicago, University of Chicago Press, 1998) ch II.

[12] JE Cohen, 'What Privacy Is For' (2013) 126 *Harvard Law Review* 1904.

[13] Allen (n 8).

[14] Rössler (n 1) 73 fn 117.

become visible – even up to the point that they have been outed against their wills by activists.[15] This illustrates the ambivalent relationship of privacy and autonomy. The constrained autonomy of being able to live the sexual life one pleases in private at the same time precludes social changes, which would enable a more far-reaching autonomy: to be able to live according to one's sexual orientation throughout many more social contexts.

Most normative theories of privacy that have been developed in the recent decades answer some of these concerns – sometimes as a direct response, sometimes due to other developments in (liberal) political philosophy. In 1975 James Rachels proposed an account of privacy that focuses on the individual as a being with social relations. Autonomy remains important, however, in the sense that it should be the individual alone to decide with whom to have what kind of relationship. This is the reason why privacy is necessary following Rachels, because it enables us 'to control who has access to us, and who knows what about us'.[16] In this sense, privacy is not about being left alone but about the possibility of determining one's position in a social world.

Jeffrey Reiman has criticised this as a 'market conception of personal intimacy'.[17] He argues that intimate or private lives are much more than just a 'resource' to invest in personal relations. Rather, he considers privacy as necessary for the development of a self 'who regards his existence – his thoughts, his body, his actions – as his own'. But again, this is a socially situated self: 'Selves' are created in social interaction rather than flowering innately from inborn seeds.' In this interaction privacy plays a pivotal role: 'Privacy is an essential part of the complex social practice by means of which the social group recognizes – and communicates to the individual – that his existence is his own.'[18] Privacy is necessary for creating persons out of infants and for the respect of the personhood for already developed selves. Reiman thus invokes autonomy in a more circumspect way as living one's own life and understanding it as one's own. This possibility, however, has a complex set of social preconditions, of which privacy is a central part.

This exchange between Rachels and Reiman implicitly turns around the interdependence of autonomy on the one hand and social relations on the other. We cannot be autonomous in a rich sense without being, or having been, in certain social relations. This is Reiman's focus. Conversely, we cannot have good relations with others without autonomy in the form of control over ourselves, our visibility, and others' access to us, which would be Rachels' point. However, I would agree with Reiman that this does not suffice – but as we will see below, neither does Reiman's account.

This entanglement of autonomy and social relations is the subject of an important strand of discussion regarding autonomy itself – rather than privacy. Marilyn Friedman has engaged with the emphasis on social relationships advanced by feminist critics of liberal theory. She argues that advanced theories of autonomy within liberal thought actually concede and integrate the necessity of social preconditions for autonomy.

[15] LP Gross, *Contested Closets: The Politics and Ethics of Outing* (Minneapolis, University of Minnesota Press, 1993).

[16] J Rachels, 'Why Privacy Is Important' (1975) 4 *Philosophy & Public Affairs* 323, 329.

[17] JH Reiman, 'Privacy, Intimacy, and Personhood' (1976) 6 *Philosophy & Public Affairs* 26, 32.

[18] ibid 39.

This includes genealogical conditions, like upbringing and education, but also the acceptance of a local – socially and historically dependent – morality.[19] However, autonomy is preserved by a procedural or content-neutral way in which an individual can relate to these social conditions and determine their own actions or way of life. These strands of thought have been developed further in the debates on relational autonomy.[20]

Beate Rössler takes up most of these discussions in her comprehensive study 'The Value of Privacy'. This book is, in my view, the most circumspect approach to reconstructing a theory of privacy within liberal theory in light of the concerns and objections that critics of privacy and autonomy advance.[21] Rössler clearly states that the value of privacy is to enable autonomy. However, she qualifies this in several regards. First, she argues that the individual value of autonomy does not suffice, but that equal autonomy is necessary.[22] This answers the objection that, eg, in a family, often only the adult male members are autonomous. That way the individual value of autonomy is hedged by a social criterion of justice. Second, she conceives of autonomy itself in a socially embedded way. She starts with a rather strong notion of authenticity: 'To describe a person as self-determined, we expect her desires and actions to be authentically hers, in the sense that she can in principle identify with her desires and actions as her own.'[23] Yet, these desires and actions have social origins. Autonomy is about the possibility to distance oneself enough from one's desires and social roles to acknowledge that this is what one really wants. Such self-reflection is a particular form of relation to oneself, which has to be learned and maintained. This is not just a matter of education or the development of a self in general. In contrast, persons are in exchange with others, and 'in light of interpretations by these others [they] interpret themselves'. Thus, 'what is at stake is not merely the formation of a self or the learning of self-determination but rather the non-stop reappropriation of self-determination, a constant updating, that is autonomy as a process.'[24]

Such a socially situated form of autonomy needs privacy. First of all, an appropriate development of self-relations needs protection, as Reiman already argued. Second, the reappropriation of self-determination is only possible, according to Rössler, if we have undisturbed spaces where we can develop a distance from the social interpretations of our acts and our person as well as from influences such as demands, cues, or incentives to do specific things and ask ourselves which of these we can authentically identify with. In addition, we need the recognition that certain aspects of our lives are just ours to determine, and certain decisions are just ours to take, eg, which religion to adhere to

[19] Friedman (n 10).

[20] J Christman and J Anderson (eds), *Autonomy and the Challenges to Liberalism: New Essays* (Cambridge, Cambridge University Press, 2009); C Mackenzie and N Stoljar (eds), *Relational Autonomy: Feminist Perspectives on Automony, Agency, and the Social Self* (New York, Oxford University Press, 1999).

[21] Another important text in this regard is JC Cohen, 'Redescribing Privacy: Identity, Difference, and the Abortion Controversy' (1992) 3 *Columbia Journal of Gender and Law* 1. However, Cohen's discussion is very much imbricated in the particular situation of the US Constitution and Supreme Court legislation.

[22] Rössler (n 1) 41.

[23] ibid 53.

[24] ibid 133.

or with whom to have an intimate relationship. Finally, we need privacy even in social interaction in order to control our relations to others. It is

> an intrinsic part of their self-understanding as autonomous individuals to have control over their self-presentation, that is control of how they want to present or stage themselves, to whom they want to do so and in which contexts, control over how they want to see themselves and how they want to be seen.[25]

In short, once we have taken the decision of which life to live or which actions to take, we also need the possibility to act them out. This leads to Rössler's encompassing definition of privacy as control over access to certain spaces, to certain decisions, and to particular pieces or forms of information, all of which she considers necessary for autonomy.[26]

J David Velleman adds another important aspect to this discussion. For him, '[p]rivacy is made possible by the ability to choose in opposition to inclination'.[27] Thus, in his view, privacy is precisely the realm where we are not always in control of ourselves, where impulse rules. However, privacy allows one to hide this beneath an 'outward face', which is consciously composed for an audience. Appearing to others as an autonomous person, according to this view, is not based on complete self-transparency and self-control. Rather, we have impulses but manage to keep them private, thus hiding moments where we are not in control. In consequence,

> [t]hreats to your standing as a self-presenting creature are thus a source of deep anxiety, and anxiety about the threatened loss of that standing is, in my view, what constitutes the emotion of shame. The realm of privacy is the central arena for shame, I think, because it is the central arena for threats to your standing as a social agent.[28]

According to this view, we are not only shamed because of the respective details of our private lives that come to the fore. Primarily, we are shamed because our entire standing as a social agent, that is, as an individual that is in control of self-presentation, is challenged. In line with the second group of concerns mentioned above, Velleman acknowledges that private life is not just rational and conscious self-reflection and deliberation. He also shows that self-presentation is an inherent social activity. Yet, he ties privacy – and the self in general – to a very strong notion of self-determination. It reacts to socially prescribed norms – particularly those regarding privacy – but a failure to present oneself accordingly is inherently a failure of the self-controlled individual.[29]

While Velleman's emphasis on emotions is important, he uses a very naturalist and sexist account of emotion when he roots the origins of shame in the outward visibility of male arousal through erections.[30] Empirically speaking, it is also apparent that the way Velleman describes self-control is only one particular socially and culturally situated form. Post-pandemic influencers, who proudly broadcast from their private kitchens

[25] ibid 116.
[26] ibid 71.
[27] JD Velleman, 'The Genesis of Shame' (2001) 30 *Philosophy & Public Affairs* 27, 35.
[28] ibid 37.
[29] ibid 43, 48.
[30] ibid 39.

their intimate relationships with their cosseted and personally named sourdoughs, form a strange alliance with Donald Trump-style politicians whose 'authenticity' is very much based on letting emotions flow freely in public. This does not mean that formerly private things become public. All of this is as much an outward presentation as Velleman's well-composed male citizen. This just illustrates that Velleman reintroduced an aspect into privacy debates that feminist thinkers knew all along, ie, privacy is not about the separation of rationality and emotion but is constituted by complex negotiations of both. Yet he did not take up the rich knowledge on the unequal requirements that are put on differently socially situated subjects in this regard, which feminist thought had also established long before his text appeared.[31]

## III. Relative Privacy: Privacy as Social Structure

All the aforementioned accounts consider privacy as a necessary condition for self-determination. They illustrate that in order to enable self-determination, privacy needs to be more than just a boundary between social or public life and the individual. Rather, privacy itself is a complex structure of social life. This move from privacy as a boundary between individual and society to privacy in society, as it were, is made explicit to varying degrees in the accounts I have discussed so far. Yet, all emphasise that in order to be able to present ourselves according to various social demands or distance ourselves from them, in order to engage in various relationships, and in order to selectively disclose elements of our lives, there has to be the possibility of different relations and social contexts in the first place. These contexts, however, are part of our social lives; thus, we are not just in one paradigmatic instance of self-presentation several times. The very sense of privacy protection is that we can stage ourselves differently on different occasions. Once we did this, however, on one occasion, our control on further occasions does not just depend on privacy in the sense of how we relate to the others who are present on further occasions. It also depends on the fact that our appearance from the first occasion stays there, so to speak. If the way we staged ourselves on one occasion transpires to another occasion, this limits the possibilities of self-presentation. In consequence, the different moments where a person is staged need to be protected against each other.

This issue has been at the attention of research in the social sciences under the rubric of 'context collapse'. It has been diagnosed particularly regarding the use of social networking sites and other social media like YouTube.[32] Context collapse describes the phenomenon when our appearance in one context suddenly is revealed in other contexts. For example, what someone told the fellow members of the sports team might suddenly appear at our workplace. The openly homosexual life of a person in a big city might be revealed to friends and family back home, who disapprove of this and

[31] L Berlant, 'The Subject of True Feeling: Pain, Privacy, and Politics' in A Sarat and TR Kearns (eds), *Cultural Pluralism, Identity Politics, and the Law* (Ann Arbor, Michigan University Press, 1999).

[32] AE Marwick and D Boyd, 'Networked Privacy: How Teenagers Negotiate Context in Social Media' (2014) 16 *New Media & Society* 1051; M Wesch, 'Youtube and You: Experiences of Self-Awareness in the Context Collapse of the Recording Webcam' (2009) 8 *Explorations in Media Ecology* 19.

thus have been kept in the dark regarding this aspect of life. Children and teenagers usually experience a dreadful collapse of contexts when their parents or teachers appear on social media. Most of these contexts, like sports teams, the workplace, and behaviour in a big city, are not traditionally regarded as parts of private life. Yet, many who experience such context collapses call this a violation of their privacy. Accordingly, the authors of one pertinent study coined the term 'networked privacy'.[33] In part, this fits the intuition of the theories of privacy discussed in section III. If privacy concerns – at least in part – our ability to control our staging or self-presentation, or the possibility to act autonomously at least locally (eg, in the city compared to home), prevention of context collapses is clearly a necessary condition for such control. Otherwise, regardless of our social competence and individual privacy protection in one context, we would constantly have to fight off our appearance from other contexts.

For similar reasons, Rössler and Mokrosinska argue for the necessity of protecting the privacy of social relations, in addition to the privacy of the individuals engaged in these relations.[34] In contrast to the discussions on context collapse, their main concern is information leaving the context of the relationship. While such information might not pertain directly to the privacy of the person involved, this still could lead to 'poor' or even 'defective role performance' of the persons involved.[35] The authors show this with regard to professional relations like psychotherapist and patient or employer and employee[36] but also the family or friends[37] or the relations among strangers.[38]

These case studies and arguments thus refer to privacy as a complex social construct that regulates how different contexts or occasions in people's lives relate to each other. Clearly, not all appearances of persons can be separate. Otherwise, no stable personalities could emerge. Still, the question of whether something is a matter of privacy depends on the relation of two different contexts, that is, the social settings, times, and places of an individual's appearance. Relative to the workplace, exchanges between the members of a sports team are private. Relative to family and friends back home, even kissing one's partner in Times Square might be a matter of privacy. This is why I will call this form of privacy as social structure 'relative privacy' for the rest of this chapter.

The problem does not only pertain to situations where context collapse in fact happens. Especially Michael Wesch's emphasis in his study of broadcasting videos online lies on the inability to judge the context one is in. Just the impossibility of estimating one's audience and their knowledge about oneself inhibits our control or possibility of exercising self-presentation. Self-presentation – since it is socially situated – is based on an expected audience. Goffman has argued that we both consciously and unconsciously adapt the way we stage ourselves regarding the audience we are confronted with.[39] Again, such judgements can only be sensibly made if a certain amount of

[33] Marwick and Boyd (n 32).

[34] B Rössler and D Mokrosinska, 'Privacy and Social Interaction' (2013) 39 *Philosophy & Social Criticism* 771, 779.

[35] ibid 781.

[36] ibid 780.

[37] ibid 774.

[38] ibid 782.

[39] E Goffman, *The Presentation of Self in Everyday Life* (Garden City, Doubleday, 1959).

relative privacy exists. Since social media bring about context collapses, they make such judgements difficult to impossible. Yet, they are not the only reason for such concerns – another one, for example, is (hidden) surveillance.[40]

In a sense, the debates on context collapse only illustrate the tip of a much bigger problem that is based on the reuse of data. This is particularly salient in the huge data collections by both state and private actors that are then fed into all kinds of algorithmically driven analysis. In this regard the notions of 'context' and 'context collapse' begin to lose their meaning. This reuse of data by algorithms is not only based on moving data from one context to the other, where these contexts would remain rather stable environments. Rather, these algorithmically driven forms of analysis bestow new forms of meaning on the data, which has the consequence that even established concepts change. For example, today, one can become a suspect just through a movement pattern recorded by a smartphone or browsing behaviour online. This is quite different from earlier forms of suspicious behaviour.[41] However, such algorithmic surveillance technologies would not be fully understood without acknowledging that they were created as suspicion machines, which continue some aspects of earlier forms of surveillance and suspicion.[42] This complex interplay between continuity and shifts in the meaning of political and ethical concepts that is brought about by algorithms forms new challenges to privacy that go way beyond collapsing contacts. Rather, the very threats to privacy that we have come to know, such as surveillance, change themselves. Theories of privacy have to reflect not just collapsing contexts but also these complex forms of reuse of data and information. In consequence, relative privacy is not just about the relationship of contexts but of single instances of collecting and using data that cut across and shift known social contexts.

## IV. Autonomy and Relative Privacy

Regarding the discussion so far, relative privacy extends what is necessary for privacy on a socio-technical level, but the normative structure stays the same. Privacy, including relative privacy, is seen as instrumental for some form of autonomy. This would also conform to some influential data protection legislation internationally. A case in point is when Facebook (now Meta) had bought the popular messaging service WhatsApp and wanted to merge the data of the users of WhatsApp with their own. Note that this concerns users who had been clients of both companies before the acquisition. Nevertheless, German data protection authorities forbade merging the data, since the consent to use the data given to either company does not entail consent regarding the new profile that would emerge if both contexts of data use were to collapse.[43]

[40] Regarding this ability to estimate the knowledge others have about oneself, relative privacy is implicitly required in Rössler's discussion of informational privacy, especially in regard to surveillance. (n 1) 116–117.

[41] T Matzner, 'Beyond Data as Representation: The Performativity of Big Data in Surveillance' (2016) 14 *Surveillance & Society* 197.

[42] S Browne, *Dark Matters: On the Surveillance of Blackness* (Durham, Duke University Press, 2015).

[43] M Scott, 'Facebook Ordered to Stop Collecting Data on WhatsApp Users in Germany' (*The New York Times*, 27.09.2016), www.nytimes.com/2016/09/28/technology/whatsapp-facebook-germany.html.

Here, regulating relative privacy is seen as necessary to uphold the legal guarantee of individual choices about personal data.

In a similar manner, Rössler and Mokrosinska argue that norms of privacy 'protect the autonomy of individual subjects and, in so doing, facilitate their different social relationships; and they regulate the social relationships themselves, insofar as these norms are a necessary condition for such relationships'.[44] Thus, privacy regarding relationships themselves rather than individuals is necessary for the relationships to be possible, but it should still be the autonomous individual to choose in which of these relationships to engage.

Some passages in the studies of context collapse also lend themselves to the reading that relative privacy is just a necessary amendment of earlier views on privacy that ground privacy in autonomy.

In summary, relative privacy is considered a necessity for individuals to autonomously direct their self-presentations or to make choices about their lives that certainly have social preconditions but should still be choices that the individuals can identify with as their own. Yet, while all of these discussions include elements of answering to the critiques of autonomy summarised in section III, I will show in the remainder of this section that some problems with autonomy as the essential value of privacy remain. In the next section, I will show that the value of relative privacy can also be ascertained by referring to a more general notion of freedom that requires fewer presuppositions than the notions of autonomy.

The first problem mainly concerns arguments that tie privacy to autonomous self-presentation or the avoidance of context collapses. Both usually refer in some form to Goffman's seminal studies.[45] He firmly established that 'playing roles', ie, being different persons at different times and places, opposite different audiences, is not insincere or malicious. To the contrary, this is how society works, and not conforming to these roles would be considered improper or deviant behaviour.[46] Yet, accordingly, most of the times we play these roles rather unknowingly or unconsciously.[47] People just conform to the roles they have been learning in social life. What is more, role behaviour is often also invested with power. Maybe the most discussed case is the victim blaming that female persons often experience when they follow social roles (which also means social pressure if that role is invested with power relations). This pressure often includes demands to be rather exhibitive both online and offline. If that is abused (eg, by distributing privately shared pictures), often the female actors are blamed for being so exhibitive. In a narrow conception of privacy, one could indeed consider this as a problem of an individual choice giving up one's privacy – and having to face the consequence. From the viewpoint of the social preconditions of relative privacy, however, it becomes clear that such behaviour is not so much of a choice but something people do due to the power structures that pervade society.[48] Thus, actions that an old-fashioned account of

[44] Rössler and Mokrosinska (n 34) 778.

[45] Wesch (n 32) 22; AE Marwick and D Boyd, 'I Tweet Honestly, I Tweet Passionately: Twitter Users, Context Collapse, and the Imagined Audience' (2011) 13 *New Media & Society* 114, 123.

[46] Goffman (n 39) 35, 56, 71–75. *Cf* also E Goffman, *Interaction Ritual: Essays on Face-to-face Behavior* (New York, Pantheon Books, 1982) ch 1.

[47] Goffman (n 39) 74.

[48] J Ringrose et al, 'Teen Girls, Sexual Double Standards and "Sexting": Gendered Value in Digital Image Exchange' (2013) 14 *Feminist Theory* 305.

privacy would consider as giving up privacy actually can be seen as deserving of privacy protection. Following this line of argument, the problem is the person who shares the images by violating the privacy of the person in the picture. In consequence, acts that are also not autonomously chosen but rather done due to either social pressure or just unreflectively deserve privacy protection.

This argument is tied to a second problem. Feminists and other critical scholars have emphasised that while social pressure and heteronomy are indeed problems, there are quite different, even empowering ways to relate to them.[49] There are situations where people seem to enjoy a certain form of heteronomy in the staging of their personalities, which they cannot fully get under control or in critical distance. Sometimes, people enjoy their appearance becoming visible and getting (a bit) out of control. In her pointedly titled study of webcams, 'Empowering Exhibitionism', Hille Koskela argues that making oneself visible to an inestimable audience addresses a 'pleasure to be seen' but also a refusal to be humble. She also paraphrases this as a refusal 'to play the game of bad conscience', thus rebelling against social norms that relegate particular aspects of life to privacy, which Koskela reads as a form of social control.[50] The decision to broadcast significant parts of one's life online is conceived as a conscious decision. Yet, it takes place under conditions which the aforementioned authors discuss as a problem for autonomy. First, it is impossible to know one's audience and how persons will react to the way one stages oneself and which norms and views will be applied. Second, the interactive nature of the internet provides a backchannel, where viewers can reach back and expose the person who is visible in the broadcast to the viewers' version of what they perceived and whatever reaction they think they would be entitled to because of that. Koskela discusses a well-known case from the 1990s where a college girl with a webcam was harassed online and eventually blackmailed by hackers to be more revealing on her webcam.[51] Nevertheless, it is this active renunciation of aspects of autonomy, of inviting a significant part of heteronomy in the way a person appears to others, that allows Koskela to analyse this as a courageous and rebellious act.

One can disagree with that appraisal. However, it is important to notice that such hybrids of autonomy and heteronomy are the defining element of the appearance of persons online. Several studies discuss social networking sites in a similar manner. They illustrate that they consist of a profile, which conforms to the ideal of individual self-presentation, where the user fills out information, posts self-created pictures, etc. The increasingly more important parts, however, are 'timelines' or 'comment sections' where other users contribute content.[52] The currently most successful social networking sites, Instagram and TikTok, have reduced the element of the profile to a large extent,

[49] J Butler, *Gender Trouble: Feminism and the Subversion of Identity* (New York, Routledge, 1990).

[50] H Koskela, 'Webcams, TV Shows and Mobile Phones: Empowering Exhibitionism' (2004) 2 *Surveillance & Society* 199, 203, 210.

[51] ibid 207.

[52] L McNeill, 'There Is No "I" in Network: Social Networking Sites and Posthuman Auto/Biography' (2012) 35 *Biography* 65; R Cover, 'Performing and Undoing Identity Online: Social Networking, Identity Theories and the Incompatibility of Online Profiles and Friendship Regimes' (2012) 18 *Convergence: The International Journal of Research into New Media Technologies* 177. It is important to note that the profile is also structured by a form of heteronomy, that is the requirement to fit one's own self-presentation into the given fields and formats. While all stagings of a person have to react to the material setting and cultural presuppositions, the centralised power of the site's programmers enforce one uniform standard on the sometimes billions of users from all over the world that populate the more successful sites.

compared to older sites such as Facebook. On these newer sites, who the person who holds an account 'is' depends on what happens in the content of the feed. This includes comments or reactions by other users and algorithmically selected content. The 'owners' of the account have limited (technical) control of these elements. However, they can – or feel obliged to – react to it or exhibit a behaviour which invites certain contributions from others. This heteronomous element is decisive for the way a person appears online to others – often it is the central element of the site. Yet, this does not seem to shy away users – in contrast, it is one of the elements that constitute the widespread allure of such services. In consequence, Donath and Boyd argue that we rely on others to constitute and confirm our identities.[53]

Privacy scholars tend to see such phenomena critically, sometimes as a naïve or paradoxical forfeiting of privacy,[54] sometimes as falling for the psychologically informed design of digital media meant to trigger affective reactions that preclude a reflected use.[55] Those are important worries. However, they do not tell the whole story. Historians of privacy have argued that the modern liberal or bourgeois individual, who has learnt to constitute a rich and socially accepted self mainly in a self-reflective manner and in relative solitude, is a historically contingent phenomenon.[56] From the seventeenth century onwards, new affordances in the home, like a study or a library; new forms of self-relation, like writing diaries or reading novels; and increased social demand to separate private and business identities led to self-reflexivity as the main form of constituting the self. Thus, what seems to be the autonomous ideal, free from heteronomous influences, actually answers to a particular set of social, material, and technological mediations. Current forms of subjectivity that follow from contemporary preconditions such as digital media and distributed networked ways of performing the self are discussed by political and social analysts in a spectrum that reaches from new forms of liberty and solidarity to large parts of society just following neoliberal ideologies of ever more demands of flexibility and work on oneself.[57] I do not want to take a stance on these debates here. The takeaway for privacy is simply that if all such behaviours would be considered too heteronomous compared to the ideal of autonomy that grounds the value of privacy, a guarantee of privacy would greatly diminish contemporary socio-political possibilities and spaces. At least, a normative theory that ties the reason of privacy to practices and situations that seem to be largely absent in many people's lives should be treated with care.

This is related to the next problem of autonomy as a theoretical starting point. Often, autonomy is linked to a certain idea of authenticity. An act can be socially conditioned and dependent, but it is considered autonomous if the actor authentically wants it or

[53] J Donath and D Boyd, 'Public Displays of Connection' (2004) 22 *BT Technology Journal* 71.

[54] T Matzner et al, 'Do-It-Yourself Data Protection – Empowerment or Burden?' in G Serge, R Leenes and P De Hert (eds), *Data Protection on the Move: Current Developments in ICT and Privacy/Data Protection*, Issues in Privacy and Data Protection 24 (Dordrecht, Springer, 2016) 277–279.

[55] For a summary and critique see P Helm and T Matzner, 'Co-Addictive Human–Machine Configurations: Relating Critical Design and Algorithm Studies to Medical-Psychiatric Research on "Problematic Internet Use"' (2023) 26 *New Media & Society* 7295.

[56] D Vincent, *Privacy: A Short History* (Cambridge, Polity Press, 2016) ch 2.

[57] A Reckwitz, *The Society of Singularities* (Cambridge, Polity Press, 2020).

if it conforms to the life that is authentically the actor's.[58] Yet, in light of the critique mentioned in the beginning, but also concerning the considerations on relative privacy, it may seem questionable if such a level of authenticity can be reached. That, however, would make defending the necessity of privacy much more difficult if its value is tied to an unachievable state. Particularly the intimate life, or the life of the house, is considered as a space for authentic life. Often sexual relations are discussed as the most intimate and honest form of private interaction. A quick glance at the wide range of products, from lingerie to cosmetics and self-help books, immediately shows how much this is a performance itself. One might deride this as an inauthentic, commodified version of a real intimate relationship. Many theorists would take issue with such an idealism, even arguing that authenticity itself is just yet another performance or capitalist ideology.[59] Again, this debate is not my point here. It is important to note that even such a staged and 'inauthentic' sexual relationship clearly deserves privacy, and just this possibility and not only the potential of the private life becoming authentic should be enough to defend the value of privacy. This theoretical restraint might also have normative benefits. It evades importing expectations into the situation protected by privacy, which are increasingly problematic.

Apart from these more socio-cultural considerations, there are also issues with the relationship between privacy and autonomy that stem more from the technical and material aspects of contemporary digital technologies. Most importantly, this concerns the precondition that an autonomous actor has a good estimate (even if not total control) of the audience of the act and of its consequences. Concerning contemporary technology, this would need a profound understanding of the technical details of information technologies to estimate the possibilities of storing, transferring, and using the data. The increasing leaks and mishaps even at the biggest technology companies in the world illustrate that such considerations are a challenge even for experts.[60] Second, such a grasp of one's audience would entail predicting the behaviour of many persons, not all of whom share one's own norms, views, or levels of consideration and care. For such reasons, one study on context collapses concludes that the 'individualistic model of privacy', where an individual decides how to stage oneself, reaches its limits. Accordingly, the authors suggest remedies like 'co-constructing the architecture of the systems' or aiming at 'shared social norms over information-sharing'.[61] Leaving feasibility aside, it remains unclear whether this is meant as a necessary social attempt to re-establish individual autonomy or if they aim at a more social model of subjectivity altogether. In any case, my discussion on algorithmic data analysis above has illustrated that a society permeated with surveillance cameras, smartphones, all kinds of networked devices in the 'internet of things', and many more sensors soon to be present in 'smart cities' filled with self-driving cars introduces a necessary element of heteronomy that far exceeds the necessity to estimate audiences even in the most contextualised and networked manner. It would mean assessing the possibilities of

[58] B Rössler, *Autonomy: An Essay on the Life Well Lived* (Cambridge, Polity Press, 2021).

[59] E Illouz, *Emotions as Commodities: Capitalism, Consumption and Authenticity* (Abington, Routledge, 2018).

[60] T Matzner, *Algorithms: Technology, Culture, Politics* (Abington, Routledge, 2024) ch 5.

[61] Marwick and Boyd (n 32) 1063.

algorithmic data analysis (not just now but also in the future), which even its programmers often do not know but just try out.[62] These developments have been at the core of many recent discussions of the need to re-establish privacy under these conditions. If that entails, however, arguing for regaining full control of the individual over the usage of their data, this would eventually mean arguing for a right that is void in the sense that no one could sensibly exercise it. Thus, the question remains how to justify the value of privacy, if not to enable autonomy.

Consequently, I want to show that a substantial part of what we claim when asking for privacy can be normatively grounded without recourse to such a notion of autonomy – and in fact, taking heteronomous situations into account. This is not to say that a revision of theories of autonomy could not answer many of the problems discussed here. What is more, autonomy can be an important value to demand and defend – it just does not necessarily cover all cases for which the value of privacy should be established. In fact, what I present below is fully compatible with most notions of autonomy that have been mentioned in this text. My perspective can include the socially situated idea of autonomy, which figures in the theories above, as a special case among the many possible configurations of autonomy and heteronomy that I discuss in the next section. In this sense autonomy need not be replaced but could just be amended as the normative ground for privacy. Albeit, my perspective also speaks to the many theories that are critical of autonomy on an empirical or normative level. Thus, I do not want to take a stand on autonomy itself, but rather detach the value of privacy from autonomy.

## V. Relative Privacy and its Value

With the introduction of all kinds of socio-technical conditions for both subjects themselves and their actions, privacy theories have incorporated these conditions despite their being sources of heteronomy. Privacy, in these theories, is a means to configure such conditions in a way that they still permit some relative autonomy, while acknowledging that these conditions cannot be completely warded off since they are necessary for sensible forms of action or subjectivity itself. This is what I have called relative privacy above. In the last section, I have shown that some problems still remain with the idea to take even that situated, relative form of autonomy as the normative grounds for privacy. In this section, I want to show that it suffices to demand a quite minimal freedom to change rather than autonomy to ground the value of privacy. Importantly, this freedom to change does not make any claims about why the change happens – by autonomous decision or maybe yielding to social pressure or by inviting a particular form of heteronomy, as in the cases discussed in the last section. This new form of grounding the value of privacy is in practice much less about the essential opposition of autonomy vs. heteronomy but rather about the configuration of different forms of heteronomy.

[62] Matzner (n 60) 124.

This is maybe most easily explained using the example of context collapses. The gist of that theory is that in many contexts one is not private in the old-fashioned sense of the term, but a form of privacy is still necessary that keeps the present context separate from other contexts. What this means is that one context (eg, work) is a source of heteronomy relative to another context (eg, going out with friends). What matters here – as far as (relative) privacy is concerned – is not how autonomous one is among one's friends but mainly to keep that source of heteronomy from the other context away. In fact, the possibility of giving up self-control in the presence of one's friends is very much dependent on curtailing such other sources of heteronomy.

A similar argument can be made for theories of self-presentation. Here, the function of relative privacy is to make sure that the audience forms *their* verdict based on the presentation of an individual itself and not based on other sources of information about that individual, which in that sense would form a source of heteronomy for the self-presentation that is currently happening. Again, it is less important if the self-presentation in any given instance happens autonomously or, for example, because of the demands of neoliberal self-fashioning – at least as far as relative privacy is concerned.

Generalising from these observations, norms and conditions of privacy contribute in an important way to the possibilities to appear (or not to appear) in a particular situation. They determine which other appearances of a person can be related to the current context and thus structure or influence the current appearance. As my discussion of algorithms above has shown, it is necessary to redescribe relative privacy not as a separation of contexts but as a more fine-grained limit on the possibilities of collecting, using, and reusing data. In consequence, I consider relative privacy as negotiating which other appearances of a person influence an appearance of the same person (at a different time and place) and which appearances are blocked from this influence – regardless of in which 'context' these appearances happen. Appearance here could also denote being recorded on a camera or being tracked, or in general should not be thought of as face-to-face interaction only (which still implicitly structures especially the Goffman-inspired privacy theories.) Rather, all kinds of mediated appearances are included. Also, the influence of one appearance on another can be highly mediated. For example, it could mean that an algorithm uses some data collected at a former occasion in order to suggest to a possible employer to whom someone applies – the current appearance – how to judge that person.[63]

In consequence, a person does not just move among contexts but continuously becomes the person that has also appeared in other contexts. Norms of privacy thus touch the fundamental social negotiation of personal identity in regulating which other appearances of a person become relevant or irrelevant for the current one. This is of course also a core element in the theories of privacy discussed above. While these attempt to carve out spaces of autonomy in such negotiations, I will show that the value

[63] In this regard it is important that such algorithmic judgements usually are made using data from many persons and not just the one who is judged. This, however, touches the complex question whether such a protection of one's data from being used to judge – or discriminate against – others still is a matter of privy, to which I return at the end of this text.

of privacy can also be defended just by the necessity of privacy for such negotiations to be possible in the first place – even if not or not fully autonomously.

Of course it is very important to remain wary of the dangers of elements of heteronomy that emanate from the socio-technical conditions of subjectivity. Yet, the antidote concerning relative privacy need not be an autonomous choice but the regulation of heteronomy. Privacy then does not necessarily give a person autonomy but rather guarantees that no single heteronomous view of a person becomes hegemonic. This is the real threat that (relative) privacy today has to ward off: a single view or account of who we are trumps all others, eg, an algorithmic verdict is all there is, and neither a person's own future appearances nor testaments by others can change or challenge this. Relative privacy thus regulates the power that different sources of heteronomy have by limiting their influence on the current and further appearances of a person.

Such forms of regulating the availability of appearances can be distinguished in two groups. The first contains privacy norms that aim at an appearance at one place and time not becoming known in more or less specified other locations and points in time. This concerns most issues usually grouped under bodily, spatial, and informational privacy. For example, the spatial configuration of houses, bars, and other places that 'afford some privacy' achieves the effect that the persons interacting there do not appear elsewhere. Also the privacy settings of internet services, encryption, and similar technical means try to achieve similar protection.

The second group concerns appearances that become known but should be disregarded in one's account of a person. Some of them concern informational privacy as well. A case in point is the well-known legislation against Google in Spain, where a 'right to be forgotten' was conceived.[64] This pertains to articles or other documents online, which clearly had some visibility, but this should not be extended by the increased visibility a search engine provides. Another case, which unites spatial and informational privacy, is the anonymity of the masses, eg, in a big city. Here a lot is appearing to others, but it is usually not noticed or should not be linked to other encounters with that person. Sociology of cities has discussed a similar phenomenon as 'ethics of indifference',[65] and Goffman has described it as 'civil inattention'[66] in his study of relations in public.

The more complex cases in this latter group, however, pertain to decisional privacy. Following Rössler, decisional privacy means that some decisions, like one's religion or sexual life, are inherently private and no one has the right to interfere. This means that the public has to accept such a life, but that also objections from family or friends can be refused by asking them not to meddle with their private affairs. These are cases in which others perceive the act, attitude, or decision, eg, the religion one practices, but are asked to refrain from 'objections, comments, or judgements'.[67] This aspect of privacy extends the usual discussion of self-presentation and focuses on the autonomy

[64] E Frantziou, 'Further Developments in the Right to Be Forgotten: The European Court of Justice's Judgment in Case C-131/12, Google Spain, SL, Google Inc v Agencia Espanola de Proteccion de Datos' (2014) 14 *Human Rights Law Review* 761.

[65] F Tonkiss, 'The Ethics of Indifference: Community and Solitude in the City' (2003) 6 *International Journal of Cultural Studies* 297.

[66] E Goffman, *Relations in Public: Microstudies of the Public Order* (New York, Harper & Row, 1977) 304.

[67] Rössler (n 1) 81.

of individual acts. Yet, these aspects can still be grasped with a view that takes the socio-technical co-constitution of subjects and their appearances (and not just role-based self-presentation) as its starting point. In that view, the demand for decisional privacy could be reformulated as follows: the issue at hand, eg, the religion, appears but has to be disregarded in further accounts of who appears to an audience. This includes individual reactions to this appearance. Since the reactions of others feed a subject's appearance back to it and derive claims from it, these parts of the appearance are not meant to figure here. They should also be excluded from accounts about the person that are passed on to others. However, my mapping of decisional privacy to the disregard of certain appearances or aspects thereof shows that such disregard can also be asked for in 'private' or intimate relationships. In this regard, it is also important to remember that following the discussion in the last section, privacy does not just concern rational decisions but should also be a means to protect emotional, affective, or impulsive reactions.

As the example of religion illustrates, however, this claim to disregard certain aspects of appearances never pertains to all others. In this case, for example, one probably could want the other members of the religious community to take that aspect particularly into account when interacting with this person. Again, the important element is which forms of heteronomy need to be curtailed relative to others that are acceptable or even wanted.

The value of relative privacy as moderation of different sources of heteronomy lies in protecting the plurality of perspectives in a situation and, in consequence, in society, which in turn is necessary for the possibility to change, to develop one's personality, to try things, and to maybe err, but not only if this happens by autonomous decisions or to eventually enable autonomous decisions. The situation in which others perceive us and form 'their' verdict can only arise if others – figuratively speaking – do not already know us from other sources. Even if such verdicts form another source of heteronomy, it is still important that they can be made. As stated above, the aim of privacy is not to prevent heteronomy per se but to make sure that no single source of heteronomy becomes too powerful or even hegemonic.

This is a more fundamental precondition to the situation discussed above: that we can confront a new audience with a new form of self-presentation. Every such situation certainly implies this condition, because without such a plurality of perspectives and audiences, there would be no different possibilities of staging oneself to choose from in the first place. My account, however, shows that there are many more situations which are equally worthy of privacy protection in the sense that the individual who appears there should not appear elsewhere or at another time or should be disregarded in certain aspects in the present situation. This wards off the danger that individuals will be confined to former appearances. Essentially relative privacy is still protecting freedom – the freedom to change.

Without such privacy, neither the individuals themselves nor the plurality of others in a society can attain a decisive influence on who individuals in this society are. While the first part is central to all accounts of privacy, I want to include the latter. For often it is not individual claims to be someone else that oppose the threat of a few persons' or an institution's judgements becoming too constricting a force on subjects. Very often it is the (probably solidary but still heteronomous) claim of some others: you should be someone else; for us, you are someone else; we want you to be someone else; here, with us, you can be someone else; and so on. In cases where individuality is structured by less friendly forms of heteronomy, relative privacy curtails the power others have in this situation, in the sense that their perspective regarding who has appeared to them will determine only a limited amount of other appearances. Again, this is necessary to maintain the possibility of plurality and change, even if the other appearance is yet another situation structured by heteronomy – but opposite different others. Finally, this form of relative privacy enables impulsive reactions and makes it possible to expose oneself to the determination of others, to let control go, without surrendering the influence over too many of all of the future appearances of that person to these others.

This view entails that privacy will remain a contested and problematic issue. The worry remains that individuals are forced to appear just in the locally necessary or opportune manner, without anything appearing beyond this economic or social necessity. Here, Rachels' concern against a market conception of the individual finds its place without the necessity to engage a true, authentic self. Rather, this means that privacy will remain contested regarding the right amount of heteronomy and, in particular, the right sources of heteronomy. The protection that relative privacy affords is necessary but at the same time inherently ambivalent. Although I extend the function of privacy from shielding autonomy to moderating different configurations of heteronomy, relative privacy still has a limiting function on heteronomy. It limits, however, the influence of particular others compared to different others, rather than the influence of generalised others in opposition to the autonomous individual. The particular limiting function of heteronomy that I ascribe to privacy still comes with a de-politicising effect. Privacy either means that some appearances are limited and thus do not spread to a wider public, or it means that they should be disregarded and thus are at least de-politicised in personal interaction. In contrast, concerning a political matter, objection and judgement would clearly be warranted – if not even called for.

In consequence, the third group of objections discussed in section III as problems of de-politicisation partly remain. Relative privacy allows a more complex view because it can differentiate various localised forms of politicisation and de-politicisation – overcoming the duality of something being an individual matter or not. Albeit, at least locally, privacy is inherently de-politicising. For without having this effect, privacy would not have its protective function either. In a sense, de-politicisation is too narrow a term, since this problem also pertains to many issues of morality. In fact, most claims to respect privacy could be replaced by a morally or politically 'laden' claim. For example, a homosexual person could ask that an interlocutor disregard or not know about this because it is private – or that person could demand that the interlocutor stop reacting in a homophobic manner. A person could ask that another person disregard or not know that she had an abortion – or she could demand that this person stop patriarchal attempts to influence her. It is an important feature of privacy that it allows persons to evade problems without having always to take on the full force of the moral or political configuration. Thus, relative privacy regulates which kind of concrete heteronomy by which kind of others is effective and how far it reaches. In this sense relative privacy still protects the individual for the sake of the individual. Relative privacy is necessary so that individuals can change and plurality is protected – in particular in morally and politically problematic conditions.[68]

In consequence, relative privacy is necessary, but it must remain one of several alternatives to regulate heteronomy. Relative privacy is thus one of many social norms which regulate the availability of appearances, and it does so in a de-politicszing and de-moralising way. Privacy thus protects against the coercion that emanates from the accounts others have of us and their respective reactions. The form of decisional privacy Cohen and Rössler have in mind goes beyond that; in particular, it wards off strong coercion by the state. This, however, is a political issue, to be precise, a problem of the extent of liberty itself. Of course, the discourse in the liberal tradition gives Rössler and Cohen every right to call this privacy. I would, however, suggest keeping different ways of protecting against heteronomy separated by different names. Following this suggestion, a privacy-based solution would mean that the state as a powerful other should not know or disregard that someone wants or had an abortion. And in many regards this is the right solution, eg, when hiring, etc. In some regards, however, the state should precisely not be ignorant of that fact; those are the cases that are necessary to provide substantial support and which should not be de-politicised – what the privacy-based solution would entail.[69] This also pertains to the immense power that algorithmic predictions have – particularly because they are not just using one person's data to predict one person's behaviour but are combining immense amounts of data from all kinds of persons in order to build predictive models.[70] Attempting to curtail these powers with recourse to each of these individuals' privacy is maybe a viable hack where more adept political and legal measures are lacking. Yet, again, this is a matter of configuring socio-economic and political powers and thus again a deeply political issue that cannot be adequately addressed with the individualising and de-politicising means of privacy. Issues of heteronomy regarding the extent of freedom and equality in the sense of which actions are possible in a society at all, however, transcend the question of the availability of appearances and are thus generic political issues which should not be confounded with problems of privacy.

[68] This is not to imply that an ideal situation where privacy was no longer needed was possible – as some rather naïve proponents of a transparent society claim.

[69] DE Roberts, 'Punishing Drug Addicts Who Have Babies: Women of Color, Equality, and the Right of Privacy' in K Crenshaw et al (eds), *Critical Race Theory – The Key Writings that Formed the Movement* (New York, The New Press, 1996).

[70] T Matzner, 'Why Privacy Is Not Enough Privacy in the Context of "Ubiquitous Computing" and "Big Data"' (2014) 12 *Journal of Information, Communication and Ethics in Society* 93.

# INDEX

www.ingramcontent.com/pod-product-compliance
Ingram Content Group UK Ltd.
Pitfield, Milton Keynes, MK11 3LW, UK
UKHW020230290926
15470UKWH00002B/452